T0338408

Market Momentum

Market Momentum

Theory and Practice

By

STEPHEN SATCHELL
and
ANDREW GRANT

WILEY

This edition first published 2021

© 2021 Stephen Satchell and Andrew Grant

Registered office
John Wiley & Sons Ltd, The Atrium, Southern Gate, Chichester, West Sussex, PO19 8SQ, United Kingdom

For details of our global editorial offices, for customer services and for information about how to apply for permission to reuse the copyright material in this book please see our website at www.wiley.com.

Wiley publishes in a variety of print and electronic formats and by print-on-demand. Some material included with standard print versions of this book may not be included in e-books or in print-on-demand. If this book refers to media such as a CD or DVD that is not included in the version you purchased, you may download this material at http://booksupport.wiley.com. For more information about Wiley products, visit www.wiley.com.

Designations used by companies to distinguish their products are often claimed as trademarks. All brand names and product names used in this book are trade names, service marks, trademarks or registered trademarks of their respective owners. The publisher is not associated with any product or vendor mentioned in this book.

Limit of Liability/Disclaimer of Warranty: While the publisher and author have used their best efforts in preparing this book, they make no representations or warranties with respect to the accuracy or completeness of the contents of this book and specifically disclaim any implied warranties of merchantability or fitness for a particular purpose. It is sold on the understanding that the publisher is not engaged in rendering professional services and neither the publisher nor the author shall be liable for damages arising herefrom. If professional advice or other expert assistance is required, the services of a competent professional should be sought.

Library of Congress Cataloging-in-Publication Data

Names: Grant, Andrew Robert, 1982- author. | Satchell, Stephen Ellwood, 1949- author.
Title: Market momentum : theory and practice / Andrew Robert Grant, Stephen Ellwood Satchell.
Description: First Edition. | Hoboken : Wiley, 2020. | Series: The wiley finance series | Includes index.
Identifiers: LCCN 2020020406 (print) | LCCN 2020020407 (ebook) | ISBN 9781119599326 (hardback) | ISBN 9781119599470 (adobe pdf) | ISBN 9781119599371 (epub)
Subjects: LCSH: Investment analysis. | Securities—Prices. | Economics—Psychological aspects.
Classification: LCC HG4529 .G73 2020 (print) | LCC HG4529 (ebook) | DDC 332.63/2042—dc23
LC record available at https://lccn.loc.gov/2020020406
LC ebook record available at https://lccn.loc.gov/2020020407

Cover Design: Wiley
Cover Image: ©palamatic/shutterstock

Set in 10/12pt, SabonLTStd by SPi Global, Chennai, India.

Printed and bound by CPI Group (UK) Ltd, Croydon, CR0 4YY

10 9 8 7 6 5 4 3 2 1

Abstracts

1 Andrew Grant

This chapter examines the behavioural finance argument for the existence of momentum profits. From a behavioural finance perspective, asset prices may deviate from fundamental values, which can persist if market frictions prevent a prompt correction to mispricing. As risk, in the form of a Fama-French three-factor model, has been shown to provide a poor explanation for momentum returns, academics have sought psychology-inspired reasons for the phenomenon. We review the literature on behavioural finance and momentum, starting with the theoretical studies of the late 1990s, which have become highly influential. Following on from this, we discuss the recent empirical evidence supporting predictions such as slow information diffusion, incorrect updating of beliefs, trading at the 52-week high, individual investor trading and market-wide sentiment. Among the key insights is that behavioural finance can help provide an explanation for statistical patterns that generate momentum portfolios (as in Chapter 2) and may help practitioners in identifying themes for enhancing their investment portfolios.

2 Steve Satchell

In this chapter we look at different momentum strategies and their properties. Many of the empirical results of momentum strategies can be seen to result from the structure of return processes and the design of the strategy. In particular, considering simple cases, we investigate the return distributions of what are the major momentum strategies which are cross-sectional momentum (CSM), time-series momentum (TSM), relative strength strategies (RSS) and cross-asset momentum. For the case of two assets, we can say a great deal about the structure and properties of returns. From a statistical perspective, behavioural analysis will determine the magnitude of model parameters along with, in some cases, the specification of the model itself. Taking these as given, the statistical analysis will determine the properties of the strategy returns. In this form of analysis, we are interested in the population moments such as the mean, variance, skewness and kurtosis but also the time-series moments of the momentum process. It is hoped that the relatively simple analysis in this chapter will help the reader in later chapters.

3 Nick Baltas and Robert Kosowski

Motivated by studies of the impact of frictions on asset prices, we examine the effect of key components of time-series momentum strategies on turnover and performance. We show that more efficient volatility estimation and price-trend detection can significantly reduce portfolio turnover by more than one-third, without causing a statistically significant performance degradation. We propose a novel implementation of the strategy that incorporates the pairwise signed correlations by means of a dynamic leverage mechanism. The correlation-adjusted variant outperforms the naïve implementation of the strategy and the outperformance is more pronounced in the post-2008 period. Finally, using a transaction costs model for futures-based strategies that separates costs into roll-over and rebalancing costs, we show that our findings remain robust to the inclusion of transaction costs

4 Jose Menchero and Lei Ji

In this chapter, we study the risk and return of momentum in developed equity markets. We construct factor portfolios by cross-sectional regression. Univariate regression results in 'simple' factor portfolios that contain 'incidental' bets on other factors. Multivariate regression results in 'pure' factor portfolios that are neutral to all factors except momentum. We compare performance of simple and pure momentum factors across various developed markets. We find that simple and pure factors have virtually identical long-term performance within each equity market. The pure factors, however, achieve this performance with considerably lower volatility, resulting in higher risk-adjusted performance. We also study the volatilities and correlations of momentum factors across time. We find that these quantities peaked during the Internet Bubble and the Financial Crisis. Finally, we show that for most periods, momentum has been negatively correlated with the market, thus offering attractive diversification opportunities.

5 Dan diBartolomeo and Bill Zieff

Price momentum exposure is a familiar concept to anyone who has studied equity return factors. Less addressed in the literature is how momentum effects in one asset class manifest in other asset classes. Theories of corporate finance that link equity and bond returns through their common dependence on the value of the firm have been known for some time, but these theories do not address the dynamics between debt and equity in a time-series context. Cross-Asset momentum provides a parsimonious description of such dynamics. We describe theoretical underpinnings and empirical results for several cross-asset class momentum effects. Included is a discussion of equity momentum impact into fixed income, selected momentum effects in illiquid assets, such as real estate and private equity, and momentum results pertaining to commodities. Implications for active management in asset allocation and active management within asset classes are explored and highlighted.

6 Katharina Schwaiger and Muhammad Massood

Momentum as an investment strategy is a well-known component of systematic strategies. With the rise of exchange-traded funds (ETFs) and smart beta, momentum strategies are available to a broad range of clients including retail via a fully transparent rules-based index strategy. The indices are built to weight and select stocks from an equity universe with high momentum exposure or high past returns. Those ETFs aim to offer momentum factor exposure at a competitive fee. In this chapter we shed light on the momentum ETF landscape and discuss how much momentum is in momentum ETFs. We find that momentum indices exhibit momentum characteristics despite differences in the underlying index methodologies, lack of leverage and infrequent rebalancing.

7 Oliver Williams

This chapter reviews time-series momentum (TSM) strategies as commonly used by Commodity Trading Advisers (CTAs). We compare TSM with cross-sectional momentum (CSM) and describe examples of various methods used for TSM signal generation, showing that there are certain essential similarities in TSM approaches although the degree of technical complexity varies considerably across methods. We note various stylized facts of CTA investing (e.g. relatively low Sharpe ratio and positive skewness) and highlight practically relevant results from existing literature concerning characteristics of TSM returns. Throughout the chapter we use simple market models to illustrate our points and we derive an expression for the correlation between TSM and CSM returns in this setting, which may be useful when contemplating asset allocation between these strategies.

8 Anders Petterson and Oliver Williams

In this chapter we apply momentum returns models in a non-traditional setting: the valuation of contemporary art. Specifically, we consider whether a momentum model is useful at predicting auction outcomes based on changes in subjective valuation opinions observed over a short period prior to the auction. We use a novel data set (supplied by ArtForecaster.com) that contains multiple valuations of the same piece of art provided by individual forecasters at approximately the same time. Combined with auctioneers' estimates and hammer prices this data can be used to estimate a simple dynamic model of valuation changes. We fail to find significant evidence of time-series momentum in these valuation changes, but a forecasting strategy based on cross-sectional momentum appears to be effective. This implies that subjective opinion is more informative when considered on a relative basis (one work of art versus another) rather than outright, and we conjecture this may be due to a sub-conscious bias on the part of art market participants towards positive rather than negative sentiment. We conclude that momentum models can provide a useful framework for analysis of information and behaviour outside traditional financial markets.

9 Yang Gao

This chapter explores the interaction between momentum and volatility. The literature has shown that momentum strategies using volatility as the conditioning variable strongly outperform plain momentum strategies by reporting higher alphas, increased Sharpe ratios and improved skewness. These volatility-managed momentum strategies benefit from the use of volatility, which has the potential to better forecast future returns. We empirically review the various volatility-managed momentum strategies that are proposed in the academic literature. Our findings show strong outperformance of both the time-series (TSVM) and cross-sectional volatility-managed momentum strategies

(CSVM) in the USA, Europe and Australia. We document interesting evidence that the TSVM strategy seems to work in the Chinese and Japanese markets where traditional momentum or CSVM does not work well. We further discuss the role of leverage constraints, turnover and short-selling constraints in the practical use of volatility-managed momentum strategies. Last, we examine how volatility manages momentum risk and suggest that momentum is not only related to its own volatility.

10 Andrew Grant, Oh Kang Kwon and Steve Satchell

The selection of assets based on the rankings of one or more of their attributes over a prior period is a standard practice in the construction of portfolios in both academic and practitioner finance. Momentum is a familiar example of this activity. Although the properties of returns from these portfolios have been the subject of considerable empirical research, there is only limited literature investigating their theoretical properties. In this chapter, we address this gap by deriving analytically the distributional properties of these portfolio returns under the assumption that asset attributes and returns are jointly multivariate normal. We show that prior sorting of asset attributes induces non-normality in the portfolio returns and that the returns depend on the order and nature of sorting The analysis looks at two fundamental types of sorting, both commonly used by practitioners, and the authors show that the method of sorting influences the pattern of returns under commonly encountered circumstances.

11 Stefano Cavaglia, Vadim Moroz and Louis Scott

The research presented in this chapter extends and corroborates the findings of Scott and Cavaglia (2016) who first illustrated the potential benefits of a factor premia overlay to an inter-temporal wealth accumulation strategy that is fully invested in equities. We examine a panel of 5 local factor premia (inclusive of momentum) in each of 21 developed equity markets and 5 regions. In nearly all instances we find that wealth accumulation is significantly enhanced by a time invariant, equal weighted allocation to these premia. The enhancement is driven in part by the mean return of the premia but more importantly by their generally positive payoff in adverse market environments. The quality and momentum factor premia are the largest contributors to this result. Applying conventional measures of risk aversion we quantify the importance of downside protection to supporting the attainment of investors' goals; the utility-based evidence suggests that some factor premia are valued by investors even when their expected return is zero.

12 Christopher Polk, Mo Haghbin and Alessio de Longis

Factor cyclicality can be understood in the context of factor sensitivity to aggregate cash-flow news. Factors exhibit different sensitivities to macroeconomic risk, and this heterogeneity can be exploited to motivate dynamic rotation strategies among established factors: size, value, quality, low volatility and momentum. A timely and realistic identification of business cycle regimes, using leading economic indicators and global risk appetite, can be used to construct long-only factor rotation strategies with information ratios nearly 70% higher than static multifactor strategies. The rules introduced here are simple to apply and can be interpreted as a macroeconomic regime-switching model without the cumbersome technology that such models usually involve. Hidden regimes are absent and, in this framework, we know what regime we are in. Results are statistically and economically significant across regions and market segments, also after accounting for transaction costs, capacity and turnover.

13 Ron Bird, Xiaojun (Kevin) Gao and Danny Yeung

Momentum is one of numerous market anomalies highlighted over the last 30 or more years, bringing into question the efficiency of markets around the world. However, the question is left open as to whether the apparent profit opportunities offered by time-series and cross-sectional investment strategies are exploitable. With the incorporation of transaction costs and risk, the 'typical' implementation of both momentum strategies yields profits in only a handful of markets. However, we demonstrate that the performance of the momentum portfolios is very much dependent on the extent to which implementation rules chosen are in synchronicity with the periodicity of the market.

14 Shivam Ghosh, Steve Satchell and Nandini Srivastava

Artificial Intelligence (AI) and Machine Learning (ML) has seen unprecedented growth over the past decade with applications across healthcare, robotics, data security and automotive industries to name a few. Penetration of AI in finance has been slower; primarily due to the intrinsic nature of markets – non-stationarity of financial processes and lack of sufficient training data. We make a foray into applying ML to finance by training a range of models to trade Momentum – a systematic strategy that benefits from persistence of trends in markets. Our findings suggest that a class of ML algorithms like Random Forests and Neural Nets produce Sharpe ratios close to optimal vanilla time-series momentum (TSMOM). However, correlation between ML and vanilla TSMOM signals is low allowing us to harvest fruits of diversification by creating hybrid vanilla – ML TSMOM strategies. We find such hybrid portfolio Sharpe ratios to be twice as high as vanilla TSMOM.

15 Byoung-Kyu Min

One of the important linkages in financial economics is between the world of macroeconomics and the returns of individual companies. Whilst this is usually hard to identify empirically, it is nevertheless possible to find causality between macroeconomics and strategy returns. Furthermore, such causal relationships are of great interest to practitioners and constitute a key part of what is described as active quantitative fund management.

Recent empirical literature shows that *time variation* in the profitability of momentum strategies is critical to understanding the source of momentum. This chapter presents direct evidence that momentum strategies deliver significantly negative profits during 'bad' economic states in which investors demand the highest market risk premium, suggesting that momentum strategies expose investors to greater downside risk. It also reviews the literature investing whether momentum profits are related to various economic states, including business cycles, market state and investor sentiment, and discusses explanations for these findings.

16 Chris Tinker

Momentum has been considered a market anomaly and treated as a behavioural phenomenon. While generally regarded as a standalone trading strategy as a consequence, growing interest in factor-based investing and the emergence of Alternative Risk Premia (ARP), argues for a more integrated, investment-based analysis of momentum. Under a systematic, stock level, time-series forecast framework we argue that it is possible to identify a clear fundamental – and therefore risk-based factor structure.

We treat momentum as a fundamental phenomenon, driven by news-flow related changes to stock level, and expected returns of fundamentalist investors. We model two investor groups – short term and long term – sharing similar, but not always consistent views of fundamental value. The occasional, but sometimes significant, variance in their respective implied Sharpe ratios provides the trigger for a momentum phase, while their realignment signals its end. A third investor group, momentum traders, do not participate in the establishment, duration or ending of the momentum phase. This group are passive bystanders who, nonetheless, would benefit from knowledge of the signals generated.

Results generated from this analysis on the S&P500 stock universe from 2004 to 2019 confirm the outperforming nature of a momentum strategy based on this signal with high hit rates and annualised returns at the stock level and clear signs of convexity in the returns, consistent with the requirements of any ARP-based momentum portfolio. As a means of evaluating risk at the individual stock level and as a framework for systematic stock selection of momentum-based factor portfolios, the treatment of momentum as a stock level risk factor suggests that an implied Sharpe-ratio-based signal adds value to the decision-making processes of both traders and investors.

17 Stefano Cavaglia, Louis Scott, Kenneth Blay and Vincent de Martel

This chapter examines the use of commodity factors in a portfolio context, aimed at customising a portfolio for specific clients. A critical question is whether the inclusion of a factor overlay, such as momentum, carry or value, or a combination of these factors, can improve outcomes for aspiring retirees, compared to the simple approach of investing in a portfolio of equities and/or bonds. Using a bootstrap simulation approach, allowing for alternative scenarios for the performance of the assets and factors, it is found that the incorporation of a single factor overlay enhances the likelihood of an aspiring retiree achieving her goal. A combination of factors in the overlay provides additional diversification benefits for the more risk-averse retiree. It is argued that, due to time diversification over the business cycle, factor overlays enhance accumulated wealth net of costs

Contents

Contributors

Andrew Grant is a Sydney University academic whose areas of expertise are behavioural finance, individual investor decision making and betting markets, focusing on preference and belief-based asset allocation and asset-pricing decisions. He has also been engaged with industry, with studies of alternative finance and marketplace lending in the Asia-Pacific. He has appeared as a guest commentator in print, radio and on television, discussing issues such as gambling market and banking regulation, personal savings and asset allocation model evaluation.

Stephen Satchell is a fellow of Trinity College; he has consulted to a large number of financial institutions and published many papers. He believes that financial research should go beyond the normal offerings and he enjoys collaborating with scholars of other disciplines to advance his understanding of markets. He was the editor of *Journal of Asset Management* and is the co-founder of Quantess, an all women quant group as well as Head of Credit Research at Imagine, a fintech start-up offering imaginative mortgage products.

Nick Baltas, PhD, is a managing director and head of R&D of the Systematic Trading Strategies Group at Goldman Sachs. He is also a visiting researcher at Imperial College Business School and the executive editor of the *Journal of Systematic Investing*. In the past, he has held several positions both in the finance industry and in academia. His academic research has received numerous awards and has been published in peer-reviewed finance journals and books.

Ron Bird recently retired from both the University of Technology Sydney and Waikato University. His research interests have most recently concentrated on the mysteries of the funds management and retirement income industries. He has published widely in journals such as *Management Science*, the *Journal of Portfolio Management* and the *Australian Journal of Management*.

Kenneth Blay is Head of Thought Leadership for the Invesco Investment Solutions team. Prior to joining Invesco, Mr. Blay was the advisory research manager in the portfolio and risk research group at State Street Associates. Previously, he served as director of research at 1st Global. Mr. Blay earned a BBA in finance from the University of Texas at San Antonio. He has co-authored and published various works on asset allocation with Nobel Laureate Harry Markowitz.

Stefano Cavaglia holds a PhD in Finance from the Chicago Booth School of Business. Throughout his career, he has applied state-of-the-art finance theory. His early work led to the restructuring of the UBS global equity platform and the founding of a $1.3b hedge fund he managed at UBS O'Connor, Chicago. Presently, he is co-developing, with Invesco, novel multi-asset, factor-based completion portfolios. His research is widely cited in the CFA community and financial press.

Alessio de Longis is a Senior Portfolio Manager for the Invesco Investment Solutions division. He leads the group's tactical asset allocation, including factor and currency strategies. He joined Invesco from OppenheimerFunds, where he was team leader and senior portfolio manager of the multi-asset team. He earned an MSc in financial economics and econometrics from University of Essex, and MA/BA in economics from the University of Rome. He is a CFA Charterholder.

Vincent de Martel, CFA, is Senior Solutions Strategist with the Invesco Investment Solutions team. Prior to joining Invesco, Mr. de Martel was head of product strategy for BlackRock's multi-asset risk parity/factor suite. Previously, he served as head of European LDI strategy at Barclays Global Investors. He earned an MA degree in accounting and financial economics from the University of Essex, as well as an MBA from EDHEC with a concentration in market finance.

Dan diBartolomeo is President and founder of Northfield Information Services, Inc. Based in Boston since 1986, Northfield develops quantitative models of financial markets. He sits on boards of numerous industry organizations include IAQF and CQA, and is past president of the Boston Economic Club. His publication record includes 35 books, book chapters and research journal articles. In January of 2018, he became co-editor of the *Journal of Asset Management*. Dan spent numerous years as a Visiting Professor at Brunel University. In 2010 he was given the 'Tech 40' award by *Institutional Investor* magazine in recognition of his role in the discovery of the Madoff hedge fund fraud. He has also been admitted as an expert witness in litigation matters regarding investment management practices and derivatives in both US federal and state courts.

Kevin Gao is an experienced Business Intelligence Consultant with a demonstrated history of working in the information technology and services industry. He has analytical skills, and skills in quantitative research, data mining, banking, accounting and teaching. He has a PhD focused in Applied Finance, and degrees in mathematics and computer science.

Yang Gao joined Huazhong University of Science and Technology as assistant professor in June 2019 after obtaining his PhD from the University of Sydney. His research interests lie in the area of empirical asset pricing including trading strategies and market anomalies. He has been invited to present his work in multiple conferences including the American Finance Association annual meeting and the Goldman Sachs Asia Conference. Yang is also interested in corporate finance related studies with a focus on corporate governance.

Shivam Ghosh completed his PhD in Theoretical Physics at Cornell University in 2014 after obtaining a BA and MA in Natural Sciences (Physics) at the Cavendish Laboratory, University of Cambridge, UK. Shivam is now a Director Research at JPMorgan, London specialising in building tradable systematic risk premia strategies in credit. Previously, he was a fixed income portfolio manager at the Chief Investment Office, JPMorgan in New York. Shivam has published papers in top peer-reviewed journals including *Physical Review B* and *Physical Review Letters*.

Mo Haghbin, CFA, CAIA, serves as the Chief Operating Officer for the Invesco Investment Solutions team, which develops and manages customized multi-asset investment strategies. Mo Haghbin joined Invesco in 2019 when the firm combined with OppenheimerFunds, where he served as senior vice president and head of product for the Beta Solutions business. At OppenheimerFunds, he led the firm's entrance into factor investing, having launched a suite of equity factor strategies including one of the industry's first dynamic multi-factor ETFs.

Lei Ji is a senior quantitative analyst at Bloomberg. Before joining Bloomberg in 2015, Lei was a global quantitative portfolio manager at Tudor Investments. Prior to that, he was a founding member of the quantitative hedge fund GSB Podium Advisors. Before that, Lei served as a systematic proprietary trader at Bank of America, Merrill Lynch and Lehman Brothers. Lei received a PhD in Financial Economics from the University of Pennsylvania.

Robert Kosowski is Professor of Finance at Imperial College Business School and Head of Quantitative Research at Unigestion. He is also a research fellow at the Centre for Economic Policy Research (CEPR) and an associate member of the Oxford-Man Institute of Quantitative Finance at Oxford University. Robert is on the editorial board of the *Journal of Alternative Investments* and the *Journal of Systematic Investing*. Robert holds a BA (First Class Honours) and MA in Economics from Trinity College, Cambridge University (UK), and a MSc in Economics and PhD from the London School of Economics (UK).

Oh Kang Kwon is a senior lecturer in the Discipline of Finance at The University of Sydney. He holds a PhD in pure mathematics from MIT and a PhD in quantitative finance from UTS. He has held academic positions at various universities in Australia, and has also worked in the role of senior quantitative analyst with all four major banks in Australia. His research interests include quantitative finance, computational finance and derivative pricing. He has recently been working in the areas of corporate finance and strategy analysis

Muhammad Masood is a researcher in the iShares Product Development team at BlackRock. He is involved in the research and design of smart beta, ESG, thematic and fixed income ETF products. His work on smart beta include single- and multi-factor strategies that are constructed in a systematic manner. Muhammad holds a master's degree in Finance and Economics from the Warwick Business School and an undergraduate degree from the American University of Paris.

Jose Menchero serves as Head of Portfolio Analytics Research at Bloomberg. Prior to joining Bloomberg, he was Head of Equity Factor Model Research at MSCI Barra. Jose has roughly 40 finance publications in leading practitioner journals. Before entering finance, Jose was Professor of Physics at the University of Rio de Janeiro, Brazil. Jose holds a PhD in theoretical physics from the University of California at Berkeley and is a CFA Charterholder

Byoung-Kyu Min's primary research interests are in the areas of asset pricing and investments. His research aims to understand determinants of cross-sectional differences in stock returns, predictability of stock returns and its implication for trading strategies, and how financial markets and the macroeconomy (such as business cycles) are related and their implications for asset pricing. He proposes multiple explanations for financial market anomalies, including risk-based explanation, lottery preference and sentiment.

Vadim Moroz holds a PhD in Applied Mathematics from Northwestern University. He was co-founder and co-PM for the $1.3b UBS O'Connor Global Equity Long/Short strategy. Subsequently he managed high-frequency trading strategies at Tudor Capital,

Citadel and JP Morgan. He is presently working as a Data Scientist supporting investment management functions. He was a co-recipient of the INQUIRE Europe prize for best research in 2003.

Anders Petterson began his career at JP Morgan and went on to set up ArtTactic in 2001. ArtTactic has become one of the leading art market research companies and a pioneer in using crowd-sourcing techniques for gathering and processing intelligence on the art market. Anders Pettersson is a regular lecturer on the art market for universities and businesses. He is also a founding board member of Professional Advisors to the International Art Market (www.paiam.org)

Christopher Polk is Department Head and Professor of Finance at the London School of Economics. He has published extensively in leading academic journals, receiving numerous professional awards including paper of the year twice at the *Journal of Financial Economics*. Polk has advised asset managers, central banks and regulators on topics related to his research. He holds a PhD in finance from the University of Chicago where he studied under 2013 Nobel Laureate Eugene Fama.

Katharina Schwaiger, PhD, is an investment researcher within the Factor-based Strategies Group at BlackRock. Her research responsibilities include macro and style factor research. Prior to joining BlackRock she worked as a Financial Engineer in the City of London, as a Quantitative Researcher at a London-based hedge fund and as a Lecturer at the London School of Economics. She received a BSc in Financial Mathematics and a PhD in Operational Research from Brunel University.

Louis Scott is the founder of Kiema Advisors, a research consultancy. He is currently working with Dr Cavaglia on research projects for Invesco. He was previously Head of FactSet's Risk and Quantitative Research. Louis has managed a global equities hedge fund at Old Mutual Asset Managers, US equities at Citigroup and currencies at PanAgora – each at over 1 billion in AUM. He is a member of the London Quant Group's management committee.

Nandini Srivastava completed her PhD at the Faculty of Economics, University of Cambridge in 2013 is now a Director at JPMorgan Asset Management, London, UK. She focuses on asset allocation research where her role involves quantitatively analysing the impact of macroeconomic and financial factors across a range of asset classes and developing strategies based on these for portfolio allocation. Nandini has been a referee at a number of academic journals and continues to publish in academic forums.

Christopher (Chris) Tinker is a founding partner of Libra Investment Services, an FCA regulated independent equity market research company. With more than 30-years experience in the Financial Services industry, he began his career as an Equity markets economist in the City of London before moving onto research roles in fixed income, credit, currency and money markets and as an international equity strategist in London and Hong Kong. He has a BA in Economics from Manchester University.

Danny Yeung is a lecturer at the UTS Business School. Danny's research interests concentrate in the area of investment, with particular emphasis on the impact of ambiguity and emotions on investor decision making, mutual fund performance and the impact of institutional investors in capital markets. He has published widely in international peer-reviewed journals including the *Journal of Banking and Finance*, the *Pacific-Basin Finance Journal* and the *International Review of Financial Analysis*.

Oliver J. Williams began his career at Boston Consulting Group, then worked in derivatives at JPMorgan and Credit Suisse before joining Markham Rae as partner, portfolio manager and lead architect/developer in systematic trading. He holds an MA in computer science and management studies, MPhil and PhD in financial economics from Cambridge University and MSc in mathematics from Birkbeck. He has co-authored several articles in investment management and is co-inventor of a software patent in network analytics

William E. (Bill) Zieff is Director at Northfield Information Services and was Managing Director, Chief Investment Officer and Portfolio Manager of Global Structured Products Group at Evergreen Investment Management Company. Previously, Bill was the Managing Director and Co-Chief Investment Officer of the Global Asset Allocation Group at Putnam Investments. He also served as a Director of Asset Allocation at Grantham, Mayo, Van Otterloo. Bill obtained a BSc in Economics and Mathematics from Brown University and an MBA from the Harvard Business School

Introduction

There are numerous definitions of momentum, which as an investment strategy is likely to be of great antiquity. Some authors credit Richard Driehaus with popularising the strategy, indeed he was described in the American Association of Individual Investors as the father of momentum investing. The concept of relative strength investing motivated Jegadeesh and Titman (1993) to analyse the momentum effect. Their basic finding showed that 'winners' (the top decile of performers) over the past three to twelve months continue to outperform 'losers' (the bottom decile) over the subsequent three to twelve months.

This return persistence phenomenon was initially documented through the following process. First, stocks are sorted each month into deciles based on performance over the past J months (the 'formation' or 'ranking' period). We might typically think of 'Portfolio 10' being that of the winning stocks, 'Portfolio 9' containing the second-best decile of performers, and so on down to 'Portfolio 1' containing the worst performing decile of stocks, 'losers'.[1]

The momentum strategy involves holding ranked portfolios of the chosen stocks for the next K months (the 'holding' period). The version advocated by Jegadeesh and Titman involves taking a long position in the winners and shorting the losing stocks. Documented profits for an overlapping version of the strategy were estimated to be about 12% per year when J and K range between 6 and 12 months. In the opinion of Jegadeesh and Titman (2011, p. 494) the sustained and consistent magnitude of returns to a momentum strategy are too large to be explained by risk factors.

However, as this book will show, there are many different definitions of momentum, and we are attempting to understand them all within a common framework. Focusing on the above definition of momentum, it is clear that we can vary both the formation period and the holding period. There may also be an intervening period between of length M between the two. Such a strategy could be defined by the triplet (J, M, K), where the usual convention is for periods of J, K and M months. However, any unit of time could be used. Further immediate generalisations could move from deciles to n-tiles. One standard convention is that the portfolio is self-financing. This means that if you were to hold $100 million in winning stocks, you would short $100 million in losers.

---

[1]This is the ordering used in Ken French's data, although Jegadeesh and Titman (1993) use reverse number ordering.

I.1. HOW HAS MOMENTUM PERFORMED?

In Figure I.1, we present returns of value-weighted portfolios of US stocks using data from Ken French's website.[2] The figure plots returns for two overlapping time periods, (i) the full sample period from January 1927 until November 2019, and (ii) the 30 year period from December 1989 until November 2019. The latter period coincides approximately with the timeframe since early versions of Jegadeesh and Titman's work became available.

To construct portfolios based on prior returns, stocks are sorted based on prior returns from month −12 to month −2. A month's return is withheld, and returns are reported on a monthly basis, which are then annualised and averaged. Using the above notation, we consider this an $(11, 1, 1)$ strategy. We note that as we move from Losers

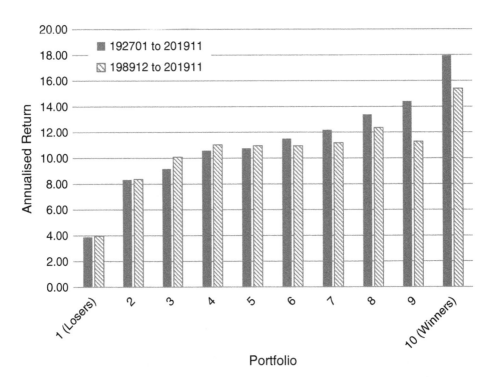

FIGURE I.1 Annualised monthly returns for value-weighted portfolios formed based on prior returns (11,1,1). The figure reports the average returns to portfolios sorted on prior returns (where portfolio 1 is the portfolio of worst performing stocks, and portfolio 10 is the portfolio of best-performing stocks) over the period from January 1927 to November 2019 (solid bars) and December 1989 to November 2019 (striped shading).

---

[2]https://mba.tuck.dartmouth.edu/pages/faculty/ken.french/data_library.html. We thank Ken French for making the data available for researchers. The data used specifically is '10 Portfolios Formed on Momentum', with value weighted monthly returns.

TABLE I.1 Moments and percentiles of momentum portfolio returns over the period January 1927 to November 2019. Panel A reports average, standard deviations, skewness and the ratio of average returns to standard deviation (Ave/Std. Dev) for each of the 10 portfolios plus the momentum 'Winner – Loser' portfolio. Panel B reports monthly portfolio return percentiles for each of the portfolios.

Portfolio	1 (Losers)	2	3	4	5	6	7	8	9	10 (Winners)	Winner – Loser
Panel A: Moments (Annualised)											
Average	3.87	8.33	9.17	10.57	10.75	11.49	12.17	13.38	14.39	17.94	14.07
Std. Dev	33.63	27.69	24.01	21.84	20.42	19.94	18.85	18.34	19.29	22.31	26.93
Skewness	0.50	0.51	0.42	0.42	0.36	0.23	0.02	0.00	−0.09	−0.14	−0.67
Ave/Std. Dev	0.11	0.30	0.38	0.48	0.53	0.58	0.65	0.73	0.75	0.80	0.52
Panel B: Percentiles of Monthly Returns											
1st	−25.51	−21.16	−19.45	−17.55	−15.64	−14.49	−14.07	−13.78	−15.57	−16.79	−20.07
5th	−13.79	−9.94	−8.52	−7.99	−7.94	−7.85	−7.36	−7.15	−7.76	−9.05	−10.05
25th	−3.85	−2.75	−2.01	−1.95	−1.76	−1.64	−1.77	−1.71	−1.62	−1.96	−1.78
50th	0.25	0.62	0.86	1.06	1.14	1.29	1.32	1.34	1.61	1.79	1.51
75th	4.13	3.98	3.74	3.70	3.68	3.86	3.93	3.97	4.44	5.50	5.05
95th	13.59	10.83	9.67	9.06	8.32	7.87	8.51	8.71	8.60	10.48	11.57
99th	25.99	23.55	17.29	13.82	13.47	15.01	14.68	13.97	14.34	17.07	20.03

(Portfolio 1) to Winners (Portfolio 10), the returns are virtually monotonically increasing in the ranking decile. The difference between the full sample period (solid shading in Figure I.1) and the 30-year period from the end of 1989 (striped columns in Figure I.1) appears to mainly be driven by the weakened performance of winners. Annual return to winners have declined by around 2.5% per annum (from approximately 18 to 15% pa), while losers have averaged approximately 4% per annum over both sample periods. Interestingly, there has been substantial 'flattening' of the portfolio returns in the remaining deciles. In the recent 30-year period, Portfolios 2 through 9 have averaged between 8 and 12% per annum.

Even though the spread between prior winners and prior losers has declined, this would be seen by practitioners as evidence of a good strategy, and would act as useful marketing material if one wanted to sell momentum investing.

Table I.1 presents statistics relating to momentum portfolio returns over the period from January 1927 until November 2019. Panel A reports the annualised average, standard deviation, skewness, and ratio of mean to standard deviation for each of the 10 value-weighted portfolios, as well as the 'Winner–Loser' portfolio constructed from the returns to decile 10 less the returns to decile 1 within each month. The returns to the momentum portfolio are evident from the fact that Winners have outperformed Losers over this full sample period by around 14% per annum.

The higher returns to the Winner portfolio do not appear to be a result of a higher level of risk, at least when measured according to standard deviations. Of the set of 10 decile-sorted portfolios, Losers exhibited by far the highest standard deviation (33.63% per annum). Notably, the Winner portfolio has substantially lower risk (22.31% per annum) despite earning a 14% higher return.

There is a monotonically increasing trend of the ratio of average returns to standard deviations across the ten portfolios, a measure of the risk-return trade-off. Historically, prior losers have represented not only the worst performing stocks on a returns basis, but also a risk-adjusted basis.

Arguably, standard deviation does not provide a full understanding of the level of risk of momentum portfolio. Panel A of Table I.1 reports the skewness of the returns to each portfolio; a portfolio exhibiting positive skewness can be considered to hold potential upside relative to downside. In contrast, a portfolio with negative skewness may experience large crashes from time to time. It is evident that skewness decreases as we move from the losing portfolio to winning portfolio; the momentum portfolio itself exhibits a large degree of negative skewness. Thus, the positive returns to a momentum strategy on average come with a drawback; occasional periods of large negative returns.

In Panel B of Table I.1, percentiles of monthly returns to each of the portfolios are reported. At the 50th percentile (median) returns, we observe median momentum profits of 1.51% per month. The other percentiles of the distribution provide some useful insights into the return distribution. For example, the loser portfolio exhibited a 5th percentile monthly return of −13.79%. In other words, in only 5% (or 56 of 1,115) months did the loser portfolio exhibit a monthly return below −13.79%. From this, we can see that the loser portfolio tends to perform poorly up to the third quartile. However, at the 95th percentile, the loser portfolio is the best performing portfolio; in 5% of cases the loser portfolio earns more than 13.59% in a month. Where losing stocks are short sold, the large potential upside for losers results in a poor performance for the overall momentum portfolio.

These percentiles may be useful from a risk-management perspective (for example in Value at Risk calculations), but do not necessarily paint the complete picture. Indeed, the distribution of returns appear rather symmetric across the portfolio deciles (rather than skewed in either direction).

Figure I.2 is a histogram of the value-weighted returns to the momentum (Winner–Loser) portfolio over the period from January 1927 to November 2019. The distribution of returns is unimodal, centred around a slightly positive mean, consistent with the results reported in the final column of Table I.1. The left-tail of the distribution shows the occurrence of extreme losses that have occurred. On eight occasions, the momentum portfolio has exhibited in excess of 30% within a single month, which would not have been identified even with the analysis of the 1st percentile in Table I.1. Two of these eight extreme losses to momentum arose during the recovery from the credit crisis in 2009, driven by extreme rebounding from the loser portfolio. Much of the recent research on momentum has focused on these so-called 'momentum crashes' (Daniel and Moskowitz, 2016), and scaling momentum strategies with market volatility is one of the practical considerations discussed in this book.

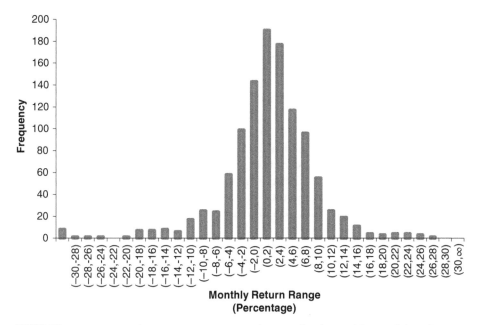

FIGURE I.2 Histogram of momentum returns, value-weighted monthly portfolio of Winners minus Losers, January 1927 to November 2019.

I.2. WHY SHOULD WE WRITE THIS BOOK?

There are many existing books on momentum, and an extraordinarily large number of academic and practitioner articles detailing stylised empirical facts about momentum. However, most of the books are of a certain variety; they often describe momentum as a near-mystical formula that will lead to unimaginable riches for those persons who purchase the book.

Our book takes a different approach. We think of the many variations of momentum as a family of strategies and we outline their strengths and weaknesses. Readers of this book may well build better investment strategies as a consequence; we do not guarantee massive enhancements in personal wealth.

On the academic side, there is a surprising absence in the analysis of momentum returns. Much of the analysis of momentum as we have defined it above (formally cross-sectional momentum) is actually analysed in terms of relative strength strategies. Whilst these are similar in some respects, they are sufficiently different as to have quite unalike statistical properties. This is a point we refer to in numerous places. We provide such an analysis. Often this involves some quite challenging mathematics. We do not restrict the scope of our analysis to equity; we have great interest in the application of momentum investing to alternative assets (for example, art). We also are interested in the construction of momentum portfolios (for example, Exchange-Traded Funds [ETFs]) for any asset class (such as credit). Furthermore, we do not exclude empirical analysis of momentum returns from this book and have included a number of recent studies that address key issues.

Given the voluminous literature on the subject, we raise the question as to who carries out the investment strategy described above, where there is zero net exposure. The answer is: virtually nobody. Firstly, institutional investors would often be prohibited from taking such extreme short positions. Retail investors would find it difficult for reasons of cost and availability of products. Versions that one finds in the market consist of products with names like '130/30' funds. One version of a momentum 130/30 fund would involve holding US$100 million in the benchmark/index, US$30 million in winning stocks, and shorting US$30 million in losers. The momentum component would have to lose a large amount of money for the 130/30 fund to fail. If we move beyond equity, then using futures contracts, it is actually quite straightforward to build and hold momentum strategies. For the example of the 130/30 strategy, in principle a market index futures contract could be shorted to leave only the momentum exposure (i.e. a 30/30 strategy). A second version might consider 130 momentum long and 30 momentum short. Clearly this is riskier relative to benchmark.

We have not described the actual investment strategy in too much detail as yet. Implicitly, for the stocks chosen in the long portfolio, we are holding them in equal money amounts. However, we may wish to hold them in proportion to their capitalisation (i.e. in value-weighted terms). Practitioners might take a different approach. They could take the constituent names in the list of winners as a universe of stocks and feed it through an optimiser, subject to various investment constraints. Optimisers are typically software programs that maximise expected returns for a given level of risk; returns are usually linear in portfolio weights while risk is quadratic, and such software is readily available commercially. The investment constraints might relate to turnover, maximum position in a given stock or industry, liquidity, and so on. They might do the same, separately, for the loser portfolio. They might even attempt the more sophisticated exercise of feeding both these portfolios (the winner and the loser portfolios) through the optimiser. Each of these exercises will lead to different patterns of returns. Unless we specify otherwise, we will typically assume equal weighting.

Who might find momentum investing attractive? From an academic perspective, the answer to this question can be couched in an expected utility framework. Conventional theory argues that investors like first- and third-moments, and dislike second- and fourth-moments of returns. This means that they like higher expected returns and skewness, and dislike variance and kurtosis. One of the points that the book will address is the distributional properties of momentum returns. A common feature of the long-short portfolio returns is that they typically have positive expected returns and negative skewness. Because its net exposure is zero, we can rescale our holdings to adjust the volatility, but this will of course also scale the expected return. From the above discussion, an investor who would like momentum would be fairly tolerant of negative skewness relative to expected returns. Academic evidence and practitioner experience records phenomena known as 'momentum crashes' (e.g. Daniel and Moskowitz, 2016). Whilst these are consistent with negative skewness in momentum returns, this is also related to the tail behaviour of assets, about which much has been written. It is a goal in momentum research to design momentum strategies that are relatively robust to momentum crashes.

Behavioural finance takes quite a different perspective from expected utility theory. Here, momentum arguably arises as individual investors prefer to sell winning, but not losing stocks (e.g. Grinblatt and Han, 2005). Consider the case of a winning stock. The tendency to sell a winning stock and lock in a capital gain delays price movement to the stocks' fundamental value, which could be different from the current price. The preference to not sell losing stocks similarly slows down the impact of negative news. This type of behaviour can be modelled (as in Grinblatt and Han, 2005) to explain the dynamics of momentum returns.

We can also consider the link between financial bubbles and momentum investing. This question has been addressed in various ways. One particular reference of interest is by Condorelli (2018), who argues that a high level of price momentum (as measured by the relative strength index) typically precedes a price bubble. Practitioners share this view. In 2018 John Hughman wrote the following in *Investors Chronicle*: [3]

> *If, as some academics suggest, widespread momentum investing also leads to the formation of bubbles, then the dangers are further pronounced – as well as investors attracted generally to rising share prices, the identification of momentum as a key factor in returns has led to the creation of numerous smart-beta exchange traded funds (ETFs) based on the strategy, sucking in billions of dollars. When the party stops, huge numbers of investors will be looking to exit extremely overbought positions simultaneously, and optimism will swing quickly towards pessimism . . .*

I.3. UBIQUITY

Many academic papers have been published demonstrating the presence of good momentum returns in virtually all countries, across most asset classes. Rouwenhorst (1998), among others, finds evidence of a momentum effect in many European countries. Asness, Moskowitz and Pedersen (2013) demonstrate the pervasiveness of momentum effects in international equities and other asset classes, such as government bonds, commodity futures and foreign currencies. Practitioners sometimes remark that 'momentum does not work in Japan', and there are quite likely to be other examples, but this ubiquity raises many questions.

Firstly, does momentum always work because of the human condition (i.e. is it driven by behavioural forces)? Alternatively, is it a consequence of the statistical structure of the data? Of course the second explanation may not be in contradiction with the first. That is to say, in the determination of the dynamic price process, human behaviour will enter into both demand and supply, and therefore into the model parameters.

Secondly, what refinements are possible in momentum portfolios? The classical approach of purchasing winners and selling losers is straightforward, and perhaps therein lies part of the appeal. A portfolio manager might use this overlay in their portfolio construction, and then aim to identify certain winners that are more likely to persist upwards, or losers that are less likely to rebound in the near term. For instance,

---

[3]The article is available at https://www.investorschronicle.co.uk/the-editor/2018/10/12/momentum-misery/

Sagi and Seasholes (2007) discuss the fact that firms with high market-to-book ratios (e.g. 'growth' stocks) exhibit higher momentum returns. They argue that a firm's growth options lead to increased return autocorrelation. Similarly, firms with relatively low costs of goods sold, and firms with high revenue volatility are shown by Sagi and Seahsoles (2007) to generate higher momentum returns. Combining momentum with fundamental analysis, market conditions or other strategies may yield obvious benefits.

I.4. SUMMARY OF CHAPTERS

We now present a summary of the contribution of each chapter.

In Chapter 1, Andrew Grant reviews the strong links between behavioural finance and momentum. This analysis can be understood at various levels; its link with Chapter 2, which contains discussion on the mathematics of momentum, is that, inter alia, it is providing psychological explanations as to why there is autocorrelation in the data. However, perhaps a more interesting viewpoint is what one might call agent-based modelling. The focus is on individuals and the psychology of their decision-making. One might argue that this approach is a part of micro-economics and certainly it moves away from *homo economicus*, that tired individual largely discredited by the global financial crisis. The chapter provides a thorough review of the literature and an analysis of more recent empirical work that is written about momentum and behavioural finance.

In Chapter 2, Steve Satchell presents an overview of the strategies that fall under the broad remit of momentum strategies. In preparation for the rather demanding later chapters where more detail is indulged, he presents relatively simple mathematical arguments that allow us to understand the mathematical properties of the various strategies. Much of the returns to momentum can be understood within this chapter in terms of two stories. The first is that momentum is riskier and therefore has a higher expected return; what we might call an efficient market-consistent explanation. The second version is that momentum is capturing the presence of autocorrelation in the data and is, essentially, acting as a robust forecasting tool.

Chapter 3, by Nick Baltas and Robert Kosowski, is motivated by studies of the impact of frictions on asset prices. The focus here is on time-series momentum. The authors examine the effect of key components of time-series momentum on turnover and performance. They show that more efficient volatility estimation and price-trend detection can significantly reduce portfolio turnover by more than one-third, without causing statistically significant performance. One is reassured to note that there is a payoff to improved econometrics; whilst this should be true, it is often not evident in applied research.

The authors offer a novel implementation of the strategy that incorporates the pairwise signed correlations by means of a dynamic leverage mechanism. The correlation-adjusted variant outperforms the naïve implementation of the strategy and the outperformance is more pronounced in the post-2008 period. Finally, using a transaction costs model for futures-based strategies that separates costs into roll-over and rebalancing costs, they show that their findings remain robust to the inclusion of transaction costs.

This approach takes many recent academic developments but implements them in a practical context. Such an implementation reflects the strong academic and commercial accomplishments of the authors.

In Chapter 4, Jose Menchero and Lei Ji take a detailed approach to the implementation of cross-sectional momentum strategies. This chapter, in addition to its intrinsic research interest, would make an excellent basis for lecturers to better graduate students as the mathematics is very neatly expressed and accessible. Furthermore, there are a great number of practical tips for those starting in their professional lives as Quants. The authors include an analysis of cross-sectional momentum in the context of risk and diversification. These are more traditional quantitative virtues, sometimes neglected in the excitement of behavioural revelation.

We are delighted to have a contribution from Dan diBartolomeo and Bill Zieff who have been industry professionals, as well as researchers, for many years. They provide us with Chapter 5, where they focus on what one might describe as the 'practical causes' of momentum and do this by analysing different asset classes. As a first example, one might consider the impact of smoothing on real-estate data. This can be modelled by a first-order autocorrelation process leading to momentum characteristics in the observed data, but not necessarily in the true underlying process. One might think of this as phantom momentum. They also note the link between how equity has behaved and the subsequent return to the same firm's corporate bonds, usually referred to as cross-asset momentum. They posit that this link can be modelled by applications of the Merton/ Leland approach to corporate finance, which essentially treats equity and bonds as derivative contracts on the underlying value of the firm. Other applications they discuss are the role of tax-harvesting around the end of the fiscal year and its ability to explain the January effect, the dependence of sovereign credit-worthiness on the nation's underlying assets and productive processes and much more. In fact, this chapter, in common with several others, could easily have become a book in its own right.

Chapter 6 has been written by Katharina Schwaiger and Muhammad Massood who both research on ETFs for Blackrock. They present expert analysis of momentum ETFs and discuss their merits as investment products for both retail and institutional investors. They also discuss construction methodology and also ETF AUM. We are pleased to learn that Blackrock and Invesco are the two largest momentum ETF providers, both of whom have contributed to this book. Finally, there is a useful analysis of performance and factor exposures, which clarifies the nature of these products and to paraphrase their conclusion dispels many of the myths of the limitations of such products.

Chapter 7 by Oliver Williams examines momentum strategies as implemented by Commodity Trading Advisers (CTAs). CTAs are defined to be managers/investors who invest at asset class level and who use derivatives. However, as Oliver points out, the term's more common usage refers to investors who are trend-followers. Such investors tend to have a high degree of mathematical sophistication although, at least in the UK, it is by no means clear that the return to these high levels of human capital have been positive as CTA investing as a whole has had some fairly volatile returns. The chapter reviews a number of strategies and provides some careful analysis of their properties. This is an area where there are very few analytical results and the ones provided here make a welcome addition to the literature. One of the technical problems that is addressed here is that the portfolio weights used in these strategies are often themselves stochastic so that simple returns become quadratic in random variables and second moments become quartic in random variables. The consequences for deriving expressions for such simple quantities as the Sharpe ratio, for example, are dire in general but the author looks at a number of tractable cases.

Chapter 8 by Anders Petterson and Oliver J. Williams, is 'Overreaction and Faint Praise: Short-Term Momentum in Contemporary Art', which as a title can only be described as gnomic. This is, essentially, an analysis of how momentum arises in art prices. Here, the informational structure is less complex than, say, an exchange-traded equity environment. The authors, who have acknowledged expertise in this field, are able to analyse the principal players and informational announcements that cause price movements. There is much to take away from this chapter for financial market analysts, as many of the processes that are clear to see in the art market – such as the predictive consequences of expert opinion – may well occur in financial environments, but are much harder to detect. Williams and Petterson also note that professional pressures inhibit outright condemnation in the art market, hence the title's mention of faint praise. One equivalent in equity and bond markets can be seen in emerging markets where advice by an analyst to investors to exit a market in a country with a dictatorial leadership can lead to personal threats against the analyst involved, but faint praise does not apply in that setting.

In Chapter 9, Yang Gao explores the interaction between momentum and volatility. The literature has shown that momentum strategies using volatility as the conditioning variable strongly outperform plain momentum strategies by reporting higher alphas, increased Sharpe ratios, and improved (positive) skewness. He reviews the various volatility-managed momentum strategies that are proposed in the academic literature presenting empirical analysis. He further examines how volatility conditioning manages momentum risk and discusses the role of volatility in momentum risk management. It is interesting to observe that the academic practices described in this chapter have been taken up by some well-informed Quant managers.

In Chapter 10, Andrew Grant, Oh Kang Kwon and Steve Satchell investigate the link between the nature of portfolio sorting techniques and the statistical properties of portfolio returns. They identify two families of sorting methodologies, namely independent and sequential sorting. Independent sorts are those typically used in the academic literature, each attribute of the asset is sorted independently of the other attributes. Sequential sorts are more commonly employed by practitioners. A decision is made as to which attribute is sorted first, then conditional on that sort, a second attribute is ranked and so forth. There is an importance in the order of sorting in sequential sorting; typically, the most important attribute is sorted first, followed by the second-most important and so on.

Whilst cross-sectional momentum is a one-dimensional sort, based on ranking returns in the formation period, many of the strategies available on Ken French's website (a leading data source) involve multi-dimensional sorts (e.g. on size and past returns). In this sense, these strategies are an extension of momentum strategies. These portfolios are called by the authors *Fama-French Portfolios*. They derive expressions for the distributions and moments of Fama-French Portfolios, which will of course include cross-sectional momentum as a special case. Although these formulae are rather complicated, they nevertheless inform as to why momentum returns are generically non-normal, even when the original asset returns are assumed to be multivariate normal

Chapter 11, by Stefano Cavaglia, Vadim Moroz and Louis Scott, looks at a family of strategies within which one could argue, momentum might sit. This family of strategies is the broad class of overlay portfolios, momentum being an example, which can be used judiciously to enhance returns in many contexts; especially in the case of global asset allocation portfolios. The authors bring decades of high-level experience to this topic and provide sound practical advice to institutional investors without weakening the intellectual quality of their arguments.

In Chapter 12, Christopher Polk, Mo Haghbin and Alessio de Longis explore how asset pricing factors, such as value, growth and momentum, exhibit different sensitivities to macroeconomic risks. The authors construct dynamic factor rotation strategies following leading economic indicator and global risk appetite signals. Momentum is shown to exhibit higher beta with respect to cash flows during economic expansions, and lower beta in contractions. Among other strategies, value and size have relatively large cash-flow betas while low-volatility and quality have relatively low cash-flow betas. The authors demonstrate that significant improvements to portfolio returns can be realised via factor rotation. Using FTSE 1000 Russell Factor Indexes, Polk, Haghbin and de Longis show that a dynamic (long-only) strategy that rotates into high cash-flow beta strategies during predicted expansions and into low cash-flow beta strategies during slowdowns or contractions outperforms a static strategy by about 2% per annum over the period 1989–2018. Given the low transaction costs incurred, these returns are economically significant, and provide useful insight into the application of leading indicators into a factor rotation strategy.

In Chapter 13, Ron Bird, Kevin Gao and Danny Yeung examine whether momentum trading strategies can be implemented profitably, in a practical (rather than statistical) sense. They analyse both cross-sectional and time-series momentum strategies, covering equity markets in 24 countries, with multiple combinations of formation and holding periods (3, 6, 9 and 12 months). Alternatives for return measurement (buy and hold abnormal returns, and cumulative abnormal returns) and portfolio weighting schemes are considered, presenting a total of 192 combinations of both time-series and cross-sectional momentum in each country. After using appropriate measures to estimate transaction costs, the authors aim to draw some conclusions on the implementation of a battery of momentum tests. Firstly, they find that time series momentum works well, with the best of the 192 implementations generating positive returns in 19 countries after transaction costs. In comparison, cross-sectional momentum generates positive and significant returns in 20 countries after transaction costs. The authors then discuss characteristics of the portfolios and the relative merits of a time-series versus cross-sectional momentum in a practical, global setting.

In Chapter 14, Shivam Ghosh, Steve Satchell and Nandini Srivastava examine whether artificial intelligence methods are applicable to momentum investing, and describe various arcane methods in machine learning and how to apply them. This is a very readable chapter that helps explain what is to many readers a black box. Random forests, neural networks and other techniques are carefully explained. The results applied to time-series momentum look very promising. There is also some discussion on what artificial intelligence might actually mean. It is quite clear that one could produce an edited volume on this topic alone.

Most informed momentum investors are concerned about strategy timing. Whilst value investing is known to benefit from periods of falling interest rates and economic expansion, less is known about momentum investing and the wider economy.

Chapter 15, by Byoung-Kyu Min, addresses the topic of momentum and business cycles. Recent empirical literature shows that *time variation* in the profitability of momentum strategies is critical to understanding the source of momentum. This chapter presents direct evidence that momentum strategies deliver significantly negative profits during 'bad' economic states in which investors demand the highest market risk premium, suggesting that momentum strategies expose investors to greater downside risk. It also reviews the literature investing whether momentum profits are related to various economic states, including business cycles, market state and investor sentiment, and discusses explanations for these findings.

In Chapter 16, Chris Tinker argues that momentum is a risk factor rather than an anomaly and can be treated as a factor at the individual stock level. The justification for this approach comes from an interesting agent-based model of the market with trend followers and fundamentalists engaged in a price-setting equilibrium which is observed, and acted upon, by the momentum trader. Agent-based models, whilst frequently used in an academic context, are rarely, if ever, utilised by practitioners and we have felt that they have a great deal of potential for informing financial management.

Chapter 17, by Stefano Cavaglia, Louis Scott, Kenneth Blay and Vincent de Martel, examines the use of commodity factors in a portfolio context, aimed at customising a portfolio for specific clients. The authors aim to determine whether the inclusion of a factor overlay, such as momentum, carry, or value, or a combination of these factors, can improve outcomes for aspiring retirees, compared to the simple approach of investing in a portfolio of equities or bonds. Using a bootstrap simulation approach, allowing for alternative scenarios for the performance of the assets and factors, the authors find that the incorporation of a single factor overlay enhances the likelihood of an aspiring retiree achieving their goal. A combination of factors in the overlay provides additional diversification benefits. The authors argue that due to time diversification over the business cycle, factor overlays enhance accumulated wealth over a long time-horizon. Moreover, there appears to be benefits of utilising a factor overlay in both the 'transition' to retirement phase, and the decumulation phase.

REFERENCES

Asness, C.S., Moskowitz, T.J. and Pedersen, L.H. (2013) Value and momentum everywhere. *Journal of Finance*, **68**, 929–985.

Condorelli, S. (2018) Price momentum and the 1719–20 bubbles: A method to compare and interpret booms and crashes in asset markets. Working Paper, Centre for Global Studies, Bern University.

Daniel, K. and Moskowitz, T.J. (2016) Momentum crashes. *Journal of Financial Economics*, **122**, 221–247.

Grinblatt, M. and Han, B. (2005) Prospect theory, mental accounting, and momentum. *Journal of Financial Economics*, **78**, 311–339.

Jegadeesh, N. and Titman, S. (1993) Returns to buying winners and selling losers: Implications for market efficiency. *Journal of Finance*, **48**, 65–91.

Jegadeesh, N., and Titman, S. (2011) Momentum. *Annual Review of Financial Economics*, **3**, 493–509.

Rouwenhorst, K.G. (1998) International momentum strategies. *Journal of Finance*, **53**, 267–284.

Sagi, J.S. and Seasholes, M.S. (2007) Firm-specific attributes and the cross-section of momentum. *Journal of Financial Economics*, **84**, 389–434.

Market Momentum

CHAPTER 1

Behavioural Finance and Momentum

ANDREW GRANT

1.1 INTRODUCTION

Behavioural finance aims to provide explanations for observed market phenomena outside the neo-classical view of financial markets. Proponents of efficient markets may argue that behaviourally biased traders will not affect prices in equilibrium, as they will make incorrect decisions and be driven out by rational arbitrageurs. Indeed, the 'no free lunch' or 'economic' approach to market efficiency suggests that, by and large, it should be difficult to profit from a simple trading strategy – such as momentum – without access to superior information. Under an alternative definition of market efficiency (e.g. Fama, 1970) asset prices should reflect fundamental value. A limits-to-arbitrage (Shleifer and Vishny, 1997) viewpoint contends that asset prices may not necessarily trade at fundamental levels because rational arbitrageurs face constraints that make it costly or risky to correct mispricing.

To provide an example, equity analysts play a crucial role in information production, and stocks without sufficient focus from market participants may not be correctly valued. Similarly, stocks with other trading frictions, such as low liquidity, high levels of idiosyncratic volatility, low levels of institutional investor ownership (making short-selling difficult) and high levels of valuation uncertainty (growth or technology stocks) are likely to experience stronger trading frictions. Indeed, much of the evidence shows that momentum is particularly prevalent among stocks that are subject to these trading frictions.

Other chapters in this book seek to explain momentum as a purely statistical phenomenon, for example, arising from autocorrelation, or statistical properties of sorted portfolios. In this chapter, we take a contrasting view, seeking to understand why the return processes may hold these properties to begin with. Behavioural finance helps provide insight into momentum returns by considering psychological explanations, including overreaction, underreaction, slow information diffusion, anchoring and sentiment. A common theme among these phenomena is that mispricing – or a temporary deviation from fundamental value – spurs momentum.

The approach taken in this chapter is not that momentum is solely driven by behavioural biases, but that a consideration of investor psychology may help to partially explain the prevalence of momentum profits or may be used to enhance the returns of a momentum strategy. A strict definition of what is categorised as 'behavioural finance' is not imposed, but I will consider issues that appear to be underpinned by either non-traditional investor preferences or beliefs, retail vs. institutional investors, or market-wide sentiment.

The behavioural approach mainly gained traction with the advent of the three-factor model of Fama and French (1996), and the noted inability of beta, firm size, and the value effect to explain short-term momentum returns. Following this, three highly influential models utilising various aspects of investor psychology were developed by Barberis, Shleifer and Vishny (1998), Daniel, Hirshleifer and Subrahmanyam (1998), and Hong and Stein (1999). These models have formed the basis for many empirical tests of momentum from the behavioural finance perspective. This chapter first examines the failure of risk-based explanations, then considers some of the predictions from the theoretical behavioural models, and then explores some empirical tests relating to these models.

One of the key insights of the Hong and Stein (1999) model is that slow information diffusion among market participants can lead to momentum. Empirical work by Hong, Lim and Stein (2000) has demonstrated momentum is particularly prevalent in small stocks, for example, supporting this notion. Chen and Lu (2017) use option markets, which are likely to be the choice of trading venue for informed traders, to infer the speed of information diffusion. They find that momentum is more pronounced in stocks that exhibit large changes in option implied volatility (where information is likely incorporated in the option but not stock market) exhibit stronger momentum than those that exhibit small changes in implied volatility.

The return pattern or price path taken by a stock, including large price movements – or an absence of large price movements – has also been shown to lead to continuation (momentum in returns), as investors may not efficiently impound information into stock prices. Recent evidence (Atilgan et al., 2020) suggests this is particularly an issue for downward price movements, where investors appear to underreact to potential risks of further price declines.

Closely related to momentum, the 52-Week High effect, as first documented by George and Hwang (2004), states that firms trading near the highest point over the previous year tend to continue upwards. Grinblatt and Han (2005) suggested that stocks near the 52-Week high are in the domain of gains for investors with prospect-theoretic preferences. Preference to sell winners (also known as the disposition effect) induces uninformed selling pressure by such investors, which consequently may lead to return continuation, supporting the contention of underreaction or delayed reaction driving momentum.

The issue of who 'creates' momentum can also be considered a behavioural issue. Unlike most other asset pricing anomalies, institutional investors appear to trade 'with' momentum strategies (Edelen, Ince and Kadlec, 2016). The counterparties, therefore are likely to be individual investors, selling out winners before price increases (as per the predictions of Grinblatt and Han, 2005), and similarly buying losers. While in the short-term, Kaniel, Saar and Titman (2008) argue that individuals are compensated for providing liquidity, at longer horizons, they tend to underperform institutional investors.

The final issue that is addressed in this chapter relates to investor sentiment. Recent attempts to operationalise behavioural finance have led to the construction of 'top-down' sentiment indices (e.g. Baker and Wurgler, 2006). The main idea of a sentiment index is to capture excessive mispricing (either over- or under-valuation), by combining factors such as IPO first-day returns that likely indicate excessive optimism or pessimism. Stocks that are difficult to value or difficult to arbitrage are most likely to load positively on a sentiment index. Momentum strategies appear to be mainly profitable during periods of high sentiment, but not during periods of low sentiment (e.g. Stambaugh, Yu and Yan, 2012; Antoniou, Doukas and Subrahmanyam, 2013). This is arguably driven by investor preferences but may also be driven by liquidity.

1.2 THE FAILURE OF RISK-BASED EXPLANATIONS

The inability to explain the returns to a momentum strategy was described as the 'prime embarrassment' of the three-factor model by Fama and French (1996, p. 75). After all, the value (High book-to-market value Minus Low book-to market value [HML]) factor in a three-factor model predicts that losing stocks will outperform winning stocks, consistent with long-term reversals but not with short-term momentum. Later, Carhart (1997) added the UMD (Up minus Down) factor to assess whether a portfolio's returns are consistent with those of a momentum strategy.

Other researchers have attempted to provide a risk-based explanation for momentum returns. Chordia and Shivakumar (2002), Cooper, Gutierrez and Hameed (2004) and Stivers and Sun (2010) all argue that momentum profits are strong during macroeconomic expansions but largely non-existent during recessions. Chapter 15 of this book discusses issues of momentum across the business cycle in more detail. Daniel and Moskowitz (2016) demonstrate that momentum performed particularly poorly during the recovery period from the financial crisis and argue that negative skewness in momentum returns (small positive returns most of the time, but occasional large crashes) is consistent with risk-based explanation. While I will not argue that these viewpoints are invalid, the fact that momentum has been a profitable trading strategy fairly consistently indicates that alternative (i.e. behavioural) explanations may be necessary to complete the picture.

1.3 BEHAVIOURAL MODELS OF MOMENTUM

Several key studies (e.g. Jegadeesh and Titman, 1993; Fama and French, 1996; Grundy and Martin, 2001; Griffin, Ji, and Martin, 2003) failed to find a satisfactory risk-based explanation for momentum profits, which led to the development of behavioural-based explanations. Three studies are considered seminal works in this area; Barberis et al. (1998, henceforth BSV), Daniel et al. (1998, henceforth DHS), and Hong and Stein (1999, henceforth HS). Each of these seeks to explain the existence of both momentum returns at a 6–12 month horizon, followed by the subsequent long-term reversals (as in DeBondt and Thaler, 1985). The seminal works of BSV, DHS and HS warrant a brief review. Many of the empirical studies of momentum have built upon components of one or more of the models.

While not specifically focused on momentum, the model of DeLong, Shleifer, Summers and Waldmann (1990) seeks to explain 'noise-trader risk' and why asset prices might deviate from fundamental values. They argue that the correlated trades of individuals, combined with constraints faced by institutional investors (either due to time horizons or risk aversion) means that stock prices can deviate from fundamental values for an extended period of time.

In short, informed arbitrageurs might understand that a stock is overvalued, but can be unwilling (or unable) to rectify the situation. Betting against sentiment-prone investors is costly (short-selling stocks is more expensive than buying stocks) and risky (it is difficult to tell when corrections to market prices will occur). These effects are exacerbated for hard-to-value stocks, or those that are particularly likely to be prone to sentiment-based mispricing.

It is from this background that Shleifer and Vishny (1997) developed the concept of 'limits to arbitrage'. Under this paradigm, stocks are generally priced at efficient levels, but may deviate from fundamental values based on the inability or unwillingness of arbitrageurs to correct the mispricing. The motivation for momentum from the behavioural finance perspective is that limits to arbitrage either cause overreaction or underreaction in prices. Disparity in information, combined with variations in transaction costs, may lead stocks away from fundamental value without immediate correction, leading to momentum opportunities.

In the BSV model, investors react to earnings surprises, with the belief that earnings are generated under one of two regimes. In the first regime, earnings are mean-reverting; a positive earnings surprise is likely to be followed by a negative earnings surprise and vice-versa. In the second regime, earnings move in a trend, a positive surprise is more likely to follow a positive surprise. The representative investor in the model uses Bayes' rule to update their beliefs about which earnings regime is in place. However, the investor exhibits tendencies of representativeness, leading them to reduce their reliance on probability laws in some circumstances, and conservatism, causing them to update their beliefs slowly in other situations. The result is underreaction to earnings surprises when investors believe earnings to be mean reverting, but a streak of positive or negative earnings has occurred. When the streak of consecutive earnings is broken by a change in sign, the representative investor overreacts, leading to large reversal.

The DHS model similarly produces momentum and reversals, but relies on a different structure to the BSV model. The representative investor is overconfident, meaning that they believe too strongly in the precision of their own private information. The investor also suffers from biased self-attribution, whereby they attribute too much significance to signals that confirm their prior belief – making them more overconfident – while downplaying or ignoring the impact of signals that contradict their prior belief.

The DHS model has two main features. The first relates to the price response function related to a private signal. If the signal is positive, informed investors immediately overreact and the security becomes overpriced. Because of biased self-attribution, the overpricing will be exacerbated with the arrival of public information thereafter. However, as public information continues to arrive, investors will see that their initial overconfidence was unjustified, leading to a correction phase. Thus, overconfidence drives momentum in the initial phase, and the longer-term reversal as investors are slow to realise their mistakes.

The second feature of the DHS model focuses on how the market responds to public or private information. In the model, investors may underreact to private information about a firm without the subsequent drift occurring. This would be the case when public information is known to all parties simultaneously. However, if there is a more gradual release of information (information either diffuses more slowly or is 'leaked' to some parties) then the underreaction by investors may result in price drift.

The HS model does not rely on specific behavioural elements, such as overconfidence or representativeness. It instead utilises the interaction between two groups of traders; 'newswatchers' who trade on the basis of public information (without worrying about past prices) and 'technical analysts' who trade on the basis of trends without consideration of fundamental values. Crucially to the model, newswatchers base their trades on information that diffuses slowly through the trading population. This leads to underreaction by newswatchers to fundamental information, which subsequently drives price drift. This drift is noticed by technical analysts who then follow the trend and push prices even further in their initial direction, leading to overpricing. Newswatchers re-enter the market to correct the overpricing, leading to a cycle of overreaction and reversals.

Shefrin (2008) argues that there are issues with each of these models. For example, both the BSV and DHS models seek to explain returns to the cross-section of stocks, yet feature only one security. In the HS model, newswatchers are inconsistent in how they develop trading plans. They trade with technical analysts on the upward-moving phase, and again on the downward-moving phase. Under the DHS model, investors overreact to private (rather than public) information, although Odean (1998b) argues that investors are more likely, in practice, to overreact to salient, attention-grabbing events. Similarly, the momentum build-up arises in the DHS model from an investor purchasing additional amounts of shares they already hold, as public information confirms the results of an investor's private signal. However, Odean (1999) finds, to the contrary, that investors prefer to purchase additional amounts of stocks that have declined, rather than increased, in price. In fact, due to the disposition effect (Shefrin and Statman, 1985), investors prefer to sell winning stocks and hold on to losers.

1.4 SLOW INFORMATION DIFFUSION

A critical aspect of the theoretical studies is that information diffuses slowly throughout the economy, at least to some participants. This may come from erroneous adjustments of beliefs (in the case of the BSV model, due to representativeness or conservatism) or through different reactions to public and private information (in the case of the DHS model).

Empirically, Hong et al. (2000) sorted stocks in terms of the expected speed of information diffusion. Using both firm size and analyst coverage as proxies, they find that momentum profits are, in fact, stronger in smaller stocks (excluding the very smallest size quintile, where liquidity issues dominate) and stocks with lower analyst coverage. In the tercile of stocks with the lowest expected analyst coverage (i.e. analyst coverage adjusted for firm size), momentum profits are 60% greater than for the tercile of stocks with high expected analyst coverage. Moreover, the effect of analyst coverage appears to be most pronounced in losing stocks; low-coverage stocks 'seem to react more sluggishly to bad news' (Hong et al., 2000, p. 268). The authors postulate that this is because, in the absence of outside analyst coverage, managers have the incentive to disseminate positive news (through increased disclosures) but not to broadcast negative news. Analyst coverage appears to help extract negative news from management.

A more recent theoretical contribution to the literature by Andrei and Cujean (2017) explores the role of information diffusion in generating patterns of momentum and reversal. Using a (non-behavioural) rational expectations framework, Andrei and Cujean (2017) derive an information arrival 'shape' that is necessary for momentum to arise, namely that private information must flow at an increasing rate. Using 'word-of-mouth' communication as an example, the authors demonstrate that it is possible for returns to continue (and subsequently reverse), even if traders are rational and risk-averse, and not subject to behavioural biases.

Chen and Lu (2017) use options markets to dynamically examine the speed of information diffusion in stocks. The logic is as follows: informed traders may prefer to use option rather than stock markets for reasons such as leverage or short sales constraints. Thus, for stocks with slow information diffusion, some traders will prefer to trade in the options markets to realise superior information. The authors utilise the information in options markets to identify those stocks with information yet to be incorporated into prices. Specifically, for winner stocks, if we also observe an increase in the price of call options, informed options traders believe that there is information to be impounded into the price. The same logic applies to loser stocks: informed option traders can sell call options if they think that the negative information associated with those loser stocks has not been fully incorporated in the stock prices.

Chen and Lu (2017) implement an enhanced momentum strategy based on information diffusion speed, taking a long position in winners with the largest growth in call option implied volatility, and shorting loser stocks with the largest drop in call option volatility. The strategy generates a return of 1.78% per month over the 1996–2011 period, whereas the return to a standard momentum strategy earned around 0.80% per month over the same period.

1.5 PATTERNS IN INFORMATION ARRIVAL

A recent strand of literature focuses on the type of information arrival that leads to underreaction or overreaction by investors. Following a large price change, for example, investors may need to drastically update their beliefs regarding expected future realisations of the stock. Cognitive psychology, from which much of behavioural finance is based, demonstrates that individuals are inefficient at updating probabilistic beliefs in response to new information (e.g. Camerer, 1987; Hogarth and Einhorn, 1992). Numerous experiments conducted by (among others) Tversky and Kahneman (1982) demonstrate that relative to the correct 'Bayesian' updating of beliefs, individuals tend to neglect or underweight the base-rate (prior probability) and overweight the new information (likelihood). This effect is systematic, and in aggregate implies that there would be an overreaction to large price movements, and underreaction to small price movements.

Consistent with the base-rate neglect hypothesis, Da, Gurun and Warachka (2014) argue that momentum arises because investors underreact to information arriving in small bits much like the proverbial 'frog in a pan' that does not notice as the water is slowly brought to boil. Da et al. (2014) show that stocks where past returns accumulate gradually exhibit more momentum than stocks where returns are accumulated in a lumpy fashion.

Savor (2012), following related work by Pritamani and Singal (2001) and Chan (2003), compares the price reaction to major price movements that are likely information-driven or non-information driven (a liquidity or sentiment shock, for example) where an accompanying analyst report is used as a proxy for information. Savor (2012) finds that information-driven price events are followed by a continuation in returns and non-information driven price events are followed by reversals. He argues that investors underreact to news about fundamentals but overreact to other shocks.

Chen, Yu and Wang (2018) examine the 'acceleration' of momentum profits, where the acceleration measure is calculated by regressing previous daily prices during the formation period on an ordinal time variable and the square of the ordinal time variable for each stock. The coefficient of the quadratic term ('convexity') measures the level of acceleration of returns. The authors find that buying winners with positive convexity (where returns are 'speeding up' during the formation period) and selling losers with negative convexity (accelerating downwards) outperforms a standard momentum strategy by 51.5% (0.95% per month vs. 0.63% per month). The authors attribute the performance differential to naïve extrapolation and also present an overreaction explanation.

Jiang and Zhu (2017) explore whether the market underreacts to large, discontinuous price movements ('jumps'). Using jumps in stock prices as a proxy for large information shocks, the authors provide evidence consistent with short-term underreaction in the US equity market. Jiang and Zhu construct a metric based on cumulative jump returns, and sorting on this they find that a strategy that takes a long position stocks with positive lagged (one- or three-month) jump returns and a short position in stocks with negative lagged jump returns earns significantly positive returns over the next one to three months.

In a thorough study, Atilgan et al. (2020) demonstrate that there is a significant negative cross-sectional relationship between expected downside risk and stock returns. Using proxies including Value at Risk (VaR) and Expected Shortfall (ES), the authors argue that investors underestimate the persistence in downside risk, and hence overprice stocks that have exhibited large recent losses. A value-weighted portfolio that takes a long position in stocks with low VaR and short in stocks with high VaR earns a one-month return of 0.78% per month in US equities over the period from 1962–2014. This return is not explained by a Fama-French five-factor model, nor illiquidity, coskewness or downside beta factors. Instead, it appears to be (i) most pronounced in stocks with low institutional ownership, suggesting a relationship with limits to arbitrage, (ii) in stocks with high retail investor participation and subject to low investor attention, and (iii) present and persistent across countries over the period 1988 to 2014. Atilgan et al. (2020) suggest that, unlike with upward movements, 'the elusive nature of left-tail risk makes the investors' attention constraints more likely to be binding', and argue that negative price shocks are harder to interpret by average investors.

1.6 THE 52-WEEK HIGH AND CAPITAL GAINS OVERHANG

The price path taken by a stock may also influence the speed of reaction to news. Some investors prefer to sell stocks that have increased in value from a reference point, such as the purchase price. This tendency, known as the disposition effect (Odean, 1998a), leads to an increase in the frequency of non-informational sales, as investors prefer to realise gains, rather than losses.

The 52-week high, a salient figure from both financial press and brokerage information, is a statistic showing the highest price a stock has traded at in the past year. Investors may compare the current stock price to the 52-week high and decide that the 52-week high represents a useful signal to sell, perhaps as they are anchored to the 52-week high. As an investor who is holding a stock near the 52-week high is also likely in the domain of gains, both biases work together to dampen the impact of good news on stocks near the 52-week high.

The examination of the 52-week high effect by George and Hwang (2004) demonstrates this point, finding that stocks trading close to the 52-week high exhibit returns of a similar magnitude to those of the classical Jegadeesh and Titman (1993) momentum strategies. George and Hwang (2004) demonstrate that the components of portfolios selected using the standard momentum approach differs from that of the 52-week high approach, thus the 52-week high effect does not strictly replicate the effect of constructing momentum profits based on past returns.

Future work has sought to shed light on the 52-week high effect. For example, Bhootra and Hur (2013) construct a related measure called 'recency rate', indicating the number of days since a stock has been at its 52-week high. Stocks that have recently been at their 52-week high tend to outperform stocks that have been at their 52-week highs in the distant past, by approximately 0.70% per month. Moreover, a strategy combining 'nearness' and 'recency' to the 52-week high outperforms one examining nearness alone, suggesting that the effects work in combination.

The 52-week high effect is closely related to the 'capital gains overhang' (CGO) effect described in Grinblatt and Han (2005). To explain CGO, suppose that, in aggregate, investors hold prospect theory preferences, and, due to mental accounting, they separate winning stocks from losing stocks based on price changes from a reference price (typically chosen as the purchase price). Under prospect theory, investors are risk-averse in the domain of winners and risk-seeking in the domain of losses, which leads them to prefer to sell winners and hold onto losers. Grinblatt and Han (2005) argue that momentum arises from the systematic preference by investors to sell winners over losers, which impedes price movements to fundamental values. Consider, for instance, a stock in the domain of gains. As investors rush to lock in gains based on price increases from the purchase price – a non-informational reason – it delays the shift upwards to funda-mental value. In the domain of losses, a reluctance to sell losing stocks can delay the impounding of information into stock prices, leading to a downward continuation.

The key measure constructed by Grinblatt and Han (2005), the CGO, is constructed using an estimate of the mean reference price distribution. The mean of the reference point distribution is estimated as the weighted moving average of past prices, with weights determined by turnover rates. The weight associated with a given price is the turnover rate probability that a share was last purchased a particular past date, and has not been traded since that time. Thus, 'winners' will have a current price exceeding the reference price, and 'losers' will have a current price below the reference price. The per-centage difference between the current price, and the reference point is defined as the capital gains overhang, so winners exhibit positive CGO, and losers exhibit negative CGO. Weighting the reference price by past turnover rates means that actively traded stocks tend to exhibit lower absolute levels of CGO, as more recent prices exhibit a higher weight in the calculation of the reference point.

In a study of common shares traded on the NYSE and AMEX exchanges between 1962 and 1996 (with NASDAQ firms excluded because of the dealer structure) Grinblatt and Han (2005) regress the week t return of stock k on past cumulative returns (1 month, 12 months and 36 months), market capitalisation, average weekly turnover and the capital gains overhang. They find that the inclusion of CGO as an explanatory variable renders the 12-month past return insignificant, suggesting that momentum is broadly driven by the tendency of investors to realise gains rather than losses.

One of the advantages of the CGO metric, compared with other measures requiring the use of reference prices is that it simply employs past price and volume data in its construction. Other studies of individual investor behaviour (e.g. Odean, 1998a; Feng and Seasholes, 2005) examine whether investors prefer to realise gains rather than losses relative to some reference point (usually taken as the purchase price). Of course, the actual reference price (or price that investors internally use to decide whether they are in the domain of gains or losses) used by investors cannot be determined. Moreover, whether investors prefer to purely seek gains or losses without regard to their size is debatable (Ben-David and Hirshleifer, 2012), and the CGO may provide a more robust measure of aggregate profit-taking trade motivations.

Some other studies have used the principles of Grinblatt and Han's (2005) CGO with further refinements to test asset pricing implications. For example, Goetzmann and Massa (2008) examine whether the proportion of disposition-prone investors holding a stock dampens returns and volatility. They find that the disposition effect is not only present at the stock level, but aggregates to the market level, creating a common factor that disperses stock returns.

Hur, Pritamani and Sharma (2010), in order to refine the CGO metric, weigh past prices by the proportion of share turnover that is attributable to individual investors. Even though they use a proxy metric, such as the proportion of shares not owned by institutions (residual institutional ownership), or the proportion of trades in a stock below \$10,000 dollars (e.g. Hvidkjaer, 2008; Barber, Odean and Zhu, 2009), to iden-tify turnover due to individuals, they find that a CGO-momentum trading strategy can be enhanced by focusing on stocks with a higher level of individual trading activity. In a (6, 1, 6) momentum strategy, for instance, in their sample of US stocks from 1980 to

2005, Hur et al. (2010) find that winners with high individual presence (based on CGO measures constructed from residual institutional ownership) outperform winners with low individual presence by 0.206% per month. Across the same time frame, losers with low individual presence underperform losers with high individual presence by 0.351% per month. The general result taken from Hur et al. (2010) is that CGO measures constructed based on residual institutional ownership appear to identify persistent losers, while CGO measures constructed using small-trade turnover help identify persistent winners.

Hur and Singh (2019) further investigate the relationship between capital gains overhang and the anchoring effect of the 52-week high. While they represent similar behaviour from individuals, Hur and Singh (2019) note that the realisation of capital gains is an effect driven by existing shareholders, while the 52-week high is relevant also to prospective shareholders. The two effects appear to be complementary; in their empirical study covering US stocks over the period 1963 to 2013, Hur and Singh (2019) find that there is a correlation of 0.56 between the two measures. The authors perform double sorts (into terciles) on the CGO and 52-week high measures, finding that stocks with high levels of capital gains overhang and close to the 52-week high return earn an average of 1.07% per month (in the six months following portfolio formation) more than stocks with low levels of CGO and far from the 52-week high. This compares favourably with decile-sorted portfolios of the 52-week high alone (which earn around 0.82% per month) but similarly to stocks sorted on CGO (which earn around 1.10% per month). In further tests, the authors find that the strategy can be enhanced by considering portfolios with high residual institutional investor ownership, low analyst coverage and high levels of illiquidity.

1.7 INSTITUTIONAL TRADING AND MOMENTUM PROFITS

Edelen et al. (2016) explore the role of institutional investors in contributing to stock market anomalies. They argue that institutions tend to make trades against the prescribed direction of most anomalies, doing so because institutional investors would prefer to hold stocks of 'good companies' with the aim of outperforming a benchmark. As it is the overvalued (i.e. the prescribed short leg) of most anomaly portfolios that institutions buy, the authors argue that institutions are not sophisticated arbitrageurs (contrary to Shleifer and Vishny's [1997] limits to arbitrage theory). Rather, they appear to be affected by institutional constraints, or agency biases.

For example, institutions prefer to load up on growth (low book-to-market) rather than value (high book-to-market) stocks and fail to earn the value premium. Only two of the anomalies of the seven they consider (gross profitability and momentum) lead to institutions increasing their holdings in the long-leg portfolio (winner stocks in the case of momentum). Thus, institutions actually contribute to the existence of momentum profits by purchasing recent winners, leading to continued upwards drift.

Vayanos and Woolley (2013) build a theoretical model in which momentum arises as a consequence of delegated portfolio management. Their argument is as follows.

Suppose that a negative shock hits the fundamental value of some assets. Investment funds holding these assets realise low returns, triggering outflows by investors who update negatively about the efficiency of the managers running these funds. As a consequence of the outflows, funds sell assets they own, and this further depresses the prices of the assets hit by the original shock. Momentum arises if the outflows are gradual, and if they trigger a gradual price decline and a drop in expected returns. Reversal arises because outflows push prices below fundamental values, and so expected returns eventually rise.

Baltzer, Jank and Smajlbegovic (2019) examine a unique data set (covering the period 2005–2012) from the German centralised registry (the Securities Holding Statistics, SHS), which reports trades made by all financial institutions and their customers at the quarterly level. Customers' securities holdings are further broken down by investor sector and customer nationality. The authors form winner and loser portfolios (top and bottom 30% of stocks based on the prior four-quarter performance), with a one-month holding period. A momentum strategy works well in Germany over the time period covered.

Examining ownership changes over the holding period, it is found that foreign investors (who are mainly institutions) tend to be momentum traders (similar to the result found in Grinblatt and Keloharju's [2000] study of Finnish investors), mainly through their sales of losing stocks than purchasing winners. Mutual funds are also momentum traders, but to a lower extent.

Domestic households, therefore, tend to be the counterparty to these trades, with a tendency to act as contrarian investors, buying losers and selling winners. Household contrarian trading has been demonstrated in a number of other studies, although typically at shorter horizons. Perhaps the most well-known example is from Kaniel et al. (2008), who demonstrate that individuals earn short-term (one month) returns from providing liquidity by selling to institutional investors. Barrot, Kaniel and Sraer (2016) demonstrate, using a large sample of French investors, that individuals are contrarians at the daily, weekly, and monthly horizons. Due to their holding periods, they argue that individuals do not actually earn the liquidity premiums from Kaniel et al. (2008), as the profits reverse after two months, and individuals tend to have longer holding periods.

1.8   SENTIMENT AND MOMENTUM

Sentiment, as broadly defined in the behavioural finance literature, is any non-fundamental factor that affects asset prices. Baker and Stein (2004) note that, if it is cheaper to open long positions than to enter into a short position, as it is in practice, the willingness of individual investors to trade represents a form of sentiment. Overconfidence, as in the DHS model, leads biased investors to over-weight their own private signal of security values. In the presence of short-sales constraints, such investors are willing to purchase, but not short stocks. In Baker and Stein's (2004) model, therefore, liquidity provides a measure of investor sentiment. Empirically, Baker and Stein (2004) find low future returns follow shocks to a turnover-based measure of liquidity, supporting the case.

Baker and Wurgler (2006), explaining that sentiment is difficult to measure, construct an index of investor sentiment, based on principal components analysis on proxy measures of optimism and pessimism, such as the average first-day returns on IPOs, and the share of equity issuance over total security issuance. Baker and Wurgler (2006) demonstrate that small, young, currently unprofitable, potentially profitable stocks, with high value uncertainty (such as an internet start-up in the dot-com bubble of the late 1990s) are particularly prone to sentiment risk. By definition, sentiment is mean-reverting, and so such stocks are overpriced in periods of high market-wide sentiment and under-priced in periods of low sentiment.

The linkage between sentiment and momentum was first discussed in Antoniou et al. (2013). Using a fundamental adjusted version of the Michigan Consumer Sentiment Index as a proxy for market-wide sentiment, Antoniou et al. (2013) find that momentum profits are only reliably positive in periods of high sentiment. The authors argue that, due to cognitive dissonance, losing stocks continue to underperform in periods of high-sentiment as investors pay less attention to the disappointing performance of losing stocks in overly optimistic periods. In US equities over the period 1967–2008, they find that a (6, 1, 6) momentum strategy earns a significant monthly return of 2.00% following optimistic periods, and an insignificant 0.34% per month following pessimistic periods. The sentiment momentum effects appear stronger for small capitalisation stocks, suggesting that the influence of sentiment is more pronounced in smaller companies that are harder to value and hence more prone to subjective evaluations. Further analysis of order flow in Antoniou et al. (2013) shows that small investors are slow to sell losers during optimistic periods, which prolongs the pricing of bad news, and supports the argument of cognitive dissonance.

Stambaugh et al. (2012) argue that overpricing (due to short-sales constraints) is more prevalent than underpricing, and demonstrate that several anomalies, including momentum, are profitable following periods of high sentiment. Stambaugh et al. (2012) show that the short leg of momentum earns significantly negative returns of −1.24% per month following periods of high sentiment (where 'high' sentiment is above the median level of Baker and Wurgler [2006]) in US equities over the period 1965–2007. However, the short-leg returns (positive) 0.34% per month following periods of low sentiment. Overall, they find that momentum is nearly twice as profitable following periods of high sentiment (2.03% per month) against low sentiment (1.09% per month).

1.9   DISCUSSION

Momentum has proven to be a profitable strategy, for the most part, for an extended period of time. Investor psychology has been used to explain a portion of the persistence of the phenomenon in the presence of seemingly efficient markets.

From the evidence presented in this chapter, the speed of information diffusion plays a key role in prices deviating from fundamental values, which is when momentum appears to arise. The reasons that information diffuses slowly may not be entirely driven by investor sentiment or behavioural biases. It does, however, seem likely that incorporating features such as individual investor trading around price anchors such as the 52-week high, the level of a sentiment index or the path taken by a stock to achieve its status as a winner or loser can help to enhance a momentum strategy.

As markets continue to evolve, some of the behavioural biases of individuals in equity trading may be attenuated. For example, with a larger focus on passive trading through ETFs (exchange traded funds), some of the noise is likely to be removed from individual stocks. Information may diffuse more quickly, and momentum may become more of a short-term strategy. Specifically, it should be possible to use the behavioural information discussed in this chapter by adjusting the magnitude of the formation period in a dynamic fashion.

REFERENCES

Andrei, D. and Cujean, J. 2017. Information percolation, momentum, and reversal, *Journal of Financial Economics*, **123**, 617–645.

Antoniou, C., Doukas, J.A., and Subrahmanyam, A. 2013. Cognitive dissonance, sentiment, and momentum. *Journal of Financial and Quantitative Analysis*, **48**, 245–275.

Atilgan, Y., Bali, T.G., Demirtas, K.O., and Gunaydin, A.D. 2020. Left-tail momentum: Under-reaction to bad news, costly arbitrage and equity returns. *Journal of Financial Economics*, **135**(3), 725–753.

Baker, M. and Stein, J. C. 2004. Market liquidity as a sentiment indicator. *Journal of Financial Markets*, 7, 271–299.

Baker, M. and Wurgler, J. 2006. Investor sentiment and the cross-section of stock returns. *Journal of Finance*, **61**, 1645–1680.

Baltzer, M., Jank, S., and Smajlbegovic, E. 2019. Who makes momentum? *Journal of Financial Markets*, **42**, 56–74.

Barber, B.M., Odean, T., and Zhu, N. 2009. Do retail trades move markets? *Review of Financial Studies*, 22, 151–186.

Barberis, N., Shleifer, A., and Vishny, R. 1998. A model of investor sentiment. *Journal of Financial Economics*, **49**, 307–43

Barrot, J.-N., Kaniel, R., and Sraer, D. 2016. Are retail traders compensated for providing liquidity? *Journal of Financial Economics*, **120**, 146–168.

Ben-David, I. and Hirshleifer, D. 2012. Are investors really reluctant to realize their losses? Trading responses to past returns and the disposition effect. *Review of Financial Studies*, 25, 2485–2532.

Bhootra, A. and Hur, J. 2013. The timing of 52-week high price and momentum. *Journal of Banking and Finance*, 37, 3773–3782

Camerer, C.F. 1987. Do biases in probability judgments matter in markets? Experimental evidence. *American Economic Review*, 77, 981–997.

Carhart, M.M. 1997. On persistence in mutual fund returns, *Journal of Finance*, **52**, 57–82.

Chan, W.S. 2003. Stock price reaction to news and no-news: Drift and reversal after headlines. *Journal of Financial Economics*, 70, 223–260.

Chen, L.-W., Yu, H.-S., and Wang, W.-K. 2018. Evolution of historical prices in momentum investing. *Journal of Financial Markets*, 37, 120–135.

Chen, Z. and Lu, A. 2017. Slow diffusion of information and price momentum in stocks: Evidence from options markets. *Journal of Banking and Finance*, 75, 98–108.

Chordia, T. and Shivakumar, L. 2002. Momentum, business cycle and time-varying expected returns. *Journal of Finance*, 57, 985–1019.

Cooper, M., Gutierrez, R., and Hameed, A. 2004. Market states and momentum. *Journal of Finance*, **59**, 1345–1365

Da, Z., Gurun, U., and Warachka, M. 2014. Frog in the pan: continuous information and momentum. *Review of Financial Studies*, 27, 2171–2218.

Daniel, K., Hirshleifer, D., and Subrahmanyam, A. 1998. Investor psychology and security market under and overreactions. *Journal of Finance*, 53, 1839–86.

Daniel, K. and Moskowitz, T.J. 2016. Momentum crashes. *Journal of Financial Economics*, **122**, 221–247.

DeBondt, W.F.M. and Thaler, R.H. 1985. Does the stock market overreact? *Journal of Finance*, **40**, 793–805.

DeLong, J.B., Shleifer, A., Summers, L.H. and Waldmann R.J. 1990. Noise trader risk in financial markets, *Journal of Political Economy*, **98**, 703–738.

Edelen, R.M., Ince, O.S. and Kadlec, G.B. 2016. Institutional investors and stock return anomalies, *Journal of Financial Economics*, **119**, 472–488.

Fama, E.F. 1970. Efficient capital markets: A review of theory and empirical work. *Journal of Finance*, **25**, 383–417.

Fama, E. and French, K. 1996. Multifactor explanations of asset pricing anomalies. *Journal of Financial Economics*, **51**, 55–84.

Feng, L. and Seasholes, M.S. 2005. Do investor sophistication and trading experience eliminate behavioral biases in financial markets? *Review of Finance*, **9**, 305–351.

George, T.J. and Hwang, C.-Y. 2004. The 52-week high and momentum investing. *Journal of Finance*, **59**, 2145–2176.

Goetzmann, W.M. and Massa, M. 2008. Disposition matters: Volume, volatility, and the price impact of a behavioral bias. *Journal of Portfolio Management*, **34**, 103–125.

Griffin, J.M., Ji, X., and Martin, J.S. 2003. Momentum investing and business cycle risk: Evidence from pole to pole. *Journal of Finance*, **58**, 2515–2547.

Grinblatt, M. and Han, B. 2005. Prospect theory, mental accounting, and momentum. *Journal of Financial Economics*, **78**, 311–339.

Grinblatt, M. and Keloharju, M. 2000. The investment behavior and performance of various investor types: a study of Finland's unique data set. *Journal of Financial Economics*, **55**, 43–67.

Grundy, B.D. and Martin, J.S. 2001. Understanding the nature of risks and the sources of rewards to momentum investing. *Review of Financial Studies*, **14**, 29–78.

Hogarth, R.M. and Einhorn, H.J. 1992. Order effects in belief updating: The belief-adjustment model. *Cognitive Psychology*, **24**, 1–55.

Hong, H., Lim, T., and Stein, J.C. 2000. Bad news travels slowly: Size, analyst coverage, and the profitability of momentum strategies, *Journal of Finance*, **55**, 265–295.

Hong, H. and Stein, J. 1999. A unified theory of underreaction, momentum trading and overreaction in asset markets. *Journal of Finance*, **54**, 2143–2184.

Hur, J., Pritamani, M., and Sharma, V. 2010. Momentum and the disposition effect: The role of individual investors. *Financial Management*, **39**, 1155–1176.

Hur, J. and Singh, V. 2019. How do disposition effect and anchoring bias interact to impact momentum in stock returns? *Journal of Empirical Finance*, **53**, 238–256.

Hvidkjaer, S. 2008. Small trades and the cross-section of stock returns. *Review of Financial Studies*, **21**, 1123–1151.

Jegadeesh, N. and Titman, S. 1993. Returns to buying winners and selling losers: Implications for stock market efficiency. *Journal of Finance*, **48**, 65–91.

Jiang, G.J. and Zhu, K.X. 2017. Information shocks and short-term market underreaction. *Journal of Financial Economics*, **124**, 43–64.

Kaniel, R., Saar, G., and Titman, S. 2008. Individual investor trading and stock returns. *Journal of Finance*, **63**, 273–310.

Odean, T. 1998a. Are investors reluctant to realize their losses? *Journal of Finance*, **53**, 1775–1798.

Odean, T. 1998b. Volume, volatility, price and profit when all traders are above average. *Journal of Finance*, **53**, 1887–1934.

Odean, T. 1999. Do investors trade too much? *American Economic Review*, **89**, 1279–1298.

Pritamani, M. and Singal, V. 2001. Return predictability following large price changes and information releases. *Journal of Banking and Finance*, **25**, 631–656.

Savor, P.G. 2012. Stock returns after major price shocks: The impact of information. *Journal of Financial Economics*, **106**, 635–659.

Shefrin, H. 2008. *A Behavioral Approach to Asset Pricing* (2e), Amsterdam: Elsevier.

Shefrin, H. and Statman, M. 1985. The disposition to sell winners too soon and ride losers too long: Theory and evidence. *Journal of Finance*, **40**, 777–790.

Stambaugh, R.F., Yu, J., and Yuan, Y. 2012. The short of it: Investor sentiment and anomalies. *Journal of Financial Economics*, **104**, 288–302.

Shleifer, A. and Vishny, R.W. 1997. The limits of arbitrage. *Journal of Finance*, **52**, 35–55.

Stivers, C. and Sun, L. 2010. Cross-sectional return dispersion and time-variation in value and momentum premia. *Journal of Financial and Quantitative Analysis*, **45**, 987–1014

Tversky A. and Kahneman D. 1982. Evidential impact of base-rates. In: Kahneman, D., Slovic, P., and Tversky, A., editors. *Judgment under Uncertainty: Heuristics and Biases*. Cambridge: Cambridge University Press, 153–160.

Vayanos, D. and Woolley, P. 2013. An institutional theory of momentum and reversal. *Review of Financial Studies*, **26**, 1087–1145.

CHAPTER 2

A Taxonomy of Momentum Strategies

STEVE SATCHELL

2.1 INTRODUCTION

In this chapter we look at different momentum strategies and their properties. Many of the empirical results of momentum strategies can be seen to result from the structure of return processes and the design of the strategy. The usual explanation for momentum out-performance is based on behavioural arguments, which are discussed in Chapter 1. The approach in this chapter is an alternative to the behavioural approach but the two approaches are not incompatible. From a statistical perspective, behavioural analysis will determine the magnitude of model parameters along with, in some cases, the specification of the model itself. Taking these as given, the statistical analysis will determine the properties of the strategy returns. In this form of analysis, we are interested in population moments such as the mean, variance, skewness and kurtosis but also the time-series moments of the momentum process. Where possible, determining the probability density function of momentum returns is of great interest. Usually this is either intractable or very complicated and we will resort to looking at cases where we assume there are a small number of assets. An alternative would be to resort to Monte Carlo methods to arrive at numerical calculations. Either approach will give us new insights into the behaviour of momentum returns and justify the necessary mathematical investment required.

Momentum-based investment strategies typically rely on there being some form of persistence, either a trend or autocorrelation in underlying asset returns, over successive holding periods. For example, cross-sectional momentum portfolios take long positions in the past outperformers and short positions in the past underperformers, with the belief that their relative performances will carry over to the next period. Since variations of such strategies usually result in small positive returns, they have found widespread popularity and adoption by practitioners. Despite the level of interest in momentum-based strategies, there is surprisingly little research that provides theoretical explanations for the observed properties of their returns.

We shall define various momentum strategies firstly investigating relative-strength (RS) portfolios in Section 2.2. We then look at research by Moskowitz, Ooi and Pedersen (2012) on time-series momentum (TSM) in Section 2.3. We investigate cross-sectional momentum (CSM) drawing upon theoretical results from Kwon and Satchell (2018) in Section 2.4. Finally, in Section 2.5, we discuss research on momentum spillovers, also known as cross-asset momentum. There are similarities in design and structure in these various strategies and some authors have used some of the simpler strategies, such as RS to mimic the properties of the more complex ones.

2.2   RELATIVE STRENGTH STRATEGIES

Let $r_{i,t+1}$ be the rate of return from holding asset i from time t to time $t+1$. We shall assume a universe of N assets so $i = 1, \ldots, N$. Next, let the vector of all asset rates of return at time $t+1$ be denoted by R_{t+1}. This N by 1 vector has ith element $r_{i,t+1}$.

We start our description with RS portfolios as these are the easiest analytically. Early work in this area was carried out by Lo and MacKinlay (1990), Jegadeesh and Titman (1993) and Lewellen (2002). We note that the basic idea behind RS portfolios is that the weight of asset i held at time t depends in a linear way upon past performance in the asset either absolutely or relative to some benchmark such as a market proxy.

To avoid excessive mathematics without losing any of the essential features, we shall assume that

$$\omega_{i,t} = r_{i,t} - r_{b,i,t} \tag{2.1}$$

Here $r_{b,i,t}$ is some benchmark weight, possibly constant across i; initially we shall set $r_{b,i,t}$ equal to zero so that we can define the RS portfolio rate of return as

$$r_{p,t+1} = \sum_{i=1}^{N} \omega_{i,t} r_{i,t+1} = \sum_{i=1}^{N} r_{i,t} r_{i,t+1} = R_t' R_{t+1} \tag{2.2}$$

Equation (2.2) is particularly useful in determining the properties of RS portfolios. For example,

$$E(r_{p,t+1}) = E(R_t' R_{t+1}) = E(R_t)' E(R_{t+1}) + tr(cov(R_t, R_{t+1})) \tag{2.3}$$

where $cov(R_t, R_{t+1})$ is the N by N covariance matrix of first-order autocovariances of each asset with itself and with the other assets. The trace operator sums the diagonals of a square matrix, and is denoted $tr(A)$ for matrix A.

Equation (2.3) tells us that RS portfolios have high expected rates of return if the assets have positive own-autocorrelation but that cross autocorrelations do not enter into the picture. Of course, if we included a moving average of past rates of return in (2.1) higher-order autocorrelations would enter the picture. If the weights were set to be relative to a benchmark, the formula becomes more complex. This case is discussed in Lo and MacKinlay (1990) and subsequently in this chapter.

Another case analysed in the literature is when we specify a particular process for R_{t+1}. This allows us to parameterise the expressions in Equation (2.3). Suppose that R_{t+1} follows a vector autoregressive process of order 1. Then we can write

$$R_{t+1} = \alpha + \beta R_t + V_{t+1}, \qquad (2.4)$$

where V_{t+1} is an independently identically distributed (i.i.d.) stochastic process with mean 0 and some non-singular covariance matrix and α is an N by 1 vector of constants, while β is an N by N matrix. If we assume stationarity,

$$E(R_{t+1}) = E(R_t) = (I - \beta)^{-1}\alpha. \qquad (2.5)$$

The conditions for weak stationarity guarantee the existence of the matrix inverse in Equation (2.5). The relevant conditions are discussed in Harvey (1981). He shows that the roots of the matrix polynomial $I - \beta L$ must lie outside the unit circle for the process to be stationary; here I is the N by N identity matrix and L is the lag operator. This condition means that all eigenvalues of $I - \beta$ are non-zero so that the matrix will be invertible.

Another similar calculation allows us to derive $cov(R_t, R_{t+1})$

$$cov(R_t, R_{t+1}) = \beta cov(R_t, R_t),$$

where $cov(R_t, R_t)$ is the covariance matrix of the rate of returns. One can then express $tr(cov(R_t, R_{t+1}))$ in terms of individual elements of β, where the individual element is denoted β_{ij}, and individual elements of $Cov(R_t, R_t)$, with element σ_{ij}

$$tr(cov(R_t, R_{t+1})) = \sum_{i=1}^{N} \sum_{j=1}^{N} \beta_{ij}\sigma_{ij}$$

This is about as far as one can go without introducing additional distributional assumptions. Computing the portfolio variance, for example, involves specifying fourth moments, which in turn requires making specific assumptions about their nature. Even in the special case where we assume that β is zero, which corresponds to asset returns being *i.i.d.*, the analysis is still complicated.

Notwithstanding the above caveats, analysis of RS expected returns is relatively straight forward as we do not sort the assets when we determine asset weights. As we will see, sorting the assets complicates the derivations of the distributions and the distributions themselves.

2.3 TIME-SERIES MOMENTUM STRATEGIES

Before getting into the mathematical detail, it will be worthwhile discussing some of the broad features of time-series momentum (TSM). TSM is, essentially, a univariate time-series modelling exercise. Moskowitz et al. (2012) regress the excess return of an asset (in their paper, a futures contract) on lagged excess returns of that asset. In their work, each asset is scaled by an estimate of its volatility, adjusted to avoid look-ahead bias. Thus, we might assume a model such as a univariate version of Equation (2.4).

$$r_{i,t+1} = \alpha_i + \beta_i r_{i,t} + v_{i,t+1},$$

Such an equation could be estimated by a variety of methods, and a forecast could be constructed based on the estimated equation

$$\widehat{r}_{i,t+1} = \widehat{\alpha}_i + \widehat{\beta}_i r_{i,t}.$$

This should make clear that we are calculating univariate forecasts, while it is also clear that we can construct a large variety of trading strategies. A simple approach used by Moskowitz et al. (2012) is to take a long position in assets with positive forecasts, and short in those assets with negative forecasts.

We shall not investigate the exact properties of TSM as its auto-regressive nature will lead to complexities, but we can see when this structure may do well. To do this, we assume a two-period structure, and we notice that all features of TSM can be described in terms of the univariate process for the asset. In other words, cross autocorrelations do not enter into the forecast construction. So, such a strategy might be expected to perform well (relative to other strategies) if we can build good forecasts based on the asset's past history, and we can ignore the past behaviour of other assets.

Thus, TSM could be expected to do relatively well across futures markets or emerging markets relative to say, a universe made up of stocks from a particular industry involving both suppliers and their clients (e.g. Paatela, Noschis and Hameri, 2017). Moreover, if the universe of assets has a common factor structure that explains a high proportion of overall asset volatility, TSM would not be expected to do well. An example here might be US large-cap equity. If the universe of assets has its volatility largely explained by idiosyncratic components (e.g. Grant and Satchell, 2016), TSM might do relatively well; this could be the case for emerging markets.

Another reason this strategy might work is that, by focusing on univariate processes, we can build forecasts that have relatively low estimation error. In comparison, CSM implicitly uses all information in the formation period of the other assets. Estimating many small, insignificant, parameters, and incorporating these estimates into a forecast is likely to lead to volatile forecasts; TSM avoids this.

We should stress that our discussion of CSM, TSM and RS strategies differs in some respects from Moskowitz et al. (2012). They state (p. 241), '[W]e can formally write down the relationship between time series (TSMOM) and cross-sectional (XSMOM) momentum.' They define the XSMOM weight to asset i as,

$$\omega_t^{XS,i} = r_{t-12,t}^i - r_{t-12,t}^{EW},$$

where $r_{t-12,t}^i$ is the return to asset i over the last twelve months and $r_{t-12,t}^{EW}$ is the average return for all N assets over the prior twelve months. This can be thought of as treating the last 12 months as the formation period. Similarly, they define the TSMOM weight as

$$\omega_t^{TS,i} = r_{t-12,t}^i.$$

These weights capture relative strength against an equal-weighted benchmark, and relative strength against a zero benchmark, respectively. Assuming stationarity for underlying returns, and that $\Omega = cov(R_{t-12,t}, R_t)$, where R is a vector of returns, i a vector of ones, and σ_u^2 is the cross-sectional variance of expected returns (constant under stationarity), we can compute moments of

$$r_{XS,t+1} = \sum_{i=1}^{N} \omega_t^{XS,i} r_{i,t+1} = \sum_{i=1}^{N} (r_{t-12,t}^i - r_{t-12,t}^{EW}) r_{i,t+1}.$$

Practitioners will recognise this as the population analogue of squared cross-sectional volatility, which is routinely calculated as an indicator of active management opportunity. Calculating the expected return to cross-sectional momentum yields the following

$$E(r_{XS,t+1}) = tr(\Omega) + 12N\sigma_u^2 - \frac{i'\Omega i}{N} \tag{2.6}$$

which is increasing in cross-sectional volatility. Following the same argument as in Equation (2.3),

$$E(r_{XS,t+1}) = tr(\Omega) + 12\mu'\mu \tag{2.7}$$

where $\mu = E(R_{t+1})$. The difference between Equation (2.6) and Equation (2.7) is largely due to the final term in Equation (2.6), $\frac{i'\Omega i}{N}$. Following this example, this would say that if asset returns over the last 12 months were positively correlated with current asset returns in the other assets, we would expect $E(r_{XS,t+1})$ to be smaller than $E(r_{TS,t+1})$.

Moskowitz et al. (2012) decompose Equations (2.6) and (2.7) in various interesting ways to characterise why and when these strategies do well or badly. However, the extent to which these two portfolios actually characterise TSM and CSM is highly debatable. In particular, $\omega_t^{XS,i} = r_{t-12,t}^i - r_{t-12,t}^{EW}$ captures that aspect of CSM that compares the returns of an asset in the holding period with all other asset returns, but fails to capture the ranking in the holding period which is an essential feature of CSM. Indeed, according to our taxonomy, the example above is a comparison between two RS portfolios with different benchmarks.

2.4   CROSS-SECTIONAL MOMENTUM STRATEGIES

In the previous section, we argued that the characterisation of cross-sectional momentum (CSM) strategies presented in the TSM literature is incomplete. In this section we describe CSM and the additional complexities not captured by RS interpretations of CSM. CSM is described by three periods, a formation period, a short period (typically of one observation) which is omitted, and a third period in which certain assets are held, long or short, referred to as the holding period.

In the formation period, asset returns are ranked and the first m ranked assets, say, are selected to form the long portfolio. The long portfolio will be based on the m assets with highest returns during the ranking period. The bottom m ranked assets become the short portfolio. These will be based on the m assets with the lowest returns. Clearly $N \geq 2m$. In addition, we can choose weights in whatever way we think appropriate. Likewise, data can be at any chosen frequency, although the literature is largely based on using monthly returns and equal portfolio weights. The choice of m is usually based on top and bottom deciles or quintiles using either number of assets or market capitalisation; in the latter case, the number of assets in the long portfolio can differ from the number of assets in the short portfolio. If we ranked over rank $t - 1$ to $t - 13$, omitted the last month ($t - 1$ to t) and held the resulting CSM portfolio for one month (t to $t + 1$), we could describe the strategy as $(12, 1, 1)$.

To progress analysis, we let R_{t+1} be the returns over the holding period and R_t be the returns over the formation period. As before, both are N by 1 vectors. We make the following assumption.

Assumption 1. $(R_{t+1}, R_t)'$ follows a $2N$ by 1 multivariate normal distribution with means $(\mu_{t+1}, \mu_t)'$, N by N covariance matrices $(\Lambda_{t+1,t+1}, \Lambda_{t,t})'$ and an N by N cross-covariance matrix $\Lambda_{t,t+1}$.

Some comments are in order. Firstly, it could be argued that these assumptions are restrictive; a point we readily concede. We note, however, that analysis can be carried out under alternative multivariate specifications, as is done in Chapter 10 of this book.

If we assume that $(R_{t+1}, R_t)'$ are weakly stationary, then $\mu_{t+1} = \mu_t = \mu$, and $\Lambda_{t+1,t+1} = \Lambda_{t,t} = \Lambda$ whilst $\Lambda_{t,t+1} = \Delta$; the above conditions, holding for all t.

Of course, the above information does not describe the full stochastic process, but the above information is sufficient for our purposes. We can think of this specification as providing a description of stochastic processes observed over two periods. Here the length of the two periods relate to the length of the formation and holding periods. If these lengths are f and h respectively, then in the context of this section, and assuming we omit the month from $t - 1$ to t, $R_t = R_{t-1,t-1-f}$ and $R_{t+1} = R_{t+h,t}$. We see that if we required stationarity for formation and holding returns and if the underlying per period returns were assumed to be stationary, then we would require $f = h$. Interestingly, many of the strategies in the empirical literature are of the form $(f, 1, f)$.

Kwon and Satchell (2018) provide a general solution for the density and moments of CSM returns. They provide a discussion of the connection between theoretical and empirical results. Many of the theoretical arguments used can be found in Chapter 10 of this book.

As in Kwon and Satchell (2018), we consider the special case of $N = 2$ assets and $m = 1$ so that we take a long position in the asset with the highest return in the formation period, and go short the asset with the lowest return in the formation period. If we do not assume stationarity, the model as specified in Assumption 1 will have eighteen distinct parameters. However, under stationarity, we only need to specify nine parameters, two means, two variances and five correlations. The five correlations are the contemporaneous correlations between the returns of assets 1 and 2, two own autocorrelations (one for each asset), and the cross autocorrelations between the return of asset 1 at time

t and asset 2 at time $t+1$ and vice-versa. We now define various parameters for the stationary case when $N = 2$:

$$E(r_{1,t}) = E(r_{1,t+1}) = \mu_1$$
$$E(r_{2,t}) = E(r_{2,t+1}) = \mu_2$$
$$Var(r_{1,t}) = Var(r_{1,t+1}) = \sigma_1^2$$
$$Var(r_{2,t}) = Var(r_{2,t+1}) = \sigma_2^2$$
$$cov(r_{1,t}, r_{2,t}) = cov(r_{1,t+1}, r_{2,t+1}) = \rho\sigma_1\sigma_2$$
$$cov(r_{1,t}, r_{2,t+1}) = \rho_{12}\sigma_1\sigma_2$$
$$cov(r_{1,t+1}, r_{2,t}) = \rho_{21}\sigma_1\sigma_2$$
$$cov(r_{1,t}, r_{1,t+1}) = \rho_{11}\sigma_1^2$$
$$cov(r_{2,t}, r_{2,t+1}) = \rho_{22}\sigma_2^2$$

Using these parameters, we can define the difference between the expected returns on the two assets (in both periods) as γ, where

$$\gamma = \mu_1 - \mu_2$$

Then we have
$$E(r_{1,t} - r_{2,t}) = E(r_{1,t+1} - r_{2,t+1}) = \gamma$$

and
$$Var(r_{1,t} - r_{2,t}) = Var(r_{1,t+1} - r_{2,t+1}) = \omega^2.$$

So, from the expressions for variances and covariance, we can write

$$\omega = \sqrt{\sigma_1^2 + \sigma_2^2 - 2\rho\sigma_1\sigma_2},$$
$$cov(r_{1,t} - r_{2,t}, r_{1,t+1} - r_{2,t+1}) = \rho_{11}\sigma_1^2 + \rho_{22}\sigma_2^2 - (\rho_{12} + \rho_{21})\sigma_1\sigma_2,$$

and

$$corr(r_{1,t} - r_{2,t}, r_{1,t+1} - r_{2,t+1}) = \frac{\rho_{11}\sigma_1^2 + \rho_{22}\sigma_2^2 - (\rho_{12} + \rho_{21})\sigma_1\sigma_2}{\omega} = \varrho.$$

We denote the density of a random variable X by $pdf(x)$ and the conditional density, conditional on event A by the notation $pdf(x|A)$. If A and B are mutually exclusive and exhaustive events, and we define $Prob(A)$ as the probability that A occurs, then the law of total probability tells us that

$$pdf(x) = pdf(x|A)Prob(A) + pdf(x|B)Prob(B).$$

Then, let X be the return to CSM at time $t+1$, and A be the event $(r_{1,t} > r_{2,t})$, and B be the event $(r_{1,t} \leq r_{2,t})$. Let Φ and ϕ represent the standardised normal distribution and density functions respectively. Utilising these definitions, we obtain the following expressions for $Prob(A)$ and $Prob(B)$

$$Prob(A) = Prob(r_{1,t} > r_{2,t}) = \Phi\left(\frac{\mu_1 - \mu_2}{\omega}\right),$$

$$Prob(B) = Prob(r_{1,t} \leq r_{2,t}) = \Phi\left(\frac{\mu_2 - \mu_1}{\omega}\right).$$

We can similarly define the conditional densities, for the event X, given that either event A or B has occurred

$$pdf(x|A) = pdf(r_{1,t+1} - r_{2,t+1} = x|r_{1,t} > r_{2,t}),$$

$$pdf(x|B) = pdf(r_{1,t+1} - r_{2,t+1} = x|r_{1,t} \leq r_{2,t})$$

$$= pdf(r_{1,t+1} - r_{2,t+1} = x|r_{1,t} - r_{2,t} \leq 0).$$

Bayes theorem can then be applied to reverse the conditioning:

$$pdf(x|B) = \frac{Prob(B|x)pdf(x)}{Prob(B)}$$

Perhaps the simplest expressions come from considering the bivariate normal case. If $X = r_{1,t+1} - r_{2,t+1}$ is the difference in returns during the holding period, and $Y = r_{1,t} - r_{2,t}$ is the difference in returns during the formation period, with $(X, Y)'$ bivariate normal with means $(\gamma, \gamma)'$ and variances (ω^2, ω^2) and covariance equal to $\rho\omega^2$.

Inputting these expressions yields

$$pdf(x|A) = pdf(r_{1,t+1} - r_{2,t+1} = x|r_{1,t} > r_{2,t})$$

$$= pdf(X = x|Y > 0)$$

$$= \frac{pdf(X = x, Y > 0)}{Prob(Y > 0)}$$

$$= \frac{Prob(Y > 0|X = x)pdf(X = x)}{Prob(Y > 0)}$$

Now, under the bivariate normal assumption,

$$pdf(Y|X = x) \sim N(\gamma + \rho(x - \gamma), \omega^2(1 - \rho^2)),$$

and substituting, we obtain

$$Prob(Y > 0| X = x) = \Phi\left(\frac{\gamma + \rho(x - \gamma)}{\sqrt{\omega^2(1 - \rho^2)}}\right),$$

$$pdf(x|A) = \frac{\Phi\left(\frac{\gamma + \rho(x-\gamma)}{\sqrt{\omega^2(1-\rho^2)}}\right)\phi\left(\frac{x-\gamma}{\omega}\right)}{\Phi\left(\frac{\gamma}{\omega}\right)}.$$

Similarly,

$$pdf(x|B) = \frac{\Phi\left(\frac{-(\gamma+\varrho(x-\gamma))}{\sqrt{\omega^2(1-\varrho^2)}}\right)\phi\left(\frac{x+\gamma}{\omega}\right)}{\Phi\left(\frac{-\gamma}{\omega}\right)}.$$

so we can obtain the expression for $pdf(x)$

$$pdf(x) = \Phi\left(\frac{\gamma+\varrho(x-\gamma)}{\sqrt{\omega^2(1-\varrho^2)}}\right)\phi\left(\frac{x-\gamma}{\omega}\right) + \Phi\left(\frac{-(\gamma+\varrho(x-\gamma))}{\sqrt{\omega^2(1-\varrho^2)}}\right)\phi\left(\frac{x+\gamma}{\omega}\right) \quad (2.8)$$

Putting it back in terms of fundamental parameters, we obtain

$$pdf(x) = \phi\left(\frac{x-(\mu_1-\mu_2)}{\omega}\right)\Phi\left(\frac{(\mu_1-\mu_2)+\varrho(x-(\mu_1-\mu_2))}{\omega\sqrt{1-\varrho^2}}\right)$$

$$+\phi\left(\frac{x+(\mu_1-\mu_2)}{\omega}\right)\Phi\left(\frac{-(\mu_1-\mu_2)+\varrho(x+(\mu_1-\mu_2))}{\omega\sqrt{1-\varrho^2}}\right)$$

It is worth reversing the cancellation step used in deriving (2.8). This yields the following

$$pdf(x) = \frac{\phi\left(\frac{x-(\mu_1-\mu_2)}{\omega}\right)\Phi\left(\frac{(\mu_1-\mu_2)+\varrho(x-(\mu_1-\mu_2))}{\omega\sqrt{1-\varrho^2}}\right)}{\Phi\left(\frac{\mu_1-\mu_2}{\omega}\right)}\cdot\Phi\left(\frac{\mu_1-\mu_2}{\omega}\right)$$

$$+\frac{\phi\left(\frac{x+(\mu_1-\mu_2)}{\omega}\right)\Phi\left(\frac{-(\mu_1-\mu_2)+\varrho(x+(\mu_1-\mu_2))}{\omega\sqrt{1-\varrho^2}}\right)}{\Phi\left(\frac{\mu_2-\mu_1}{\omega}\right)}\cdot\Phi\left(\frac{\mu_2-\mu_1}{\omega}\right) \quad (2.9)$$

Equation (2.9) allows us to see that the pdf of CSM returns is in fact a mixture of two probability density functions, each of which can be recognised as a version of the unified skew-normal (SUN) family. See Arellano-Valle and Azzalini (2006) for full definitions; in particular, their equations 9 and 10. The mixing coefficients (probabilities) are $\Phi\left(\frac{\mu_1-\mu_2}{\omega}\right)$ and $\Phi\left(\frac{\mu_2-\mu_1}{\omega}\right)$. They correspond to the events $Y > 0$ ($r_{1,t} - r_{2,t} > 0$) and $Y \leq 0$ ($r_{1,t} - r_{2,t} \leq 0$), respectively.

It turns out that these results generalise to the non-stationary case and to arbitrary N and m. We note that if $\varrho = 0$, the density further simplifies to a mixture of normals;

$$pdf(x) = \phi\left(\frac{x-(\mu_1-\mu_2)}{\omega}\right)\Phi\left(\frac{\mu_1-\mu_2}{\omega}\right) + \phi\left(\frac{x+(\mu_1-\mu_2)}{\omega}\right)\Phi\left(\frac{\mu_2-\mu_1}{\omega}\right) \quad (2.10)$$

There are several immediate consequences of Equations 2.9 and (2.10). Firstly, it is obvious that CSM returns will be non-normal and that the returns will be both skewed and kurtotic. Secondly, we can see conditions under which normality of CSM returns prevail. Whilst there are a number of different circumstances, we note that setting $\Phi\left(\frac{\mu_1 - \mu_2}{\omega}\right)$ to be close to one (or zero) in Equation (2.10) will make $pdf(x)$ close to normal. This will be near one if $\frac{\mu_1 - \mu_2}{\omega}$ is very large, and so will occur if the mean of asset 1 is much greater than the mean of asset 2 and ω is relatively small. The standard deviation of relative returns, ω, will be small if the standard deviations are approximately similar and ρ, the cross-sectional correlation, is large. Of course, such a situation points to a certain degree of mispricing in the sense that the two assets have similar risks, very different returns and are strongly positively correlated. Such a situation is ideal for pairs trading, of which this can be considered an example. Indeed, much of the analysis described in this section in the $N = 2$ case could be interpreted an analysis of pairs trading.

Thirdly, the obvious case when Equation (2.9) reduces to Equation (2.10) is based on the assumption that returns at time t are uncorrelated with returns at time $t + 1$, a popular notion of market efficiency. However, we see a more interesting case when we inspect the formula for $cov(r_{1,t} - r_{2,t}, r_{1,t+1} - r_{2,t+1})$ which was shown to be equal to $\rho_{11}\sigma_1^2 + \rho_{22}\sigma_2^2 - (\rho_{12} + \rho_{21})\sigma_1\sigma_2$. This expression could be zero if the weighted sum of own autocorrelations was equal to the weighted sum of cross autocorrelations. This may happen in practice and helps to provide an understanding of circumstances in which a CSM strategy may not be effective. In particular, if own autocorrelations were large whilst cross autocorrelations were large and overall ρ was small, we would have a situation where TSM would do well and CSM might do badly.

We now turn to the moments of CSM when $N = 2$. Using the formula in Theorem 1 for $E(X)$ in Kwon and Satchell (2018), and simplifying, we see that

$$E(X) = (\mu_1 - \mu_2)\left(2\Phi\left(\frac{\mu_1 - \mu_2}{\omega}\right) - 1\right) + 2\rho\omega\phi\left(\frac{\mu_1 - \mu_2}{\omega}\right)$$

Now, suppose we re-parameterise this by replacing the three fundamental parameters, $(\mu_1 - \mu_2)$, ρ, and ω by SR, ρ, and ω. Here SR$=\frac{(\mu_1 - \mu_2)}{\omega}$ can be interpreted as a Sharpe ratio for a long-short portfolio. Our choice here is largely dictated by the popularity of the Sharpe ratio with practitioners. The re-parameterised version of E(X) is given below.

$$E(X) = SR\omega(2\Phi(SR) - 1) + 2\rho\omega\phi(SR) \tag{2.11}$$

We see, immediately, that if SR is positive and ρ is positive, then $E(X)$ is positive. Also $\frac{\partial E(X)}{\partial \rho} = 2\omega\phi(SR)$ which is unambiguously positive. Therefore, increasing the auto-correlation between the differenced returns in the two periods is always good for expected CSM returns. Likewise

$$\frac{\partial E(X)}{\partial SR} = 2\omega\phi(SR)SR(1 - \rho) + \omega(2\Phi(SR) - 1)$$

This tells us that if SR is positive, then $E(X)$ is increasing in SR whilst if SR is negative, then $E(X)$ is decreasing in SR so that $E(X)$ must have a minimum when SR $= 0$, that is when $\mu_1 = \mu_2$.

Suppose now that the world was stationary and that an investor knew with certainty that $\mu_1 > \mu_2$. Such an investor might always enter a long position in asset 1 and short asset 2. In such a circumstance, the investor's return would be $r_{1,t+1} - r_{2,t+1}$, which would be Gaussian with mean $\mu_1 - \mu_2$ and variance ω^2. How would this compare with a CSM strategy? We could call this investor the perfect pairs trader. Intuitively, it would seem difficult to beat the perfect pairs trader. The difference in their expected returns will be

$$\mu_1 - \mu_2 - E(X) = 2(\mu_1 - \mu_2)\left(1 - \Phi\left(\frac{\mu_1 - \mu_2}{\omega}\right)\right) - 2\varrho\omega\phi\left(\frac{\mu_1 - \mu_2}{\omega}\right) \qquad (2.12)$$

This is clearly positive if $\varrho \leq 0$ but it may well be possible to extend this result using inequalities on Mill's ratios.

Define the Mill's ratio evaluated at $SR = \dfrac{(\mu_1 - \mu_2)}{\omega}$ as

$$M\left(\frac{\mu_1 - \mu_2}{\omega}\right) = \frac{\left(1 - \Phi\left(\frac{\mu_1 - \mu_2}{\omega}\right)\right)}{\phi\left(\frac{\mu_1 - \mu_2}{\omega}\right)}$$

It is known from Sampford (1952) that

$$M(SR) < \frac{4}{3SR + \sqrt{8 + SR^2}}.$$

We can write Equation (2.12) as

$$\mu_1 - \mu_2 - E(X) = 2\omega\phi(SR)(SR\, M(SR) - \varrho)$$

which is less than

$$\mu_1 - \mu_2 - E(X) = 2\omega\phi(SR)\left(\frac{4}{3SR + \sqrt{8 + SR^2}} - \varrho\right).$$

Kwon and Satchell (2019) use this upper bound to identify situations when CSM beats perfect pairs trading in expected returns. It turns out that we can beat the perfect pairs trader as long as we can forecast the return spread reasonably well and as long as the underlying Sharpe ratio of the pairs trader is not too large.

In the context of Equation (2.10), should CSM lead to profitable opportunities? We can answer this by examining Equation (2.11) and setting $\varrho = 0$. In this case, $E(X) = SR\omega\,(2\Phi(SR) - 1)$, and as long as $\mu_1 - \mu_2 > 0$, and we can identify this ordering during the formation period, we should expect CSM to be profitable on average. This does not automatically contravene any notion of financial efficiency as $\mu_1 - \mu_2 > 0$ could well be compatible with equal risk-adjusted returns.

2.5 CROSS-ASSET MOMENTUM

There is a large literature on investment strategies that consider the ranking period based on a firm's equity and the holding period being based on the same firm's debt. This literature mainly considers investment grade (IG) debt. This is usually referred to as a 'momentum spillover'. Jostova et al. (2013) also present evidence of a similar effect in non-investment grade (HY) bonds, while Lee, Naranjo and Sirmans (2019) show that a momentum spillover exists between credit default swaps and individual stocks. A similar approach can be implemented at the index level, where the reverse strategy obtains. Geczy and Samonov (2015), in turn, study cross-asset momentum in a sample of country-level bond and equity indexes from 1800 to 2014, and show that sorting equity indexes into winner and loser portfolios based on past bond index returns yields a significant winner minus loser spread of 0.59% per month.

Gebhardt, Hvidkjaer and Swaminathan (2004), Pospisil and Zhang (2010) and Jostova et al. (2013) all document that bond momentum is weaker in IG bonds and significantly stronger in HY bonds. More recent work, see for example Maitra, Salt and Satchell (2018), modifies the bond momentum signal to capture overreaction and improves the efficacy of the bond momentum signal, even within IG bonds.

If we look back to Section 2.4 and consider the analysis in the $N = 2$ case, we see that we are essentially defining a four-dimensional multivariate normal process. We could repeat the analysis for momentum spillovers in that the problem remains very similar and again we get a four-dimensional normal process. The difference now is that stationarity will not lead to any parameter reduction as it would seem highly unrealistic to assume that the equity returns distribution at time t will be the same as the bond return distribution at time $t + 1$.

Recent versions have considered cross-asset time-series momentum as discussed in Section 2.3 where a country or firm's current equity or bond returns are based on a time-series regression of past equity and bond returns.

The results for cross-asset momentum seem to persist as found by Maitra et al. (2018). Their study of equity momentum in bonds (EMB) shows significant predictability of corporate-bond credit returns using lagged equity momentum. They use deciles or quintiles and implement a long-short strategy. Maitra et al. (2018) show that equity momentum predicts not only credit performance, but also rating downgrades more effectively than other forms of co-quantile momentum, such as spreads or rating momentum. By co-quantile momentum we mean that the holding period need not necessarily be own-asset class returns but other attributes of the firm. That is, we might rank on something other than returns.

These ideas generalise to cross-asset momentum in the sense that we can sort on any variable or attribute of a firm and examine the returns or indeed any other attribute in the following period. In fact, we need not just confine ourselves to single sorts in the formation period, but we could have multiple sorts as well. Generalising further, we need not restrict ourselves to firms but could also consider industries or countries as well. Indeed, cross-asset momentum simply needs some form of indexing, which allows associating a variable in the formation period with a variable in the holding period.

It becomes apparent that that the holding and formation period could become the same period. If so, using the same variable in formation and holding in the same period gives us order statistics. If we have different variables in the holding and formation periods which are the same period, we get concomitants. The above discussion covers many variable construction procedures that are used throughout finance.

Concluding, it seems that momentum – however defined – performs well when there is autocorrelation in the data such that holding and formation returns – however defined – are positively correlated. Although not discussed in detail here, it is quite possible that expected returns to momentum could well be positive because we are taking more risk in which case there is no immediate challenge to market efficiency. Examples of such results compatible with market efficiency should be familiar to readers, the capital asset pricing model would predict higher returns on average for assets with higher betas. To this point, in the formula for $E(X) = SR\omega (2\Phi(SR) - 1)$, there is another formula for its standard deviation not discussed and both can be increasing functions of SR and ω.

REFERENCES

Arellano-Valle, R. B. and Azzalini, A. 2006. On the unification of families of skew-normal distributions. *Scandinavian Journal of Statistics*, 33(3), 561–574.

Gebhardt, W. R., Hvidkjaer, S., and Swaminathan, B. 2005. Stock and bond market interaction: Does momentum spill over? *Journal of Financial Economics*, 75(3), 651–690.

Geczy, G. and Samonov, M. 2015. 215 years of global multi-asset momentum: 1800–2014 (Equities, sectors, currencies, bonds, commodities and stocks). *SSRN Electronic Journal*. https://doi.org/10.2139/ssrn.2607730.

Grant, A. and Satchell, S. 2016. Theoretical decompositions of the cross-sectional dispersion of stock returns. *Quantitative Finance*, 16(2), 169–180.

Harvey, A. C. 1981. *Time Series Models*. Oxford: Philip Allan; Atlantic Highlands, NJ: Humanities Press.

Jegadeesh, N. and Titman, S. 1993. Returns to buying winners and selling losers: Implications for stock market efficiency. *The Journal of Finance*, 48(1), 65–91.

Jostova, G., Nikolova, S., Philipov, A., and Stahel, C. 2013. Momentum in corporate bond returns. *The Review of Financial Studies*, 26(7), 1649–1693

Kwon, O. K. and Satchell, S. 2018. The distribution of cross-sectional momentum returns. *Journal of Economic Dynamics and Control*, 94, 225–241.

Kwon, O. K. and Satchell, S. 2019. *When Does Cross-Sectional Momentum Outperform Pairs Trading?* Mimeo, University of Sydney Business School.

Lee, J., Naranjo, A., and Sirmans, S. (2019). CDS momentum: slow moving credit ratings and cross-market spillovers. Mimeo, University of Florida. Online at: http://dx.doi.org/10.2139/ssrn.2423371 (accessed 24 June 2020).

Lewellen, J. 2002. Momentum and autocorrelation in stock returns. *The Review of Financial Studies*, 15(2), 533–564.

Lo, A. W. and MacKinlay, A. C. 1990. When are contrarian profits due to stock market overreaction? *The Review of Financial Studies*, 3(2), 175–205.

Maitra, A., Salt, M., and Satchell, S. 2018. Equity momentum in corporate bonds. LOIM research paper. Online at: https://am.lombardodier.com/files/live/sites/am/files/news/AM_news/2019/January/20190121/Equity%20Momentum%20in%20Bonds_21Jan19.pdf

Moskowitz, T. J., Ooi, Y. H., and Pedersen, L. H. 2012. Time series momentum. *Journal of Financial Economics*, **104**(2), 228–250.

Paatela, A., Noschis, E., and Hameri, A. -P. 2017. Abnormal stock returns using supply chain momentum and operational financials. *Journal of Portfolio Management*, **43**(2), 50–60.

Pospisil, L. and Zhang, J. 2010. Momentum and reversal effects in corporate bond prices and credit cycles. *The Journal of Fixed Income*, **20**(2), 101–115.

Sampford, M. R. 1952. Some inequalities on Mill's Ratio and related functions. *The Annals of Mathematical Statistics*, **24**(1), 130–132.

CHAPTER 3

Demystifying Time-Series Momentum Strategies: Volatility Estimators, Trading Rules and Pairwise Correlations

NICK BALTAS and ROBERT KOSOWSKI

Managed futures funds, also known as Commodity Trading Advisors (CTAs), constitute a significant part of the hedge fund industry. Using BarclayHedge estimates at the end of 2018, managed futures funds manage a total of US$355bn of assets, which is about 11% of the US$3.2tr hedge fund industry. These funds typically trade futures contracts on assets in various asset classes (equity indices, commodities, government bonds and FX rates) and profit from systematic price trends by means of time-series momentum strategies; Moskowitz, Ooi and Pedersen (2012) are the first to comprehensively study these strategies in the academic literature, whereas Hurst, Ooi and Pedersen (2013) and Baltas and Kosowski (2013) provide statistical evidence that managed futures and CTA funds do employ such strategies.

Time-series momentum strategies are constructed using long and short positions based on a simple momentum-based trading rule, which is typically the sign of the past 12-month return. The portfolio weights are inversely proportional to realised volatility (Moskowitz et al. 2012), as the correlation structure of the portfolio constituents is not typically incorporated in the weighting scheme. These strategies have recently received considerable investor attention for two reasons. On the one hand, they provided impressive diversification benefits during the global financial crisis (GFC) of 2008, but on the other hand, they have exhibited rather poor performance in the subsequent post-crisis period. One of the reasons for this recent underperformance has been claimed to be the recent increase in the level of correlations across markets and asset classes (Baltas and Kosowski 2013, Georgopoulou and Wang 2017).

The objective of this chapter is threefold. First, we focus on the portfolio turnover implications of the two key inputs in time-series momentum strategies, namely the volatility estimator that is used to scale the asset positions and the trading rule that is used to identify the price trends. In particular, we explore the turnover reduction benefits from employing more efficient volatility estimates and from identifying more accurately the strength of price trends by means of alternative trading rules. Second, the chapter studies the dependence of the performance of time-series momentum strategies on the level of asset pairwise correlations, with special attention paid to their under-performance following the GFC. In an attempt to improve the diversification of the strategy and therefore its performance during periods of increased asset co-movement, we introduce a dynamic leverage adjustment at the overall portfolio that reduces the employed leverage in such periods. Finally, we introduce a new transaction costs model for futures-based investment strategies that separates costs into roll-over costs and rebalancing costs. We use this model to evaluate the economic magnitude of the various methodological innovations mentioned in this paragraph. For our empirical analysis, we construct time-series momentum strategies using futures data on 56 assets across four asset classes (commodities, equity indices, currencies and government bonds) for a 30-year period between January 1983 and February 2013.

Starting from the turnover reduction analysis, we first document the economic value of using a volatility estimator with desirable theoretical properties. In the spirit of Fleming, Kirby and Ostdiek (2003), we hypothesise that more efficient and accurate estimators, than those constructed using daily close-to-close returns (standard deviation of past daily returns), can reduce excessive rebalancing and therefore substantially reduce the turnover of a time-series momentum strategy. Using a range-based estimator (constructed using open-high-low-close prices), such as the one proposed by Yang and Zhang (2000), we empirically find that the turnover of the strategy is statistically strongly reduced by 17% (t-statistic of 5.33) without causing any statistically sizeable performance penalty. Importantly, the benefit in the turnover reduction is not due to a small number of portfolio constituents, but instead it is found to be pervasive across all portfolio constituents from all asset classes, without a single exception.

The second part of our turnover reduction analysis focuses on the trading rule of the time-series momentum strategy. The typical momentum trading rule in the literature is binary (−1 or +1), based on the signs of the past 12-month asset returns (Moskowitz et al. 2012). Intuitively, the frequency at which a trading rule switches between long and short positions can dramatically affect the portfolio turnover. Put differently, avoiding the excessive position changes when no significant price trend exists can substantially reduce the turnover. Using an alternative trading rule that takes a continuum of values between −1 and +1 as a function of the statistical strength of daily futures log-returns over the past 12 months, we find that the turnover of the strategy can be reduced by roughly 24% (t-statistic of 8.49) without causing any statistically sizeable performance penalty to the strategy. Importantly, as in the case of the alternative volatility estimator, the benefit is pervasive across all portfolio constituents from all asset classes.

Taken together, we find that these two methodological amendments can lead to statistically strong turnover gains of more than one-third (36.23%, t-statistic of 13.19), without having any statistically strong impact on the performance of the strategy. The strategies before and after employing these amendments are statistically indistinguishable. This is an important result as time-series momentum – as any momentum strategy – is a high-turnover strategy,[1] and therefore requires frequent rebalancing in order to capture emerging price trends and move away from trends that have already materialised. Put differently, one can only do so much in terms of turnover reduction, before the actual performance of the strategy starts falling significantly. The fact that our results show a turnover reduction of more than one-third without a material impact on the actual performance of the strategy is therefore noteworthy. In addition, it is also worth noting that lower turnover generally allows for scalability and capacity in terms of capital invested and is therefore always welcome by investors.

Our second objective is to study the dependence of the performance of the time-series momentum strategy on the level of pairwise correlations of portfolio constituents. This analysis is motivated by the findings in Baltas and Kosowski (2013), who, apart from documenting the business cycle performance of the strategy, also highlight its poor performance after 2008. The authors explain that the underperformance can be due to (i) capacity constraints in the futures markets, (ii) a lack of trends for each asset, or (iii) increased correlations across assets, which is, in turn, closely related to a fall in diversification benefits. They find no evidence of capacity constraints based on two different methodologies, but they do show that correlations between futures markets have experienced a significant increase in the period from 2008 to 2013 (also in line with Georgopoulou and Wang 2017).

We show that incorporating the pairwise *signed* correlations of the constituent assets into the weighting scheme of the strategy not only sheds light on its return drivers, but can also significantly improve its performance, especially in periods of increased co-movement. We investigate the interplay between the pairwise signed correlations – hence incorporating the fact that some of the assets command a short position in the portfolio – of portfolio constituents and portfolio volatility and extend the formulation of the standard time-series momentum strategy by introducing a correlation factor in the weighting scheme that increases (decreases) the leverage of portfolio constituents in periods of low (high) average pairwise signed correlation. This adjustment improves the risk-adjusted performance of the strategy, both over the entire sample period, but most importantly over the most recent post-crisis period 2009–2013 during which pairwise correlations across assets and asset classes dramatically increased. The improvement is primarily due to the fact that the correlation-adjusted strategy safeguards against downside risk.

Nevertheless, the performance benefit of the correlation adjustment does not come at no cost. The turnover of the strategy increases statistically significantly by about 23% (t-statistic of 3.98), all else being equal. However, when the correlation adjustment is paired with the turnover reduction techniques discussed earlier, the net effect turns positive, as the overall turnover of the strategy compared to its default specification (Moskowitz et al. 2012) falls by 23% (t-statistic of 6.34).

---

[1] The high levels of turnover and therefore the associated costs have been claimed to significantly reduce the profitability of cross-sectional momentum equity strategies; indicatively see Korajczyk and Sadka (2004), Lesmond, Schill and Zhou (2004), Menkhoff, Sarno, Schmeling and Schrimpf (2012) and Novy-Marx and Velikov (2016).

In order to evaluate the economic magnitude of the various methodological amendments suggested in this chapter – in particular that of turnover reduction – we introduce a new transaction costs model for futures-based investment strategies that separates the costs into two main distinct sources: (i) roll-over costs of futures contracts and (ii) rebalancing costs. The roll-over costs are incurred when a futures contract approaches maturity and rollovers to the next-to-mature contract and are only related to the gross weight of each asset in the overall portfolio (in line with Barroso and Santa-Clara 2015a). Conversely, the rebalancing costs are incurred when the strategy rebalances and are therefore directly related to the turnover of the strategy and the change in the net weight of each asset at each rebalancing date.

Using our transaction costs model, we estimate annualised trading costs of 163 basis points for the default specification of the time-series momentum strategy (as per Moskowitz et al. 2012), which roughly represent 10% of the strategy's gross annualised performance of 16.12% over our sample period. In line with our earlier findings on turnover reduction, a more efficient volatility estimator and a more robust trading rule can substantially reduce these costs by 13% and 25% respectively, or up to 35% when both are employed (costs fall to 105 basis points without causing a statistically significant fall in the Sharpe ratio of the strategy). Most importantly, the performance benefit of the correlation adjustment – which, when considered in isolation, actually increases the trading costs by about 13% to 185 basis points – can still come with a substantial costs reduction of about 28%, down to 118 basis points, when combined with the turnover reduction techniques discussed above. This translates to better after costs risk-adjusted returns for the strategy, partly due to the performance benefit of the correlation adjustment and partly due to the overall turnover reduction. The impact becomes even more pronounced in the post-GFC period, when the default specification of the strategy exhibits negative after-costs Sharpe ratio.

This chapter is related to and complements several streams of the literature. First, it is related to work on the economic value of volatility-timing and the importance of volatility estimation efficiency on dynamic portfolio construction and turnover. Fleming, Kirby and Ostdiek (2001), Ilmanen and Kizer (2012), Kirby and Ostdiek (2012) and Hallerbach (2012) highlight the benefits of volatility-timing, while Barroso and Santa-Clara (2015b), Daniel and Moskowitz (2016), and Moreira and Muir (2017) examine the effect of volatility-scaling on the performance of cross-sectional equity momentum and other factor premia. Fleming et al. (2003) investigate the performance and turnover benefits for a mean-variance portfolio from using more efficient estimates of volatility. Second, this chapter is related to recent work by Dudler, Gmür and Malamud (2015) and Levine and Pedersen (2016) on alternative trading rules for time-series momentum strategies and their impact on strategy performance and turnover. Finally, this chapter is related to Baltas (2015), who attempts to introduce pairwise correlations in the portfolio construction methodology of the time-series momentum strategy using a long-short risk-parity framework. Although our objective is the same, our methodology differs from Baltas's (2015) methodology in that we introduce a portfolio leverage control mechanism that is driven by the level of the average pairwise signed correlations.

The rest of the chapter is organised as follows. Section 3.1 provides an overview of the dataset. Section 3.2 describes the construction of the time-series momentum strategy, explores the dependence of the strategy's turnover on the volatility estimator and trading rule and introduces the correlation adjustment. Section 3.3 presents the empirical results of the effects of the volatility estimator and trading rule on the turnover of time-series momentum strategies. Section 3.4 discusses the recent underperformance of the time-series momentum strategies and presents our empirical results on the effect of incorporating pairwise signed correlations in the weighting scheme onto the performance of these strategies. Section 3.5 reports the transaction cost implications of all the methodological alterations that are presented in the chapter. Section 3.6 concludes.

3.1 DATA DESCRIPTION

The dataset that we use is obtained from Tick Data and consists of daily opening, high, low and closing futures prices for 56 assets across all asset classes: 25 commodities, 14 developed country equity indices, 6 currencies and 11 government bonds; see Table 3.1. Since the contracts of different assets are traded on various exchanges each with different trading hours and holidays, the data series are appropriately aligned by filling forward any missing prices. Finally, for equity indices, we also obtain spot prices from Datastream and backfill the respective futures series for periods prior to the availability of futures data.[2]

The overall sample period of the dataset is from December 1974 to February 2013. However, not all contracts start in December 1974; Table 3.1 reports the starting month and year of each contract and Figure 3.1 presents the number of assets per asset class that are available at the end of each month. At the beginning of the sample period the cross-section is relatively small, containing only nine assets and no government bonds. The composition becomes significantly broader after 1983, when the number of assets increases to 25, including the first government bonds. Because of this, the empirical analysis in this chapter focuses on the period that starts in January 1983. As we explain later in the chapter, the momentum signals are based on the most recent 12-month returns and, therefore, the first monthly returns of the time-series momentum strategy become available in January 1984.[3]

Futures contracts are short-lived instruments and are only active for a few months until the delivery date. Additionally, entering a futures contract is, in theory, a free-of-cost investment and in practice only implies a small (relative to a spot transaction) initial margin payment, hence rendering futures highly levered investments. These features of futures contracts give rise to two key issues that we carefully address below, namely (a) the construction of single continuous price time-series per asset suitable for backtesting and (b) the calculation of holding period returns.

First, in order to construct a continuous series of futures prices for each asset, we appropriately splice together different contracts. Following the standard approach in

---

[2]de Roon, Nijman and Veld (2000) and Moskowitz et al. (2012) find that equity index returns calculated using spot price series or nearest-to-delivery futures series are largely correlated. In unreported results, we confirm this and find that our results remain qualitatively unchanged without the equity spot price backfill.

[3]Our results remain qualitatively unchanged if we include the period prior to 1983. These results are available upon request from the authors.

TABLE 3.1 Summary statistics for futures contracts.

	Exchange	From	Mean	t-stat	Vol.	Skew	Kurt.	SR
CURRENCIES								
AUD/USD	CME	Feb-1987	5.07	2.11	11.67	−0.40	4.94	0.44
CAD/USD	CME	Feb-1977	0.90	0.79	6.88	−0.31	8.12	0.13
CHF/USD	CME	Dec-1974	0.77	0.36	12.55	0.05	3.81	0.06
EUR/USD	CME	Dec-1974	0.58	0.30	11.37	−0.08	3.55	0.05
GBP/USD	CME	Oct-1977	1.69	0.85	10.70	0.04	4.96	0.16
JPY/USD	CME	Apr-1977	0.69	0.31	11.97	0.49	4.46	0.06
EQUITIES								
NASDAQ 100	CME	Feb-1983	9.29	1.91	25.40	−0.31	4.29	0.37
S&P 500	CME	Dec-1974	5.76	2.20	15.35	−0.48	4.62	0.38
Russell 2000	ICE	Feb-1988	7.06	1.75	19.17	−0.49	4.01	0.37
FTSE 100	NYSE Liffe	Feb-1978	4.41	1.75	16.05	−0.76	5.76	0.28
DAX	Eurex	Dec-1974	4.64	1.33	20.07	−0.48	5.00	0.23
CAC 40	NYSE Liffe	Aug-1987	3.88	0.88	20.64	−0.32	4.12	0.19
IBEX 35	MEFF	Feb-1987	4.92	1.10	22.23	−0.47	4.89	0.22
AEX	NYSE Liffe	Feb-1983	4.81	1.19	20.33	−0.73	5.38	0.24
SMI	Eurex	Aug-1988	6.18	1.66	16.68	−0.56	4.27	0.37
MIB 30	BI	Jan-1998	−0.56	−0.09	22.87	0.00	3.80	−0.02
S&P Canada 60	MX	Feb-1982	4.39	1.38	15.75	−0.68	5.85	0.28
Nikkei 225	CME	Dec-1974	0.60	0.19	19.45	−0.22	4.20	0.03
ASX SPI 200	ASX	Jun-1992	2.75	0.81	13.58	−0.66	3.70	0.20
Hang Seng	SEHK	Dec-1974	13.01	2.82	28.73	−0.26	5.71	0.45
INTEREST RATES								
US Treasury Note 2Yr	CBOT	Feb-1991	1.65	3.73	1.75	0.28	3.44	0.95
US Treasury Note 5Yr	CBOT	Aug-1988	3.23	3.56	4.23	0.05	3.66	0.76
US Treasury Note 10Yr	CBOT	Feb-1983	4.82	3.77	6.90	0.15	3.98	0.70
US Treasury Bond 30Yr	CBOT	Nov-1982	5.93	3.18	10.55	0.25	4.46	0.56
Euro/German Schatz 2Yr	Eurex	Apr-1997	1.00	2.43	1.39	0.08	3.59	0.72
Euro/German Bobl 5Yr	Eurex	Feb-1997	2.71	2.94	3.29	−0.02	2.70	0.83
Euro/German Bund 10Yr	Eurex	Feb-1997	4.17	2.98	5.35	0.08	2.88	0.78
Euro/German Buxl 30Yr	Eurex	Oct-2005	5.53	1.28	12.64	1.02	4.83	0.44
UK Long Gilt	NYSE Liffe	Aug-1998	2.96	1.82	5.97	0.28	3.59	0.50
Canadian 10Yr	MX	May-1990	4.76	3.88	5.87	−0.04	3.23	0.81
Japanese 10Yr	TSE	Aug-2003	1.75	2.02	2.99	−0.73	4.99	0.59
COMMODITIES								
ENERGY								
Light Crude Oil	NYMEX	Feb-1987	13.22	1.71	34.13	0.40	5.46	0.39
Brent Crude Oil	NYMEX	Sep-2003	15.45	1.22	31.37	−0.63	4.81	0.49
Heating Oil	NYMEX	Feb-1984	13.53	2.09	33.75	0.49	4.84	0.40
Natural Gas	NYMEX	Feb-1993	0.01	0.00	61.39	1.03	5.77	0.00
RBOB Gasoline	NYMEX	Oct-1987	22.10	2.99	36.24	0.36	5.45	0.61
METALS								
Copper	COMEX	Jan-1990	9.47	1.48	26.45	−0.05	5.46	0.36
Gold	COMEX	Feb-1984	1.88	0.72	15.42	0.31	4.12	0.12

TABLE 3.1 (*Continued*)

	Exchange	From	Mean	t-stat	Vol.	Skew	Kurt.	SR
Palladium	NYMEX	Feb-1994	14.37	1.60	35.29	0.34	5.68	0.41
Platinum	NYMEX	Aug-2003	11.83	1.19	27.03	−0.81	7.33	0.44
Silver	COMEX	Jan-1984	2.71	0.56	27.80	0.26	4.17	0.10
MEAT								
Feeder Cattle	CME	Feb-1978	2.46	1.04	14.52	−0.38	5.20	0.17
Live Cattle	CME	Dec-1974	4.66	1.70	16.51	−0.13	4.39	0.28
Live Hogs	CME	Dec-1974	3.32	0.83	25.57	−0.04	3.31	0.13
GRAINS								
Corn	CBOT	Aug-1982	−0.92	−0.19	25.95	0.64	6.02	−0.04
Oats	CBOT	Aug-1982	−1.02	−0.16	34.68	2.76	25.57	−0.03
Soybean Oil	CBOT	Aug-1982	2.26	0.48	26.29	0.58	6.13	0.09
Soybean Meal	CBOT	Aug-1982	8.70	1.90	25.19	0.24	3.88	0.35
Soybeans	CBOT	Aug-1982	4.43	1.08	23.53	0.13	4.13	0.19
Wheat	CBOT	Aug-1982	−2.98	−0.68	25.47	0.36	4.92	−0.12
SOFTS								
Cocoa	ICE	Aug-1986	−3.81	−0.76	29.17	0.58	4.14	−0.13
Coffee	ICE	Feb-1987	−2.04	−0.26	37.86	1.00	5.69	−0.05
Cotton	ICE	Feb-1987	1.42	0.24	26.01	0.28	3.78	0.05
Lumber	CME	Dec-1974	−3.43	−0.68	29.17	0.29	3.67	−0.12
Orange Juice	ICE	Aug-1987	2.87	0.47	32.25	0.68	4.57	0.09
Sugar	ICE	Aug-1986	8.77	1.34	33.10	0.33	3.81	0.27

Source: Nick Baltas and Robert Kosowski; based on data from Tick Data. The table presents summary statistics for the 56 futures contracts of the dataset, which are estimated using monthly fully collateralised excess return series. The statistics are: annualised mean return in %, Newey and West (1987) t-statistic, annualised volatility in %, skewness, kurtosis and annualised Sharpe ratio (SR). The table also indicates the exchange that each contract is traded at the end of the sample period (February 2013) as well as the starting month and year for each contract. All but seven contracts have data up until February 2013. The EUR/USD contract is spliced with the DEM/USD (Deutsche Mark) contract for dates prior to January 1999 and the RBOB Gasoline contract is spliced with the Unleaded Gasoline contract for dates prior to January 2007, following Moskowitz et al. (2012).

the literature (e.g. de Roon et al. 2000, Miffre and Rallis 2007, Moskowitz et al. 2012), we use the most liquid futures contract at each point in time and we roll over contracts so that we always trade the most liquid contract. The most liquid contract is typically the nearest-to-delivery ('front') contract up until a few days/weeks before delivery, when the second-to-delivery ('first-back') contract becomes the most liquid one and a rollover takes place.

An important issue for the construction of continuous price series of a futures contract is the price adjustment on a roll date. The two contracts that participate in a rollover do not typically trade at the same price. If the time-series of these contracts were to be spliced together without any further adjustment, then an artificial non-traded return would appear on the rollover day, which would bias the mean return upwards or downwards for an asset that is on average in contango or backwardation respectively.

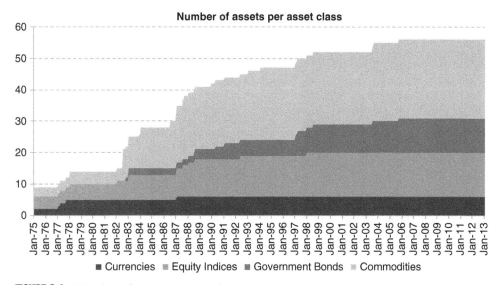

FIGURE 3.1 Number of assets per asset class.
Source: Nick Baltas and Robert Kosowski; based on data from Tick Data. The figure presents the number of assets for each asset class that are available in the dataset at the end of every month. The sample period is from December 1974 to February 2013.

For that purpose, we backwards ratio-adjust the futures series at each roll date, that is, we multiply the entire history of the asset by the ratio of the prevailing futures prices of the new and the old contracts. Hence, the entire price history up to the roll date is scaled accordingly so that no artificial return exists in the continuous data series.[4]

Second, having obtained single price data series for each asset, we need to calculate daily excess returns. As already mentioned, calculating futures holding period returns is not as straightforward as it is for spot transactions and requires additional assumptions regarding the margin payments. For that purpose, let $F_{t,T}$ and $F_{t+1,T}$ denote the prevailing futures prices of a futures contract with maturity T at the end of months t and $t + 1$ respectively. Additionally, assume that the contract is not within its delivery month, hence $t < t + 1 < T$. Entering a futures contract at time t implies an initial margin payment of M_t that earns the risk-free rate, r_t^f during the life of the contract. During the course of a month, assuming no variation margin payments, the margin account will have accumulated an amount equal to $M_t(1 + r_t^f) + (F_{t+1,T} - F_{t,T})$. Therefore, the

---

[4]Another price adjustment technique is to add/subtract to the entire history the level difference between the prevailing futures prices of the two contracts involved in a rollover (backwards difference adjustment). The disadvantage of this technique is that it distorts the historical returns as the price level changes in absolute terms. In fact, the historical returns are upwards or downwards biased for contracts that are on average in backwardation or contango respectively. Instead, backwards ratio adjustment only scales the price series, hence it leaves percentage changes unaffected and results in a tradable series that can be used for backtesting.

holding period return for the futures contract in *excess* of the risk-free rate is:

$$r_{t,t+1}^{margin} = \frac{[M_t\,(1 + r_t^f) + (F_{t+1,T} - F_{t,T})] - M_t}{M_t} - r_t^f = \frac{F_{t+1,T} - F_{t,T}}{M_t} \tag{3.1}$$

If we assume that the initial margin requirement equals the prevailing futures price, i.e. $M_t = F_{t,T}$ then we can calculate the fully collateralised return in excess of the risk-free rate as follows:

$$r_{t,t+1} = \frac{F_{t+1,T} - F_{t,T}}{F_{t,T}} \tag{3.2}$$

Interestingly, the excess return calculation for a fully collateralised futures transaction takes the same form as a total return calculation for a cash equity spot transaction.

In practice, the initial margin requirement is a fraction of the prevailing futures price and is typically a function of the historical risk profile of the underlying asset. If we therefore express the initial margin requirement as the product of the underlying asset's volatility and its futures price, i.e. $M_t = \sigma_t \cdot F_{t,T}$, we can deduce from Equation (3.1) a levered holding period return in excess of the risk-free rate as follows:

$$r_{t,t+1}^{lev} = \frac{F_{t+1,T} - F_{t,T}}{\sigma_t \cdot F_{t,T}} = \frac{1}{\sigma_t} \cdot r_{t,t+1} \tag{3.3}$$

This result can also be interpreted as a long-only constant-volatility strategy, with the target level of volatility being equal to 100%.

Using Equation (3.2), we construct daily excess close-to-close fully collateralised returns, which are then compounded to generate monthly returns.[5] Table 3.1 presents summary monthly return statistics for all assets and asset classes. In line with the futures literature (e.g. see de Roon et al. 2000, Moskowitz et al. 2012), we find that there is a large cross-sectional variation in the return distributions of the different assets. In total, 49 out of 56 futures contracts have a positive unconditional mean excess return, 21 of which are statistically significant at the 10% level. Currency and commodity futures have insignificant mean returns with only a few exceptions. All but two assets have leptokurtic return distributions (fat tails) and, as expected, all equity futures have negative skewness. More importantly, the cross-sectional variation in volatility is substantial. Commodity and equity futures exhibit the largest volatilities, followed by the currencies and lastly by the bond futures, which have the lowest volatilities in the cross-section.

---

[5] This procedure is fairly standard in the futures literature. Among others, see Bessembinder (1992; 1993), Gorton and Rouwenhorst (2006), Gorton, Hayashi and Rouwenhorst (2007), Miffre and Rallis (2007), Pesaran, Schleicher and Zaffaroni (2009), Fuertes, Miffre and Rallis (2010) and Moskowitz et al. (2012).

3.2   METHODOLOGY

3.2.1   Time-series Momentum Strategies

A time-series momentum (TSMOM, hereafter) strategy, also known as a trend-following strategy, is formed as the average of volatility-scaled long and short positions in a universe of assets:

$$r_{t,t+1}^{TSMOM} = \frac{1}{N_t} \sum_{i=1}^{N_t} X_t^i \cdot \sigma_{tgt} \cdot r_{t,t+1}^{i,lev} \tag{3.4}$$

$$= \frac{1}{N_t} \sum_{i=1}^{N_t} X_t^i \cdot \frac{\sigma_{tgt}}{\sigma_t^i} \cdot r_{t,t+1}^i \tag{3.5}$$

where X denotes the trading rule that captures the asset's recent performance over some predetermined lookback period, σ_{tgt} denotes a desired volatility target for each individual asset, and N_t is the number of available assets at time t. The volatility of the portfolio is expected to be relatively lower that σ_{tgt} due to diversification. By construction, the volatility of the portfolio can only be equal to σ_{tgt}, if all the assets are perfectly correlated, which is not typically the case.

In its simplest form, the trading rule takes the form of the sign of the past 12-month return (as in Moskowitz et al. 2012, Hurst et al. 2013, Baltas and Kosowski 2013), i.e. $X_t^i = sign\left[r_{t-12,t}^i\right]$:

$$r_{t,t+1}^{TSMOM} = \frac{1}{N_t} \sum_{i=1}^{N_t} sign\left[r_{t-12,t}^i\right] \cdot \frac{\sigma_{tgt}}{\sigma_t^i} \cdot r_{t,t+1}^i \tag{3.6}$$

3.2.2   Turnover Dynamics

The TSMOM strategy requires rebalancing because either (i) the volatility of the portfolio constituents changes or (ii) the trading rule of some assets changes from positive to negative and vice versa, due to the change in the direction of price trends. We next disentangle these two channels through which portfolio turnover is affected. In order to facilitate the exposition of the effects, we assume a single-asset paradigm and a single trading period defined by two rebalancing dates $t - 1$ and t.

First, consider a single-asset TSMOM, whose trading rule at dates $t - 1$ and t remains unchanged (either long or short). The turnover of the strategy is then proportional to the change of the reciprocal of volatility:

$$turnover_{vol}(t - 1, t) \propto \left| \frac{1}{\sigma_t} - \frac{1}{\sigma_{t-1}} \right| = \left| \Delta \left(\frac{1}{\sigma_t} \right) \right| \tag{3.7}$$

The smoother the transition between different states of volatility, the lower the turnover of a strategy. However, volatility is not directly observable, but is instead estimated with error, that is $\hat{\sigma}_t = \sigma_t + \varepsilon_t$, where ε_t denotes the estimation error. Consequently, the turnover of the strategy is not only a function of the underlying volatility path, but more importantly of the error inherent in the estimation of the unobserved volatility path.

Larger in magnitude time-varying estimation errors result in over-trading and therefore in increased turnover in line with Fleming et al. (2003). Consequently, we hypothesise that a more efficient volatility estimator can significantly reduce the turnover of the TSMOM strategy and hence improve the performance after accounting for transaction costs.

The rebalancing of the TSMOM strategy could alternatively be due to the switching of a position from long to short or vice versa. In order to focus on the marginal effect of the trading rule, assume that the volatility σ of an asset stays unchanged between the rebalancing dates $t - 1$ and t, but the position switches sign. The marginal effect of a trading rule on the turnover of a single-asset TSMOM strategy is illustrated by the following relationship:

$$turnover_{rule}(t - 1, t) \propto \left| \frac{X_t}{\sigma} - \frac{X_{t-1}}{\sigma} \right| = \frac{|\Delta X_t|}{\sigma} \qquad (3.8)$$

For a binary trading rule, such as the sign of the past return, $|\Delta X_t| = 2$, when the position switches sign. In a more general setup that the trading rule has more than two states or even becomes a continuous function of past performance, the turnover of the TSMOM strategy largely depends on the speed at which the trading rule changes states. The effect is expected to be magnified for lower volatility assets, such as interest rate futures, since volatility appears in the denominator of Equation (3.8). This leads to the conjecture that a trading rule that avoids frequent swings between long and short positions and smooths out the transition between the two can significantly reduce the turnover of the TSMOM strategy and therefore improve its performance after accounting for transaction costs.

We empirically test the hypotheses relating to portfolio turnover reduction based on either the volatility estimator or the trading rule in Section 3.

3.2.3   Incorporating Pairwise Correlations

The construction of the TSMOM strategy in equations (3.5) and (3.6), which follows the standard specification used in the literature (Moskowitz et al. 2012, Hurst et al. 2013, Baltas and Kosowski 2013) does not explicitly model the pairwise correlations between the futures contracts as part of the weighting scheme. This potentially constitutes an important limitation for the strategy, especially in periods of increased asset co-movement, like the post-GFC period. One of the main methodological contributions of this chapter is the extension in the formulation of the TSMOM strategy by taking into account the average pairwise correlation of portfolio constituents in an effort to improve the portfolio risk-return characteristics.

We first investigate the interplay between the portfolio volatility and the pairwise correlations of portfolio constituents. Assume a portfolio of N assets with weights and volatilities denoted by w_i and σ_i for $i = 1, \cdots, N$ respectively. To facilitate the notation, we drop the dependence on time in the following derivations. The portfolio volatility,

σ_P, is defines as follows:

$$\sigma_P = \sqrt{\sum_{i=1}^{N} w_i^2 \sigma_i^2 + 2 \sum_{i=1}^{N} \sum_{j=i+1}^{N} w_i w_j \sigma_i \sigma_j \rho_{i,j}} \tag{3.9}$$

where $\rho_{i,j}$ denotes the pairwise correlation between assets i and j. In the TSMOM specification in equations (3.5) and (3.6) each asset has a net leveraged weight equal to $(X_i \cdot \sigma_{tgt})/(N \cdot \sigma_i)$, where $X_i = \pm 1$. Substituting the portfolio weights in Equation (3.9) yields:

$$\sigma_P = \sigma_{tgt} \sqrt{\sum_{i=1}^{N} \frac{X_i^2}{N^2} + 2 \sum_{i=1}^{N} \sum_{j=i+1}^{N} \frac{X_i \cdot X_j}{N^2} \rho_{i,j}}$$

$$= \frac{\sigma_{tgt}}{N} \sqrt{N + 2 \sum_{i=1}^{N} \sum_{j=i+1}^{N} X_i \cdot X_j \cdot \rho_{i,j}} \tag{3.10}$$

The *signed* double summation $\sum_{i=1}^{N} \sum_{j=i+1}^{N} X_i \cdot X_j \cdot \rho_{i,j}$ is effectively the sum of all the elements of the upper right triangle of the correlation matrix of the assets, after taking into account the type of position (long or short) that each asset is going to have over the holding period. Normalising this quantity by the number of pairs formed by N assets, that is $\frac{N(N-1)}{2}$, results in the average pairwise *signed* correlation of the universe, ρ:

$$\bar{\rho} = 2 \frac{\sum_{i=1}^{N} \sum_{j=i+1}^{N} X_i \cdot X_j \cdot \rho_{i,j}}{N(N-1)} \tag{3.11}$$

Solving for the double summation and substituting back into Equation (3.10) yields:

$$\sigma_P = \sigma_{tgt} \sqrt{\frac{1 + (N-1)\bar{\rho}}{N}} \tag{3.12}$$

The above result lies at the heart of diversification. Given that $\bar{\rho} \le 1$, we deduce that $\sqrt{\frac{1+(N-1)\bar{\rho}}{N}} \le 1$, and therefore that $\sigma_P \le \sigma_{tgt}$. Trivially, when correlation falls, diversification benefits increase and portfolio volatility drops further.

Using this result, we next introduce the average pairwise correlation as a factor that controls the target level of volatility of each asset. When average pairwise signed correlation increases (decreases) we would optimally lower (increase) the per asset target level of volatility. Solving Equation (3.12) for a dynamic level of target volatility $\sigma_{tgt}(\bar{\rho})$ for each asset results in:

$$\sigma_{tgt}(\bar{\rho}) = \sigma_P \cdot CF(\bar{\rho}) \tag{3.13}$$

where $CF(\overline{\rho}) = \sqrt{\frac{N}{1+(N-1)\overline{\rho}}}$ denotes a correlation factor (CF) that adjusts the level of leverage applied to each portfolio constituent as a function of the overall average pairwise signed correlation.

Following the above, the generalised TSMOM strategy of Equation (3.5) can be accordingly adjusted by replacing the volatility target for each asset, σ_{tgt} with a time-varying target level of volatility that is determined by a target level of volatility for the *overall* strategy, $\sigma_{P,tgt}$ and a measure of the contemporaneous average pairwise signed correlation of the assets. This gives rise to the correlation-adjusted time-series momentum strategy (TSMOM-CF):

$$r_{t,t+1}^{TSMOM-CF} = \frac{1}{N_t} \sum_{i=1}^{N_t} X_t^i \cdot \frac{\sigma_{P,tgt}}{\sigma_t^i} \cdot CF(\overline{\rho}_t) \cdot r_{t,t+1}^i \qquad (3.14)$$

We empirically study the effect of the correlation adjustment in Section 3.4, with a particular focus on the post-GFC period, when pairwise correlations across assets and asset classes increased significantly, thus diminishing any diversification benefits.

It is important to highlight that, in parallel to our work, a recent paper by Baltas (2015) introduces pairwise correlations between constituents in the portfolio construction methodology of the TSMOM strategy using a long-short risk-parity framework in order to improve the diversification and therefore its performance in periods of increased correlation. Although our objective is the same, our methodology differs from Baltas's (2015) methodology in that we introduce a portfolio leverage control mechanism that is driven by the level of the average pairwise signed correlation. We therefore consider our methodology and findings as complementary to those of Baltas (2015).

3.3 TURNOVER REDUCTION

The purpose of this section is to investigate empirically the turnover implications of the two key determinants of a TSMOM strategy, namely the volatility estimator and the trading rule. As motivated in the previous section, more efficient volatility estimators and more robust trading rules can be expected to reduce the turnover of the strategy.

3.3.1 The Effect of the Volatility Estimator

Fleming et al. (2003) show that increasing the efficiency of volatility estimates can result in significant economic benefits for a risk-averse investor that dynamically rebalances a mean-variance optimised portfolio. The efficiency gain is achieved by switching from daily to high-frequency returns in order to estimate the conditional covariance matrix that is used in the optimisation. Extending this finding, we hypothesise that more efficient volatility estimates can significantly reduce portfolio turnover and consequently improve the net of transaction costs profitability of a TSMOM strategy.

A typical measure of volatility is the standard deviation of past daily close-to-close returns (SD, hereafter), which, even though an unbiased estimator, it only makes use of daily closing prices and therefore is subject to large estimation error when compared to volatility estimators that make use of intraday information. In the absence of high-frequency data in our dataset, we attempt to improve the estimation efficiency by using intraday open, high, low and close daily prices. The volatility estimators that make use of such prices are known in the literature as range estimators and have been shown to offer additional robustness against microstructure noise such as bid-ask bounce and asynchronous trading (Alizadeh, Brandt and Diebold 2002).

A multitude of range estimators have been suggested in the literature by Parkinson (1980), Garman and Klass (1980), Rogers and Satchell (1991), and Yang and Zhang (2000), which have been empirically shown to reduce the estimation error of a conventional daily volatility estimator, like the standard deviation of past returns (Brandt and Kinlay 2005, Shu and Zhang 2006). Out of these estimators, the Yang and Zhang (2000) estimator (YZ, hereafter) is the most efficient and the only to be independent of both the overnight jump (i.e. the price change between the previous day's close and the next day's opening price) and the drift of the price process. For that reason and for the purposes of our analysis we focus solely on the added benefit of more efficient volatility estimates, as these are offered by the YZ estimator.[6]

The YZ estimator is defined as a linear combination of three volatility estimators: the standard deviation of past overnight (close-to-open) logarithmic returns, the standard deviation of open-to-close logarithmic returns and the Rogers and Satchell (1991) (RS, hereafter) range estimator.[7] In particular, the YZ volatility of an asset at the end of month t (assuming some estimation period) is given by:

$$\sigma_{YZ}^2(t) = \sigma_{OJ}^2(t) + k \cdot \sigma_{OC}^2(t) + (1 - k) \cdot \sigma_{RS}^2(t) \tag{3.15}$$

where $\sigma_{OJ}(t)$ denotes the overnight jump estimator, and $\sigma_{OC}(t)$ denotes the open-to-close estimator. The parameter k is chosen so that the variance of the estimator is minimised and is shown by Yang and Zhang (2000) to be a function of the number of days used in the estimation.[8] The YZ estimator is $1 + \frac{1}{k}$ times more

---

[6]In undocumented results, we have additionally evaluated the performance of the less efficient range estimators by Parkinson (1980), Garman and Klass (1980) and Rogers and Satchell (1991). These results are available upon request.

[7]Rogers and Satchell (1991) are the first to introduce an unbiased estimator that allows for a non-zero drift in the price process, but their estimator does not account for the overnight jump (see also Rogers, Satchell and Yoon 1994). Their estimator is 6.2 times more efficient than SD. The RS volatility of an asset over the course of a single day τ is given by:

$$\sigma_{RS}^2(\tau) = h(\tau)[h(\tau) - c(\tau)] + l(\tau)[l(\tau) - c(\tau)]$$

where $h(\tau)$, $l(\tau)$ and $c(\tau)$ denote the logarithmic difference between the high, low and closing prices respectively and the opening price. The RS volatility of an asset at the end of month t, assuming a certain estimation period is equal to the average daily RS volatility over this period.

efficient than SD; this expression is maximised for a 2-day estimator, when YZ is almost 14 times more efficient than SD. For our purposes, a monthly YZ estimator with -on average- 21 daily returns would be 8.2 times more efficient than the monthly SD estimator.

Performance Evaluation We start our analysis by exploring the effects of a more efficient volatility estimator on the turnover of a TSMOM portfolio that is constructed as in equation (3.6). Following Moskowitz et al. (2012) and Baltas and Kosowski (2013) we use $\sigma_{tgt} = 40\%$. This choice is motivated in these studies, because it generates ex-post TSMOM portfolio volatilities that are comparable to those of commonly used factors such as those by Fama and French (1993) and Asness, Moskowitz and Pedersen (2013).

Table 3.2 presents out-of-sample performance statistics for TSMOM strategies that employ different volatility estimators and trading signals.

Looking across the "SIGN" column, where the sign of past returns is used as the trading signal, we find that the two different volatility estimators, SD and YZ, do not have a statistically significantly different economic effect on the performance of the TSMOM strategy. The Sharpe ratios are around 1.15 for both estimators and are statistically indistinguishable from each other as deduced by the large p-value of the Ledoit and Wolf (2008) statistical test.[9] However, when focusing on portfolio turnover, we find that the more efficient estimator reduces the turnover by roughly 17%, with the estimate being statistically significant at the 1% level. This result is in line with our conjecture and the turnover benefit comes without any significant performance penalty.

We next investigate whether the turnover reduction is pervasive across all portfolio constituents. For that reason, we use monthly SD and YZ volatility estimates for all 56 future contracts of our dataset and calculate the time-series average absolute first order difference in the reciprocal of volatility estimates, which is a quantity that, as shown in Equation (3.7), directly affects the turnover of the strategy. For that purpose, we call this statistic the "Volatility Turnover":

Volatility Turnover(i, estimator)

$$
= \frac{1}{\#months} \sum_{\forall m} \left| \frac{1}{\sigma_{i,\text{estimator}}(t_m, t_{m+1})} - \frac{1}{\sigma_{i,\text{estimator}}(t_{m-1}, t_m)} \right| \tag{3.16}
$$

where estimator = {SD, YZ}. In principle, a more efficient volatility estimator should reduce the volatility turnover statistic for each asset. Panel A in Figure 3.2 presents the

---

[8]

The parameter k is chosen using the following equation:

$$
k = \frac{0.34}{1.34 + \frac{N_D+1}{N_D-1}}
$$

where N_D denotes the number of days in the estimation period.

[9]We use the Ledoit and Wolf (2008) bootstrap methodology for time-series data. The optimal block size is estimated to be $b = 10$ and the bootstrap p-values are computed using $M = 4999$ bootstrap samples.

TABLE 3.2 Time-series momentum strategies and the effects of the volatility estimator and the trading rule.

Trading Rule	SIGN		TREND	
Volatility Estimator	SD	YZ	SD	YZ
Average Return (%)	16.12	15.70	13.00	12.72
Volatility (%)	14.01	13.82	11.69	11.60
Skewness	−0.13	−0.21	−0.47	−0.52
Kurtosis	3.46	3.56	3.93	4.37
Sharpe Ratio	1.15	1.14	1.11	1.10
LW Boot-TS p-value	H_0	0.53	0.43	0.37
Average Leverage	4.02	3.84	2.87	2.74
Monthly Turnover (%)	170.0	141.4	128.6	108.4
Relative Turnover change (%)				
– due to volatility		−16.81		−15.67
(t-stat)		(−5.33)		(−5.95)
– due to trading rule			−24.37	−23.34
(t-stat)			(−8.49)	(−8.07)
– joint				−36.23
(t-stat)				(−13.19)

Source: Nick Baltas and Robert Kosowski; based on data from Tick Data. The table presents performance statistics for time-series momentum strategies that differ between each other in the momentum trading rule – sign of past return (SIGN) or trend strength (TREND) – and the volatility estimator used – standard deviation of past one-month returns (SD) or the Yang and Zhang (2000) estimator (YZ). The reported statistics are: annualised average return in %, annualised volatility in %, skewness, kurtosis, annualised Sharpe ratio, Ledoit and Wolf (2008) bootstrap time-series (Boot-TS) p-value for the null hypothesis of equality of Sharpe ratios between all different strategies against the strategy that uses the SIGN trading rule and the SD volatility estimator, average leverage, monthly turnover in % and relative turnover change from switching between volatility estimators, trading rules or both ("joint"); for the relative turnover change, the table reports the respective two-sample t-statistics for the equality in the turnover of the respective strategies. The dataset covers the period January 1984 to February 2013.

percentage drop in the volatility turnover statistic when switching from the SD estimator to the YZ estimator, i.e. $100 \cdot \left(\frac{\text{VolatilityTurnover}(i,\text{YZ})}{\text{VolatilityTurnover}(i,\text{SD})} - 1 \right)$ for each asset i.

The evidence is very strong. Without a single exception, the volatility-induced turnover is reduced when the more efficient volatility estimator is used. The effects are more pronounced for low volatility assets, such as the interest rate contracts, but even for equities the average drop is above 10%. These results suggest that the large error variance of the SD estimator contributes significantly to the excess trading in the TSMOM strategy.

3.3.2 The Effect of Trading Rule

We next turn to the mechanics of two different trading rules and investigate how they affect the turnover and performance of the TSMOM strategy. In particular, we compare

Panel A: The effect of the Volatility Estimator

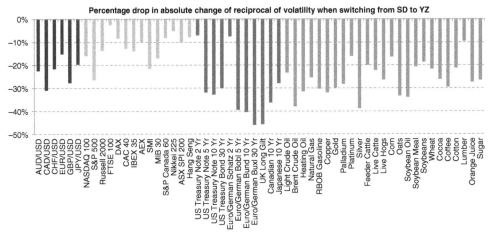

Panel B: The effect of the Trading Rule

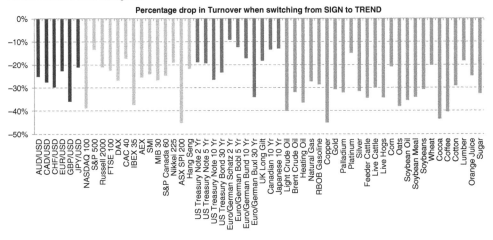

FIGURE 3.2 Effect of volatility estimator and trading rule on turnover.
Source: Nick Baltas and Robert Kosowski; based on data from Tick Data. Panel A in the figure presents the percentage drop of the average absolute change in the reciprocal of volatility for each asset of the dataset when switching from the standard deviation of past returns (SD) volatility estimator to the Yang and Zhang (2000) estimator (YZ). Panel B in the figure presents the percentage drop in the turnover of each univariate time-series momentum strategy when switching between SIGN and TREND trading rules. The one-month SD volatility estimator is used across all strategies for this part of the analysis. The specific sample period of each contract is reported in Table 3.1.

the standard rule (sign of the past return) with a rule that adjusts the gross exposure to each asset based on the strength of the respective price trend.

Return Sign (SIGN): The ordinary measure of past performance that has been used in the literature (Moskowitz et al. 2012, Hurst et al. 2013, Baltas and Kosowski 2013) as well as in this chapter so far is the sign of the past 12-month return. A positive (negative) past return dictates a long (short) position:

$$\text{SIGN}_t^{12M} = sign[r_{t-12,t}] = \begin{cases} +1, & r_{t-12,t} \geq 0 \\ -1, & \text{otherwise} \end{cases} \tag{3.17}$$

Trend Strength (TREND): The SIGN trading rule maps past performance into ± 1 without considering the statistical properties and strength of the price path. An alternative way to capture the trend of a price series is by looking at the statistical strength of the realised return. In particular, we use the Newey and West (1987) t-statistic of the average daily log-return over the past 12 months and accordingly scale the exposure to the various assets. In order to safeguard against extreme allocations, the trading rule is capped at ± 1, when the t-statistic exceeds a certain threshold, which for our analysis is set equal to ± 1:

$$\text{TREND}_t^{12M} = \begin{cases} +1, & \text{if } t(r_{t-12,t}) > +1 \\ t(r_{t-12,t}), & \text{otherwise} \\ -1, & \text{if } t(r_{t-12,t}) < -1 \end{cases} \tag{3.18}$$

Apart from the statistical nature of the t-statistic, it also conveniently bears an economic interpretation as well, as it coincides with the realised annualised Sharpe ratio of the asset over the past 12 months (adjusted both for heteroskedasticity and serial correlation following Newey and West [1987]).

The TREND rule introduces a sigmoid response function that suggests a reduction in the gross exposure for the assets that do not exhibit a certain level of statistical and economic strength in their past realised price path. As price trends switch over time between upward to downward and vice versa, this trading rule is expected to smooth out the transition between 100% long and 100% short and therefore reduce the turnover of the TSMOM strategy. The sigmoid nature of the TREND rule resembles the delta of an option straddle (as shown by Hamill, Rattray and Van Hemert 2016), which in turn establishes the link between the profitability of TSMOM strategies and that of lookback option straddles (Fung and Hsieh 1997, Fung and Hsieh 2001).

As explained above, the signal strength directly impacts the gross exposure for each asset and therefore the collective signal strength across assets and asset classes determines the leverage that is employed at the overall portfolio level. The portfolio leverage at any point in time (L_t) is defined as the sum of the gross weights of all assets:

$$L_t = \sum_{i=1}^{N_t} \frac{|X_t^i|}{N_t} \cdot \frac{\sigma_{tgt}}{\sigma_t^i} \tag{3.19}$$

Given the binary nature of the SIGN rule, $|X_t^i| = 1$ for all assets. Conversely, $|X_t^i| \leq 1$ for the TREND rule and therefore $L_t^{SIGN} \geq L_t^{TREND}$ at any point in time. Put differently, the TREND rule introduces a dynamic leverage reduction mechanism that reduces the overall gross exposure of the TSMOM strategy following periods of collectively weak price trends.

Statistically, in the absence of serial correlation and cross-sectional dependence, a t-statistic is larger than +1 or less than −1, which maps into a TREND rule being +1 or −1 respectively, with probability 31.7%. Any empirical deviation from this threshold constitutes evidence of serial correlation (return continuation if the probability is higher than 31.7%, or return reversal – or, equivalently, lack of return continuation – if the probability is lower than 31.7%) and/or evidence of cross-sectional clustering of these serial correlation effects among assets. Figure 3.3 graphically illustrates this.

Panel A in Figure 3.3 shows the proportion of time for each asset that we document a TREND trading rule being either +1 or −1 (what we call a *strong* trend) and its relationship to asset volatility. The evidence shows that across almost all assets of all asset classes this proportion of time generally exceeds 31.7%. This, in turn, suggests the existence of sizeable return serial correlation (which reduces the standard error, hence inflating the t-statistics). We return to such persistent price trends and the statistical detection of time-series momentum patterns in the next subsection. Most importantly, there does not seem to exist any strong relationship between the underlying volatility of an asset and its respective time-series momentum behaviour. Put differently, the time-series momentum dynamics are neither asset class-specific nor volatility-specific.

Panel B in Figure 3.3 presents the time-series part of the analysis by showing the proportion of assets that exhibit a strong TREND trading rule at the end of each month. As in Panel A, in the absence of any time-series and cross-sectional dependence, we would expect a flat line at 31.7% across time. Conversely, for the most part of the sample period, a larger proportion of assets exhibit a strong TREND rule, which is again an indication of time-series momentum behaviour. One of the most interesting observations is that the number of assets with a strong TREND trading rule has fallen –more than any other historical period– during and after the GFC. We return to this point at a later stage in this chapter, in Section 4.

Parallel to our work, a few other papers have looked at alternative definitions for the TSMOM trading rule, but all of these studies have maintained the rule's binary nature. Dudler et al. (2015) construct a daily rebalanced "risk-adjusted" momentum strategy using the sign of a number of averages of volatility-adjusted daily returns over the look-back period; a similar signal is also used by Lempérière et al. (2014). The risk-adjusted momentum strategy is shown to outperform the typical TSMOM strategy and to reduce portfolio turnover. Levine and Pedersen (2016) focus on the relationship between the basic TSMOM trading rule (SIGN) and moving average cross-over rules.

Performance Evaluation   We next examine the turnover implications from switching the SIGN trading rule for the TREND rule in a TSMOM strategy; Table 3.2 reports the relevant statistics.

The results show that the SIGN trading rule generates a slightly higher Sharpe ratio than the TREND trading rule; using the SD volatility estimator, the Sharpe ratio of the TSMOM strategy is 1.15 for SIGN and 1.11 for TREND. However, the Ledoit and Wolf (2008) p-value shows that these Sharpe ratios are not statistically indistinguishable from each other.

In order to further study this insignificant change in the Sharpe ratio of the strategy, Figure 3.4 contains an event study that presents the 12 months prior to portfolio formation and the 36 month post portfolio formation, separately, for assets with a strong

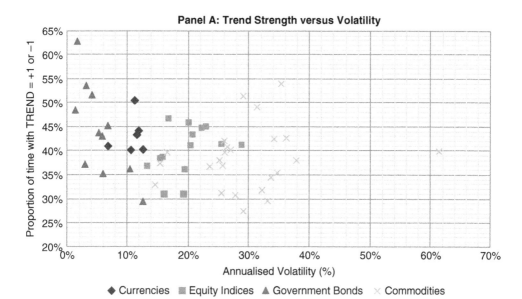

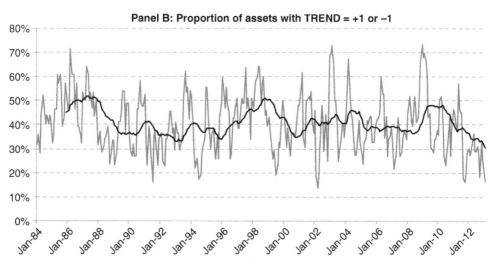

FIGURE 3.3 The statistics of the TREND trading rule.
Source: Nick Baltas and Robert Kosowski; based on data from Tick Data. Panel A presents a scatterplot between the volatility of an asset and the proportion of time that the TREND rule of this asset is either +1 or −1. The specific sample period of each asset of each asset class is reported in Table 3.1. Panel B presents the percentage of available contracts at the end of each month for which the TREND rule is either +1 or −1; the 24-month moving average of this value is also superimposed. The lookback period for which the rules are generated is 12 months and the sample period is January 1983 (first observation in January 1984) to February 2013.

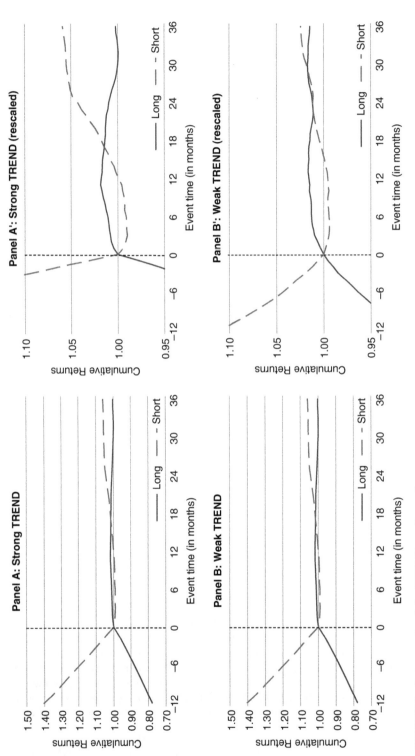

FIGURE 3.4 Event study of the TREND trading rule.

Source: Nick Baltas and Robert Kosowski; based on data from Tick Data. The figure presents an event study across all assets and across time for the period between 12 months before and 36 months after the portfolio formation date (event time '0'). Panel A contains the cumulative performance of all asset-month pairs with a TREND rule of +1 or −1 ('Strong'), whereas Panel B contains the respective performance of all asset-month pairs with a positive TREND rule strictly less than one or a negative TREND rule strictly larger than −1 ('Weak'). All returns are standardised in order to have zero mean across time and across the four groups (long or short, strong or not strong) for comparison purposes. Panels A′ and B′ present rescaled versions of Panels A and B respectively. The specific sample period of each asset class that is used in the analysis is reported in Table 3.1.

TREND rule (±1) in Panels A and A′, and for assets with a weak TREND rule (between −1 and +1) in Panels B and B′. For comparison purposes, all returns are standardised so to have a zero mean across time and across the four groups (long or short, strong or not strong) as in Moskowitz et al. (2012).

During the 12 months prior to portfolio formation, the assets with strong TREND exhibit – by construction – more persistent price trends compared to the assets with weak TREND. However, during the first months after portfolio formation both assets with strong TREND and assets with weak TREND realise their time-series momentum behaviour in equal sizes (Panels A′ and B′ make this easier to illustrate). This is in line with our finding of a statistically insignificant difference in the performance of the TREND rule (which scales down the exposure to assets with weak TREND) versus the SIGN rule (which assumes equal exposure to all the assets of the universe).

Following the first year after portfolio formation, all assets start experiencing reversals. However, the assets with strong TREND experience much stronger reversals both for their long and short positions; in fact, the reversals for the short positions start slightly earlier, at around six months after portfolio formation. This evidence appears complementary to the findings of Lou and Polk (2013) and Baltas (2019), who find that a cross-sectional equity momentum strategy experiences stronger reversals after periods of increased momentum activity over the portfolio formation period. They measure momentum activity as the average pairwise correlation of stocks in the winner or the loser portfolio, after accounting for the exposure to the Fama and French (1993) factors. Hence, high momentum activity implies a stronger co-movement of assets during the portfolio formation period, which, to a certain extent, can be related to having a strong TREND rule across the assets. We therefore consider our analysis in Figure 3.4 as the multi-asset complement the analyses of Lou and Polk (2013) and Baltas (2019).

Going back to our analysis on the impact of the TREND rule on the properties of the TSMOM strategy in Table 3.2, we note that, contrary to the actual risk-adjusted performance that remains quantitatively almost unchanged when switching the trading rule, the turnover reduction is both sizeable and statistically strong. We report a portfolio turnover reduction of roughly 24% (statistically significant at 1%) when the TREND rule is used. This implies that the TREND rule leads to a similar Sharpe ratio, while requiring one quarter less rebalancing.[10]

As in the case of the volatility estimator, the documented turnover reduction at the strategy level is pervasive across all portfolio constituents. Panel B in Figure 3.2 presents the percentage turnover change for univariate TSMOM strategies for each asset of our universe when switching between these rules. Without a single exception, the turnover reduction is pronounced across all assets and asset classes.

3.3.3 The Joint Benefit and a Discussion on the Importance of Turnover Reduction

Taken together, the switch in the volatility estimator and the trading rule can lead to turnover gains of more than one third (36.23%, with a t-statistic of 13.19, as shown in

---

[10]Dudler et al. (2015) report a similar turnover reduction for their daily-rebalanced risk-adjusted momentum strategy. For a lookback period of 12 months, the turnover reduction is around 30%.

the last rows of Table 3.2), without any significant performance drop in the TSMOM strategy. This is a remarkable result, as without causing any performance degradatiion, the turnover of the strategy has been significantly reduced. In Section 3.5, we investigate the economic benefit of this turnover reduction in terms of trading cost reduction. It is worth noting the importance of turnover reduction on its own merit.

The TSMOM strategy – as any momentum strategy – is a high-turnover strategy.[11] Using the estimates from Table 3.2, the default setup of the strategy (using SD volatility estimates and the SIGN trading rule) exhibits a monthly turnover, after leverage, of 170%. The profitability of the strategy is therefore largely dependent on how quickly the portfolio is rebalanced so as to capture the latest emerging price trends and move away from previous trends that have already materialised. This, in turn, means that one can only do so much in terms of turnover reduction, before the actual performance of the strategy starts falling significantly. There is an obvious trade-off: a momentum strategy cannot be turned into a low-turnover strategy without an impact on its performance. The fact that our results show a reduction in the turnover of more than one-third without a material impact on the actual performance of the strategy is therefore noteworthy.

Looking at the practical implications on the implementation of a trading strategy, a portfolio manager would welcome such a sizeable and statistically strong reduction in the turnover. Investors typically face turnover constraints, either because of mandate and regulation and/or just because they want to avoid having a significant price impact when turning over their portfolios. A lower turnover strategy is therefore more likely to be employed by such investors. Additionally, low turnover allows for scalability and capacity in terms of capital invested.

As we shall show in the next section, the turnover reduction that has been achieved can permit changes in the strategy design that focus on performance improvement, which generally come at the cost of higher turnover.

3.4 THE RECENT UNDERPERFORMANCE OF TIME-SERIES MOMENTUM STRATEGIES AND THE EFFECT OF PAIRWISE CORRELATIONS

The purpose of this section is to investigate the dependence of the performance of the TSMOM strategy on the level of the pairwise signed correlations of portfolio constituents and shed light on the poor performance of the strategy after 2008. Our analysis is motivated by the results of Baltas and Kosowski (2013), who, after finding no significant evidence of capacity constraints in the performance of the strategy, argue that the underperformance can potentially be attributed to the lack of significant price trends or an increased level of correlation across assets of different asset classes in the post-GFC period (also argued by Georgopoulou and Wang 2017). We first empirically document evidence supporting these two claims, namely the relative lack of strong price trends

---

[11]Academic evidence even suggests that such high turnover and the associated costs can strongly squeeze the performance of cross-sectional momentum; see Korajczyk and Sadka (2004), Lesmond et al. (2004), Menkhoff et al. (2012) and Novy-Marx and Velikov (2016).

over the most recent period and the increase in the pairwise correlations. Subsequently, we investigate the benefit from incorporating pairwise correlations in the weighting scheme of the TSMOM strategy, as a way to improve its performance in periods of heightened correlations.

3.4.1 Price Trend Strength and Pairwise Correlations

As already shown in Panel B of Figure 3.3, the number of assets with a strong TREND rule has fallen significantly during the post-GFC period. This absence of strong momentum patterns could, therefore, be one reason for the recent performance drop of the TSMOM strategy.

In order to shed more light on this, Panel A of Figure 3.5 presents the average (unsigned) pairwise correlation across all assets over our sample period using a three-month rolling estimation window. In addition to this, Panel B of Figure 3.5 presents the average signed pairwise correlation across all contracts, as defined in Equation (3.11). The unsigned correlations are useful in identifying periods of regime shifts in the co-movement across assets and asset classes, whereas the signed correlations are useful in identifying periods of systematic clustering of time-series momentum trading rules. During periods of significant signed co-movement between assets, portfolio diversification can be impacted, hence rendering the portfolio construction methodology that is typically employed in TSMOM strategies suboptimal.

Looking first at the average unsigned pairwise correlation across all assets in Panel A of Figure 3.5, it is visually clear that this has increased significantly over the last decade of our sample period, in two distinct phases.

The first shift, which has been the milder of the two, seems to have taken place after 2004 and is more likely to be related to the introduction of the Commodity Futures Modernization Act (CFMA) in 2000. This Act effectively rendered the futures market accessible for investors as a way to hedge commodity price risk. This led to significant capital flows into commodity futures contracts as well as into newly introduced – at the time – exchange traded funds (ETF) tracking the performance of commodity indices, like the Goldman Sachs Commodity Index (GSCI) or the Bloomberg Commodity (BCOM) index (formerly Dow Jones UBS Commodity index). These capital flows gave rise initially, post-2004, to higher levels of correlations within commodities (Tang and Xiong 2012) and subsequently, post-GFC, between commodities and other asset classes (Silvennoinen and Thorp 2013), in what is widely referred to as the financialisation of commodities. The financialisation of commodities has recently been a very active research field (Irwin and Sanders (2011), Singleton (2013), Cheng and Xiong (2014), Büyükşahin and Robe (2014), Henderson, Pearson and Wang (2015), Hamilton and Wu (2015) and Basak and Pavlova (2016)).

The second shift in the average pairwise correlation, which is the more pronounced of the two, has occurred after the GFC. In the post-GFC period, assets became more closely related, not only within the same asset class, but most importantly across asset classes; see Silvennoinen and Thorp (2013) for the part of this increase that is due to the already discussed financialisation of commodities and Baltas (2015) for a broader analysis across all asset classes. These higher levels of co-movement have substantially

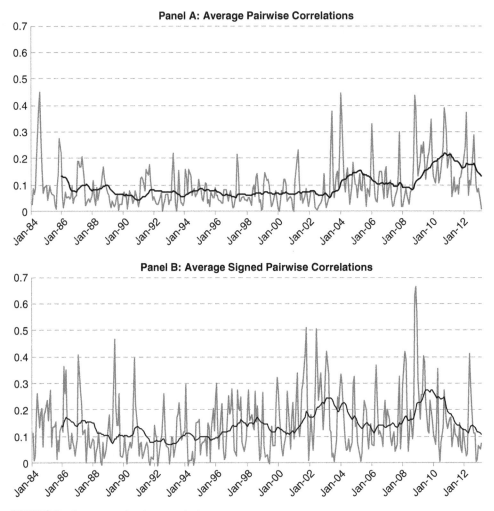

FIGURE 3.5   Average pairwise correlations.
Source: Nick Baltas and Robert Kosowski; based on data from Tick Data. The figure presents
the three-month raw (Panel A) and signed (Panel B) average pairwise correlation of the
available contracts at the end of each month; 24-month moving averages of these estimates are
superimposed. The sample period is from January 1984 to February 2013.

reduced the diversification benefits of the investable universe and can explain the common grouping of all tradable assets into "Risk On" and "Risk Off" assets by market
participants.

Looking at the signed pairwise correlations in Panel B of Figure 3.5, the patterns are
relatively similar to the unsigned correlations, but generally stronger and larger in magnitude. This effectively means that, in addition to the higher level of asset co-movement,
a higher level of clustering of time-series momentum trading rules has recently been
exhibited. To give an example of how this can happen, let us consider two assets that are

negatively correlated. On an unsigned basis, this negative correlation, in fact, reduces the overall level of the average unsigned correlation. However, if the time-series momentum trading rule suggests taking a short position in one of these two assets then their signed correlation turns positive and therefore contributes positively to the average pairwise signed correlation.

To summarise, during the last decade of our sample period, and most importantly in the post-GFC period, the assets of our universe have exhibited significantly higher levels of correlation compared to the more distant past, and their TSMOM trading rules have exhibited higher levels of clustering. We could therefore hypothesise that this increased level of signed co-movement has reduced the diversification benefits of the multi-asset universe and this could have, in turn, reduced the profitability potential of the TSMOM strategy over that period (as also claimed by Baltas and Kosowski 2013, Georgopoulou and Wang 2017). Hence, we investigate whether incorporating information from the signed correlation matrix of the assets into the portfolio construction could render the TSMOM strategy more robust in periods of increased signed co-movement.

As presented in Section 3.2, this can be achieved by using the level of the average pairwise signed correlation to dynamically adjust the target level of volatility of each asset in the TSMOM strategy. The correlation-adjusted TSMOM strategy of Equation (3.14) is repeated below for convenience:

$$
r^{TSMOM-CF}_{t,t+1} = \frac{1}{N_t} \sum_{i=1}^{N_t} X^i_t \cdot \frac{\sigma_{P,tgt}}{\sigma^i_t} \cdot CF(\overline{\rho}_t) \cdot r^i_{t,t+1} \tag{3.20}
$$

Incorporating the correlation factor (CF) would call for a reduction in the leverage when pairwise signed correlations increase and diversification benefits diminish. We next evaluate the performance of the correlation-adjusted TSMOM strategy.

3.4.2 Performance Evaluation

Table 3.3 reports performance statistics for the default specification of the TSMOM strategy (using SD volatility estimates and the SIGN trading rule) with a per asset target level of volatility $\sigma_{tgt} = 40\%$ and for various specifications of the correlation-adjusted strategy (using SD or YZ volatility estimates and the SIGN or TREND trading rules) with a portfolio target level of volatility $\sigma_{P,tgt} = 12\%$. These choices of asset and portfolio target volatility are inconsequential and are justified by the arguments of Moskowitz et al. (2012), who similarly choose the asset target level of volatility to be 40%, so that the overall TSMOM strategy exhibits an ex-post portfolio volatility of 12% for their respective sample period (1985–2009), which, in turn, matches roughly the level of volatility of the Fama and French (1993) and Asness et al. (2013) factors. Panel A covers the entire sample period, whereas Panel B focuses on the post-GFC period, which was shown above to have been characterised by elevated levels of co-movement across asset classes and therefore by diminished diversification benefits.

Over the entire sample period, the correlation adjustment achieves an increase in the Sharpe ratio from 1.15 to 1.19. The performance improvement is much stronger in the post-GFC period with the Sharpe ratio increasing from 0.01 to 0.11 (or even up to

TABLE 3.3 Time-series momentum strategies and the effect of correlations.

| Trading Rule | SIGN | SIGN | | TREND | |
Volatility Estimator	SD	SD	YZ	SD	YZ
Correlation Adjustment	No	Yes	Yes	Yes	Yes
Average Return (%)	16.12	15.13	14.85	12.20	12.03
Volatility (%)	14.01	12.68	12.60	10.32	10.32
Skewness	−0.13	0.23	0.16	−0.10	−0.13
Kurtosis	3.46	4.36	4.32	3.80	4.01
Sharpe Ratio (Mean/Volatility)	1.15	1.19	1.18	1.18	1.17
LW Boot-TS p-value	H_0	0.56	0.73	0.68	0.85
Sortino Ratio (Mean/Downside Vol.)	2.08	2.31	2.25	2.16	2.11
Calmar Ratio (Mean/Max Drawdown)	0.73	1.03	1.02	0.88	0.80
Average Leverage	4.02	3.72	3.56	2.60	2.48
Monthly Turnover (%)	170.0	208.6	190.1	144.7	130.2
Relative Turnover change (%)		+22.71	+11.82	−14.88	−23.41
(t-stat)		(3.98)	(2.16)	(−3.73)	(−6.34)
Average Return (%)	0.14	1.32	1.32	1.26	1.51
Volatility (%)	15.68	11.57	10.98	9.49	9.00
Skewness	−0.28	−0.28	−0.31	−0.49	−0.53
Kurtosis	3.73	3.52	3.69	3.97	4.14
Sharpe Ratio (Mean/Volatility)	0.01	0.11	0.12	0.13	0.17
LW Boot-TS p-value	H_0	0.56	0.57	0.56	0.55
Sortino Ratio (Mean/Downside Vol.)	0.01	0.16	0.17	0.19	0.24
Calmar Ratio (Mean/Max Drawdown)	0.01	0.09	0.09	0.09	0.13
Average Leverage	5.06	4.73	4.36	3.47	3.17
Monthly Turnover (%)	197.5	230.5	196.7	167.5	137.7
Relative Turnover change (%)		+16.71	−0.41	−15.19	−30.28
(t-stat)		(0.95)	(−0.02)	(−1.18)	(−2.46)

Source: Nick Baltas and Robert Kosowski; based on data from Tick Data. The table presents performance statistics for correlation-adjusted time-series momentum strategies that differ between each other in the momentum trading rule – sign of past return (SIGN) or trend strength (TREND) – and the volatility estimator used – standard deviation of past one-month returns (SD) or the Yang and Zhang (2000) estimator (YZ). The correlation factor is estimated using the average past three-month pairwise signed correlation. For comparison, the first column of the table contains performance statistics for the time-series momentum strategy that uses the SIGN trading rule, the SD volatility estimator and employs no correlation adjustment ('benchmark strategy'). The reported statistics are: annualised average return in %, annualised volatility in %, skewness, kurtosis, annualised Sharpe ratio, Ledoit and Wolf (2008) bootstrap time-series (Boot-TS) p-value for the null hypothesis of equality of Sharpe ratios between all different strategies against the benchmark strategy, Sortino ratio, Calmar ratio, average leverage, monthly turnover in % and relative turnover change from the introduction of the correlation adjustment; for the relative turnover change, the table reports the respective two-sample t-statistics for the equality in the turnover of the respective strategies. Panel A covers the entire sample period from January 1984 to February 2013, whereas Panel B covers the period following the financial crisis, from January 2009 to February 2013.

0.17, when all methodological amendments suggested in this chapter are incorporated, as seen in the far right column of the Table – YZ estimator, TREND rule and correlation adjustment).

Given the dynamic leverage nature that is introduced by the correlation factor (reducing leverage in times of large asset signed co-movement), the benefit in the performance of the TSMOM strategy becomes much more pronounced when considering crash/downside risk. This is evidenced by the relatively larger values of performance ratios that measure risk using downside volatility (the so-called Sortino ratio; see Sortino and Van Der Meer 1991) or by the maximum drawdown (the so-called Calmar ratio; see Young 1991). As an example, the Sortino ratio increases from 2.08 to 2.31 over the entire sample period, and from 0.01 to 0.16 for the post-GFC period. These findings are in line with our hypothesis; that is, taking into account signed pairwise correlations positively affects the diversification benefits of the portfolio and improves the risk-adjusted performance especially in periods of higher asset co-movement, like the post-GFC period. This outcome is in line with Baltas (2015), who, as already discussed earlier, introduces a TSMOM strategy that incorporates pairwise correlations in portfolio construction by means of a long-short risk-parity framework and shows that this strategy performs significantly better in periods of heightened asset co-movement.

As expected, the performance benefit does not come without a cost. The effect of modelling and incorporating correlations in portfolio construction leads to more frequent and larger adjustments in portfolio leverage, which, in turn, increases portfolio turnover; all else being equal, the turnover of the standard TSMOM strategy increases after the correlation adjustment from 170% up to 208.6%, an increase that is statistically significant at 1% level (t-statistic of 3.98).

However, as shown earlier in Section 3.3, the additional turnover burden could theoretically be alleviated – if not completely contained – by the use of a more efficient volatility estimator and/or trading rule. Applying both (YZ volatility estimates and TREND trading rule), in fact, leads to an overall turnover reduction compared to the original setup of the TSMOM strategy, even after applying the correlation adjustment (130.2% down from 170%; the reduction is statistically significant at 1% level).

In a nutshell, our results highlight the role that the increased pairwise signed correlations have played in the recent performance of simple unadjusted TSMOM strategies. The implication for fund managers and investors is two-fold. First, allowing signed correlations to determine portfolio weights and dynamically adjust the level of leverage that is employed can be beneficial during periods of high co-movement and trading rule clustering. Second, adjusting for correlation can increase turnover and therefore trading costs. However, other methodological adjustments that have been suggested in this chapter, such as a more efficient volatility estimator or a trading rule that becomes informed of the statistical strength of the price trends, can counteract and contain this increased turnover. The next section of the chapter introduces a new trading costs model for futures-based strategies and provides a set of after-costs results for the variants of the TSMOM strategy.

3.5   TRADING COSTS IMPLICATIONS

Our results so far have shown that different volatility estimators, trading rules and correlation adjustments can substantially impact portfolio turnover, which, as a result, can potentially affect the performance of a strategy after accounting for transaction costs. In this section, we present a detailed model for the approximation of transaction costs for futures-based trading strategies and evaluate the after-costs performance of the various variants of the TSMOM strategy.

Transaction costs have several components and these are typically classified into implicit and explicit transaction costs (Harris 2002). Explicit transaction costs include brokerage commissions, market fees, clearing and settlement costs, and taxes/stamp duties. Implicit transaction costs refer to costs that are not explicitly included in the trade price and therefore have to be estimated. They mainly consist of bid-ask spreads, market impact, operational opportunity costs, market timing opportunity costs and missed trade opportunity costs.

Market participants estimate implicit transaction costs using specified price benchmark methods and econometric transaction cost estimation methods (Harris 2002). These costs depend primarily on the characteristics of any given trade relative to prevailing market conditions and include factors such as the order size as well as the asset's daily trading volume and volatility. Several papers focus on estimating transaction costs in cash equities (see for example Jones and Lipson 1999) using institutional equity order data. Frazzini, Israel and Moskowitz (2015) use proprietary data of a large institution on portfolio holdings and execution prices for the construction and rebalancing of various equity factor portfolios (e.g. momentum, value) and estimate the respective average market impact costs. A similar analysis of the costs and therefore of the respective capacity of equity factor portfolios is conducted by Novy-Marx and Velikov (2016).

Our purpose is to study the trading costs of a futures-based strategy, but, unfortunately, we do not have access to datasets similar to those used in the papers discussed above. For that reason, as opposed to looking at the implicit and explicit costs of a TSMOM strategy, we introduce a transaction costs model that separates the costs into two main distinct sources: (i) roll-over costs of futures contracts and (ii) rebalancing costs. We explain in detail the dynamics for both sources below.

3.5.1   Roll-over Costs

The roll-over costs are incurred when a futures contract approaches maturity and rolls over to the next-to-mature (back) contract. Such costs incur even if there is no change in the notional allocation to an asset; one can think of the roll-over costs as a type of maintenance costs. As an example, if an asset has a 20% weight and a roll-over is imminent because the front contract approaches maturity, there is a cost to pay in order to close down the existing position on the front futures contract and to open a new position of the same notional size on the back contract. One can contrast this against a buy and hold strategy in the spot market, where no additional cost is required to maintain the portfolio.

The roll-over costs are typically quoted in basis points per annum for maintaining a position of 100% gross exposure to an asset. To continue the previous example, if the asset of interest has roll-over costs of 10 basis points per annum, then maintaining a constant 20% weight over a year would incur roll-over costs of $20\% \times 10 = 2$ basis points. As it becomes obvious, the roll-over costs are only a function of the gross weight of each asset. Furthermore, roll-over costs are directly impacted by the leverage that is employed at the overall portfolio level. Assuming that the above example relates to an unlevered portfolio (so that the sum of the gross weights equals to 100%), then a leverage of 3x would triple all roll-over costs, as the gross weight of the asset, after leverage, would be 60% and the respective roll-over costs equal to 6 basis points.

Our universe contains a broad list of assets across asset classes with different futures maturity schedules. For our empirical analysis, we assume different levels of roll-over costs for each asset class, which is a rather realistic assumption, as commodity futures are relatively more expensive to roll-over than FX or bond futures.

Denoting by θ_i the roll-over costs for asset i, the roll-over costs of the overall portfolio between rebalancing times t and $t + 1$, denoted by $RO_{t,t+1}$, are calculated as follows:

$$RO_{t,t+1} = \sum_{i=1}^{N_t} |w_t^i| \cdot \theta_i \qquad (3.21)$$

where $w_t^i = \frac{X_t^i}{N_t} \cdot \frac{\sigma_{tgt}}{\sigma_t^i}$ for the TSMOM strategy with no correlation adjustment and $w_t^i = \frac{X_t^i}{N_t} \cdot \frac{\sigma_{P,tgt} \cdot CF(\rho_t)}{\sigma_t^i}$ for the correlation-adjusted TSMOM strategy.

3.5.2 Rebalancing Costs

The other part of the transaction costs, namely the rebalancing costs, relate directly to the turnover of the portfolio. As the TSMOM strategy rebalances on a monthly basis, these costs incur on a monthly basis and describe the costs from changing the net allocation to the various assets due to potential changes in their volatility or trading rule.

Contrary to the roll-over costs, the rebalancing costs are directly related to the net weight of each asset and therefore reflect any position rebalancing between long and short exposure. As an example, if an asset has an unchanged net weight of 20% long over a rebalancing date, it incurs no rebalancing costs (even though it might still incur roll-over costs if a roll-over takes place, as explained earlier). Conversely, if there is a position switch and the net weight shifts from 20% long to 20% short, then there are rebalancing costs relating to $| 20\% - (-20\%) | = 40\%$ of gross exposure.

The rebalancing costs are typically quoted in basis points per gross position change of 100% over a rebalancing date. To continue the example used earlier in the last paragraph, if the asset of interest has rebalancing costs of 10 basis points, then the transition from 20% long to 20% short would incur rebalancing costs of $40\% \times 10 = 4$ basis points.

For the purposes of our analysis, we assume different levels of rebalancing costs for each asset class. Denoting by η_i the rebalancing costs for asset i, the rebalancing costs of the overall portfolio between rebalancing times t and $t + 1$, denoted by $RB_{t,t+1}$, are calculated as follows:

$$RB_{t,t+1} = \sum_{i=1}^{N_t} |w_{t+1}^i - w_t^i| \cdot \eta_i \tag{3.22}$$

3.5.3 Transaction Costs Model

Taken together, both types of costs reduce the profitability of a TSMOM strategy. The after-costs performance of the strategy between rebalancing times t and $t+1$ is therefore given by:

$$r_{t,t+1}^{TSMOM,\text{aftercosts}} = r_{t,t+1}^{TSMOM} - RO_{t,t+1} - RB_{t,t+1} \tag{3.23}$$

$$= \sum_{i=1}^{N_t} [w_t^i \cdot r_{t,t+1}^i - |w_t^i| \cdot \theta_i - |w_{t+1}^i - w_t^i| \cdot \eta_i] \tag{3.24}$$

As the rebalancing costs are solely driven by portfolio turnover, they are directly impacted by the choice of the volatility estimator, the choice of the trading rule and the correlation adjustment. Conversely, the roll-over costs are solely related to the gross exposure of the assets and are therefore mostly impacted by the choice of the trading rule (as a reminder, the TREND rule – but not the SIGN rule – scales the exposure to the various assets as a function of their realised Sharpe ratio of daily returns over the past 12 months) and the correlation adjustment (the overall leverage of the strategy is adjusted in response to signed correlation shifts); the choice of the volatility estimator hardly alters the roll-over costs (in the long run), as long as the different volatility estimators are unbiased (for our analysis, both SD and YZ estimators are unbiased).

Before presenting the empirical analysis on transaction costs, it is worth comparing our costs model to the one used by Barroso and Santa-Clara (2015a). The TSMOM strategy (or any other futures-based strategy) incurs, as already explained, two different types of costs that are distinctly different and that are incurred at different times; roll-over costs are incurred when a futures contract rolls-over from the front to the back, whereas rebalancing costs are incurred when the overall portfolio is rebalanced (on a monthly basis in our formulation). Contrary to TSMOM, Barroso and Santa-Clara's (2015a) FX carry strategy is rebalanced on a monthly basis and trades one-month FX forward contracts, which are then settled at next month's spot FX rate before a new set of weights is generated and new positions on one-month FX forward contracts are employed. This means that they only have to consider rebalancing costs.

Following the above discussion, we consider our transaction costs model as an extension of Barroso and Santa-Clara's (2015a) costs model that can be applied to futures-based portfolios whose rebalancing and roll-over schedules do not necessarily coincide.

3.5.4 Time-series Momentum and Trading Costs

Using our trading costs model, we next look at the costs estimates of the various TSMOM specifications that have been studied so far in this chapter. For this analysis,

TABLE 3.4 Levels of transaction costs per asset class.

	Roll-over Costs basis points per annum	Rebalancing Costs basis points per transaction
Currencies	8	3
Equity Indices	10	5
Government Bonds	8	4
Commodities	20	6

Source: Nick Baltas and Robert Kosowski. The table presents the levels of roll-over costs and rebalancing costs for every asset class. The roll-over costs are measured in basis points per annum for maintaining a position of 100% gross exposure to an asset. The rebalancing costs are measured in basis points per gross position change of 100% over a rebalancing date.

and based on discussion with market participants, we use realistic levels of roll-over and rebalancing costs for each asset class, reported in Table 3.4.

Table 3.5 reports pre-costs performance statistics, annual costs estimates and after-costs performance statistics for all combinations of volatility estimator, trading rule and correlation adjustment, over the entire sample period (Panel A) and over the post-GFC period (Panel B). Our focus is on the marginal relative reduction or increase of trading costs from the various TSMOM methodological amendments suggested in this chapter. In order to facilitate these comparisons, the Table contains a three-digit binary code system for every TSMOM specification: the first digit represents the trading rule 0/1: SIGN/TREND, the second digit represents the volatility estimator 0/1: SD/YZ, and the third digit represents the correlation adjustment 0/1: without/with. As an example, the strategy 101 uses the TREND rule, the SD volatility estimator and employs the signed correlation adjustment. The left-most column of the Table contains the default TSMOM specification in the literature (coded as 000), whereas the right-most column of the Table contains the TSMOM specification that incorporates all methodological amendments that have been introduced (coded as 111).

Overall, the results from the costs analysis are very much in line with our earlier findings. The use of the more efficient volatility estimator, YZ, or the more robust TREND trading rule reduces the trading costs of the strategy by about 13% and 25% respectively, whereas taken together these two amendments manage to reduce the trading costs by more than a third (35%), from 163 basis points per annum, down to 105 basis points (comparing codes 000 to 110). This is a sizeable reduction.

Conversely, the correlation adjustment always increases the trading costs due to the higher associated turnover. As an example, the costs of the default TSMOM specification increase by about 13%, from 163 basis points per annum to 185 basis points (comparing codes 000 to 001). Interestingly though, when combined with the more efficient volatility estimator and the trading rule that accounts for price trend strength, the net effect is still a sizeable costs reduction of about 28%, from 163 basis points per annum, down to 118 basis points (comparing codes 000 to 111).

How do these estimates translate into after-costs performance? Comparing pre- and after-costs Sharpe ratios in Panel A of Table 3.5, one can argue that the benefits

TABLE 3.5 Transaction costs analysis.

Trading Rule	SIGN		TREND		SIGN		TREND	
Volatility Estimator	SD	YZ	SD	YZ	SD	YZ	SD	YZ
Correlation Adjustment	No	No	No	No	Yes	Yes	Yes	Yes
	(000)	(010)	(100)	(110)	(001)	(011)	(101)	(111)
Panel A: Full sample (1984–2013)								
Before Costs								
Average Return (%)	16.12	15.70	13.00	12.72	15.13	14.85	12.20	12.03
Volatility (%)	14.01	13.82	11.69	11.60	12.68	12.60	10.32	10.32
Sharpe Ratio	1.15	1.14	1.11	1.10	1.19	1.18	1.18	1.17
Monthly Turnover (%)	170.0	141.4	128.6	108.4	208.6	190.1	144.7	130.2
Annual Costs								
Roll-over (%)	0.45	0.43	0.31	0.30	0.42	0.40	0.29	0.28
Rebalancing (%)	1.18	0.97	0.90	0.75	1.43	1.30	1.01	0.90
Total (%)	1.63	1.41	1.22	1.05	1.85	1.70	1.29	1.18
Relative cost reduction/increase (%)								
due to volatility: (x0x) to (x1x)		−13.77		−13.31		−8.01		−9.14
due to rule: (0xx) to (1xx)			−25.46	−25.06			−30.07	−30.92
due to vol. & rule: (00x) to (11x)				−35.38				−36.46
due to correlation: (xx0) to (xx1)					+13.41	+20.98	+6.39	+11.51
due to all: (000) to (111)								−27.94
After Costs								
Average Return (%)	14.49	14.29	11.78	11.67	13.28	13.15	10.91	10.86
Sharpe Ratio	1.03	1.03	1.01	1.01	1.05	1.04	1.06	1.05
Panel B: Post-GFC (2009–2013)								
Before Costs								
Average Return (%)	0.14	−0.02	−0.66	−0.52	1.32	1.32	1.26	1.51
Volatility (%)	15.68	14.79	12.66	11.91	11.57	10.98	9.49	9.00
Sharpe Ratio	0.01	0.00	−0.05	−0.04	0.11	0.12	0.13	0.17
Monthly Turnover (%)	197.5	145.8	154.5	112.9	230.5	196.7	167.5	137.7
Annual Costs								
Roll-over (%)	0.49	0.45	0.36	0.33	0.45	0.42	0.32	0.29
Rebalancing (%)	1.05	0.78	0.80	0.59	1.21	1.04	0.86	0.71
Total (%)	1.54	1.23	1.16	0.92	1.66	1.46	1.18	1.00
After Costs								
Average Return (%)	−1.39	−1.26	−1.81	−1.44	−0.34	−0.13	0.08	0.51
Sharpe Ratio	−0.09	−0.08	−0.14	−0.12	−0.03	−0.01	0.01	0.06

Source: Nick Baltas and Robert Kosowski; based on data from Tick Data. The table presents a transaction costs analysis for various specifications of the time-series momentum strategy using (a) two different momentum trading rules – sign of past return (SIGN) or trend strength (TREND), (b) two different volatility estimators – standard deviation of past one-month returns (SD) or the Yang and Zhang (2000) estimator (YZ), and (c) the pairwise signed correlations. To identify each combination of specifications, the fourth row of the table presents a three-digit binary code in the form of (xxx), where the first digit corresponds to the trading rule, the second digit corresponds to the volatility estimator and the third digit corresponds to the correlation adjustment. The reported statistics are: annualised average return in %, annualised volatility in %, annualised Sharpe ratio, monthly turnover in %, roll-over costs, rebalancing costs, total costs (the sum of roll-over and rebalancing costs), and finally annualised average return in % and Sharpe ratio after costs. Panel A covers the entire sample period from January 1984 to February 2013, whereas Panel B covers the most recent period following the financial crisis, from January 2009 to February 2013.

in terms of costs reduction are not strongly reflected. This does have an interpretation. Starting from the default TSMOM specification, we find that the estimated trading costs of 163 basis points per annum represent about 10% of the pre-costs average annualised returns of the strategy (16.12%). All else being equal, any turnover and therefore costs reduction, can only impact this 10% of annualised performance, so in total in can only be a small proportion of the overall strategy performance.

However, as already discussed in paragraph 3.3, this should not undermine the importance of our findings. Turnover and costs reduction without any performance drop, especially for a strategy like TSMOM that generally demands high levels of turnover in order to achieve profitability, increases the overall capacity of the strategy in terms of capital invested and therefore improves the potential for scalability.

Focusing in the post-GFC period at Panel B of Table 3.5, the results relating to the absolute levels of trading costs as well as the relative gains or losses due to the various alternative specifications of the TSMOM strategy are generally similar to those of the full sample analysis. However, it is worth emphasising the importance of incorporating the pairwise signed correlations in the portfolio construction of a TSMOM strategy, especially in this period of increased level of co-movement across asset classes. When the trading costs are incorporated, the Sharpe ratio of the default setup of the TSMOM strategy turns negative and it is equal to -0.09 (0.01 before costs). After incorporating the various methodological amendments suggested in this chapter and most importantly after incorporating the correlation adjustment the Sharpe ratio of the TSMOM strategy remains positive and equal to 0.06 (0.17 before costs).

In absolute terms, these estimates of the Sharpe ratio before and after costs in the post-GFC period are much lower compared to historical standards. However, this highlights two important issues. First, the TSMOM strategy has indeed suffered from significant underperformance in this most recent period as already discussed several times throughout the chapter. Second, this underperformance has been partly due to the increased level of co-movement between assets and asset classes over this period, which, however, when taken into account in the design of the strategy by the means of the correlation factor leads to relatively better performance that remains marginally positive even after incorporating the respective trading costs.

3.6 CONCLUDING REMARKS

This chapter contributes to the literature on time-series momentum in three ways related to reduction of turnover, improvement of diversification potential, and estimation of trading costs, respectively.

First, we show that the turnover of the strategy can be significantly reduced with the use of more efficient volatility estimates like the ones suggested by Yang and Zhang (2000) or the use of alternative trading rules that depart from the typical binary setup (+1: long, and −1: short). The turnover gains can reach levels of up to approximately 36% (for our sample period and underlying universe), when both methodological amendments are employed, without causing a statistically significant performance penalty.

Second, we provide new empirical evidence to shed light on the post-GFC under-performance of the strategy and the increased level of asset co-movement in this period. This finding subsequently motivates the introduction of a modified implementation of the strategy in a way that incorporates the pairwise signed correlations between portfolio constituents by means of a dynamic leverage mechanism. This mechanism effectively reduces the employed leverage in periods of increased co-movement. We find that the correlation-adjusted variant of the strategy outperforms its naive implementation and the outperformance is more pronounced in the post-GFC period. Importantly, the higher turnover due to dynamic leverage is fully counter-balanced when the earlier turnover reduction techniques are also employed.

Finally, in order to evaluate the economic magnitude of these methodological innovations, we introduce a novel transaction costs model for futures-based investment strategies that separates costs into roll-over costs and rebalancing costs. While roll-over costs are only determined by the gross exposure to the various futures contracts, the rebalancing costs are directly related to the turnover of the strategy. Over our 30-year sample period, we estimate that the trading costs of a time-series momentum strategy roughly represent 10% of its gross return. In line with our earlier findings on turnover reduction, more efficient volatility estimates and more robust trading rules can substantially reduce these costs. In addition, the performance benefit of the correlation adjustment –which, when considered in isolation, actually increases trading costs– can still come with a substantial cost reduction when combined with the turnover reduction techniques discussed above. As a result, the strategy delivers better after costs risk-adjusted returns, benefitting both from the performance benefit of the correlation adjustment and the overall turnover reduction.

Overall, the findings of this chapter have important implications for the academic literature on and investors in time-series momentum trading. By shedding light on the drivers of the recent underperformance of CTA funds, we indicate ways to improve the performance of time-series momentum strategies either by estimating volatility and price trends more efficiently or by improving the diversification properties of the portfolio.

ACKNOWLEDGEMENTS

Comments by Yoav Git, Mark Hutchinson, Nadia Linciano, Pedro Saffi, Mark Salmon, Stephen Satchell, Laurens Swinkels and participants at the UBS Annual Quantitative Conference (April 2013), the IV World Finance Conference (July 2013), the 67th European Meeting of the Econometric Society (August 2013), the FMA Hedge Fund Consortium (November 2014) and the FMA European Conference (June 2015) are gratefully acknowledged. Financial support from INQUIRE Europe is gratefully acknowledged. The views expressed in this chapter are those of the authors only and no other representation to INQUIRE Europe should be attributed. The chapter has been previously circulated with the title 'Improving Time-Series Momentum Strategies: The Role of Volatility Estimators and Trading Signals'.

REFERENCES

Alizadeh, S., Brandt, M. W. and Diebold, F. X.: 2002, Range-based estimation of stochastic volatility models, *Journal of Finance* **57**(3), 1047–1091.

Asness, C. S., Moskowitz, T. J. and Pedersen, L. H.: 2013, Value and momentum everywhere, *Journal of Finance* **68**(3), 929–985.

Baltas, N.: 2015, Trend-following, risk-parity and the influence of correlations, *in* E. Jurczenko (ed.), *Risk-based and Factor Investing*, ISTE Press & Elsevier, chapter 3, pp. 65–96.

Baltas, N.: 2019, The impact of crowding in alternative risk premia investing, *Financial Analysts Journal* **75**(3), 89–104.

Baltas, N. and Kosowski, R.: 2013, Momentum strategies in futures markets and trend-following funds, *SSRN eLibrary*.

Barroso, P. and Santa-Clara, P.: 2015a, Beyond the carry trade: Optimal currency portfolios, *Journal of Financial and Quantitative Analysis* **50**(5), 1037–1056.

Barroso, P. and Santa-Clara, P.: 2015b, Momentum has its moments, *Journal of Financial Economics* **116**(1), 111–120.

Basak, S. and Pavlova, A.: 2016, A model of financialization of commodities, *Journal of Finance* **71**(4), 1511–1556.

Bessembinder, H.: 1992, Systematic risk, hedging pressure, and risk premiums in futures markets, *Review of Financial Studies* **5**(4), 637–667.

Bessembinder, H.: 1993, An empirical analysis of risk premia in futures markets, *Journal of Futures Markets* **13**(6), 611–630.

Brandt, M. W. and Kinlay, J.: 2005, Estimating historical volatility, *Research Article*, Investment Analytics .

Büyükşahin, B. and Robe, M. A.: 2014, Speculators, commodities and cross-market linkages, *Journal of International Money and Finance* **42**, 38–70.

Cheng, H. and Xiong, W.: 2014, Financialization of commodity markets, *The Annual Review of Financial Economics* **6**, 419–41.

Daniel, K. and Moskowitz, T. J.: 2016, Momentum crashes, *Journal of Financial Economics* **122**(2), 221–247.

de Roon, F. A., Nijman, T. E. and Veld, C.: 2000, Hedging pressure effects in futures markets, *Journal of Finance* **55**(3), 1437–1456.

Dudler, M., Gmür, B. and Malamud, S.: 2015, Momentum and risk adjustment, *Journal of Alternative Investments* **18**(2), 91–103.

Fama, E. F. and French, K. R.: 1993, Common risk factors in the returns on stocks and bonds, *Journal of Financial Economics* **33**(1), 3–56.

Fleming, J., Kirby, C. and Ostdiek, B.: 2001, The economic value of volatility timing, *Journal of Finance* **56**(1), 329–352.

Fleming, J., Kirby, C. and Ostdiek, B.: 2003, The economic value of volatility timing using realized volatility, *Journal of Financial Economics* **67**(3), 473–509.

Frazzini, A., Israel, R. and Moskowitz, T. J.: 2015, Trading costs of asset pricing anomalies, *SSRN eLibrary pp.* **14–05**.

Fuertes, A., Miffre, J. and Rallis, G.: 2010, Tactical allocation in commodity futures markets: Combining momentum and term structure signals, *Journal of Banking and Finance* **34**(10), 2530–2548.

Fung, W. and Hsieh, D. A.: 1997, Empirical characteristics of dynamic trading strategies: The case of hedge funds, *Review of Financial Studies* **10**(2), 275–302.

Fung, W. and Hsieh, D. A.: 2001, The risk in hedge fund strategies: Theory and evidence from trend followers, *Review of Financial Studies* **14**(2), 313.

Garman, M. B. and Klass, M. J.: 1980, On the estimation of security price volatilities from historical data, *Journal of Business* **53**(1), 67–78.

Georgopoulou, A. and Wang, J. G.: 2017, The trend is your friend: Time-series momentum strategies across equity and commodity markets, *Review of Finance* **21**(4), 1557–1592.

Gorton, G. B., Hayashi, F. and Rouwenhorst, K. G.: 2007, The fundamentals of commodity futures returns, *NBER Working Paper*.

Gorton, G. and Rouwenhorst, K. G.: 2006, Facts and fantasies about commodities futures, *Financial Analysts Journal* **62**(2), 47–68.

Hallerbach, W. G.: 2012, A proof of the optimality of volatility weighting over time, *Journal of Investment Strategies* **1**(4), 87–99.

Hamill, C., Rattray, S. and Van Hemert, O.: 2016, Trend following: equity and bond crisis alpha, *Available at SSRN*.

Hamilton, J. D. and Wu, J. C.: 2015, Effects of index-fund investing on commodity futures prices, *International Economic Review* **56**(1), 187–205.

Harris, L.: 2002, *Trading and Exchanges: Market Microstructure For Practitioners*, Oxford University Press.

Henderson, B. J., Pearson, N. D. and Wang, L.: 2015, New evidence on the financialization of commodity markets, *Review of Financial Studies* **28**(5), 1285–1311.

Hurst, B., Ooi, Y. H. and Pedersen, L. H.: 2013, Demystifying managed futures, *Journal of Investment Management* **11**(3), 42–58.

Ilmanen, A. and Kizer, J.: 2012, The death of diversification has been greatly exaggerated, *Journal of Portfolio Management* **38**(3), 15–27.

Irwin, S. H. and Sanders, D. R.: 2011, Index funds, financialization, and commodity futures markets, *Applied Economic Perspectives and Policy* **33**(1), 1–31.

Jones, C. and Lipson, M.: 1999, Execution costs of institutional equity orders, *Journal of Financial Intermediation* **8**(3), 123–140.

Kirby, C. and Ostdiek, B.: 2012, Its all in the timing: simple active portfolio strategies that outperform naive diversification, *Journal of Financial and Quantitative Analysis* **47**(02), 437–467.

Korajczyk, R. A. and Sadka, R.: 2004, Are momentum profits robust to trading costs?, *Journal of Finance* **59**, 1039–1082.

Ledoit, O. and Wolf, M.: 2008, Robust performance hypothesis testing with the Sharpe ratio, *Journal of Empirical Finance* **15**(5), 850–859.

Lempérière, Y., Deremble, C., Seager, P., Potters, M. and Bouchaud, J.-P.: 2014, Two centuries of trend following, *Journal of Investment Strategies* **3**(3), 41–61.

Lesmond, D. A., Schill, M. J. and Zhou, C.: 2004, The illusory nature of momentum profits, *Journal of Financial Economics* **71**(2), 349–380.

Levine, A. and Pedersen, L. H.: 2016, Which trend is your friend?, *Financial Analysts Journal* **72**(3), 51–66.

Lou, D. and Polk, C.: 2013, Comomentum: Inferring arbitrage activity from return correlations, Working Paper.

Menkhoff, L., Sarno, L., Schmeling, M. and Schrimpf, A.: 2012, Currency momentum strategies, *Journal of Financial Economics* **106**(3), 660–684.

Miffre, J. and Rallis, G.: 2007, Momentum strategies in commodity futures markets, *Journal of Banking and Finance* **31**(6), 1863–1886.

Moreira, A. and Muir, T.: 2017, Volatility-managed portfolios, *Journal of Finance* **72**(4), 1611–1644.

Moskowitz, T., Ooi, Y. H. and Pedersen, L. H.: 2012, Time series momentum, *Journal of Financial Economics* **104**(2), 228 – 250.

Newey, W. K. and West, K. D.: 1987, A simple, positive semi-definite, heteroskedasticity and autocorrelation consistent covariance matrix, *Econometrica* **55**(3), 703–708.

Novy-Marx, R. and Velikov, M.: 2016, A taxonomy of anomalies and their trading costs, *Review of Financial Studies* **29**(1), 104–147.

Parkinson, M.: 1980, The extreme value method for estimating the variance of the rate of return, *Journal of Business* **53**(1), 61–65.

Pesaran, M., Schleicher, C. and Zaffaroni, P.: 2009, Model averaging in risk management with an application to futures markets, *Journal of Empirical Finance* **16**(2), 280–305.

Rogers, L. C. G. and Satchell, S. E.: 1991, Estimating variance from high, low and closing prices, *Annals of Applied Probability* **1**(4), 504–512.

Rogers, L. C. G., Satchell, S. E. and Yoon, Y.: 1994, Estimating the volatility of stock prices: a comparison of methods that use high and low prices, *Applied Financial Economics* **4**(3), 241–247.

Shu, J. and Zhang, J. E.: 2006, Testing range estimators of historical volatility, *Journal of Futures Markets* **26**(3), 297–313.

Silvennoinen, A. and Thorp, S.: 2013, Financialization, crisis and commodity correlation dynamics, *Journal of International Financial Markets, Institutions and Money* **24**, 42–65.

Singleton, K. J.: 2013, Investor flows and the 2008 boom/bust in oil prices, *Management Science* **60**(2), 300–318.

Sortino, F. A. and Van Der Meer, R.: 1991, Downside risk, *Journal of Portfolio Management* **17**(4), 27–31.

Tang, K. and Xiong, W.: 2012, Index investment and the financialization of commodities, *Financial Analysts Journal* **68**(5), 54–74.

Yang, D. and Zhang, Q.: 2000, Drift-independent volatility estimation based on high, low, open, and close prices, *Journal of Business* **73**(3), 477–491.

Young, T.: 1991, Calmar Ratio: A smoother tool, *Futures* **20**(1), 40.

CHAPTER 4

Risk and Return of Momentum in Developed Equity Markets

JOSE MENCHERO and LEI JI

4.1 INTRODUCTION

There is ample academic evidence to suggest that past returns can serve as an effective predictor of future stock performance. For example, De Bondt and Thaler (1985) showed that stocks that performed poorly over the trailing three to five years tended to outperform stocks that performed well over the same trailing window. A possible explanation for this effect is that investors overreact to a long string of bad news, which pushes stock prices down below their fair market value. Hence, these stocks tend to outperform as they eventually revert to their fair market value. This effect is known as long-term reversal.

Another form of reversal occurs over the recent past. Jegadeesh (1990) found that stocks that outperformed over the trailing week or month tended to underperform over the subsequent period. This effect is known as short-term reversal. One possible explanation is that investors overreact to recent bad news, which pushes stock prices down. As investors realize their 'mistake,' the stock price quickly recovers. Another possible explanation, however, is that the effect is due to illiquidity. Namely, as investors buy large positions in individual stocks, illiquidity causes the stock price to rise, which subsequently is reversed.

Yet another return pattern exists over the medium term. Jegadeesh and Titman (1993) showed that stocks that performed well over the trailing 3 to 12 months tended to outperform stocks that performed poorly over the same historical window. Furthermore, they found that the performance differential was enhanced if they added a one-week lag (to remove the negative impact of short-term reversal). This medium-term return pattern is known as 'relative strength', or momentum. A possible explanation for this effect is that investors tend to *underreact* to news and information over the medium term.[1]

In their seminal paper, Fama and French (1992) did not include momentum as an explanatory variable. Instead, they used three factors: market, value and size. The value factor (also known as *high minus low*, or HML) was defined as the return difference between a portfolio of high book-to-market stocks and a portfolio of low book-to-market stocks. Similarly, the size factor (also known as *small minus big*, or SMB) was defined as the return difference between a portfolio of small-cap stocks and a portfolio of large-cap stocks.

Carhart (1997) extended the Fama-French model by adding momentum as a fourth explanatory variable. Carhart constructed his momentum factor using trailing 12-month returns with a one-month lag. The factor return (also known as *up minus down*, or UMD) was computed as the return difference between past 'winners' and 'losers'.

In this chapter, we study the performance of momentum factors across multiple developed markets. We form our factor-replicating portfolios using cross-sectional regression. One approach we consider is to construct the momentum factor portfolio in isolation. This leads to the concept of a 'simple' factor portfolio, which goes long positive-momentum stocks and goes short negative-momentum stocks (similar to UMD). Simple factor portfolios have many 'incidental' exposures to other factors known to drive stock returns (e.g., industries or other styles). Hence, using simple factor portfolios, it is difficult to know if the observed performance was intrinsic to momentum or due to incidental exposures to other factors.

The cross-sectional regression framework is particularly powerful when applied to multiple factors, as it neatly disentangles the return contributions from each factor. More specifically, the 'pure' momentum factor portfolios have zero exposure to each industry, country and other styles. Hence, pure factor portfolios allow us to isolate the intrinsic impact of the momentum.

The remainder of this chapter is organized as follows. In the next section we present our definition of momentum and show how to standardize the exposures. Next, we describe how to form 'simple' factor portfolios. We then describe our multifactor structure, which is followed by a description of 'pure' factor portfolios. Finally, we compare the risk and return characteristics of momentum pure factor portfolios across the different developed equity markets.

4.2 DEFINITION OF MOMENTUM

Updating momentum exposures on a monthly frequency is adequate for most academic studies. Practitioners, on the other hand, require momentum exposures to be updated on a daily basis to properly manage their portfolios. Moreover, it is important to construct

---

[1]The critical reader may wonder why investors would overreact to news over the long run and over the short run, but underreact to news over the medium term. Such questions are beyond the scope of this paper.

the factor in such a way as to avoid spurious 'jumps' in momentum exposure when extreme stock returns enter or exit the window.

In this section, we describe our construction of momentum factor exposures. Our approach is similar to the traditional definition (i.e., trailing 12m return with a 1m lag), except for two modifications: (1) exposures are updated daily, and (2) spurious jumps in exposure are mitigated.

The raw momentum exposure M_{nt} of stock n at the start of day t is given by the weighted sum of lagged log returns,

$$M_{nt} = \sum_{l=1}^{L} \lambda_{t-l} \ln(1 + r_n^{t-l}), \tag{4.1}$$

where r_n^{t-l} is the return of stock n (in the local currency) on day $t - l$, λ_{t-l} is the weight assigned to day $t - l$, l is the lag number, and $L = 252$ is the total number of lags.

To remove the effects of short-term reversal, we assign zero weight ($\lambda_{t-l} = 0$) for the most recent month($l \leq 21$). For the next month($21 < l \leq 42$), we use linearly increasing weights. The linear weighting means that the raw momentum exposure does not suddenly 'jump' when a large daily return enters the window. Instead, it will be smoothly phased in. For the next nine months ($42 < l \leq 231$) we use constant weights. Finally, for the 12th month($231 < l \leq 252$), we use linearly decreasing weights, thereby ensuring that momentum exposures do not suddenly change when a large return exits the rear window. The momentum-weighting scheme is illustrated in Figure 4.1.

It is important to use log returns when computing raw momentum values. An alternative approach would be to use arithmetic returns. This alternative definition, however, has a potentially serious flaw, as illustrated by the following example. Suppose that a stock falls by 50% in a single day and subsequently rebounds by 100% over the next day. The two-day return of the stock is exactly zero. However, the aggregated arithmetic returns would be 50%, suggesting that the stock had performed extremely well. By contrast, the aggregated log return would be exactly zero, consistent with reality.

To compute returns for the momentum factor, we must first specify an estimation universe. For each country, at the start of each day, we rank stocks according to market capitalization. We then include the N largest stocks that collectively comprise 97% of the total market cap for each country. While the number of stocks varies over time, the average number of stocks across time is roughly 1,900 for the US, 300 for the UK, 1,000 for Europe, 1,500 for Japan, and 400 for Canada.

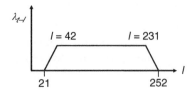

FIGURE 4.1 Return-weighting scheme for constructing momentum factor.

Equation (4.1) provides the raw exposures to the momentum factor. Next, these factor exposures are standardized as z-scores. Suppressing the time subscript, the cap-weighted raw momentum exposure on any given day is

$$\overline{M} = \sum_{n=1}^{N} w_n M_n, \tag{4.2}$$

where w_n is the cap weight of stock n. The standardized momentum exposure is given by

$$X_n = \frac{M_n - \overline{M}}{\sigma_M}, \tag{4.3}$$

where σ_M is the equal-weighted cross-sectional standard deviation. Note that the market portfolio, by design, is style-neutral (i.e., zero standardized exposure). Hence, a stock whose performance matched that of the broad market would have zero exposure to the standardized momentum factor, while a stock whose raw momentum exposure M_n was one standard deviation above the mean would have an exposure of 1.0 to the standardized factor.

4.3 SIMPLE FACTOR PORTFOLIOS

Let r_n denote the return of stock n, and let X_n be the standardized stock exposure to the momentum factor. To form the simple factor portfolio, we perform a univariate cross-sectional regression of stock returns against the momentum factor exposures (including an intercept term),

$$r_n = f_M + X_n f_S + e_n, \tag{4.4}$$

Where f_M is the slope coefficient of the intercept term, f_S is the slope coefficient of the momentum factor, and e_n is the unexplained residual. As discussed later, we interpret f_M to be the return of the market factor, and f_S to be the return of the momentum simple factor portfolio. Note that the return of the style factor depends on whether or not an intercept is included, since the style exposures are generally not orthogonal to the intercept term on a regression-weighted basis.

It proves convenient to write Equation (4.4) in matrix form,

$$\mathbf{r} = \mathbf{Yb} + \mathbf{e}, \tag{4.5}$$

where $\mathbf{r}$ is an $N \times 1$ vector of stock returns, N is the number of stocks in the estimation universe, $\mathbf{e}$ is an $N \times 1$ vector of residual returns, $\mathbf{b}$ is a 2×1 vector of slope coefficients ($\mathbf{b}' \equiv [f_M\ f_S]$), and $\mathbf{Y}$ is an $N \times 2$ exposure matrix,

$$\mathbf{Y} \equiv \begin{bmatrix} 1 & X_1 \\ 1 & X_2 \\ \vdots & \vdots \\ 1 & X_N \end{bmatrix}. \tag{4.6}$$

The textbook solution using weighted least squares (WLS) is given by

$$\mathbf{b} = (\mathbf{Y'VY})^{-1}\mathbf{Y'Vr}, \tag{4.7}$$

where $\mathbf{V}$ is an $N \times N$ diagonal matrix of regression weights v_n. From an econometric perspective, the optimal regression weights are inversely proportional to the residual variance, as these minimize the sampling error of the factor return estimate. In practice, the square root of market cap is often used as a proxy for inverse residual variance, and this is the convention that we adopt in this paper.

The regression weights sum to unity, which implies that matrix $\mathbf{V}$ has a trace of 1. For ease of derivation, we momentarily assume that the style factor exposures are standardized to be *regression-weighted* mean zero,

$$\sum_n v_n X_n = 0, \tag{4.8}$$

with *regression-weighted* unit variance, i.e.,

$$\sum_n v_n X_n^2 = 1. \tag{4.9}$$

In this case, the slope coefficients can be easily solved by hand using Equation (4.7). The slope coefficient for the intercept term is given by

$$f_M = \sum_n v_n r_n, \tag{4.10}$$

which represents the return of the regression-weighted market portfolio. Similarly, the slope coefficient for the style factor is given by

$$f_S = \sum_n (v_n X_n) r_n. \tag{4.11}$$

Hence, the weight of stock n in the simple factor portfolio is given by the product of the regression weight v_n and the style exposure X_n. Note that by Equation (4.8), these stock weights sum to zero, which implies that the simple style factor portfolio is strictly dollar neutral.

The portfolio exposure to the style factor is given by the weighted average of the individual stock exposures, i.e., $\sum_n (v_n X_n) X_n$, which is equal to 1.0 by Equation (4.9). Hence, the simple factor portfolio has unit exposure to the momentum factor.

Simple factor portfolios effectively consider the style factor in isolation. For instance, if the technology sector has recently outperformed the market, then the momentum simple factor portfolio will have a net long position in the technology sector. Similarly, if large-cap stocks have recently outperformed the market, then the momentum simple factor portfolio will likely make a positive tilt on the size factor. In this case, it is unclear whether the return of the momentum simple factor portfolio is intrinsically due to momentum, or perhaps due to 'incidental' exposures to other factors (e.g., technology or size).

Equation (4.10) and Equation (4.11) were derived under the assumption that the exposures were regression-weighted mean zero and regression-weighted unit standard deviation. We now relax these two assumptions. First, suppose that we use style exposures $\widetilde{X}_n$ that have been rigidly shifted by some constant Δ relative to the original exposures. In this case, the regression becomes

$$r_n = \widetilde{f}_M + \widetilde{X}_n \widetilde{f}_S + \widetilde{e}_n, \tag{4.12}$$

where $\widetilde{X}_n = X_n + \Delta$. Note that the factors in Equation (4.12) span the same space as the original factors in Equation (4.4). Hence, the residuals must be equal, i.e., $e_n = \widetilde{e}_n$. Substituting $\mathbf{Y} = [\mathbf{1}\ \widetilde{\mathbf{X}}]$ into Equation (4.7), after a few lines of algebra, we find that the style factor returns are invariant, i.e., $\widetilde{f}_S = f_S$. The market factor returns, on the other hand, become $\widetilde{f}_M = f_M - f_S \Delta$, which can be interpreted as the return of the regression-weighted market portfolio net of the return contribution explained by the style factor.

Next, we consider the effect of scaling the standard deviation, while keeping the shift Δ fixed. Any desired standard deviation can be obtained by scaling the style exposures by a constant a, i.e., $\widetilde{X}_n \rightarrow a\widetilde{X}_n$. In this case, it is easy to show that the market factor return is invariant, while the style factor returns scale as $\widetilde{f}_S = \widetilde{f}_S / a$. In other words, scaling the style exposures by a constant a is equivalent to delevering the style factor portfolio by a factor of $1/a$. Empirically, for the momentum factor, we find that $\Delta \approx 0$ and $a \approx 1$. Hence, Equation (4.10) is an excellent approximation to the market factor return $\widetilde{f}_M$, while Equation (4.11) is an excellent approximation to the style factor return $\widetilde{f}_S$.

4.4 MULTIFACTOR STRUCTURE

Conceptually, as described by Menchero and Lee (2015), factors can be grouped into two categories. 'Alpha' factors explain the *mean* of asset returns (i.e., they are associated with return premia), whereas 'risk' factors explain the *variability* and *comovement* of asset returns.

Using this terminology, according to the Capital Asset Pricing Model (CAPM) as described by Sharpe (1964), the only 'alpha' factor is market beta, since no other factor should have a return premium associated with it. Nevertheless, Fama and French (1992) showed that in the US equity market the return to the market beta factor was flat, contrary to the CAPM.

Moreover, academics have identified several factors that according to CAPM 'should not' have a return premium, but in fact appear effective at explaining expected returns. These represent the so-called 'pricing anomalies' (e.g., value, momentum, size, low volatility and quality). Most academics and practitioners agree that the number of independent 'alpha' factors is very small.

While the CAPM asserts that there is only one alpha factor, it is silent on how many risk factors may exist. In fact, the number of risk factors is typically much larger than the number of alpha factors. For instance, a portfolio that is concentrated in a single industry or country tends to be far more volatile than a portfolio that is diversified across industries and countries. Hence, industries and countries are important risk factors, although this does not imply that there is a return premium associated with particular industries or countries. Another example of an excellent risk factor is given by market beta. For instance, a dollar-neutral portfolio that is long the top quintile of beta stocks and short the bottom quintile will be far more volatile than a portfolio that randomly takes long/short positions in individual stocks. Again, this does not imply that there is a return premium associated with market beta, consistent with Fama and French.

We now describe the factor structure used to construct our multifactor models. We construct models for the following developed equity markets: US, UK, Europe, Japan and Canada. All of the models are associated with individual countries, except Europe, which contains multiple countries.

All models contain an intercept term, which is associated with the market factor. All stocks have unit exposure to the market factor.

All models include industry factors, which we treat as dummy variables. That is, the stock exposure is equal to 1 if the stock belongs to the industry, whereas it is equal to zero otherwise. Industry factors are based on the Bloomberg Industry Classification System (BICS).

To determine industry structure for a given model, we empirically test which combinations of BICS industries maximize the explanatory power of the model (i.e., R^2), while retaining the statistical significance of the factor returns. In order to have high statistical significance of factor returns, we must avoid thin industries (which are 'noisy' and hence dominated by idiosyncratic risk). Broad markets with large numbers of stocks that span multiple industries (e.g., US) tend to have a richer industry factor structure than those with a smaller numbers of stocks (e.g., Canada). The number of industry factors contained in our models are: US (42), UK (12), Europe (26), Japan (36), and Canada (12).

All models include the same set of 14 style factors: beta, residual volatility, size, momentum, earnings yield, mid-cap, liquidity, long-term reversal, growth, variability, profitability, valuation, dividend yield and leverage. The four most important style factors for purposes of explaining risk are: beta, residual volatility, size, and momentum. Raw beta is defined as the slope coefficient of a time-series regression of daily stock returns against the daily market return. The look-back window for the regression was 252 days with a 126-day half-life parameter. Raw residual volatility is defined as the realized volatility of the residuals in the same time-series regression. Raw size is given by the log of market cap. Finally, raw momentum is defined as in Equation (4.1).

With the style factors thus defined, the raw exposures are converted into z-scores. As shown in Equation (4.3), all style factors are standardized to be cap-weighted, mean zero and equal-weighted, standard deviation 1 across their respective estimation universes.

The European model contains individual country factors for each country in the model. Again, country exposures are expressed as dummy variables, which are equal to 1 if the stock has country of risk associated with the factor, and zero otherwise. The European model spans the following 15 developed markets: Austria, Belgium/Luxembourg, Denmark, Finland, France, Germany, Greece, Ireland, Italy, Holland, Norway, Portugal, Spain, Sweden and Switzerland.

As a concrete example, the German automaker BMW would have unit exposure to the European market factor, unit exposure to the Germany factor, and unit exposure to the European automobile factor. In addition, it would have exposures to all of the European style factors.

4.5 PURE FACTOR PORTFOLIOS

Suppose there are N stocks in the estimation universe and we use K factors to explain their returns, as described in the previous section. The multi-variate cross-sectional regression used to estimate factor returns is written as,

$$\mathbf{r} = \mathbf{Xf} + \mathbf{u}, \tag{4.13}$$

where now $\mathbf{X}$ is an $N \times K$ factor exposure matrix, $\mathbf{f}$ is a $K \times 1$ vector of factor returns, and $\mathbf{u}$ is an $N \times 1$ vector of residual returns. An issue with this model specification is that the factor exposure matrix contains an exact collinearity. More specifically, since each stock has unit exposure to a single industry factor, the sum of all industry columns is a column of 1's, which is identical to the intercept term. In other words, while matrix $\mathbf{X}$ contains K columns, the vector space spans only $K - 1$ dimensions.

Hence, we need to impose a single constraint to obtain a unique regression solution. The constraint can be expressed in the following form,

$$\mathbf{f} = \mathbf{Rg}, \tag{4.14}$$

where $\mathbf{R}$ is a constraint matrix containing K rows and $K - 1$ columns, and $\mathbf{g}$ is a column vector of $K - 1$ constrained variables.

As shown by Menchero (2010), the factor returns are given by

$$\mathbf{f} = \mathbf{R}(\mathbf{R}'\mathbf{X}'\mathbf{VXR})\mathbf{R}'\mathbf{X}'\mathbf{Vr}, \tag{4.15}$$

where again $\mathbf{V}$ is a diagonal matrix of regression weights. The constraint we impose is that the cap-weighted industry factor returns sum to zero each period,

$$\sum_{i=1}^{K_I} w_i f_i = 0, \tag{4.16}$$

where w_i is the cap-weight of industry i, f_i is the industry factor return, and K_I is the total number of industry factors.

The constraint equation is best illustrated by example. Suppose that there are three industry factors and the weighted sum is set equal to zero, i.e., $w_1 f_1 + w_2 f_2 + w_3 f_3 = 0$. In this case, the constraint equation is

$$\begin{bmatrix} f_1 \\ f_2 \\ f_3 \end{bmatrix} = \begin{bmatrix} 1 & 0 \\ 0 & 1 \\ -(w_1/w_3) & -(w_2/w_3) \end{bmatrix} \begin{bmatrix} g_1 \\ g_2 \end{bmatrix}. \tag{4.17}$$

For any set of values g_1 and g_2, it is easily verified that $w_1 f_1 + w_2 f_2 + w_3 f_3 = 0$ is always satisfied.

Multi-country models also contain country factors, which introduces a second exact collinearity in the factor structure of such models. In this case, we must impose an additional constraint to obtain a unique regression solution. Specifically, we set the cap-weighted country factor returns sum to zero,

$$\sum_{c=1}^{K_C} w_c f_c = 0, \tag{4.18}$$

where w_c is the cap weight of country C, and K_C is the total number of country factors. The general form for the restriction matrix for multi-country models is

$$\mathbf{R} = \begin{bmatrix} \mathbf{I} & \mathbf{0} & \mathbf{0} \\ \mathbf{0} & \mathbf{R}_I & \mathbf{0} \\ \mathbf{0} & \mathbf{0} & \mathbf{R}_C \end{bmatrix}, \tag{4.19}$$

where $\mathbf{R}_I$ is a $K_I \times (K_I - 1)$ constraint matrix for industries, $\mathbf{R}_C$ is a $K_C \times (K_C - 1)$ constraint matrix for countries, and $\mathbf{I}$ is the identity matrix of dimension $(K - K_I - K_C)$. Note that the market factor and the style factors map onto block $\mathbf{I}$, and the matrix $\mathbf{R}$ has K columns and $K-2$ rows.

Let $\mathbf{Q}$ denote the $K \times N$ matrix that is formed by multiplying all of the matrices to the left of the return vector in Equation (4.15). That is, $\mathbf{Q} \equiv \mathbf{R}(\mathbf{R}'\mathbf{X}'\mathbf{V}\mathbf{X}\mathbf{R})\mathbf{R}'\mathbf{X}'\mathbf{V}$. The rows of matrix $\mathbf{Q}$ give the weights of the stocks in the pure factor portfolios. As described by Menchero (2010), pure style factor portfolios have unit exposure to their respective factor, and zero exposure to all other factors. Hence, the pure momentum factor portfolio is long high momentum stocks, short low-momentum stocks, and is dollar neutral within each industry and country.

4.6 EMPIRICAL RESULTS: MOMENTUM PERFORMANCE

In Figure 4.2, we plot the cumulative log returns of the US momentum factor (estimated using monthly regressions). We first consider the pure factor portfolio, whose cumulative performance is given by the dashed line. The pure factor had very strong performance for the first six years of the sample period. For instance, from Jan-1995 to Dec-2000, the pure factor was up nearly 50%. However, from Dec-2000 to Feb-2018, the factor had roughly zero cumulative return.

The US simple factor portfolio also performed strongly in the first part of the sample period, as indicated by the solid red line. For example, from Jan-1995 to Feb-2000, the portfolio was up more than 50%. Since Feb-2000, while the factor has exhibited large swings, it was essentially flat through Feb-2018.

Interestingly, the cumulative performance over the full sample period was virtually identical for the simple and pure factor portfolios. Note that the simple and pure factor

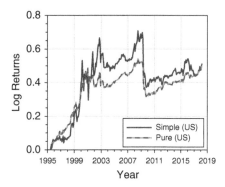

FIGURE 4.2 Cumulative log returns of simple and pure momentum factor for the US equity market.

portfolios both have the same unit exposure to the momentum factor. This implies that the return premium associated with the simple factor portfolio was entirely explained by the pure momentum factor. In other words, there was not a return premium associated with the 'incidental' exposures to other risk factors.

The other item worth noting is that the simple factor portfolio had considerably greater volatility than the pure factor portfolio. This additional risk was attributable to the 'incidental' bets placed by the simple factor.

A prominent feature for both the simple and pure factor portfolios is the momentum crash that started in April 2009. The pure factor portfolio dropped 10.47% in a single month, while the simple factor dropped 17.42%. Note that the momentum crash coincided with the rebound of the global equity markets following the Global Financial Crisis.

Daniel and Moskowitz (2016) showed that momentum strategies are prone to crashes when a market rebounds after suffering severe losses, such as occurred in April 2009. They showed that this was due to negative momentum stocks (past losers) having spectacular performance, not from positive momentum stocks (past winners) crashing. They also documented this effect in the US equity market going back to the Great Depression. For instance, they found that in the market rebound of July/August 1932, the return of the bottom decile (losers) was 232%, whereas the top decile (winners) returned only 32%. Similarly, from March to May of 2009, the bottom decile gained 163%, whereas the top decile returned only 8%. The basic mechanism at work is that at the height of the panic, the losers are severely underpriced. When market sentiment turns positive, these stocks exhibit a spectacular recovery.

In Figure 4.3, we plot cumulative log returns for simple and pure momentum factors in the UK equity market. Qualitatively, the UK shares many of the same features as momentum in the US market. In particular, we find: (a) both simple and pure factor portfolios performed very well through February 2000, (b) the simple factor was considerably more volatile than the pure factor, (c) the cumulative returns of simple and pure factors were similar, and (d) the momentum crash of April 2009 is a prominent feature. While there are many similarities with US momentum, a notable difference is that the

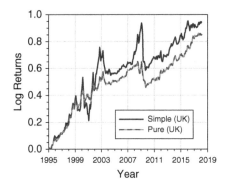

FIGURE 4.3 Cumulative log returns of simple and pure momentum factor for the UK equity market.

UK factor had considerably stronger cumulative performance. While the US momentum factor was mostly flat over the period 2000-2018, the UK factor was up sharply over this same period. As a result, UK momentum had much stronger performance over the full sample period than its US counterpart.

In Figure 4.4, we report cumulative returns to the simple and pure momentum factors in Europe. The behavior of momentum in Europe is qualitatively similar to its UK counterpart. In particular, the cumulative performance was quite strong in both markets. Moreover, the cumulative returns of the Europe simple and pure factors were virtually identical, showing that there was not a return premium associated with the 'incidental' exposures of the simple factor portfolio. Finally, the momentum crash of April 2009 is clearly evident.

In Figure 4.5, we show cumulative returns of the Japan simple and pure momentum factor portfolios. Anecdotally, many practitioners hold the view that momentum 'doesn't work' in Japan. Figure 4.5 suggests that the reality is a bit more nuanced. While

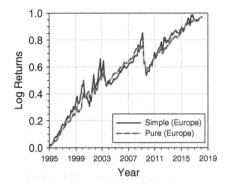

FIGURE 4.4 Cumulative log returns of simple and pure momentum factor for the Europe equity market.

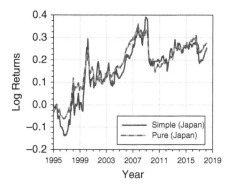

FIGURE 4.5 Cumulative log returns of simple and pure momentum factor for the Japan equity market.

it is true that the cumulative returns were smaller than in other markets, the net returns over the sample period were still positive. Another difference between Japan and the other equity markets is that momentum in Japan performed quite poorly over the first two years of the sample period.

While there are many differences between Japan momentum and that in other markets, there are also some important similarities. For instance, the simple and pure factor portfolios had similar cumulative returns, again showing that there was not a return premium associated with the incidental exposures of simple momentum. Finally, the momentum crash of April 2009 is readily apparent.

In Figure 4.6, we plot the cumulative returns of the simple and pure momentum factor portfolios in Canada. The most striking feature of this plot is the strong historical performance. From January 1995 through February 2018, both simple and pure factor were up roughly 160% (in log returns). Converting this into conventional returns ($e^{1.6} - 1$) yields a cumulative return of nearly 400%.

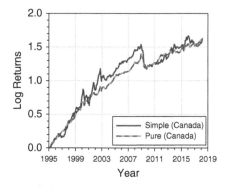

FIGURE 4.6 Cumulative log returns of simple and pure momentum factor for the Canada equity market.

Momentum in Canada also shared many similarities with momentum in other developed equity markets. For instance, as in other markets, the cumulative returns of simple and pure factors were again very similar over the full sample period. Moreover, the simple factor portfolio had considerably higher volatility than the pure factor portfolio. Finally, the momentum crash of April 2009 is clearly visible.

4.7 EMPIRICAL RESULTS: MOMENTUM RISK

In Figure 4.7, we plot the trailing 24-month volatility (annualized) of the monthly pure factor returns versus time. The mean volatility is the equal-weighted average volatility across the five factors. The minimum and maximum curves represent the highest and lowest volatility of the five factors at any point in time.

Note that the mean volatility exhibits one distinct valley surrounded by two distinct peaks. The first peak, which lasted from roughly 2000 to 2004, corresponded to the Internet Bubble period and its aftermath. The second peak, which lasted roughly from 2009 to 2011, coincided with the end of the Global Financial Crisis. We have seen from the performance charts that all momentum factors crashed in early 2009. Hence, it is not surprising that volatility also spikes following a momentum crash.

The period of lowest mean volatility occurred from roughly 2006 to 2008, where the mean volatility was roughly 2.0% annualized. Since 2012, the mean volatility has ranged from 3 to 4%, which was still well below the historical long-term average.

The minimum-volatility factor from Jan-1997 through Feb-2002 was Europe momentum. By contrast, the highest-volatility factor from Jan-1997 to Nov-1999 was Japan momentum. From Mar-2002 to Apr-2005, however, Japan momentum had the

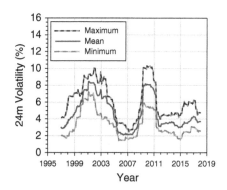

FIGURE 4.7 Trailing 24-month volatility of pure momentum factor versus time. Mean is the equal-weighted average across five models (US, UK, Europe, Japan and Canada). Maximum and minimum represent the largest and smallest values, respectively, among the five models.

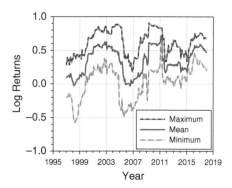

FIGURE 4.8 Trailing 24-month correlation of pure momentum factors versus time. Mean is the equal-weighted average across ten pairs of momentum factors. Maximum and minimum represent the largest and smallest correlations, respectively, among the ten factor pairs.

lowest volatility. Except for a few short windows, Canada momentum had the highest volatility roughly from Dec-2008 to Mar-2011.

An interesting, but not surprising, feature of Figure 4.7 is that momentum volatilities tend to rise and fall in relative unison. For instance, during the two sub-periods of peak volatility, even the lowest-volatility factor was well above the long-term average (4.7%) across factors. Similarly, during the low-volatility period of 2006 to 2008, even the highest volatility factor was below the long-run average across all factors.

In Figure 4.8, we plot the rolling 24-month correlation of monthly momentum pure factor returns across different markets. The five momentum factors lead to 10 pairwise correlations. We plot the mean, minimum, and maximum of these 10 correlations versus time. The mean correlation averaged across time was 0.34. For two brief periods, in 1998 and 2006, the mean correlation was close to zero (and even slightly negative). Mean correlations exceeded 0.5 during three periods. The first of these periods (2001–2004) corresponded to the bursting of the Internet Bubble. From Figure 4.7, we see that this was a time of high volatility for momentum. The second of these periods (2009–2011) is associated with the rebound from the Global Financial Crisis; again, this was a period of high momentum volatility. The last of these periods (2016–2018), by contrast, was not associated with any crisis and momentum volatility was relatively subdued during this period, as shown in Figure 4.7.

From Figure 4.8, we see that there were two times when the minimum correlations became strongly negative. The first occurred in 1998, when the minimum correlation was -0.57 (between UK and Japan). The second time this happened was in 2005, when the minimum correlation reached -0.49 (between US and Japan). In January 2011, the minimum correlation was 0.58 (between UK and Canada).

The maximum correlation contained two strong peaks and one distinct valley. In Oct-2004, the trailing 24m correlation reached 0.89 (between the UK and Europe). The

TABLE 4.1 Mean log return, volatility and information ratio of simple and pure factor portfolios in different equity markets. All variables are expressed on an annualized basis. Sample period is from January 1995 to February 2018. A statistically significant information ratio over the sample period of 23.2 years is approximately 0.41.

	US		UK		Europe		Japan		Canada	
Variable	Simple	Pure	Simple	Pure	Simple	Pure	Simple	Pure	Simple	Pure
Return	2.21%	2.14%	4.08%	3.68%	4.20%	4.19%	1.09%	1.20%	6.97%	7.06%
Volatility	9.78%	5.09%	9.48%	5.52%	7.84%	4.34%	7.88%	4.56%	10.17%	5.80%
IR	0.23	0.42	0.43	0.67	0.54	0.97	0.14	0.26	0.69	1.22

second peak was in Jun-2009, at which time the correlation between the US and Europe was 0.91. In late 2006, it was about 0.18, between (between US and Japan).

In Table 4.1, we report mean annual log returns, annualized volatilities, and information ratios for the simple and pure factor portfolios across the five developed equity markets considered here. The first observation from Table 4.1 is that within each market, the mean log returns were very similar for simple and pure factor portfolios. This result is consistent with the previous figures that charted cumulative returns. Again, we interpret this to mean that there was no return premium associated with the 'incidental' exposures of the simple factor portfolio.

The second observation from Table 4.1 is that the pure factor portfolios had considerably lower volatility than their simple factor portfolio counterparts. In fact, in each market, the volatility of the simple factor portfolio was approximately 80% higher than the volatility of the corresponding pure factor portfolio. Finally, due to their lower volatility, we observe that the information ratios of the pure factor portfolios were considerably higher than the simple factor portfolios in each of the equity markets. All pure factor portfolios, except Japan, had statistically significant information ratios over the full sample period.

In Table 4.2, we report the correlation matrix for the momentum factors in the five developed equity markets considered here. Correlations were estimated over the full sample period (Jan-1995 to Feb-2018) using monthly factor returns. All of the correlations were strongly positive and statistically significant. Not surprisingly, Japan tended to have the lowest correlations with the other markets. In fact, four of the five lowest

TABLE 4.2 Correlation matrix of pure momentum factors across different equity markets. Sample period is from January 1995 to February 2018.

Market	US	UK	Europe	Japan	Canada
US	1.00	0.52	0.61	0.40	0.54
UK	0.52	1.00	0.60	0.35	0.34
Europe	0.61	0.60	1.00	0.40	0.47
Japan	0.40	0.35	0.40	1.00	0.30
Canada	0.54	0.34	0.47	0.30	1.00

correlations were associated with Japan. The exception was Canada, which had a correlation of 0.34 with the UK. The two highest correlations were US/Europe (0.61) and UK/Europe (0.60).

4.8 DIVERSIFICATION BENEFITS

Next, we consider the diversification benefits of combining momentum strategies across multiple developed markets. In Figure 4.9, we plot the cumulative log return of the equal-weighted mean return of pure momentum factors across the five developed equity markets. Visually, the diversified momentum strategy appears to have excellent risk-adjusted performance. The mean log return (annualized) of the diversified momentum strategy was 3.79%, with a cumulative log return of roughly 0.88. The annualized volatility was approximately 3.79%. Hence, the information ratio of the diversified momentum strategy was approximately 1.0, which is higher than the risk-adjusted performance of any individual momentum strategy, except Canada.

Also in Figure 4.9, we plot the equally weighted mean cumulative log return of the five market factors. The cumulative log market return over the entire sample period (23.2 years) was roughly 2.0. This represents an annualized log return of 8.62% (equivalently, an annualized mean geometric return of 9.0%). The realized volatility of the mean market factor was 13.3%. Hence, the return-to-risk ratio was roughly 0.65. Note, however, that this number cannot be interpreted as a Sharpe Ratio, since the market

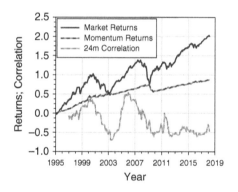

FIGURE 4.9 Mean cumulative log returns for market factor and momentum factor, plotted together with mean trailing 24-month correlation between momentum factor and market factor. Mean values were computed as the equal-weighted averages across the five models (US, UK, Europe, Japan and Canada).

returns were not computed net of the risk-free rate. For instance, over the sample period considered here, the US risk-free rate was approximately 3% on average. Note that the risk-free rate has no effect on the return of the momentum factor, since the portfolio is dollar-neutral.

The diversified momentum strategy exhibited strong positive returns throughout, with the exception being the 2009 momentum crash. It is interesting to note that the momentum crash coincided with the rebound of the equity markets. This nicely illustrates the benefit of diversification. Namely, the market portfolio performed extremely well precisely when the momentum strategy suffered a major drawdown.

Finally, we plot the trailing 24-month correlation between the mean momentum return and the mean market return. Over most of the sample period, the correlations were negative. Since both the market factor and the momentum factor earned positive returns over the sample period and were negatively correlated, the diversification benefit was very strong. The correlations were positive only during two brief periods. The first period occurred from 1999 to 2001. The second period spanned 2005 to 2008.

4.9 SUMMARY

We have analyzed the risk and return of momentum factors for five developed equity markets. We studied both simple factor portfolios (with many 'incidental' tilts), and pure factor portfolios (tilting only on momentum). In each of the five developed equity markets, the cumulative returns of the simple and pure factors were virtually identical, indicating that there did not appear to be a return premium associated with incidental momentum tilts. We also found that the incidental tilts added significant risk to the simple factor portfolios. In fact, on average, they were nearly 80% more volatile than the pure factors.

We found many similarities and several differences between the behaviors of momentum factors across the five developed equity markets. All momentum factors exhibited positive returns over the sample period. All pure factor portfolios had statistically significant information ratios, except for Japan. The strongest performance was in Canada, where momentum earned an annualized return of 7.06%, with an annualized volatility of 5.80%. The mean correlation between all momentum factors was approximately 0.34. The maximum correlation observed was 0.91, which occurred in June 2009 between US and Europe momentum.

We also investigated the benefit of diversifying across momentum factors. We found that the diversified momentum strategy had a higher information ratio than any individual momentum factor, except for Canada. Finally, we found that momentum tended to have a strong negative correlation with the equal-weighted market factor. Hence, adding the diversified momentum strategy as an overlay on the market portfolio tended to increase returns, while simultaneously reducing risk. The diversification benefits were particularly striking in 2009, when the momentum factor crashed while the market initiated a spectacular recovery.

REFERENCES

Carhart, Mark. 1997. 'On Persistence in Mutual Fund Performance'. *Journal of Finance* **52**(1): 57–82.

Daniel, Kent and Tobias J. Moskowitz. 2016. 'Momentum Crashes'. *Journal of Financial Economics* **122**(2): 221–247.

De Bondt, Werner and Richard Thaler. 1985. 'Does the Stock Market Overreact?' *Journal of Finance* **40**(3): 793–805.

Fama, Eugene and Kenneth French. 1992. 'The Cross-Section of Expected Returns'. *Journal of Finance* **47**(2): 427–465.

Jegadeesh, Narasimhan. 1990. 'Evidence of Predictable Behavior of Security Returns'. *Journal of Finance* **45**(3): 881–898.

Jegadeesh, Narasimhan and Sheridan Titman. 1993. 'Returns to Buying Winners and Selling Losers: Implications for Stock Market Efficiency'. *Journal of Finance* **48**(1): 65–91.

Menchero, Jose. 2010. 'The Characteristics of Factor Portfolios'. *Journal of Performance Measurement* **15**(1): 52–62.

Menchero, Jose and Jyh-Huei Lee. 2015. 'Efficiently Combining Multiple Sources of Alpha'. *Journal of Investment Management* **13**(4): 71–86.

Sharpe, William. 1964. 'A Theory of Market Equilibrium under Conditions of Risk'. *Journal of Finance* **19**(3): 425–442.

CHAPTER 5

Momentum Across Asset Classes

DAN diBARTOLOMEO and WILLIAM E. ZIEFF

P rice momentum exposure is a familiar concept to anyone who has studied equity return factors. Less addressed in the literature is how momentum effects in one asset class manifest in other asset classes.

We begin with consideration of cross-asset class momentum between equities and fixed income. The contingent-claims framework of Merton (1974) provides a clear theoretical link between equity returns and the returns of corporate bonds of corresponding issuers. This serves as a foundation for a cross-asset class momentum relationship between equities and fixed income. We describe the theoretical link and examine empirical results of equity market momentum and its relationship to fixed income markets, both in the literature and from our own research.

In addition to fixed income, we explore empirical results and theoretical underpinnings for cross-asset class momentum relationships in real estate, private equity and commodities. Real estate is obviously 'geographically bounded', and we describe how this contributes to linkages between equity markets and real estate. The relationship between private equity markets and publicly traded equities also is examined, and included in this review is consideration of whether the 'number of deals' and 'capital allocated' in private equity markets, rather than returns, contain economically useful information for investors. As inputs to global production, changes in commodity prices have a clear and direct impact on production costs and profitability of firms. Beyond a direct effect, we highlight research suggesting that since commodity prices reflect global supply and demand, commodities are informative to investors in all asset classes, and this can be observed in equity markets.

The structure of markets, the tax environment, and the role of financial intermediaries in implementing active management strategies also create apparent momentum effects, and the review here includes a discussion of several of these.

5.1 MEASURING MOMENTUM

The concept of 'momentum' in financial markets has been around for a long time. Momentum implies that securities that have outperformed a universe of peer securities are likely to continue to do so. More precisely, momentum suggests positive first order autocorrelation in relative returns. It is important to highlight early in this discussion that positive autocorrelation causes observed volatility to be downward biased relative to expectations of random movement. This can be particularly important in examining illiquid markets for which 'prices' are not be observed from actual transactions but are estimated or appraisal-based.

There is a vast array of research papers written with a range of definitions of momentum in equity markets and apparent related market outcomes. Many people would point to the seminal papers of Jegadeesh and Titman (1993, 2011). The most widely used definition of momentum comes from Carhart (1997), which uses a one-year sample period to measure the effect. The Carhart definition of momentum is frequently combined with the equity factors defined by Fama and French (1992). More recent studies include those of Novy-Marx (2012, 2015) which argue that price momentum is a manifestation of momentum in the fundamental profitability of firms.

A nuance in the definition of momentum is that this attribute of a security is often also referred to as a 'factor', as used in the parlance of 'smart beta' investment strategies. Framed as a factor, the most widely used description of the factor return to momentum is calculated by forming quantile groups (e.g. quintiles) of securities by momentum rank and observing differences in return between the quintile groups with highest and lowest ranks (e.g. quintile one minus quintile five). Importantly, to the extent the security composition of the quantile groups have other differences (e.g. industry composition), the measure of return being attributed to momentum may be influenced significantly by other security attributes.

In many widely used risk and linear factor models, cross-sectional regressions are used to estimate the return impact of momentum, net of the influence of other security attributes. Whereas returns to momentum calculated by grouping as described previously can be considered simple or in 'raw' form, momentum returns estimated through regression may be considered in 'pure' or orthogonalised form. In many cases, the times series of returns using the two methods are highly correlated, but this need not always be the case, and the specifics of the measure of momentum must be considered in any study. In the example in Figure 5.1, the correlation of the two series is .82.

5.2 FRAMEWORK: EQUITY MOMENTUM AND CORPORATE CREDIT RISK

Merton's pioneering work on contingent claims in corporate capital structure published in *Journal of Finance* in 1974 took advantage of options constructs, but the underlying linkage between equity and fixed income of a firm can be thought about in a simple way. As the value of a firm's stock goes up, it becomes easier for a firm to sell new equity shares, raise cash, and use the cash to pay off debt. This implies that both absolute and relative equity returns should have a measurable impact on the perceived credit risk of corporate bonds and financial institutions (as counterparties).

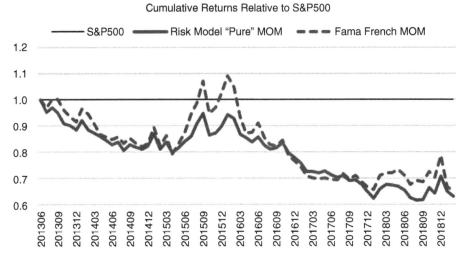

FIGURE 5.1   Cumulative returns relative to S&P500.
Sources: Northfield; Ken French Data Library

The contingent claims literature began with Merton posing the equity of a firm as a European call option on the firm's assets, with a strike price equal to the face value of the firm's debt. Similarly, lenders are short a put on the firm assets. In the original construct, default on corporate debt can occur only at the time of maturity.

Subsequent extensions and enhancements to Merton's work were made to reflect the reality of markets more accurately. Black and Cox (1976) provide a 'first passage' model. Default in this model is permitted at any time before debt maturity, essentially changing the option structure from a European to an American option. Firm extinction is assumed if asset values hit a boundary value (i.e. specified by bond covenants). Papers by Leland (1994), and Leland and Toft (1996) take this further and account for additional 'real world' nuances such as the tax deductibility of interest payments and administration costs of bankruptcy. The key element of these papers is to estimate a boundary value for which residual equity value is maximized subject to apparently exogenous effects in bankruptcy (for example, legal fees and court costs).

diBartolomeo (2010) reverses the order of operations of the Merton approach to estimate a *market implied expected life of the firm* as a description of corporate sustainability. As in the original Merton treatment, the underlying asset of the option is the firm's assets. However, in the expected life approach the volatility of the assets is exogenously estimated from an equity factor risk model. This is done by asking the question, 'What would the volatility of the company's stock be if the firm had no debt?' By equating the option value to the stock price, the implied expiration date of the option can be solved numerically, and this value can be taken as an indication of the expectation of the survival time of the firm. It should be pointed out that methods for valuing long-term options ought to include a term structure of interest rates so that as the implied expiration date moves around, the interest rate changes appropriately. Even better are more complex option models that allow for stochastic interest rates.

Formalizing the linkage to fixed income, to estimate the impact of an equity factor (or multiple equity factors) on the return of a corporate bond, the 'equity beta' of the bond is estimated. This value is approximately the fraction of a bond's value that is expected to be lost in the event of default (LGD, loss given default). The LGD percentage value can be derived from the 'moneyness' of the Merton put and call options. Alternatively, a simple approximation formula is available.

$$LGD = -\left(\frac{E}{B}\right) \times \left(\frac{\Delta_{put}}{\Delta_{call}}\right) \tag{5.1}$$

where E is the market value of the firm's equity, B is the market value of the firm's debt, Δ_{put} is the delta of the Merton put option, and Δ_{call} is the delta of the Merton call option.

5.3 EMPIRICAL STUDIES: MOMENTUM AND CREDIT RISK

As momentum is a popular factor tilt for 'smart beta' equity strategies, a literature has developed describing potential investment strategies for 'smart beta corporate bond' portfolios that assert momentum in stock returns as an alpha source in bonds. Numerous related studies have come forward in the research literature. We review several of these studies.

The first body of research covers three related studies by Bektic et al. (2017), Bektic et al. (2019), and Bektic (2019). The 2017 study considered whether the well-known Fama-French (FF) equity factors have explanatory power over corporate bond returns. The empirical results over a sample period from 2000 to 2016 suggest that the FF factors are indeed explanatory to a statistically significant degree. Intuitively, the effects are strongest in 'high yield' bonds where both the likelihood of default and expected loss given default are highest, and hence the 'equity betas' of these bonds are also highest. Bektic et al. (2019) adds momentum to the set of factors studied in 2017, and it provides a Merton-based explanation of the operative mechanism of the relationship.

Bektic (2019) focuses specifically on 'spillover' of equity momentum effects into corporate bond credit risk. Momentum, as defined by relative equity returns, is shown to have significant explanatory power incrementally beyond that of simple total equity returns in explaining bond returns.

Kaufmann and Messow (2019) examine equity momentum spillover effects on bonds for European investment grade and high yield bonds in the Industrials, Utilities and Financials sectors over the period 2000 to 2018. Several different look back horizons were examined for constructing an equity momentum factor ranging, from one month to twelve months. In addition, a composite score combining one, three, and six-month horizons for momentum was reviewed. The research reveals equity momentum spillover into bonds including after accounting for what the authors consider conservative estimates for transaction costs.

In a related working paper Kaufmann (2019) shows simulation results for a multi-factor alpha forecast model for bonds that includes an equity momentum factor along with four bond factors: value, size, quality and carry. In the investment grade segment, the cross-sectional correlations of the equity momentum score with each of the other factors were low, the most pronounced being between momentum and carry at only −.07. Similar low correlations were reported in high yield. For example, in high yield, the cross-sectional correlation between the momentum and carry scores was only −0.2, though it was statistically significant. Interestingly, when equity momentum and carry scores were used individually as alphas in simulations, the time series correlation of the two simulation results was −0.5, somewhat stronger than the cross-sectional correlation on average. Still, the work offers evidence that in the European universe and time period studied positive equity momentum scores contributed to excess returns and improved risk-adjusted returns in the bond portfolio beyond that which would come from bond only factors.

Some researchers, such as Jostova et. al. (2013) document a within fixed-income-bond momentum effect in US corporate bonds when tested from 1973 to 2011. The results, however, were identified primarily in the US high-yield segment.

Maitra, Salt and Satchell (2019) show in a working paper that using three-month trailing equity momentum as a sorting factor leads to positive bond portfolio alpha in US investment grade and high-yield bonds between 2000 and 2018. In addition, the results indicate excess returns are unexplained by other bond-momentum strategies, such as spread momentum and ratings momentum. From among the factors examined in the study, ratings change momentum is highlighted as the strongest determinant of variation in the bond portfolio results derived from three-month trailing equity momentum. As a result, the authors posit that a trailing equity momentum factor may best be considered as a responsive 'change in fundamentals' indicator.

Slimane and de Jong (2018) focus on both the cross-section of corporate bond returns and the estimation of risk in corporate bond markets. The paper has extensive empirical simulations of various equity related strategies that have been proposed in the 'smart bond' literature. The results suggest that equity-related style factors do have statistically significant explanatory power in bond returns, but the impact of traditional credit rating changes (upgrades and downgrades) continues to have a profound effect on bond returns. We speculate that the persistent importance of traditional credit ratings may relate to regulatory injunctions on some large institutions (e.g. banks) holding 'non-investment grade' bonds.

If credit risk in bonds, and therefore bond returns resulting from changes in credit risk premiums in pricing, can be reliably related to equity factors such as momentum, then it should be possible to hedge the risk of volatility in credit-related yield spreads via equity options. Avino and Salvador (2018) address this issue. They show that changes in credit-related yield spreads as defined by credit default swaps can be efficiently hedged using equity options. The hedge ratios are defined by a clever 'compound option' model, and interestingly, the hedging process presented is shown to be less costly than previous proposals that focus on hedging actual dollar losses associated with potential defaults on corporate bonds (Beinstein et al., 2006). Recent working papers by Lin (2019) and Xiao (2019) extend research on how to assess and hedge credit risk through the mechanism of equity put options.

5.4 OUR RESEARCH ON EQUITY MOMENTUM AND BOND RETURNS

Whereas to date most research in equity momentum spillover has tended to use simple portfolio construction rules (e.g. top quintile momentum for selection, equally weighted securities for portfolio construction), our research has focused on using optimized equity portfolios to establish bond portfolio weights. The intent is to contribute to the growing body of work by examining whether 'smart beta' equity portfolio strategies can inform corresponding 'smart beta' bond portfolios in a practical and implementable way. As in the published research previously discussed, we do find evidence of equity momentum spillover to bonds. In addition, we have found that just as in equities, for which single factor excess returns can persist positively or negatively for extended periods, smart beta portfolio excess returns can display similar effects, at least over the period studied. Some of our research in this area is still underway.

Our colleagues MacQueen and Mostovoy (2018) studied potential 'smart beta' bond strategies based upon four equity style factors for the period from 2013 to 2017, including momentum. The process first created optimized smart beta equity portfolios using only companies that had bonds outstanding. Two weighting schemes were tested for bond portfolios. In the first, bond position weights were taken as company weights from the optimized equity portfolios. In the second, the bond portfolio weights were adjusted for expectations of 'loss given default' as representation of the equity properties of the respective corporate bonds expressed through the structural linkage.

Over the sample period, momentum driven bond portfolios performed well even though the equity momentum strategies did not exhibit significant positive alpha. In terms of investor utility, the bond portfolio outperformed the Barclay's Aggregate Bond Index by around 1% per annum, assuming a mean-variance risk aversion (i.e. lambda) of 10. The choice of risk aversion was inferred from the 'discretionary wealth hypothesis' put forward in Wilcox (2003).

In 2019, research on the momentum factor expanded the historical period with updated data and evaluated the results relative to a custom bond benchmark. In the newer study the historical period examined was from January 2013 to January 2019. The purpose of the custom benchmark was to isolate bond returns coming purely from credit risk effects in a more refined manner.

As in the earlier work an optimized 'smart beta' equity momentum portfolio was created first. The security weights from the equity portfolio were then used to establish the weight of a corresponding representative bond of each issuing company to create the bond momentum portfolio – 'smart beta' bond portfolio.

To get a more refined measure of pure credit effects, instead of measuring excess returns relative to a conventional benchmark index (e.g. Barclay's Aggregate), a custom benchmark was created. Each month, a benchmark portfolio was created comprised of a matching US Treasury bond of equal duration and equal position weight for each holding in the smart bond portfolio. Using this method, any difference between the bond portfolio returns and the custom benchmark can be attributed solely to changes in credit risk.

Two results deserve mention. While the creation of the bond portfolio was done using past equity momentum up until each date of portfolio formation, the subsequent contemporaneous monthly correlation between the bond portfolio return and the equity portfolio that was used for its weights was negative. This does not contradict the spillover concept, but it raises interesting questions about time series attributes and evolution (i.e. term structure) of the factor returns in each of the asset classes. In addition, the average excess return over the entire is the result of underperformance in the first of half of the study period offset by strong outperformance in the second half of the study period. Thus, at least as far as for the approach taken in this research, and for the period studied, sustained periods of over and underperformance appear, just as can occur in equity factor return strategies. Both results warrant further study over a longer period within the context of optimized portfolios.

5.5   GEOGRAPHICALLY BOUND ASSETS

Many types of financial assets are geographically bound, and this establishes linkages that can be observed in capital markets and across asset classes. For example, the economic prosperity of a given country may be inferred from local equity market returns and hence a relation to sovereign credit risk is apparent. Similarly, demand for commercial real estate in a given region is closely tied to the economic activity in that area. Again, an inference can be made that equity market returns are indicative of expectations on local real estate returns. Creditworthiness of municipal bonds can then be linked to real estate values as taxes on real property are the primary source of local government revenues in most countries. The creditworthiness of mortgage-backed securities both residential and commercial are at least partially dependent on the value of underlying real estate.

To the extent that equity market momentum is observable at the company or sector level we can use this information to predict returns in other asset classes. For example, if oil company stocks are showing momentum, this bodes well for the sovereign creditworthiness of oil producing countries such as Saudi Arabia, Norway and the Gulf Cooperation Council (GCC) countries. Belev and diBartolomeo (2019) provide a Merton-based approach to assessing sovereign credit risk. Each country's economy is defined by its respective 'national portfolio' which includes known local equity market plus nationalized resources (e.g. oil production) and financial reserve assets. As the various sectors in the national portfolio show positive absolute returns or incremental momentum returns, *this information is translated into expectations of government tax revenues and thereby the creditworthiness of the sovereign state.*

Another asset class where equity momentum effects are used in a predictive fashion is real estate and property-related securities. The most transparent example of this situation would be the case of momentum effects being observed in the performance of portfolios of Real Estate Investment Trusts (REITs). Numerous papers such as Liang et al. (1996), Chatrath and Liang (1998) and Clayton and MacKinnon (2001) all estimate the unobservable return on 'brick and mortar' real estate as the residual return of REITS after hedging away what they believe is the influence of the general equity market.

To the extent we describe the concept of momentum as positive first order serial correlation (i.e. AR(1)) in abnormal returns, there is an extensive literature in real estate.

The seminal work in this area is a whole series of papers by Geltner (1989, 1991, 1993) which assert that autocorrelated returns arise from 'appraisal bias' in the way that property values are estimated rather than observed through frequent transactions. The effect of these biases is to 'smooth' the time series of returns that are reported to investors. Lin and Liu (2008) show that the appraisal bias causes reported returns on real estate to be overstated and volatility understated.

To the extent that valuation-based returns are smoothed, one might naturally want to 'de-smooth' a known time series of returns to obtain a more realistic representation. A very thorough investigation of this issue was presented in Chaplin (1997) which provides an encyclopedic treatment of prior research and a proposed analytical solution. A very simple technique was put forward by Geltner (1993) for estimating the 'de-smoothed' returns.

$$C_t = \frac{R_t - R_{t-1}\rho}{(1 - \rho)} \tag{5.2}$$

where C_t is the estimated corrected return for period t, R_t is the reported return for period t and ρ is the first-order autocorrelation coefficient for the return series.

From this relationship we can derive a simple expression for the appropriate adjustment to the volatility of the observed return time series

$$\sigma_a = \sigma \left[\frac{(1 + \rho)}{(1 - \rho)} \right]^5 \tag{5.3}$$

where σ_a is the estimated adjusted volatility (or standard deviation), and σ is the observed volatility of the return time series.

The impact of this correction on the reported volatility of real estate (or other illiquid assets) is very substantial. When we reviewed the autocorrelation coefficients for commercially available real-estate indices, the first order auto-correlation coefficients ranged from 0.7 to 0.9. If we take the midpoint between these coefficients (that is, 0.8) and plug it into Equation 5.2 we obtain a *corrected volatility that is three times that of the observed standard deviation.*

To the extent that observed volatility understates the true volatility, the expectation of long-term returns is upward biased as the effect of return variance on the difference between arithmetic mean and geometric mean returns is muted. For more detail on this relationship see Messmore (1995).

Demand for commercial real estate in a given region is closely tied to the economic activity in that region. Again, an inference on effects on local real-estate returns can be drawn from the relative momentum of equity market sector returns. In Gold (2018) and Belev and Gold (2018a) this is done by linking equity sector momentum and the portion of local employment in the respective economic sector.

Several studies confirm the linkage between equity market returns and the relative performance of housing prices in given regions based on a local economic profile. Bahmani-Oskooee and Ghodsi (2018) find significant explanatory power at the level of individual US states. Intuitively, US states with greater concentration in the financial services sector are more impacted and states with high agricultural activity are less so. Belev and Gold (2018b) show that times series variation in housing prices by region can replicated with portfolios of liquid securities. To the extent that the replicating portfolio shows equity momentum this spills over into abnormal returns for housing prices.

5.6 MOMENTUM IN OTHER ILLIQUID ASSETS

Like real estate, private equity (PE) is an illiquid asset class where reported returns are often positively serially correlated, which can be described as momentum. Two related papers have been written based on a proprietary data set compiled by State Street Bank. Kritzman, Kinlaw and Mao (2014) assert that a material portion of the alpha (abnormal return) associated with private equity investing is based on private equity managers ability to make efficient allocations of capital across economic sectors. They argue that the return momentum in private equity sector returns can be replicated in publicly traded securities such as sector ETFs and is therefore distinct from any liquidity related effects.

Like in real estate, but unlike publicly traded assets, private equity managers have wide discretion to estimate the '*fair market value*' of their private holdings. Cocoma, Czasonis, Kritzman and Turkington (2017) argue that apparent return effects (e.g. momentum) may result from bias in the 'mark-to-market' of private equity.

We observe other interesting momentum-like properties in a private equity dataset provided by *Prequin*. Over a sample period of 2006 to 2018, the number of PE deals done in each quarter exhibits positive serial correlation (i.e. momentum) to a statistically significant degree in both total and by economic sector. This is not entirely surprising as the level of 'deal flow' might be expected to be positively correlated as PE firms invest material effort and capital to operate their firms, as well as addressing the ongoing need to provide investor capital to external enterprises. As such, PE firms tend to maintain some level of routine activity irrespective of variations in the opportunity set at each moment in time.

Interestingly, the average size of PE deals appears unrelated to the timeline. Average deal size varies little, so the time variation in the dollar amount of investor capital committed to private equity seems wholly related to the number rather than the size of deals. This is a different result than has been asserted by Kyle and Obizhaeva (2016) for public markets where time variation in trading volume appears related to both number of transactions and typical size of transactions.

Other illiquid asset classes also exhibit various forms of autocorrelated behavior. For non-traditional investments such as fine art and other collectible assets, sellers often choose to withdraw items from potential sale in perceived periods of 'weak prices' and bring more items to market during periods of perceived 'strong prices'. The relatively fewer transactions when prices are down and higher numbers of transactions when prices are up biases transaction-based return indices as discussed in Korteweg, Kraussl and Verwijmeren (2016). So, even for transaction-based indices that may exist for illiquid assets, without continuously posted quotations of bona fide bids and offers (for example, real estate, or PE) concerns about significant bias are justified.

5.7   CROSS-ASSET CLASS EFFECTS OF COMMODITIES

Price momentum in commodities has been studied and researched for a long time. Market participants and researchers have explored price and return time series information using the less scientific approaches of technical analysis and charting, as well as with more disciplined time series analysis and econometrics. In addition, due to the role of commodities as inputs in production and as end products (for example in agriculture and energy), economists often use commodity prices in models of the overall economy, industrial production, inflation and other macro-economic variables.

With respect to cross-asset class momentum, one recent contribution to the body of research in this area is Alves and Szymanowska (2019), which examined the predictiveness of commodity momentum on stock market returns globally. The authors analysed the impacts of six commodity sectors on 70 countries, including both developed and developing markets. They report that in all but five of the countries stock market returns are predicted by commodity futures returns of at least one commodity sector, and in more than half, the stock markets are predicted by two to four of the six commodity sectors.

Even though commodities are important direct factors of production, the authors find that cross-country differences in the predictability of commodity momentum on country stock markets are not captured by differences in trade dependence between countries and the corresponding input/output cost channels through trade. Instead, the authors conclude that their results support the idea that all commodity sectors provide economically important information about the global economy including macro-economic fundamentals such as inflation and that, as a result, commodity prices contribute to price discovery in other asset classes.

5.8   MOMENTUM EFFECTS AND TAXABLE INVESTORS

Momentum effects across all asset classes can be especially important to entities subject to the payment of capital gain taxes upon liquidation of an investment asset. Such entities include private households, corporate investors (e.g. insurance companies) and some institutional investors such as 'superannuation' funds in Australia.

To the extent that the simple basis of momentum strategies is that securities that have provided superior returns to their respective markets will continue to provide superior returns, then the expectation of continuing superior returns will bias such investors toward holding on to securities that have appreciated more than others. Pursuing momentum-related strategies would also imply the opposite which would be to bias investors to more readily liquidate securities that have underperformed.

If the cross-sectional dispersion of security returns within an asset class is large relative to the average returns of the security universe, a momentum strategy naturally realizes less tax costs for investors who hold what has gone up more and sell what has gone up less (or down) in value. In effect, investors are able to reduce realization of taxable gains when rebalancing their portfolio. The economic benefit of reductions in rebalancing related tax costs is explored in Balvers and Mitchell (2000).

In recent years, an extensive literature has developed around the concept of 'tax loss harvesting' which proposes to consistently liquidate security positions with capital losses in an effort to 'bank' tax losses that can be used later to offset taxable gains generated in subsequent transactions. Recent studies of the economic value of tax loss harvesting include Goldberg (2017) and Chadhuri, Burnham and Lo (2019). It can be inferred that at least a portion of the 'tax alpha' reported in these studies would arise naturally from pursuit of momentum strategies in any liquid asset class.

It is often asserted that the response of taxable investors to negative momentum effects (i.e. losses) is a contributing factor in the 'January' anomaly in securities prices. Studies such as Haug and Hirschey (2006), and Boehmer and Kelley (2009) suggest that in December near the end of tax relevant fiscal year investors sell securities that have fallen in value to claim the related capital loss tax deduction in the current tax year. This concentrated selling depresses prices temporarily leading to abnormally positive returns in the subsequent January.

An alternative rationale for the January anomaly is that institutional investors may wish to avoid drawing attention to the individual securities that they held that materially underperformed (i.e. negative momentum). To the extent that nearly all mutual funds and asset managers produce a year-end statement of the value of portfolios, negative momentum securities may be sold just before the end of year to avoid inclusion of the poorly performing securities, a practice commonly known as 'window dressing'.

Research studies such as Folliott (2007) have observed the January effect across numerous financial markets including countries where the fiscal year for investor taxation is different from the calendar year. This result suggests that while tax selling may contribute, 'window dressing' may be a more globally pervasive contributor.

5.9 ACTIVE MANAGEMENT AND MOMENTUM EFFECTS

In the pursuit of above average superior returns that characterize active management, decisions made by portfolio managers as well as those of ultimate investors can translate into observed momentum effects.

Momentum effects at the asset class level often arise out of dynamic asset allocation strategies. For example, the process of 'Constant Proportion Portfolio Insurance' (CPPI) proposes that investors synthesise a put option on an asset class by selling as prices fall. To the extent that a large number of investors pursue such a strategy, the obvious 'knock-on' effect is that the resulting further declines in the prices of the subject assets induce continued selling under the CPPI regime. This again leads to continuation of price declines, and establishes a reinforcing cycle. Seminal papers in the area include Leland and Rubinstein (1976), Perold (1986), Black and Rouhani (1989), and Black and Perold (1992).

The mechanical nature and reinforcing cycle of CPPI and related strategies was widely blamed for the 19 October 1987 crash of global equity markets when prices fell an average of 20% in a single trading day. However, the subsequent US government study called the 'Report of the Presidential Task Force on Market Mechanisms' (popularly known as the Brady Commission Report) found several additional factors in the way equity and stock index futures trades were conducted and cleared that contributed greatly to this singular event. A summary of the report can be found in diBartolomeo (1988).

To the extent that dynamic allocation strategies are meant to synthesize option positions, the distribution of returns to the investor's portfolio will exhibit higher moments (skew and kurtosis). The calculation and economic implications of higher moments for portfolio return and risk are presented in Hall and Satchell (2013).

When dealing with semi-liquid asset classes (e.g. high-yield bonds), there is an interesting counter argument to the prior discussion regarding how momentum affects downward bias volatility in illiquid markets. If an asset market is liquid enough to allow for trading over time frames of days rather than months or years, the presence of statistically-significant momentum effects should allow active managers to predict future returns. To the extent that future returns on an asset class are predictable, active managers may consider the asset class less uncertain and, therefore, less risky than would a passive investor. The active manager could choose to reduce exposure to the asset class when predicted returns are less favorable, whereas a passive allocation would fully participate in future return outcomes. An example of the effect of autocorrelation on the perception of volatility is presented in diBartolomeo (2013). Such tactical allocation changes are obviously unavailable in fully illiquid asset classes.

Active management would have no purpose if all the securities produced the same returns at the same times. The basis of active management within a universe of securities is that the returns have cross-sectional dispersion or 'variety' that is distinct from time series volatility. To the extent that momentum effects are evident, the cross-sectional dispersion of the individual security returns increases faster than would arise out of a 'random walk' process. If active managers believe that momentum effects are evident in a given universe of securities, conventional methods for defining the opportunity set for active management such as Grinold (1989) need to be adjusted accordingly. A large study of mutual fund performance by Elton, Gruber and Blake (1995) found that while active fund managers produced positive risk-adjusted returns or 'alpha', the magnitude of alpha declined with portfolio turnover, which is consistent with the idea that managers may misjudge the relative opportunity of investing with a shorter or longer holding period.

There is a complex 'two-sided' relationship between momentum effects and the investment choices undertaken by actual investors, as opposed to decisions undertaken by portfolio managers managing assets at financial intermediaries. The movement of capital initiated by investors to move their investments from one agent-managed fund at a financial intermediary to another fund is generally referred to as 'fund flows'. These flows may arise from either the actions of retail investors (e.g. mutual funds or unit trusts) or institutional investors moving capital between managers (or broad security allocations such as by country). The bidirectional relationship is that retail investors in particular tend to 'chase returns' and so move their funds into those vehicles which have had the best recent performance. There is broad statistical evidence that retail mutual fund flows are therefore highly serially correlated. To the extent that a fund manager who is receiving inflows is content with an existing portfolio composition, this will induce new purchases of the same or similar securities, which as just described have recently performed well, purportedly contributing to the existence of momentum effects.

The relationships between fund flows and asset performance have been extensively studied. An obvious concern about all fund-flow-based explanations of asset prices is that for a given fund to purchase or sell securities that are undertaken due to investor fund flows, some other investors outside the subject fund must be on the other side of those trades. If flows are presumed to be predictive of future asset performance, there must be some implicit hypothesis that some investors are 'smarter' than others so as to more (less) successfully move money from one fund to another. Alternatively, one could argue that investors who move their money from fund to fund do so erroneously with trades based only on 'noise' and that other market participants have learned to take advantage and profit from this pointless activity.

Vayanos and Wooley (2013) argue that time delays in fund flows generate momentum effects, while fund flows into certain securities create imbalances that move market prices away from fundamental values. In Lou (2012), the concept of 'smart money' is introduced and assertion is again made about explanation of momentum effects. More recently, Srimurthy, Shen and Smallbach (2019) argue that fund flows of US mutual funds and ETFs investing internationally are predictive of country by country equity market returns and that this effect is far stronger than when local investors and funds are excluded from the analysis. In a more recent paper, Ben-David et al. (2019) argue that retail mutual fund investors are ignorant of systematic risk and factor effects, leading to the myopic chasing of past performance information distributed by industry sources (e.g. Morningstar). In a related paper by Huang, Song and Xiang (2019) it is reported that fund flows are highly explanatory of returns to the familiar set of equity attributes known as the Fama-French factors. This paper also suggests that the time series volatilities of the factor returns are highly influenced by the time series variation in fund flows.

5.10   CONCLUSIONS

While momentum effects have been widely studied in equity markets, the literature of momentum in other asset classes and more specifically in cross-asset class momentum is comparatively sparse. In credit risk, the Merton (1974) model provides a clear theoretical link between factor effects (e.g. momentum) in equity markets and corresponding effects in corporate bond markets. Multiple recent empirical studies (including our internal research) broadly support the legitimacy of the Merton process for formulating expectations of credit risk and the operation of 'smart beta' bond portfolio strategies.

Equity market momentum can also be interpreted as indication of the general prosperity of nations, or sectors of the economy (whether local, national or global). The Merton concept has been extended to assert a linkage between equity market momentum and the creditworthiness of sovereign debt.

In illiquid markets such as real estate and private equity, what we might describe as momentum effects arise from two sources. The first is the actual effects of economic growth with equity market momentum being the evidence that investors anticipate future prosperity. The second source of positive serial correlation is a mathematical artefact of the fact that returns for these assets are estimated rather than observed. The effect is that conventional calculations of returns will be upward-biased and the volatility of returns will be downward-biased.

Commodities as factors of production naturally have a direct impact on countries and firms directly through trade and input costs. Nonetheless, beyond any direct effect, to the extent commodity prices provide new information about the global economy and economic fundamentals relevant to price discovery broadly, commodity momentum may translate into price momentum in other asset classes indirectly through an information channel.

The review here has described momentum effects across asset classes in a range of contexts including those arising from structural economic linkages, market dynamics in illiquid assets, and decisions by market participants. Momentum effects offer opportunities for active managers to 'bet' on the continuation of such effects across time. Therefore, recognition and understanding of the drivers of momentum are important for active managers who seek opportunities to increase return while managing risk relative to passive allocations. Viewed in this light, consideration of momentum can be seen to impact the process of active asset allocation across asset classes as well as the active management of individual security portfolios within an asset class.

REFERENCES

Alves, R. and Szymanowska, M. (2019). The Information Content of Commodity Futures Markets. Erasmus University Rotterdam Working Paper, https://papers.ssrn.com/sol3/papers.cfm?abstract_id=3352822

Avino, D. and Salvador, E. (2018). Contingent Claims and Hedging of Credit Risk with Equity Options. University of Liverpool Working Paper, https://papers.ssrn.com/sol3/papers.cfm?abstract_id=3184004

Bahmani-Oskooee, M. and Ghodsi, S. (2018). Link between Housing and Stock Markets: Evidence from OECD Using Asymmetry Analysis. *International Real Estate Review*, **21**(4), 447–472.

Balvers, R. and Mitchell, D. (2000). Efficient gradualism in intertemporal portfolios. *Journal of Economic Dynamics and Control*, **24**(1), 21–38.

Beinstein, E., Scott, A., Graves, B., Sbityakov, A. and Le, K. (2006). JPMorgan Credit Derivatives Handbook,

Bektic, D. (2019). Residual Equity Momentum Spillover in Global Corporate Bond Markets. *Journal of Fixed Income*, **28**(3), 46–54.

Bektic, D., Neugebauer, U., Wegener, M. and Wenzler, J. (2017). Common Equity Factors in Corporate Bond Markets, in Jurczenko, E. (Ed.), *Factor Investing: From Traditional to Alternative Risk Premia*, ISTE Press, 207–226.

Bektic, D., Wenzler, J., Wegener, M., Schiereck, D. and Spielmann, T. (2019). Extending Fama-French Factors To Corporate Bond Markets. *Journal of Portfolio Management*, **45**(3), 141–158.

Belev, E. and diBartolomeo, D. (2019). Finance Meets Macroeconomics: A Structural Model of Sovereign Credit Risk, in Crouhy, M., Galai, D. and Wiener, Z. (Ed.), *World Scientific, Contingent Claims Analysis in Corporate Finance*, World Scientific, 433–461.

Belev, E. and Gold, R. (2018a). Face Off: The Factor Model vs. the Commercial Real Estate Risk Premiums. Northfield Webinar Presentation Series, https://www.northinfo.com/documents/838.pdf

Belev, E. and Gold, R. (2018b). Replication of Residential Real Estate Returns Using Liquid Market Instruments and Managing Housing Market-Related Investment Risk. *Real Estate Finance*, **35**(2), 136–152.

Ben-David, I., Li, J., Rossi, A. and Song, Y. (2019). What Do Mutual Fund Investors Really Care About? Fisher College of Business Working Paper No. 2019-03-005. https://papers.ssrn.com/sol3/papers.cfm?abstract_id=3292317

Black, F. and Cox, J. (1976). Valuing Corporate Securities: Some Effects of Bond Indenture Provisions. *The Journal of Finance*, **31**(2), 351–367.

Black, F. and Perold, A. (1992). Theory of Constant Proportion Portfolio Insurance. *Journal of Economic Dynamics and Control*, **16**(3–4), 403–426.

Black, F. and Rouhani, R. (1989). Constant Proportion Portfolio Insurance and the Synthetic Put Option: A Comparison, in Fabozzi, F. (Ed.), *Institutional Investor Focus on Investment Management*, Ballinger, 695–708.

Boehmer, E. and Kelley, E. (2009). Institutional Investors and the Informational Efficiency of Prices. *Review of Financial Studies*, **22**(9), 3563–3594.

Carhart, M. (1997). On Persistence in Mutual Fund Performance. *Journal of Finance*, **52**(1), 57–82.

Chadhuri, S., Burnham, T. and Lo, A. (2019). An Empirical Evaluation of Tax-Loss Harvesting Alpha, MIT Working Paper, https://papers.ssrn.com/sol3/papers.cfm?abstract_id=3351382

Chaplin, S. (1997). Unsmoothing Valuation-Based Indices Using Multiple Regimes. *Journal of Property Research*, **14**(3), 189–210.

Chatrath, A. and Liang, Y. (1998). REITs and Inflation: A Long-Run Perspective. *Journal of Real Estate Research*, **16**(3), 311–326.

Clayton, J. and MacKinnon, G. (2001). The Time-Varying Nature of the Link between REIT, Real Estate and Financial Asset Returns. *Journal of Real Estate Portfolio Management*, 7(1), 43–54.

Cocoma, P., Czasonis, M., Kritzman, M. and Turkington, D. (2017). Facts about Factors. *Journal of Portfolio Management*, **43**(5), 55–65.

diBartolomeo, D. (1988). Computers and the Crash: Did the Machines Really Do It? *Computer Update*, Sep/Oct, 19–21.

diBartolomeo, D. (2010). Equity Risk, Credit Risk, Default Correlation, and Corporate Sustainability. *The Journal of Investing*, **19**(4), 128–133.

diBartolomeo, D. (2013). The Volatility of Financial Assets Behaving Badly, The Example of the High Yield Bond Market. *Northfield News*. https://www.northinfo.com/documents/546.pdf

Elton, E., Gruber, M. and Blake, C. (1995). The Persistence of Risk-Adjusted Mutual Fund Performance. *Journal of Business*, **69**(2), 133–157.

Fama, E. and French, K. (1992). The Cross-Section of Expected Stock Returns. *The Journal of Finance*, **47**(2), 427–465.

Folliott, T. (2007). The January Effect: A Global Perspective. Simon Fraser University Working Paper. https://core.ac.uk/download/pdf/56372543.pdf

Geltner, D. (1989). Bias in Appraisal-Based Returns. *Real Estate Economics*, **17**(3), 338–352.

Geltner, D. (1991). Smoothing in appraisal-based returns. *Journal of Real Estate Finance and Economics*, **4**(3), 327–345.

Geltner, D. (1993). Temporal Aggregation in Real Estate Return Indices. *Real Estate Economics*, **21**(2), 141–166.

Gold, R. (2018). Why Location Still Matters for Real Assets – Integrating Public and Private Market Information. *Northfield News*. https://www.northinfo.com/documents/794.pdf

Goldberg, L. (2017). The Tax-Loss Harvesting Life Cycle. Northfield Research Conference, Vermont, USA, **2017**. https://www.northinfo.com/documents/755.pdf

Grinold, R. (1989). The Fundamental Law of Active Management. *Journal of Portfolio Management*, **15**(3), 30–37.

Hall, A. and Satchell, S. (2013). The Anatomy of Portfolio Skewness and Kurtosis. University of Technology, Sydney, Working Paper 2013-7.

Haug, M. and Hirschey, M. (2006). The January Effect. *Financial Analysts Journal*, **62**(5), 78–88.

Huang, S., Song, Y. and Xiang, H. (2019). Fragile Factor Premia. University of Hong Kong Working Paper. https://ssrn.com/abstract=3312837

Jegadeesh, N. and Titman, S. (1993). Returns to Buying Winners and Selling Losers: Implications for Stock Market Efficiency. *Journal of Finance*, **48**(1), 65–91.

Jegadeesh, N. and Titman, S. (2011). Momentum. *Annual Review of Financial Economics*, **3**, 493–509.

Jostova, G., Nikolova, S., Philipov, A. and Stahel, C. (2013). Momentum in Corporate Bond Returns. *Review of Financial Studies*, **26**(7), 1649–1693.

Kaufmann, H. (2019). Factor Investing in Credit. Northfield Research Conference, Washington, DC, USA. https://www.northinfo.com/Documents/913.pdf

Kaufmann, H. and Messow, P. (2019). Equity Momentum in European Credits. Quoniam Asset Management Working Paper. https://papers.ssrn.com/sol3/papers.cfm?abstract_id=3436776

Kinlaw, W., Kritzman, M. and Mao, J. (2014). The Components of Private Equity Performance: Implications for Portfolio Choice. MIT Sloan Research Paper No. 5084-14.

Korteweg, A., Kräussl, R. and Verwijmeren, P. (2016). Does it Pay to Invest in Art? A Selection-Corrected Returns Perspective. *Review of Financial Studies*, **29**(4), 1007–1038.

Kyle, A. and Obizhaeva, A. (2016). Market Microstructure Invariance: Empirical Hypotheses. *Econometrica*, **84**(4), 1345–1404.

Leland, H. (1994). Corporate Debt Value, Bond Covenants, and Optimal Capital Structure. *Journal of Finance*, **49**(4), 1213–1252.

Leland, H. and Rubinstein, M. (1976). The Evolution of Portfolio Insurance, in Luskin, D (Ed.), Portfolio Insurance: A Guide to Dynamic Hedging, Wiley.

Leland, H. and Toft, K. (1996). Optimal Capital Structure, Endogenous Bankruptcy, and the Term Structure of Credit Spreads. *Journal of Finance*, **51**(3), 987–1019.

Liang, Y., Chatrath, A. and Webb, J. (1996). Hedged REIT Indices. *Journal of Real Estate Literature*, **4**(2), 175–184.

Lin, M. (2019). What Drives the Price Convergence Between Credit Default Swap and Put Option: New Evidence. De Montfort University (UK) Working Paper.

Lin, Z. and Liu, Y. (2008). Real Estate Returns and Risk with Heterogeneous Investors. *Real Estate Economics*, **36**(4), 753-776.

Lou, D. (2012). A Flow-Based Explanation of Return Predictability, *Review of Financial Studies*, **25**(12), 3457–3489.

MacQueen, J. and Mostovoy, D. (2018). Smart Beta Corporate Bond Portfolios. Northfield Asia Seminar Series, **2018**. https://www.northinfo.com/documents/841.pdf

Maitra, A., Salt, J. and Satchell, S. (2019). Equity Momentum in Corporate Bonds. Working paper, https://am.lombardodier.com/files/live/sites/am/files/news/AM_news/2019/January/20190121/Equity Momentum in Bonds_21Jan19.pdf

Merton, R. (1974). On the Pricing of Corporate Debt: The Risk Structure of Interest Rates. *Journal of Finance*, **29**(2), 449–470.

Messmore, T. (1995). Variance Drain. *Journal of Portfolio Management*, **21**(4), 104–110.

Novy-Marx, R. (2012). Is Momentum Really Momentum? *Journal of Financial Economics*, **103**(3), 429–453.

Novy-Marx, R. (2015). Fundamentally, Momentum is Fundamental Momentum. NBER Working Paper No. 20984. https://www.nber.org/papers/w20984

Perold, A. (1986). Constant Proportion Portfolio Insurance. Harvard Business School Working Paper. https://www.hbs.edu/faculty/Pages/item.aspx?num=4800

Slimane, M. and de Jong, M. (2018). The Cross-Section of Corporate Bond Returns. Northfield Research Conference, Maine, USA, **2018**. https://www.northinfo.com/Documents/826.pdf

Srimurthy, V., Shen, S. and Smallbach, M. (2019). Fund Flows as Country Allocator. *Journal of Alternative Investments*, **21**(3), 87–95.

Vayanos, D. and Wooley, P. (2013). An Institutional Theory of Momentum and Reversal, *Review of Financial Studies*, **26**(5), 1087–1145.

Wilcox, J. (2003). Harry Markowitz and the Discretionary Wealth Hypothesis. *Journal of Portfolio Management*, **29**(3), 58–65

Xiao, X. (2019). Implied Volatility Changes and Corporate Bond Returns. Erasmus University at Rotterdam Working Paper.

CHAPTER 6

Momentum in Momentum ETFs

KATHARINA SCHWAIGER and MUHAMMAD MASOOD

6.1 INTRODUCTION

Momentum investing, i.e. buying the recent winners and selling the recent losers has been a popular investment strategy for systematic and for fundamental portfolio managers alike. Portfolios comprised of higher-momentum stocks have exhibited persistent outperformance versus market cap weighted benchmarks through time and across global markets. One of the easiest ways for retail investors to get exposure to such a strategy is via Exchange Traded Funds (ETFs). An ETF is an investment fund that aims to track the performance of a specific index by holding a basket of securities (equities, commodities or fixed income). ETFs themselves have gained popularity since the early 2000s, but smart beta ETFs and in particular momentum ETFs have hit their peak in recent years. One gauge of consumer demands is Google Trends. Figure 6.1 shows how popular the search terms: 'Smart beta', 'Exchange-traded fund' and 'Momentum ETF' are, i.e. volumes of searches have been compared to the search volume of different queries over time (see https://trends.google.com/trends/). According to Google, momentum ETFs have reached a new all-time high of hits at the end of 2018, while Smart beta has been trending slightly earlier since mid-2011 and ETFs more in general have been increasing their popularity since inception of the Google Trend tool in 2004.

In this chapter we look at the growing trend of momentum equity ETFs and what characteristics they bring with them. In Section 6.2 we summarise the growth in assets under management of momentum ETFs and their performance over the past twenty years. Taking the largest momentum ETF as example we examine risk and performance drivers of momentum indices in Section 6.3 before looking at the effects of leverage constraints on performance in Section 6.4. Although momentum ETFs have faced several myths, we find evidence that most of their characteristics such as risk and return are driven by their targeted momentum exposure.

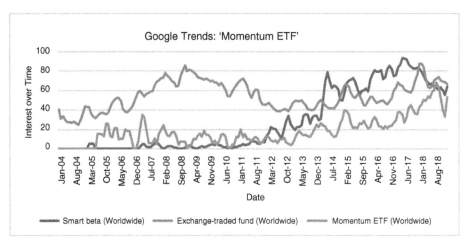

FIGURE 6.1   Popularity in momentum ETFs.
Source: Google: https://trends.google.com/trends/, September 2019

6.2   WHY ARE MOMENTUM ETFS SO POPULAR?

Momentum as an equity investment strategy has been discussed in Chapter 2. One of the first extensive studies on momentum can be found in Jegadeesh and Titman (1993) and a comprehensive literature review on factor investing including momentum investing in Ang (2014). Momentum is one of the most popular investment strategies. With the increased adoption of exchange traded funds (ETFs) momentum strategies have also gained popularity as a smart beta ETF which aims to give momentum exposure at a low fee with full transparency via tracking an index. Full transparency includes availability of the index methodology, daily fund holdings and performance via the internet.

The total assets under management (AUM) in momentum ETFs globally increased four-fold over the past five years: from $2.95 billion in 2014 to $12.265 billion end of 2018 (Figure 6.2). The total AUM is dominated by one asset manager, namely Black-Rock and its ETFs under the iShares brand. In particular, one ETF accounts for the largest share, namely the iShares Edge MSCI USA Momentum Factor ETF, which has an AUM over $8 billion. The second largest asset manager is Invesco. Almost 80% of the AUM are dominated by two asset managers. The total AUM in momentum ETFs is still minute compared to the AUM and growth in ETFs globally: global ETFs grew at an organic annualised rate of 19% from 2009 through 2017, to $4.7 trillion AUM in 2018.

Aside from full transparency, another key component that drives the growth in ETFs is their attractive fees. Figure 6.3 looks at the assets under management of individual momentum ETFs and their respective fee (total expense ratio – TER). Fees range from 12 bps to 90 bps with an average of 35 bps. Global ETFs tend to have a higher fee than USA or Europe ETFs and other smart beta ETFs tend to be similarly priced to momentum ETFs. Unlike active funds, ETFs do not charge an additional performance fee.

Momentum indices tend to vary in their construction methodologies. We find that a common approach is to consider short to medium term price returns as a signal – that is

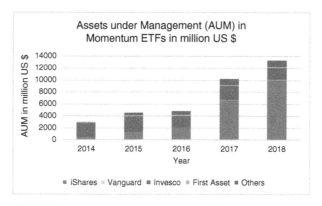

FIGURE 6.2 Assets under management (AUM) in momentum ETFs.
Source: BlackRock, December 2014 to December 2018.

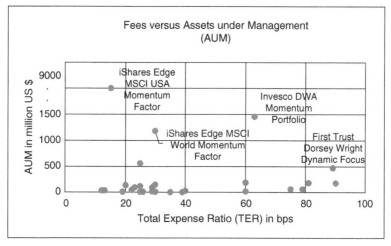

FIGURE 6.3 Assets under management (AUM) and fees of momentum ETFs.
Source: BlackRock, December 2018.

selecting stocks with the highest 6- to 12-month past performance. In some cases, such as the Invesco S&P 500 Momentum and iShares Edge MSCI World Momentum Factor ETFs, the underlying volatility of the stock is also taken into consideration. In these instances, the strategy is seeking those stocks that have delivered a better price return adjusted for their level of risk. Most of the ETFs we look at in Table 6.1 weight securities based on a combination of market capitalization weight and the respective momentum factor score. Such weighting schemes help avoid excessive turnover and maintain sufficient capacity. Lastly, we observe that the rebalancing of these strategies is done either quarterly or semi-annually. Those frequencies are chosen to be a good compromise between maintaining exposure to the momentum factor and the transaction costs of rebalancing more frequently.

TABLE 6.1 Index methodology of momentum indices. Please note: These are summary index methodologies to provide some insight on key construction steps. Methodologies of the respective indices may vary depending on the underlying starting universe. For more details please refer directly to the index provider's methodology documents

	MSCI Momentum index	FTSE Russell Momentum Factor Index	S&P Momentum index	Dorsey Wright Technical Leaders Index	Fidelity Momentum Factor index
ETFs tracking these methodologies	*iShares Edge MSCI World Momentum Factor*	*Oppenheimer Russell 1000 Momentum*	*Invesco S&P 500 Momentum Portfolio*	*Invesco DWA Momentum Portfolio*	*Fidelity Momentum Factor ETF*
Momentum Signal Definition	Using both 6- and 12-month local currency price return (excluding most recent month) divided by historical standard deviation	12-month total return in local currency	12-month local currency price return (excluding most recent month) divided by the standard deviation of daily local price returns over one year	All securities in the Index universe are ranked using a proprietary relative strength (momentum) measure. Each security's score is based on intermediate and long-term price movements relative to a representative market benchmark	Composite score using the following metrics is calculated: - 12-month total return (excluding most recent month) - Volatility-adjusted 12-month total return (excluding most recent month) - Comparison of EPS estimate from twelve months ago to actual EPS - 12-month Average Short Interest (favour stocks with low short interest)

(*continued*)

TABLE 6.1 (*Continued*)

	MSCI Momentum index	FTSE Russell Momentum Factor Index	S&P Momentum index	Dorsey Wright Technical Leaders Index	Fidelity Momentum Factor index
Stock selection	A target number of stocks are selected, which differs based on the underlying universe. This target number of stocks is calculated taking both capacity and exposure to the momentum factor into consideration	Stocks with the least contribution to the targeted factors are removed whilst monitoring the impact on diversification, capacity and factor exposure	Securities ranked in the top quintile based on momentum signal are selected	Top 100 securities by momentum score are selected	Select highest ranked stocks within each sector (number of stocks selected per sector varies by the number of stocks within the sector. Either top decile, quintile or tercile are selected for broader to more concentrated sectors respective) .
Weighting	Product of market capitalisation and momentum score	Product of market capitalisation and momentum score, with country and industry constraints	Product of market capitalisation and momentum score	Weight is determined by momentum score. Securities with higher scores get a higher weight	Sector weights reset to be sector-neutral (for starting universe) at each reconstitution

(*continued*)

TABLE 6.1 (*Continued*)

	MSCI Momentum index	FTSE Russell Momentum Factor Index	S&P Momentum index	Dorsey Wright Technical Leaders Index	Fidelity Momentum Factor index
Reconstitution/ Rebalancing frequency	Semi-annual, with conditional rebalances if the underlying market volatility is significantly high	Semi-annual	Semi-annual	Quarterly	Quarterly
Number of stocks versus starting universe	350 out of 1650 stocks (global universe)	600 out of 1000 stocks (US universe)	100 out of 500 stocks (US universe)	100 out of 1000 stocks (US universe)	100 out of 3000 stocks (US universe)

Source: Bloomberg, December 1999 to December 2018. World, USA and Europe refer to MSCI World, MSCI USA and MSCI Europe, respectively. All other smart beta indices reference MSCI smart beta indices.

One of the main differences in index methodology is the targeted number of stocks within each index. This can range from a relatively concentrated number of stocks such as around 100 for the S&P, Dorsey Wright and Fidelity index to around 350 stocks for the MSCI index, and up to 600 stocks for the FTSE Russell index.

In the academic literature, momentum strategies have been characterised as being susceptible to larger drawdowns (for example in Daniel and Moskowitz [2016]). This has been adjusted for by all index methodologies described earlier by adjusting the momentum exposure by a measure of volatility which leads to overweighting stocks that have a high momentum exposure but a lower stock price volatility. We examine the effects on performance in a subsequent section, but found that the volatility adjustment reduced historical drawdowns.

A key feature of smart beta indices is their lower turnover which is achieved by rebalancing the index in most cases either quarterly or semi-annually. In Section 6.3 we look at the effects of less frequent rebalancing on the momentum exposures within the index.

For the next section we focus on the largest momentum ETF: the iShares Momentum ETFs. The ETFs under consideration tend to track the underlying index very well and hence we will use the underlying MSCI momentum indices and their holdings from now on for our analysis.

An attractive feature of momentum ETFs for investors has been their strong performance. They have achieved strong absolute performance but also outperformed market cap weighted benchmarks. Table 6.2 compares the absolute performance of momentum indices as represented by iShares Momentum ETFs to other smart beta indices (other

TABLE 6.2 Performance statistics of smart beta indices.

		Annualised return (%)	Annualised risk (%)	Return/ Risk	Maximum drawdown (%)
World	World	3.39	15.00	0.23	54.03
	World Min Vol	6.00	10.72	0.56	43.48
	World Momentum	5.38	14.94	0.36	52.79
	World Quality	4.86	14.29	0.34	50.67
	World Size	5.81	16.24	0.36	55.65
	World Value	6.74	17.10	0.39	58.24
USA	USA	4.04	14.62	0.28	51.12
	USA Min Vol	7.45	11.68	0.64	44.84
	USA Momentum	6.55	15.17	0.43	52.01
	USA Quality	4.76	13.70	0.35	44.34
	USA Size	6.65	17.49	0.38	55.08
	USA Value	7.27	16.54	0.44	55.56
Europe	Europe	1.88	14.88	0.13	54.10
	Europe Min Vol	5.34	10.95	0.49	46.30
	Europe Momentum	4.74	14.14	0.34	53.21
	Europe Quality	3.76	13.73	0.27	50.06
	Europe Size	3.82	16.66	0.23	61.54
	Europe Value	4.23	16.93	0.25	58.00

TABLE 6.3 Relative performance statistics of smart beta indices.

		Annualised active return (%)	Annualised tracking error (%)	Information ratio
World	World Min Vol	4.09	7.31	0.56
	World Momentum	3.22	7.76	0.41
	World Quality	2.44	2.96	0.82
	World Size	3.83	4.70	0.82
	World Value	5.10	5.64	0.90
USA	USA Min Vol	5.57	6.66	0.84
	USA Momentum	4.28	7.79	0.55
	USA Quality	1.38	2.99	0.46
	USA Size	4.43	6.75	0.66
	USA Value	5.32	5.55	0.96
Europe	Europe Min Vol	4.40	6.38	0.69
	Europe Momentum	3.69	7.80	0.47
	Europe Quality	2.48	3.27	0.76
	Europe Size	2.55	5.48	0.47
	Europe Value	3.07	4.82	0.64

Source: Bloomberg, December 1999 to December 2018.

iShares smart beta ETFs) and to the market cap weighted index. Annualised returns of the momentum indices have been between 4.7% and 6% with risk (volatility) of 15%. The return/risk ratios of around 0.4 for all three regions is comparable to the other smart beta indices. In particular versus the size and the value indices, the momentum indices have a lower annualised return with lower annualised volatilities, which lead to similar return/risk ratios.

In relative terms the momentum indices achieved, over the last ten years, annualised excess return of around 3% with tracking errors versus the market cap weighted index of almost 8%. The high ex-post tracking error is comparable with active funds whose objective is to invest in a concentrated set of stocks and is also the highest active risk among the other smart beta indices. The information ratios of the momentum indices are positive and statistically significant across all three regional exposures (Table 6.3).

Figure 6.4 shows the historical performance of various factor strategies compared to that of MSCI World. In general, the performance metrics of these factors are in line with expectations. We find that defensive factors such as minimum volatility and quality showed better performance during market downturns (early 2000s and 2008 for example). By contrast, value and size tended to do better during market rallies, in particular after periods of market downturns. Momentum returns have been strong during

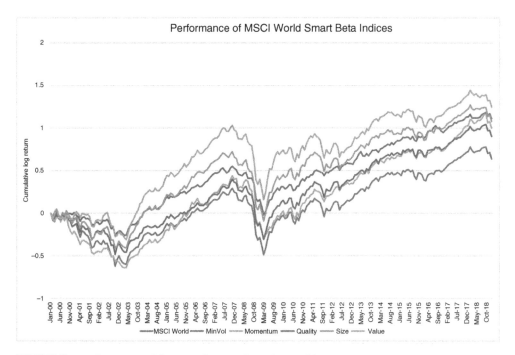

FIGURE 6.4 Performance of factor indices and MSCI World.
Source: iShares, December 1999 to December 2018.

periods of sustained equity market performance. Using excess returns versus the market cap weighted benchmark (MSCI World) the negative correlation of the momentum index to the value factor index is also noticeable historically. There are also periods where momentum can be correlated with defensive factors such as minimum volatility and quality; 2009 is a good example of this.

One of the main criticisms of momentum strategies has been their susceptibility to large drawdowns (see Daniel and Moskowitz, 2016). To address that additional risk, most of the index methodologies adjust the momentum score by volatility, i.e. high momentum stocks with high volatility get penalised compared to a stock with similar momentum exposure but lower volatility. Figure 6.5 charts the performance drawdowns of MSCI World and MSCI World smart beta indices.

Coming out of the dotcom bubble in the late 1990s, momentum stocks were mainly defined as internet-based companies. In 2001 and through 2002 when the dotcom bubble burst and equities entered a bear market, the momentum index saw the largest drawdown relative to the market cap index (MSCI World) and to the other smart beta indices. However, the largest drawdown experienced since the late 1990s has been during the global financial crises. Global indices drew down more than 50% with the exception of minimum volatility due to its low-beta characteristics. The momentum index, however, despite its perceived drawdown characteristics, fared slightly better than the value and size indices. Partially this behaviour is due to the index adjusting stocks momentum exposure by volatility.

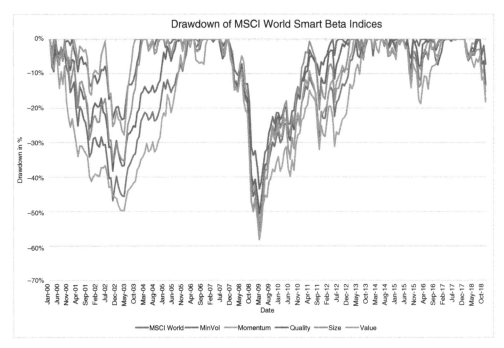

FIGURE 6.5 Drawdown profile of factor indices and MSCI World.
Source: iShares.

6.3 WHAT IS IN A MOMENTUM ETF?

Section 6.2 looked at reasons why momentum ETFs have gained in popularity and how they are constructed. In the following section we examine further characteristics of momentum indices.

One way to measure momentum characteristics of a portfolio is to look at a risk factor analysis. Fundamental risk factor models decompose risk into country, sector, factor and idiosyncratic risk drivers. Factor exposures include momentum, value, volatility or small cap exposures. Risk factor exposures are typically measured by cross-sectional z-scores ranging from [-3, +3]. An active momentum exposure is relative to a market cap weighted benchmark – a positive (negative) active exposure suggests a higher (lower) momentum tilt than the benchmark. We would expect momentum indices to have a constantly positive and significant tilt versus benchmark. Since the momentum indices rebalance mostly on a quarterly or semi-annual basis, one of the criticisms of momentum indices has been around potential factor decays over time and in particular during intra rebalance periods. In Figure 6.6. we plot the active momentum exposure of MSCI momentum indices just after rebalance, as well as one to five months after rebalance. The index itself rebalances semi-annually, which suggests that the sixth month incurs a new rebalance. At all rebalance dates historically, the momentum index has a positive exposure and meaningfully above zero. As months pass the active exposures decrease. Nevertheless, with the exception of some outliers, the momentum index always exhibits a higher momentum exposure than the benchmark. This is true for all three regions.

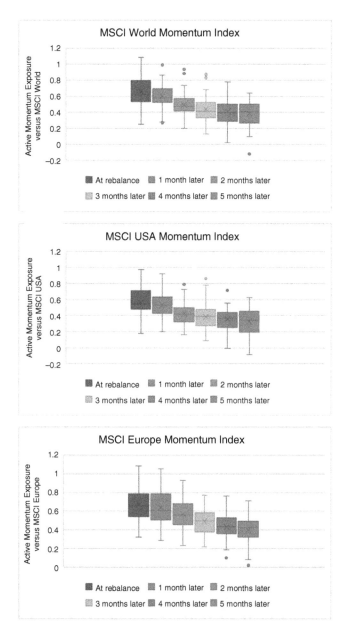

FIGURE 6.6 Momentum exposure of momentum indices.
Source: iShares.

Active exposures are a way to measure a portfolio's characteristics. An additional useful measure is to understand how much of the active risk (tracking error) can be attributed to a particular characteristic. In the next section we look at how much active risk comes from being exposed to the momentum factor versus other factors such as style factors, industries or stock specifics.

6.4 WHICH FACTORS DRIVE ACTIVE RISK FOR MOMENTUM ETFS?

This section explores the active risk levels of momentum indices versus their respective parent benchmarks (ex-ante and ex-post) and looks at risk decompositions over time. Across all three regional exposures of World, USA and Europe, Figures 6.7, 6.8 and 6.9 show that ex-ante active risk in general fluctuates between 3 and 6%, with some periods of exceptionally higher levels. The active risk numbers are lower than the ex-post tracking errors seen in the previous section. This is mainly skewed by the global financial crises period where risk models were underestimating portfolio risk.

The drivers of active risk vary over time. On average we find that the momentum factor itself explains around 20–25% of the ex-ante active risk. This is followed by exposure to industries. The other style factors, such as value, volatility or small cap, contribute less and their importance in driving active risk can vary over time.

An interesting observation concerns the contribution of the beta factor towards ex-ante active risk. While mostly it is quite low, in certain years such as 2002 and 2009, it becomes the largest driver of ex-ante active risk across all three regional indices. One explanation for this is based on the relationship of momentum strategies with the low-volatility factor during certain phases of the market. In particular, when equity markets experienced negative returns, momentum strategies can move into more defensive / low volatility securities as those securities usually would have had the best relative performance. This skews the exposure of the momentum strategy towards lower beta, hence contributing more towards active risk.

In this section we conclude that momentum indices do exhibit a positive and statistically significant momentum exposure, even after taking into account their infrequent rebalancing. Additionally, we show that a large proportion of the active risk is driven by the targeted momentum factor exposure, which should also be an indication of return

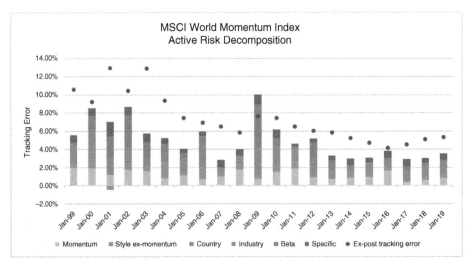

FIGURE 6.7   MSCI World momentum index: active risk decomposition.
Source: iShares, December 1998 to December 2018.

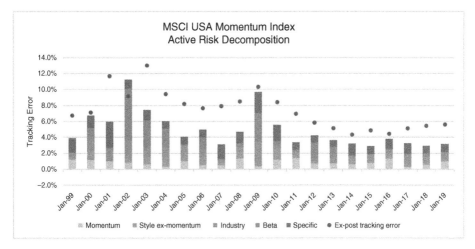

FIGURE 6.8 MSCI USA momentum index: active risk decomposition.
Source: iShares, December 1998 to December 2018.

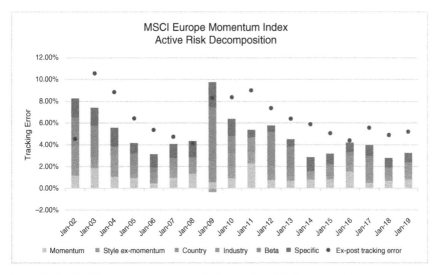

FIGURE 6.9 MSCI Europe momentum index: active risk decomposition.
Source: iShares, December 2001 to December 2018.

drivers. One way to examine what drives returns of a momentum index is by taking a look at its contribution to return by each style factor. This decomposition analysis excludes other return drivers such as country, sector or idiosyncratic effects and is useful in understanding how much the momentum exposure contributes to return versus the other style factors. Figures 6.10, 6.11 and 6.12, respectively, present the cumulative return contributions by factor for the MSCI World, MSCI USA, and MSCI Europe.

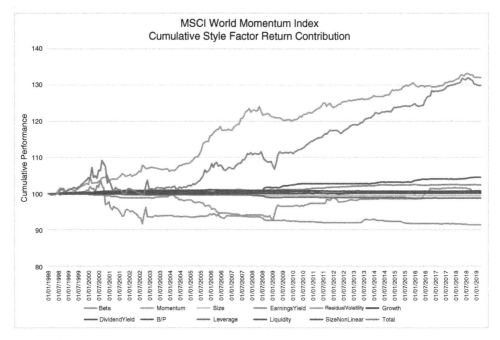

FIGURE 6.10   MSCI World momentum index: style factor return decomposition.
Source: iShares, December 1998 to December 2018.

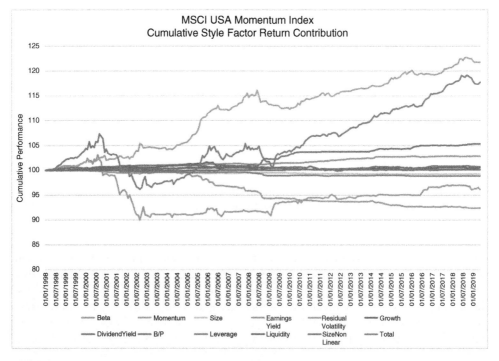

FIGURE 6.11   MSCI USA momentum index: style factor return decomposition.
Source: iShares, December 1998 to December 2018.

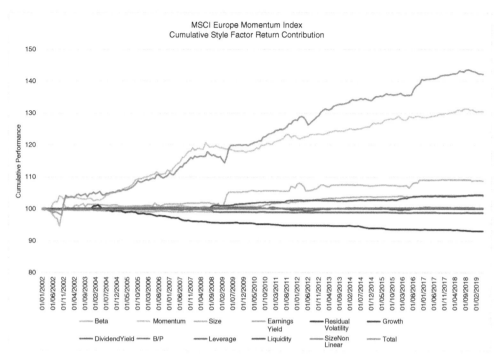

FIGURE 6.12 MSCI Europe momentum index: style factor return decomposition.
Source: iShares, December 2001 to December 2018.

For all three regional momentum indices, momentum is the strongest positively contributing style factor. The other two style factors that contribute to the excess performance versus the market cap index are residual volatility and beta. Residual volatility detracts across all three regions while beta contributes within Europe but detracts from the USA and global momentum index. The magnitude is however small compared to the momentum factor contribution. This is another confirmation that momentum ETFs load positively on momentum characteristics and their risk and return contributions are dominated by the momentum style factor.

6.5 FROM CONSTRAINED TO UNCONSTRAINED STRATEGIES

Momentum ETFs aim to track low-turnover (lower turnover compared to long-short momentum strategies), long-only and fully transparent indices that aim to tilt into high momentum stocks. ETFs are one choice of investment vehicle. We next discuss other hypothetical options of investment strategies that can be seen as less constrained and examine their risk/return profiles. Active momentum funds tend to be less constrained and can take on leverage, rebalance more frequently and only publicly distribute selective information. With the addition of leverage, those active momentum strategies can additionally short the past losers alongside being long the past winners. A higher rebalancing frequency enables those funds to have a consistently high momentum exposure without seeing a significant decay during intra-rebalance periods. We examine three cases: a) a leveraged long-short strategy, b) a leveraged long-short strategy with a maximum of 30% shorting ability and c) an unleveraged long-only strategy. As an empirical illustration we create momentum strategies based on 12-month price momentum from a global equity universe. Unlike the transparent indices, those strategies rebalance monthly and use an optimisation to determine the portfolio weights. The leveraged strategy is market neutral (i.e. it maintains a market beta close to zero) and the long-only strategy is beta neutral versus a market cap weighted benchmark.

The addition of shorting stocks within a momentum strategy can benefit the performance of those strategies. In Figure 6.13 we compare the excess performance of the long-only strategy to the long-only strategy with modest leverage (130/30 strategy) to the absolute performance of a long-short strategy. Although the long-only strategy delivers the lowest long-term performance out of the three implementations, it also typically would be offered at a lower fee and it can be accessed by all types of investors, while the others cannot.

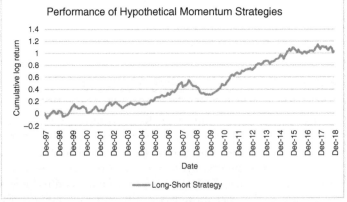

FIGURE 6.13 Hypothetical backtest of a momentum strategy:
a) Long-only, b)130/30 and c) Long-short.
Source: BlackRock, December 1997 to December 2018.

6.6 CONCLUSIONS

Given increased investor interest in the momentum ETFs, we examined in this chapter the key characteristics of such investment strategies. It is widely believed that smart beta products such as momentum ETFs tracking rules-based indices cannot capture truly dynamic characteristics of a momentum strategy due to: a) their infrequent rebalancing, b) simplistic and transparent index construction and c) long-only portfolio implementation. We sought to dispel these myths in our paper by taking a closer look at index construction, time-varying style factor exposure, as well as risk and return drivers.

REFERENCES

Ang, A. (2014) *Asset Management: A Systematic Approach to Factor Based Investing*. New York: Oxford University Press.

Daniel, K. and T. J. Moskowitz (2016) 'Momentum Crashes', *Journal of Financial Economics*, **122**(2), 221–247.

Jegadeesh, N. and S. Titman (1993) 'Returns to Buying Winners and Selling Losers: Implications for Stock Market Efficiency', *Journal of Finance*, **48**(1), 65–91.

CHAPTER 7

CTA Momentum

OLIVER J. WILLIAMS

7.1 INTRODUCTION

The term Commodity Trading Adviser (CTA) dates back to the 1974 United States legislation setting up the Commodities Futures and Trading Commission (CFTC). The definition applies to firms advising investors on strategies encompassing various derivative products (across all asset classes), but in common market parlance it has become almost universally used to refer to investment management firms that aim to profit from *trends* in market prices, irrespective of where they are domiciled, which regulatory regime they fall under and whether or not they trade commodities. Indeed it is not unusual for CTA portfolios to be dominated by financial contracts, as trend-following strategies are generally statistically driven, asset class agnostic and many commodity markets present liquidity challenges for larger funds.[1]

At first glance the CTA strategy may seem similar to cross-sectional momentum (CSM) which is discussed elsewhere in this volume: both are predicated on the thesis that past returns have some predictive power over future returns, and both seek to profit from this using portfolios with long and short positions, however the CTA strategy typically relies on predictions computed using the history of an instrument's *own* price and is therefore better described as time-series momentum (TSM).[2] In comparison, in cross-sectional momentum strategies past returns of an instrument *relative to a benchmark* are used to predict its future returns. Also, CSM tends to be focused on equities, whereas TSM is actively applied across all asset classes.

Although the operational difference between TSM and CSM is well-defined, if an investor believes in momentum effects (either for structural or behavioural reasons)

---

[1]In the fourth quarter of 2018 BarclayHedge estimated total assets under management of USD 355.1 billion in CTA funds, which is generally leveraged to some extent.
[2]Baltas and Kosowski (Chapter 3, this volume) rigorously demonstrate the relationship between CTAs and TSM strategies using benchmark portfolios and index data.

it may not be immediately clear to them whether their views are better reflected by a TSM or CSM strategy, or perhaps even a combination of both. We believe that in such cases it would be helpful to have a framework in which to compare these based on observable market characteristics, e.g. the correlation structure of returns, rather than reaching conclusions based on more qualitative or thematic grounds. However this endeavour is complicated by the fact that there are numerous alternative forms of TSM and CSM models in commercial use, each with subtly different properties.[3]

The contribution of this chapter is to review the mechanics of TSM in more detail, then present a simple model in which specific forms of TSM and CSM are combined in the same portfolio. We address two specific sets of questions:

1. What are the statistical properties of TSM returns in our model?
2. What is the correlation between our TSM and CSM returns?

To be clear, throughout this chapter we tackle CSM in the form of the 'weighted relative strength strategy' which enables us to obtain tractable results, although (as emphasised by Kwon and Satchell [2019]) this differs from original CSM definitions such as those proposed by Jegadeesh and Titman (1993) and Carhart (1997). Our aim is to err towards intuitive insights rather than technical detail.

The chapter is organised as follows: Section 7.2 sets the scene with examples of alternative approaches to trend-following, Section 7.3 introduces our simplified strategy returns models, Section 7.4 considers the statistical properties of TSM returns in our model (focusing on Sharpe ratio and skewness) and Section 7.5 addresses portfolio combinations of TSM and CSM. Section 7.6 concludes.

7.2 TIME-SERIES MOMENTUM (TSM)

Trend-following traders use a wide range of methods to convert historic price information into long/short position sizes per instrument. Although methods differ in terms of their intellectual foundations they can often be decomposed into some form of filter that generates an informative signal from a historic price series, along with a position-sizing function that translates this signal into a long or short amount of the underlying instrument.

Although a plethora of different methods can be used, a stylised fact of CTA investing is that instrument-level positions tend to be highly similar across funds (at least in terms of longs and shorts, although not necessarily individual portfolio weights) and correlations between fund returns are often very high. Therefore dispersion in fund returns is to some extent driven by differences in asset class weightings, sizing functions or risk management policies (e.g. stop loss rules) rather than radically differing sets of directional signals.

---

[3]Kwon and Satchell (2019) discuss various CSM formulations (including the so-called 'weighted relative strength strategy' which we use in this chapter).

Various other stylised facts have become established as regards TSM, for instance:

- TSM provides option-like payoffs with positive skewness (Fung and Hsieh, 2001; Potters and Bouchaud, 2006; Till and Eagleeye; 2011);
- performance tends to have a low Sharpe ratio (which is sometimes viewed as the price to be paid for positive skewness); and
- TSM is a useful addition to a portfolio of long-only equity or hedge funds (e.g. Kat, 2005).

We will return to these themes later in this chapter, but first for background we briefly describe some alternative approaches to the TSM signal generation and position-sizing stages.

7.2.1 Signal generation

For the purpose of example we describe two approaches that are conceptually quite different but (in certain circumstances) may nevertheless lead to similar trading decisions. This underlines our point that instrument-level positions may be similar across CTA funds despite quite dramatic differences in the investment process. This also encourages us to use a simple TSM returns model later in the chapter to capture the essence of the CTA process without burdensome technicality. An encyclopaedic review of a wide range of alternative filtering methods is provided by Bruder et al. (2011), including nonlinear methods and techniques from machine learning.

Technical analysis Technical analyses can be viewed as heuristic forecasting methods without an explicit stochastic model for prices or returns. These include quasi-geometric techniques intended to identify informative patterns in prices (e.g. the famous *head-and-shoulders* and less famous *Andrews pitchfork*) as well as variations on basic summary statistics (typically involving averages or ranges).

Among the most common technical analysis methods used for trend-following are rules based on various forms of moving averages of prices (e.g. *moving average crossover* and the *moving average convergence divergence* (MACD) technique). Zakamulin (2017) provides a detailed analysis of such rules. These are commonly deployed by professional money managers and also form the basis of various mechanical TSM replication systems or research tools (such as the SG Trend Indicator (Société Générale, 2016).

In the case of moving average crossover, the trader computes two moving averages which are updated on a regular basis (e.g. daily), one of which (the 'slow' average) covers a longer period than the other (the 'fast' average). The averages may be weighted equally or exponentially. There is no well-defined theory to guide the choice of these averages, and they are typically selected by some form of back-testing. The slow average is subtracted from the fast average to generate a predictive trend signal; the most basic associated trading rule maintains a long position when the signal is positive (indicating an upward trend) and a short position when the opposite is true, with various functions applied for position-sizing (e.g. the linear systems described by Martin and Zou, 2012).

In typical moving average systems the overall signal can be expressed as a weighted sum of lagged price observations and we show example sets of weights in Figures 7.1(a) (equal weights) and 7.1(b) (exponential weights). In both cases the

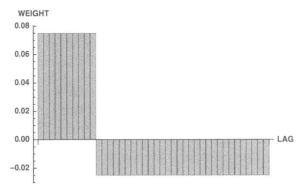

(a) Moving average crossover (10 days versus 40 days)

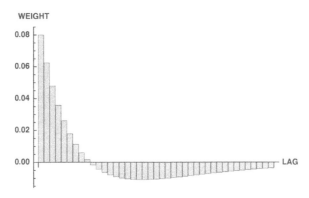

(b) Dual exponentially-weighted moving averages; infinite window with weight at lag τ given by $(1 - \lambda)\lambda^\tau$ ($\lambda_{slow} = 0.93$, $\lambda_{fast} = 0.85$).

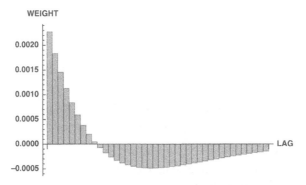

(c) Optimal weights (w_s) for extraction of trend slope using Wiener-Kolmogorov approach applied to model in sectiona

FIGURE 7.1 Price weights as a function of lag for three alternative signal generation formulations.

signal is the net of positive and negative weighted values, and although the exact profile of weights is noticeably different in each case, we see some similarity in that a block of positive weights is followed by a block of negative weights.

7.2.1.2 Signal processing One drawback of moving average approaches is that parameters are usually specified in terms of 'numbers of days', which are hard to intuitively relate to statistical quantities that are commonly used elsewhere in financial modelling, e.g. volatilities and correlations used in risk management, portfolio optimisation or option pricing. Various alternative approaches to filter design arise from the fields of time-series analysis and signal processing; these have the benefit that they involve explicit statistical modelling of price dynamics and derivation of associated optimal forecasting functions.

By way of example we summarise here the Wiener-Kolmogorov (W-K) approach to signal extraction as described by Whittle (1963). In this case the observed price series is a formally specified stochastic process that can be defined in terms of an underlying price trend plus some additive noise. A standard method can be applied to determine the filter weights that will compute a minimum mean squared error prediction of underlying trend from observed prices. The pattern of these weights will depend on the exact structure of the process and all associated parameters (noise variances, coefficients, etc.).

As a specific example, suppose observed price p_t is composed of an underlying trend q_t plus noise $\varepsilon_t \sim N(0, \sigma^2)$, and the underlying trend has an AR(1) slope s_t with noise $\eta_t \sim N(0, \sigma_\eta^2)$:

$$p_t = q_t + \varepsilon_t \tag{7.1}$$

$$q_t = \theta q_{t-1} + s_t \tag{7.2}$$

$$s_t = \zeta s_{t-1} + \eta_t. \tag{7.3}$$

If the components are mutually independent stationary stochastic processes with zero mean, then the autocovariance generating function of p_t is the sum of the autocovariance generating functions of its two components[4]

$$g_{pp}(z) = g_{qq}(z) + g_{\varepsilon\varepsilon}(z)$$

and optimal filter weights for estimation of q_t are given by the coefficients of the z-transform

$$w_q(z) = \frac{1}{\sigma^2 B_p(z)} \left[\frac{g_{qq}(z)}{B_p(z^{-1})} \right]_+ \tag{7.4}$$

where $g_{qq}(z)$ is the autocovariance generating function of q_t and $g_{\varepsilon\varepsilon}(z) = \sigma^2$. The notation $[\cdot]_+$ denotes the set of terms z^k where $k \geq 0$ and $B_p(z)$ is a factor of $g_{pp}(z)$ found from the Cramér-Wold factorisation:

$$g_{pp}(z) = \sigma^2 B_p(z) B_p(z^{-1}). \tag{7.5}$$

---

[4]For example purposes, we choose to work with zero mean processes. For greater generality p_t could be interpreted as a deviation from some fixed reference level, or a log transform of price.

One benefit of this approach is that once the optimal filter weights have been found it is straightforward to determine the filter's frequency response $H(\omega)$ as follows

$$H(\omega) = w_q(z)|_{z=e^{i\omega}} = w_q(e^{i\omega})$$

which provides a way of quantifying the lag of the strategy (a typical drawback of trend-following strategies).

From a practical perspective, determining $w_q(z)$ involves several steps:

1. specifying a structure for the stochastic process p_t;
2. determining parameter estimates (e.g. coefficients and variances);
3. finding the Cramér-Wold factorisation (Equation [7.5]);
4. performing the polynomial division inside the square brackets; and
5. inversion of the z-transform in Equation (7.4) to determine weights as a function of lag.

Steps 1 and 2 can be achieved by a conventional process of model selection and maximum likelihood estimation. Step 3 requires an appropriate algorithm, such as Laurie's (1982) Fortran subroutine AS175 which provides the Cramér-Wold factorisation (Equation [7.5]) given the coefficients of the Laurent series representation of $g_{pp}(z)$. We denote these coefficients by $\gamma_{pp}(\tau)$ and following Nerlove et al. (2014) they can be determined by complex integration as follows:

$$\gamma_{pp}(\tau) = \frac{1}{2\pi i} \oint_{|z|=1} \frac{g_{pp}(z)}{z^{\tau+1}} dz \qquad \tau = 0, \pm 1, \pm 2, \ldots \tag{7.6}$$

where

$$g_{pp}(z) = \frac{\sigma_\eta^2}{(1 - \zeta z)(1 - \zeta z^{-1})(1 - \theta z)(1 - \theta z^{-1})} + \sigma^2.$$

Step 4 requires division of

$$g_{qq}(z) = \frac{\sigma_\eta^2}{(1 - \zeta z)(1 - \zeta z^{-1})(1 - \theta z)(1 - \theta z^{-1})}$$

by $B_p(z^{-1})$ followed by discarding the terms with negative powers, and finally the inversion in step 5 can be performed by another application of complex integration (similar to Equation [7.6]).

If we make the standard assumption that $\theta = 1$ then the process becomes non-stationary, suggesting that the W–K approach is inapplicable, however in this case we recognise that for trading purposes it may be more useful to extract an estimate of the slope s_t (rather than trend q_t) and this can be done by differencing Equation (7.1) to obtain the stationary process

$$p_t - p_{t-1} = d_t = s_t + (\varepsilon_t - \varepsilon_{t-1}).$$

These components are mutually independent stationary stochastic processes and hence the W–K method can be applied:[5]

$$w_s(z) = \frac{1}{\sigma^2 B_d(z)} \left[\frac{g_{ss}(z)}{B_d(z^{-1})} \right]_+ \tag{7.7}$$

where $B_d(z)$ is found from the Cramér-Wold factorisation of $g_{dd}(z)$ and

$$g_{ss}(z) = \frac{\sigma_n^2}{(1 - \zeta z)(1 - \zeta z^{-1})}.$$

Figure 7.1(c) shows the weights for extraction of estimated slope s_t from observed prices p_t by applying the method above to the model (Equations [7.1], [7.2] and [7.3]) with $\theta = 1, \zeta = 0.9, \sigma^2 = 10^{-2}$ and $\sigma_\eta^2 = 10^{-6}$ (these parameters were chosen for example purpose only, to give a broad sense of the shape of the weighting function). The exact profile of weights is somewhat different from the cases of both technical analysis rules (Figures 7.1(a) and 7.1(b)) but there are some striking similarities, despite significant differences in computational complexity across the three methods.

Hence technical analysis might be viewed by a signal processing enthusiast as an ad hoc approximation to an optimal signal extraction solution. By contrast, a technical analyst might view the signal processing approach as an over-engineered solution to an ill-posed problem. Nevertheless, anecdotal and empirical evidence suggests that both are likely to come to much the same conclusion if given a time series of historical prices and asked whether they would prefer to buy or sell December expiry Brent crude futures. Where traders and analysts may differ more widely is on the question of position size.

7.2.2 Position-sizing

There are various ways in which a signal can be extracted, but the statistical properties of overall returns are heavily dependent on how these signals are translated into long or short positions in the traded asset. Simplistic approaches include an 'always in the market' unit long or short position, where position size is constant irrespective of signal strength (although likely to be scaled based on some form of volatility prediction). More sophisticated approaches involve the typical range of portfolio optimisation tools used elsewhere in asset management, with expected returns and volatility forecasts determined by systematic methods.

Underlining the impact of the position sizing decision, Martin and Zou (2012) focus on the skewness of returns which results when holding a position in an asset that is directly proportional to a trending indicator. In particular they consider linear systems where position is a weighted sum of prior returns (such as the moving average methods described earlier). They make assumptions about the first three moments of asset returns but do not require normality. Importantly they show that even if daily returns are independent and non-skewed, the trend-following strategy return will be positively

---

[5]Further details are provided by Pollock (2009).

skewed; they also show that skewness initially increases as a function of the length of the return period (M), reaching a maximum and then decaying as $\frac{1}{\sqrt{M}}$.

7.3 STRATEGY RETURN MODELS

Our approach to modelling strategy returns builds on the framework used by Lo and MacKinlay (1990), Lewellen (2002) and Moskowitz et al. (2012) among others. This involves expressions for TSM and CSM portfolio returns in terms of sums of products of correlated random variables, which will allow us to obtain closed-form expressions for moments under the assumption of multivariate normality.

We assume portfolios consist of N instruments, with weightings decided at time t based on actual returns observed during the prior period (represented by $r_{t-1,t}$) and we consider the return realised over the subsequent period $(r_{t,t+1})$. For concise notation we assume that both periods have the same length, while recognising that, in general, momentum strategies will involve weights based on various historical return periods and time horizon for future returns will depend on context.

We define vectors of expected returns

$$\mu = (\mu_1, \mu_2, \ldots, \mu_N),$$

actual returns from time τ_1 to τ_2

$$R_{\tau_1,\tau_2} = (r^1_{\tau_1,\tau_2}, \ r^2_{\tau_1,\tau_2}, \ldots, r^N_{\tau_1,\tau_2})$$

and matrix of cross-covariances

$$\Omega = E[(R_{t-1,t} - \mu)(R_{t,t+1} - \mu)].$$

7.3.1 Time-series momentum (TSM)

For the time-series momentum strategy the weight of each instrument $w_t^{TS,i}$ is directly proportional to its prior period return $r_{t-1,t}$:

$$w_t^{TS,i} = \frac{1}{N} r^i_{t-1,t}$$

hence the N-instrument TSM portfolio return is given by

$$r_{TS} = \sum_{i=1}^{N} w_t^{TS,i} r^i_{t,t+1}$$

$$= \frac{1}{N} \sum_{i=1}^{N} r^i_{t-1,t} r^i_{t,t+1} \qquad (7.8)$$

and it is straightforward to show that

$$E[r_{TS}] = \frac{\text{tr}(\Omega)}{N} + \frac{\mu'\mu}{N}. \tag{7.9}$$

Thinking in terms of Figure 7.1, we might describe this as loosely similar to using a signal computed with a weight of +1 at lag 0 (the most recent observed price) and −1 at lag 1, thereby computing the historic arithmetic return, combined with a trivial position size function. Although simplistic, this does incorporate the realistic feature that position sizes are influenced by expected returns (the historic return can be viewed as a crude estimate of future return assuming some implicit [unspecified] autoregressive returns model).

7.3.2   Cross-sectional momentum (CSM)

In our version of the cross-sectional momentum strategy each instrument weight is directly proportional to the difference between its historical return and the equally-weighted average historical return across all N instruments. This formulation was proposed by Lo and MacKinlay (1990) and referred to as the 'weighted relative strength strategy' by Jegadeesh and Titman (2002).

Hence we define

$$r_{t-1,t}^{EW} = \frac{1}{N} \sum_{i=1}^{N} r_{t-1,t}^{i}$$

$$w_{t}^{CS,i} = \frac{1}{N}(r_{t-1,t}^{i} - r_{t-1,t}^{EW})$$

and

$$r_{CS} = \sum_{i=1}^{N} w_{t}^{CS,i} r_{t,t+1}^{i}$$

$$= \frac{1}{N} \sum_{i=1}^{N} (r_{t-1,t}^{i} - r_{t-1,t}^{EW}) r_{t,t+1}^{i}$$

which gives

$$E[r_{CS}] = \frac{\text{tr}(\Omega)}{N} - \frac{1'\Omega 1}{N^2} + \sigma_{\mu}^2. \tag{7.10}$$

We emphasise that this weight function is not intended to be a high-fidelity representation of methods used in real-world CSM portfolios (such as modelled in greater detail by Kwon and Satchell [2019]), but it is a tractable means of incorporating key structural aspects with minimal notation; this enables us to focus on the high level concepts that are common to both TSM and CSM.

7.3.3 Comparing the strategies

As pointed out by Moskowitz et al. (2012), expected CSM returns in Equation (7.10) can be decomposed into components corresponding to autocovariance (predictability from *own price*), cross-covariance (predictability from *other prices*) and cross-sectional variation in unconditional mean returns. In comparison, expected TSM returns in Equation (7.9) can be decomposed into effects of autocovariance and magnitude of expected returns with no dependence on cross-sectional variation. We will shortly scrutinise these differences more closely.

Importantly, cross-covariance $\frac{1'\Omega 1}{N^2}$ has a negative sign in Equation (7.10). As observed by Lewellen (2002), negative cross-serial covariance between returns on instruments i and j will tend to contribute positively to CSM portfolio performance: as an example, if i delivers a relatively high historic return (compared to j) and is included as a long position (while j is a short position) this negative correlation leads us to expect that a positive realisation of return i will tend to be associated with a negative realisation of return j, both profitable in the portfolio. Hence *negative* cross-serial correlation reinforces autocorrelation in each instrument's own returns.

It is informative to compare r_{TS} and r_{CS} in some special cases. While considering these we will make simplifying covariance assumptions. In all our subsequent examples we will assume that all instrument returns have the same variance σ^2 and that contemporaneous correlation in returns is equal for all pairs of instruments (denoted by ϕ). We will also occasionally assume that autocorrelation is equal across all instruments (denoted by ρ) and that cross-correlations are equal and symmetric across all pairs (denoted η).

That said, the requirement that the covariance matrix must be positive definite places restrictions linking all correlation values and such simplifications must be made with caution. Determining appropriate restrictions for arbitrary sized matrices is straightforward but time-consuming, so in Appendix A we present sufficient conditions for the example case of two assets to give some sense of the nature of the constraints involved.

7.3.3.1 Perfect contemporaneous correlation

As an introductory extreme example we assume contemporaneous returns are perfectly correlated, hence $\phi = 1$ and for consistency with this we further assume $\eta = \rho$ (autocorrelation equals cross-correlation).[6] We also assume that expected returns are equal across all instruments hence $\sigma_\mu^2 = 0$. Although this is a somewhat pathological extreme it is nevertheless useful for intuition. In this case it is trivially apparent that expected CSM returns will be zero.

Symbolically:

$$\Omega = E[(R_{t-1,t} - \mu)(R_{t,t+1} - \mu)$$

$$= \begin{bmatrix} \rho\sigma^2 & \rho\sigma^2 & \cdots & \rho\sigma^2 \\ \rho\sigma^2 & \rho\sigma^2 & \cdots & \rho\sigma^2 \\ \vdots & \vdots & \ddots & \vdots \\ \rho\sigma^2 & \rho\sigma^2 & \cdots & \rho\sigma^2 \end{bmatrix}$$

---

[6]In Appendix A we show that $\eta = \rho$ will ensure positive definiteness for the case of two assets when $\phi \approx 1$ and this extends intuitively to the case of larger portfolio sizes although we do not prove this explicitly.

with

$$E[r_{CS}] = \rho\sigma^2 - \frac{N^2\rho\sigma^2}{N^2} + \sigma_\mu^2 = \sigma_\mu^2 = 0$$

and

$$E[r_{TS}] = \rho\sigma^2 + \mu^2.$$

This arises because $r_{t-1,t}^i = r_{t-1,t}^{EW}$ for all instruments $i \in \{1 \ldots N\}$ and so each instrument has a weight of zero in the portfolio. However in more realistic cases of very high correlation slightly below 1 it is likely that $r_{t-1,t}^i \neq r_{t-1,t}^{EW}$ for at least some instruments so positions will be split between longs and shorts and in this case any profitable positions (whether long or short) will tend to be largely offset by losing positions in the opposite direction because all instrument prices are tending to move together.

The key point is that even in a market when assets have rallied (or fallen) almost in tandem, the CSM portfolio will hold some counter-trend positions (e.g. short positions in assets which did not rally as much as the average), whereas the TSM portfolio will never hold counter-trend positions by deliberate design. This slavish devotion to holding both long and short positions will inevitably come at the expense of performance.

7.3.3.2 General contemporaneous correlation In this case we consider general values of $\phi < 1$, while assuming that η and ρ are common across pairs of instrument returns. Although we consider general values of ϕ we must be mindful of the fact that positive definiteness places associated constraints on η and ρ as considered in Appendix A (e.g. if $\phi = 0$ with two instruments we see that a sufficient condition for positive definiteness is $|\eta| < \sqrt{1 - \rho^2}$).

In this case,

$$\Omega = E[(R_{t-1,t} - \mu)(R_{t,t+1} - \mu)]$$

$$= \begin{bmatrix} \rho\sigma^2 & \eta\sigma^2 & \cdots & \eta\sigma^2 \\ \eta\sigma^2 & \rho\sigma^2 & \cdots & \eta\sigma^2 \\ \vdots & \vdots & \ddots & \vdots \\ \eta\sigma^2 & \eta\sigma^2 & \cdots & \rho\sigma^2 \end{bmatrix}$$

with

$$E[r_{CS}] = \frac{N-1}{N}(\rho - \eta)\sigma^2 + \sigma_\mu^2$$

and

$$E[r_{TS}] = \rho\sigma^2 + \mu^2.$$

In these conditions the momentum portfolio is more likely to generate overall positive returns with contributions from short positions as well as long positions (compared to extreme perfect correlation described in the previous section). More dispersed levels of expected returns across instruments (σ_μ^2) will further contribute to higher returns at portfolio level.

We also see that contemporaneous correlation ϕ does not appear in expected returns for either TSM or CSM, however expected returns for CSM increase with the difference $\rho - \eta$ (loosely speaking this is *own* autocorrelation minus autocorrelation with *others*). Although ϕ does not feature explicitly it is nevertheless relevant for CSM because it constrains the relationship between ρ and η (due to positive definiteness).

7.4 TIME-SERIES MOMENTUM

7.4.1 Return mean and variance (single instrument)

In this section we focus on statistical properties of TSM returns, applying our model to the simplest possible case: a single instrument ($N = 1$). For general distributions and trading rules this is a complex problem with relatively little prior literature (examples include Acar and Satchell [1997]) however our simplifying assumptions allow for tractable results. Also, despite its apparent triviality, the single instrument version of Equation (7.8) is not entirely unrealistic because signals in a conventional TSM strategy often depend on the prior returns of each instrument in isolation. Hence we will focus on the following expression:

$$r_{TS} = w_t r_{t,t+1}$$

$$= r_{t-1,t} r_{t,t+1}$$

and therefore

$$E[r_{TS}] = \rho \sigma^2 + \mu^2. \tag{7.11}$$

Note that this is the return for an investment of one unit of money in a portfolio with weighting $r_{t-1,t}$ in the instrument; the unit of money is not fully invested (assuming that $r_{t-1,t} < 1$) so there is no special significance to the fact that $E[r_{TS}]$ is likely to be less than μ here.

For returns variance we require the following helpful lemma:

Lemma 1. Goodman (1960). For two normal random variables $x \sim N(\mu_x, \sigma_x)$ and $y \sim N(\mu_x, \sigma_y)$ with correlation ρ, the variance $V(xy)$ of the product xy is equal to

$$V(xy) = \mu_x^2 \sigma_y^2 + \mu_y^2 \sigma_x^2 + 2\mu_x \mu_y \rho \sigma_x \sigma_y + (1 + \rho^2) \sigma_x^2 \sigma_y^2.$$

Applying Lemma 1 to our single instrument case:

$$V[r_{TS}] = \sigma^2 (2\mu^2 (1 + \rho) + \sigma^2 (1 + \rho^2)) \tag{7.12}$$

which we will now use to compute the Sharpe ratio.

7.4.2 Sharpe ratio

By combining Equations (7.11) and (7.12) we can determine the single-period single-instrument TSM Sharpe ratio for our particular position-sizing function w_t (on the assumption that the risk-free rate is zero):

$$\text{Sharpe}_{TS} = \frac{E[r_{TS}]}{\sqrt{V[r_{TS}]}} = \frac{\rho \sigma^2 + \mu^2}{\sigma(2\mu^2(1 + \rho) + \sigma^2(1 + \rho^2))^{0.5}}. \tag{7.13}$$

When $\rho = 0$ (no trending) this reduces to

$$\text{Sharpe}_{TS}|_{\rho=0} = \frac{E[r_{TS}]}{\sqrt{V[r_{TS}]}}$$

$$= \frac{\mu^2}{\sigma(2\mu^2 + \sigma^2)^{0.5}}$$

$$= \frac{\mu}{\sigma} \frac{\mu}{(2\mu^2 + \sigma^2)^{0.5}}$$

$$< \frac{\mu}{\sigma} \frac{1}{\sqrt{2}}.$$

This is an intriguing result which supports the stylised fact that CTA strategies tend to have a low Sharpe ratio: assuming $\mu > 0$, when there is no predictability (no trend) our particular TSM strategy has a risk/reward ratio which is strictly worse than an outright long position in the same instrument. In such conditions TSM involves taking random long and short positions period-by-period, thereby *on average* incurring losses on short positions where the positive expected return will act as a chronic drag.

In order to focus attention on returns due to the actively managed nature of TSM we now allow ρ to be unconstrained and make the assumption instead that $\mu = 0$. Over short term horizons it is plausible that $\mu \approx 0$ and indeed for several important asset classes traded by CTAs it is unclear how to determine μ in any case (e.g. commodities, short term interest rate contracts, etc.).

When $\mu = 0$ the Sharpe ratio (Equation [7.13]) reduces to

$$\text{Sharpe}_{TS} = \frac{E[r_{TS}]}{\sqrt{V[r_{TS}]}} = \frac{\rho}{\sqrt{1 + \rho^2}} \leq \frac{1}{\sqrt{2}}.$$

7.4.3 Skewness

Assuming zero means, the exact distribution of the product of two correlated normal random variables was derived by Williams (2008).[7] Applying this to our setting, the exact density of single instrument TSM return will be

$$f(r_{TS}) = \frac{\exp\left(\frac{\rho \, r_{TS}}{(1-\rho^2)\sigma^2}\right) K_0\left(\frac{|r_{TS}|}{(1-\rho^2)\sigma^2}\right)}{\pi\sqrt{1-\rho^2} \; \sigma^2}$$

where K_0 denotes the modified Bessel function of the second kind. Craig (1936) presented an early approximation for this density together with formulas for cumulants and we use these to obtain

$$\text{Skew}(r_{TS}) = \frac{2\rho(3 + \rho^2)}{(1 + \rho^2)^{\frac{3}{2}}}$$

---

[7]This was also independently derived by Nadarajah and Pogány (2016).

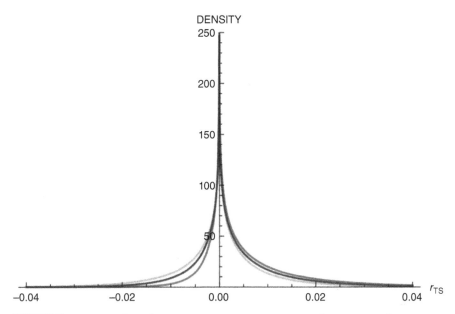

FIGURE 7.2 Density of single instrument TSM returns r_{TS} with $\sigma = 0.1$ and $\rho = 0.0$ (green), $\rho = 0.3$ (blue) and $\rho = 0.6$ (red).

which is illustrated by various example density plots in Figure 7.2 for the case of $\sigma = 0.1$ and selected values of ρ.

Evidently skewness will be positive if $\rho > 0$ and we emphasise that this is a consequence of our particular weighting function $w_t = r_{t-1,t}$ (in comparison it is easy to show that a more naive TSM rule using a fixed positive/negative weight scheme would have skewness of zero).

Our model includes only a single period of uncertainty and skewness arises here directly from the assumed correlation in underlying returns. This differs from the more general result presented by Martin and Zou (2012) who demonstrate positive skewness in trend-following returns even if correlation is zero (although when underlying returns are independent with zero-mean their result shows zero skewness over a single period, consistent with the expression above).

7.5 TSM MEETS CSM WITH TWO INSTRUMENTS

7.5.1 Return mean and variance

We now consider how a two instrument TSM portfolio compares with a CSM portfolio trading the same instruments. This has practical relevance for various reasons, e.g. fund managers with a TSM allocation may analyse their risk using a factor model, in which case it may be helpful to understand the effect of TSM on their CSM factor exposure; alternatively, a multi-asset manager may be interested in optimal weightings for a TSM and CSM combination.

We assume that $N = 2$ and therefore

$$r_{TS} = \frac{1}{2}[r_{TS_1} + r_{TS_2}]$$

$$= \frac{1}{2}[r_{t-1,t}^1 r_{t,t+1}^1 + r_{t-1,t}^2 r_{t,t+1}^2]$$

and

$$r_{CS} = \frac{1}{2}\left[\left(r_{t-1,t}^1 - \frac{1}{2}(r_{t-1,t}^1 + r_{t-1,t}^2)\right)r_{t,t+1}^1 + \left(r_{t-1,t-}^2 - \frac{1}{2}(r_{t-1,t}^1 + r_{t-1,t}^2)\right)r_{t,t+1}^2\right]$$

$$= \frac{1}{4}[(r_{t-1,t}^1 - r_{t-1,t}^2)r_{t,t+1}^1 + (r_{t-1,t}^2 - r_{t-1,t}^1)r_{t,t+1}^2].$$

As in previous sections we also assume $\mu = 0, \rho_1 = \rho_2 = \rho$ and $\eta = \eta_{12} = \eta_{21}$ to keep the focus on correlations at a high level of abstraction.

Applying results from Section 7.3.3.2 gives the following expected returns

$$E[r_{TS}] = \rho\sigma^2$$

$$E[r_{CS}] = \frac{\sigma^2}{2}[\rho - \eta].$$

(In passing we emphasise that these returns are not directly comparable with each other without appropriate risk adjustment.)

In Appendix B we derive variances and covariance for these two strategy returns and summarise the results below:

$$\Omega_{TS\&CS} = E[(r_{TS} - \mu_{TS}, r_{CS} - \mu_{CS})(r_{TS} - \mu_{TS}, r_{CS} - \mu_{CS})]$$

$$= \frac{\sigma^4}{2}\begin{bmatrix} 1 + \rho^2 + \phi^2 + \eta^2 & \dfrac{(1-\phi)^2 + (\rho-\eta)^2}{2} \\ \dfrac{(1-\phi)^2 + (\rho-\eta)^2}{2} & \dfrac{(1-\phi)^2 + (\rho-\eta)^2}{2} \end{bmatrix}.$$

We note that TSM variance increases in the absolute values of all correlations, while CSM variance decreases in contemporaneous correlation and increases in the *difference* between 'own return' autocorrelation and 'other return' cross-correlation.

We are now able to address the practically interesting matters of Sharpe ratios and the correlation between CSM and TSM portfolio returns, all of which are relevant to an investor's asset-allocation decision.

7.5.2 Sharpe ratios

When *two* instruments are available the Sharpe ratio for the TSM strategy is:

$$\text{Sharpe}_{TS} = \frac{E[r_{TS}]}{\sqrt{V(r_{TS})}}$$

$$= \sqrt{2}\frac{\rho}{\sqrt{1 + \rho^2 + \phi^2 + \eta^2}}.$$

If both instruments are the same then we have $\phi = 1$ and $\eta = \rho$ so this reduces to $\frac{\rho}{\sqrt{1+\rho^2}}$ which we have seen earlier for the single instrument case.

For cross-sectional momentum we have

$$\text{Sharpe}_{CS} = \frac{E[r_{CS}]}{\sqrt{V(r_{CS})}}$$

$$= \frac{\rho - \eta}{\sqrt{(1-\phi)^2 + (\rho - \eta)^2}}$$

$$= \frac{\rho - \eta}{\sqrt{(1 - 2\phi + \phi^2 + \rho^2 - 2\rho\eta + \eta^2}}.$$

7.5.3 TSM and CSM correlation

$$Corr(r_{TS}, r_{CS}) = \frac{COV(r_{TS}, r_{CS})}{\sqrt{V(r_{TS})V(r_{CS})}}$$

$$= \frac{(1 - \phi)^2 + (\rho - \eta)^2}{2\sqrt{(1 + \rho^2 + \phi^2 + \eta^2)\frac{(1-\phi)^2 + (\rho-\eta)^2}{2}}}$$

$$= \frac{1}{\sqrt{2}} \sqrt{\frac{(1 - \phi)^2 + (\rho - \eta)^2}{1 + \rho^2 + \phi^2 + \eta^2}}$$

$$= \frac{1}{\sqrt{2}} \sqrt{\frac{1 + \rho^2 + \phi^2 + \eta^2 - 2\phi - 2\eta\rho}{1 + \rho^2 + \phi^2 + \eta^2}}.$$

As special cases, we known that when $\phi = 1$ by Appendix A we must have $\eta = \rho$ and hence correlation in this case will be zero (and from Section 7.3.3.1 we know that the expected return to CSM will also be zero). At the opposite extreme, when $\phi = 0$

$$Corr(r_{TS}, r_{CS}) = \frac{1}{\sqrt{2}} \sqrt{\frac{1 + \rho^2 + \eta^2 - 2\eta\rho}{1 + \rho^2 + \eta^2}};$$

assuming $\rho > 0$ this will be either less than or greater than $\frac{1}{\sqrt{2}}$ depending on whether η is positive or negative respectively, however assuming relatively small magnitudes of η and ρ it seems plausible that the correlation will lie fairly close to $\frac{1}{\sqrt{2}}$ either way.

7.6 CONCLUSIONS

Our purpose in this chapter was to consider statistical properties of simplified TSM returns and how TSM and CSM might coexist in the same portfolio. To that end we have presented and extended analysis from existing literature (particularly the model used by Moskowitz et al. [2012] and others) and showed how various well-known characteristics of TSM returns can arise (e.g. positive skewness and relatively low Sharpe ratio).

We have also demonstrated a simple approach to analysis of correlation between TSM and CSM strategies. In our two-asset model with $\phi \approx 0$ and $\eta \approx 0$, the correlation between these strategy returns will be approximately $\frac{1}{\sqrt{2}}$ which is relatively high (as one might intuitively expect) but comfortably less than one. However TSM returns tend to be positively-skewed (compared to the negative skewness of CSM which is well-established in the literature) which underlines the potential usefulness of allocating to a TSM strategy despite the high correlation and low Sharpe ratio.

In future work we look forward to generalising these results to larger portfolios and less constrained correlation structures.

APPENDIX

7.A.1   APPENDIX A: CORRELATION PARAMETER RESTRICTIONS

In this section we determine sufficient conditions for positive definiteness of the overall covariance matrix of the returns vector

$$(r^1_{t-1,t}, \quad r^1_{t,t+1}, \quad r^2_{t-1,t}, \quad r^2_{t,t+1}).$$

We make various simplifying assumptions and aim only for sufficiency for example purposes. In particular we are interested in relationships that must hold among the correlation parameters ϕ, ρ, η with returns variance fixed as a common constant σ^2 throughout the chapter. We approach this by applying Kreindler and Jameson (1972), who provide conditions under which a partitioned matrix is positive definite.

We shall make the initial assumption that all cross-correlations are equal to η, hence the covariance matrix in question is

$$\text{COV}[(r^1_{t-1,t} \quad r^1_{t,t+1} \quad r^2_{t-1,t} \quad r^2_{t,t+1}), (r^1_{t-1,t} \quad r^1_{t,t+1} \quad r^2_{t-1,t} \quad r^2_{t,t+1})]$$

$$= \sigma^2 \begin{bmatrix} 1 & \rho_1 & \phi & \eta \\ \rho_1 & 1 & \eta & \phi \\ \phi & \eta & 1 & \rho_2 \\ \eta & \phi & \rho_2 & 1 \end{bmatrix}.$$

For positive definiteness of this matrix we require positive definiteness of

$$\begin{bmatrix} 1 & \rho_1 \\ \rho_1 & 1 \end{bmatrix} - \begin{bmatrix} \phi & \eta \\ \eta & \phi \end{bmatrix} \begin{bmatrix} 1 & \rho_2 \\ \rho_2 & 1 \end{bmatrix}^{-1} \begin{bmatrix} \phi & \eta \\ \eta & \phi \end{bmatrix}$$

$$= \begin{bmatrix} 1 & \rho_1 \\ \rho_1 & 1 \end{bmatrix} - \frac{1}{1-\rho_2^2} \begin{bmatrix} \phi & \eta \\ \eta & \phi \end{bmatrix} \begin{bmatrix} 1 & -\rho_2 \\ -\rho_2 & 1 \end{bmatrix} \begin{bmatrix} \phi & \eta \\ \eta & \phi \end{bmatrix}$$

$$= \begin{bmatrix} 1 & \rho_1 \\ \rho_1 & 1 \end{bmatrix} - \frac{1}{1-\rho_2^2} \begin{bmatrix} \phi & \eta \\ \eta & \phi \end{bmatrix} \begin{bmatrix} \phi - \rho_2\eta & \eta - \rho_2\phi \\ \eta - \rho_2\phi & \phi - \rho_2\eta \end{bmatrix}$$

$$= \begin{bmatrix} 1 & \rho_1 \\ \rho_1 & 1 \end{bmatrix} - \frac{1}{1-\rho_2^2} \begin{bmatrix} \phi^2 - 2\phi\rho_2\eta + \eta^2 & 2\eta\phi - \rho_2\phi^2 - \rho_2\eta^2 \\ 2\eta\phi - \rho_2\phi^2 - \rho_2\eta^2 & \phi^2 - 2\phi\rho_2\eta + \eta^2 \end{bmatrix}.$$

Considering the first leading principal minor:

$$1 - \frac{1}{1 - \rho_2^2}(\phi^2 - \phi\rho_2\eta + \eta^2 - \phi\rho_2\eta) > 0$$

$$\phi^2 - 2\phi\rho_2\eta + \eta^2 < 1 - \rho_2^2$$

$$(\phi\rho_2 - \eta)^2 + \phi^2 - \phi^2\rho_2^2 < 1 - \rho_2^2$$

$$(\phi\rho_2 - \eta)^2 + \phi^2(1 - \rho_2^2) < 1 - \rho_2^2$$

$$(\phi\rho_2 - \eta)^2 < (1 - \rho_2^2)(1 - \phi^2).$$

This is an intuitively reasonable condition in itself: cross-correlation has to lie near to the product of inter-temporal correlation and contemporaneous correlation; the amount of freedom we have in η depends on both the other two correlations: if either are particularly high we face a tight constraint, e.g. if considering a portfolio of two highly correlated products with $\phi \approx 1$ we require $\rho_2 = \eta$; however if both ϕ and are close to zero then this is not a particularly demanding constraint.

We now make the strong assumption that $\eta = \phi\rho_2$ (which will ensure compliance with the condition above) and consider the second leading principal minor:

$$\begin{bmatrix} 1 & \rho_1 \\ \rho_1 & 1 \end{bmatrix} - \frac{1}{1 - \rho_2^2} \begin{bmatrix} \phi^2 - 2\phi\rho_2\eta + \eta^2 & 2\eta\phi - \rho_2\phi^2 - \rho_2\eta^2 \\ 2\eta\phi - \rho_2\phi^2 - \rho_2\eta^2 & \phi^2 - 2\phi\rho_2\eta + \eta^2 \end{bmatrix}$$

$$= \begin{bmatrix} 1 & \rho_1 \\ \rho_1 & 1 \end{bmatrix} - \frac{1}{1 - \rho_2^2} \begin{bmatrix} \phi^2 - \phi^2\rho_2^2 & \phi^2\rho_2 - \phi^2\rho_2^3 \\ \phi^2\rho_2 - \phi^2\rho_2^3 & \phi^2 - \phi^2\rho_2^2 \end{bmatrix}$$

$$= \begin{bmatrix} 1 & \rho_1 \\ \rho_1 & 1 \end{bmatrix} - \begin{bmatrix} \phi^2 & \phi^2\rho_2 \\ \phi^2\rho_2 & \phi^2 \end{bmatrix}$$

$$= \begin{bmatrix} 1 - \phi^2 & \rho_1 - \phi^2\rho_2 \\ \rho_1 - \phi^2\rho_2 & 1 - \phi^2 \end{bmatrix}.$$

This will be positive definite if

$$(1 - \phi^2)^2 - (\rho_1 - \phi^2\rho_2)^2 > 0$$

which can be simplified somewhat, e.g. if $\rho_1 > \rho_2$ (to ensure positivity of the right-hand side) then

$$1 - \phi^2 > \rho_1 - \phi^2\rho_2$$

$$\rho_1 + \phi^2(1 - \rho_2) < 1$$

$$\phi^2 < \frac{1 - \rho_1}{1 - \rho_2}.$$

Hence for example purposes if we define ρ_1 as the larger of the two intertemporal correlations and we set $\eta = \phi\rho_2$ then we have positive definiteness as long as $\phi^2 < \frac{1-\rho_1}{1-\rho_2}$.

7.A.2   APPENDIX B: PROOFS OF VARIANCES AND COVARIANCE

Throughout this section we assume $\mu = 0$ is common to both instruments 1 and 2 and make use of the following helpful result (in addition to Lemma 1 introduced earlier in the text):

> **Lemma 2.** Bohrnstedt and Goldberger (1969). For four jointly-normal random variables $u \sim N(\mu_u, \sigma_u)$, $v \sim N(\mu_v, \sigma_v)$, $x \sim N(\mu_x, \sigma_x)$ and $y \sim N(\mu_y, \sigma_y)$, the covariance COV(xy,uv) of the products xy and uv is equal to
>
> $$COV(xy, uv) = \mu_x \mu_u COV(y, v) + \mu_x \mu_v COV(y, u) + \mu_y \mu_u COV(x, v)$$
> $$+ \mu_y \mu_v COV(x, u) + COV(x, u)COV(y, v) + COV(x, v)COV(y, u).$$

We begin with the TSM portfolio:

$$r_{TS} = \frac{1}{2} \ [r^1_{t-1,t} r^1_{t,t+1} + r^2_{t-1,t} r^2_{t,t+1}]$$

$$= \frac{1}{2}[r_{TS_1} + r_{TS_2}]$$

Applying Lemmas 1 and 2 gives

$$V(r_{TS}) = \frac{1}{4}V(r_{TS_1}) + \frac{1}{4}V(r_{TS_2}) + \frac{1}{2}COV(r_{TS_1}, r_{TS_2})$$

$$= \frac{\sigma^4}{2} \ [1 + \rho^2 + \phi^2 + \eta^2]. \tag{7.14}$$

Next for the CSM portfolio:

$$r_{CS} = \frac{1}{2} \ \left[\left(r^1_{t-1,t} - \frac{1}{2}(r^1_{t-1,t} + r^2_{t-1,t}) \right) r^1_{t,t+1} + \left(r^2_{t-1,t} - \frac{1}{2}(r^1_{t-1,t} + r^2_{t-1,t}) \right) r^2_{t,t+1} \right]$$

$$= \frac{1}{4} \ [(r^1_{t-1,t} - r^2_{t-1,t})r^1_{t,t+1} + (r^2_{t-1,t} - r^1_{t-1,t})r^2_{t,t+1}]$$

$$= \frac{1}{2}[r_{TS} - r_{CC}]$$

where we define
$$r_{CC} = \frac{1}{2} \ [r^2_{t-1,t} r^1_{t,t+1} + r^1_{t-1,t} r^2_{t,t+1}]$$

which is similar to the expression for TSM portfolio return except weightings are based on the prior performance of the *other* instrument in each case; this means that $V(r_{CC})$ can be computed most easily by exchanging ρ with η in Equation (7.14) which gives us the identical expression:

$$V(r_{CC}) = \frac{\sigma^4}{2} \ [1 + \rho^2 + \phi^2 + \eta^2].$$

Now by repeated application of Lemma 2 for each pair of products we obtain the intermediate result

$$\text{COV}(r_{CC}, r_{TS}) = \text{COV}\left(\frac{1}{2}(r^2_{t-1,t}r^1_{t,t+1} + r^1_{t-1,t}r^2_{t,t+1}), \; \frac{1}{2}(r^1_{t-1,t}r^1_{t,t+1} + r^2_{t-1,t}r^2_{t,t+1})\right)$$

$$= \sigma^4(\phi + \rho\eta)$$

which enables us to write

$$\text{COV}(r_{CS}, r_{TS}) = \text{COV}\left(\frac{1}{2}[r_{TS} - r_{CC}], \; r_{TS}\right)$$

$$= \frac{1}{2}\text{V}(r_{TS}) - \frac{1}{2}\text{COV}(r_{CC}, \; r_{TS})$$

$$= \frac{\sigma^4}{4}(1 + \rho^2 + \phi^2 + \eta^2) - \frac{\sigma^4}{2}(\phi + \rho\eta)$$

$$= \frac{\sigma^4}{4}(1 + \rho^2 + \phi^2 + \eta^2 - 2\phi - 2\rho\eta)$$

$$= \frac{\sigma^4}{4}((1 - \phi)^2 + (\rho - \eta)^2)$$

and

$$\text{V}(r_{CS}) = \frac{1}{4}\text{V}(r_{TS} - r_{CC})$$

$$= \frac{1}{4}\text{V}(r_{TS}) + \frac{1}{4}\text{V}(r_{CC}) - \frac{1}{2}\text{COV}(r_{TS}, r_{CC})$$

$$= \frac{\sigma^4}{4}(1 + \rho^2 + \phi^2 + \eta^2) - \frac{\sigma^4}{2}(\phi + \rho\eta)$$

$$= \frac{\sigma^4}{4}(1 - 2\phi + \phi^2 + \rho^2 + \eta^2 - 2\rho\eta)$$

$$= \frac{\sigma^4}{4} ((1 - \phi)^2 + (\rho - \eta)^2).$$

REFERENCES

Acar, E. and Satchell, S. E. (1997). A theoretical analysis of trading rules: an application to the moving average case with Markovian returns, *Applied Mathematical Finance* 4(3): 165–180.

Bohrnstedt, G. W. and Goldberger, A. S. (1969). On the exact covariance of products of random variables, *Journal of the American Statistical Association* 64(328): 1439–1442.

Bruder, B., Dao, T.L., Richard, J.C. and Roncalli, T. (2011). Trend filtering methods for momentum strategies, SSRN, www.ssrn.com/abstract=2289097.

Carhart, M. M. (1997). On persistence in mutual fund performance, *Journal of Finance* 52(1): 57–82.

Craig, C. C. (1936). On the frequency function of xy, *The Annals of Mathematical Statistics* 7(1): 1–15.

Fung, W. and Hsieh, D. A. (2001). The risk in hedge fund strategies: theory and evidence from trend followers, *Review of Financial Studies* 14(2): 313–341.

Goodman, L. A. (1960). On the exact variance of products, *Journal of the American Statistical association* 55(292) : 708–713.

Jegadeesh, N. and Titman, S. (1993). Returns to buying winners and selling losers: implications for stock market efficiency, *Journal of Finance* 48: 65–91.

Jegadeesh, N. and Titman, S. (2002). Cross-sectional and time-series determinants of momentum returns, *Review of Financial Studies* 15(1): 143–157.

Kat, H. M. (2005). Managed futures and hedge funds: a match made in heaven, The World of Hedge Funds: *Characteristics and Analysis*, World Scientific, pp. 129–139.

Kreindler, E. and Jameson, A. (1972). Conditions for nonnegativeness of partitioned matrices, *IEEE Transactions on Automatic Control* 17(1): 147–148.

Kwon, O.K. and Satchell, S (2019). The analytics of momentum, *The Journal of Asset Management*, 20(6): 433–441.

Laurie, D. (1982). Algorithm AS 175: Cramer-wold factorization, Journal of the Royal Statistical Society. Series C (Applied Statistics) 31(1): 86–93.

Lewellen, J. (2002). Momentum and autocorrelation in stock returns, *The Review of Financial Studies* 15(2): 533–564.

Lo, A. W. and MacKinlay, A. C. (1990). When are contrarian profits due to stock market over-reaction?, *The Review of Financial Studies* 3(2): 175–205.

Martin, R. and Zou, D. (2012). Momentum trading: 'skews me, *Risk*. https://www.risk.net/derivatives/structured-products/2194247/momentum-trading-skews-me

Moskowitz, T. J., Ooi, Y. H. and Pedersen, L. H. (2012). Time series momentum, *Journal of Financial Economics* 104(2): 228–250.

Nadarajah, S. and Pogány, T. K. (2016). On the distribution of the product of correlated normal random variables, *Comptes Rendus Mathematique* 354(2): 201–204.

Nerlove, M., Grether, D. M. and Carvalho, J. L. (2014). *Analysis of Economic Time Series: A Synthesis*, Academic Press.

Pollock, D. S. G. (2009). Statistical signal extraction and filtering: a partial survey, in D. A. Belsey and E. J. Kontoghiorghes, eds., *Handbook of Computational Econometrics*, Wiley, pp. 321–376

Potters, M. and Bouchaud, J.-P. (2006). Trend followers lose more often than they gain, *Wilmott Magazine* 26: 58–63.

Société Générale (2016). *SG Trend Indicator Construction Methodology*. https://wholesale.banking.societegenerale.com/fileadmin/indices_feeds/SG_Trend_Indicator_Methodology_Summary.pdf

Till, H. and Eagleeye, J. (2011). A hedge fund investor's guide to understanding managed futures, EDHEC Risk Institute.

Whittle, P. (1963). *Prediction and Regulation by Linear Least-Square Methods*, English University Press.

Williams, O. J. (2008). *Asset Pricing with Heterogeneous Skilled Agents*, PhD Dissertation, Faculty of Economics, University of Cambridge.

Zakamulin, V. (2017). *Market Timing with Moving Averages*, Palgrave Macmillan.

CHAPTER 8

Overreaction and Faint Praise – Short-Term Momentum in Contemporary Art

ANDERS PETTERSON and OLIVER J. WILLIAMS

'Talk is cheap.'

P.T. Barnum

8.1 INTRODUCTION

Price dynamics in collectible asset markets have intrigued connoisseurs and speculators for centuries. Spieth (2019) describes the emergence of collectors, dealers and auctions in seventeenth-century Flanders, Huemer (2004) describes 'fever of speculation' in nineteenth-century Paris, where 'paintings were treated like stocks', and Bayer and Page (2015) present a meticulous analysis of art investment and speculation in Victorian England.

The academic study of collectible investments has evolved considerably in recent years; an extensive and rapidly growing literature covers art as an alternative investment (Mei and Moses, 2002; Campbell, 2008), price index computation (Ginsburgh et al., 2006; Renneboog and Spaenjers, 2013), auction structures (Ashenfelter and Graddy, 2003), valuation of art as collateral (McAndrew and Thompson, 2007), analysis of expert opinion (Petterson and Williams, 2014) and numerous other related topics.

In this chapter we focus on short-term changes in the perceived value of specific works of contemporary art at auction. This is a particularly challenging segment of the collectible market – objective measurement of 'quality' is essentially impossible, and economic value cannot be computed using any standard asset valuation approach such as present value of future cash flows. Instead, as observed by Hutter and Frey (2010), the 'cultural value' of art can be assessed in terms of non-financial metrics, such as 'audience

141

applause, expert reviews, prizes, or length of text and footage dedicated in print and broadcast media'; further examples include backing by private collectors, institutional endorsement (such as museum exhibitions and acquisitions for permanent collections) and gallery representation. We very much follow their view that the 'cultural value of certain items determines their economic value', and hence valuation can be highly sensitive to subjective and behavioural factors, some of which we deliberately set out to capture in this work.

When analysing drivers of art prices and values, anecdotal experience from domain experts (such as auctioneers, museum curators, galleries, collectors, art advisers and dealers) suggests numerous hypotheses for testing, however a consistent obstacle is the inherent heterogeneity of art works and the lack of significant liquidity in all but very few special cases, meaning that data for repeat sales is extremely sparse.

For example, without a richer understanding of market context (and many qualitative influences) the fact that Alexander Calder's mobile *Two Horizontals and Nine Verticals* sold for USD 2.05m at Phillips, New York in November 2016 does not provide any significant *quantitative* insight into why the same artist's larger work *Polychrome from One to Eight* realised USD 5.55mm at Christie's, New York in May 2019. Indeed, even when a repeat sale does take place, demand conditions may have changed considerably over the intervening period (for example Cecily Brown's painting *Lady with a Little Dog* sold for USD 550,000 at Sotheby's, New York in November 2013, before subsequently achieving USD 1.58mm when re-sold at Christie's, London in October 2017). Our analysis sidesteps such difficulties by using a unique data set with multiple alternative valuations of the same specific works over relatively short periods.

There are various groups for whom understanding art price dynamics is relevant. Most obvious are those with a direct material stake in the market, e.g. serious collectors (whether individuals or institutions), investors, gallerists, dealers, auction guarantors or bankers (accepting art as collateral against borrowing). There is also an increasing focus around fractional ownership of art and collectible assets (in some cases supported by blockchain technology)[1] which suggests that forms of derivative instruments may eventually develop, potentially improving liquidity and making shorter term investment strategies more common.

However, *exposure* to art market developments extends much further, encompassing a broad community of commentators, analysts, appraisers and other miscellaneous experts. Individuals in this broader community repeatedly opine on the qualities and prospects of particular artists or works. Their views are increasingly easy to access via social media, and some are particularly influential. We conjecture that their long-term economic welfare depends on delivering non-trivial predictive insight to their 'followers', sufficiently differentiated to remain 'interesting' and retain an audience. Those who presciently endorse appreciating artists can derive enhanced reputation, while sceptics who correctly forecast declines in value or popularity can receive kudos for their foresight (especially if their views are contrarian or counter-trend).

Such intangibles can be monetised, and hence tipping potential winners and identifying potential losers becomes commercially relevant in its own right. In effect, such forecasters can be viewed as running 'fantasy' art portfolios with long and short

---

[1]Examples of commercial enterprises in this area include Masterworks.io and LookLateral.

positions based on their forecasts, and we suggest that their utilities can be proxied by the financial returns which would be experienced, were these portfolios to be actually tradable.[2]

With this in mind, our approach in this chapter is to investigate short-term art market dynamics by assessing the effectiveness of alternative prediction strategies. The broad spectrum of potential strategies includes pure intuitive judgement (or 'gut feel'), quantitative models (e.g. fundamental analysis of factors which lead to artist popularity), relative value analysis and systematic techniques based on recent price dynamics for the same or comparable work. We focus on the last of these, in particular the use of returns *momentum* to forecast future outcomes, borrowing and adapting methods commonly used in liquid financial markets.

Specifically we analyse the evolution of valuation estimates for particular lots over the days leading up to sales at major auction houses. These valuations are a combination of auctioneers' estimates, forecasts by independent experts and enthusiasts (submitted to the ArtForecaster competition[3]) and actual final auction prices. Although we consider a short time-scale, these are informationally-rich periods of price discovery, when the market is actively discussing and closely scrutinising valuations due to imminent auction activity, and hence we would expect a relatively good chance of interesting shifts in opinion and valuation.[4]

We will assess the viability of systematic momentum-based forecasting strategies from the perspective of a forecaster who cares about predictive accuracy *and* also strives to maintain a reputation for insightful analysis. This gives rise to a subtle hypothesis test for each strategy: are the returns significantly better than those which would be generated by an unskilled forecaster who randomly makes *both positive and negative predictions*? The final clause is important: we view diversity of forecast direction as a necessary condition of any skilful prediction strategy; we ignore the strategy of indiscriminate tipping of all auction lots on the basis that this does not display conspicuous skill (and from a practical perspective monotonous predictions seem likely to lead to a loss of followers and influence).

The structure of the chapter is as follows: Section 8.2 sets the scene with an overview of some relevant structural aspects of the contemporary art market, Section 8.3 describes the unique ArtForecaster data set that underpins our analysis, Section 8.4 discusses and tests the alternative forecasting strategies that we consider and Section 8.5 concludes.

---

[2]Naturally there are many important differences between forecasting and fund management. For example: fund managers combine prediction with portfolio construction techniques to take advantage of diversification so that (for instance) many incorrect predictions with small average losses are completely acceptable if outweighed by a smaller number of instances of much larger average profits. In comparison, forecasters tend to be evaluated based on unweighted accuracy metrics (e.g. a directional hit-rate or correlation measurement). Inter alia this makes it hard or impossible to judge forecasters based on the levels of confidence which they may have in their individual predictions.

[3]www.artforecaster.com

[4]This is somewhat related to the concept of a 'stochastic clock' used in mathematical finance to model the changing speed of trading activity and corresponding news flow, as described by Geman (2008).

8.2   CONTEMPORARY ART MARKET ECOSYSTEM

Since our model is heavily based on subjective valuations rather than actual traded prices we first provide a high-level overview of key players and structures in the contemporary art market. The aim is to shed some light on the question of 'What is good art, and who decides?' This topic was discussed in detail by Petterson (2014) and we summarise some key observations from that text below.

Notions of skill and craftsmanship are central to traditional approaches to art valuation. Within contemporary art these aspects remain relevant, but they sit alongside a focus on ideas and concepts (which often question the very nature of art itself). This move away from craftsmen and makers towards idea generators and thinkers has made long-established tools of evaluating 'good' or 'bad' art somewhat redundant. Largely aesthetic considerations have been replaced by aspects of philosophy and art theory – specialist areas of knowledge in which only a few art market participants are genuinely well-versed.

These conditions create an opportunity for individual experts and institutions to act as translators, explaining language and making the context and meaning of work accessible to potential buyers. Naturally these players are not only communicating facts and figures, they are also adding their own subjective interpretations. We describe them as 'tastemakers' as in many cases they have a significant influence over what the market considers to be 'good' or 'bad' art.

The credibility of a tastemaker is highly dependent on earning (or being granted) some commonly recognised rank or status by their peers. Once accepted by the community, the tastes and preferences of a tastemaker can influence the cultural value of an artist, increasing the probability that the artist will be successful in future and, as discussed by Hutter and Frey (2010), higher cultural value can translate into higher economic value due to conventional market forces (e.g. demand for the artist's work by galleries, museums and collectors).

From a structural perspective, the contemporary art market can be viewed as an international ecosystem with subsets consisting of national, regional and local sub-markets. While we observe many important geographical differences in diversity and complexity (often due to the maturity of the local market), the Western contemporary art market provides examples of many of the most important categories of tastemakers, specifically:

- Producers (artists)
- Educators (art schools, academics)
- Media and commentators (art critics and reviewers, magazines and other media [social and non-social])
- Market intermediaries (auction houses, dealers and art advisors)
- Cultural intermediaries (museums, Kunsthalle, biennales)
- Agents and promoters (commercial galleries, artist-run spaces)
- Interpreters (art historians, curators and art critics)
- Consumers (private buyers and collectors, corporate collections and public institutions)

These tastemakers use various alternative channels to communicate their views, both formally and informally. Social media, in particular Instagram, is actively used for promotional purposes and, importantly, collectors are more inclined to use this channel to show off their acquisitions (and influence their followers) in a more public manner than the more 'secretive' collecting habits of the past. For example, collector Yusaku Maezawa paid USD 110.5m for Basquiat's *Untitled* (1982) at Sotheby's in 2017 and announced his acquisition on Instagram soon afterwards (he has approximately 390,000 followers at time of writing). On an institutional level, Sotheby's has built up one million followers on Instagram and actively publishes posts about work coming up for sale at future auctions.

Finally we also note that the art market is not regulated to the same detailed extent as financial markets, hence tastemakers are subject to relatively few constraints regarding the material and comments that they may publish.

8.3   ARTFORECASTER DATA

8.3.1   Structure of quizzes

Our data set consists of auction price forecasts submitted by players of the ArtTactic ArtForecaster competition. This is a regular public contest (open to any individual at no cost) in which players make interval forecasts of the final auction prices of a set of lots chosen in advance by the organisers. Each set of lots is referred to as a 'quiz', and we have data from 942 quizzes run between February 2014 and July 2019, covering 4,083 individual lots which encompass painting, sculpture, works on paper, photography, prints and editions.

Quizzes are synchronised with major sales at prominent auction houses (most frequently Christie's, Sotheby's and Phillips in London and New York), therefore the chosen lots tend to be relatively high profile pieces; as an indication of typical values: average final prices over the period covered by our data set were GBP 1.0m (for GBP-denominated lots) and USD 2.1m (for USD-denominated lots).

Typically quizzes contain five questions relating to lots included in a sale (or sales) which take place within the following week. Each quiz closes a few hours before the sale takes place, so for analytical purposes we consider quiz responses to be a group of contemporaneous forecasts immediately prior to the auction.

Once the quiz has closed, the distribution of players' forecasts is published and we view the average forecast as an indicator of market sentiment for the work.[5] Players are scored and ranked on the basis of predictive accuracy as a means to incentivise participation (although we do not use these metrics in the analysis in this chapter).

In Table 8.1 we present example quiz submissions relating to one particular lot: *Brother's Sausage* (1983) by Jean-Michel Basquiat, offered for sale at Sotheby's

---

[5]Although we doubt that publication of forecasters' opinions has any direct market impact, we recognise the possibility that some participants may skew their forecasts in order to influence the market.

TABLE 8.1 ArtForecaster quiz submissions for *Brother's Sausage* (1983) by Jean-Michel Basquiat, Sotheby's Contemporary Art Evening Auction, 17 November 2016, New York.

Price Range (USD m)	Assumed Value[6] (USD m)	Forecasts	r_1
(a) No Sale	8.75	4	−50.0%
(b) Less than 8.75	8.75	0	−50.0%
(c) 8.75 to 12.4	10.575	1	−39.6%
(d) 12.4 to 17.5	14.95	21	−14.6%
(e) 17.5 to 24.7	21.10	29	+20.6%
(f) 24.7 to 35.0	29.85	10	+70.6%
(g) Greater than 35.0	35.00	0	+100.0%
Weighted Average	19.54	65	+11.2%

Contemporary Art Evening Auction, on 17 November 2016 in New York. The auctioneer's estimate for this work was USD 15m–20m (hence we define mid-estimate to be USD 17.5m) and final price was USD 16.5m.

We highlight some important technical considerations:

1. *Handling interval forecasts*: intervals are based on a logarithmic scale, with the auctioneer's mid-estimate used as a central point. For the purposes of our analysis we map intervals onto their mid-points (except for extreme low and high intervals) and we use these mid-points to compute an average forecast across players.

2. *Extreme low and high intervals*: forecasts and actual outcomes in these intervals are relatively infrequent. While there is scope to use estimated tail distributions to determine appropriate conditional means this is limited by the sparsity of empirical data (especially when conditioned on a particular artist and/or type of work), therefore in our current analysis we simply map the extreme high (low) intervals onto their the minimum (maximum) values as illustrated in Table 8.1.

3. *Bought-in lots ('no sales')*: these can be treated as having unknown values which are below their corresponding reserve prices. Although reserve prices are not disclosed to the public it is known that they will not be higher than the lower end of the auctioneer's estimated price range. Based on published research and our private surveying we estimate that the reserve price typically lies at around 75% to 80% of the low estimate (although this will vary from lot to lot). McAndrew and Thompson (2007) propose a method for imputing a value for bought-in lots based on fitting a left-censored lognormal distribution, however for the purposes of this chapter (in the interests of transparency and simplicity) we make the strong assumption that bought-in lots are valued at 50% of the auctioneer's mid-estimate.

---

[6]For (a) we use 50% of low estimate, for (c) to (e) we use the midpoint of the interval, for (b) we use the maximum value in the interval, and for (g) we use the minimum value.

TABLE 8.2 Sequence of valuation events

Time	Activity	Transactable
t_0	$p_{estimate}$ is published by auctioneer	✗
t_1	$p_{forecast}$ is determined by ArtForecaster	✗
t_2	auction takes place and p_{final} is determined	✓

TABLE 8.3 Definitions of returns for lot i

Period	Return	Formula
t_0 to t_1	$r_{1,i}$	$p_{forecast}/p_{estimate} - 1$
t_1 to t_2	$r_{2,i}$	$p_{final}/p_{forecast} - 1$

TABLE 8.4 Correlation matrix of valuations

	$p_{estimate}$	$p_{forecast}$	p_{final}
$p_{estimate}$	1	0.996	0.957
$p_{forecast}$	0.996	1	0.955
p_{final}	0.957	0.955	1

8.3.2 Summary of data

We summarise the steps involved in the forecasting process in Table 8.2, and in Table 8.3 we show how the various valuations are converted into stylised investment returns for the purposes of our analysis. Return r_1 is observable by forecasters once the ArtForecaster quiz has closed, while r_2 is the relative difference between the average ArtForecaster valuation and the final auction outcome.

By way of introduction to the data, we first present the correlation matrix between various prices and values in Table 8.4. Auctioneer estimates tend to have a strong anchoring effect on forecasts and since auctioneers have considerable expertise it is unsurprising to find high correlations across the matrix.

The distributions of r_1 and r_2 are presented in Figure 8.1 and provide further helpful context. Considering r_1: the distribution of the relative difference between average forecast and auctioneer estimate is relatively symmetric (skewness approximately 0.9) with a slightly negative mean (-0.5%) and median (-1.8%). This gives the impression that forecasts can be viewed as a somewhat noisy version of auctioneer estimates, however we will shortly see that this unconditional picture obscures useful informational content which we find when we analyse forecasts on a quiz-by-quiz basis.

In comparison we see a notably different shape for r_2 (relative difference in final auction price compared to average forecast): this distribution is heavily positively-skewed (skewness approximately 3.8) with a mean of $+5.8\%$ but median of -11.7%. In other words we find that our average forecast overestimates final auction price more often

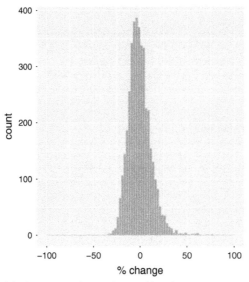

(a) *r*1: percent change from mid estimate to average
    forecast (mean −0.5%, median −1.8%, skewness 0.9)

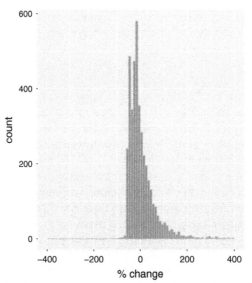

(b) *r*2: percent change from average forecast to final
    price (mean +5.8%, median −11.7%, skewness 3.8)

FIGURE 8.1   Percent changes over both the two time
periods exhibit positive skewness, but this is more
pronounced when dependent on the final hammer
price (panel (b)) rather than subjective estimates
(panel (a)).

than not, but on average the final price is above the average forecast, driven by fairly frequent extreme surprises on the upside.

In passing we emphasise that the peak in the r_2 distribution around the -50% point is partly influence by our assumption that bought-in lots ('no-sales') are valued at 50% of the auctioneer's mid estimate (as discussed in section 8.3.1).

Importantly we note that the significant positive skew in r_2 suggests that making negative predictions require a strong stomach. A forecaster can suffer serious reputational damage by taking a strong negative view on a work such as Ilya Chashnik's *The Seventh Dimension, Suprematist Relief* which sold for GBP 2.4m at Sotheby's, London in November 2016, following a mid-estimate of only GBP 125,000.

Finally we report that the Pearson correlation between r_1 and r_2 is 0.064, indicating negligible serial correlation.

8.4   SYSTEMATIC FORECASTING STRATEGIES

We now proceed to test the efficacy of alternative momentum strategies which might be used consciously (or subconsciously) by a forecaster, specifically time-series momentum (TSM) and cross-sectional momentum (CSM). In both cases we assume that a forecaster observes the auctioneer's estimate and the average forecast of ArtForecaster participants at time t_1, and hence computes the relative change between these valuations:

$$r_1 = p_{\text{forecast}}/p_{\text{estimate}} - 1.$$

A forecaster then uses these r_1 values to decide whether to 'support' or 'deprecate' various lots over the period from t_1 until the auction result is revealed at t_2. The precise methodology used to make decisions based on r_1 depends on whether TSM or CSM is being used as we shall shortly explain.

We consider 'support' to be equivalent to a hypothetical investment (or long position) in the work, and 'deprecation' to be a hypothetical short-sale of the work, with all trading done at the average forecast price (p_{forecast}) and corresponding returns (hypothetically) realised based on the final auction price.

In this 'fantasy' art market we make several other expeditious assumptions to remove distractions from our core purpose: (1) all works of art are infinitely divisible, (2) there are no costs of borrowing for short sales, (3) our forecaster has access to a suitably large pool of cash collateral for borrowing purposes, (4) all interest rates are zero.

The return metric enables us to evaluate the performance of a forecasting strategy by reference to the proxy investment portfolio. In the following sections we will frequently refer to a forecaster's *portfolio*, its *return* (in percentage terms) and the long and short positions which it contains. These should all be understood to refer to the hypothetical constructs explained above.

Implicit in this approach is the view that magnitudes of forecast returns are relevant. Predicting a 500% price move is 100 times as impressive as predicting a 5% move. This is clearly an arbitrary assumption, but one which is straightforward to adjust.

In the subsequent sections we analyse TSM and CSM in more detail. Loosely speaking, TSM treats each lot in its own right and extrapolates a performance forecast from the first period return r_1 independently of the returns of other lots, while CSM bases forecasts on first period returns of all lots in the same quiz ranked against each other. In certain particular conditions the two strategies will support/deprecate the same works of art, but in general recommendations will differ. In Figure 8.2 we sketch some diagrams to draw attention to key differences, assuming a simplified setting where all quizzes involve only two lots.

The TSM strategy will tend to be successful on average if there is non-trivial positive autocorrelation between r_1 and r_2. We have already noted that autocorrelation in our data set is close to zero (approximately 0.06) and hence we analyse this strategy first (expecting that its returns will be poor) primarily as a benchmark for comparison with CSM. We will see a significant performance difference between the two strategies, and understanding potential reasons for this focuses our attention on interesting aspects of valuation dynamics which we will discuss in detail.

As a validation step for both strategies we test the hypothesis that returns were achieved by chance rather than skill. We do this by comparing mean return across all quizzes in our data set against a simulated distribution of returns which would be generated by a 'zero-skill' forecaster who chooses long/short positions by random guessing.

8.4.1 Time-series momentum (TSM) strategy

8.4.1.1 Skilled TSM strategy A forecaster who deploys the Time-Series Momentum (TSM) strategy chooses to support works where $r_1 > 0$ and deprecate works where $r_1 < 0$. They take the view that if the average forecast $p_{forecast}$ is at least as large as the auctioneer's estimate $p_{estimate}$ then this presages a *further* increase to the final auction price such that $p_{final} > p_{forecast}$.

In terms of Figure 8.2, a TSM forecaster is more likely to believe that real-world valuation trajectories follow scenarios (b) and (c) rather than scenarios (d) and (e).

We assume that a forecaster who uses this strategy will diversify their portfolio across all works in every quiz, i.e. they will hold either a long or short position in every lot, with lot i generating a return

$$r_{TSM,i} = \text{sign}(r_{1,i})r_{2,i}.$$

and their mean return across all lots will be given by

$$\bar{r}_{TSM} = \frac{1}{n_{lots}} \sum_{i=1}^{n_{lots}} \text{sign}(r_{1,i})r_{2,i}.$$

where n_{lots} is the total number of auction lots across all quizzes (across our entire data set we have $n_{lots} = 4,083$).

We present the distribution of $r_{TSM,i}$ returns in Figure 8.3. As highlighted earlier, autocorrelation between r_1 and r_2 is 0.064, suggesting an almost negligible degree of predictability, and indeed we find that the TSM strategy delivered $\bar{r}_{TSM} = -0.5\%$.

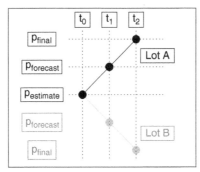

(a) If the sign of returns from t_0 to t_1 differs between lots then TSM and CSM will both lead to the same position at t_1 and will yield the same return at t_2.

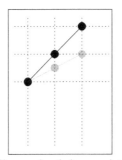

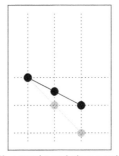

(b) If general optimism persists, TSM outperforms CSM.

(c) If general pessimism persists, TSM outperforms CSM.

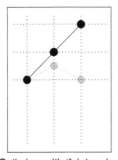

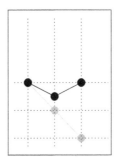

(d) Optimism with 'faint praise'; CSM outperforms TSM.

(e) Pessimism with some overreaction; CSM outperforms TSM.

FIGURE 8.2 Valuation trajectory scenarios for two lots (black and grey).

8.4.1.2 Zero-skill TSM strategy   For the case of TSM our null hypothesis is that the actual TSM return is generated by randomly selecting a long or short position in each work across all quizzes. To carry out this test we simulate a distribution of mean return across n_{lots} lots where long or short positions in each lot are chosen with 50% probability each, irrespective of r_1.

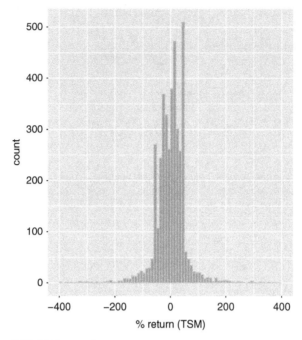

FIGURE 8.3 Per-lot returns to time-series momentum strategy: long lots with $r_1 > 0$, short lots with $r_1 < 0$; mean +1.2%, sd 66.0% (4,083 lots).

We present the simulated distribution in Figure 8.4 with the actual mean return shown as an overlaid vertical line. It is clear that the TSM strategy actually performed worse on average than random guessing.

8.4.2 Cross-sectional momentum (CSM) strategy

8.4.2.1 Skilled CSM strategy A forecaster who deploys the Cross-Sectional Momentum (CSM) strategy compares valuation changes across works in each quiz and supports the single work which had the largest relative valuation increase between auctioneer's estimate (at t_0) and average forecast (at t_1), i.e. the largest r_1, and deprecates the single work which had the smallest relative valuation change (or largest negative relative valuation change) over the same period (the smallest r_1).

To be clear: a CSM forecaster will support work which seems to be performing well relative to peers (the largest r_1 per quiz) versus deprecating work which underperforms peers (the lowest r_1 per quiz) even if the underperforming work itself sees a positive value uplift between auctioneer's estimate and ArtForecaster valuation. In terms of Figure 8.2, they believe the world works like scenarios (d) and (e), rather than (b) or (c).

We assume that the forecaster hypothetically invests a total of 1 unit of money in all supported works and that total short sales amount to an exactly equal amount of money.

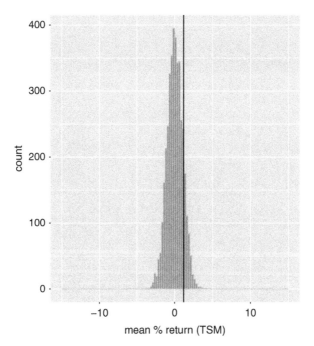

FIGURE 8.4 Simulated distribution of mean return for zero-skill time-series momentum strategy: long lots with $r_1 > 0$, short lots with $r_1 < 0$; mean 0.0%, sd 1.0%. (4,000 simulations).

Therefore we can define a hypothetical portfolio return as follows:

$$r_{\mathrm{CSM}} = \frac{1}{n_{\mathrm{long}}} \sum_{i=1}^{n_{\mathrm{long}}} r_{2,i} - \frac{1}{n_{\mathrm{short}}} \sum_{i=1}^{n_{\mathrm{short}}} r_{2,i}$$

where n_{long} and n_{short} are numbers of long and short positions respectively, and $r_{2,i}$ is the return for work i between t_1 and t_2.

From a computation perspective, we group forecast data quiz-by-quiz so that we obtain sets of forecasts which are contemporaneous, and for each quiz we choose a single long position (the work with the largest associated r_1) and a single short position (the work with the lowest associated r_1). Hence the return generated in respect of a single quiz will involve $n_{\mathrm{long}} = n_{\mathrm{short}} = 1$:

$$r_{\mathrm{CSM},j} = r_{2,j}^{\mathrm{max}_1} - r_{2,j}^{\mathrm{min}_1}$$

where $r_{2,j}^{\mathrm{max}_1}$ is the period 2 return of the work with the maximum value of r_1 in quiz j, and $r_{2,j}^{\mathrm{min}_1}$ is the period 2 return of the work with minimum r_1 in quiz j.

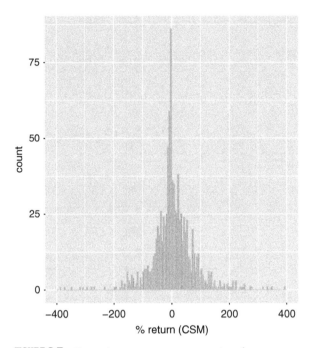

FIGURE 8.5   Per-quiz returns to cross-sectional momentum strategy: long the best performer, short the worst performer; mean +6.1%, sd 86.7% (942 quizzes).

Mean return across all quizzes is therefore

$$\bar{r}_{CSM} = \frac{1}{n_{quizzes}} \sum_{j=1}^{n_{quizzes}} r_{CSM,j}$$

where $n_{quizzes} = 942$.

We present the distribution of $r_{CSM,j}$ in Figure 8.5 and note that across quizzes the CSM strategy delivers better mean (+6.1%) and median (0%) returns than indiscriminately backing all pieces (+5.8% mean and -11.7% median). In addition, we reiterate that CSM involves taking both long and short positions, and therefore has greater scope to generate 'interesting' recommendations over time.

8.4.2.2   Zero-skill CSM strategy   We now test the significance of the CSM return versus a 'zero-skill' strategy where in each quiz a forecaster chooses one piece of work to support and one to deprecate, both selected at random. This simplifies the portfolio return (per quiz) to

$$r_{port} = r_{2,long} - r_{2,short}.$$

In Figure 8.6 we present our simulated distribution of mean return generated under the null hypothesis that a forecaster is deploying this zero skill strategy. The actual

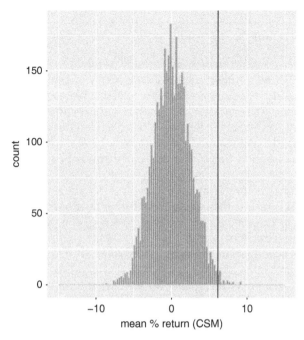

FIGURE 8.6   Simulated distribution of mean per-quiz return of the zero-skill strategy; mean 0.0% sd 2.5% (4,000 simulations).

mean CSM return is overlaid as a vertical line at +6.1%. We find the empirical p-value is approximately 0.6% and therefore reject the null hypothesis, concluding that our evidence supports the hypothesis that the CSM strategy is skillful.

8.4.3   Behavioural interpretation

Our results support the view that momentum effects are helpful to explain short-term art valuation movements, but the key determinant is *relative* performance of a piece of work (the ingredient to the CSM strategy) rather than its individual performance (as used by the TSM strategy).

In terms of Figure 8.2, the strong outperformance of CSM versus TSM suggests that – loosely-speaking – scenarios (d) and (e) are more characteristic of our setting than scenarios (b) and (c). It appears that sentiment which is uniformly positive or negative across lots tends not to persist; instead modest changes in valuation (either positive or negative) tend to be over-reactions influenced by the prevailing mood, while more extreme changes continue (at least directionally).

We lack detailed evidence to probe causality or behaviour more deeply, but these observations seem intuitively reasonable. The relevance of over-reaction to momentum strategies is already well-documented (e.g. Daniel et al., 1998) but in our particular context we hypothesise that additional behavioural factors might be 'faint praise' and/or 'silent negativity' (as illustrated by our example in Figure 8.2(d)).[7] These are relevant when background sentiment is generally positive. Our reasoning is as follows:

- Our data set is concentrated on high value works of art in sales at leading auction houses. We view these auctions as 'edited', in the sense that these auction houses are less likely to accept works by an artist that has been performing poorly. The majority of ArtForecaster players are industry insiders, students or collectors who may (on average) be prone to over-confidence in the merits of work which has already been edited by auctioneers. Hence it is plausible that there will often be a background of positive sentiment towards all lots which are actually for sale.
- The right-skewed nature of auction outcomes (as shown in the distribution of r_2 in Figure 8.1(b)) means that predictions below auctioneer estimates are relatively risky (from a forecaster's reputational perspective) compared to predictions in the other (positive) direction.
- We view players' valuation forecasts as a barometer of sentiment. Given these positive background influences we conjecture that expressions of negative sentiment (if/when they arise) may be cloaked in somewhat ambiguous language; we recall the words of Alexander Pope:

> *Damn with faint praise, assent with civil leer,*
> *And without sneering, teach the rest to sneer;*
> *Willing to wound, and yet afraid to strike,*
> *Just hint a fault, and hesitate dislike.*[8]

This translates into relatively small valuation upticks *above* estimates (positive contributions to r_1) for work which is less favoured, rather than more aggressive forecasts *below* estimates (which would constitute negative contributions to r_1). However such 'faint praise' seems unlikely to find its way into an actual price paid at auction by a buyer who is 'putting their money where their mouth is', hence we would expect a tendency for negative r_2 in this case.

- Similarly, among commentators and the media, unpopular work may be edited out of the conversation completely, so that negativity is not expressed explicitly but by silence. This may be partly due to the emotional aspect of owning art and the fact that there may often be personal relationships between tastemakers and artists. In the words of Oscar Wilde:

> *There is only one thing in the world worse than being talked about, and that is not being talked about.*[9]

---

[7]Harris et al. (2013) discuss the concept of 'faint praise' within a probabilistic setting.
[8]from *Epistle to Dr Arbuthnot* (1735)
[9]from *The Picture of Dorian Gray* (1890)

The effect of such 'silent negativity' is that forecasters' valuations of such lots may be modestly buoyed-up by background positive sentiment pre-sale (which supports r_1) but this does not follow through to the transaction stage where we see a reversal (negative r_2).

8.5 CONCLUSIONS

This chapter has considered various systematic momentum-based methods which a forecaster could use in order to make positive and negative predictions about art auctions, taking advantage of the information incorporated in a broad survey of subjective valuations from those with a professional or personal interest in the market (the ArtForecaster data set).

Art auction outcomes are significantly positively-skewed and therefore as a general rule being positive about every lot is a strategy which will, from time to time, result in spectacularly correct predictions, while reducing the risk of embarrassment due to negative pronouncements which end up being extremely off-side. However, we view a monotonous succession of positive predictions as unsuitable for a tastemaker who seeks to enrapture their followers, so we have deliberately ignored such a strategy and focused on approaches where predictions will be a mixture of positives and negatives.

A casual preliminary analysis of our data set suggests that forecaster opinions have only weak predictive power over auction outcomes: autocorrelation is close to zero and we could not find evidence to support a simple 'trend-following' forecasting strategy based on time-series momentum. However we have shown that a cross-sectional momentum strategy does exhibit strong performance which is significantly better than what could be achieved by random guessing, and we have speculated about potential behavioural explanations for this.

We reiterate that our framework departs substantially from standard financial momentum models because a real transaction is only possible at a single point in time and we otherwise deal with non-tradable valuations. Nevertheless we believe these valuations do have non-trivial connections to more concrete economic objects, e.g. (1) the earning capacity of tastemakers depends on reputation which may be partially linked to forecasting prowess, (2) evolution of valuation over short periods before auctions may be relevant when formulating auction bidding strategies, (3) valuations may become more tradable in future if/when fractional ownership becomes more prevalent.

Throughout the analysis we have deliberately used simple statistical methods to present data and test hypotheses so that we keep the focus on central concepts. However there are many areas in which econometric methods could be refined, e.g. estimation of the value of bought-in lots, more sophisticated methods of handling forecasters' interval predictions and weighting individual forecasters' contributions based on the level of predictive accuracy which they have demonstrated over time. It may also be feasible to more directly test our behavioural hypotheses of 'faint praise' and 'silent negativity' – we look forward to addressing these issues in future work.

In conclusion, we believe our results are an interesting example of how momentum concepts from financial markets can have broader applicability. This may be relevant in other non-traded domains when assessing the value of sentiment-driven forecasts. Our final thought is that in a world of noisy influencers, *relative* opinion may be more insightful than a dominant trend.

Or as Henri Matisse put it:

I don't paint things, I only paint the difference between things.[10]

All statistical analysis in this chapter has been performed using anonymised quiz data provided by artforecaster.com, supplemented by public records of auction result data as gathered on a best-efforts basis by artforecaster.com. No warranty is provided as to the completeness or accuracy of these data sources.

REFERENCES

Ashenfelter, O. and Graddy, K. (2003). 'Auctions and the Price of Art', *Journal of Economic Literature*, **41**, pp. 763–788.

Bayer, T.M. and Page, J.R. (2015) *The Development of the Art Market in England: Money as Muse, 1730–1900, Financial History*, Routledge.

Campbell, R.A.J. (2008) 'Art as a Financial Investment', *The Journal of Alternative Investments*, Spring, pp. 64–81.

Daniel, K., Hirshleifer, D. and Subrahmanyam, A. (1998) 'Investor Psychology and Security Market Under- and Overreactions', *Journal of Finance*, **53**(6), pp. 1839–1885.

Delectorskaya, L., Matisse, H. and Monod-Fontaine, I. (1996) *Henri Matisse: contre vents et marées: peinture et livres llustrés de 1939 à 1943*, Editions Irus et Vincent Hansma.

Geman, H. (2008) Stochastic Clock and Financial Markets. In: Yor, M. (ed.) *Aspects of Mathematical Finance*. Springer, Berlin, Heidelberg

Ginsburgh, V., Mei, J. and Moses, M. (2006) 'On the Computation of Price Indices', in Ginsburgh V. and Throsby, J. (eds.) *Handbook of Economics Art and Culture, 1*, Amsterdam: Elsevier North-Holland

Harris, A.J.L., Corner, A. and Hahn, U. (2013) 'James is Polite and Punctual (and Useless): A Bayesian Formalisation of Faint Praise', *Thinking and Reasoning*, **19** (3–4), pp. 414–429.

Huemer, C. (2004) 'Charles Sedelmeyer's Theatricality: Art and Speculation in Late 19th-Century Paris,' in Bakoš, J. (ed.) *Artwork through the Market, The Past and Present*, Bratislava: VEDA, pp. 109–123.

Hutter, M. and Frey, B.S. (2010) 'On the Influence of Cultural Value on Economic Value', *Revue d'Economie Politique*, **120**(1), pp. 35–46.

McAndrew, C. and Thompson, R. (2007) 'The Collateral Value of Fine Art' *Journal of Banking and Finance*, **31**, pp. 589–607.

Mei, J. and Moses, M. (2002) 'Art as an Investment and the Underperformance of Masterpieces', *American Economic Review*, **92**(5), pp. 1656–1668.

---

[10]Delectorskaya et al. (1996)

Petterson, A. (2014) 'Value, Risk and the Contemporary Art Ecosystem', in Dempster, A.M. (ed.) Risk and Uncertainty in the Art World, A&C Black Business Information and Development.

Petterson, A. and Williams, O. (2014) 'Quantifying Expert Opinion: The Role of Tastemakers in Contemporary Art', in *Rudd, A.* and Satchell, S. (eds.) *Quantitative Approaches to High Net Worth Investment*, Risk Books.

Renneboog, L. and Spaenjers, C. (2013) 'Buying Beauty: On Prices and Returns in the Art Market', *Management Science*, **59**(1): pp. 36–53.

Spieth, D.A. (2019) '*Art Markets*' *Oxford Art Online*, https://www.oxfordartonline.com/page/art-markets (accessed 3 December 2019).

CHAPTER 9

Volatility-Managed Momentum

YANG GAO

9.1 INTRODUCTION

One of the holy grails for academics and practitioners in investments research has been to find trading strategies that consistently beat the market. Since the late 1960s, scholars have questioned the efficient market hypothesis following observations of deviations in the patterns or trends of stock price returns away from the widely-accepted random walk theory. Jegadeesh and Titman (1993) and Chan, Jegadeesh, and Lakonishok (1996) suggest that by buying the past best performing stocks and shorting the worst performing stocks over short to medium horizons, such strategies are able to generate significant abnormal returns in the US equity markets. Following studies have shown that this strategy, named the momentum strategy, is profitable in various asset classes across different time periods globally. The literature has further shown that momentum interacts with various business conditions including volatility (see, for example, Ang, Chen, and Xing, 2001; Daniel, Jagannathan, and Kim, 2012; Min and Kim, 2016; Ji, Martin, and Yao, 2017).

However, as summarized by Daniel and Moskowitz (2016), momentum strategies face a serious issue – their vulnerability to crashes. Gao, Leung, and Satchell (2018, 2019) further indicate that both winner and winner-minus-loser portfolios suffer from negative skewness. Thus, a typical pattern for momentum is frequent gains with occasional large losses as the conventional momentum strategy fails to adjust its overall exposure according to distinct market states. Thus, Barroso and Santa-Clara (2015) and Daniel and Moskowitz (2016) propose cross-sectional volatility-managed momentum strategies that scale the risk exposure of momentum portfolios and outperform the conventional momentum strategy.

In this chapter, we first examine the outperformance of four representative volatility-managed momentum strategies that are documented in the existing literature. Volatility-managed momentum strategies have the ability to increase their risk exposure when volatility is low and reduce their risk exposure when volatility is high. Our focus

160

is the nature of the improvement compared to conventional momentum and how volatility forecasts future returns. We next explore the impact of various volatility measures on momentum. There are quite a few volatility measures that are used to manage momentum risk. For instance, Barroso and Santa-Clara (2015) pick realized volatility whilst Daniel and Moskowitz (2016) utilize expected variance. We illustrate the importance of choosing the correct volatility measure. We suggest that momentum is not only correlated with its own volatility, but also with market volatilities. Further analyses indicate that the outperformance of volatility-managed momentum strategies remains after controlling for country-specific risks and transaction costs.

The rest of this chapter is organized as follows. The next section describes the data and how we construct a conventional momentum portfolio; then we briefly introduce four volatility-managed momentum strategies and compare their performances in and outside the US equity markets; we further explore the practical issues faced by these strategies followed by an investigation on the choice of various volatility measure; the last section concludes.

9.2 DATA AND MOMENTUM PORTFOLIO CONSTRUCTION

Our data are sourced from the Center for Research in Security Prices (CRSP). We obtain daily and monthly data of all firms listed on NYSE, Amex, and Nasdaq (CRSP exchange code 1, 2 or 3) over a time period from January 1927 to April 2019. We first restrict our sample stocks to the primary common stocks of all US-headquartered firms. We further require that a valid sample stock should have a share price and the number of shares outstanding at the construction date and also should have at least eight monthly observations over the past twelve months. Then we compute the adjusted return of all valid sample stocks based on the close price on the last trading day in any given month.

We follow the conventional approach to construct our plain momentum portfolio. We first rank all valid sample stocks in a descending order based on their past cumulative return over an eleven-month formation period from t-12 to t-2 and then sort them into one of the ten portfolios with an equal number of NYSE stocks. This approach, using NYSE break-points rather than all-firm break-points, focuses on the large and liquid stocks, and consequently, seems more practical. The one-month gap between the formation period and the holding period is to avoid the short-term reversal. We then long (short) the winner (loser) portfolio that contains the best (worst)-performing stocks with the highest (lowest) past cumulative returns over the formation period. We next hold the winner and loser portfolios for one month and rebalance all momentum decile portfolios on the last trading day of each month. It's possible that a few stocks might be delisted or suspended during the holding period. Thus, we check the stocks in the winner and loser portfolios for their trading status on a daily basis during the holding period. Once the stocks are no longer available for trading, we close out their positions immediately.

We use the value-weighted index of all valid sample stocks and the 1-month Treasury bill rate as a proxy for the market portfolio and the risk-free rate, respectively. The 1-month Treasury bill rate is collected from the Kenneth R. French Data Library over the same period as that of the US equity data.

9.3   VOLATILITY-MANAGED MOMENTUM STRATEGIES

Asness, Moskowitz and Pedersen (2013) have shown that the conventional momentum strategy is generally profitable in international equity markets, across multiple asset classes and during various time periods. However, as argued by Chordia and Shivakumar (2002), Cooper, Gutierrez, and Hameed (2004) and Avramov, Cheng, and Hameed (2016), the profitability of momentum is subject to an expansionary, persistent and liquid market state. Daniel and Moskowitz (2016) further argue that momentum portfolios suffer from a negative skewness, and consequently, crash during periods when markets rebound. Although momentum gains are still large in the long run, the huge negative returns during crash periods could neutralize momentum profits over a significant short-time period.

Thus, momentum, a trend-capturing strategy, might be better reconstructed as a risk-managed strategy so that it has the ability to further adjust its risk exposure according to the different states of the market and make the strategy unappealing to risk-averse/loss-averse investors. We propose four representative volatility-managed momentum strategies taken from the existing literature, one time-series volatility-managed momentum strategy (Moskowitz, Ooi and Pedersen, 2012); and three cross-sectional volatility-managed momentum strategies (Barroso and Santa-Clara, 2015; Daniel and Moskowitz, 2016; and Gao, Leung and Satchell, 2017). All these strategies benefit from the use of a target volatility to scale returns of plain momentum portfolios.

In this section, we follow Gao et al. (2018) who summarize the above volatility-managed momentum strategies and compare their performances in the US equity markets, whilst we note that our discussions in this chapter are mainly from a cross-sectional perspective.

9.3.1   Cross-sectional volatility-managed momentum

Barroso and Santa-Clara (2015) and Daniel and Moskowitz (2016) suggest that by managing the risk exposure of plain momentum, the cross-sectional volatility-managed momentum trading strategy (henceforth, VM) outperforms the plain momentum strategy. The main difference between these two methodologies lies in the choice of their target volatilities. Barroso and Santa-Clara (2015) uses a constant volatility target at 12% (annualized), whilst Daniel and Moskowitz (2016) pick a time-varying (expected) volatility estimate. We name these two VM strategies as VM_C and VM_TV, respectively. VM_C compares the target volatility with the six-month average realized volatility of momentum return; VM_TV, however, benefits from the conditional mean and variance. The returns for VM strategies are computed as follows:

$$W_t^{VM\_C} = \frac{\sigma_{target}^{VM\_C}}{\sqrt{21 \sum_{j=0}^{125} r_{WML,d_{t-1-j}}^2 / 126}}, \tag{9.1}$$

$$W_t^{VM\_TV} = \left(\frac{1}{2\sigma_{target}^{VM\_TV}} \right) \frac{\mu_{WML,t}}{\sigma_{WML,t}^2}, \tag{9.2}$$

$$VM_t = W_t r_{WML,t}, \tag{9.3}$$

where $r_{WML,t}$ and VM_t are the returns of plain and risk-managed momentum returns in month t, respectively; $\sigma_{target}^{VM\_C}$ and $\sigma_{target}^{VM\_TV}$ are the target volatility and a level of 12% and 19% are chosen for the VM_C and VM_TV strategies, respectively; $\mu_{WML,t}$ and $\sigma_{WML,t}^2$ are the conditional expected return and the conditional variance of the plain momentum portfolio; W_t is the scaling weight on the return of plain momentum.

9.3.2 Partial moment momentum

The VM strategies in Barroso and Santa-Clara (2015) and Daniel and Moskowitz (2016) have been suggested to better manage the risk of plain momentum and consequently, outperform plain momentum. However, both VM strategies fail to differentiate between upside and downside risk. Further, as we could see from equation 9.3, the VM strategies also do not separately scale the weights of the winner and loser portfolios.

Gao et al. (2017) propose partial moment momentum strategies (henceforth, PMM) which distinguish between upside and downside risk exposure and treat the winner and loser portfolios separately. This method benefits from the decomposition of the realized variance, RV_t, into upper partial moment RPM_t^+ and lower partial moment RPM_t^-, as

$$RPM_t^+ = \sum_{i=1}^{n} r_{i,t}^2 I(r_{i,t} \geq 0), \tag{9.4}$$

$$RPM_t^- = \sum_{i=1}^{n} r_{i,t}^2 I(r_{i,t} < 0), \tag{9.5}$$

where $I()$ is the indicator function, these being sample lower and upper partial moments of order 2 with truncation at zero in both cases, $r_{i,t}$ is the return of stock i in day t, and n is the number of valid sample stocks in day t. There is an identity,

$$RV_t = RPM_t^- + RPM_t^+, \tag{9.4}$$

In addition to the scaled winner and loser portfolios, the PMM strategies also include a cash portfolio to make the overall position net-zero. This helps to minimize the overall risk exposure of the portfolio. The weights and the returns of the unconstraint PMM strategies are computed as follows.

$$W_{winner,t+1}^{PMM} = \frac{2\sigma_{target}^{PMM}}{\sqrt{RV_t}} \left(\frac{RPM_t^+}{RPM_t^+ + RPM_t^-} \right), \tag{9.5}$$

$$W_{loser,t+1}^{PMM} = \frac{2\sigma_{target}^{PMM}}{\sqrt{RV_t}} \left(\frac{RPM_t^-}{RPM_t^+ + RPM_t^-} \right), \tag{9.6}$$

$$W_{cash,t+1}^{PMM} = W_{winner,t+1}^{PMM} - W_{loser,t+1}^{PMM}, \tag{9.7}$$

$$PMM_t = W_{winner,t}^{PMM} r_{winner,t} - W_{loser,t}^{PMM} r_{loser,t} - W_{cash,t}^{PMM} r_{cash,t} \tag{9.8}$$

where $r_{winner,t}$, $r_{loser,t}$, and $r_{cash,t}$ are the returns at time t to the winners, losers and cash portfolios, respectively; σ_{target}^{PMM} is the target volatility at a level of 12% (annualized).

The authors further introduce a leverage-constraint PMM strategy with 200% leverage being the upper bound. The details of this strategy can be further found in Section 5 of Gao et al. (2017).

9.3.3 Time-series volatility-managed momentum

We also briefly describe the time-series momentum. Moskowitz et al. (2012) propose the time-series volatility-managed momentum trading strategy (henceforth, TSVM). In the time-series model, whether a security is performing well or bad is only subject to its own past returns. For a security s in the construction month t, if the sign of its accumulative excess return over the past one-year formation period is positive, then one might long this security and hold it for one month, and vice versa. The TSVM return for an individual security is given as follows:

$$TSVM_{t,t+1}^s = sign(r_{t-12,t}^s) \frac{40\%}{\sigma_t^s} r_{t,t+1}^s, \tag{9.4}$$

The authors choose an annualized volatility of 40% for any individual security as they argue that the equally weighted portfolio of all securities reports a similar level of annualized volatility around 12% compared to other factor portfolios. Further, the weight of the security is inversely proportional to the security's ex-ante annualized volatility, σ_t^s. The market TSVM return is the equally-weighted average of all securities in the market.

9.3.4 Performance comparison

We report the performance of the above volatility-managed momentum strategies in Table 9.1. Results show that apart from TSVM of Moskowitz et al. (2012), all the other volatility-managed momentum strategies outperform the plain momentum strategy by reporting higher returns, increased Sharpe ratios, modified skewness, and reduced kurtoses. Specifically, the VM_TV strategy of Daniel and Moskowitz (2016) doubles the Sharpe ratio of the plain momentum strategy from 0.15 to 0.29. These results suggest that momentum interacts with volatility and in particular, using volatility as the conditioning variable significantly improves the performance of plain momentum. Further, in Figure 9.1, which is partly sourced from Gao et al. (2018), we plot the cumulative returns of three volatility-managed momentum strategies, TSVM, VM_C, and PMM

TABLE 9.1   Performance of volatility-managed momentum strategies

	Market	Risk-free	Plain momentum	Volatility-managed momentum			
				Moskowitz et al. (2012)	Barroso and Santa-Clara (2015)	Daniel and Moskowitz (2016)	Gao et al. (2017)
Return (%)	0.93	0.27	1.16	0.61	1.38	1.37	1.43
t-statistics	(5.83)***	(35.96)***	(4.97)***	(2.52)**	(9.77)***	(10.26)***	(13.93)***
Sharpe Ratio	0.14	0.00	0.15	0.11	0.29	0.31	0.39
Skewness	0.15	1.10	-2.33	-0.73	-0.23	-0.20	0.26
Kurtosis	7.82	1.33	17.50	3.11	2.06	2.73	2.02

Notes: The table reports the performance of four volatility-managed momentum strategies with the plain momentum, the market portfolio and the risk-free asset from January 1927 to April 2019, respectively. For plain momentum, we follow a conventional construction strategy which constructs momentum portfolios using an eleven-month formation period, a one-month holding period, and a one-month gap between the formation and holding periods; for volatility-managed momentum strategies, we follow the same methodologies as they appeared in the respective literature; for market portfolio and risk-free asset, we use the value-weighted index of all firms in CRSP and the 1-month treasury bill rate as the proxy, respectively. All series are monthly. *, ** and *** denote the significance level of 10%, 5% and 1%, respectively.

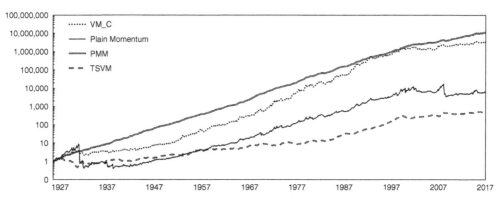

FIGURE 9.1   Cumulative performance of volatility-managed momentum strategies.
Notes: The figure plots the cumulative returns of three volatility-managed momentum strategies with the plain momentum given a $1 initial investment in January 1927 over an investment period of 1927 to 2017. For plain momentum, we follow a conventional construction strategy which constructs momentum portfolios using an eleven-month formation period, a one-month holding period, and a one-month gap between the formation and holding periods. For volatility-managed momentum strategies, we follow the same methodologies as they appeared in the respective literature. TSVM, VM_C and PMM represent the volatility-managed momentum strategies proposed by Moskowitz (2012), Barroso and Santa-Clara (2015) and Gao et al. (2017), respectively.

with the plain momentum over 1927 to 2017. If one invests \$1 in January 1927 and then closes out all positions in December 2017, the PMM and VM_C strategies generate a cumulative revenue of around \$10,000,000 and \$4,000,000, respectively. Of course, the above gains are under some extreme conditions, for instance, without the consideration of trading costs; we therefore do not claim that either institutional or individual investors would profit that much from a similar investment. The reason these strategies work is that there is abundant evidence that volatility is forecastable (see, for instance, Lamoureux and Lastrapes, 1990; Bollerslev, Chou, and Kroner, 1992; Andersen, Bollerslev, Diebold, and Ebens, 2001).

The literature has documented that momentum is subject to country-specific risk as it works extremely well in some equity markets, for example, the Australian market, but does not work well in some other equity markets, for example, the Chinese and Japanese markets. We also report the performance of three volatility-managed momentum strategies in four major non-US equity markets in Table 9.2. The international equity data is obtained from Compustat over a shorter period of 1996 to 2013 and we follow the same methodology to construct the portfolios. Results show that apart from the TSVM of Moskowitz et al. (2012), the other two volatility-managed momentum strategies outperform the plain momentum strategy in Australia and Europe, where the plain momentum works well. However, in the Japanese and the Chinese markets, neither does the plain momentum nor the volatility-managed momentum make money. This might be due to the unique country-specific risks these markets possess, which require further examination.

9.4   SOME POTENTIAL PRACTICAL ISSUES

The existing volatility-managed momentum strategies have been shown to possess good performance compared to the well-known Jegadeesh and Titman (1993) plain momentum. However, these strategies experience some practical issues that require special attention. In this work, we follow Moreira and Muir (2017) but we extend their analyses.

9.4.1   Leverage constraints

Volatility-managed momentum strategies use the notion of the use of target volatility to scale momentum returns to produce risk-managed momentum returns. Hence, whether an investor can benefit from these volatility-managed momentum strategies even under a tight leverage constraint is crucial from a practical perspective (Moreira and Muir, 2017; Gao et al., 2018).

We first report the distribution of the weights of three cross-sectional volatility-managed momentum strategies in Table 9.3. Results show that the median weights are slightly higher than the means which are around 1. However, if we turn to the upper distribution of the weights of these strategies, the 90th percentiles are near 1.9 and all the 99th percentiles exceed 2.1. Additionally, Figure 9.2 shows that the weights of the VM_C strategy fluctuate wildly from year to year. According to the authors, the weights 'range between the values of 0.13 and 2.00' over the 1927 to 2011 period whilst the

TABLE 9.2 Performance of volatility-managed momentum strategies, the international evidence

Panel A: Australia

	Plain momentum	Volatility-managed momentum		
		VM_C	TSVM	PMM
Return (%)	1.52	1.43	0.97	1.46
t-statistics	(5.79)***	(6.53)***	(3.41)***	(6.67)***
Sharpe Ratio	0.33	0.38	0.20	0.39
Skewness	-0.22	0.17	-0.32	0.21
Kurtosis	4.35	2.97	6.10	2.92

Panel A: China

	Plain momentum	Volatility-managed momentum		
		VM_C	TSVM	PMM
Return (%)	-0.79	-0.96	0.27	-0.87
t-statistics	(-1.52)	(-1.61)	(1.73)*	(-1.58)
Sharpe Ratio	-0.10	-0.08	0.13	-0.11
Skewness	-2.13	-1.79	-1.95	-1.83
Kurtosis	5.73	4.92	5.04	4.35

Panel A: Europe

	Plain momentum	Volatility-managed momentum		
		VM_C	TSVM	PMM
Return (%)	0.68	0.71	0.50	0.93
t-statistics	(3.69)***	(5.03)***	(2.36)**	(7.97)***
Sharpe Ratio	0.20	0.28	0.13	0.42
Skewness	-1.59	0.13	-2.26	0.76
Kurtosis	5.12	1.95	13.67	1.99

Panel A: Japan

	Plain momentum	Volatility-managed momentum		
		VM_C	TSVM	PMM
Return (%)	-0.30	-0.46	0.15	-0.39
t-statistics	(-0.97)	(-0.63)	(1.67)*	(-0.56)
Sharpe Ratio	-0.15	-0.13	0.12	-0.13
Skewness	-0.90	-0.94	-1.32	-0.86
Kurtosis	4.51	4.30	9.75	4.49

Notes: The table reports the performance of three volatility-managed momentum strategies with the plain momentum in four non-US equity markets from January 1996 to December 2013. VM_C, TSVM and PMM represent the volatility-managed momentum strategies proposed by Barroso and Santa-Clara (2015), Moskowitz et al. (2012) and Gao et al. (2017), respectively. Panels A, B, C and D report the performances of these strategies in Australia, China, Europe and Japan, respectively. All series are monthly. *, ** and *** denote the significance level of 10%, 5% and 1%, respectively.

TABLE 9.3   Leverage of volatility-managed momentum strategies

| | | | | Weights | | | | |
Strategy	Leverage constraints	Leg	Description	Mean	Median	SD	P90	P99
VM_C	No	Both	Realized	0.91	0.95	0.33	1.89	2.11
VM_TV	No	Both	Expected	0.93	0.97	0.34	1.93	2.35
PMM	No	Long	Realized	1.33	1.44	0.57	2.07	4.64
		Short	Realized	0.94	1.02	0.31	1.86	2.72
	Yes	Long	Realized	1.06	1.10	0.39	2.00	2.00
		Short	Realized	0.77	0.83	0.26	1.75	1.84

Notes: The table reports some distribution statistics for three cross-sectional volatility-managed momentum strategies over a sample period from January 1927 to April 2019. VM_C, VM_TV and PMM represent the volatility-managed momentum strategies proposed by Barroso and Santa-Clara (2015), Daniel and Moskowitz (2016) and Gao et al. (2017), respectively. Specifically, the PMM strategies scale the weights of the winner and loser portfolios separately and there is a particular version of PMM with a 200% leverage constraint; see Gao et al. (2017) for more details. SD, P90 and P99 report the standard deviation, 90th percentile and 99th percentile of the values of weights, respectively. All series are monthly.

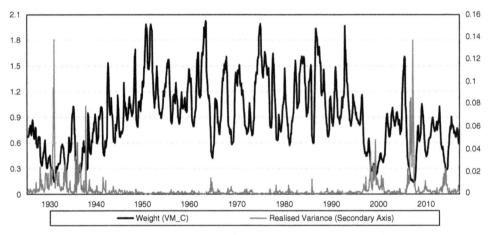

FIGURE 9.2   Weights of the VM_C strategy.
Notes: The figure plots the weights of the VM_C strategy proposed by Barroso and Santa-Clara (2015) over an extended sample period from March 1927 to December 2017. The VM_C strategy scales the plain momentum portfolio (WML) using the realized volatility in the past six months. This figure also plots the realized variance in the secondary axis. See Equation (9.1) and Section 4 of Barroso and Santa-Clara (2015) for more details.

leverage is negatively correlated with the weights. We can see clearly from this figure that the weights during market downturns or momentum crashing periods, for instance, the Great Depression and the Global Financial Crisis period, are extremely low. Combining all these results, we might argue that the volatility-managed portfolio utilizes moderate leverage generally with rather substantial leverage when the volatility is extreme high or low. Consequently, the leverages of volatility-managed momentum strategies seem realistic.

9.4.2 Turnover and transaction costs

As argued by Korajczyk and Sadka (2004), plain momentum strategies survive trading costs but at an expensive cost that reduces the abnormal returns to almost half the amount as before. Hence, plain momentum itself is already a turnover-heavy strategy. What makes things worse is that the volatility-scaling increases the amount of turnover in the volatility-managed portfolio, due to the dynamic nature of leverage. We now test the turnover and transaction costs for all variants of volatility-managed momentum strategies for the practical employment of the various volatility-momentum adjustments.

Portfolio turnover is calculated by taking either the total amount of new securities purchased, or the amount of existing securities sold (whichever is greater) over a particular period, divided by the total net asset value (NAV) of the portfolio. By using such a measure, we are able to have a broad picture of the holding time of the various portfolios. For transaction costs, we use three measures, effective spreads, quoted spreads and the 10-bps approach from Frazzini et al. (2015) to evaluate the impact of trading costs on volatility-managed momentum strategies. The results in Table 9.4 indicate that the profits of the volatility-managed momentum strategies are robust to transactions costs in all three distinct regimes. In particular, the alphas of these strategies drop after controlling for trading costs, however, are still significantly larger than the alphas of plain momentum.

9.4.3 The short leg

Momentum purports to benefit by longing the winners and shorting the losers. However, it is known that short selling is not easily implemented in equity markets relative to derivative markets. In the Australian equity markets, Gao and Leung (2017) examine the impact of short selling (restrictions) on momentum using the actual Approved Daily Short Sales Report issued by the Australian Securities and Investments Commission. The authors suggest that even during calm market periods, only a small group of the stocks is allowed to be covered short sold at a non-substantial amount. But even so, the trading activities of whoever has recently shorted in the equity market are being monitored by the authorities. Moreover, at least in the Australian markets, one cannot guarantee that a stock that is approved for being short sold on the portfolio construction day will also be able to be bought back later as the stock could be banned/restricted for short selling during the holding period. Whichever stocks are approved to be short sold change each trading day. Therefore, the unclosed short positions could be a huge issue for momentum in practice.

Does it mean that momentum profits would drop dramatically without the short leg? Gao et al. (2019) further explore the performance comparison between the winner and loser portfolios. The authors indicate that the short leg actually dilutes momentum gains as in general, the loser portfolio produces positive return.

TABLE 9.4   Turnover and transaction costs for volatility-managed momentum strategies

Panel A: Turnover

Strategy	Turnover
WML	58.23
VM_C	63.70
VM_TV	65.29
PMM	67.85

Panel B: Transaction costs

Strategy	A	α after transaction costs		
		Effective spreads	Quoted Spreads	10bps
WML	1.57	0.82	0.77	1.16
VM_C	3.17	1.76	1.63	2.38
VM_TV	3.50	1.95	1.79	2.57
PMM	3.79	1.96	1.80	2.81

Notes: The table reports the turnover and transaction cost statistics for three volatility-managed momentum strategies with the plain momentum over a sample period of 1990 to 2017. In Panel A, portfolio turnover is calculated by taking either the total amount of new securities purchased, or the amount of existing securities sold (whichever is greater) over a particular period, divided by the total net asset value (NAV) of the portfolio. This measure shows how long a portfolio holds stocks on average. For instance, a portfolio turnover of 25% for a fund is equivalent to holding a stock for 4 months on average. The turnover of a strategy is the summation of the turnover for all portfolios within the strategy. In Panel B, we use three transaction costs, effective spreads, quoted spreads and 10 bps from Frazzini, Israel and Moskowitz (2015) to evaluate the impact of trading costs on volatility-managed momentum strategies. The alphas are annualized. All figures are in percentages.

So, a long-only momentum strategy or a 130/30 portfolio might be better than a conventional momentum with zero-net position.

9.5   THE BEST VOLATILITY MEASURE FOR MOMENTUM?

We have shown in the previous sections the good performances of volatility-managed momentum strategies are robust to transaction costs and practical issues such as the leverage constraints. In this section, we explore whether there exists a universal volatility measure that works well for momentum. We choose the VM_C strategy in Barroso and Santa-Clara (2015) as the benchmark strategy. The authors compute their weights using the past six months realized volatility of the returns of momentum.

We investigate five alternative implementations and report the results in Table 9.5. First, we use realized volatility of the market portfolio rather than that of the momentum portfolio. From our economic intuition, it seems that the alternative strategy using market volatility should produce very different results compared to the strategy using momentum volatility, as when market rallies/crashes, momentum does not rally/crash

TABLE 9.5 The choice of volatility in volatility-managed momentum strategies

w_t	Description	Ret (%)	Sharpe	Statistics of weights w				
				Mean	SD	P50	P90	P90
$\dfrac{c}{RV_t}$	Realized volatility	1.38	0.29	0.91	0.33	0.95	1.89	2.11
$\dfrac{c}{RV_t^{mkt}}$	Realized volatility (Mkt)	1.40	0.30	0.92	0.35	0.93	1.87	2.15
$\dfrac{c}{RV_t^2}$	Realized variance	1.49	0.27	0.97	0.46	0.87	2.34	5.30
$\dfrac{c}{E[RV_{t+1}^2]}$	Expected variance	1.56	0.28	1.05	0.41	1.16	2.20	4.12
$\dfrac{c}{RV_t^+}, \dfrac{c}{RV_t^-}$	Upside vs. downside vol	1.38	0.29	0.37	0.10	0.29	0.95	1.32
$\min\left\{\dfrac{c}{RV_t}, 1.5\right\}$	150% leverage constraint	1.25	0.26	0.76	0.23	0.95	1.50	1.50

Notes: The table reports the six volatility-managed momentum strategies using different volatility measures with their respective returns, Sharpe ratios and some distribution statistics for the weights over a sample period from January 1927 to April 2019. The benchmark strategy is the VM_C strategy in Barroso and Santa-Clara (2015) which is reported in the first row. This strategy scales momentum using the past six months realized volatility of plain momentum returns and chooses a 12% annualized volatility as the target. In the following rows, we report five alternative VM_C strategies. Rather than using the realized volatility of the plain momentum portfolio, we use the realized volatility of the market, realized variance, expected variance, realized upper and lower volatility and realized volatility but with a 150% leverage constraint, respectively. The letter c in the numerator represents the value of a target volatility/variance. All series are monthly.

simultaneously. This phenomenon has been well documented in the existing literature, for instance, Barroso and Santa-Clara (2015) find that momentum variance is better forecasted than market variance and that the most predictable component of momentum variance is the specific risk and not the part attributed to market risk (see their Tables 2 and 4); Daniel and Moskowitz (2016) argue that momentum crashes following market stress scenarios, for instance, when the market rebounds. And these findings justify their use of momentum volatility for their volatility-managed momentum strategies. However, it is interesting to see that these two strategies report almost identical results from the first two rows of Table 9.5. Not surprisingly, Barroso and Santa-Clara (2015) also state in their robustness checks section that 'In unreported results, we find that forecasting the risk of momentum with the realized variance of the market in the previous six months produces very similar results'. This might be related to the findings of Cooper et al. (2004) and Daniel and Moskowitz (2016) that the past market return positively leads contemporaneous momentum gains. As for why momentum and market volatility/variance produce very similar results requires further investigation.

Second, we find that using realized variance rather than realized volatility also report almost identical results. However, using realized variance instead of realized volatility makes the weights far more extreme, with the 90th percentile around five instead of two. This finding is consistent with Moreira and Muir (2017). Third, following Daniel and Moskowitz (2016), we utilize expected variance to scale momentum.

Results show that the weights are also amplified but not as extreme as those using realized variance. Also, this approach produces the highest nominal return among all six strategies whilst we note that this result requires further investigation to explore the impact of forecasting errors. We next use decomposed volatility to scale winner and loser portfolios separately according to upside and downside risks. This approach reports the lowest overall exposure with an average around 0.4 whilst its overall performance is not reduced. The merits of this methodology also include its negative aggregate exposure when the downside risk becomes overwhelming (Gao et al., 2017). Last, we introduce a 150% leverage constraint. Both the nominal return and Sharpe ratio are reduced and are, on average, the lowest among all six strategies.

Overall, using variance rather than volatility slightly improves the performance whilst that approach suffers from some extremely large weights. The decomposed approach with a reasonable leverage constraint seems better. However, we note that the returns and Sharpe ratios of all these alternative strategies do not change much in our sample.

9.6 CONCLUDING REMARKS

In this chapter, we demonstrate the importance of volatility to momentum. We first show that volatility-managed momentum strategies produce good returns and increased Sharpe ratios. These strategies benefit from the use of volatility which has the potential to better forecast future returns. In particular, scaling the weights of momentum using volatility information assists these strategies to adjust their risk exposure and consequently, outperforms the conventional approaches. Moreover, we find that the time-series volatility-managed momentum strategy seems to work in the Chinese and Japanese markets where traditional momentum does not work well. Second, we analyze volatility choice and the practical issues of the existing strategies. Results show that the outperformance of volatility-managed momentum strategies are robust to the various volatility measures. We also find no evidence that momentum is only related to its own volatility. This finding raises the question whether market volatility is better forecasted than momentum volatility.

REFERENCES

Andersen, T.G., Bollerslev, T., Diebold, F.X. and Ebens, H. 2001. The Distribution of Realized Stock Return Volatility. *Journal of Financial Economics*, **61**, pp. 43–76.

Ang, A., Chen, J. and Xing, Y. 2001. Downside Risk and the Momentum Effect. Unpublished working paper. National Bureau of Economic Research.

Asness, C.S., Moskowitz, T.J. and Pedersen, L.H. 2013. Value and Momentum Everywhere. *The Journal of Finance*, **68**(3), pp. 929–985.

Avramov, D., Cheng, S. and Hameed, A. 2016. Time-varying Liquidity and Momentum Profits. *Journal of Financial and Quantitative Analysis*, **51**, pp. 1897–1923.

Barroso, P. and Santa-Clara, P. 2015. Momentum Has its Moments. *Journal of Financial Economics*, **116**(1), pp. 111–120.

Bollerslev, T., Chou, R.Y. and Kroner, K.F. 1992. ARCH Modeling in Finance: A Selective Review of the Theory and Empirical Evidence. *Journal of Econometrics*, **52**, pp. 5–59.

Chan, L. K., Jegadeesh, N. and Lakonishok, J. 1996. Momentum Strategies. *The Journal of Finance*, **51**, pp. 1681–1713.

Chordia, T. and Shivakumar, L. 2002. Momentum, Business Cycle, and Time-varying Expected Returns. *The Journal of Finance*, 57(2), pp. 985–1019.

Cooper, M. J., Gutierrez, R. C. and Hameed, A. 2004. Market States and Momentum. *The Journal of Finance*, **59**, pp. 1345–1365.

Daniel, K., Jagannathan, R. and Kim, S. 2012. *Tail Risk in Momentum Strategy Returns. Unpublished working paper.* Cambridge, MA: National Bureau of Economic Research.

Daniel, K. and Moskowitz, T. 2016. Momentum Crashes. *Journal of Financial Economics*, **122**, pp. 221–247.

Frazzini, A., Israel, R. and Moskowitz, T. 2015. *Trading Costs of Asset Pricing Anomalies*, Unpublished Working Paper, AQR Capital Management.

Gao, Y. and Leung, H. 2017. Impact of Short Selling Restrictions on Informed Momentum Trading: Australian Evidence. *Pacific-Basin Finance Journal*, **45**, pp. 103–115.

Gao, Y., Leung, H. and Satchell, S. 2017. Partial Moment Momentum. The University of Sydney, Finance Discussion Paper Series, DP-2017-002.

Gao, Y., Leung, H. and Satchell, S. 2018. A Critique of Momentum Strategies. *Journal of Asset Management*, **19**, pp. 341–350.

Gao, Y., Leung, H. and Satchell, S. 2019. Momentum Winners and Losers: A Joint Approach. Unpublished Working Paper.

Jegadeesh, N. and Titman, S. 1993. Returns to Buying Winners and Selling Losers: Implications for Stock Market Efficiency. *The Journal of Finance*, 48(1), pp.5–91.

Ji, X., Martin, J. S. and Yao, Y. 2017. Macroeconomic Risk and Seasonality in Momentum Profits. *Journal of Financial Markets*, **36**, 76–90.

Korajczyk, R.A. and Sadka, R. 2004. Are Momentum Profits Robust to Trading Costs? *The Journal of Finance*, **59**, pp. 1039–1082.

Lamoureux, C.G. and Lastrapes, W.D. 1990. Heteroskedasticity in Stock Return Data: Volume versus GARCH Effects. *Journal of Finance*, **45**, pp. 221–229.

Min, B.K. and Kim, T.S. 2016. Momentum and Downside Risk. *Journal of Banking and Finance*, **72**, pp. S104–S118.

Moreira, A. and Muir, T. 2017. Volatility-anaged Portfolios. *The Journal of Finance*, 72(4), pp. 1611–1644.

Moskowitz, T.J., Ooi, Y.H. and Pedersen, L.H. 2012. Time Series Momentum. *Journal of Financial Economics*, 104(2), pp. 228–250.

CHAPTER 10

Theoretical Analysis of the Fama-French Portfolios

ANDREW GRANT, OH KANG KWON and STEVE SATCHELL

10.1 INTRODUCTION

Sorting asset attributes over a prior period and constructing portfolios based on these rankings is a technique widely used by both academics and practitioners. Although it was recognised that selecting portfolios this way has consequences for subsequent returns and examination of their properties has been the focus of considerable empirical research, there is surprisingly little commensurable theoretical analysis of the returns. In particular, the analytical properties of returns from portfolios constructed by double or treble sorting on asset attributes have not been researched to the best of our knowledge and we provide such an analysis in this chapter.

Cross-sectional momentum (CSM) refers to the persistence in the ordering of asset returns, and the empirical properties of 'winner minus loser' portfolios that seek to exploit this anomaly have been much studied in the academic literature. While it is widely reported that returns from such CSM portfolios exhibit small positive returns and negative skewness, there was an absence of statistical theory justifying these empirical observations. This was addressed in part by Kwon and Satchell (2018) who introduced a theoretical framework to analyse CSM portfolios and analytically derived many properties of CSM portfolio returns reported in the empirical literature. For example, it was shown that the distribution of CSM portfolio returns are mixtures of so-called unified skew normal (SUN) distributions, and that the skewness of CSM portfolio returns during times of financial crises can become very large and negative. In this chapter, we extend their framework to consider sorting of assets on multiple attributes over a ranking period and derive the distributional properties of resulting portfolio returns over a subsequent holding period. It will be shown that the expressions for the distributional properties of portfolio returns become significantly more involved with the introduction of additional attributes for sorting. This is more so for sequential sorting for which

174

the probability density function for portfolio returns can only be expressed in terms of iterated integrals involving multivariate cumulative normal density functions.

To motivate subsequent analysis and to place the contribution of this chapter within the context of extant research, we provide a brief review of the literature on sorting and the key empirical findings.

10.1.1 The rationale of sorting

While sorting stocks based on one or more dimensions has a long history in finance, closer considerations of the motivation to do so have also been discussed. Black and Scholes (1974) sorted stocks on dividend yield and then beta, while Banz (1981) also employed sequential sorting, first on size, then on beta.

Black et al. (1972) argue that sorting stocks into portfolios helps to provide a powerful test of the capital asset pricing model (CAPM), arguing that stocks should be grouped into portfolios sorted on beta with large cross-sectional differences in expected returns across portfolios. Berk (2000) notes that this emphasis on 'between groups' variation is aimed at mitigating the 'within group' variation. As such, an asset pricing test that examines a model within a pre-sorted portfolio of known factors will tend to reject the model. This follows because, within any group, there will not be sufficient variation in the data to carry out meaningful statistical testing.

Kan (1999) and Berk (2000) both describe the procedure of sorting and its role in testing asset pricing models. The aim is to eliminate within-portfolio variation (that is, by sorting on the first dimension) and to maximise the between-portfolio variation. By sorting on a variable known to be correlated with returns (for example, size), Lo and MacKinlay (1990) argue that a data-snooping bias is induced. Kan (1999) finds that the practice of testing asset pricing models based on portfolios does not provide useful information for firm-level pricing. He concludes that any asset pricing model test is really an examination of the variable used to sort stocks into portfolios.

Lambert and Hübner (2013) propose sequential sorting in their examination of higher comoments in asset pricing. Following the argument of Hwang and Satchell (1999), who suggest that higher moment factors exhibit collinearities, Lambert and Hübner (2013) produce portfolios sorted on covariance, coskewness and cokurtosis. Controlling for the covariance, for example, by implementing it as the first-sorting dimension, then sorting on coskewness or cokurtosis, allows for an examination of the coskewness premium while mitigating potential correlations between the higher comoments. They also argue that independent, rather that sequential (conditional) sorts are necessary because moderate correlation between sorting variables can induce unbalanced or even empty portfolios (as we previously noted). Moreover, Lambert and Hübner (2013, p. 194) also claim that sequential sorting is closer to reality when it comes to the decision-making process of investors.

There are a number of explanations for multiple sorting that stem from arguments about univariate sorting which we shall discuss first. Cattaneo et al. (2019) posit a relationship between returns (R_{it}), a vector of conditioning variables (X_{it}) and a vector of characteristics (z_{it}) which constitute a non-linear regression, see their Equation (10.5) on page 10, which we reproduce below.

$$R_{it} = \mu(z_{it}) + X'_{it} + e_{it} \tag{10.1}$$

Here $\mu(z_{it})$ is some smooth unknown function to be estimated non-parametrically. Sorting into n-tiles is treated by the authors as a 'bandwidth' problem in the non-parametric estimation of $\mu(z_{it})$. More details and technical arguments are provided in their paper. The practitioner approach to sorting has several strands; we address an argument to models similar to Equation (10.1). These are based on linear factor models of the form

$$R_{it} = \beta'_{it}f_t + e_{it}, \tag{10.2}$$

where f_t is a vector of unobservable factors such as value, momentum, and so on. We cannot observe the stock i's exposures to these factors, but we believe that z_{it} is an adequate vector of proxies for these unknown exposures. By using these characteristics as regressors, we can estimate implied factor returns by cross-sectional regression. In line with this approach, sorting on a characteristic is a way of ranking exposures to that particular factor, and allows us to build portfolios that implicitly have high or low exposure to value.

Turning now to sequential sorts, say size and then momentum; how could this be interpreted in terms of the above ideas? Knight et al. (2013) note that if the two factors are positively correlated then regressing on, say size first, then saving the residuals and using them as the dependent variable in a second regression on momentum leads to larger size exposures than by running a joint regression. They also provide analytical arguments to support this.

Thus, we can interpret sequential sorting as a technique that emphasises the relative importance of the variables to the portfolio builder. Nicholas Rabener from FactorResearch in a private communication with the authors presented the following practitioner's viewpoint.[1]

Regarding the factor sequence: Most practitioners have a certain investment philosophy. For example, they may be value investors. If they use the sequential model, but don't define Value as the first factor, then the portfolio won't necessarily contain Value stocks. For example, if an investor first ranks for Momentum and then Value, then it will be a portfolio of stocks that are rising and cheap within the universe of Momentum stocks, but can still be expensive compared to all stocks.

The first two sorts are operated on the 'control risk' dimensions. The third sort is conducted on the risk dimension to be priced. We argue that such a conditional way of ranking stocks is closer to the way investors are approaching an asset allocation problem. Investors generally deal with one problem at a time, and we therefore expect them to consider sequentially the different dimensions of risk.

---

[1]This is discussed in greater detail at https://www.factorresearch.com/research-multi-factor-models-101

10.1.2 Independent versus sequential sorting

In this subsection, we review independent and sequential sorting of asset attributes, or factors, most commonly used in portfolio construction. Distributional properties of corresponding portfolio returns will then be derived in subsequent sections.

Independent Sorts: Consider the example where the factors by which assets are sorted are momentum and size. Independent sorts would take stocks sorted on past returns from high to low (momentum) and rank them. The same universe of stocks would also be ranked on size (for example, from large to small). We would then choose 'breakpoints' which can be defined in various ways, typically as quantiles of the current universe or quantiles of some past universe. In many examples, size is sorted into two groups (big and small) and momentum is sorted into three groups (winners and losers taking the extremes of high and low returns). This would give us six groups, and each stock would then be allocated to one of the groups or buckets. There is no guarantee that the numbers in each group would be equal, or indeed, we cannot rule out the possibility that some groups could be empty.

Sequential Sorts: To deal with the problems associated with the variability of group size in independent sorts, as the name implies, sequential sorts first rank stocks on one attribute, and then on a second. If we set the breakpoints at the 30th and 70th percentile (as in the construction of the HML factor on Ken French's website), and we did this in both dimensions for 1000 stocks, we would get a table that would look like Table 10.1.

Independent sorting is most common in academic work whilst sequential sorting is more prevalent among practitioners. The reason for the latter, as will become clear in what follows, is that sequential sorting allows you to control the number of assets in each portfolio, which is important for diversification and portfolio construction generally. Independent sorting will lead to varying numbers in each cell and so portfolio size is subject to the vagaries of the multivariate empirical distribution function.

TABLE 10.1

	30	40	30
30	90	120	90
40	120	160	120
30	90	120	90

$$\mathcal{F}_{l,u,\tau} = \{3, 4\} \qquad\qquad \mathcal{F}_{l,u,\tau} = \{4\}$$

FIGURE 10.1 Example with $n = (6,6,6)$, $l = (3,2,1)$, and $u = (6,4,4)$, where the first entries of l and u refer to the top row and the final entries refer to the bottom row.

10.1.3   Critiquing Fama-French sorting

Ken French hosts an excellent and widely used data library for finance researchers.[2] Numerous factors from different countries are provided at different frequencies, with factors sorted on one, two and even three dimensions. There are hundreds of data series in this library. We believe most, if not all, to be independent sorts. Precise details of the sorting procedures are described in the library. For example, the 2 × 3 sort on size and momentum for US stocks, based on monthly data is described thus:

> **Construction:** The portfolios, which are constructed monthly, are the intersections of 2 portfolios formed on size (market equity, ME) and 3 portfolios formed on prior (2-12) return. The monthly size breakpoint is the median NYSE market equity. The monthly prior (2-12) return breakpoints are the 30th and 70th NYSE percentiles.

> **Stocks:** The six portfolios constructed each month include NYSE, AMEX, and NAS-DAQ stocks with prior return data. To be included in a portfolio for month t (formed at the end of month $t - 1$), a stock must have a price for the end of month $t - 13$ and a good return for $t - 2$. In addition, any missing returns from $t - 12$ to $t - 3$ must be −99.0, CRSP's code for a missing price. Each included stock also must have Market Equity for the end of month $t - 1$.

French also notes: 'The momentum... portfolios are reconstituted monthly and the other research portfolios are reconstituted annually. We reconstruct the full history of returns each month when we update the portfolios. (Historical returns can change, for example, if CRSP revises its database.) Although the portfolios include all NYSE, AMEX, and NASDAQ firms with the necessary data, the breakpoints use only NYSE firms'.

The use of NYSE breakpoints, but equities across multiple exchanges, means that the first column in the table will not (generally) have the same number of elements as the second (big stocks are 'big' across all exchanges, in other words). We next discuss some academic research in which sorting has been identified as pertinent.

Lambert and Hübner (2014) present a critique of the sorting methods of Fama-French, arguing that the value premium may be mis-specified, and is driven by the sorting rather than as compensation for risk. They prefer a procedure that is based on conditioning arguments, which leads to alternative estimates of risk premia. The key change in the context of this chapter is the replacement of independent sorting with sequential sorting.

Cremers et al. (2012) discuss differences between practitioner-oriented studies (that primarily use broad index-based benchmarks) and academic studies (that prefer to use Fama-French factor model benchmarks). For instance, Cremers et al. (2012) examine the return to the S&P500 index (a common benchmark for mutual funds) against a Carhart four-factor benchmark, and find a positive and significant annual alpha of

---

[2]The Data Library is at https://mba.tuck.dartmouth.edu/pages/faculty/ken.french/data_library .html.

0.82% p.a. for the period 1980 to 2005. They attribute this finding to three sources. Firstly, in the 2×3 size/book-to-market independent sorts in the Fama-French data set, portfolios are equally weighted when constructing SMB and HML factors. This over-weights small stocks relative to a market capitalization-weighted index.

Secondly, the market index is proxied by the CRSP value-weighted index, which includes assets outside the universe of US Common stocks (such as Real Estate Investment Trusts [REITs] and American Depositary Receipts [ADRs]), which have underperformed the S&P500. Cremers et al. (2012) also suggest that index rebalancing effects of broad stock indices exacerbate return differences compared with the CRSP index. The main finding of the Cremers et al. (2012) study is that by using appropriate weighting schemes (value weighting stocks within portfolios) and investable bench-marks, out-of-sample tracking error volatility is reduced substantially. This reflects the fact that, in part, desirable criteria of a model used for asset pricing purposes (i.e. linear factor models) are not identical to those of a model used as a benchmark for fund managers (where the hurdle is the passive investment return).

Stambaugh et al. (2015) and Liu et al. (2018) advocate averaging over different sorts, a tactic frequently used by practitioners when employing multiple models. Their approach is to average percentile ranks over multiple pricing anomalies in the construc-tion of a 'mispricing index'. This alleviates the need for multi-dimensional sorting, but does not ensure that extremes of a particular attribute are included in the final sorted sample. To an extent, this can be interpreted as a mitigation of model risk.

From the documentation on Robert Stambaugh's website, where asset growth is used as one sorting variable (among a total of 11):

> We … rank firms each month by asset growth, and those with the highest growth receive the highest rank. The higher the rank, the greater the relative degree of overpricing according to the given anomaly variable. A stock's mis-pricing measure (MISP), ranging between 0 and 100, is the arithmetic average of its ranking percentile for each of the 11 anomalies. According to this mea-sure, the stocks with the highest values of MISP are the most 'overpriced', and those with the lowest values are the most 'underpriced'.

10.2 STRATEGIES, NOTATION AND PRELIMINARIES

We now move to a more technical discussion. For the convenience of the reader, we introduce in this section the notation that will be used throughout the chapter, and present some known results that will be relied upon in subsequent sections.

10.2.1 Notation

For any $x \in \mathbb{R}^n$, we will write x_i for the i-th coordinate of x, and given $y \in \mathbb{R}^n$ write $x \prec y$ if and only if $x_i < y_i$ for all $1 \le i \le n$. Similarly, given a matrix $M \in \mathbb{R}^{m \times k}$, we will write $M_{i,j}$ for the (i, j)-th entry of M, and the transpose of a vector or a matrix will be denoted by the superscript $'$. For any $1 \le i \le n$, we will denote by $x_{-i} \in \mathbb{R}^{n-1}$ the vector obtained from x by omitting the i-th component, and likewise negative subscripts for matrices will indicate omission of a row or column depending on the position of the subscript. For example, if $1 \leq i, j \leq n$, then $M_{-i,j} \in \mathbb{R}^{(n-1) \times n}$ is the j-th column of M with the i-th entry removed, while $M_{-i,-j} \in \mathbb{R}^{(n-1) \times (n-1)}$ is the submatrix of M with i-th row and j-th column removed. Given a subset $A \in \mathbb{R}^n$, we will denote by $\mathbb{1}_A$ the indicator function on A.

For a random vector, X, with values in a region $\mathcal{D}_X \subset \mathbb{R}^n$, we will write $f_X(x)$ and $F_X(x)$ for the probability density and the cumulative density functions of X respectively. Moreover, given another random vector Y, with values in $\mathcal{D}_Y \subset \mathbb{R}^m$, we will denote by $f_{X|Y}(x|y)$ and $F_{X|Y}(x|y)$ the conditional probability density and conditional cumulative density functions of X given $Y = y$ respectively.

For any $n \in \mathbb{N}$, let $[n] = \{1, 2, \ldots, n\}$ and let S_n be the set of permutations of $[n]$. We will denote the permutation that maps $1 \mapsto i_1, 2 \mapsto i_2, \ldots, n \mapsto i_n$ by a sequence $(i_1, i_2, \ldots, i_n)$, and given any $\tau \in S_n$ write $\tau(i)$ for the image of i under τ so that if $\tau = (1, 3, 2)$, for example, then $\tau(1) = 1$, $\tau(2) = 3$, and $\tau(3) = 2$. More generally, given $m \in \mathbb{N}$, and $n = (n_1, n_2, \ldots, n_m) \in \mathbb{N}^m$, let $\mathbb{R}^n = \prod_{i=1}^{m} \mathbb{R}^{n_i}$, and denote by S_n the Cartesian product

$$S_n = \prod_{i=1}^{m} S_{n_i} = \left\{ (\tau_1, \tau_2, \ldots, \tau_m) | \tau_i \in S_{n_i} \quad \text{for} \quad 1 \leq i \leq m \right\}. \tag{10.3}$$

10.2.2 Multivariate normal distributions

The density of an n-dimensional normal distribution with mean μ and covariance Σ at $x \in \mathbb{R}^n$ will be denoted $\phi_n(x; \mu, \Sigma)$, and the corresponding cumulative density function will be denoted $\Phi_n[x; \mu, \Sigma]$. In general, given random variables $X_1, \ldots, X_n$, their joint probability density function will be denoted $f_{X_1, \cdots, X_n}$, and we will write $F_{X_1, \cdots, X_n}$ for the cumulative density function.

Theorem 1. Let $n_1, n_2 \in \mathbb{N}$ and suppose $X \sim \mathcal{N}_{n_1 + n_2}(\mu, \Sigma)$, where

$$X = \begin{bmatrix} X_1 \\ X_2 \end{bmatrix}, \quad \mu = \begin{bmatrix} \mu_1 \\ \mu_2 \end{bmatrix}, \quad \Sigma = \begin{bmatrix} \Sigma_{1,1} & \Sigma_{1,2} \\ \Sigma_{2,1} & \Sigma_{2,2} \end{bmatrix}, \tag{10.4}$$

with $X_i, \mu_i \in \mathbb{R}^{n_i}$ and $\Sigma_{i,j} \in \mathbb{R}^{n_i \times n_j}$ for $1 \leq i, j \leq 2$, and Σ positive definite. Then the conditional distribution of X_1 given X_2 is normal with mean and covariance

$$\mu_{X_1 | X_2} = \mu_1 + \Sigma_{1,2} \Sigma_{2,2}^{-1} (X_2 - \mu_2), \tag{10.5}$$

$$\Sigma_{X_1 | X_2} = \Sigma_{1,1} - \Sigma_{1,2} \Sigma_{2,2}^{-1} \Sigma_{2,1}, \tag{10.6}$$

respectively, and $\phi_{n_1 + n_2}(x; \mu, \Sigma)$ decomposes as

$$\phi_{n_1 + n_2}(x; \mu, \Sigma) = \phi_{n_1}(x_1; \mu_{X_1 | X_2}, \Sigma_{X_1 | X_2}) \phi_{n_2}(x_2; \mu_2, \Sigma_{2,2}). \tag{10.7}$$

Proof. Refer to Muirhead (1982) Theorem 1.2.11.   □

Given a n-dimensional random vector X and $p = (p_1, \ldots, p_m) \in \{1, 2, \ldots, n\}^m$, we will denote by $\mu_p(X)$ the p-th moment of X so that

$$\mu_p(X) = \mathbb{E}\left[\prod_{i=1}^{m} X_{p_i}\right]. \tag{10.8}$$

Theorem 2. Let $X \sim \mathcal{N}_n(\mu, \Sigma)$, where $n \in \mathbb{N}$, $\mu \in \mathbb{R}^n$ and $\Sigma \in \mathbb{R}^{n \times n}$ is positive definite. Then for any $p = (p_1, \ldots, p_m) \in \{1, 2, \ldots, n\}^m$, we have

$$\mu_p(X) = \sum_{\substack{k, l \in \mathbb{N} \\ k + 2l = m}} \sum_{\tau \in Q(k, 2l)} \left(\prod_{i=1}^{k} \mu_{p_{\tau_i}}\right)\left(\prod_{i=1}^{l} \Sigma_{p_{\tau_{k+2i-1}}, p_{\tau_{k+2i}}}\right). \tag{10.9}$$

Proof. Refer to Withers (1985) Theorem 1.1. □

An alternative expression for $\mu_p(X)$, where X is multivarite normal, is given in Kan (2008) Proposition 2.

Corollary 1. Let $X \sim \mathcal{N}_1(\mu, \sigma^2)$. Then for any $m \in \mathbb{N}$, the m-th moment of X is given by

$$\mu_m(X) = \sum_{\substack{i=0 \\ m \\ i\,\text{even}}} m_i (i-1)!!\sigma^i \mu^{m-i}, \tag{10.10}$$

where $k!! = \prod_{i=0}^{\frac{k}{2}}(k - 2i)$ is the double factorial of $k \in \mathbb{N}$.

Proof. Follows immediately from Theorem 2, since the inner sum in Equation (10.9), corresponding to $2l = i$, consists of $\binom{m}{i}(i - 1)!!$ identical terms all equal to $\sigma^i \mu^{m-i}$. □

10.2.3 Multivariate skew normal and unified skew normal family of distributions

It transpires that, and is shown in Kwon and Satchell (2018), that sorting multivariate data leads to skew-normal distributions, which we define next. Multivariate skew-normal (SN) distributions are an extension of the multivariate normal distributions that accommodate non-zero skewness through the introduction of an additional parameter. In the original formulation introduced in Azzalini and Valle (1985), the density of the n-dimensional SN distribution with location parameter $\xi \in \mathbb{R}^n$, positive definite covariance matrix $\Sigma \in \mathbb{R}^{n \times n}$, and skewness parameter $\alpha \in \mathbb{R}^d$ is given by:

$$\varphi(x) = 2\phi_n(x; \xi, \Sigma)\Phi_1\left[\alpha' \Delta^{-1}(x - \xi)\right], \tag{10.11}$$

where $\Delta \in \mathbb{R}^{n \times n}$ is the diagonal matrix with the non-zero entries $D_{i,i} = \sqrt{\Sigma_{i,i}}$. Since their introduction, the multivariate SN distributions have been the subject of considerable interest with several variants subsequently being introduced with apparently different representations. For a detailed discussion of these variants, refer to Arellano-Valle and Azzalini (2006).

The seemingly disparate distributions related to the multivariate SN distributions were brought together under the umbrella of the so-called unified skew-normal (SUN) family of distributions in Arellano-Valle and Azzalini (2006), where it was shown that the SUN family contains many of these skew-normal variants as special cases. Given $n_i \in \mathbb{N}$, $\mu_i \in \mathbb{R}^{n_i}$, $\Sigma_{i,j} \in \mathbb{R}^{n_1 \times n_2}$ for $1 \leq i \leq j$, where $\Sigma'_{2,1} = \Lambda_{1,2}$ and $\Sigma_{i,i}$ are positive definite, let

$$\begin{bmatrix} X_1 \\ X_2 \end{bmatrix} \sim \mathcal{N}_{n_1 + n_2} \left(\begin{bmatrix} \mu_1 \\ \mu_2 \end{bmatrix}, \begin{bmatrix} \Sigma_{1,1} & \Sigma_{1,2} \\ \Sigma'_{1,2} & \Sigma_{2,2} \end{bmatrix} \right).$$

Then the probability density function of an n_2-dimensional SUN distributed random variable U associated with $(X'_1, X'_2)'$ is given by

$$f_U(u) = \frac{\phi_{n_2}(u; \mu_2, \Sigma_{2,2}) \Phi_{n_1}[0; -\mu_1 - \Sigma_{1,2}\Sigma_{2,2}^{-1}(u - \mu_2); , \Sigma_{1,1;2}]}{\Phi_{n_1}[0; -\mu_1, \Sigma_{1,1}]}. \tag{10.12}$$

where $\Sigma_{1,1;2} = \Sigma_{1,1} - \Sigma_{1,2}\Sigma_{2,2}^{-1}\Sigma_{2,1}$. Moreover, the moment generating function of U is known and is given by

$$m_U(t) = \frac{\Phi_{n_1}[\mu_1 + \Sigma_{1,2}t; 0, \Sigma_{1,1}]}{\Phi_{n_1}[\mu_1; 0, \Sigma_{1,1}]} \exp\left(\mu'_2 t + \frac{1}{2} t' \Sigma_{2,2} t \right) \tag{10.13}$$

The key characteristic of $f_U(u)$ is that it is a product of an n_2-dimensional normal density and an n_1-dimensional cumulative normal density with the variable u appearing as the main variable in the former and in the mean of the latter. As will be seen, the densities of Fama-French portfolio returns will be a mixture of these SUN densities.

10.3 DISTRIBUTION OF FAMA-FRENCH FACTORS

In this section, we develop the theoretical framework and obtain some key results for analysing the properties of the returns on Fama-French portfolios, or more generally Fama-French factors, that we define in a mathematically precise manner in Subsection 10.3.2. We begin with a brief discussion on investment strategies.

10.3.1 Strategies

In this subsection, we discuss the relation of sorting to strategy construction. Before we do, we shall define a concomitant, which is a set of order statistics based on sorting on one variable and recording the values of the second variable. An example would be sorting on value and then recording future returns.

In the case of concomitants, strategies are straightforward. The ranking period provides a clear ordering on the assets; these can be grouped into quantiles and linear combinations, such as long the first quantile or long the first and short the n-th, can be constructed as portfolio strategies.

In higher dimensions, the problem is less clear. We discuss the case $m = 2$, but the treatment is general. We can consider two attributes, both deemed desirable with respect to top quantiles such as size (small) and value (cheap). This gives us two univariate rankings but no sense of multivariate rankings. We recognize here the problem of multivariate order statistics for which there is a vast but rather inconclusive literature, see Weller and Eddy (2015) for a comprehensive review of the existing literature. Our discussion follows Belloni and Winkler (2011) in that we consider partial orderings. In the context of size and value, this could imply that $(i_1, i_2) \geq (i_1 + \Delta_1, i_2 + \Delta_2)$ for $\Delta_1, \Delta_2 \geq 0$. However, such an ordering does not provide a total ordering in the sense that it does not allow us to rank (1,2) and (2,1) for example. Given such a partial ordering, we may wish to long (1,1) and short (2,3) which would be longing small and cheap stocks and shorting large and over-priced stocks.

10.3.2 Fama-French factors

We now provide a mathematically precise definition of the Fama-French factors. These are portfolios whose composition depends on the ordering of assets by possibly multiple attributes (typically one or two) over the ranking period. The portfolio may typically be weighted equally, by value, or indeed by any non-negative weight scheme.

Let $n = (n_1, n_2, \ldots, n_m) \in \mathbb{N}^m$, and let $l = (l_1, l_2, \ldots, l_m) \in \mathbb{N}^m$ and $u = (u_1, u_2, \ldots, u_m) \in \mathbb{N}^m$ such that $1 \leq l_i < u_i \leq n_i$ for $1 \leq i \leq m$. The purpose of l_i and u_i is to specify the lower and upper positions of a quantile upon sorting the elements of X_i. Note that for each $1 \leq i \leq m$, the permutation $\tau_i \in S_{n_i}$ naturally induces an ordering on $[n_i]$, viz. $(\tau_i(1), \tau_i(2), \ldots, \tau_i(n_i))$, and we will write

$$\mathcal{F}_{l_i, u_i, \tau_i} = \{\tau_i(l_i), \tau_i(l_i + 1), \ldots, \tau_i(u_i)\}, \tag{10.14}$$

$$\mathcal{F}_{l, u, \tau} = \cap_{i=1}^{m} \mathcal{F}_{l_i, u_i, \tau_i}, \tag{10.15}$$

where $\tau = (\tau_1, \tau_2, \ldots, \tau_m) \in S_n$. We will refer to the sets of the form $\mathcal{F}_{l, u, \tau}$ as *Fama-French intersection indices* corresponding to l, u, and τ. For most practical applications, it will be the case that $n = (n, n, \ldots, n)$, and it should be noted that for a given $\tau \in S_n$, it may be the case that $\mathcal{F}_{l, u, \tau} = \emptyset$. An example of the case with $n = (6,6,6)$, $l = (3,2,1)$, and $u = (6,4,4)$ is given in Figure 1. For the figure on the left, considering the first attribute corresponding to $i = 1$, the permutation τ_1 in this case is $(6,5,2,4,3,1)$, and the subset of indices between the $l_1 = 3$ and the $u_1 = 6$ positions is $\mathcal{F}_{l_1, u_1, \tau_1} = \{1,2,3,4\}$. For $i = 2$ and $i = 3$, corresponding to second and third attributes, the relevant subset of indices are $\mathcal{F}_{l_2, u_2, \tau_2} = \{2,3,4\}$ and $\mathcal{F}_{l_3, u_3, \tau_3} = \{1,3,4,5\}$ respectively, and so the Fama-French intersection indices associated with the left figure is $\mathcal{F}_{l, u, \tau} = \{3,4\}$. Similar calculation gives the Fama-French intersection indices for the right figure as $\mathcal{F}_{l, u, \tau} = \{4\}$.

Definition 1. Let $m \in \mathbb{N}$, $n = (n, n, \ldots, n) \in \mathbb{N}^m$, $X = (x_1, \ldots, x_m) \in \mathbb{R}^{mn}$, $Y \in \mathbb{R}^n$, and let $l, u \in \mathbb{N}^m$ such that $1 \leq l_i \leq u_i \leq n$ for all $1 \leq i \leq m$. Moreover, for each $\tau \in S_n$

define $D_{X,\tau} \subset \mathbb{R}^{mn}$ by

$$D_{X,\tau} = \{(x_1 \ldots x_m) \in \mathbb{R}^{mn} | x_{i,\tau_i(1)} > x_{i,\tau_i(2)} > \cdots > x_{n,\tau_i(n)} \text{ for } 1 \le i \le m\}, \qquad (10.16)$$

and let $w_\tau \in \mathbb{R}^n$ be given by

$$w_{\tau,i} = \begin{cases} \dfrac{1}{|\mathcal{F}_{l,u,\tau}|}, & \text{if } \mathcal{F}_{l,u,\tau} \ne \varnothing \text{ and } i \in \mathcal{F}_{l,u,\tau}, \\ 0, & \text{otherwise,} \end{cases} \qquad (10.17)$$

where $|\mathcal{F}_{l,u,\tau}|$ denotes the number of elements of the set $\mathcal{F}_{l,u,\tau} \ne \varnothing$. Then the *Fama-French factor* associated with (m, n, X, Y, l, u) is the random variable $Z \in \mathbb{R}$ given by

$$Z = \sum_{\tau \in S_n} \mathbb{1}_{D_{X,\tau}}(X) w_\tau' Y. \qquad (10.18)$$

In the above definition, the components of the vector $x_i \in \mathbb{R}^n$, where $1 \le i \le m$, represent the i-th attribute of the assets being ranked over the formation period, and the components of the vector Y are the corresponding attributes of the assets being recorded over the holding period. Each $\tau \in S_n$ determines an ordering of the m asset attributes over the ranking period, and $w_\tau \in \mathbb{R}$ specifies the weights of the portfolio over the holding period conditional on the ranked attributes being ordered according to τ. The sets $D_{X,\tau}$ are the regions in $\mathbb{R}^{mn}$ consisting of points for which the ordering of the coordinates are determined by the same permutation τ.

We now show that the probability density function (pdf) of the Fama-French factor, Z, associated with (m, n, X, Y, l, u) can be determined explicitly, and begin with a basic lemma.

Lemma 1. *Let Z be the Fama-French factor in Equation (10.18) determined by (m, n, X, Y, l, u). Then the probability density, $f_Z(z)$, of Z is given by*

$$f_Z(z) = \sum_{\tau \in S_n} f_{w_\tau' Y}(z) \int_{x \in D_{X,\tau}} f_{X|w_\tau' Y}(x | z) \, dx. \qquad (10.19)$$

Proof. Follows from the basic properties of conditional probabilities and is given in Appendix A.1. □

We now analyse in detail the distributional properties of the generalized Fama-French factors. Denote by e_i the i-standard basis vector of $\mathbb{R}^n$ for $i \in [n]$, let

$$D_n = \begin{bmatrix} -1 & 1 & 0 & 1 & \cdots & 0 & 0 & 0 \\ 0 & -1 & 1 & 0 & \cdots & 0 & 0 & 0 \\ \cdots & \cdots & \cdots & \cdots & \cdots & \cdots & \cdots & \cdots \\ 0 & 0 & 0 & 0 & \cdots & 0 & -1 & 1 \end{bmatrix} \in \mathbb{R}^{(n-1) \times n}, \qquad (10.20)$$

and let $P_\tau \in \mathbb{N}^{n \times n}$ be the permutation matrix corresponding to $\tau \in S_n$. Moreover, let $D_{n,\tau} = D_{n-1}P_\tau$, and given $\tau = (\tau_1, \tau_2, \ldots, \tau_m) \in S_n$, define

$$
D_\tau = \begin{bmatrix}
D_{n,\tau_1} & O & O & \cdots & & O \\
O & D_{n,\tau_2} & O & \cdots & & O \\
\vdots & \ddots & \ddots & \ddots & & \vdots \\
O & O & \cdots & D_{n,\tau_{m-1}} & & O \\
O & O & \cdots & & O & D_{n,\tau_m}
\end{bmatrix},
\tag{10.21}
$$

where $O \in \mathbb{R}^{(n-1) \times n}$ is the zero matrix.

Theorem 3. Suppose $(X', Y')'$ is multivariate normal so that

$$
\begin{bmatrix} X \\ Y \end{bmatrix} \sim \mathcal{N}_{(m+1)n}\left(\begin{bmatrix} \mu_X \\ \mu_Y \end{bmatrix}, \begin{bmatrix} \Lambda_{X,X} & \Lambda_{X,Y} \\ \Lambda_{Y,X} & \Lambda_{Y,Y} \end{bmatrix} \right)
\tag{10.22}
$$

where $\mu_X = (\mu'_{X_1}, \ldots, \mu'_{X_m})' \in \mathbb{R}^{mn}$ with $\mu_i \in \mathbb{R}^n$ for $i \in [n]$, $\mu_Y \in \mathbb{R}^n$,

$$
\Lambda_{X,X} = \begin{bmatrix}
\Lambda_{X_1,X_1} & \Lambda_{X_1,X_2} & \cdots & \Lambda_{X_1,X_{m-1}} & \Lambda_{X_1,X_m} \\
\Lambda_{X_2,X_1} & \Lambda_{X_2,X_2} & \cdots & \Lambda_{X_2,X_{m-1}} & \Lambda_{X_2,X_m} \\
\vdots & \vdots & \ddots & \vdots & \vdots \\
\Lambda_{X_m,X_1} & \Lambda_{X_m,X_2} & \cdots & \Lambda_{X_m,X_{m-1}} & \Lambda_{X_m,X_m}
\end{bmatrix},
\tag{10.23}
$$

$\Lambda_{X_i,X_j} \in \mathbb{R}^{n \times n}$ for all $i, j \in [m]$,

$$
\Lambda_{Y,X} = [\Lambda_{Y,X_1} \ \Lambda_{Y,X_2} \ \cdots \ \Lambda_{Y,X_m}],
\tag{10.24}
$$

$\Lambda_{Y,X_i} \in \mathbb{R}^{n \times n}$ *for all* $i \in [m]$, *and* $\Lambda_{X,Y} = \Lambda'_{Y,X}$. *If* Z *is the associated Fama-French factor defined in Equation* (10.18), *then the probability density of* Z *is given by*

$$
f_Z(z) = \sum_{\tau \in S_n} \phi_1(z; w'_\tau \mu_Y, w'_\tau \Lambda_{Y,Y} w_\tau) \Phi_{m(n-1)}(0; \mu_{z,\tau}, \Lambda_{\tau,\tau}),
\tag{10.25}
$$

where we define $\Phi_0 \equiv 1$, and

$$
\mu_{z,\tau} = D_\tau \mu_X + \frac{z - w'_\tau \mu_Y}{w'_\tau \Lambda_{Y,Y} w_\tau} D_\tau \Lambda_{X,Y} w_\tau,
\tag{10.26}
$$

$$
\Lambda_{\tau,\tau} = D_\tau \Lambda_{X,X} D'_\tau - \frac{1}{w'_\tau \Lambda_{Y,Y} w_\tau} D_\tau \Lambda_{X,Y} w_\tau (D_\tau \Lambda_{X,Y} w_\tau)'.
\tag{10.27}
$$

Alternatively,

$$
f_Z(z) = \sum_{\tau \in S_n} \int_{\mathbb{R}^{m(n-1)}_-} \phi_1(z; \gamma_{v,\tau}, Y_{\tau,\tau}) \phi_{m(n-1)}(v; D_\tau \mu_X, D_\tau \Lambda_{X,X} D'_\tau) dv,
\tag{10.28}
$$

where

$$\gamma_{v,\tau} = w'_\tau \mu_Y + w'_\tau \Lambda_{Y,X} D'_\tau \Lambda_{X,X}^{-1} D_\tau (v - D_\tau \mu_X), \tag{10.29}$$

$$Y_{\tau,\tau} = w'_\tau \Lambda_{Y,Y} w_\tau - (D_\tau \Lambda_{X,Y} w_\tau)' \Lambda_{X,X}^{-1} D_\tau \Lambda_{X,Y} w_\tau. \tag{10.30}$$

Proof. Refer to Appendix 10.A.2. □

We note that each summand of $f_Z(z)$ in Equation (10.25) has the characteristic structure of the SUN family of distributions, viz. the product of a normal probability density and a cumulative normal density where the variable z appears in the mean term of both. In particular, based on the properties of SUN distributions, $f_Z(z)$ will generally be skewed and have excess kurtosis with the degree of skewness and kurtosis depending on the means and covariances of underlying attributes and returns.

Corollary 2. *Let $X, Y,$ and Z be as defined in Theorem 1. If X and Y are independent, then*

$$f_Z(z) = \sum_{\tau \in S_n} \Phi_{m(n-1)}(0; D_\tau \mu_X, D_\tau \Lambda_{X,X} D'_\tau) \phi_1(z; w'_\tau \mu_Y, w'_\tau \Lambda_{Y,Y} w_\tau), \tag{10.31}$$

so that $f_Z(z)$ is a weighted average of 1-dimensional normal densities. Alternatively,

$$f_Z(z) = \sum_{\tau \in S_n} \phi_1(z; w'_\tau \mu_Y, w'_\tau \Lambda_{Y,Y} w_\tau) \int_{\mathbb{R}_-^{n-1}} \phi_{m(n-1)}(v; D_\tau \mu_X, D_\tau \Lambda_{X,X} D'_\tau) dv. \tag{10.32}$$

Proof. Follows from Theorem 3 since $\Lambda_{X,Y} = O_{n \times n} = \Lambda_{Y,X}$.   □

10.3.3   Moments of Fama-French factors

In this subsection, we consider the moments of the Fama-French factor, Z, associated with the sextuplet (m, n, X, Y, l, u) as defined in Equation (10.18). Since each term, $w'_\tau Y$, that appears in the sum on the right-hand side of Equation (10.18) is linear in Y, it is useful to consider conditional expectations of products of the form $Y_{i_1} Y_{i_2} \cdots Y_{i_k}$, given $D_{X,\tau}$, where $k \in \mathbb{N}$ and $i_j \in [n]$ for $j \in [k]$. So for any given $d \in \mathbb{N}$ and $p = (p_1, p_2, \ldots, p_d) \in \{1, 2, \ldots, n\}^d$, define

$$Y_p = \prod_{i=1}^d Y_{p_i}. \tag{10.33}$$

Then the moments of the Fama-French factor, Z, are given in terms of expectations of the form $Y_p \mathbb{I}_{D_{X,\tau}}$, and we now show that it is possible to obtain explicit expressions for $\mathbb{E}[Y_p \mathbb{I}_{D_{X,\tau}}]$.

Theorem 4. *Let $(X', Y')'$ be multivariate normal as defined in Theorem 3. Then for any $d \in \mathbb{N}$ and $p = (p_1, p_2, \ldots, p_d) \in \{1, 2, \ldots, n\}^d$, we have*

$$\mathbb{E}[Y_p \mathbb{I}_{D_{X,\tau}}] = \int_{v \in \mathbb{R}_-^{m(n-1)}} \mu_{p,\tau}(Y \mid v) \phi_{m(n-1)}(v; D_\tau \mu_X, D_\tau \Lambda_{X,X} D'_\tau) dv, \tag{10.34}$$

where

$$\mu_{p,\tau}(Y|v) = \sum_{\substack{k,l \in \mathbb{N} \\ k+2l=\eta}} \sum_{v \in Q(k,2l)} \left(\prod_{i=1}^{k} \mu_Y(\tau,v)_{p_{v(i)}} \right) \left(\prod_{i=1}^{l} \Lambda_{Y,Y}(\tau)_{p_{v(k+2i-1)},p_{v(k+2i)}} \right), \quad (10.35)$$

$$\mu_Y(\tau,v) = \mu_Y + \Lambda_{Y,X} D'_\tau (D_\tau \Lambda_{X,X} D'_\tau)^{-1} (v - D_\tau \mu_X), \tag{10.36}$$

$$\Lambda_{Y,Y}(\tau) = \Lambda_{Y,Y} - \Lambda_{Y,X} D'_\tau (D_\tau \Lambda_{X,X} D'_\tau)^{-1} D_\tau \Lambda_{X,Y}. \tag{10.37}$$

In particular, if $d = 1$, so that $Y_p = Y_i$ and $\mu_{p,\tau}(Y|v) = \mu_Y(\tau,v)_i$ for some $i \in [n]$, then we have

$$\mathbb{E}[Y_i \mathbb{1}_{D_{X,\tau}}] = \mu_{Y,i} \Phi_{m(n-1)}(\mathbf{0}; D_\tau \mu_X, D_\tau \Lambda_{X,X} D'_\tau)$$

$$- \sum_{j=1}^{m(n-1)} (D_\tau \Lambda_{X,Y})_{j,i} \phi_1(0; m_j, s_j^2) \Phi_{m(n-1)-1}(\mathbf{0}; \gamma_j, \gamma_j), \quad (10.38)$$

where $\mu_{Y,i}$ is the i-entry of μ_Y, $m_j = (D_\tau \mu_X)_j$, $s_j^2 = (D_\tau \Lambda_{X,X} D'_\tau)_{j,j}$,

$$\gamma_j = (D_\tau \mu_X)_{-j} - \frac{m_j}{s_j^2}(D_\tau \Lambda_{X,X} D'_\tau)_{-j,j}, \tag{10.39}$$

$$\gamma_j = (D_\tau \Lambda_{X,X} D'_\tau)_{-j,-j} - \frac{1}{s_j^2}(D_\tau \Lambda_{X,X} D'_\tau)_{-j,j}(D_\tau \Lambda_{X,X} D'_\tau)_{j,-j}. \tag{10.40}$$

Proof. Refer to Appendix 10.A.3. □

The expression for $\mathbb{E}[Y_i \mathbb{1}_{D_{X,\tau}}]$ in Equation (10.38) allows the first moment of Z to be obtained explicitly as shown below.

Theorem 5. *Let Z be defined as in Equation (10.18). Then the first non-central moment of Z is given by*

$$\mu_1(Z) = \sum_{\tau \in S_n} \left(w'_\tau \mu_Y \Phi_{m(n-1)}(\mathbf{0}; D_\tau \mu_X, D_\tau \Lambda_{X,X} D'_\tau) \right.$$

$$\left. - \sum_{j=1}^{m(n-1)} (D_\tau \Lambda_{X,Y} w_\tau)_j \phi_1(0; m_j, s_j^2) \Phi_{m(n-1)-1}(\mathbf{0}; \gamma_j, \gamma_j) \right), \quad (10.41)$$

where m_j, s_j^2, γ_j and γ_j are as defined in Theorem 4.

Proof. Since $Z = \sum_{\tau \in S_n} \mathbb{1}_{D_{X,\tau}} w'Y = \sum_{\tau \in S_n} \sum_{i=1}^{n} w_i \mathbb{1}_{D_{X,\tau}} Y_i$, the expression for $\mu_1(Z)$ follows from Equation (10.38) by scaling by w_i and summing over i. □

10.3.4 Special case with $n = 2$ and $m = 2$

In this section, we consider in detail the distributional properties of Fama-French factors in the special case of $n = 2$, $m = 2$, $l_1 = u_1 = l_2 = u_2 = 2$, and $w_{\tau,i} = 1$ for $i \in F_{l,u,\tau}$, where it is possible to derive analytic expressions. This case corresponds to $n = 2$ assets sorted independently on $m = 2$ attributes. For each sorted attribute, indices of assets that are ranked between $l_i = 2$ and $u_i = 2$ are selected. Since $l_i = 2 = u_i$ in this case, the index of the asset that is ranked lower on each attribute is noted. If the same asset is ranked lower on both attributes, then the portfolio is constructed using that asset. However, if a different asset is ranked lower on the two attributes then the portfolio is not formed over the holding period and the holding period return is zero. Other choices of l_i and u_i can be considered in an analogous manner.

Firstly, note that $n = (2,2)$, and $S_n = S_2 \times S_2$ so that

$$S_n = \{((1,2)(1,2)), ((1,2)(2,1)), ((21)(1,2)), ((2,1)(2,1))\}.$$

The choice of l_i and u_i in this case implies that we are considering the assets that rank higher on both attributes, and we provide below that mapping from S_n to the corresponding Fama-French intersection set, assuming each attribute is ranked from lowest to highest so that the permutation $(1,2)$ for an attribute corresponds to asset 2 being ranked higher than asset 1.

$$2((1,2), (1,2)) \mapsto \{2\}, ((1,2), (2,1)) \mapsto \emptyset,$$
$$((2,1), (1,2)) \mapsto \emptyset, ((2,1), (2,1)) \mapsto \{1\}.$$

It follows that the Fama-French factor in this case is given by

$$Z = \mathbb{1}_{D_{X,((2,1),(2,1))}} Y_1 + \mathbb{1}_{D_{X,((1,2),(1,2))}} Y_2,$$

and from Equation (10.25) the pdf of Z is

$$f_Z(z) = \phi_1(z; \mu_{Y_1}, \sigma_{Y_1}^2) \Phi_2 \left(0; - \begin{bmatrix} \mu_{X_{1,1}} - \mu_{X_{1,2}} \\ \mu_{X_{2,1}} - \mu_{X_{2,2}} \end{bmatrix} - \frac{\mu_{Y_1}}{\sigma_{Y_1}^2} \begin{bmatrix} \sigma_{X_{1,1},Y_1} - \sigma_{X_{1,2},Y_1} \\ \sigma_{X_{2,1},Y_1} - \sigma_{X_{2,2},Y_1} \end{bmatrix} \right)$$
$$+ \phi_1(z; \mu_{Y_2}, \sigma_{Y_2}^2) \Phi_2 \left(0; \begin{bmatrix} \mu_{X_{1,1}} - \mu_{X_{1,2}} \\ \mu_{X_{2,1}} - \mu_{X_{2,2}} \end{bmatrix} + \frac{\mu_{Y_2}}{\sigma_{Y_2}^2} \begin{bmatrix} \sigma_{X_{1,1},Y_2} - \sigma_{X_{1,2},Y_2} \\ \sigma_{X_{2,1},Y_2} - \sigma_{X_{2,2},Y_2} \end{bmatrix} \right),$$

where μ_{Y_i} and $\sigma_{Y_i}^2$ are the expected value and the variance of Y_i respectively, $\mu_{X_{i,j}}$ is the expected value of $X_{i,j}$ and $\sigma_{X_{i,j},Y_k}$ is the covariance between of $X_{i,j}$ and Y_k.

10.4 FAMA-FRENCH FACTORS WITH SEQUENTIAL SORTING

The Fama-French portfolios we considered in previous sections are formed by first sorting the assets according to each attribute individually and then forming the intersection of the resulting buckets. In this section, we consider the alternative process in which the assets are sorted sequentially according to the given set of attributes.

10.4.1 Distributional properties of Fama-French factors with sequential sorting

Let $b, q_1, \ldots, q_m \in \mathbb{N}$, $n = b \prod_{j=1}^{m} q_j$, and for $1 \leq i \leq m$ let $n_{(i)} = b \prod_{j=i}^{m} q_j$. Denote by $S_{n:m}$ the set

$$S_{n:m} = S_{n_{(1)}} \times S_{n_{(2)}} \times \cdots \times S_{n_{(m)}}, \tag{10.42}$$

and given $\pi = (\pi_1, \pi_2, \ldots, \pi_m) \in S_{n:m}$ with $\pi_j \in S_{n_{(j)}}$, and $i = (i_1, i_2, \ldots, i_m) \in \prod_{j=1}^{m} [q_j]$, let $\mathcal{I}_k^{\circ}(\pi, i)$ be the subsequence of $[n]$ given by

$$\mathcal{I}_k^{\circ}(\pi, i) = (\pi_k((i_k - 1)n_{(k)} + 1), \pi_k((i_k - 1)n_{(k)} + 2), \ldots, \pi_k((i_k - 1)n_{(k)} + n_{(k)})) \tag{10.43}$$

for $1 \leq k \leq m$. Next, define $\mathcal{I}_k(\pi, i) \subset [n]$ recursively, for $1 \leq k \leq m$, by $\mathcal{I}_1(\pi, i) = \mathcal{I}_1^{\circ}(\pi, i)$, and given $\mathcal{I}_k(\pi, i) = (j_1, j_2, \ldots, j_{n_{(k)}})$ define

$$\mathcal{I}_{k+1}(\pi, i) = (j_{\pi_{k+1}((i_{k+1}-1)n_{(k+1)}+1)}, j_{\pi_{k+1}((i_{k+1}-1)n_{(k+1)}+2)}, \ldots, j_{\pi_{k+1}((i_{k+1}-1)n_{(k+1)}+n_{(k+1)})}) \tag{10.44}$$

and let $\mathcal{I}(\pi, i) = \mathcal{I}_m(\pi, i)$. Note that $| \mathcal{I}(\pi, i) | = b$.

For example, consider the case where $m = 2$, $b = 1$, and $q_1 = q_2 = 2$. Then $n = 4$, $n_{(1)} = 2$, $n_{(2)} = 1$, and $S_{4:2} = S_4 \times S_2$. If $(\pi_1, \pi_2) \in S_4 \times S_2$ is given by $\pi_1 = (2,3,4,1)$ and $\pi_2 = (2,1)$, and $i = (1,2)$, then we have

$$\mathcal{I}_1^{\circ}(\pi, i) = (\pi_1(1), \pi_1(2)) = (2,3),$$

$$\mathcal{I}_2^{\circ}(\pi, i) = (\pi_2(1)) = (2),$$

$$\mathcal{I}_1(\pi, i) = (2,3) = (j_1, j_2),$$

$$\mathcal{I}_2(\pi, i) = (j_{\pi_2(2)}) = (j_1) = (2).$$

Note that each $\pi_1 \in S_4$ defines an ordering $a_{1,2} < a_{1,3} < a_{1,4} < a_{1,1}$ of the first attribute, and partitioning into $q_1 = 2$ buckets gives asset indices in the $i_1 = 1$ bucket as $\mathcal{I}_1(\pi, i) = (2,3)$. Similarly, π_2 defines an ordering $a_{2,3} < a_{2,2}$ of the second attribute for the assets in $\mathcal{I}_1(\pi, i)$, and taking the $i_2 = 2$ sub-bucket gives the asset index resulting from sequential sorting as $\mathcal{I}_2(\pi, i) = (2)$.

For simplicity, we assume equal weighting for the recorded attributes $r_{j_1}, \ldots, r_{j_b}$ in each bucket $\mathcal{I}(\pi, i)$, for all $i = (i_1, i_2, \ldots, i_m) \in \prod_{j=1}^{m} [q_j]$ and $\pi \in S_{n:m}$, and define

$$r_i = \frac{1}{b} \sum_{\pi \in S_{n:m}} \sum_{j \in \mathcal{I}(\pi, i)} r_j. \tag{10.45}$$

Now, for $1 \leq k \leq m$, denote by $a_k(\pi, i)$ the random vector

$$a_k(\pi, i) = (a_{k,j_1}, a_{k,j_2}, \ldots, a_{k,j_{n_{(k)}}}), \tag{10.46}$$

where $j_l = I_k(\pi, i)_l$ for $1 \leq l \leq n_{(k)}$, and let $\mathcal{R}_k(\pi, i) \subset \mathbb{R}^{n_{(k)}}$ be the subset

$$\mathcal{R}_k(\pi, i) = \{x_k \in \mathbb{R}^{n_{(k)}} \mid x_{k,1} < x_{k,2} < \cdots < x_{k,n_{(k)}}\}. \tag{10.47}$$

Note that by setting $z_{k,l} = x_{k,l} - x_{k,l+1}$ for $1 \leq l < n_{(k)}$, the region $\mathcal{R}_k(\pi, i)$ can be parametrized alternatively as

$$\mathcal{R}_k(\pi, i) = \{(x_{k,1}z_k) \in \mathbb{R} \times \mathbb{R}^{n_{(k)}-1} = \mathbb{R}^{n_{(k)}} \mid x_{k,1} \in \mathbb{R} \text{ and } z_k \prec 0\} \tag{10.48}$$

If we denote by $f_{r_i}(r)$ the density of r_i, then

$$f_{r_i}(r) = \sum_{\pi \in S_{n:m}} \int_{\mathcal{R}_m(\pi,i)} \int_{\mathcal{R}_{m-1}(\pi,i)} \cdots \int_{\mathcal{R}_1(\pi,i)} f_{a_1(\pi,i),\ldots,a_m(\pi,i),r_{\pi,i}}(x_1, x_2, \ldots, x_m, r) dx_1 \ldots dx_m,$$

where $x_k \in \mathbb{R}^{n_{(k)}}$ and $r_{\pi,i} = \sum_{j \in I(\pi,i)} r_j$. Standard properties of conditional probabilities imply

$$f_{a_1(\pi,i),\ldots,a_m(\pi,i),r_{\pi,i}}(x_1, x_2, \ldots, x_m, r) = f_{a_1(\pi,i)\mid a_2(\pi,i),\ldots,a_m(\pi,i),r_{\pi,i}}(x_1 \mid x_2, \ldots, x_m, r)$$

$$\cdot f_{a_2(\pi,i)\mid a_3(\pi,i),\ldots,a_m(\pi,i),r_{\pi,i}}(x_2 \mid x_3, \ldots, x_m, r)$$

$$\cdots$$

$$\cdot f_{a_m(\pi,i)\mid r_{\pi,i}}(x_m \mid r) f_{r_{\pi,i}}(r).$$

Denoting by $\mathcal{I}_k$ the integral involving the term $f_{a_k(\pi,i)\mid a_{k+1}(\pi,i)\ldots,a_m(\pi,i),r_{\pi,i}}(x_k \mid x_{k+1}, \ldots, x_m, r)$, we have

$$\mathcal{I}_k = \int_{\mathcal{R}_k(\pi,i)} f_{a_k(\pi,i)\mid a_{k+1}(\pi,i),\ldots,a_m(\pi,i),r_{\pi,i}}(x_k \mid x_{k+1}, \ldots, x_m, r) dx_k$$

$$= \int_{z_k \prec 0} \int_{x_{k,1} \in \mathbb{R}} f_{a_k(\pi,i)_1,z_k(\pi,i)\mid a_{k+1}(\pi,i),\ldots,a_m(\pi,i),r_{\pi,i}}(x_{k,1}, z_k \mid x_{k+1}, \ldots, x_m, r) dz_k dx_{k,1}$$

$$= \int_{z_k \prec 0} \int_{x_{k,1} \in \mathbb{R}} f_{a_k(\pi,i)_1\mid z_k(\pi,i),a_{k+1}(\pi,i),\ldots,a_m(\pi,i),r_{\pi,i}}(x_{k,1} \mid z_k, x_{k+1}, \ldots, x_m, r) dx_{k,1}$$

$$f_{z_k(\pi,i)\mid a_{k+1}(\pi,i),\ldots,a_m(\pi,i),r_{\pi,i}}(z_k \mid x_{k+1}, \ldots, x_m, r) dz_k.$$

Noting that the inner integral ranges over the entire domain of the variable $x_{k,1}$, we note that it evaluates to 1, and so that

$$\mathcal{I}_k = \int_{z_k \prec 0} f_{z_k(\pi,i)\mid a_{k+1}(\pi,i),\ldots,a_m(\pi,i),r_{\pi,i}}(z_k \mid x_{k+1}, \ldots, x_m, r) dz_k.$$

Substituting the integrals with the resulting expressions gives

$$f_{r_i}(r) = \sum_{\pi \in S_{n:m}} f_{r_{\pi,i}}(r) \int_{z_m < 0} f_{z_m(\pi,i)|r_{\pi,i}}(z_m, r)$$

$$\int_{z_{m-1} < 0} f_{z_{m-1}(\pi,i)|z_m(\pi,i),r_{\pi,i}}(z_{m-1} | z_m, r)$$

$$\vdots$$

$$\int_{z_1 < 0} f_{z_1(\pi,i)|z_2(\pi,i),\dots,z_m(\pi,i),r_{\pi,i}}(z_1 | z_2, \dots, z_m, r) dz_1 \cdots dz_m. \quad (10.49)$$

Since conditional densities $f_{z_k(\pi,i)|z_{k+1}(\pi,i),\dots,z_m(\pi,i),r_{\pi,i}}(z_k | z_{k+1}, \dots, z_m, r)$ are multivariate normal and $f_{r_{\pi,i}}(r)$ is normal, each term that appears in the sum for the density $f_{r_i}(r)$ is a product of a univariate normal density and a term that is an iterated integral involving multivariate cumulative normal densities. We provide some insights into this expression using a simple example in the next subsection where the density, $f_{r_i}(r)$, can be written explicitly without integrals.

10.4.2 Special case where $b = 1$, $m = 2$, $q_1 = q_2 = 2$, and $n = 4$

We consider in detail an example where $n = 4$ assets are sorted sequentially on $m = 2$ attributes. Quantile $q_1 = 1$, containing two assets ranked highest on the first attribute, is further sorted on the second attribute and the asset with the higher second attribute is then used to construct the portfolio over the holding period. It follows that there is $b = 1$ asset in the resulting portfolio in this example.

Let $a_1 = (a_{1,1}, \dots, a_{1,4})$ be the first attribute ranked, $a_2 = (a_{2,1}, \dots, a_{2,4})$ the second attribute ranked, and let $r = (r_1, \dots, r_4)$ the recorded attribute. For each $i = (i_1, i_2) \in \{1,2\} \times \{1,2\}$, let r_i be the recorded attribute in the i-th bucket after the two attributes are sorted in sequence. If we define $r_{\pi,i}$ by

$$r_{\pi,i} = r_{\pi_1(2(i_1-1)+\pi_2(i_2))}, \quad (10.50)$$

and the density of $r_{\pi,i}$ by $f_{\pi,i}(r)$, then we have

$$r_i = \sum_{\pi \in S_{4:2}} r_{\pi,i} = \sum_{\pi \in S_{4:2}} r_{\pi_1(2(i_1-1)+\pi_2(i_2))}, \quad (10.51)$$

and the density of r_i, denoted f_i for simplicity, is given by

$$f_i(r) = \sum_{\pi \in S_{4:2}} f_{\pi,i}(r) \int_{x_2 < 0} f_{z_2(\pi,i)|r_{\pi,i}}(x_2 | r) \int_{x_1 < 0} f_{z_1(\pi,i)|z_2(\pi,i),r_{\pi,i}}(x_1 | x_2, r) dx_1 dx_2$$

$$= \sum_{\pi \in S_{4:2}} f_{\pi,i}(r) \int_{(x'_1,x_2)' < 0} f_{z_1(\pi,i),z_2(\pi,i)|r_{\pi,i}}(x_1, x_2 | r) dx_1 dx_2$$

$$= \sum_{\pi \in S_{4:2}} f_{\pi,i}(r) \int_{x<0} f_{z(\pi,i)|r_{\pi,i}}(x \mid r)\, dx, \tag{10.52}$$

where $x = (x_1', x_2)'$ and

$$z_1(\pi, i) = (a_{1,\pi(1)} - a_{1,\pi(2)}, a_{1,\pi(2)} - a_{1,\pi(3)}, a_{1,\pi(3)} - a_{1,\pi(4)}),$$

$$z_2(\pi, i) = a_{2,\pi_1(2(i_1-1)+\pi_2(1))} - a_{2,\pi_1(2(i_1-1)+\pi_2(2))},$$

$$z(\pi, i) = (z_1'(\pi i), z_2(\pi, i))'.$$

Define $Q_1(\pi, i) = [\delta_{1,i_1} I_2 \;\; \delta_{2,i_1} I_2] P_{\pi_1} \in \mathbb{R}^{2\times4}$ and $Q_2(\pi, i) = [\delta_{1,i_2} \;\; \delta_{2,i_2}] P_{\pi_2}$, where $I_2 \in \mathbb{R}^{2\times2}$ is the identity matrix, $P_{\pi_k} \in \mathbb{R}^{n(k)\times n_{(k)}}$ is the permutation matrix corresponding to π_k for $1 \le k \le 2$, and let $Q(\pi, i) = Q_2(\pi, i) Q_1(\pi, i)$. Then we have

$$r_{\pi,i} = Q(\pi, i) r,$$

$$z_1(\pi, i) = D_3 P_{\pi_1} a_1,$$

$$z_2(\pi, i) = D_1 P_{\pi_2} Q_1(\pi, i) a_2,$$

where $D_k \in \mathbb{R}^{k\times(k+1)}$ is given by

$$
D_k = \begin{bmatrix}
1 & -1 & 0 & 0 & \cdots & 0 & 0 & 0 \\
0 & 1 & -1 & 0 & \cdots & 0 & 0 & 0 \\
\cdots & \cdots & \cdots & \cdots & \cdots & \cdots & \cdots & \cdots \\
0 & 0 & 0 & 0 & \cdots & 0 & 1 & -1
\end{bmatrix},
$$

and so

$$
\begin{bmatrix} z_1(\pi, i) \\ z_2(\pi, i) \\ r_{\pi,i} \end{bmatrix} =
\begin{bmatrix}
D_3 P_{\pi_1} & O_{3\times4} & O_{3\times4} \\
O_{1\times4} & D_1 P_{\pi_2} Q_1(\pi, i) & O_{1\times4} \\
O_{1\times4} & O_{1\times4} & Q(\pi, i)
\end{bmatrix}
\begin{bmatrix} a_1 \\ a_2 \\ r \end{bmatrix}
$$

$$
\begin{bmatrix} z(\pi, i) \\ r_{\pi,i} \end{bmatrix} =
\begin{bmatrix}
A(\pi, i) & O_{4\times4} \\
O_{1\times8} & Q(\pi, i)
\end{bmatrix}
\begin{bmatrix} a \\ r \end{bmatrix},
$$

where $z(\pi, i) = (z_1'(\pi i), z_2(\pi i))'$, $a = (a_1', a_2')'$, and

$$
A(\pi, i) = \begin{bmatrix}
D_3 P_{\pi_1} & O_{3\times4} \\
O_{1\times4} & D_1 P_{\pi_2} Q_1(\pi, i)
\end{bmatrix}
$$

We remark that we have not made any assumptions on the joint distributional properties of the underlying asset attributes and returns. However, to provide a relatively simple analytic expression for $f_i(r)$, we assume in the remainder of this subsection that

$$
\begin{bmatrix} a \\ r \end{bmatrix} \sim \mathcal{N} \left(\begin{bmatrix} \bar{a} \\ \bar{r} \end{bmatrix}, \begin{bmatrix} \Lambda_{a,a} & \Lambda_{a,r} \\ \Lambda_{r,a} & \Lambda_{r,r} \end{bmatrix} \right),
$$

then it follows that

$$
\begin{bmatrix} z(\pi, i) \\ r_{\pi,i} \end{bmatrix} \sim \mathcal{N} \left(\begin{bmatrix} \bar{z}(\pi i) \\ \bar{r}_{\pi,i} \end{bmatrix}, \begin{bmatrix} A(\pi i)\Lambda_{a,a}A(\pi i)' & A(\pi i)\Lambda_{a,r}Q(\pi i)' \\ Q(\pi i)\Lambda_{r,a}A(\pi i)' & Q(\pi i)\Lambda_{r,r}Q(\pi i)' \end{bmatrix} \right),
$$

and

$$
z(\pi, i) \mid r_{\pi,i} \sim \mathcal{N} \left(\bar{z}(\pi i) + \frac{\Lambda_{z,r}(\pi i)(r_{\pi,i} - \bar{r}_{\pi,i})}{\sigma^2_{\pi,i}}, \Lambda_{z,z}(\pi, i) - \frac{\Lambda_{z,r}(\pi i)\Lambda_{r,z}(\pi i)}{\sigma^2_{\pi,i}} \right),
$$

where for notational convenience we have defined

$$
\bar{z}(\pi, i) = A(\pi, i)\bar{a},
$$

$$
\bar{r}_{\pi,i} = Q(\pi, i)\bar{r},
$$

$$
\Lambda_{z,z}(\pi, i) = A(\pi, i)\Lambda_{a,a}A(\pi, i)',
$$

$$
\Lambda_{z,r}(\pi, i) = A(\pi, i)\Lambda_{a,r}Q(\pi, i)',
$$

$$
\sigma^2_{\pi,i} = Q(\pi, i)\Lambda_{r,r}Q(\pi, i)'.
$$

It follows from Equation (10.52) and the definitions introduced above that

$$
f_i(r) = \sum_{\pi \in S_{4:2}} \phi_1(r; \bar{r}_{\pi,i}, \sigma^2_{\pi,i})\Phi_4(0; \mu_{\pi,i}(r), \Lambda_{\pi,i}),
$$

where

$$
\mu_{\pi,i}(r) = A(\pi, i)\bar{a} + \frac{A(\pi, i)\Lambda_{a,r}Q(\pi, i)'(r - \bar{r}_{\pi,i})}{\sigma^2_{\pi,i}},
$$

$$
\Lambda_{\pi,i} = A(\pi, i)\Lambda_{a,a}A(\pi, i)' - \frac{A(\pi, i)\Lambda_{a,r}Q(\pi, i)'Q(\pi, i)\Lambda_{r,a}A(\pi, i)'}{\sigma^2_{\pi,i}}.
$$

In this special case, we find that $f_i(r)$ once again decomposes as a sum of SUN densities, and the expression for $f_i(r)$ comprises of $4! \times 2! = 48$ such terms corresponding to the permutations in $S_{4:2}$. However, examination of Equation (10.49) shows that $f_i(r)$ will not decompose as a sum of SUN densities in general due to the iterated integrals involving multivariate cumulative normal distributions. This is in contrast to the returns on independently sorted portfolios considered in Section 10.3 where it was possible to decompose the pdf of the holding period portfolio returns as a sum of SUN densities.

It should also be noted that the number of terms that appear in $f_i(r)$ increases very quickly with the number of assets and the attributes on which the assets are sorted. For example, with $n = 1,000$ assets, $m = 2$ attributes, $n_{(1)} = 1,000$, and $n_{(2)} = 500$, there would be $1,000! \times 500! \approx 10^{6,471}$ terms which is not computationally feasible even with modern computers. However, it is possible to obtain accurate numerical approximations of $f_i(r)$ using Monte Carlo simulation even in such cases.

10.5   CONCLUSION

The somewhat formidable analysis presented in this chapter has a practical consequence. If we start with the simplifying assumption that our financial data are multivariate normal, then the act of sorting will mean that the consequent holding period returns will be non-normally distributed. Furthermore, the nature of sorting can be seen to influence the structure of the return distributions as we demonstrate explicitly. Broadly speaking, they will be mixtures of unified skew-normal (SUN) distributions, which are generically skewed and kurtotic. Recognition of this fact goes a long way to understanding why momentum crashes occur, as reported for example by Daniel and Moskowitz (2016), and this chapter provides an alternative explanation to macroeconomic explanations such as rebounding of loser stocks following a recession.

APPENDIX A. PROOFS

10.A.1   PROOF OF LEMMA 1

Firstly, since $D_{X,\tau} \cap D_{X,\nu} = \emptyset$ if $\tau \neq \nu$, and $\cup_{\tau \in S_n} D_{X,\tau} = \mathbb{R}^{mn}$ almost surely, it follows that $\{D_{X,\tau} | \tau \in S_n\}$ is a partition of $\mathbb{R}^{mn}$. So using the relationship between joint and marginal densities, we obtain

$$f_Z(z) = \int_{x \in \mathbb{R}^{mn}} f_{X,Z}(x, z) dx = \sum_{\tau \in S_n} \int_{x \in D_{X,\tau}} f_{X,Z}(x, z) dx.$$

But since $Z = w'_\tau Y$ on $D_{X,\tau}$, it follows that

$$f_Z(z) = \sum_{\tau \in S_n} \int_{x \in D_{X,\tau}} f_{X,w'_\tau Y}(x, z) dx = \sum_{\tau \in S_n} f_{w'_\tau Y}(z) \int_{x \in D_{X,\tau}} f_{X|w'_\tau Y}(x | z) dx,$$

which is Equation (10.19).

10.A.2   PROOF OF THEOREM 3

Firstly, for any $\tau = (\tau_1, \dots, \tau_m) \in S_n$, considering the map $\varphi_\tau = (\varphi_{\tau_1}, \dots, \varphi_{\tau_m})$, where $\varphi_{\tau_i} : \mathbb{R}^n \to \mathbb{R}^n$ are given by

$$\varphi_{\tau_i}(x_i) = \begin{bmatrix} 1 & O_{1\times(n-1)} \\ O_{(n-1)\times 1} & D_{\tau_i} \end{bmatrix} x_i,$$

and applying the arguments similar to those used in the proof of the Kwon and Satchell (2018) Theorem 2 gives

$$\int_{x \in D_{X,\tau}} f_{X|w'Y}(x|z)dx = \int_{v \in \mathbb{R}^{m(n-1)}_-} f_{D_\tau X|w'Y}(v|z)dv,$$

where $D_\tau \in \mathbb{R}^{m(n-1)\times mn}$ is as defined in Equation (10.21). Next, since $(X, Y')'$ is multivariate normal as given by Equation (10.22), if $w_\tau \neq 0$ then $w_\tau' Y \sim \mathcal{N}_1(w_\tau' \mu_Y, w_\tau' \Lambda_{Y,Y} w_\tau)$, and by Theorem 1

$$D_\tau X \mid w_\tau' Y \sim \mathcal{N}_{m(n-1)}(\mu_{w'Y,\tau}, \Lambda_{\tau,\tau}),$$

where $\mu_{w'Y,\tau}$ and $\Lambda_{\tau,\tau}$ are as defined in Equations (10.26) and (10.27) respectively. Finally, it follows from Lemma 1 that

$$f_Z(z) = \sum_{\tau \in S_n} \int_{x \in D_{X,\tau}} f_{X|w_\tau'Y}(x|z) f_{w_\tau'Y}(z)dx$$

$$= \sum_{\tau \in S_n} f_{w_\tau'Y}(z) \int_{v \in \mathbb{R}^{m(n-1)}_-} f_{D_\tau X|w_\tau'Y}(v|z)dv,$$

$$= \sum_{\tau \in S_n} \phi_1(z; w_\tau' \mu_Y, w_\tau' \Lambda_{Y,Y} w_\tau) \Phi_{m(n-1)}(0; \mu_{w'Y,\tau}, \Lambda_{\tau,\tau}),$$

which is Equation (10.25). The alternative expression Equation (10.28) follows from similar arguments by rewriting in Lemma 1

$$f_Z(z) = \sum_{\tau \in S_n} \int_{x \in D_{X,\tau}} f_{X,w'Y}(x,z)dx = \sum_{\tau \in S_n} \int_{v \in \mathbb{R}^{m(n-1)}_-} f_{w'Y|D_\tau X}(z|v) f_{D_\tau X}(v)dv, \qquad (10.53)$$

and using the fact that $D_\tau X \sim \mathcal{N}_{m(n-1)}(D_\tau \mu_X, D_\tau \Lambda_{X,X} D_\tau')$ and $w'Y \mid D_\tau X \sim \mathcal{N}_1(\gamma_{D_\tau X,\tau}, \tau,\tau)$, where $\gamma_{D_\tau X,\tau}$ and $Y_{\tau,\tau}$ are as defined in Equations (10.29) and (10.30) respectively.

10.A.3   PROOF OF THEOREM 4

Since $(X', Y')'$ is multivaraite normal as described in Equation (10.22), we have that for any $\tau \in S_n$

$$\begin{bmatrix} Y \\ D_\tau X \end{bmatrix} \sim \mathcal{N}_{n+m(n-1)} \left(\begin{bmatrix} \mu_Y \\ D_\tau \mu_X \end{bmatrix}, \begin{bmatrix} \Lambda_{Y,Y} & \Lambda_{Y,X} D_\tau' \\ D_\tau \Lambda_{X,Y} & D_\tau \Lambda_{X,X} D_\tau' \end{bmatrix} \right), \tag{10.54}$$

and so using the expression for $f_Z(z)$ from Equation (10.54) we have

$$Y \mid D_\tau X \sim \mathcal{N}_n(\mu_Y(\tau D_\tau X), \Lambda_{Y,Y}(\tau)), \tag{10.55}$$

where $\mu_Y(\tau, v)$ and $\Lambda_{Y,Y}(\tau)$ are as defined in Equations (10.36) and (10.37) respectively. Applying Theorem 2, we obtain

$$\mu_p(Y|D_\tau X) = \sum_{\substack{k,l \in \mathbb{N} \\ k+2l = \eta}} \sum_{v \in Q(k,2l)} \left(\prod_{i=1}^k \mu_Y(\tau, D_\tau X)_{v(i)} \right) \left(\prod_{i=1}^l \Lambda_{Y,Y}(\tau)_{v(k+2i-1),v(k+2i)} \right),$$

and so using the expression for $f_Z(z)$ from Equation (10.28) gives

$$\mathbb{E}[Y_p \mathbb{I}_{D_{X,r}}] = \sum_{v \in S_n} \int_{v \in D_{X,r}} \left(\int_{y \in \mathbb{R}^n} y_p f_{Y|D_\tau X}(y \mid v) \, dy \right) \mathbb{I}_{D_{X,r}}(x) f_X(x) \, dx$$

$$= \int_{v \in \mathbb{R}_-^{m(n-1)}} \mu_p(Y \mid v) \phi_{m(n-1)}(v; D_\tau \mu_X, D_\tau \Lambda_{X,X} D_\tau') \, dv.$$

Now, considering the special case where $d = 1$, so that $Y_p = Y_i$ for some $i \in [n]$, we have

$$\mathbb{E}[Y_i \mathbb{I}_{D_{X,r}}] = \int_{v \in \mathbb{R}_-^{m(n-1)}} \mu_{(i),\tau}(Y \mid v) \phi_{m(n-1)}(v; D_\tau \mu_X, D_\tau \Lambda_{X,X} D_\tau') \, dv,$$

where, on defining $\alpha_{i,\tau} = (D_\tau \Lambda_{X,X} D_\tau')^{-1} D_\tau \Lambda_{X,Y} e_i$, we have from Equation (10.36)

$$\mu_{(i),\tau}(Y \mid v) = \mu_{Y_i} + \alpha_{i,\tau}'(v - D_\tau \mu_X).$$

Substituting $\mu_{(i),\tau}(Y \mid v)$ into the expression for $\mathbb{E}[Y_i \mathbb{I}_{D_{X,r}}]$ gives

$$\mathbb{E}[Y_i \mathbb{I}_{D_{X,r}}] = \mu_{Y_i} \Phi_{m(n-1)}(0; D_\tau \mu_X, D_\tau \Lambda_{X,X} D_\tau')$$

$$+ \int_{v \in \mathbb{R}_-^{m(n-1)}} \alpha'_{i,\tau}(v - D_\tau \mu_X) \phi_{m(n-1)}(v; D_\tau \mu_X, D_\tau \Lambda_{X,X} D_\tau') \, dv.$$

Denoting by $\mathcal{I}$ the integral term on the right-hand side, we note from the expression for $\alpha_{i,\tau}$ that

$$\mathcal{I} = -e_i' \Lambda_{X,Y}' D_\tau' \int_{v \in \mathbb{R}_-^{m(n-1)}} \nabla_v \phi_{m(n-1)}(v; D_\tau \mu_X, D_\tau \Lambda_{X,X} D_\tau') dv$$

$$= -\sum_{j=1}^{m(n-1)} (D_\tau \Lambda_{X,Y} e_i)_j \int_{v \in \mathbb{R}_-^{m(n-1)}} \frac{\partial}{\partial v_j} \phi_{m(n-1)}(v; D_\tau \mu_X, D_\tau \Lambda_{X,X} D_\tau') dv$$

$$= -\sum_{j=1}^{m(n-1)} (D_\tau \Lambda_{X,Y})_{j,i}$$

$$\int_{v_{-j} \in \mathbb{R}_-^{m(n-1)-1}} \int_{v_j \in \mathbb{R}_-} \frac{\partial}{\partial v_j} \phi_{m(n-1)}(v; D_\tau \mu_X, D_\tau \Lambda_{X,X} D_\tau') dv_{-j}$$

$$= -\sum_{j=1}^{m(n-1)} (D_\tau \Lambda_{X,Y})_{j,i} \int_{v_{-j} \in \mathbb{R}_-^{m(n-1)-1}} [\phi_{m(n-1)}(v; D_\tau \mu_X, D_\tau \Lambda_{X,X} D_\tau')]_{-\infty}^0 dv_{-j}$$

$$= -\sum_{j=1}^{m(n-1)} (D_\tau \Lambda_{X,Y})_{j,i} \int_{v_{-j} \in \mathbb{R}_-^{m(n-1)-1}} \phi_{m(n-1)}(v; D_\tau \mu_X, D_\tau \Lambda_{X,X} D_\tau')_{v_j=0} dv_{-j}.$$

Now, applying Theorem 1 with $X = v$, $X_1 = v_{-j}$, and $X_2 = v_j \in \mathbb{R}$, gives

$$\phi_{m(n-1)}(v; D_\tau \mu_X, D_\tau \Lambda_{X,X} D_\tau') = \phi_{m(n-1)-1}(v_{-j}; \gamma_j^\star(v_j), Y_j)\phi_1(v_j; m_j, s_j^2),$$

where m_j, s_j^2, and Y_j are as defined in Theorem 3.3, and

$$\gamma_j^\star(v_j) = (D_\tau \mu_X)_{-j} + \frac{v_j - m_j}{s_j^2}(D_\tau \Lambda_{X,X} D_\tau')_{-j,j},$$

so that γ_j defined in Equation (10.39) corresponds to $\gamma_j^\star(0)$. It follows that

$$\mathcal{I} = -\sum_{j=1}^{m(n-1)} (D_\tau \Lambda_{X,Y})_{j,i}\phi_1(0; m_j, s_j^2) \int_{v_{-j} \in \mathbb{R}_-^{m(n-1)-1}} \phi_{m(n-1)-1}(v_{-j}; \gamma_j^\star(0), Y_j) dv_{-j}$$

$$= -\sum_{j=1}^{m(n-1)} (D_{\tau\tau} \Lambda_{X,Y})_{j,i}\phi_1(0; m_j, s_j^2)\Phi_{m(n-1)-1}(0; \gamma_j, Y_j),$$

and so

$$\mathbb{E}[Y_i \mathbb{1}_{D_{X,\tau}}] = \mu_{Y_i} \Phi_{m(n-1)}(0; D_\tau \mu_\tau, D_\tau \mu_\tau \Lambda_{X,X} D_\tau' \mu_\tau)$$

$$- \sum_{j=1}^{m(n-1)} (D_\tau \Lambda_{X,Y})_{j,i}\phi_1(0; m_j, s_j^2)\Phi_{m(n-1)-1}(0; \zeta_j, \Xi_j).$$

REFERENCES

Arellano-Valle, R. B. and Azzalini, A. (2006), 'On the Unification of Families of Skew-normal Distributions', *Scandinavian Journal of Statistics* **33**, 561–574.

Azzalini, A. and Valle, A. D. (1985), 'The Multivariate Skew-normal Distribution', *Biometrika* **83**, 715–726.

Belloni, A. and Winkler, R. L. (2011), 'On Multivariate Quantiles under Partial Orders', *Annals of Stochastics* **39**(2), 1125–1179.

Berk, J. B. (2000), 'Sorting out Sorts', *Journal of Finance* **55**(1), 407–427.

Black, F., Jensen, M. C. and Scholes, M. (1972), The Capital Asset Pricing Model: Some Empirical Tests, *in* M. C. Jensen, ed., *Studies in the Theory of Capital Markets*, Praeger Publishers, New York.

Black, F. and Scholes, M. (1974), 'The Effects of Dividend Policy on Common Stock Prices and Returns', *Journal of Financial Economics* **2**, 1–22.

Cattaneo, M. D., Crump, R. K., Farrell, M. H. and Schaumberg, E. (2019), Characteristic-Sorted Portfolios: Estimation and Inference, Staff report no. 788, Federal Reserve Bank of New York.

Cremers, K. J. M., Petajisto, A. and Zitzewitz, E. (2012), 'Should Benchmark Indices have Alpha? Revisiting Performance Evaluation', *Critical Finance Review* **2**, 1–48.

Daniel, K. and Moskowitz, T. J. (2016), 'Momentum Crashes', *Journal of Financial Economics* **122**(2), 221–247.

Hwang, S. and Satchell, S. E. (1999), 'Modelling Emerging Market Risk Premia using Higher Moments', *International Journal of Finance and Economics* **4**, 271–296.

Kan, R. (1999), On the Explanatory Power of Asset Pricing Models Across and Within Portfolios, Working paper, University of Toronto.

Kan, R. (2008), 'From Moments of Sum to Moments of Product', *Journal of Multivariate Analysis* **99**, 542–554.

Knight, J., Satchell, S. E. and Zhang, J. Q. (2013), 'Sequential Variable Selection as Bayesian Pragmatism in Linear Factor Models', *Journal of Mathematical Finance* **3**, 230–236.

Kwon, O. K. and Satchell, S. (2018), 'The Distribution of Cross Sectional Momentum Returns', *Journal of Economic Dynamics and Control* **94**, 225–241.

Lambert, M. and Hübner, G. (2013), 'Comoment Risk and Stock Returns', *Journal of Empirical Finance* **23**, 191–205.

Lambert, M. and Hübner, G. (2014), *Size Matters, Book Value Does Not! The Fama-French Empirical CAPM Revisited*, Working Paper, HEC Liège.

Liu, J., Stambaugh, R. F. and Yuan, Y. (2018), 'Absolving Beta of Volatility's Effects', *Journal of Financial Economics* **128**(1), 1–15.

Lo, A. and MacKinlay, C. (1990), 'When are Contrarian Profits Due to Stock Market Overreaction?', *Review of Financial Studies* **3**(2), 175–205.

Muirhead, R. J. (1982), *Aspects of Multivariate Statistical Theory*, John Wiley & Sons, New Jersey.

Stambaugh, R. F., Yu, J. and Yuan, Y. (2015), 'Arbitrage Asymmetry and the Idiosyncratic Volatility Puzzle', *Journal of Finance* **70**, 1903–1948.

Weller, G. B. and Eddy, W. F. (2015), 'Multivariate Order Statics: Theory and Application', *Annual Review of Statistics and Application* **2**, 237–257.

Withers, C. S. (1985), 'The Moments of the Multivariate Normal', *Bulletin of Australian Mathematics Society* **32**, 103–107.

CHAPTER 11

Exploiting the Countercyclical Properties of Momentum and other Factor Premia – A Cross-Country Perspective

STEFANO CAVAGLIA VADIM MOROZ and LOUIS SCOTT

11.1   INTRODUCTION

Smart beta- or factor premia-based strategies are traditionally motivated as sources of return that can be 'manufactured' relatively cheaply and in large scale as they are linked to a behavioural or a structural inefficiency.[1] Cochrane (1999) argues that investors will hold varying quantities of factor premia in their portfolio as a means of hedging recession and other risks; hence he suggests that investors will want to hold multifactor efficient rather than mean-variant efficient portfolios.[2]

Robert Merton, one of finance's pioneering giants, has recently championed the view that the investment management industry may need to refocus the objectives of products developed for an aspiring retiree (Artee henceforth).[3] Indeed the merits of products and strategies are often evaluated in terms of the expected return and risk they deliver; risk is generally measured by the volatility of returns. Though this measure may suffice for one period portfolio construction problems, it has limited relevance in a multi-period context. Plan sponsors, industry funds and wealth managers are typically concerned with delivering to their constituents a *future* income stream with a high degree of certainty upon retiring. Large drawdowns are a significant risk to achieving

---

[1] An excellent review of the practical implementation of factor-based investment strategies can be found in Bender et al. (2013).
[2] Fama provides a comprehensive analytical framework in Fama (1996).
[3] See Merton (2007).

this objective.[4] Indeed, the often-touted benefits of return compounding are limited if Artee's wealth is struck by a series of drawdowns during his accumulation path. Though constructing investment strategies that generate high risk adjusted returns is an important part of helping Artee meet his/her objectives, managing downside risk is essential for success. It follows that the co-variation of investment strategies plays a critical role in achieving investment success in a multi-period context.[5]

In this chapter, we extend and corroborate the findings of Scott and Cavaglia (2016) who first illustrated the potential benefits of a factor premia overlay to an inter-temporal wealth accumulation strategy that is fully invested in global equities. We examine a panel of five local factor premia in each of twenty-one developed equity markets and five regions. The premia considered span the equity asset class and include size, value, momentum, low beta and quality. In all instances we find that wealth accumulation is significantly enhanced by a time invariant, equal weighted allocation to these premia. The enhancement is driven in part by the mean return of the premia but more importantly by their generally positive payoff in adverse market environments – particularly relevant to momentum, 'betting against beta' (BAB) and to quality. Applying conventional measures of risk aversion we quantify the importance of downside protection to supporting the attainment of investors' goals. We provide robust, cross-country evidence that both momentum and quality are value enhancing overlays even when these premia exhibit a zero expected return.

Our work is presented in three sections. In Section 11.2, we outline our methodology. In Section 11.3 we examine alternative investment strategies across countries and regions. In Section 11.4 we provide a utility-based framework for quantifying the hedging value of a factor premia overlay. Our concluding section summarizes the results and suggests areas for further investigation.

11.2 METHODOLOGY

Artee's retirement income problem is often presented as determining the level of contributions to a specific investment programme that will result in an *expected* wealth level at retirement; this expected wealth level can then be translated into an equivalent annuity.[6] Clearly the problem becomes more complex when one allows for time variation in the investment program as for instance with a dynamic asset allocation strategy.

---

[4]Investors often exit the market at the trough and miss the reversion in asset prices. Sequencing risk however only compounds the impact of large drawdowns.

[5]Alternatively one can introduce active asset allocation strategies that produce the same effect. Basu et al. (2011) show that traditional target date retirement strategies can be enhanced by tactically de-risking part of Artee's accumulated wealth.

[6]We understand that there are numerous strategies in the marketplace that aim to deliver an 'income' stream by investing in high yielding stocks. We adopt a total return approach where income yield follows naturally from the solution rather than being an explicit choice variable. We also note that our characterisation of the retirement income problem is a simplification of more sophisticated specifications of the problem. An elegant statement of the problem can be found in Das et al. (2018a, 2018b).

Investment 'calculators' are often used to support these analyses; however, seldom do they report the full distribution of outcomes that might come about or the assumptions that underlie the 'calculations'.

In order to simplify our illustration that factors matter, we will consider a baseline investment strategy comprised of a passive, fully invested exposure to equities over a 20-year horizon. We will then examine the effect of adding an overlay of factor premia to the distribution of terminal wealth. An empirically fitted utility function will then be used to quantify the hedging benefits of the factor premia to the baseline investment strategy. This is examined on a country by country basis for each of twenty-one markets and five regions. We obtain from the AQR public website returns on equity indexes and premia for size, value, momentum, and quality.[7] This is complemented by data for the BAB premium maintained by Frazzini.[8]

Many investment calculators rely on Monte Carlo simulations of asset returns. Unfortunately such techniques assume independence of observations and this may not be consistent with some of the observed empirical regularities in the data. Clearly serial correlation and conditional covariation of investment strategies are important dynamics to capture when one is concerned with drawdown risk. We provide descriptive summary statistics that illustrate the qualitative attributes of our data for the period 31 July 1996 to 31 July 2019.[9]

In Table 11.1 we provide the monthly average returns and standard deviation of returns for the premia. Given the breadth of the data set we examine, our qualitative assessment is limited to being broad brushed. We note that:

- Historical returns for the size premium, over the period analysed, are negative across nearly every country except the USA, Austria and the Netherlands, thus confirming recent scepticism for this factor.
- Historical returns on value, momentum, BAB and quality have been quite high relative to those of the equity market. The returns to momentum, BAB, and quality at the regional level exceed those of the equity market.
- Nationally, factor premia tend to have larger volatilities than when aggregated at the regional level. This suggests that the factors have both local and global drivers at work and that local effects are not synchronized across countries.[10]

The cross-country evidence presented here-in provides convincing support for the view that risk premia offer an interesting alternative source of return to the conventional exposure to the equity or the bond market.

---

[7]The construction of these factors is outlined in Asness, Frazzini and Pedersen (2017); the data is obtained on https://www.aqr.com/Insights/Datasets/Quality-Minus-Junk-Factors-Monthly

[8]The construction of this factor is outlined in Frazzini and Pedersen (2014); the data is obtained on Andrea Frazzini's home page http://people.stern.nyu.edu/afrazzin/data_library.htm

[9]The length of history available varies across countries and factors. To mitigate the effect of global factors on country specific effects, we limit the analysis to one global common time period.

[10]This is more formally examined in Griffin (2002) and Griffin, Ji and Martin (2003).

TABLE 11.1 Descriptive statistics

	Equity Mkt		Size		Value		Momentum		BAB		Quality	
	mean (%)	stdv (%)	mean (%)	stdv (%)	mean (%)	stdv (%)	mean (%)	stdv (%)	mean (%)	stdv (%)	mean (%)	stdv (%)
Australia	0.69	6.79	−0.19	3.39	0.13	3.55	1.54	4.29	1.25	4.41	0.45	2.66
Austria	0.35	6.79	0.19	3.74	0.63	4.63	0.39	5.67	0.58	6.75	0.26	4.27
Belgium	0.58	5.60	−0.23	3.56	0.27	4.31	0.77	4.87	0.46	4.61	0.00	3.88
Canada	0.35	5.18	−0.11	2.60	0.05	4.36	1.17	5.35	1.55	4.28	0.78	4.00
Switzerland	0.53	4.95	−0.09	2.71	−0.01	3.53	0.69	4.55	0.52	4.52	0.46	3.89
Germany	0.34	5.92	−0.48	3.00	0.26	4.24	1.00	5.24	0.78	4.95	0.59	2.79
Denmark	0.67	5.36	−0.10	3.45	−0.37	4.39	1.05	4.50	0.59	4.85	0.25	3.70
Spain	0.59	6.66	−0.41	3.82	0.16	4.11	0.59	5.12	0.54	4.81	0.26	4.22
Finland	0.59	7.66	−0.22	4.40	0.23	6.21	0.80	6.17	0.80	6.28	−0.19	4.83
France	0.51	5.81	−0.15	3.00	0.14	3.89	0.62	4.65	1.20	4.66	0.46	3.24
UK	0.39	5.00	−0.24	3.47	0.14	3.84	0.92	4.54	0.32	4.56	0.38	2.57
Hong Kong	0.64	7.92	−0.20	4.71	0.45	4.57	0.33	5.50	1.42	6.22	0.56	5.65
Ireland	0.46	7.54	−0.24	5.81	−0.32	7.09	0.61	9.98	0.15	10.43	0.32	10.25
Italy	0.22	6.88	−0.26	3.41	−0.11	4.65	0.70	4.86	0.60	3.97	0.74	4.05
Japan	0.11	5.94	−0.01	2.64	0.74	3.29	0.01	4.62	0.31	4.15	0.24	2.96
Netherlands	0.53	5.42	0.02	3.19	0.10	4.83	0.27	5.16	0.75	4.55	0.12	4.41
Norway	0.57	7.27	−0.12	3.59	−0.15	5.19	0.90	6.04	0.83	5.81	0.38	4.30
New Zealand	0.57	6.62	−0.03	3.59	−0.50	5.31	1.02	4.37	0.98	5.81	0.07	3.25
Singapore	0.55	7.01	−0.14	3.92	0.38	4.36	0.26	5.88	1.00	3.80	0.28	4.26
Sweden	0.65	6.97	−0.27	3.62	0.06	5.39	0.65	5.93	0.92	5.54	0.56	3.68
USA	0.51	5.27	0.17	2.92	0.25	4.01	0.58	4.96	0.64	3.26	0.35	2.15
Global	0.48	4.41	−0.07	1.93	0.25	2.78	0.57	3.79	0.74	2.91	0.45	2.08
Gbl Ex USA	0.29	4.82	−0.07	1.93	0.37	2.75	0.63	3.59	0.76	2.78	0.50	1.97
Europe	0.42	5.06	−0.20	2.18	0.11	3.00	0.84	3.83	0.75	3.26	0.43	2.32
N America	0.58	4.46	−0.06	2.54	0.05	3.41	0.55	4.57	0.76	3.68	0.47	2.54
Pacific	0.33	5.98	−0.05	2.33	0.66	2.89	0.30	4.08	0.59	3.45	0.36	2.49

Source: Statistics are derived from data that are sourced as follows: The time series for the size, value, momentum and quality factors are obtained from Asness, Frazzini and Pedersen (2017). Quality Minus Junk, Monthly, Excel Sheet (2019), https://www.aqr.com/Insights/Datasets/Quality-Minus-Junk-Factors-Monthly. The time series for the BAB factor is outlined in Frazzini and Pedersen (2014). BAB equity factors, monthly (2019), http://people.stern.nyu.edu/afrazzin/data_library.htm

In Table 11.2, we report the conditional returns of the factors across different market environments; the regimes we consider are favourable (positive) or unfavourable (negative) equity market returns. For the period analysed we note that:

- The Size factor tends to be procyclical which is in line with the view that small cap stocks provide high market beta exposures.
- Momentum, BAB and quality tend to have counter-cyclical return payoffs; namely in adverse market conditions the return to these premia is significantly positive.

TABLE 11.2 Descriptive statistics (conditional returns)

	Equity Mkt		Size		Value		Momentum		BAB		Quality	
	Mkt Down (%)	Mkt Up (%)	Mkt Down (%)	Mkt Up (%)	Mkt Down (%)	Mkt Up (%)	Mkt Down (%)	Mkt Up (%)	Mkt Down (%)	Mkt Up (%)	Mkt Down (%)	Mkt Up (%)
Australia	−5.09	4.13	−0.87	0.05	0.22	0.10	1.89	1.39	0.04	1.81	1.69	−0.34
Austria	−5.08	4.43	1.08	−0.57	0.05	1.09	1.00	0.14	1.23	0.19	1.51	−0.75
Belgium	−4.27	4.07	−0.08	−0.33	−0.13	0.31	2.07	−0.03	0.72	0.01	1.49	−1.14
Canada	−4.47	4.30	−0.66	0.29	0.44	−0.28	1.89	0.98	0.63	3.09	2.61	−0.46
Switzerland	−3.75	3.64	0.15	0.05	−0.43	0.28	1.87	0.01	2.01	−0.50	2.38	−0.99
Germany	−4.78	4.16	0.33	−1.04	0.06	0.34	3.01	0.02	2.03	0.34	1.94	−0.40
Denmark	−4.28	3.96	0.68	−0.68	0.24	−0.71	1.34	1.11	0.53	0.84	0.61	0.00
Spain	−5.16	4.87	0.24	−0.57	−0.48	0.52	2.18	−0.62	1.45	0.07	2.50	−1.56
Finland	−6.03	5.48	1.10	−1.52	1.94	−1.32	1.78	0.21	1.52	0.49	−0.61	−0.15
France	−4.74	4.08	0.65	−0.78	−0.07	0.42	2.10	−0.20	2.44	0.71	2.19	−0.86
UK	−3.71	3.36	−0.63	0.00	−0.34	0.65	2.07	0.11	−0.11	0.66	1.72	−0.59
Hong Kong	−6.17	4.85	0.27	−0.46	0.01	0.84	1.35	−0.09	2.15	1.49	3.04	−1.12
Ireland	−6.03	4.90	0.40	−0.82	−2.02	0.79	2.86	−1.44	0.33	0.26	4.08	−2.56
Italy	−5.15	4.95	0.07	−0.23	−0.75	0.38	2.22	−0.65	1.07	0.41	2.70	−0.98
Japan	−4.11	3.61	−0.11	−0.07	0.66	0.53	0.90	−0.40	1.08	−0.16	1.79	−1.06
Netherlands	−4.72	3.97	0.45	−0.09	−1.73	1.76	1.94	−0.86	1.69	0.12	2.79	−1.83
Norway	−5.63	5.31	0.72	−0.90	−1.07	0.37	2.46	0.35	1.24	0.91	1.99	−0.75
New Zealand	−4.65	4.39	0.26	0.05	−0.17	−0.54	1.50	0.94	0.15	1.70	0.30	−0.09
Singapore	−5.04	4.63	−0.95	0.40	0.17	0.87	1.63	−0.86	0.55	1.29	2.04	−1.14
Sweden	−5.12	5.10	−0.08	−0.45	0.04	−0.12	2.12	−0.01	1.80	0.49	1.73	−0.30
USA	−4.27	3.22	−0.84	0.53	−0.11	0.09	1.64	−0.38	2.09	−0.14	2.40	−0.65
Global	−3.90	3.14	−0.28	0.09	0.14	0.19	1.75	−0.09	1.76	0.27	2.11	−0.55
Gbl Ex USA	−3.87	3.38	−0.08	−0.21	0.21	0.38	1.82	0.12	1.15	0.86	1.81	−0.50
Europe	−4.05	3.76	0.01	−0.29	−0.34	0.56	2.29	−0.08	1.53	0.38	2.06	−0.79
N America	−4.26	3.25	−0.79	0.50	−0.05	0.07	1.65	−0.28	1.98	0.07	2.40	−0.61
Pacific	−4.22	3.60	−0.23	−0.07	0.67	0.41	1.12	0.07	0.93	0.74	1.72	−0.64

Source: Statistics are derived from data that is sourced as follows: The time series for the size, value, momentum and quality factors are obtained from Asness, Frazzini and Pedersen (2017). Quality Minus Junk, Monthly, Excel Sheet (2019), https://www.aqr.com/Insights/Datasets/Quality-Minus-Junk-Factors-Monthly. The time series for the BAB factor is outlined in Frazzini and Pedersen (2014). BAB equity factors, monthly (2019), http://people.stern.nyu.edu/afrazzin/data_library.htm

■ With few country-level exceptions, the data suggests that most of the return to the momentum strategy is captured in adverse market environments. This is somewhat at odds with the commonly held view that momentum is a 'return chasing' strategy that exploits bullish market conditions.

The cross-country evidence presented provides convincing support for the view that risk premia offer payoff patterns that are conditional on market conditions as postulated in Cochrane (1999). We have merely explored one such condition.

TABLE 11.3 Descriptive statistics (conditional correlation)

	Size		Value		Momentum		BAB		Quality	
	Mkt Down	Mkt Up	Mkt Down	Mkt Up	Mkt Down	Mkt Up	Mkt Down	Mkt Up	Mkt Down	Mkt Up
Australia	0.28	0.23	−0.11	0.09	−0.01	−0.25	0.36	0.16	−0.47	−0.41
Austria	−0.06	−0.18	0.09	−0.02	−0.18	−0.28	−0.02	−0.16	−0.56	−0.30
Belgium	0.06	−0.04	0.18	0.15	−0.51	−0.39	−0.12	0.01	−0.57	−0.31
Canada	0.24	0.03	−0.17	−0.02	−0.04	−0.21	0.43	0.18	−0.41	−0.21
Switzerland	0.06	−0.15	0.03	0.21	−0.11	−0.22	−0.12	−0.06	−0.48	−0.41
Germany	−0.20	−0.15	0.04	0.22	−0.38	−0.34	−0.09	−0.22	−0.49	−0.36
Denmark	0.03	−0.01	−0.03	0.12	−0.26	−0.24	0.15	0.04	−0.40	−0.24
Spain	0.01	−0.09	0.22	0.08	−0.13	−0.25	−0.07	−0.31	−0.34	−0.53
Finland	−0.20	−0.51	−0.50	−0.27	−0.33	−0.23	−0.26	−0.32	0.38	0.01
France	0.11	−0.18	0.12	0.14	−0.23	−0.30	0.06	−0.17	−0.41	−0.33
UK	0.25	−0.08	0.00	0.33	−0.20	−0.35	0.27	−0.05	−0.44	−0.49
Hong Kong	0.33	0.04	0.03	0.14	−0.01	−0.48	0.35	−0.22	−0.51	−0.55
Italy	0.10	0.04	0.20	0.08	−0.34	−0.15	0.06	−0.07	−0.50	−0.31
Japan	0.04	−0.03	−0.21	0.08	−0.07	−0.12	0.00	0.08	−0.25	−0.49
Netherlands	0.06	−0.07	0.38	0.36	−0.32	−0.24	−0.10	−0.24	−0.51	−0.31
Norway	−0.07	−0.21	−0.10	0.10	−0.03	−0.07	0.20	0.01	−0.22	−0.26
New Zealand	−0.32	−0.04	0.19	0.16	−0.33	−0.22	0.07	0.06	−0.14	−0.20
Singapore	0.18	0.40	0.19	0.57	−0.25	−0.66	0.33	−0.25	−0.47	−0.67
Sweden	−0.06	−0.11	−0.02	−0.01	−0.23	−0.27	−0.06	−0.20	−0.40	−0.36
USA	0.25	0.08	0.09	0.17	−0.23	−0.32	−0.05	−0.38	−0.59	−0.38
Global	0.27	0.09	0.02	0.27	−0.18	−0.40	0.06	−0.36	−0.66	−0.58
Gbl Ex USA	0.15	0.01	−0.03	0.26	−0.18	−0.37	0.14	−0.17	−0.61	−0.58
Europe	0.15	−0.08	0.08	0.21	−0.29	−0.31	0.15	−0.15	−0.55	−0.47
N America	0.26	0.10	0.06	0.18	−0.20	−0.33	−0.01	−0.36	−0.59	−0.41
Pacific	0.14	0.00	−0.15	0.20	−0.02	−0.31	0.17	−0.07	−0.38	−0.58

Source: Statistics are derived from data that is sourced as follows: The time series for the size, value, momentum and quality factors are obtained from Asness, Frazzini and Pedersen (2017). Quality Minus Junk, Monthly, Excel Sheet (2019), https://www.aqr.com/Insights/Datasets/Quality-Minus-Junk-Factors-Monthly. The time series for the BAB factor is outlined in Frazzini and Pedersen (2014). BAB equity factors, monthly (2019), http://people.stern.nyu.edu/afrazzini/data_library.htm

In Table 11.3, we further explore the cyclicality of the premia by computing their correlation with the market conditional on equity market conditions. For the period analysed we note that:

- Momentum and quality are both uniformly countercyclical under the market conditions that are considered
- Value and size are broadly procyclical under the market conditions that are considered.
- BAB exhibits the only asymmetry. It is countercyclical in bullish market conditions and procyclical in adverse market conditions.

TABLE 11.4   Factor premia autocorrelation

	Size	Value	Momentum	BAB	Quality
Australia	0.18	0.10	0.21	0.16	0.00
Austria	−0.01	−0.03	0.14	0.02	0.08
Belgium	−0.05	0.15	0.20	−0.09	0.15
Canada	0.19	0.16	0.21	0.33	0.11
Switzerland	0.07	0.20	0.21	−0.02	0.11
Germany	0.01	0.24	0.07	0.05	0.02
Denmark	0.00	0.05	0.16	0.08	0.15
Spain	0.13	0.15	0.09	0.07	0.04
Finland	0.08	0.14	0.05	0.05	0.05
France	−0.05	0.15	0.10	0.01	0.16
UK	0.09	0.28	0.32	0.17	0.14
HongKong	0.18	0.13	0.23	0.28	0.00
Ireland	−0.18	0.06	0.08	−0.04	−0.01
Italy	0.08	0.10	0.09	0.17	0.05
Japan	0.06	0.16	0.13	0.01	0.01
Netherlands	−0.09	0.14	0.15	0.05	0.05
Norway	−0.11	0.06	0.02	0.08	0.16
NewZealand	0.13	0.03	0.04	0.05	−0.16
Singapore	0.08	0.14	0.28	0.20	0.23
Sweden	−0.05	0.29	0.09	0.04	0.12
USA	−0.03	0.19	0.07	0.10	0.23
Global	0.06	0.27	0.16	0.12	0.25
GblExUSA	0.09	0.31	0.28	0.14	0.18
Europe	0.05	0.32	0.23	0.08	0.17
NAmerica	−0.02	0.19	0.08	0.12	0.23
Pacific	0.07	0.21	0.24	0.08	0.06

Source: Statistics are derived from data that is sourced as follows: The time series for the size, value, momentum and quality factors are obtained from Asness, Frazzini and Pedersen (2017). Quality Minus Junk, Monthly, Excel Sheet (2019), https://www.aqr.com/Insights/Datasets/Quality-Minus-Junk-Factors-Monthly. The time series for the BAB factor is outlined in Frazzini and Pedersen (2014). BAB equity factors, monthly (2019). http://people.stern.nyu.edu/afrazzin/data_library.htm

The evidence across premia presented here-in suggests that they offer a rich menu of choices for the construction of alternative investment strategies that we will subsequently explore.

In Table 11.4, we explore the persistence of the returns of the premia by computing an AR(1) coefficient. We do not formally test the statistical significance of the coefficients but rather we highlight values that are greater than 0.3 suggesting important economic significance. For the period analysed we note that:

- Momentum, Value and Quality tend to exhibit persistence in returns
- The persistence of the momentum return is rather at odds with the often-touted view that this is a high frequency, opportunistic trading strategy.

- Persistence is strongest at the regional level suggesting that there is a global factor at work that is difficult to discern at the national/country level.

The evidence across premia presented suggests that there are important and subtle dependencies that need to be accounted for when utilizing them in the construction of multi-temporal investment strategies.

Conditional heavy tails, volatility clustering and the leverage effect are all stylized facts observed in financial data. To apply naive selection techniques in our simulations would destroy the structure present in real data (see Politis, 2003). Politis (2003) surveys the implications of ignoring as well as the means of addressing weak dependence in the data. With this in mind, we have chosen to use the circular block bootstrap of Politis and Romano (1992). In our case we randomly select a starting period and sample blocks of 3 months. The simulations preserve the AR structure present in the market and factors.

11.3   ALTERNATIVE INVESTMENT STRATEGIES

The analysis presented in this section should be viewed as descriptive; in Section 11.4 we use a utility-based framework to evaluate the results presented here.

Block bootstrap simulations are used to generate alternative histories for the market and our five factor premia. These histories can be used to generate terminal wealth distributions from investing $1 across alternative investment strategies over a 20 year horizon.[11] The strategies we consider are an investment in the local or regional equity market, an investment in the local or regional market complemented by an overlay in one risk premium (each considered independently), and an investment in the market complemented by an overlay of an equal weighted allocation to each factor premia.

We examine the effect of the overlays on mean terminal wealth as well as the distribution of terminal wealth. We also examine the sensitivity of our results to alternative assumptions about the sustainability of factor returns. The broad investment community has expressed scepticism on the sustainability of the historically high level of returns in the factors we have outlined. Our simulations can be conducted assuming that the history of returns will persist unperturbed into the future. Alternatively one can assume, somewhat arbitrarily, that mean returns will be half their historical levels. This is simulated by stripping the mean returns by half but leaving the cross-correlation structure of the data intact. Similarly one can even strip returns to an average level of zero. Though it is often argued that factor premia ought to earn a positive return as compensation for volatility, we believe that this need not be the case. A factor strategy might have zero expected return but because it is highly countercyclical, it is valuable to the end investor wishing to accumulate wealth; mitigating drawdowns allows investors to reap the benefits of compounding. Hence we will examine the extent to which risk premia that are assumed to have zero mean may be of value to the end investor.

---

[11]The length of the investment horizon is arbitrary. The broad qualitative conclusions we present would still hold; however the orders of magnitude of the statistics we present would be magnified (reduced) with longer (shorter) horizons.

In Table 11.5 we show the impact of the overlay on the terminal distribution of terminal wealth; for compactness we show only the 25th, 50th and 75th percentiles. We illustrate the layout of the table via an example. If an investor was to hold $1 in the global equity market, then 20 years hence that investment would have accumulated to a range of values: the 25th percentile of the wealth distribution would be $1.5, the 50th would be $2.6, and the 75th would be $4.2. An equal weighted overlay that assumed that historical means would persist into the future, would shift the distribution of wealth to the right. The 25th percentile for global equities with a premia overlay would shift by $3.6 shift (attaining $5.1) which is shown in the table; similarly the 50th percentile would be shifted by $5.6 (attaining $8.2), and the 75th percentile would be shifted by $8.6 (attaining $12.8). The table provides marginal contributions to terminal wealth for all assumptions about means considered. We highlight the contributions that are positive with a shaded colour.

The results presented in Table 11.5 highlight the following:

- An overlay that is entirely comprised of an exposure to the small cap factor detracts from an investor's wealth accumulation strategy.
- Conversely, overlays that are entirely comprised of exposures to momentum, value, BAB or quality produce significant positive shifts in the distribution of terminal wealth; this holds whether the premia's future mean returns are in line with historical returns or even when they are expected to be halved.
- In general when factor premia are expected to have a mean return of zero, their marginal impact on terminal wealth when added on a stand-alone basis (via an overlay) is negligible. The quality premium is however the exception; even when we assume it to have a zero expected return it is value additive for the lower tail of the distribution of terminal wealth as is evident in the differential effect for the 25th and 75th percentiles.
- An equal weighted allocation to factor premia, even in the extreme case when all premia are expected to have mean zero, is value additive to the pure equity strategy. This hold across the distribution.

Taken together, these results suggest that, in the context of Artee's wealth accumulation goals, an optimal overlay need not require assets that yield high average expected returns but rather assets that on average have positive payoffs in adverse market environments.

In Table 11.6 we report formal statistical tests for how the overlay shifts the mean of terminal wealth. We conduct a one-sided test, with the null being that the base asset (equities) plus the overlay has a mean that is lower than that of the base asset (equities). We show the p value of the test statistics and we highlight instances when we reject the null. Broadly, the results are in line with those found in Table 11.5 though BAB appears to be the significant value adding factor even when we assume mean returns to be zero. This result suggests that we ought to apply a more rigorous approach to shifts in the distribution of returns across the full distribution of wealth and its parameters. This matter is addressed Section 11.4.

TABLE 11.5 Terminal wealth distributions (delta)

		25th percentile						50th percentile						75th percentile					
		SIZE	VAL	MOM	BAB	QUAL	EQW	SIZE	VAL	MOM	BAB	QUAL	EQW	SIZE	VAL	MOM	BAB	QUAL	EQW
Australia	Hist	-1.3	0.6	83.3	15.4	5.9	6.8	-2.1	1.5	174.7	41.2	9.7	13.5	-3.3	4.1	357.8	106.2	15.3	27.8
Australia	Half	-1.1	0.0	9.5	2.3	2.5	2.0	-1.6	0.3	20.3	7.3	3.8	4.1	-2.0	1.5	42.3	20.7	5.4	8.7
Australia	Zero	-0.8	-0.4	-0.3	-0.8	0.6	-0.1	-0.9	-0.6	-0.5	-1.0	0.5	-0.2	-0.3	-0.5	-0.5	-0.3	-0.1	0.0
Austria	Hist	0.6	2.5	2.8	2.9	1.7	3.2	1.4	7.2	6.9	8.7	3.0	6.7	3.2	19.4	16.3	26.0	5.2	13.3
Austria	Half	0.2	0.4	0.7	0.4	0.9	1.1	0.6	1.7	1.9	1.6	1.4	2.3	1.4	5.2	4.6	5.9	2.0	4.4
Austria	Zero	0.0	-0.4	-0.2	-0.5	0.3	0.1	0.0	-0.6	-0.4	-0.9	0.2	0.2	0.1	-0.7	-0.6	-1.1	-0.1	-0.1
Belgium	Hist	-0.6	0.0	15.6	1.6	0.9	2.2	-1.1	0.6	30.2	3.8	1.1	3.7	-1.8	2.8	56.1	8.5	0.7	6.2
Belgium	Half	-0.5	-0.4	3.6	0.3	0.7	1.0	-0.7	-0.2	6.8	1.0	0.7	1.6	-1.0	0.9	12.5	2.7	0.1	2.4
Belgium	Zero	-0.3	-0.6	0.0	-0.4	0.5	0.2	-0.3	-0.8	0.0	-0.6	0.3	0.2	0.0	-0.6	-0.3	-0.8	-0.5	-0.2
Canada	Hist	-0.7	0.1	38.8	103.8	17.7	13.8	-1.0	0.6	99.2	326.7	32.2	28.3	-1.0	2.3	249.1	986.3	58.9	57.5
Canada	Half	-0.6	-0.2	4.6	6.4	4.4	3.3	-0.7	-0.1	12.6	22.5	7.9	6.8	-0.4	0.9	33.6	72.1	14.3	14.2
Canada	Zero	-0.5	-0.5	-0.7	-1.1	0.2	-0.1	-0.5	-0.6	-0.9	-1.4	0.2	-0.1	0.2	-0.3	-0.3	-0.4	0.1	0.2
Switzerland	Hist	0.2	-0.5	11.8	5.9	6.1	4.4	0.9	-0.3	22.8	11.2	9.2	7.0	2.4	0.3	42.9	21.1	13.5	11.0
Switzerland	Half	-0.1	-0.5	2.6	1.6	2.4	1.7	0.3	-0.5	5.4	3.2	3.4	2.7	1.3	0.1	10.5	6.4	4.7	4.1
Switzerland	Zero	-0.3	-0.6	-0.4	-0.4	0.4	0.2	-0.2	-0.6	-0.4	-0.4	0.4	0.2	0.3	-0.2	-0.2	-0.2	0.0	0.0
Germany	Hist	-0.8	0.4	36.5	14.5	6.4	5.8	-1.4	1.4	71.0	32.3	9.9	9.7	-2.6	3.8	135.6	72.8	15.5	16.2
Germany	Half	-0.5	-0.1	5.3	2.5	2.3	2.0	-0.9	0.2	10.5	6.0	3.4	3.3	-1.5	1.1	20.2	14.2	4.9	5.2
Germany	Zero	0.0	-0.5	-0.1	-0.3	0.4	0.3	0.1	-0.6	-0.1	-0.4	0.3	0.3	0.3	-0.7	-0.1	-0.2	-0.1	0.0
Denmark	Hist	-1.1	-2.0	58.4	9.1	3.7	5.7	-1.5	-3.3	113.4	26.0	6.3	11.0	-1.8	-5.3	219.6	70.9	10.8	20.2
Denmark	Half	-0.8	-1.5	9.8	1.2	1.6	2.1	-1.0	-2.3	19.3	5.5	2.5	4.1	-0.8	-3.3	38.0	18.5	4.0	7.6
Denmark	Zero	-0.6	-1.0	-0.5	-1.6	0.1	0.0	-0.4	-1.1	-0.7	-1.9	-0.1	0.0	0.4	-0.6	-0.9	-0.6	-0.7	0.0
Spain	Hist	-0.5	-0.2	5.6	5.5	2.9	2.3	-0.9	0.1	12.5	13.1	4.6	4.4	-1.2	1.6	27.5	32.5	6.7	8.5
Spain	Half	-0.4	-0.4	1.5	1.3	1.5	1.0	-0.6	-0.3	3.5	3.4	2.2	1.9	-0.5	0.5	8.0	9.2	2.8	3.5
Spain	Zero	-0.2	-0.5	-0.2	-0.3	0.6	0.2	-0.2	-0.7	-0.1	-0.3	0.6	0.2	0.3	-0.4	0.2	0.4	0.2	0.3
Finland	Hist	-0.8	1.8	16.6	18.7	-1.3	3.9	-2.1	4.0	44.8	49.8	-2.8	8.1	-5.2	8.5	118.2	127.6	-5.4	16.8
Finland	Half	-0.3	0.9	3.5	3.8	-1.1	1.9	-0.9	1.8	9.8	10.4	-2.3	3.7	-2.6	3.5	26.8	27.2	-3.8	7.1
Finland	Zero	0.4	0.2	-0.3	-0.3	-0.9	0.6	0.8	0.1	-0.3	-0.4	-1.6	0.8	1.3	-0.3	0.2	-0.3	-1.6	0.9
France	Hist	-0.6	0.5	9.9	43.6	4.6	5.9	-0.9	1.7	19.6	95.7	6.9	10.7	-1.3	4.9	37.9	217.1	10.0	18.6
France	Half	-0.4	-0.1	2.4	5.5	2.0	2.0	-0.5	0.3	4.9	12.6	2.8	3.7	-0.5	1.8	9.8	29.9	3.6	6.2
France	Zero	-0.1	-0.6	-0.2	-0.5	0.5	0.2	-0.1	-0.7	-0.2	-0.5	0.4	0.2	-0.4	-0.4	-0.1	0.1	-0.2	0.2
UK	Hist	-0.7	0.2	10.7	0.3	3.1	1.8	-1.0	1.0	21.7	2.0	4.4	3.2	-1.2	3.1	43.5	6.9	6.2	5.9
UK	Half	-0.6	-0.2	2.1	-0.2	1.3	0.6	-0.7	0.1	4.5	0.4	1.7	1.2	-0.6	1.2	9.4	2.8	2.2	2.3
UK	Zero	-0.4	-0.4	-0.3	-0.6	0.3	0.0	-0.3	-0.5	-0.2	-0.5	0.2	0.0	0.2	-0.2	0.1	0.4	-0.1	0.1
Hong Kong	Hist	-0.6	1.7	2.9	46.3	9.1	6.2	-1.0	5.4	8.6	167.8	16.0	15.0	-0.9	15.8	24.0	616.1	26.6	35.7
Hong Kong	Half	-0.6	0.2	0.7	3.3	3.3	1.7	-0.9	1.2	2.4	13.6	5.4	4.3	-0.7	4.5	7.5	54.0	8.0	10.4
Hong Kong	Zero	-0.5	-0.5	-0.3	-0.7	0.8	0.0	-0.8	-0.8	-0.4	-1.1	0.8	0.1	-0.4	-1.0	0.0	-0.4	0.4	0.4
Ireland	Hist	-0.4	-0.5	3.1	-0.1	4.7	1.7	-0.7	-1.1	9.7	1.5	9.6	3.8	-0.9	-2.1	29.1	11.5	20.5	8.4
Ireland	Half	-0.3	-0.5	0.5	-0.4	1.4	0.7	-0.6	-1.0	1.9	-0.5	2.8	1.5	-0.6	-1.8	6.6	1.8	5.8	3.3
Ireland	Zero	-0.3	-0.4	-0.3	-0.6	0.2	0.1	-0.4	-0.9	-0.4	-1.1	0.1	0.2	-0.3	-1.5	-0.3	-1.6	0.1	0.3

Source: Statistics are derived from data that is sourced as follows: The time series for the size, value, momentum and quality factors are obtained from Asness, Frazzini and Pedersen (2017). Quality Minus Junk, Monthly, Excel Sheet (2019), https://www.aqr.com/Insights/Datasets/Quality-Minus-Junk-Factors-Monthly. The time series for the BAB factor is outlined in Frazzini and Pedersen (2014). BAB equity factors, monthly (2019), http://people.stern.nyu.edu/afrazzin/data_library.htm

TABLE 11.5 Terminal wealth distributions (delta)

		25th percentile						50th percentile						75th percentile					
		SIZE	VAL	MOM	BAB	QUAL	EQW	SIZE	VAL	MOM	BAB	QUAL	EQW	SIZE	VAL	MOM	BAB	QUAL	EQW
Italy	Hist	−0.3	−0.5	5.4	3.5	8.3	2.2	−0.4	−0.7	11.3	9.4	14.3	4.5	−0.4	−1.0	24.4	24.6	24.5	8.7
Italy	Half	−0.2	−0.4	1.4	0.8	2.6	0.9	−0.2	−0.6	3.0	2.4	4.2	1.7	−0.2	−0.8	6.8	7.0	6.9	3.3
Italy	Zero	−0.2	−0.4	−0.1	−0.3	0.4	0.1	−0.2	−0.6	−0.1	−0.3	0.4	0.1	0.0	−0.6	0.1	0.2	0.2	0.2
Japan	Hist	−0.1	1.4	0.3	0.8	0.9	0.7	−0.2	2.9	0.8	1.8	1.3	1.3	−0.2	5.9	1.8	4.0	1.9	2.2
Japan	Half	−0.1	0.4	0.1	0.2	0.4	0.3	−0.1	0.8	0.2	0.6	0.6	0.5	−0.1	1.8	0.7	1.5	0.8	0.9
Japan	Zero	−0.1	−0.1	−0.1	−0.1	0.1	0.0	−0.1	−0.1	−0.1	−0.1	0.1	0.0	0.0	0.0	−0.1	0.1	0.0	0.0
Netherlands	Hist	0.3	0.0	1.9	6.9	1.5	2.5	1.0	1.2	4.4	15.2	2.0	4.7	2.9	5.9	9.6	34.2	2.4	8.6
Netherlands	Half	0.0	−0.5	0.5	1.6	1.0	1.0	0.3	−0.3	1.5	3.7	1.1	1.9	1.4	1.7	3.6	8.9	1.0	3.3
Netherlands	Zero	−0.2	−0.8	−0.2	−0.3	0.5	0.1	−0.3	−1.1	−0.2	−0.3	0.4	0.1	0.0	−0.9	−0.1	0.0	−0.2	0.1
Norway	Hist	−0.4	−0.9	31.1	11.3	4.8	4.5	−0.8	−1.7	80.8	36.1	10.1	10.9	−1.6	−2.9	202.2	116.5	21.0	24.9
Norway	Half	−0.2	−0.8	4.3	1.6	1.8	1.5	−0.4	−1.5	11.6	6.2	3.6	3.7	−0.5	−2.1	29.9	22.5	7.3	8.6
Norway	Zero	0.0	−0.7	−0.4	−0.7	0.2	0.0	0.1	−1.1	−0.7	−1.1	0.2	0.1	0.6	−1.1	−1.0	−0.4	0.1	0.4
New Zealand	Hist	0.9	−1.7	42.7	18.1	0.6	5.3	2.2	−2.8	81.3	47.9	1.3	10.3	5.0	−4.7	157.6	121.8	2.8	19.4
New Zealand	Half	0.2	−1.4	7.8	2.4	0.2	1.8	0.9	−2.1	15.0	7.9	0.5	3.6	2.3	−3.1	29.4	22.5	1.1	6.8
New Zealand	Zero	−0.3	−1.0	−0.2	−1.3	−0.2	−0.1	−0.2	−1.2	−0.1	−1.6	−0.2	−0.1	−0.2	−1.0	−0.2	−1.4	−0.2	−0.2
Singapore	Hist	−0.6	1.3	2.0	6.0	2.6	2.1	−1.0	4.2	4.3	17.4	4.4	4.6	−1.5	13.3	9.2	48.0	7.1	9.9
Singapore	Half	−0.5	0.1	0.8	1.1	1.4	0.8	−0.9	0.8	1.7	3.7	2.1	1.7	−1.1	3.5	3.6	11.0	3.0	3.7
Singapore	Zero	−0.5	−0.5	0.1	−0.3	0.5	0.0	−0.7	−0.8	0.1	−0.4	0.6	0.1	−0.6	−0.9	0.2	0.1	0.3	0.1
Sweden	Hist	−0.9	−0.4	18.8	22.0	9.9	6.2	−1.8	−0.3	45.6	55.6	18.0	12.6	−3.1	0.5	110.9	137.8	32.7	25.0
Sweden	Half	−0.7	−0.5	3.7	3.7	3.4	2.2	−1.1	−0.6	9.2	10.0	5.9	4.5	−1.6	−0.2	23.5	26.0	10.1	8.6
Sweden	Zero	−0.4	−0.6	−0.4	−0.5	0.5	0.2	−0.3	−0.9	−0.4	−0.6	0.5	0.4	0.5	−0.8	0.1	−0.3	0.0	0.3
USA	Hist	−0.3	−0.4	3.1	8.1	7.0	3.6	0.0	0.0	6.3	16.3	9.0	5.6	1.1	1.2	11.8	31.6	11.7	8.5
USA	Half	−0.4	−0.5	0.8	2.1	3.0	1.6	−0.3	−0.4	2.0	4.7	3.5	2.3	0.6	0.5	4.2	9.7	4.0	3.4
USA	Zero	−0.6	−0.7	−0.5	−0.4	0.7	0.2	−0.5	−0.7	−0.4	−0.1	0.4	0.2	0.0	−0.2	−0.2	0.6	−0.3	0.1
Global	Hist	−0.4	0.4	6.1	10.1	5.8	3.6	−0.4	1.1	11.1	19.0	7.4	5.6	−0.1	2.7	19.3	35.2	9.3	8.6
Global	Half	−0.3	0.0	1.7	2.5	2.4	1.4	−0.3	0.3	3.2	4.8	2.8	2.1	0.1	1.2	5.8	9.4	3.1	3.2
Global	Zero	−0.3	−0.4	−0.2	−0.2	0.6	0.2	−0.2	−0.4	−0.1	0.0	0.4	0.1	0.3	−0.1	0.0	0.4	−0.2	0.1
GBL ex US	Hist	−0.4	0.9	8.4	9.2	4.0	3.1	−0.6	1.9	15.4	18.7	5.6	5.1	−0.8	4.1	27.2	37.0	7.5	8.5
GBL ex US	Half	−0.2	0.2	2.0	1.9	1.6	1.1	−0.3	0.6	3.8	4.2	2.1	1.8	−0.3	1.6	6.9	8.7	2.6	3.0
GBL ex US	Zero	−0.2	−0.2	−0.1	−0.2	0.4	0.1	−0.1	−0.2	0.0	−0.1	0.3	0.1	0.2	−0.1	0.1	0.3	−0.1	0.0
Europe	Hist	−0.5	0.3	14.5	8.9	4.7	3.6	−0.7	0.9	27.3	18.7	6.5	6.2	−1.0	2.7	49.7	39.8	8.9	10.7
Europe	Half	−0.4	−0.1	3.2	2.0	2.0	1.4	−0.4	0.2	6.1	4.5	2.6	2.3	−0.3	1.0	11.2	10.1	3.1	3.8
Europe	Zero	−0.2	−0.4	−0.1	−0.3	0.6	0.1	−0.1	−0.4	0.0	−0.2	0.4	0.1	0.4	−0.2	0.1	0.4	−0.1	0.1
N America	Hist	−0.3	−0.3	4.0	10.5	7.6	4.1	0.0	0.1	8.0	21.1	10.0	6.4	1.0	1.3	15.2	41.8	13.0	9.8
N America	Half	−0.4	−0.5	1.1	2.5	3.1	1.7	−0.3	−0.3	2.5	5.5	3.8	2.6	0.5	0.5	5.1	11.7	4.3	3.8
N America	Zero	−0.5	−0.7	−0.4	−0.4	0.7	0.2	−0.5	−0.7	−0.4	−0.2	0.4	0.2	−0.2	−0.2	−0.1	0.7	−0.3	0.1
Pacific	Hist	−0.3	1.6	2.0	3.7	2.0	1.6	−0.4	3.2	3.9	8.1	2.9	2.8	−0.5	6.6	7.8	17.0	4.4	5.0
Pacific	Half	−0.2	0.4	0.6	0.8	0.9	0.6	−0.3	1.0	1.2	2.0	1.2	1.0	−0.2	2.2	2.5	4.6	1.6	1.8
Pacific	Zero	−0.1	−0.1	−0.1	−0.2	0.2	0.0	−0.1	−0.1	−0.1	−0.1	0.2	0.0	0.1	0.0	0.0	0.1	0.0	0.0

TABLE 11.6 Test Statistic for means of terminal wealth

		SIZE	VAL	MOM	BAB	QUAL	EQW
Australia	Hist	1.00	0.00	0.00	0.00	0.00	0.00
Australia	Half	1.00	0.00	0.00	0.00	0.00	0.00
Australia	Zero	0.00	0.42	0.99	0.00	1.00	0.45
Austria	Hist	0.00	0.00	0.00	0.00	0.00	0.00
Austria	Half	0.00	0.00	0.00	0.00	0.00	0.00
Austria	Zero	0.07	0.74	0.99	0.35	1.00	1.00
Belgium	Hist	1.00	0.00	0.00	0.00	0.00	0.00
Belgium	Half	1.00	0.00	0.00	0.00	0.37	0.00
Belgium	Zero	0.00	0.13	0.99	0.98	1.00	1.00
Canada	Hist	1.00	0.00	0.00	0.00	0.00	0.00
Canada	Half	0.26	0.00	0.00	0.00	0.00	0.00
Canada	Zero	0.00	0.01	0.00	0.00	0.57	0.00
Switzerland	Hist	0.00	0.00	0.00	0.00	0.00	0.00
Switzerland	Half	0.00	0.00	0.00	0.00	0.00	0.00
Switzerland	Zero	0.00	0.01	0.96	0.45	0.81	0.95
Germany	Hist	1.00	0.00	0.00	0.00	0.00	0.00
Germany	Half	1.00	0.00	0.00	0.00	0.00	0.00
Germany	Zero	0.00	0.86	0.80	0.00	0.91	0.77
Denmark	Hist	1.00	1.00	0.00	0.00	0.00	0.00
Denmark	Half	0.58	1.00	0.00	0.00	0.00	0.00
Denmark	Zero	0.00	0.23	1.00	0.00	1.00	0.66
Spain	Hist	1.00	0.00	0.00	0.00	0.00	0.00
Spain	Half	0.90	0.00	0.00	0.00	0.00	0.00
Spain	Zero	0.00	0.00	0.00	0.00	0.72	0.00
Finland	Hist	1.00	0.00	0.00	0.00	1.00	0.00
Finland	Half	1.00	0.00	0.00	0.00	1.00	0.00
Finland	Zero	0.34	1.00	0.05	0.48	0.60	0.87
France	Hist	1.00	0.00	0.00	0.00	0.00	0.00
France	Half	1.00	0.00	0.00	0.00	0.00	0.00
France	Zero	0.00	0.07	0.36	0.00	1.00	0.07
UK	Hist	1.00	0.00	0.00	0.00	0.00	0.00
UK	Half	1.00	0.00	0.00	0.00	0.00	0.00
UK	Zero	0.00	0.00	0.00	0.00	0.99	0.00
Hong Kong	Hist	0.00	0.00	0.00	0.00	0.00	0.00
Hong Kong	Half	0.00	0.00	0.00	0.00	0.00	0.00
Hong Kong	Zero	0.00	0.26	0.00	0.00	1.00	0.00
Ireland	Hist	1.00	1.00	0.00	0.00	0.00	0.00
Ireland	Half	0.24	1.00	0.00	0.00	0.00	0.00
Ireland	Zero	0.00	0.91	0.00	0.00	0.97	0.05

		SIZE	VAL	MOM	BAB	QUAL	EQW
Italy	Hist	0.36	1.00	0.00	0.00	0.00	0.00
Italy	Half	0.00	1.00	0.00	0.00	0.00	0.00
Italy	Zero	0.00	0.70	0.00	0.00	0.23	0.01
Japan	Hist	1.00	0.00	0.00	0.00	0.00	0.00
Japan	Half	0.84	0.00	0.00	0.00	0.00	0.00
Japan	Zero	0.00	0.07	0.06	0.00	0.87	0.21
Netherlands	Hist	0.00	0.00	0.00	0.00	0.00	0.00
Netherlands	Half	0.00	0.00	0.00	0.00	0.00	0.00
Netherlands	Zero	0.00	0.00	0.00	0.00	1.00	0.03
Norway	Hist	1.00	1.00	0.00	0.00	0.00	0.00
Norway	Half	0.72	0.51	0.00	0.00	0.00	0.00
Norway	Zero	0.00	0.00	0.91	0.00	0.95	0.02
New Zealand	Hist	0.00	1.00	0.00	0.00	0.00	0.00
New Zealand	Half	0.00	1.00	0.00	0.00	0.00	0.00
New Zealand	Zero	0.00	0.73	0.19	0.02	0.77	0.34
Singapore	Hist	1.00	0.00	0.00	0.00	0.00	0.00
Singapore	Half	0.50	0.00	0.00	0.00	0.00	0.00
Singapore	Zero	0.00	0.01	0.65	0.00	1.00	0.43
Sweden	Hist	1.00	0.00	0.00	0.00	0.00	0.00
Sweden	Half	1.00	0.00	0.00	0.00	0.00	0.00
Sweden	Zero	0.00	0.66	0.00	0.15	1.00	0.78
USA	Hist	0.00	0.00	0.00	0.00	0.00	0.00
USA	Half	0.00	0.00	0.00	0.00	0.00	0.00
USA	Zero	0.00	0.00	0.30	0.00	0.99	0.13
Global	Hist	0.92	0.00	0.00	0.00	1.00	0.00
Global	Half	0.04	0.00	0.00	0.00	1.00	0.00
Global	Zero	0.00	0.00	0.17	0.00	1.00	0.32
GBL ex US	Hist	1.00	0.00	0.00	0.00	0.00	0.00
GBL ex US	Half	1.00	0.00	0.00	0.00	0.00	0.00
GBL ex US	Zero	0.00	0.03	0.09	0.00	1.00	0.41
Europe	Hist	1.00	0.00	0.00	0.00	0.00	0.00
Europe	Half	1.00	0.00	0.00	0.00	0.00	0.00
Europe	Zero	0.00	0.04	0.03	0.00	1.00	0.28
N America	Hist	0.00	0.00	0.00	0.00	0.00	0.00
N America	Half	0.00	0.00	0.00	0.00	0.00	0.00
N America	Zero	0.00	0.00	0.19	0.00	0.99	0.11
Pacific	Hist	1.00	0.00	0.00	0.00	0.00	0.00
Pacific	Half	1.00	0.00	0.00	0.00	0.00	0.00
Pacific	Zero	0.00	0.08	0.24	0.00	0.99	0.23

Source: Statistics are derived from data that is sourced as follows: The time series for the size, value, momentum and quality factors are obtained from Asness, Frazzini and Pedersen (2017). Quality Minus Junk, Monthly, Excel Sheet (2019), https://www.aqr.com/Insights/Datasets/Quality-Minus-Junk-Factors-Monthly. The time series for the BAB factor is outlined in Frazzini and Pedersen (2014). BAB equity factors, monthly (2019), http://people.stern.nyu.edu/afrazzin/data_library.htm

11.4   QUANTIFYING THE UTILITY OF RISK PREMIA STRATEGIES

Thus far our analysis has supported strictly quantitative conclusions on the merits of factor premia-based strategies. We have highlighted how factor premia can reshape the distribution of outcomes relating to terminal wealth. We extend this analysis to allow for individuals' *risk preferences* and, in particular, aversion to losses. Agents will often pay a premium well above the expected value of an adverse event to insure against a large loss. Alternatively in bad times, an extra $1 of income is worth 'more' than an extra $1 in good times; understanding and quantifying how individual's *value* this trade-off in a multi-period goals-based investment problem is the key question we aim to answer.

For illustrative purposes we apply the constant relative risk aversion (CRRA) utility function with p = 2; this is in line with empirical estimates of the coefficient of relative risk aversion - see Mehra and Prescott (1985). Though this specification captures key characteristics of agents' preferences, it does not account for asymmetric preferences to gains and losses as in Kahneman and Tversky (1979). Hence our results will err on the conservative side.

We utilise the empirical distributions for terminal wealth that support Table 11.5. For each strategy considered we compute an empirically determined certainty equivalent and then obtain summary statistics that may be of interest.

We illustrate the results using the global equity market as Artee's base asset. In Table 11.7a we reference the simulations that assume historical means to persist into the future. As previously reported, $1 invested in global equities will grow on average to $3.3 over a holding period of 20 years. Due to the uncertainty of the terminal wealth, the certainty equivalent of this strategy is $1.88; we report the 'value' net of the initial investment as $0.88. Note in comparison that the equal weighted portfolio of factor premia grew to $3.0 over a holding period of 20 years; the certainty equivalent of this strategy net of the $1 initial investment is $1.91. The lower volatility and less extreme drawdowns of the risk premia overlay are valued more by our investor that an exposure to the equity market.

We next examine investors' valuation of an equity strategy combined with an overlay of risk premia. We see that the certainty equivalent net of investment for a global equity strategy with an equal weighted factor overlay is $5.25 that is far greater than the certain equivalent of the global equity strategy ($0.88). In the middle panel of Table 11.7 we colour highlight those instances when the overlay results in a 'certain' improvement to an investment in the base or local/regional equity market. Note further that there is an important interaction between the base asset and the factor premia overlay. In our illustrative example, the simple sum of the components $0.88 (global equity CE) and 1.91 (equal weighted factor overlay) is $2.79; the difference $2.46 represents an interaction effect of the strategies that combines both a mean level effect and a correlation effect. As identified in Scott and Cavaglia (2017) the interaction effect captures in part the ability of the premium to mitigate adverse market performance thus permitting additional compounding into the future. We arbitrarily scale this interaction effect by the certainty equivalent of the base asset, or $2.46/$0.88 (or 2.79), and report this in the third panel of the table. This construct is not intended to have any economic interpretation; it merely aims to provide orders of magnitude for the importance of the

TABLE 11.7a Certainty equivalent analysis (historical mean)

	CE RISK PREMIA							CE LOCAL EQY + RISK PREMIA						DIVERSIFICATION PREMIUM					
	EQY	SIZE	VAL	MOM	BAB	QUAL	EQW	SIZE	VAL	MOM	BAB	QUAL	EQW	SIZE	VAL	MOM	BAB	QUAL	EQW
Australia	1.12	-0.61	0.18	32.43	11.46	1.73	3.77	-0.47	1.63	90.53	15.15	8.48	8.69	-0.88	0.30	51.10	2.31	5.05	3.41
Austria	-0.06	0.22	2.53	0.90	1.62	0.35	2.28	0.52	1.93	2.75	1.94	2.17	3.45	-5.84	-8.66	30.76	6.09	30.23	19.86
Belgium	0.58	-0.48	0.01	4.36	0.70	-0.18	0.99	-0.25	0.23	19.03	2.23	1.94	3.24	-0.61	-0.62	24.44	1.65	2.68	2.90
Canada	0.97	-0.33	-0.25	13.91	86.82	5.14	7.76	-0.09	0.84	36.73	70.91	22.06	15.98	-0.75	0.12	22.60	-17.46	16.50	7.50
Switzerland	1.33	0.13	-0.21	3.81	2.07	1.40	1.70	1.46	0.62	15.05	8.51	8.99	6.75	0.00	-0.37	7.46	3.85	4.72	2.81
Germany	0.47	-0.70	0.23	13.43	7.92	2.81	3.20	-0.50	0.72	43.42	15.68	8.44	7.58	-0.57	0.06	62.70	15.49	10.95	8.30
Denmark	2.76	-0.41	-0.66	11.99	2.98	0.45	1.53	1.36	0.37	68.89	8.98	7.30	9.47	-0.36	-0.63	19.58	1.17	1.48	1.87
Spain	0.45	-0.49	-0.08	2.18	2.78	0.48	1.27	-0.25	-0.09	6.48	5.92	4.13	3.13	-0.47	-1.02	8.47	5.92	7.03	3.09
Finland	0.74	-0.69	-0.34	4.32	5.15	-0.67	1.05	-0.01	2.72	15.50	16.69	-0.63	5.19	-0.07	3.15	14.15	14.65	-0.94	4.62
France	0.90	-0.42	0.31	3.26	21.46	1.27	2.86	0.14	1.10	12.64	45.23	6.82	8.03	-0.38	-0.13	9.37	25.28	5.13	4.72
UK	0.35	-0.56	0.27	5.17	0.54	1.48	1.51	-0.58	0.47	12.68	0.14	4.17	2.38	-1.04	-0.44	20.49	-2.15	6.70	1.49
Hong Kong	0.13	-0.53	1.48	0.69	31.90	1.69	4.57	-0.65	1.36	2.33	24.38	11.49	6.26	-1.95	-1.89	11.58	-58.76	74.18	12.03
Ireland	-0.37	-0.66	-0.82	-0.57	-0.61	-0.43	1.01	-0.83	-0.94	1.82	-0.93	5.03	1.35	-0.52	0.69	7.53	0.11	15.93	1.94
Italy	0.13	-0.28	-0.45	2.45	3.29	3.63	1.80	-0.28	-0.48	6.10	3.46	10.42	2.75	-0.94	-1.24	26.83	0.33	50.76	6.32
Japan	-0.39	-0.25	2.44	0.21	1.23	0.76	1.17	-0.55	1.33	-0.01	0.43	0.76	0.56	-0.21	-1.86	0.43	-1.07	0.98	-0.58
Netherlands	0.42	0.23	0.52	0.29	3.52	-0.01	1.58	0.68	-0.22	2.37	7.54	2.41	3.36	0.08	-2.77	3.98	8.59	4.79	3.26
Norway	0.32	-0.43	-0.64	13.32	7.71	1.26	2.63	-0.09	-0.59	28.92	6.87	5.44	4.66	0.07	-0.85	47.63	-3.61	12.03	5.31
New Zealand	1.95	0.21	-0.70	13.18	8.00	0.08	2.10	2.86	-0.25	52.99	17.85	2.72	8.10	0.36	-0.77	19.40	4.04	0.35	2.08
Singapore	-0.01	-0.51	1.95	-0.19	7.10	0.43	1.91	-0.69	0.71	2.37	5.31	3.30	2.32	19.26	-138.26	290.41	-201.76	325.51	47.58
Sweden	0.94	-0.55	-0.43	4.87	8.34	2.54	2.44	-0.20	0.22	19.52	20.76	12.68	7.75	-0.62	-0.30	14.67	12.27	9.84	4.68
USA	1.58	0.00	-0.16	0.51	2.87	1.67	1.35	1.06	0.92	5.21	10.74	10.13	6.00	-0.33	-0.31	1.97	3.98	4.36	1.95
Global	0.88	-0.16	0.28	2.31	5.81	2.01	1.91	0.36	1.26	8.37	12.64	7.83	5.25	-0.41	0.11	5.87	6.74	5.59	2.79
GBL ex US	0.33	-0.33	0.83	4.92	8.54	2.08	2.45	-0.20	1.36	10.56	10.75	5.27	4.15	-0.59	0.59	15.88	5.61	8.54	4.09
Europe	0.64	-0.35	0.27	6.08	6.00	1.70	2.19	-0.05	0.80	18.14	9.85	6.41	5.02	-0.53	-0.17	17.72	4.97	6.31	3.40
N America	1.53	-0.02	-0.14	0.82	4.03	1.88	1.58	0.98	0.97	6.23	13.28	10.90	6.51	-0.35	-0.27	2.52	5.02	4.88	2.21
Pacific	-0.16	-0.32	2.03	1.76	5.36	1.52	2.02	-0.48	1.73	2.19	3.90	2.36	1.86	0.01	-0.90	3.74	-8.24	6.35	0.00

Source: Statistics are derived from data that is sourced as follows: The time series for the size, value, momentum and quality factors are obtained from Asness, Frazzini and Pedersen (2017). Quality Minus Junk, Monthly, Excel Sheet (2019), https://www.aqr.com/Insights/Datasets/Quality-Minus-Junk-Factors-Monthly. The time series for the BAB factor is outlined in Frazzini and Pedersen (2014). BAB equity factors, monthly (2019), http://people.stern.nyu.edu/afrazzin/data_library.htm

TABLE 11.7b Certainty equivalent analysis (historical means halved)

	CE RISK PREMIA							CE LOCAL EQY + RISK PREMIA						DIVERSIFICATION PREMIUM					
	EQY	SIZE	VAL	MOM	BAB	QUAL	EQW	SIZE	VAL	MOM	BAB	QUAL	EQW	SIZE	VAL	MOM	BAB	QUAL	EQW
Australia	1.12	−0.47	−0.10	3.43	2.03	0.52	1.14	−0.29	1.02	11.16	2.89	4.28	3.35	−0.84	0.00	5.93	−0.22	2.37	0.98
Austria	−0.06	−0.06	0.44	−0.17	−0.10	−0.08	0.66	0.17	0.19	0.65	0.00	1.15	1.24	−4.74	−3.07	14.10	2.63	20.89	10.44
Belgium	0.58	−0.36	−0.23	0.55	−0.01	−0.27	0.35	−0.09	−0.06	4.84	0.88	1.64	1.87	−0.52	−0.71	6.44	0.54	2.31	1.65
Canada	0.97	−0.26	−0.37	1.28	5.79	0.92	1.81	0.00	0.54	4.77	4.42	6.26	4.43	−0.73	−0.06	2.62	−2.42	4.52	1.71
Switzerland	1.33	−0.03	−0.25	0.58	0.36	0.28	0.56	1.11	0.55	4.28	3.22	4.37	3.48	−0.14	−0.40	1.79	1.16	2.08	1.20
Germany	0.47	−0.51	−0.17	1.49	1.12	0.77	0.94	−0.18	0.16	6.73	2.96	3.39	2.96	−0.29	−0.29	10.12	2.91	4.57	3.30
Denmark	2.76	−0.34	−0.54	1.72	0.43	0.00	0.51	−0.29	0.81	13.75	2.57	4.73	5.27	−0.29	−0.51	3.35	−0.23	0.71	0.72
Spain	0.45	−0.40	−0.24	0.26	0.42	−0.02	0.42	−0.11	−0.24	1.96	1.59	2.39	1.59	−0.37	−1.02	2.75	1.59	4.31	1.56
Finland	0.74	−0.54	−0.52	0.52	0.66	−0.57	0.32	0.48	1.73	3.71	3.76	−0.50	2.99	0.38	2.05	3.33	3.21	−0.91	2.62
France	0.90	−0.31	−0.09	0.48	2.50	0.32	0.86	0.36	0.46	3.76	6.20	3.55	3.36	−0.26	−0.40	2.62	3.09	2.57	1.76
UK	0.35	−0.44	−0.11	0.65	−0.08	0.44	0.53	−0.45	0.03	2.67	−0.32	2.00	1.06	−1.05	−0.61	4.79	−1.69	3.47	0.51
Hong Kong	0.13	−0.50	0.18	−0.25	2.08	0.15	1.17	−0.63	0.12	0.48	1.32	4.34	1.82	−2.00	−1.47	4.58	−6.81	31.22	3.98
Ireland	−0.37	−0.62	−0.79	−0.87	−0.87	−0.79	0.12	−0.81	−0.92	−0.15	−0.98	1.29	0.31	−0.46	0.63	2.97	0.69	6.68	1.52
Italy	0.13	−0.25	−0.41	0.30	0.64	0.76	0.60	−0.24	−0.45	1.67	0.70	3.34	1.14	−0.94	−1.26	9.48	−0.55	18.71	3.16
Japan	−0.39	−0.19	0.57	−0.18	0.21	0.19	0.42	−0.52	0.06	−0.33	−0.23	0.18	0.02	−0.16	−0.31	0.61	−0.13	0.99	−0.04
Netherlands	0.42	−0.02	−0.10	−0.26	0.55	−0.21	0.54	0.34	−0.54	0.93	1.93	1.72	1.60	−0.14	−2.06	1.86	2.29	3.61	1.53
Norway	0.32	−0.34	−0.57	1.51	1.08	0.16	0.80	0.06	−0.51	4.23	0.85	2.33	1.79	0.25	−0.82	7.47	−1.71	5.73	2.10
New Zealand	1.95	−0.02	−0.59	2.21	1.13	−0.07	0.71	2.11	0.03	11.27	3.44	2.20	4.01	0.09	−0.68	3.64	0.18	0.16	0.69
Singapore	−0.01	−0.43	0.32	−0.53	1.38	−0.08	0.64	−0.64	−0.24	0.96	0.83	1.76	0.86	22.18	−62.15	169.79	−60.51	209.51	26.67
Sweden	0.94	−0.42	−0.48	0.53	1.16	0.58	0.73	0.05	0.12	4.38	4.01	5.12	3.41	−0.50	−0.36	3.11	2.05	3.85	1.86
USA	1.58	−0.08	−0.25	−0.16	0.58	0.48	0.49	0.89	0.72	2.47	3.81	5.19	3.46	−0.39	−0.38	0.66	1.04	1.98	0.88
Global	0.88	−0.12	−0.01	0.39	1.33	0.63	0.67	0.42	0.75	2.96	3.66	3.79	2.60	−0.38	−0.14	1.91	1.65	2.58	1.18
GBL ex US	0.33	−0.21	0.21	0.95	1.81	0.67	0.82	−0.05	0.56	2.82	2.46	2.39	1.72	−0.52	0.05	4.58	0.92	4.17	1.68
Europe	0.64	−0.23	−0.02	1.02	1.28	0.52	0.74	0.12	0.39	4.49	2.53	3.19	2.28	−0.45	−0.36	4.38	0.94	3.13	1.39
N America	1.53	−0.09	−0.24	−0.07	0.82	0.54	0.57	0.83	0.75	2.71	4.18	5.38	3.56	−0.40	−0.36	0.81	1.19	2.15	0.95
Pacific	−0.16	−0.22	0.53	0.30	1.25	0.47	0.70	−0.40	0.38	0.51	0.72	0.96	0.61	0.17	0.02	2.29	−2.31	4.12	0.42

Source: Statistics are derived from data that is sourced as follows: The time series for the size, value, momentum and quality factors are obtained from Asness, Frazzini and Pedersen (2017). Quality Minus Junk, Monthly, Excel Sheet (2019), https://www.aqr.com/Insights/Datasets/Quality-Minus-Junk-Factors-Monthly. The time series for the BAB factor is outlined in Frazzini and Pedersen (2014). BAB equity factors, monthly (2019), http://people.stern.nyu.edu/afrazzin/data_library.htm

TABLE 11.7c Certainty equivalent analysis (historical mean set to zero)

	CE RISK PREMIA							CE LOCAL EQY + RISK PREMIA						DIVERSIFICATION PREMIUM					
	EQY	SIZE	VAL	MOM	BAB	QUAL	EQW	SIZE	VAL	MOM	BAB	QUAL	EQW	SIZE	VAL	MOM	BAB	QUAL	EQW
Australia	1.12	-0.29	-0.31	-0.42	-0.27	-0.15	-0.04	-0.05	0.55	0.59	-0.07	1.94	0.94	-0.78	-0.23	-0.09	-0.82	0.88	-0.12
Austria	-0.06	-0.27	-0.41	-0.63	-0.69	-0.38	-0.17	-0.09	-0.52	-0.28	-0.66	0.46	0.13	-3.88	-0.71	6.75	1.52	14.53	5.72
Belgium	0.58	-0.22	-0.41	-0.55	-0.42	-0.34	-0.09	0.11	-0.28	0.69	0.10	1.37	0.94	-0.41	-0.78	1.16	-0.10	1.97	0.79
Canada	0.97	-0.19	-0.47	-0.66	-0.49	-0.40	-0.10	0.10	0.28	-0.13	-0.60	1.27	0.73	-0.70	-0.22	-0.45	-1.12	0.73	-0.14
Switzerland	1.33	-0.17	-0.28	-0.49	-0.40	-0.31	-0.10	0.81	0.48	0.73	0.87	1.88	1.59	-0.26	-0.43	-0.09	-0.04	0.65	0.27
Germany	0.47	-0.21	-0.44	-0.58	-0.50	-0.18	-0.11	0.34	-0.22	0.33	-0.07	1.04	0.83	0.16	-0.52	0.92	-0.08	1.59	0.98
Denmark	2.76	-0.27	-0.39	-0.44	-0.49	-0.31	-0.10	1.92	1.41	2.08	0.27	2.96	2.75	-0.21	-0.35	-0.09	-0.73	0.18	0.03
Spain	0.45	-0.28	-0.37	-0.51	-0.47	-0.36	-0.11	0.06	-0.37	0.16	-0.03	1.24	0.62	-0.24	-1.01	0.48	-0.03	2.51	0.60
Finland	0.74	-0.32	-0.65	-0.57	-0.56	-0.43	-0.15	1.20	1.01	0.34	0.27	-0.34	1.57	1.06	1.24	0.23	0.12	-0.88	1.33
France	0.90	-0.18	-0.36	-0.49	-0.46	-0.23	-0.10	0.62	0.02	0.65	0.11	1.65	1.10	-0.11	-0.58	0.26	-0.37	1.08	0.33
UK	0.35	-0.27	-0.38	-0.56	-0.45	-0.17	-0.07	-0.29	-0.28	-0.02	-0.60	0.74	0.25	-1.06	-0.73	0.55	-1.42	1.60	-0.08
Hong Kong	0.13	-0.48	-0.44	-0.67	-0.72	-0.51	-0.16	-0.61	-0.47	-0.34	-0.79	1.28	0.09	-2.05	-1.25	1.47	-1.57	12.77	0.89
Ireland	-0.37	-0.57	-0.75	-0.96	-0.95	-0.92	-0.38	-0.79	-0.91	-0.75	-0.99	-0.14	-0.27	-0.40	0.56	1.59	0.90	3.15	1.29
Italy	0.13	-0.21	-0.38	-0.51	-0.38	-0.34	-0.09	-0.20	-0.41	0.00	-0.36	0.64	0.22	-0.93	-1.27	2.93	-0.85	6.48	1.36
Japan	-0.39	-0.13	-0.29	-0.45	-0.34	-0.20	-0.07	-0.48	-0.52	-0.55	-0.58	-0.20	-0.33	-0.09	0.40	0.74	0.38	0.99	0.32
Netherlands	0.42	-0.22	-0.46	-0.58	-0.47	-0.37	-0.09	0.07	-0.73	0.10	0.00	1.16	0.54	-0.32	-1.63	0.64	0.13	2.67	0.50
Norway	0.32	-0.23	-0.49	-0.56	-0.51	-0.40	-0.11	0.24	-0.43	-0.10	-0.57	0.71	0.38	0.47	-0.79	0.46	-1.19	2.47	0.52
New Zealand	1.95	-0.22	-0.44	-0.28	-0.50	-0.20	-0.06	1.50	0.42	1.76	0.04	1.75	1.76	-0.12	-0.56	0.05	-0.72	0.00	-0.07
Singapore	-0.01	-0.35	-0.41	-0.73	-0.31	-0.41	-0.08	-0.59	-0.66	0.14	-0.47	0.77	0.05	25.53	-27.55	99.32	-17.53	134.87	15.12
Sweden	0.94	-0.23	-0.52	-0.60	-0.51	-0.30	-0.13	0.37	0.03	0.40	0.14	1.73	1.22	-0.35	-0.41	0.07	-0.31	1.16	0.44
USA	1.58	-0.16	-0.33	-0.53	-0.36	-0.18	-0.05	0.72	0.54	0.94	0.96	2.44	1.83	-0.44	-0.45	-0.07	-0.17	0.66	0.19
Global	0.88	-0.08	-0.24	-0.42	-0.21	-0.12	-0.04	0.49	0.35	0.67	0.59	1.59	1.07	-0.36	-0.34	0.23	-0.10	0.94	0.25
GBL ex US	0.33	-0.07	-0.20	-0.36	-0.17	-0.10	-0.04	0.12	0.03	0.25	0.01	0.83	0.43	-0.43	-0.31	0.84	-0.45	1.79	0.41
Europe	0.64	-0.10	-0.25	-0.43	-0.26	-0.14	-0.06	0.32	0.07	0.56	0.14	1.36	0.78	-0.35	-0.51	0.54	-0.38	1.34	0.30
N America	1.53	-0.15	-0.32	-0.52	-0.34	-0.18	-0.05	0.70	0.55	0.90	0.87	2.41	1.76	-0.45	-0.43	-0.07	-0.21	0.69	0.18
Pacific	-0.16	-0.09	-0.23	-0.39	-0.21	-0.14	-0.04	-0.30	-0.31	-0.29	-0.40	0.15	-0.09	0.36	0.50	1.60	-0.18	2.82	0.67

Source: Statistics are derived from data that is sourced as follows: The time series for the size, value, momentum and quality factors are obtained from Asness, Frazzini and Pedersen (2017). Quality Minus Junk (2019). Quality Minus Junk, Monthly, Excel Sheet (2019), https://www.aqr.com/Insights/Datasets/Quality-Minus-Junk-Factors-Monthly. The time series for the BAB factor is outlined in Frazzini and Pedersen (2014). BAB equity factors, monthly (2019), http://people.stern.nyu.edu/afrazzin/data_library.htm

interaction effect. Noting that the gains from investing in equities are often touted as providing investors with significant benefits, we colour highlight those ratios that exceed 0.33; this threshold is arbitrary but aims to represent an effect of significant economic importance.

Table 11.7b provides the analogous statistics to those in Table 11.7 but utilises simulations obtained with mean returns for the factor premia rescaled to half their historical values. Table 11.7c utilises simulations obtained with mean returns for the factor premia set to zero.

Our utility-based analysis suggests the following:

- Broadly, with the exception of the size premium, risk premia overlays are value additive.
- The above result holds even when we assume that risk premia earn half of their historical average returns.
- The above holds even for the quality premium when we assume risk premia to have an expected return of zero. The large certainty equivalent additive value to the base asset suggests the importance of the pure diversification effect of this premium and corroborates the view that some investors need earn excess returns from risk premia strategies when they provide significant diversifying benefits.
- The size of the diversification premium is 'large' across countries and regions for reasonable assumptions about expected returns; it is even quite large in select instances when expected returns are assumed zero.

We acknowledge that we have greatly simplified Artee's problem to one of evaluating alternative terminal wealth distributions. Artee's problem is however far more complex; he/she must optimize consumption and savings decisions *over time* to attain the desired income goal for retirement; addressing this problem is however beyond the scope of this chapter and will be addressed in a follow-on paper.

11.5 SUMMARY AND CONCLUSIONS

This chapter links two current, topical investment themes – goals-based investment strategies and factor premia (or smart beta) investment strategies. Goals-based strategies suggest that Artee's (our representative agent's) inter-temporal investment problem is to invest his/her savings to attain a future desired level of income required to meet his/her retirement income spending needs; large drawdowns may critically impact Artee's odds of attaining these requirements. Factor premia strategies have attracted considerable attention for their apparent simplicity and high reward to cost ratio. To date there is limited but very suggestive evidence identifying the countercyclical properties of factor premia and hence their ability to mitigate drawdowns. In brief then, factor premia may enhance Artee's odds of attaining multi-period objectives and this is the issue we address.

We provide a framework for empirically estimating the benefits offered by a portfolio of conventional factor premia: value, size, momentum, BAB and quality applied to the developed global equity universe of countries and regions. We empirically simulate alternative histories of market returns and factor premia via block bootstrap methods that preserve some of the key time series characteristics of the data. The alternative histories are used to obtain an empirical distribution for terminal wealth across several investment strategies. Our baseline strategy is a fully invested exposure to local or regional equity markets. Our results show that the distribution of terminal wealth of our baseline strategy can be significantly enhanced via an overlay that allocates capital to nearly all premia considered (except size) and to an equal weighted combination of the premia. Our simulation framework further suggests that even if the means of the premia were halved, their wealth enhancing properties are preserved.

Our qualitative conclusions are more formally explored via a utility-based framework that quantifies the trade-off of $1 in a 'bad' state versus $1 in a 'good' state. Factor premia can then be evaluated like 'insurance'; in our hypothetical illustration it is insurance against a market drawdown. We consider the conventional CRRA utility function ($p = 2$) and find that the (insurance) value of the factor premia is large and significant; indeed for momentum and for quality we find the result holds even when these premia are expected to have a return of zero.

We believe that the main contribution of this chapter is to provide fairly robust 'orders of magnitude' statistics which highlight the diversification value of factor premia in a multi-period portfolio construction problem; this *diversification* value is *over and above* conventional expected return benefits that have been expounded in the smart beta literature. Our results are consistent across countries and regions providing support for the robustness of our findings.

ACKNOWLEDGEMENT

We thank Guillaume Boglioni Beaulieu, who developed all the programs necessary to produce the results of this chapter.

REFERENCES

Asness, Clifford, Frazzini A. and Pedersen, L. 2017, 'Quality minus Junk', *SSRN Working Paper No.* **2312432**.

Basu, A., Byrne, A. and Drew, M. 2011, 'Dynamic Lifecycle Strategies for Target Date Retirement Funds', *Journal of Portfolio Management*, **37**, pp. 83–96.

Bender, J., Briand, R., Melas, D. and Subramanian, R. 2013, '*Foundations of Factor Investing*', MSCI Research Insight.

Cochrane, John 1999, 'Portfolio Advice in a Multifactor World', *Federal Reserve Bank of Chicago Economic Perspectives*, **23**, pp. 59–78.

Das, Sanjiv, Ostrov, D., Radhakrishnan, A. and Srivastav, D. 2018a, 'A New Approach to Goals-Based Wealth Management', SSRN Working paper *No.* **3117765**.

Das, Sanjiv, Ostrov, D., Radhakrishnan, A. and Srivastav, D. 2018b, 'Dynamic Portfolio Allocation in Goals-Based Wealth Management', *SSRN Working Paper No.* **3111951**.

Fama, Eugene 1996, 'Multifactor Efficiency and Multifactor Asset Pricing', *Journal of Financial and Quantitative Analysis*, **31**(4), pp. 441–465.

Frazzini, Andrea and Pedersen, L. 2014, 'Betting against Beta', *Journal of Financial Economics*, **111**(1), pp. 1–25.

Griffin, John, Ji, X. and Spencer Martin, J. 2003, 'Momentum Investing and Business Cycle Risk: Evidence from Pole to Pole', *Journal of Finance*, **58**, pp. 1515–1547.

Griffin, John, 2002, 'Are the Fama and French Factors Global or Country Specific', *Review of Financial Studies*, **15**, pp. 783–803.

Kahneman, Daniel and Tversky, A. 1979, 'Prospect Theory: An Analysis of Decision under Risk', *Econometrica*, **47**(2), pp. 263–291.

Mehra, Rajnish and Prescott, E. 1985, 'The Equity Premium: A Puzzle', *Journal of Monetary Economics*, **15**(2), pp. 145–161.

Merton, Robert C. 2007, 'The Future of Retirement and Planning,' in *The Future of Life Cycle Saving and Investing* (Z. Bodie, D. McLeavey and L. B. Siegel, eds.) Research Foundation of CFA Institute, Charlottesville.

Politis, Dimitris N. 2003, 'The Impact of Bootstrap Methods on Time Series Analysis', *Statistical Science*, **18**(2), pp. 219–230.

Politis, Dimitris N. and Romano, J.P. 1992, 'A Circular Block-Resampling Procedure for Stationary Data,' in *Exploring the Limits of Bootstrap* (R. LePage and L. Billard, eds.) Wiley, New York, pp. 263–270.

Scott, L. and Cavaglia, S. 2017, 'A Wealth Management Perspective on Factor Premia and the Value of Downside Protection', *The Journal of Portfolio Management*, **43**(3) 33–41.

CHAPTER 12

Time-Series Variation in Factor Premia: The Influence of the Business Cycle

CHRISTOPHER POLK MO HAGHBIN and ALESSIO DE LONGIS

12.1 INTRODUCTION

A revolution has occurred in investment management as both academics and practitioners have recognized that quantitative stock characteristics, such as market capitalization or book-to-market equity are associated with cross-sectional variation in average returns. This has led to a boom in new investment strategies commonly referred to as 'smart or strategic beta'. Interestingly, the stocks inside portfolios designed to take advantage of these patterns move together, controlling for market movements. Consequently, these patterns represent a dimension of systematic risk different from the capital asset pricing model (CAPM) beta. We argue that understanding the economic drivers of these new systematic risks brings novel insights as to how to tilt among these factors to achieve superior returns.

This insight flows from recognizing that markets are not static but dynamic. Academic research in the 1980s highlighted that aggregate returns are too volatile compared to fundamentals such as aggregate dividends or profitability (Shiller 1981). More than two decades of academic literature have concluded that much of the variation in market returns is temporary, reflecting news about future discount rates rather than the permanent news about fundamentals that static models like the CAPM are based on.

Therefore, a potentially useful way to understand what drives variation in smart beta returns comes from disentangling temporary versus permanent movements in the aggregate stock market. Indeed, this view highlights that the sources of risk in factor returns may not be so exotic after all but simply requires decomposing the market return into these two distinct components.

Following Campbell and Vuolteenaho (2004); Campbell, Polk and Vuolteenaho (2010); Campbell, Giglio and Polk (2013); and Campbell, Giglio, Polk, and Turley

(2018), we exploit the fact that portfolios based on classic quantitative strategies load differentially on the discount-rate news and cash-flow news components of aggregate returns and use this to motivate dynamic factor strategies that generate Information Ratios that are nearly twice as large as static implementations.

Our results can be easily summarised as follows. First, consistent with the aforementioned academic studies, quantitative strategies such as value and size have relatively large cash-flow betas while other strategies such as low-volatility and quality have relatively low cash-flow betas. Momentum, consistent with the transitory nature of its signal, exhibits a relatively higher cash-flow beta in expansions and lower cash-flow beta in contractions. Importantly, these differences do not simply reflect differences in market beta.

Second, market timing strategies based on timely forecasts of aggregate economic fundamentals can be leveraged through a smart beta lens. Holding the subset of strategies with higher cash-flow beta through the recovery and expansion phases of the business cycle but rotating to the subset of strategies with lower cash-flow beta during the slowdown and contraction phases of the business cycle, outperforms a static allocation to these factors.

12.2 FACTORS AND FACTOR ROTATION

12.2.1 Cross-sectional variation in average returns: a factor view

The use of characteristic-based factor models took hold in academia with the publication of Fama and French (1993), which introduced a three-factor model of stock returns. Their model was designed to capture two well-known patterns in the cross-section of average returns that are not explained by the Capital Asset Pricing Model of Sharpe (1964) and Lintner (1965), the size and book-to-market effects.[1] Since then, Fama and French (2015) have expanded their model to capture two patterns related to two additional firm characteristics, investment and profitability.[2]

In financial practice, these findings have led to the introduction of various benchmark indices associated with these characteristics. This so-called 'smart-beta' market continues to grow with accelerated innovation in the development of non-traditional offerings. According to Morningstar, smart beta includes strategies with relatively basic style tilts, such as the Russell 1000 Value and Russell 1000 Growth but has also evolved to include a variety of alternatively weighted single-factor and multifactor approaches. In particular, there has recently been an increase in the introduction of multifactor and risk-based investment solutions. These strategies aim to provide superior risk-adjusted returns for investors by combining two or more of these factors.

---

[1]The size effect was first shown in Banz (1981), and the book-to-market effect first appeared in Stattman (1980) and subsequently in Rosenberg, Reid and Lanstein (1985).
[2]The investment effect was identified by Fairfield, Whisenant and Yohn (2003), Titman, Wei and Xie (2004), and Polk and Sapienza (2009). The profitability effect was introduced by Haugen and Baker (1996) and confirmed first in Vuolteenaho (2002) and later in Novy-Marx (2013).

12.2.2 Time-series variation in factor premia

Around the same time that a factor view of markets arose, researchers also documented time-variation in the market risk premium. Campbell and Shiller (1988a, 1988b) and Fama and French (1989) are seminal papers in this literature. As a consequence, it became natural to also investigate time-variation in factor premia. Perhaps the leading example of this line of research is Cohen, Polk and Vuolteenaho (2003), who documented that the expected return on value-minus growth strategies is relatively high when the spread in book-to-market ratios across the two legs of the strategy (which they dub the 'value spread') is relatively wide.[3]

Researchers have also identified momentum and reversal effects in factor returns (Lewellen 2002, and Teo and Woo 2004) as well as identified time-variation in factor premia related to share issuance (Greenwood and Hanson 2012), short interest (Hansen and Sunderam (2014) and factor volatility (Barroso and Santa-Clara 2015). Given the rise in the popularity of these strategies, researchers have also inquired as to whether time-variation in the profitability of factor strategies can be linked to variation in their popularity among professional investors (Lou and Polk 2013; Huang, Lou and Polk 2018; and Lou, Polk and Skouras 2019).

Linking time-variation in factor premia to the business cycle is relatively unexplored, with most studies conducted on a narrow set of factors. Cooper, Mitrache and Priestley (2016) proposed a global macroeconomic risk model for value and momentum, while Ahmerkamp, Grant and Kosowski (2012) studied the predictability of carry and momentum strategies, and found strong explanatory power in business cycle indicators. Recent studies have explored the influence of the business cycle across a wider set of equity factors (see Hodges, Hogan Peterson and Ang 2017 and Varsani and Jain 2018), providing a descriptive analysis of historical factor performance conditional on economic regimes. However, a comparison of results across these studies reveals differences between the expected cyclical properties and the actual performance of factors in each economic regime. To our knowledge, limited research has been conducted analyzing the influence of the business cycle on factor returns in a single framework. We contribute to the literature by providing a consistent fundamental framework that links the variation in factor performance to the sensitivity to aggregate cash-flow news, across the most commonly established equity factors: size, value, quality, low volatility and momentum.

12.3 FACTORS AND THE BUSINESS CYCLE

A key insight since Campbell and Shiller (1988a) is that returns on the market portfolio are comprised of two components. The market may drop in value because investors receive bad news about future cash flows, but it may also drop because, all else equal, investors increase the discount rate that they apply to these expected cash flows going

---

[3] Asness, Friedman, Krail, and Liew (2000) also document similar time-variation in value premia. Recent work by Asness, Liew, Pedersen, and Thapar (2017) and Baba-Yara, Boons, and Tamoni (2018) study these patterns in other asset classes.

forward. This distinction naturally follows from recognizing that the market risk premium varies through time.

The Campbell-Shiller log-linear present-value model facilitates that distinction. In particular, following Campbell and Shiller (1988a), Campbell (1991) shows how unexpected log returns on an asset may be decomposed written as follows:

$$r_{t+1} - E_t r_{t+1} = (E_{t+1} - E_t) \sum_{j=0}^{\infty} \rho^j \Delta d_{t+1+j} - (E_{t+1} - E_t) \sum_{j=1}^{\infty} \rho^j \Delta r_{t+1+j}$$

$$= N_{CF,t+1} - N_{DR,t+1}, \tag{12.1}$$

$N_{CF,t+1}$ reflects news about future cash flows, $N_{DR,t+1}$ reflects news about future expected returns, and ρ is a discount coefficient determined by the average log dividend yield.[4] Note that this decomposition is simply an accounting identity and not a behavioral model, taking no stance on whether variation in expected returns is rational or irrational.[5]

Differentiation between these two components of the market return is important as a large body of research starting with Shiller (1981) has shown that most of the variation in market valuations is from the latter.

Researchers have exploited this decomposition to show that different types of stocks load differently on these two components of market risk. Indeed, Campbell and Vuolteenaho (2004) propose a model where investors care more about permanent cash flow-driven movements than about temporary discount rate-driven movements in the aggregate stock market. In their model, the required return on a stock is determined not by its overall beta with the market, but by two separate betas, one with permanent cash-flow shocks to the market, and the other with temporary shocks to market discount rates.

This theoretical distinction has empirical traction as Campbell and Vuolteenaho (2004) show that small stocks and value stocks have higher cash-flow betas than their large and growth counterparts. Recent papers by Campbell, Polk and Vuolteenaho (2010) and Campbell, Giglio, Polk and Turley (2018) document rich heterogeneity in terms of exposure to aggregate cash-flow news linked to fundamental firm characteristics often associated with smart beta strategies, such as profitability and leverage.

This heterogeneity may be important in devising factor timing strategies. In particular, signals that anticipate the evolution of the business cycle can be viewed through a factor lens. If a signal is positive about future market fundamentals, then tilting towards strategies that are known to have relatively high cash-flow betas is relatively attractive. Alternatively, if a signal is negative about future market fundamentals, then tilting towards strategies that are known to have relatively low cash-flow betas is the more attractive option.

---

[4] Additionally, r stands for returns, E stands for expectations and d for dividends.
[5] Thus, this accounting identity also takes no stance on the way in which either aggregate discount rates or expected cash flows may propagate through time.

12.4   DATA AND SUMMARY STATISTICS

When vetting the ability of a particular strategy to generate additional returns over time, one can examine a few key attributes such as pervasiveness, persistence, intuitiveness, robustness and investability. Our analysis studies the FTSE Russell Factor Indices, which reference five equity factors supported by academic research, where each factor has a significant amount of theoretical research proposing explanations justifying the observed predictability. These indices represent common factor characteristics supported across different geographies and time periods, covering the following universes: US Large Cap, US Small Cap, Developed ex-US and Emerging Markets across the following factors – Value, Quality, Momentum, Low Volatility and Size. For the purpose of this chapter we use the Russell 1000 universe and the factor definitions set forth in Table 12.1.[6] Table 12.2 provides some key summary statistics.

TABLE 12.1   Factor definitions

Factor	Description	FTSE Russell Factor Definition	FTSE Russell Factor Index
Value	Stocks that appear cheap tend to perform better than stocks that appear expensive.	Equally weighted composite of cash-flow yield, earnings yield and price-to-sales ratio	Russell 1000 Value Factor Index
Quality	Higher-quality companies tend to perform better than lower-quality companies.	Equally weighted composite of profitability (return on assets, change in asset turnover, accruals) and leverage ratio	Russell 1000 Quality Factor Index
Size	Smaller companies tend to perform better than larger companies.	Inverse of full market capitalization index weights	Russell 1000 Size Factor Index
Low Volatility	Stocks that exhibit low volatility tend to perform better than stocks with higher volatility on a risk-adjusted basis.	Standard deviation of 5 years of weekly total returns	Russell 1000 Volatility Factor Index
Momentum	Stocks that rise or fall in price tend to continue rising or falling in price.	Cumulative 11-month return (last 12 months excluding the most recent month)	Russell 1000 Momentum Factor Index

Source: FTSE Russell.

---

[6] Each factor index starts with the market cap weighted Russell 1000 Index, then multiplies the market cap weight by a normalized composite score of the relevant metrics for the given factor in order to create the factor index.

TABLE 12.2 Single factor performance characteristics

	Return	Standard Deviation	Excess Return	Sharpe Ratio	Information Ratio	Max Drawdown	Skewness
Russell 1000 Low Volatility Factor Index	11.67	12.87	−0.03	0.54	−0.01	−46.90	−0.58
Russell 1000 Momentum Factor Index	12.06	15.00	0.36	0.49	0.17	−49.13	−0.62
Russell 1000 Quality Factor Index	12.09	14.91	0.38	0.49	0.13	−47.13	−0.59
Russell 1000 Size Factor Index	13.22	16.57	1.52	0.51	0.26	−53.00	−0.79
Russell 1000 Value Factor Index	12.34	14.71	0.64	0.51	0.15	−54.35	−0.72
Russell 1000 TR USD	11.70	14.81	0.00	0.47	−	−51.13	−0.67

Source: FTSE Russell as of 30/9/2018. Russell 1000 Factor Indexes inception date: 30 September 2015. The returns of the Index prior to 30/9/2015 represent hypothetical pre-inception index performance to illustrate how the Indices may have performed had they been in existence for the time period prior to 30/9/2015.

Consistent with a large body of academic research beginning at least in the 1990s, these indices have outperformed the market since inception, particularly on a risk-adjusted basis.

Table 12.3 reports the correlation matrix of factor returns. As the data show, the excess returns of the factors are not extremely correlated, suggesting the possibility of useful diversification benefits when used in combination, justifying the relatively recent move to static multifactor implementations. Our analysis emphasizes that exploiting the time variation in the expected return components of these realized returns can be beneficial, and add incremental returns over a static multifactor implementation.

TABLE 12.3 Factor excess return correlations (July 1980 to September 2018)

	Size	Value	Low Vol.	Quality	Momentum
Size	1				
Value	0.32	1			
Low Vol.	−0.42	0.30	1		
Quality	−0.27	−0.55	−0.06	1	
Momentum	−0.05	−0.44	−0.15	0.29	1

Source: FTSE Russell and FactSet as of 30/9/2018.

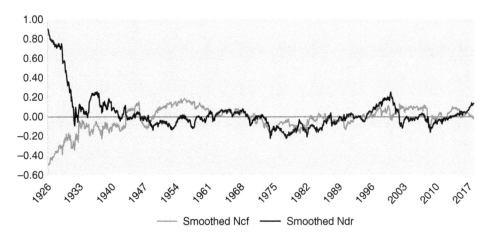

FIGURE 12.1 Smoothed components of aggregate returns (July 1926 to June 2018).

Further examination of historical returns on these factors shows they have exhibited pronounced cyclicality. For example, in some years size consistently outpaced the market, whereas in other years, low volatility was the best performing factor. This chapter analyses *ex ante* investment strategies that are designed to take advantage of predictable aspects of this apparent cyclicality. In particular, we motivate our work using the cash-flow news series introduced earlier and described in detail in the Appendix Section A.12.1. Figure 12.1 plots smoothed versions of $N_{CF,t+1}$ and $N_{DR,t+1}$. As the plot shows, $N_{CF,t+1}$ clearly better reflects movement in underlying fundamentals relative to $N_{DR,t+1}$, given even a casual understanding of the history of news about the underlying business cycle during this period. For example, the 1920s and 1930s were characterized by negative return contribution from cash-flow news, driven by the Great Depression. Similarly, negative cash-flow news contributions are registered across the major economic downturns of the following decades.

12.5   EMPIRICAL RESULTS

12.5.1   Factor exposures to cash-flow news

We first document intuitive differences in the cash-flow betas of the Russell indices by regressing the monthly returns of each factor on the aforementioned cash-flow news

TABLE 12.4　Single factor exposure to aggregated cash-flow news (July 1980 to June 2018)

	Constant	Cash Flow News Sensitivity	R^2
Russell 1000	0.01	0.97	0.19
	(5.28)	(6.98)	
Comprehensive Factor Index	0.01	0.91	0.16
	(6.75)	(6.79)	
Low Volatility	0.01	0.75	0.15
	(5.83)	(6.06)	
Quality	0.01	0.94	0.18
	(5.41)	(6.69)	
Momentum	0.01	0.99	0.17
	(5.28)	(6.71)	
Value	0.01	0.99	0.17
	(5.55)	(7.14)	
Size	0.01	1.16	0.18
	(5.37)	(7.45)	

Source: FTSE Russell as of 30/6/2018. We report *t* statistics in parentheses. Sample time-period dictated by data availability for factor indices and cash-flow news series.

variable. Following Scholes and Williams (1977) and Dimson (1979), we include lags of cash-flow news. Specifically, we estimate regressions of the form

$$R_{p,t+1} = a + \sum_{k=0}^{2} \beta_p N_{CF,t+1-k} + \varepsilon_{p,t+1} \tag{12.2}$$

and report the sum of β_p along with the associated *t* statistic.[7] For comparison, we include the Russell 1000 and the Russell 1000 Comprehensive Factor Index, which represents an equally weighted static exposure to the five factors.[8] Table 12.4 documents that the factors we study have differential exposures to aggregate cash-flow news. In particular, size, and to some degree value have sensitivities that are higher than the Russell 1000 index, and clearly higher than a static multifactor approach. Momentum also exhibits relatively higher cash-flow sensitivity. However, as it will be illustrated shortly, its relative sensitivity varies substantially across the stages of the business cycle, in line with the transitory nature of its signal definition. In stark contrast, quality and particularly low volatility have relatively low cash-flow sensitivities compared to the Russell 1000. These results are consistent with previous academic research. Next, we

---

[7]Campbell and Vuolteenaho (2004) and others rescale cash-flow sensitivities when measuring cash-flow beta so that cash-flow and discount-rate betas sum to market beta. This purely-cosmetic transformation facilitates comparison across pricing tests of two-beta and single-beta models. We simply report the raw sensitivity which is proportional to their cash-flow beta.

[8]The Russell Comprehensive Factor Index uses a common methodology to achieve controlled exposure to five target factors, whilst considering levels of diversification and capacity.

utilize a forward-looking framework to identify the different stages of the business cycle, and attempt to exploit these differential factor exposures by mapping a different factor portfolio to each macro regime.

12.5.2 Forecasting fundamental news

We classify the different stages of the business cycle based on the level and change in economic growth, and define the following four regimes:

Recovery: growth below trend and accelerating

Expansion: growth above trend and accelerating

Slowdown: growth above trend and decelerating

Contraction: growth below trend and decelerating

Figure 12.2a provides a *stylized* plot of the business cycle regimes we aim to measure. In order to forecast the evolution of the economic cycle along these regimes,

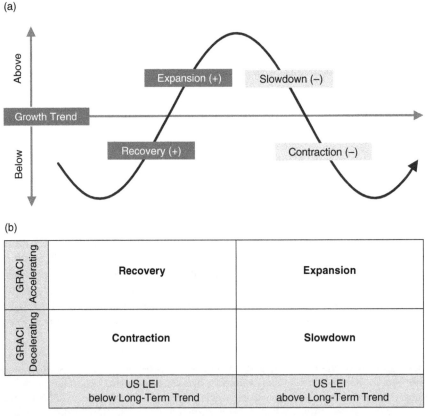

FIGURE 12.2 (a) Stylized business cycle regimes. (b) Explanation of stylized business cycle regimes.

we construct a macro regimes framework which combines the interaction between a US leading economic indicator ('US LEI') and a global risk appetite cycle indicator ('GRACI') using the following rules

$$Recovery_{t+1} : US\ LEI_t < LT\ LEI\ trend_t\ \&\ GRACI_t \geq MA\ (GRACI)_t$$

$$Expansion_{t+1} : US\ LEI_t \geq LT\ LEI\ trend_t\ \&\ GRACI_t \geq MA\ (GRACI)_t$$

$$Slowdown_{t+1} : US\ LEI_t \geq LT\ LEI\ trend_t\ \&\ GRACI_t < MA\ (GRACI)_t$$

$$Contraction_{t+1} : US\ LEI_t < LT\ LEI\ trend_t\ \&\ GRACI_t < MA\ (GRACI)_t$$

where *LT LEI trend$_t$* stands for long-term trend in the US LEI at time t, and *MA (GRACI)$_t$* stands for short-term moving average in the GRACI at time t. In other words, the forecasting rule of the four regimes is driven by whether a) the US LEI is above or below its long-term trend and b) whether GRACI is above or below its short-term moving average (i.e. accelerating or decelerating). These rules are also summarized in Figure 12.2b, where the four macro regimes are mapped to their model-based forecast rules.

In other words, we first construct a US leading economic indicator to determine whether growth is likely to be above or below trend, using the same panel of variables selected by the OECD for the US composite leading indicator.[9] However, to eliminate well-known issues of look-ahead bias in statistical filtering techniques, we use a simple z-scoring procedure to de-trend, normalize and smooth each variable. In addition, we use first vintage economic data as far back as possible, to ensure a realistic use of information available at the time.[10] Finally, these normalized variables are aggregated with equal weights into a composite index (Figure 12.3a).

Second, we estimate the future directional change in economic growth from cyclical fluctuations in global risk appetite. As is well known and consistent with our return decomposition, financial markets contain information about future economic activity, as market participants discount information affecting future fundamentals in real time. Notably, asset prices can reflect a broader set of fundamental news, such as changes in monetary conditions, fiscal policy announcements, corporate news, global financial shocks, etc. While these fundamental drivers are reflected in economic activity with a lag, market participants continuously revisit their economic outlook and adjust their propensity to take risk accordingly. Indeed, in almost all models, market premia and risk aversion are tied to the amount of risk in the economy, and both these objects have been shown to be negatively correlated with business conditions (Campbell and Cochrane, 1999, for the former and Black, 1976, and Christie, 1982 for the latter).

Thus, cyclical fluctuations in global risk premia can be used to forecast subsequent variation in economic risk and future risk premia. Polk, Thompson, and Vuolteenaho

---

[9]Information on the OECD composite leading indicators is available at https://www.oecd.org/sdd/leading-indicators/oecdcompositeleadingindicatorsreferenceturningpointsandcomponentseries.htm

[10]We source first vintage economic statistics from the Alfred database of the Federal Reserve.

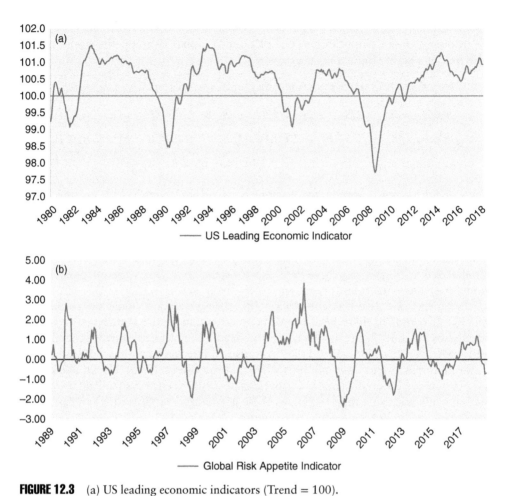

FIGURE 12.3   (a) US leading economic indicators (Trend = 100).
(b) Global risk appetite indicator.
Source: Bloomberg, OECD, Federal Reserve, Bureau of Economic Analysis as of 30/9//2018.
Sample time-period dictated by data availability.

(2006) show how cross-sectional techniques can be used to forecast time-variation in the market risk premium. Similarly, Kumar and Persaud (2002) use cross-sectional regressions of risks and returns to extract investor behavior and risk appetite, emphasizing the increasing importance of global financial markets, in addition to domestic fundamentals, given the exponential increase in trade linkages, cross-border capital flows, and portfolio contagion channels. In a related fashion, we define global risk appetite as the incremental return received by investors for taking an incremental unit of risk in global financial markets over the past year, and construct it using country-level equity, government bond and corporate bond indices across both developed and emerging markets (Figure 12.3b). Consistent with the literature, this indicator has a strong and statistically

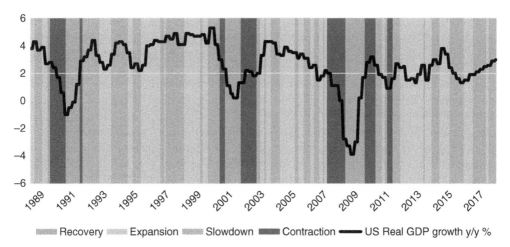

Recovery ▨ Expansion ▨ Slowdown ▨ Contraction ▬ US Real GDP growth y/y %

FIGURE 12.4 Model-predicted business cycle regimes versus realized GDP growth.
Source: Business cycle regimes are computed by the authors, based on the composite business cycle regime model outlined in Section 12.A.2 of the Appendix, using a combination of US leading economic indicators and global risk appetite indicator. US GDP time series is sourced from the Bureau of Economic Analysis as of 30/9/2018. US GDP data do not contribute to the calculation of the regimes, and they are illustrated for reference purposes only. Sample time-period dictated by data availability.

significant correlation with several proxies of the global business cycle.[11] Our US leading economic indicator and global risk appetite indicator are illustrated in Figures 12.3a and 12.3b and details of their construction methodology are reported in Appendix Section 12.A.2.

As mentioned earlier, our final composite business cycle model combines the US leading economic indicator and global risk appetite to forecast the four stages of the business cycle, as summarized in Figure 12.2b. The output of our model is illustrated in Figure 12.4, where our estimated macro regimes are plotted through time, and visually compared to realized GDP growth. Figure 12.4 is suggestive of the predictive content of our model-based regime classification versus directional changes in realized GDP growth.

12.5.3 A regime-based view: cash-flow sensitivities and relative returns

As a final step, we construct four distinct factor portfolios, one for each business cycle regime, based on our knowledge of cash-flow sensitivities of these factors, previously

---

[11]For example, our global risk appetite indicator has correlations ranging between 0.70 and 0.75 with indicators such as the Global Manufacturing PMI survey, the Global Employment PMI Manufacturing survey and global industrial production growth. These correlations are all statistically significant at the 99% confidence level. In addition, risk appetite exhibits leading properties in the identification of cyclical turning points in these variables by 2 to 3 months. See also de Longis and Ellis (2019).

shown in Table 12.4. Consistent with the literature, we expect the performance of size and value relative to the market to be pro-cyclical, while quality and low volatility to be counter-cyclical. Unlike these four factors, the momentum factor cannot be linked to persistent fundamental characteristics such as leverage or profitability. The momentum premium is based on the behavioral premise of continuation of recent prices trends, and its signal is relatively transitory. Therefore, with respect to its cyclicality, we expect momentum to outperform in the late-stage of a cyclical upturn (i.e. expansion) and late-stage of a downturn (i.e. contraction) and, conversely, to underperform in the phases following cyclical turning points (i.e. recovery and slowdown), where relative price trends are likely to change. If correct, this behavioral premise should also have implications for the exposure of momentum to cash-flow news. We measure these sensitivities relative to the Russell 1000 to confirm that these patterns do not just reflect broader patterns in the market. As the business cycle regime can change from one month to the next, and as momentum is a relatively transitory signal, we only measure contemporaneous sensitivities. Table 12.5 reports that the momentum factor exhibits clear variation in relative cash-flow sensitivity across the four regimes. Specifically, the Russell 1000 momentum strategy has a relatively high cash-flow sensitivity (0.05) during the Expansion regime and a relatively low cash-flow sensitivity (-0.09) during the Contraction regime. The difference with the respective sensitivities of the Recovery and Slowdown regime are statistically significant, and consistent with the expectation of relative outperformance of the momentum factor in late-stage regimes versus early-stage regimes.

With these facts in hand, we examine combinations of these five factors based on the regime/tilt matrix described in Table 12.6. We use these tilts as characteristic weights in the standard FTSE Russell methodology (FTSE Russell 2017).

The FTSE Russell approach utilizes a Tilt-Tilt ('Bottom-up' portfolio construction) with sequential or 'multiplicative' tilts away from market cap weighting on each factor, with the outcome independent of ordering. This creates approximately the same exposures of single-factor indexes, without the dilutive effects of other methods.

TABLE 12.5   Momentum factor's conditional cash-flow sensitivity (January 1989 to June 2018)

	Constant	Cash-Flow News Sensitivity	R^2
Unconditional (N = 354)	0.00	0.01	0.00
	(1.17)	(−0.48)	
Recovery (N = 43)	0.00	−0.04	−0.02
	(0.35)	(−0.54)	
Expansion (N = 124)	0.00	0.05	0.00
	(1.04)	(1.06)	
Slowdown (N = 131)	0.00	0.03	0.00
	(0.51)	(0.74)	
Contraction (N = 56)	0.00	−0.09	0.07
	(0.04)	(−2.24)	

Source: FTSE Russell as of 30/6/2018. We report t statistics in parentheses. Sample time-period dictated by data availability.

TABLE 12.6 Factor tilts through the business cycle

	Factor Tilts for Given Regime				
	Low Volatility	Size	Value	Momentum	Quality
Recovery	0	2	2	0	0
Expansion	0	1	1	2	0
Slowdown	2	0	0	0	2
Contraction	2	0	0	2	2
	Factor Tilts for Other Russell Indices				
Russell 1000	0	0	0	0	0
R1000 Comprehensive Factor	1	1	1	1	1

The magnitude of tilt is determined by the business cycle indicator and adjusted for implementation concerns such as liquidity, capacity, diversification and turnover.[12] Table 12.6 highlights the tilts given the regimes described above. In this matrix, a '1' indicates that we multiply a company's market cap by the factor score a single time, and a '2' indicates that we multiply by the factor score twice. A '0' indicates that the factor is not targeted. For comparison, we include both the Russell 1000 Index, which carries a '0' tilt to each factor, and the Russell 1000 Comprehensive Factor Index, which has a static single tilt to each factor.

Table 12.7 documents that the resulting regime portfolios have the predicted exposure to cash-flow news. The Recovery and Expansion portfolios are designed to load on the business cycle and both have a total cash-flow sensitivity of 1.09. In stark contrast, the Slowdown and Contraction portfolios are designed to load less on the business cycle and have total cash-flow sensitivities of 0.74 and 0.82, respectively. For a formal statistical test, we measure the cash-flow sensitivity of a composite portfolio that is long an equal-weight average of the Recovery and Expansion regime portfolios and short an equal-weight average of the Slowdown and Contraction regime portfolios. The total cash-flow sensitivity of that portfolio is 0.31 and statistically significant.

Finally, in Table 12.8, we document how the sensitivity of our composite portfolio varies across the two main types of regimes (Recovery and Expansion or Slowdown and Contraction). In the former, we want a portfolio that has relatively positive cash-flow news sensitivity. In the latter, we want a portfolio that has relatively negative cash-flow sensitivity. The exhibit confirms this is the case, as during the Recovery and Expansion regimes, the recovery and expansion portfolio has a cash-flow sensitivity that is 0.10 higher than the corresponding estimate of the slowdown and contraction portfolio. Conversely, during the Slowdown and Contraction regimes, the slowdown and

---

[12]In particular, this adjustment takes place in the expansion regime, where an otherwise desired double tilt to size and value is reduced to a single tilt, given interaction effects with a double tilt on momentum. A simultaneous double tilt to the three factors would lead to excessive concentration in less liquid, smaller capitalization stocks, with detrimental implications for turnover and transaction costs.

TABLE 12.7 Cash-flow sensitivity by regime portfolio (July 1980 to June 2018)

	Constant	Cash-Flow News Sensitivity	R^2
RecoveryPortfolio (R)	0.01	1.09	0.16
	(5.90)	(6.95)	
ExpansionPortfolio (E)	0.01	1.09	0.18
	(5.97)	(7.46)	
SlowdownPortfolio (S)	0.01	0.74	0.15
	(6.32)	(6.03)	
Contraction Portfolio (C)	0.01	0.82	0.14
	(5.94)	(6.12)	
0.5*(R+E) -0.5*(S+C)	0.00	0.31	0.03
	(1.39)	(3.81)	

Source: FTSE Russell as of 30/6/2018. We report t statistics in parentheses.

TABLE 12.8 Composite portfolio's cash-flow sensitivity (January 1989 to June 2018)

	Constant	Cash-Flow News Sensitivity	R^2
Unconditional (N = 354)	0.00	0.19	0.04
	(1.14)	(3.83)	
Recovery or Expansion (N = 167)	0.00	0.10	0.00
	(2.49)	(1.14)	
Slowdown or Contraction (N = 187)	0.00	0.23	0.07
	(−0.67)	(3.78)	

Source: FTSE Russell as of 30/6/2018. We report t statistics in parentheses. Portfolio calculations = 0.5*(R+E) −0.5*(S + C).

contraction portfolio has a cash-flow sensitivity that is 0.23 lower than the corresponding estimate of the recovery and expansion portfolio. Thus, the difference across these two quite different components of the business cycle is 0.33 and highly statistically significant.

Table 12.9 puts this all together, reporting the excess returns and associated information ratios provided by the dynamic multifactor model. The dynamic implementation strongly outperforms both the Russell 1000 Index and the static multifactor implementation of the Russell Comprehensive Factor Index, with average annual excess returns of about 4.5% and 2% over these two benchmarks. This is represented graphically in Figure 12.5. Furthermore, given an average one-way annual turnover of 150% and estimated transaction costs of 7–10bps per 100% turnover, these results are economically significant also after transaction costs. Details of the risk-adjusted performance of the strategy are reported in Table 12.10.

Finally, we apply the same model-based macro framework and factor tilts to document dynamic factor rotation strategies for the Russell 2000, FTSE Developed Markets

TABLE 12.9 Mean returns (before transaction costs) and *t* statistic (January 1989 to September 2018)

	Mean Monthly Return	Mean Monthly Excess Return over Russell 1000 Index	Mean Monthly Excess Return over R1000 Comprehensive Factor Index
Russell 1000	0.94%		
	(4.32)		
Russell Comprehensive	1.11%	0.17%	
Factor Index	(5.43)	(2.11)	
Russell 1000 Dynamic	1.26%	0.33%	0.16%
Multifactor Strategy	(6.15)	(3.71)	(1.97)

Source: FTSE Russell and Bloomberg as of 30/9/2018. Mean monthly returns, non-annualized. We report *t* statistics in parentheses. Results do not include transaction costs. Sample dictated by data availability. The Russell Comprehensive Factor Index uses a common methodology to achieve controlled exposure to five target factors, whilst considering levels of diversification and capacity.

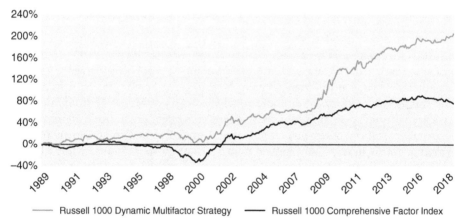

— Russell 1000 Dynamic Multifactor Strategy — Russell 1000 Comprehensive Factor Index

FIGURE 12.5 Cumulative excess returns over Russell 1000 index (January1989 to September 2018).
Source: FTSE Russell and Bloomberg as of 30/9/2018. Results do not include transaction costs. The Russell Comprehensive Factor Index uses a common methodology to achieve controlled exposure to five target factors, whilst considering levels of diversification and capacity.

ex-USA and FTSE Emerging Markets benchmarks (details reported in the Appendix). Results are broadly consistent and statistically significant, providing additional support to the robustness of this framework, and its practical relevance to global investors across regions and market segments.

TABLE 12.10 Dynamic multifactor strategy performance characteristics(January 1989 to September 2018)

	Returns	Standard Deviation	Excess Returns	Sharpe Ratio	Information Ratio	Max Drawdown	Skewness
Russell 1000 Dynamic Multifactor Strategy	15.23%	13.45%	4.52%	0.92	0.78	−43.25%	−0.29
Russell 1000 Comprehensive Factor Index	13.12%	13.33%	2.41%	0.77	0.46	−45.53%	−0.71
Russell 1000 Index	10.71%	14.20%	–	0.55	0.00	−51.13%	−0.65

Source: FTSE Russell and Bloomberg as of 30/9/2018. Average annual returns. Results do not include transaction costs. Sample dictated by data availability. The Russell Comprehensive Factor Index uses a common methodology to achieve controlled exposure to five target factors, whilst considering levels of diversification and capacity.

12.6 CONCLUSIONS

Portfolios based on quantitative characteristics such as value, momentum and quality have historically generated relatively high average returns and represent a new dimension of systematic risk. We argue that understanding the economic drivers of these new systematic risks brings novel insights as to how to time these factor bets. In particular, market timing strategies based on more timely forecasts of aggregate fundamentals can be leveraged through a smart beta lens, as these smart beta portfolios differentially load on aggregate cash-flow news. Dynamic factor strategies exploiting this insight generate information ratios nearly 70% higher than static implementations, while generating excess returns of about 4.5% per annum versus their benchmark index over the past 30 years. Results are statistically significant after accounting for transaction costs, capacity and turnover, and they are robust across market cap segments and geographies.

APPENDIX

12.A.1 DERIVATION OF CASH-FLOW NEWS SERIES

Campbell, Giglio, Polk, and Turley's (2018) (CGPT) VAR specification contains six state variables measured monthly over the period from June 1926 to June 2018. The first variable in the VAR is based on the usual proxy for aggregate wealth and is the log real return on the market, rM, the difference between the log return on the Center for Research in Security Prices (CRSP) value-weighted stock index and the log return on the Consumer Price Index. The second variable is expected market variance (EVAR),

APPENDIX TABLE 12.1   Estimation of VAR based on state variables in CGPT (2018)

	Constant	rM_{t-1}	$EVAR_{t-1}$	PE_{t-1}	$TERM_{t-1}$	DEF_{t-1}	VS_{t-1}
rM	0.0562	0.0892	0.1978	−0.0112	0.0019	−0.0003	−0.0130
	2.85	2.72	0.25	−2.10	1.19	−0.06	−2.12
EVAR	−0.0040	−0.0026	0.5036	0.0010	−0.0001	0.0015	0.0005
	−5.65	−2.16	17.33	5.41	−2.07	8.82	2.16
PE	0.0198	0.5005	0.6301	0.9930	0.0012	−0.0031	−0.0006
	1.70	25.75	1.32	316.10	1.26	−1.13	−0.17
TERM	−0.0436	−0.0477	2.6513	0.0213	0.9469	0.0676	−0.0120
	−0.36	−0.24	0.54	0.66	97.25	2.37	−0.32
DEF	0.0632	−0.7666	5.6451	−0.0174	−0.0049	0.9513	0.0227
	1.30	−9.50	2.86	−1.34	−1.25	82.27	1.51
VS	0.0142	0.1188	0.1204	0.0067	−0.0021	0.0154	0.9708
	0.71	3.57	0.15	1.24	−1.27	3.22	156.05

capturing the market return variance of market returns, σ^2, conditional on information available at time t, so that innovations to this variable can be mapped to volatility news. To construct EVAR, CGPT first create a series of within-month realized variance of daily returns, RVAR. CGPT then run a regression of RVAR on its lagged value as well as the lagged values of the other five state variables, creating a series of predicted values for RVAR, which becomes the variable EVAR. The third variable is the log price-to-smoothed-earnings ratio (PE). The fourth is the term yield spread (TERM), the difference between the log yield on the 10-year US Constant Maturity Bond and the log yield on the 3-Month US Treasury Bill. The fifth state variable is the default spread (DEF), defined as the difference between the log yield on Moody's BAA and AAA bonds. The final variable is the small-stock value spread (VS). Appendix Table 12.1 presents CGPT's estimation of the monthly VAR. Standard errors include a Newey-West adjustment based on 12 lags.

In particular, CGPT estimate a heteroskedastic VAR,

$$x_{t+1} = \bar{x} + \Gamma(x_t - \bar{x}) + \sigma_t u_{t+1}. \tag{12.3}$$

where x_{t+1} is the $n \times 1$ vector of state variables with rM as the first element, σ^2_{t+1} as the second element, $\bar{x}$ and Γ as parameters, and u_{t+1} a vector of shocks with constant variance-covariance matrix, Σ, where element 11 is equal to 1. CGPT define an $n \times 1$ vector e_1 with zero elements except for a unit first element. Their structure implies

$$N_{DR,t+1} = e'_1 \rho \Gamma (I - \rho \Gamma)^{-1} \sigma_t u_{t+1} \tag{12.4}$$

$$N_{CF,t+1} = (e'_1 + e'_1 \rho \Gamma (I - \rho \Gamma)^{-1}) \sigma_t u_{t+1} \tag{12.5}$$

CGPT follow previous academic research and set ρ to an annualized value of 0.95.

12.A.2   US LEADING ECONOMIC INDICATOR AND GLOBAL RISK APPETITE INDICATOR

Our US leading economic indicator ('LEI') is an equally weighted average of several economic variables, where each variable is de-trended, normalized and smoothed with a simple z-scoring procedure $z = \frac{x-\mu}{\sigma}$, where x is the economic variable, μ is its long-term moving average and σ its standard deviation. Finally, z is smoothed via a shorter-term moving average. The de-trending procedure is calibrated to the typical length of a business cycle, normally between 7 and 10 years.

Our global risk appetite cycle indicator ('GRACI') represents the incremental return received by investors over a one-year look-back window (i.e. between t and $t-x$) per incremental unit of risk, and it is computed as the slope β of a cross-sectional regression between excess returns over cash, r_j, and their volatility σ_j, using a large set of country-level total return indices (j) across equity and fixed income markets, from the perspective of a US dollar-based investor:

$$r_{t|t-x,j} = \alpha + \beta\sigma_{t-x,j} + \varepsilon_{tj} \tag{12.6}$$

12.A.3   DYNAMIC MULTIFACTOR STRATEGY: EXTENSION TO OTHER MARKET SEGMENTS AND REGIONS

12.A.3.1   Russell 2000 dynamic multifactor strategy

We apply the same methodology, factor definitions and macro regimes used for the Russell 1000 to the universe of stocks in the Russell 2000 index. Therefore, we use the same macro regimes derived from the intersection of the US leading economic indicator and global risk appetite indicator, illustrated in Figure 12.2a and Figure 12.2b, and the factor tilts illustrated in Table 12.6 to dynamically rotate among the same five factors within the Russell 2000 index. Results are reported in Appendix Table 12.2. The dynamic implementation strongly outperforms both the Russell 2000 Index and the static multifactor implementation of the Russell 2000 Comprehensive Factor Index, with average annual excess returns of about 4.7% and 1.7% over these two benchmarks. Furthermore, given an average one-way annual turnover of 150% and estimated transaction costs of 30–60bps per 100% turnover, these results are economically significant also after transaction costs.

12.A.3.2   FTSE developed markets ex-USA and FTSE emerging markets dynamic multifactor strategies

Using the same factor definitions (Table 12.1) and factor tilts (Table 12.6), we investigate the efficacy of our macro regime framework for the FTSE Developed Markets ex-USA and FTSE Emerging Markets benchmarks. In order to deploy our macro regime method-

APPENDIX TABLE 12.2a   Mean returns (before transaction costs) and *t* statistic (January 1989 to September 2018)

	Mean Monthly Return	Mean Monthly Excess Return over Russell 2000 Index	Mean Monthly Excess Return over R2000 Comprehensive Factor Index
Russell 2000	0.95%		
	(3.39)		
Russell 2000 Comprehensive Factor Index	1.14%	0.19%	
	(4.78)	(2.02)	
Russell 2000 Dynamic Multifactor Strategy	1.27%	0.32%	0.13%
	(5.02)	(3.30)	(1.90)

Source: FTSE Russell and Bloomberg as of 30/9/2018. Mean monthly returns, non-annualized. We report *t* statistics in parentheses. Results do not include transaction costs. Sample dictated by data availability. The Russell Comprehensive Factor Index uses a common methodology to achieve controlled exposure to five target factors, whilst considering levels of diversification and capacity.

APPENDIX TABLE 12.2b   Russell 2000 dynamic multifactor strategy performance statistics (January 1989 to September 2018)

	Returns (%)	Standard Deviation (%)	Excess Returns (%)	Sharpe Ratio	Information Ratio	Max Drawdown (%)	Skewness
Russell 2000 Dynamic Multifactor Strategy	14.82	16.59	4.69	0.72	0.73	−48.42	−0.26
Russell 2000 Comprehensive Index	13.20	15.62	3.08	0.66	0.49	−50.44	−0.60
Russell 2000 Index	10.13	18.32	0.00	0.39	0.00	−52.89	−0.53

Source: FTSE Russell and Bloomberg as of 30/9/2018. Average annual returns. Results do not include transaction costs. Sample dictated by data availability. The Russell Comprehensive Factor Index uses a common methodology to achieve controlled exposure to five target factors, whilst considering levels of diversification and capacity.

ology, we replace the US leading economic indicator with equivalent leading economic indicators for each region. Given the limited availability of first vintage economic data outside the US, both in terms breadth and history, we rely on a single indicator across countries, using country-level Markit PMI Manufacturing surveys, weighted by GDP, to create a Developed Markets ex-USA and an Emerging Markets composite leading economic indicator.[13] Finally, we combine each composite leading indicator with the same global risk appetite indicator described earlier to define the four regimes of each regional business cycle, as per the same methodology outlined in Figure 12.2a. Results are reported in Appendix Table 12.3 and Appendix Table 12.4 for the FTSE Developed Markets ex-USA and FTSE Emerging Markets benchmarks, respectively. In both cases, the dynamic factor implementation strongly outperforms both the market cap benchmarks and the static implementation of the Comprehensive factor indices, with average annual excess returns in the range of 5.8% to 6.8% versus benchmark and 2.3% to 2.5% versus the Comprehensive index. Given an average one-way annual turnover of 150%, and estimated transaction costs of 10–20bps for Developed Markets-ex USA and 25–50bps for Emerging Markets, per 100% turnover, these results are economically significant also after transaction costs.

APPENDIX TABLE 12.3a   Mean monthly returns (before transaction costs) and *t* statistics (August 1997 to September 2018)

	Mean Return	Mean Excess Return over FTSE DM ex USA Index	Mean Excess Return over FTSE DM ex USA Comprehensive Factor Index
FTSE DM ex USA	0.54%		
	(1.81)		
FTSE DM ex USA	0.85%	0.31%	
Comprehensive Factor Index	(3.31)	(3.33)	
FTSE DM ex USA Dynamic	1.05%	0.50%	0.20%
Multifactor Strategy	(3.81)	(4.51)	(2.04)

Source: FTSE Russell and Bloomberg as of 30/9/2018. Mean monthly returns, non-annualized. We report *t* statistics in parentheses. Results do not include transaction costs. Sample dictated by data availability. The Russell Comprehensive Factor Index uses a common methodology to achieve controlled exposure to five target factors, whilst considering levels of diversification and capacity.

---

[13]PMI Manufacturing surveys are well-known and commonly used leading indicators of GDP growth across countries, given their coverage of cyclical industries and timely release on a monthly basis.

APPENDIX TABLE 12.3b   FTSE DM ex USA dynamic multifactor strategy performance statistics (August 1997 to September 2018)

	Return (%)	Standard Deviation (%)	Excess Return (%)	Sharpe Ratio	Information Ratio	Max Drawdown (%)	Skewness
FTSE DM ex USA Dynamic Multifactor Strategy	12.06	15.17	6.81	0.67	1.10	−48.93	−0.10
FTSE DM ex USA Comprehensive Factor Index	9.61	14.21	4.36	0.54	0.85	−50.47	−0.74
FTSE DM ex USA Index	5.25	16.56	–	0.20	0.00	−56.32	−0.66

Source: FTSE Russell and Bloomberg as of 30/9/2018. Average annual returns. Results do not include transaction costs. Sample dictated by data availability. The Russell Comprehensive Factor Index uses a common methodology to achieve controlled exposure to five target factors, whilst considering levels of diversification and capacity.

APPENDIX TABLE 12.4a   Mean monthly returns (before transaction costs) and *t* statistics (January 2005 to September 2018)

	Mean Return	Mean Excess Return over FTSE EM Index	Mean Excess Return over FTSE EM Comprehensive Factor Index
FTSE EM	0.84% (1.72)		
FTSE EM Comprehensive Factor Index	1.07% (2.41)	0.23% (2.45)	
FTSE EM Dynamic Multifactor Strategy	1.26% (2.70)	0.42% (3.55)	0.19% (1.63)

Source: FTSE Russell and Bloomberg as of 3/9/2018. Mean monthly returns, non-annualized. We report *t* statistics in parentheses. Results do not include transaction costs. Sample dictated by data availability. The Russell Comprehensive Factor Index uses a common methodology to achieve controlled exposure to five target factors, whilst considering levels of diversification and capacity.

APPENDIX TABLE 12.4b   FTSE EM dynamic multifactor strategy performance statistics (January 2005 to September 2018)

	Return (%)	Standard Deviation (%)	Excess Return (%)	Sharpe Ratio	Information Ratio	Max Drawdown (%)	Skewness
FTSE EM Dynamic Multifactor Strategy	13.78	20.70	5.82	0.61	1.11	−53.61	0.03
FTSE EM Comprehensive Factor Index	11.42	19.79	3.46	0.52	0.83	−53.74	−0.52
FTSE EM Index	7.96	21.76	–	0.31	0.00	−61.07	−0.50

Source: FTSE Russell and Bloomberg as of 30/9/2018. Average annual returns. Results do not include transaction costs. Sample dictated by data availability. The Russell Comprehensive Factor Index uses a common methodology to achieve controlled exposure to five target factors, whilst considering levels of diversification and capacity.

ACKNOWLEDGEMENTS

The views expressed here are those of the authors alone and not of Invesco. We would like to thank Tom Koch, Karl Desmond, Christopher Clark, Dianne Ellis, Arezu Moghadam, Jesse Hurwitz, Matthew Schilling and Kenneth Blay for their contributions and helpful comments.

REFERENCES

Ahmerkamp, J., J. Grant and R. Kosowski, 2012, 'Predictability in Carry and Momentum Strategies Across Asset Classes', SSRN Working Paper.

Asness, Clifford, Jacques Friedman, Robert Krail and John Liew, 2000, 'Style timing: Value versus growth', *Journal of Portfolio Management* **26**, 50–60.

Asness, C.S., J. Liew, L.H. Pedersen and A. Thapar, 2017, 'Deep Value', AQR Capital Management Working Paper.

Baba-Yara, Fahiz, Martijn Boons and Andrea Tamoni, 2018, 'Value Return Predictability Across Asset Classes and Commonalities in Risk Premia', London School of Economics Working Paper.

Banz, Rolf W., 1981, 'The relationship between return and market value of common stocks', *Journal of Financial Economics* **9**, 103–126.

Barroso, Pedro and Pedro Santa-Clara, 2015, 'Momentum has its moments', *Journal of Financial Economics* **116**, 111–120.

Black, Fischer, 1976, Studies of stock price volatility changes. In: Proceedings of the 1976 Meetings of the American Statistical Association. *Business and Economic Statistics Section*, Washington, DC, pp. 177–181.

Campbell, John Y., 1991, 'A variance decomposition for stock returns', *Economic Journal* **101**, 157–179.

Campbell, John Y. and John Cochrane, 1999, 'By force of habit: A consumption-based explanation of aggregate stock market behavior', *Journal of Political Economy* **107**, 205–251.

Campbell, John Y., Stefano Giglio and Christopher Polk, 2013, 'Hard times', *Review of Asset Pricing Studies* **3**, 95–132.

Campbell, John Y., Stefano Giglio, Christopher Polk, and Robert Turley, 2018, 'An Intertemporal CAPM with Stochastic Volatility,' *Journal of Financial Economics* **128**, 207–233.

Campbell, John Y., Christopher Polk and Tuomo Vuolteenaho, 2010, 'Growth or glamour? Fundamentals and systematic risk in stock returns', *Review of Financial Studies* **23**, 305–344.

Campbell, John Y. and Robert Shiller, 1988a, 'The dividend-price ratio and expectations of future dividends and discount factors', *Review of Financial Studies* **1**, 195–228.

Campbell, John Y. and Robert Shiller, 1988b, 'Stock prices, earnings, and expected dividends', *Journal of Finance* **43**, 661–676.

Campbell, John Y. and Tuomo Vuolteenaho, 2004, 'Bad beta, good beta', *American Economic Review* **94**, 1249–1275.

Christie, Andrew, 1982, 'The stochastic behavior of common stock variances: Value, leverage, and interest rate effects', *Journal of Financial Economics* **10**, 407–432.

Cohen, Randolph B., Christopher Polk and Tuomo Vuolteenaho, 2003, 'The value spread', *Journal of Finance* **58**, 609–641.

Cooper, I., A. Mitrache and R. Priestley, 2016, 'A Global Macroeconomic Risk Explanation for Momentum and Value', SSRN Working Paper.

de Longis, A. and D. Ellis, 2019, 'Market Sentiment and the Business Cycle: Identifying Macro Regimes Through Investor Risk Appetite', Invesco Investment Solution White Papers.

Dimson, Elroy, 1979, 'Risk measurement when shares are subject to infrequent trading', *Journal of Financial Economics* **7**, 197–226.

Fairfield, P.M., S. Whisenant and T.L. Yohn, 2003, 'Accrued earnings and growth: Implications for future profitability and market mispricing', *Accounting Review* **78**, 353–371.

Fama, Eugene F. and Kenneth R. French, 1989, 'Business conditions and expected returns on stocks and bonds', *Journal of Financial Economics* **25**, 23–49.

Fama, Eugene F. and Kenneth R. French, 1993, 'Common risk factors in the returns on stocks and bonds', *Journal of Financial Economics* **33**, 3–56.

Fama, Eugene F. and Kenneth R. French, 2015, 'A five-factor asset-pricing model', *Journal of Financial Economics* **116**, 1–22.

FTSE Russell, 2017, 'Multi-factor indexes: The power of tilting', https://www.ftserussell.com/sites/default/files/multi-factor-indexes-the-power-of-tilting-final.pdf

Greenwood, Robin and Samuel G. Hanson, 2012, 'Share issuance and factor timing', *Journal of Finance* **67**, 761–798.

Hanson, Samuel G. and Adi Sunderam, 2014, 'The growth and limits of arbitrage: Evidence from short interest',' *Review of Financial Studies* **27**, 1238–1286.

Haugen, Robert A and Nardin L. Baker, 1996, 'Commonality in the determinants of expected stock returns,' *Journal of Financial Economics* **41**, 401-439.

Hodges, Philip, Ken Hogan, Justin Peterson and Andrew Ang, 2017, 'Factor timing with cross-section and time-series predictors', *Journal of Portfolio Management Fall*, 30–43.

Huang, Shiyang, Dong Lou and Christopher Polk, 2018, 'The booms and busts of beta arbitrage', London School of Economics Working Paper.

Kumar, Manmohan and Avinash Persaud, 2002, 'Pure contagion and investors' shifting risk appetite: Analytical issues and empirical evidence', *International Finance* **5**, 401–436.

Lewellen, Jonathan, 2002, 'Momentum and autocorrelation in stock returns', *Review of Financial Studies* **15**, 533–564.

Lintner, John, 1965, 'The valuation of risk assets and the selection of risky investments in stock portfolios and capital budgets', *Review of Economics and Statistics* **47**, 13–37.

Lou, Dong and Christopher Polk, 2013, 'Comomentum: Inferring Arbitrage Activity from Return Correlations,' London School of Economics Working Paper.

Lou, Dong, Christopher Polk and Spyros Skouras, 2019, 'A tug of war: Overnight vs. intraday expected returns,' *Journal of Financial Economics* **134**, 192–213.

Novy-Marx, Robert, 2013, 'The other side of value: The gross profitability premium', *Journal of Financial Economics* **108**, 1–28.

Polk, Christopher and Paola Sapienza, 2009, 'The stock market and corporate investment: A test of catering theory', *Review of Financial Studies* **22**, 187–217.

Polk, Christopher, Sam Thompson and Tuomo Vuolteenaho, 2006, 'Cross-sectional forecasts of the equity premium', *Journal of Financial Economics* **81**, 101–141.

Rosenberg, Barr, Kenneth Reid and Ronald Lanstein, 1985, 'Persuasive evidence of market inefficiency', *Journal of Portfolio Management* **11**, 9–17.

Scholes, Myron and Joseph Williams, 1977, 'Estimating betas from nonsynchronous data', *Journal of Financial Economics* **5**, 309–327.

Sharpe, William F., 1964, 'Capital asset prices: A theory of market equilibrium under conditions of risk', *Journal of Finance* **19**, 425–442.

Shiller, Robert, 1981, 'Do stock prices move too much to be justified by subsequent changes in dividends?' *American Economic Review* **71**, 421–436.

Stattman, Dennis, 1980, 'Book values and stock returns', *The Chicago MBA: A Journal of Selected Papers* **4**, 25–45.

Teo, M. and S. Woo, 2004, 'Style effects in the cross-section of stock returns', *Journal of Financial Economics* **74**, 367–398.

Titman, S., K.C. Wei, and F. Xie, 2004, 'Capital investments and stock returns', *Journal of Financial and Quantitative Analysis* **39**. 677–700.

Varsani, H.D. and V. Jain, 2018, 'Adaptive Multi-Factor Allocation', MSCI Factor Investing Research Paper.

Vuolteenaho, Tuomo, 2002, 'What drives firm-level stock returns?' *Journal of Finance* **57**, 233–264.

CHAPTER 13

Where Goes Momentum?

RON BIRD XIAOJUN (KEVIN) GEO and DANNY YEUNG

13.1 INTRODUCTION

In the *Journal of Financial Economics*, Vol. 6, No. 2/3 (1978), the editor (Michael Jensen) packaged seven articles that presented evidence anomalous to the Efficient Market Hypothesis (EMH). In introducing this issue, Jensen commenced by saying that 'I believe there is no other proposition in economics which has more solid empirical evidence supporting it than the Efficient Market Hypothesis'. He went on to say that the 'purpose of this special issue ... is to bring together a number of these scattered pieces of anomalous evidence regarding Market Efficiency'. He concluded by saying that 'It is my hope that bringing the(se) studies together ... will focus the attention of scholars throughout the world on these disturbing pieces of evidence and ... result in the resolution of the questions they raise'.

Undoubtedly Jensen would be pleased that he stimulated the research and debate for which he hoped by bringing the evidence on market anomalies to the attention of the academic community. However, he might be somewhat surprised by the fact that more than 35 years later we continue to see new evidence on market anomalies and no resolution as to what gives rise to them (or, indeed, whether they exist at all). As Novy-Marx and Velikov (2016) note, there have been hundreds of anomalies identified during the intervening period. Further, no closure has been reached as to whether the anomalies are indicative of true inefficiencies possibly driven by the behavioural traits of investors and the failure of arbitrage, or they are the result of data snooping, a failure to correctly incorporate risk or other reasons to suggest that the anomalies do not exist. Another issue is the extent to which the profits attributable to the anomalies persist once the anomaly has been identified. McLean and Pontiff (2016) and Chordia et al. (2014) variously estimate that between a third and a half of these apparent profits disappear once the anomaly has been identified in the literature, but this varies widely across anomalies.

A relatively small proportion of the empirical studies that have identified market anomalies have incorporated implementation costs to any meaningful extent. Several of the studies that have incorporated implementation costs have examined the momentum anomaly without coming to any consensus as to whether the apparent profits are exploitable. Lesmond et al. (2004) argue that profits associated with the momentum strategies are illusory once appropriate transaction costs are taken into account. However, Jegadeesh and Titman (1993) found that the cross-sectional momentum strategy yielded around 9% per annum in the US equity market after accounting for transaction costs. More recently, authors have extended the incorporation of transaction costs to a wider array of anomalies. Novy-Marx and Velikov (2016) evaluated 23 market anomalies using US data and found that most anomalies remain profitable provided they generate turnover of less than 50% per month and they are efficiently implemented. Frazzini et al. (2015) evaluated the robustness of three popular investment strategies (momentum, value and size) to the introduction of transaction costs. Their analysis was based upon actual transactions data obtained from a single large institutional investor with their conclusion being that each of the three strategies yield sizable after-transaction cost profits because their identified transactions are only a small fraction of those estimated in many previous studies.

What we embark on in this study is what we believe to be the most comprehensive study of a market anomaly executed to date. We believe that we learn more from a thorough analysis of one anomaly than by undertaking a less detailed analysis across a range of anomalies. The anomaly on which we concentrate is momentum which has proved the most robust, being described by Fama (1998) as the 'premier unexplained anomaly'. The profitability of the momentum strategy is calculated in the traditional way as the aggregate of the returns on a long portfolio of stocks that have recently recorded good performance (winners) and a short portfolio of stocks that have recently performed poorly (losers). We evaluate the performance of both cross-sectional momentum (Jegadeesh and Titman, 1993, 2000) and time-series momentum (Moskowitz et al., 2012?) across 24 markets under 192 implementation strategies, after taking account of implementation costs, the risk exposure of the portfolios, and the impact of restrictions on shorting stocks.

Bird et al. (2016) and Gulen and Petkova (2015) both demonstrate and provide reasons for the profitability of the time-series momentum strategy over cross-sectional momentum strategies , even though based on absolute returns both would appear to be profitable investment strategies. However, all studies of momentum performance (and also that of other anomalies) are premised on assumptions as to how these strategies are implemented. Bird et al. (2016) clearly demonstrate that the profitability of these strategies is totally dependent on choosing the 'right' implementation strategy. In this study, we demonstrate how the apparent profitability of the two momentum strategies is eroded as we sequentially introduce implementation costs, risk and restrictions on shorting stocks. When evaluated across the 24 markets, we demonstrate that there is very little evidence of either strategy offering exploitable investment opportunities for investors with average implementation skills. These findings bring into question whether momentum is an anomaly at all or simply a result of data snooping and the lack of realism within the plethora of studies that have evaluated this phenomenon.

The remainder of the chapter is organised as follows. In Section 13.2, we review the literature on viability of momentum strategies. Sections 13.3 and 13.4 discuss the data and the method employed in this study. In Section 13.5, we analyse the findings relating to the exploitability of both momentum strategies. Section 13.6 examines how risk-adjustment and short-sales constraints affect momentum profitability, while Section 13.7 provides us with the opportunity to summarise our findings.

13.2 MOMENTUM STRATEGIES

Although the momentum anomaly has been discussed and investigated over the last two decades, the literature still has not reached consensus as to whether it is exploitable once account is taken of transaction costs, risk and restrictions relating to shorting stocks. Jegadeesh and Titman (1993) find that the cross sectional momentum strategy yielded around 9% per annum in the US equity market after accounting for transaction costs.[1] However, Lesmond et al. (2004), observed that there are numerous problems associated with how the transaction costs have been calculated in this and other studies.[2] They proposed a method (which we will call the LOT method) that they claim overcomes these deficiencies,[3] and used this method to show that the profitability of the cross-sectional momentum strategy largely disappears once account is taken of the appropriate transaction costs. Goyenko et al. (2009) show that transaction cost estimates from the standard LOT model failed to precisely capture effective spread, realized spread and price impact spread.[4] In addition, Li et al. (2009) argue that by only evaluating a 6-month holding period in their study, Lesmond et al. (2004) fail to provide the full picture of the profitability from the cross-sectional momentum strategy. They demonstrate that the transaction costs are reduced by extending the holding period, for example using 12-month holding period instead of 6-month, and show that the momentum strategy is still profitable when using longer holding period. Frazzini at al. (2015) find momentum to be a highly profitable investment strategy based on transaction costs they have derived using a proprietary database provided by one institutional money manager.

---

[1]Jegadeesh and Titman (1993) based on work undertaken by Berkowitz et al. (1988) assume the cost of 0.5% per trade when calculating the after-transaction costs returns on the cross-sectional momentum strategy.

[2]First, Lesmond et al. (2004) argue that it is inappropriate to assume a single transaction cost for all stocks because these costs exhibit substantial cross-sectional variation (Keim and Madhavan, 1997). Second, they argue that the cost estimated from one period is unable to capture the time-series variations in trading costs over other time horizons (Lesmond et al., 1999). Third, they point out that most measurements of transaction costs from the extant literature, such as bid-ask spread plus commissions, fail to account for additional costs faced by investors, such as price impact costs, taxes, short-sale costs and immediacy costs.

[3]Lesmond et al. (1999) introduced a model (LOT) based on investors' behaviour to estimate transaction costs from the marginal trader's side, and claimed that the transaction cost estimates had more than 85% accuracy to measure the overall transaction costs from the buyer's side.

[4]Goyenko et al. (2009) compare the transaction cost estimates from widely used proxies with the transaction data from Trade and Quote (TAQ) and Rule 605 database in the US stock markets, and observe the estimated transaction costs from the LOT model has less accuracy compared with the results from the 'Effective Tick', 'Holden' and 'LOT Y-split' models.

There is a dearth of evidence to suggest that traditional risk-based models such as the Capital Asset Pricing Model (CAPM) or the Fama-French three-factor models explain the momentum profits (Jegadeesh and Titman, 2000; Grundy and Martin, 2001). Conrad and Kaul (1998) find that virtually all of the profits to momentum strategies can be traced to cross-sectional variation in unconditional mean returns. However, Jegadeesh and Titman (2002) dispute their findings, stating that while cross-sectional variation in unconditional mean returns is a legitimate theoretical candidate for the profits of momentum strategies, it has a trivial role to play in generating actual momentum profits. A deficiency in the analysis to date is the failure to integrate transaction costs and risk by applying the after-transaction costs returns to the risk-based models. Indeed, Lesmond et al. (2004) argue that there is no reason to consider risk once transaction costs have been introduced into the analysis.

Traditionally the momentum return is calculated as the aggregate of the returns on a long portfolio of winners and a short portfolio of losers (Jegadeesh and Titman, 1993). Market regulations vary across markets but typically they restrict the investor from shorting some or all of the stocks assigned to the short portfolio (Lesmond et al., 2004). The importance of this constraint becomes apparent when one realises that the major proportion of the momentum profits typically are attributed to the poor performance of the loser (Ali and Trombley, 2006). However, the short-sale restrictions do not necessarily prevent continuation of the momentum profit. Griffin et al. (2005) demonstrate that momentum traders could be still realise profit by only taking long positions of the winner portfolios across 40 countries in the absence of transaction costs. Fong et al. (2005) investigate the momentum strategies in 24 countries and find that only buying stocks in the winner portfolio generated significant abnormal returns after accounting for transaction costs.

The literature to date on momentum in equity markets has focused on investigating the cross-sectional momentum strategy. Bird et al. (2016) examine both strategies in developed markets and find that the time-series momentum strategy outperforms the cross-sectional momentum strategy, largely driven by the market timing element that it introduces to stock selection. This chapter seeks to establish whether the two momentum strategies still yield positive significant returns, and whether the time-series momentum strategy still outperforms the cross-sectional momentum strategy, after incorporating transaction costs, risk adjustments and restrictions on shorting

13.3 DATA

The sample consisted of the stocks in 24 developed markets over the period from 1992 to 2012. The daily and monthly returns, the market value and the book-to-market ratio for all active and dead stocks were obtained from DataStream.[5] Table 13.1 displays the

---

[5] We also conducted the analysis for the US market using CRSP data and obtained substantially the same results.

total sample size, the average number of stocks in each month, and several market indexes for each country.[6] After applying several filtering procedures,[7] our sample size consists of 22,977 stocks, with the US market having the largest number of stocks with 10,041 stocks and Hong Kong having the smallest number with 1404 stocks. The total sample size, average number of monthly observations, and the average monthly returns under each of the three weighting strategies used in constructing the portfolios: equal weights (EW), market-value weights (MW) and four sets of returns for inverse volatility weights (I-VOL).

13.4 METHOD

Following Bird et al. (2016), we set out the various implementation procedures that we examine for cross-sectional and time-series momentum strategies after transaction costs and risks. They are discussed in the following subsections in terms of the contribution that they make to the two components of the investment process: stock selection and portfolio structure.

13.4.1 Stock selection

Stock selection involves identifying the stocks to be allocated to each of the long and short portfolios. It has two components:

(i) Specifying the prior period over which to measure stock returns (the formation period): We examine four oft-used formation points (J) of 3, 6, 9 and 12 months.

(ii) *Specifying the cut-off rule that identifies stocks as being either winners or losers*: We examine cut-offs which result in 32%, 60% and 100% of stocks being allocated to one of the winner and loser portfolios. For cross sectional momentum, this involves ranking the stocks and using symmetric cut-offs (e.g. top and bottom 16% when seeking 32% of stocks). With the time-series momentum strategy, the cut-off for

---

[6]Ince and Porter (2006) report the match rate of samples in the US market from DataStream and CRSP is approximately above 70% after 1990. Samples are retrieved from 1990 to 2012 which could help to compare the results with previous literature that is either using data source from DataStream or CRSP. We leave the first two years as calculation preparing of momentum strategies. Reporting the momentum results from 1992 to 2012 could consistently compare momentum profits under different formation and holding periods across markets.

[7]For a stock to be included in our analysis, a stock should have both return and market capitalization data available at each month. Following Ince and Porter (2006), we apply several filtering procedures to our sample stocks for correcting stock returns of delisted firms, and identifying non-trading days across stock markets. In accordance with Chui et al. (2010), monthly returns will be trimmed if the market capitalization of a stock is below the bottom fifth percentile of all stocks within a given country in any month. Following McLean et al. (2009), we then winsorise daily and monthly returns within a given country at the top and bottom 1% to minimize the effects of outliers.

TABLE 13.1 Summary statistics

Country	Sample Size		Average Monthly Return (%)					
	No. of stocks		EW	MW	IVOL3	IVOL6	IVOL9	IVOL12
	Total	Ave. monthly						
Australia	2880	1141	1.53	1.14	0.82	0.88	0.91	0.91
Austria	218	96	0.43	1.14	0.31	0.28	0.31	0.32
Belgium	335	157	0.63	1.17	0.61	0.62	0.60	0.63
Canada	3020	1200	1.69	1.81	0.72	0.81	0.82	0.81
Denmark	360	195	0.59	1.55	0.57	0.57	0.60	0.59
Finland	213	106	1.19	1.85	1.10	1.14	1.17	1.19
France	1991	828	0.96	1.43	0.47	0.41	0.51	0.56
Germany	1450	663	0.47	1.33	0.28	0.34	0.31	0.35
Greece	415	224	1.07	1.39	0.91	0.82	0.93	0.94
Hong Kong	1,404	715	1.38	1.98	1.02	1.23	1.28	1.41
Ireland	131	58	1.02	1.61	1.02	0.88	0.80	0.80
Israel	843	475	1.19	1.67	0.93	0.91	0.89	0.87
Italy	543	241	0.33	1.35	0.27	0.35	0.37	0.38
Japan	2990	2096	0.27	0.71	0.03	0.12	0.16	0.18
Netherlands	304	160	0.72	1.33	0.73	0.77	0.80	0.82
New Zealand	279	115	1.05	1.47	1.55	1.00	0.97	0.98
Norway	479	165	1.22	1.91	1.05	1.06	1.04	1.06
Portugal	198	92	0.78	1.26	0.83	0.69	0.54	0.56
Singapore	792	367	1.10	1.36	0.93	0.91	0.98	0.96
Spain	281	145	0.71	1.06	0.63	0.69	0.66	0.71
Sweden	906	308	1.15	1.92	1.04	1.12	1.17	1.18
Switzerland	412	235	0.79	1.19	0.80	0.77	0.77	0.79
UK	4212	1601	0.66	1.39	0.24	0.43	0..49	0.61
US	10041	4232	1.52	1.65	1.05	0.99	1.03	1.02

This table reports the number of stocks, the average monthly number of stocks, the average monthly market returns based on equal weight (EW), market weight (MW) and inversed-volatility weight (IVOL) as measured over 3, 6 9 and 12 months. The data with are obtained from DataStream from 1990 to 2012 for the 24 markets. Australia (Australian stock exchange), Germany (Frankfurt stock exchange), Hong Kong (Hong Kong stock exchange), Japan (Tokyo stock exchange), the UK (London stock exchange) and the US (NYSE, NASDAQ and AMEX). Following Ince and Porter (2006), we clean the data for delisted firm, exclude stocks whose market capitalization is below 5% of all stocks in each month and monthly (daily) return is below the 1 percentile or above the 99 percentile of the return distribution in each month (day). All returns are reported in local currencies. The first two years of data are used in the preparation of momentum strategies and therefore all results in this chapter are from 1992 to 2012.

identifying winners and losers is an absolute number(s). To match the situation where the cut-offs under the cross-sectional momentum strategy are set at 16%, we set symmetric upper and lower cut-offs for the time-series momentum strategy which result on average in 32% of the stocks in the investment universe being classified as either a winner or a loser stock.

13.4.2 Portfolio construction

Portfolio construction involves determining at the time of each rebalancing, the proportion of the weights that are allocated to each stock in the winning and losing portfolios. There are three separate decisions that in combination determine these weights:

(i) The holding period: We examine holding periods (H) of 3, 6, 9 and 12 months.
(ii) The period for portfolio rebalancing: We examine two option: (i) a buy and hold strategy where the portfolio is rebalanced at the end of each holding period (BHAR), and (ii) monthly rebalancing which results in the portfolio being partially rebalanced each month (CAR).
(iii) The determination of the weights assigned to stocks: Once it is determined what new stocks to include in a portfolio, it is then necessary to allocate a portion of the total funds available to each stock. Three alternatives are considered: (i) equal weighting (EW), (ii) market weighting (MW), and (iii) inverse volatility weighting (I-VOL) as proposed in Moskowitz et al. (2012).

The findings reported in this chapter are based on the case where 32% of all stocks are included in either the winner or loser portfolios.[8] The decision rules associated with choosing these portfolios are summarised in Table 13.2.[9]

13.4.3 Transaction costs measurement

13.4.3.1 LOT Y – split model Lesmond et al. (1999, 2004) introduced the LOT model that infers transaction costs based on the incidence of zero daily returns for a particular stock. The proposition being that investors will only trade on new information where they see a profitable opportunity and higher transaction costs will make the incidence of such perceived opportunities less frequent. They divide the information into three regions: negative information sufficient to generate a trade; either positive or negative information insufficient to generate a trade; positive information sufficient to generate a trade. A particular advantage of the transaction cost estimates from the LOT model is that they not only include the bid-ask spread, but also take into account both the effective and realised spreads, and price impact. Goyenko et al. (2009) point out that the definition of the three regions in the LOT model significantly influenced the quality of the transaction costs estimates. They introduce an improved version called the LOT Y-split model that distributes daily stock return into three regions based on the stock return itself (R_{jt}) rather than using a combination of the stock return (R_{jt}) and the market return (R_{mt}).

Comparing the transaction costs estimates from the two models with the estimates based on the actual data from TAQ and Rule 605 in the US, the LOT Y-split model

---

[8]Bird et al. (2016) found the better performance came from the implementations that included a smaller number of stocks in the winner and loser portfolios.
[9]All combinations of these decisions rules aggregate to 192 implementations. In total we considered four cut-offs resulting is us examining 768 implementations in total.

TABLE 13.2   Implementation options for time-series and cross-sectional momentum

	Stock selection criteria	Cross-sectional momentum	Time-series momentum
Stock selection	Formation periods	J = 3, 6, 9 and 12 months	
	Cut-off Point Invest in 32% of sample	Winner/Loser portfolio contains top/bottom 16% of stocks in the entire market	Absolute cut off points of winner (loser) portfolios are calculated as the average monthly on all stocks over the entire sample market over the testing period plus/minus approximately one (half) standard deviation.
Portfolio structure	Portfolio construction	CAR(0) and CAR(1) BHAR(0) and BHAR(1)	
	Portfolio weights	Equal weight (EW) Market value weight (MW) Inversed-volatility weight (I-VOL)	
	Holding periods	H = 3, 6, 9 and 12 months	

provides a better estimate of the effective and realized spreads, and price impact.[10] Following Goyenko et al. (2009), we use the LOT Y-split model to estimate the transaction costs for each stock which in turn is then used to calculate the after-transaction cost performance of time-series and cross-sectional momentum strategies.

According to Lesmond et al. (1999), let R_{jt}^* be the true returns such that,

$$R_{jt}^* = \beta_j R_{mt} + \varepsilon_{jt}$$

where β_j is the sensitivity of stock returns (R_{jt}) to the market return on day t (R_{mt}), and the error term (ε_{jt}) indicates a public information shock on day t. This model assumes that ε_{jt} is normally distributed with mean zero and variance, σ_j^2.

Let R_{jt} be measured returns from daily returns on stocks, where j denotes the stock j and t is the trading day and the accumulated transaction cost of buying and selling a stock is α_2 and α_1, respectively. Based on the suggestion from Goyenko et al. (2009), the daily returns assign into region 0 if they equal to zero, into region 1 if they are positive and into region 2 if they are negative. The relationship between the measured return R_{jt}

---

[10]Trade and Quote (TAQ) data collects intraday transactions data (trades and quotes) for stocks listed in American stock exchange, New York stock exchange, NASDAQ, National market system and Small Cap issues. Rule 605 is the Securities and Exchange Commission's Rule 605 (formerly 11Act1-5) in the US markets. The rule mandates that stock exchanges, dealers and other market centres provide selected data on selected order executions.

and true return R_{jt}^* can be shown as

$$R_{jt} = R_{jt}^* - \alpha_{1j} \ if \ R_{jt}^* < \alpha_{1j} \tag{13.1}$$

$$R_{jt} = 0 \ if \ \alpha_{1j} < R_{jt}^* < \alpha_{2j} \tag{13.2}$$

$$R_{jt} = R_{jt}^* - \alpha_{2j} \ if \ R_{jt}^* > \alpha_{2j} \tag{13.3}$$

α_{1j} is the accumulated transaction cost of selling stock j. Similarly, α_{2j} is the accumulated transaction cost of buying stock j. The proportional round-trip transaction cost of stock j at time t for competitive marginal investor is the difference between the per cent buying and selling costs,

$$COST_j = \alpha_{2j} - \alpha_{1j}$$

To determine two threshold levels, α_{1j} and α_{2j}, Lesmond et al. (1999) develop the following maximum likelihood function to estimate four parameters $\alpha_{1j}, \alpha_{2j}, \beta_j, \sigma_j$ of the LOT model:

$$L(\alpha_{1j}, \alpha_{2j}, \beta_j, \sigma_j | R_{jt}, R_{mt})$$

$$= \prod_1 \frac{1}{\sigma_j} n \left[\frac{R_{jt} + \alpha_{1j} - \beta_j R_{mt}}{\sigma_j} \right]$$

$$\times \prod_0 \left[N \left(\frac{\alpha_{2j} - \beta_j R_{mt}}{\sigma_j} \right) - N \left(\frac{\alpha_{1j} - \beta_j R_{mt}}{\sigma_j} \right) \right]$$

$$\times \prod_2 \frac{1}{\sigma_j} n \left[\frac{R_{jt} + \alpha_{2j} - \beta_j R_{mt}}{\sigma_j} \right]$$

S.T. $\alpha_{1j} \leq 0, \alpha_{2j} \geq 0, \beta_j \geq 0, \sigma_j \geq 0$

where N(.) is the cumulative normal distribution and n(.) is the normal distribution.[11]

13.4.4 Risk adjustment

After calculating after-transaction costs returns for each of the implementations of the momentum strategies, we use two methods to calculate risk-adjusted measures of performance: the Sharpe ratio and the alpha from the Fama-French three-factor model.[12]

---

[11] Round-trip transaction costs are estimated as a percentage of cost for each stock in each calendar year. As in Liu et al. (2011), we require that stocks have at least 30% nonzero returns in a calendar year to be included in the model. We set the starting values for the estimated parameters, $\alpha_{1j}, \alpha_{2j}, \beta_j, \sigma_j$ as 0.01, 0.01, 1, and 0.1, respectively. If the procedure fails to converge, we change the alternative starting values to 0.1, 0.1, 1, and 0.1, and re-estimate.

[12] We do not extend to applying the Carhart four-factor model as deem it inappropriate to apply momentum as a factor when evaluating the performance of momentum portfolios.

13.4.4.1 The Sharpe ratio The Sharpe ratio is a risk-adjusted approach of return that is often used to assess the performance of a portfolio (Sharpe, 1998). It measures the increment in excess returns (as measured by the portfolio return minus the risk-free rate) for each additional unit of risk (as measured by the standard deviation of the portfolio returns). We use this ratio to compare the performances of different implementations of our two momentum strategies under each of the implementation approaches.

13.4.4.2 The Fama-French three-factor model The alternative common standard risk-adjusted measure used in the literature is the Fama-French three-factor model (Fama and French, 1992). We test whether the two momentum strategies yield significant positive risk-adjusted returns (or abnormal returns) as measured by the intercept term (Fama and French alpha) in the following the regression model.

$$MR_i - Rf_i = \alpha_i + \beta1_i(Rm_i - Rf_i) + \beta2_i SMB_i + \beta3_i HML_i$$

where MR_i is momentum return after transaction costs at month t, Rf_i is the risk-free rate at month t, Rm_i is market-weighted index at month t, SMB_i is 'small minus big' at month t, which is calculated as the average return for the smallest 30% of stocks minus the average return of the largest 30% of stocks in that month. HML_i is 'high minus low' at month t, which is calculated as the market average return for 50% of stocks with the highest book-to-market ratio minus market average return for 50% of stocks with the lowest book-to-market ratio.

13.5 RESULTS

The results that we report in Table 13.3 are those derived where the cut-offs used are targeted to result in 32% of the stocks being allocated to either the winner or loser portfolio.[13] In the case of cross-sectional momentum, this meant that the cut-offs were set so as to include 16% of stocks in the each of the winner and loser portfolios at the time of each rebalancing. In the case of time-series momentum it involved determining sets of upper and lower cut-offs for each of the 24 markets designed to ensure that 32% of stocks are assigned to either the winner or loser portfolio over the entire sample period. For example, in the case of Australia, the upper bound was set at 5.99% and the lower bound at −4.14%. This meant that any stock returning over 5.99% over any formation period was classified as a winner and returning less than −4.14% was classified as a loser.

We analysed 192 implementations for each of cross-sectional and time-series momentum but report in Table 13.3 for each market, the performance under three of these implementations: the best, median and worst implementations. In order to identify these portfolios, we aggregated the net returns for both the momentum strategies under each of the 192 implementations, ranked them and then report the one with the highest (best), median and lowest (worst) returns.

---

[13] We focus on these cut-offs as Bird et al. (2016) found the momentum profits fall as the cut-offs are extended.

TABLE 13.3 After–transaction costs momentum monthly returns

COUNTRY		JxH	Weight	Construction	TSM Momentum Raw return (%)	TSM Cost – Loser (%)	TSM Cost – Winner (%)	TSM Loser (%)	TSM Winner (%)	TSM Momentum Net return (%)	CSM Momentum Raw return (%)	CSM Cost – Loser (%)	CSM Cost – Winner (%)	CSM Loser (%)	CSM Winner (%)	CSM Momentum Net return (%)	DIFFERENCE NET RETURN TSM – CSM (%)
Australia	best	9x6	MW	BHAR(0)	2.38[1]	0.58[1]	0.47[1]	0.55	1.88[1]	1.33[1]	1.54[1]	0.53[1]	0.45[1]	0.68	1.25[1]	0.57	0.76
	median	12x6	IVOL	BHAR(0)	0.51	0.53[1]	0.48	1.36[1]	0.85[5]	-0.51	0.72[10]	0.44[1]	0.48[1]	1.03[1]	0.84[5]	-0.20	-0.31
	worst	3x3	EW	CAR(0)	0.24	1.25[1]	1.23[1]	2.40[1]	0.16	-2.24[1]	0.22	1.09[1]	1.10[1]	2.15[1]	0.17	-1.97[1]	-0.27[10]
Austria	best	9x12	EW	BHAR(0)	1.33[1]	0.15[1]	0.25[1]	-0.39	0.66[10]	1.05[5]	1.17[1]	0.12[1]	0.12[1]	-0.27	0.66[10]	0.93[1]	0.12
	median	6x6	IVOL	BHAR(0)	1.05[5]	0.27[1]	0.25[1]	-0.21	0.32	0.52	0.90[1]	0.25[1]	0.24[1]	0.00	0.41	0.41	0.11
	worst	3x3	MW	BHAR(0)	0.33	0.49[1]	0.47[1]	1.39[1]	0.75	-0.63	-0.11	0.46[1]	0.44[1]	1.32[1]	0.31	-1.01[5]	0.37
Belgium	best	3x6	MW	BHAR(1)	0.86	0.23[1]	0.18[1]	0.13	0.59	0.46	0.57	0.18[1]	0.17[1]	0.51	0.72[5]	0.22	0.24
	median	6x3	EW	BHAR(1)	1.53[1]	0.39[1]	0.37[1]	-0.05	0.72[5]	0.77[5]	1.29[1]	0.29[1]	0.27[1]	0.14	0.86[1]	0.73[1]	0.04
	worst	3x9	MW	BHAR(0)	-0.03	0.17[1]	0.14[1]	0.53	019	-0.34	-0.49	0.14[1]	0.12[1]	0.99[5]	0.24	-0.75	0.41
Canada	best	6x9	MW	BHAR(0)	3.06[1]	0.42[1]	0.36[1]	0.13	2.41[1]	2.28[1]	1.86[1]	0.38[1]	0.35	0.47	1.60[1]	1.13[10]	1.14[1]
	median	12x3	IVOL	CAR(1)	1.63[1]	0.86[1]	0.70[1]	1.34[1]	1.41[1]	0.07	1.34[1]	0.69[1]	0.57[1]	1.31[1]	1.40[1]	0.09	-0.02
	worst	3x3	EW	BHAR(0)	0.89[5]	1.49[1]	1.46[1]	2.95[1]	0.90[10]	-2.06[1]	0.66[10]	1.30[1]	1.27[1]	2.83[1]	0.92[10]	-1.91[1]	0.15
Denmark	best	6x12	IVOL	BHAR(0)	1.64[1]	0.18[1]	0.15[1]	-0.23	1.07[1]	1.30[1]	1.50[1]	0.17[1]	0.16[1]	-0.03	1.15[1]	1.18[1]	0.12
	median	9x3	MW	CAR(0)	1.65[1]	0.58[1]	0.38[1]	0.74	1.43[1]	0.69	1.63[1]	0.44[1]	0.29[1]	0.59	1.49[1]	0.90[10]	-0.21
	worst	3x3	MW	BHAR(0)	0.71	0.68[1]	0.56[1]	1.26[1]	0.73[10]	-0.53	0.80[10]	0.61[1]	0.49[1]	1.31[1]	1.01[1]	-0.30	-0.23
Finland	best	12x6	MW	BHAR(0)	2.85[1]	0.24[1]	0.22[1]	0.25	2.64[1]	2.38[1]	1.72[5]	0.24[1]	0.22[1]	0.47	1.73[5]	1.25	1.13[10]
	median	12x3	IVOL	BHAR(1)	1.39[5]	0.42[1]	0.40[1]	0.71	1.28[1]	0.57	1.08[1]	0.34[1]	0.32[1]	0.80	1.22[1]	0.42	0.16
	worst	3x3	EW	BHAR(0)	0.79	0.70[1]	0.69[1]	1.07[10]	0.47	-0.60	0.42	0.64[1]	0.62[1]	1.37[1]	0.52	-0.84[5]	0.24
France	best	9x9	IVOL	BHAR(0)	1.12[1]	0.24[1]	0.21[1]	0.48	1.16[1]	0.67[1]	0.99[1]	0.21[1]	0.20[1]	0.53	1.10[1]	0.58[10]	0.09
	median	6x9	EW	BHAR(0)	0.67[5]	0.26[1]	0.24[1]	0.67[10]	0.83[1]	0.16	0.40	0.22[1]	0.22[1]	0.80[5]	0.75[1]	-0.04	0.20
	worst	3x3	MW	BHAR(0)	-0.53	0.69[1]	0.65[1]	2.05[1]	0.18	-1.87[1]	-0.61	0.64[1]	0.62[1]	1.74[1]	-0.13	-1.87[1]	0.00
Germany	best	6x12	EW	BHAR(0)	1.43[1]	0.23%[1]	0.20	0.08	1.07[5]	1.00[10]	1.47[1]	0.20[1]	0.19[1]	-0.09	0.99[5]	1.07[1]	-0.08
	median	6x12	EW	CAR(0)	0.80[1]	0.24	0.22[1]	-0.13	0.22	0.35	0.83[1]	0.20[1]	0.19[1]	-0.09	0.34	0.44[10]	-0.09
	worst	3x3	EW	BHAR(0)	1.12[1]	1.04[1]	0.98[1]	0.55	-0.36	-0.90[5]	0.72[5]	0.90[1]	0.91[1]	0.62	-0.47	-1.09[1]	0.19
Greece	best	3x12	MW	BHAR(1)	1.71[5]	0.15[1]	0.16[1]	-0.25	1.15	1.40[10]	1.38	0.14[1]	0.12[1]	0.46	1.58	1.12	0.28
	median	3x9	MW	CAR(1)	-0.05	0.24[1]	0.27[1]	0.65	0.09	-0.56	0.40	0.20[1]	0.20	0.45	0.45	0.00	-0.57
	worst	12x12	EW	BHAR(1)	-0.93	0.21[1]	0.18[1]	1.17	-0.14	-1.32[10]	-0.91	0.19[1]	0.18[1]	1.50[10]	0.23	-1.27[1]	-0.05
Hong Kong	best	9x9	MW	BHAR(0)	1.35[5]	0.37[1]	0.33[1]	1.20[10]	1.86[1]	0.65	0.51	0.34[1]	0.28[1]	1.07[10]	0.95	-0.12	0.77
	median	3x6	EW	CAR(0)	0.69[1]	0.61[1]	0.62[1]	1.27[5]	0.73	-0.54[5]	0.29	0.52[1]	0.53[1]	1.48[1]	0.73	0.75[1]	0.22
	worst	3x3	EW	BHAR(1)	0.06	1.32%[1]	1.29[1]	2.23[1]	-0.31	-2.55[1]	-0.11	1.14[1]	1.11[1]	2.34[1]	-0.02	-2.36[1]	-0.19
Ireland	best	6x12	MW	BHAR(0)	3.52[1]	0.18[1]	0.17[1]	-1.08	2.09[1]	3.17[1]	2.36[5]	0.18[1]	0.16[1]	-0.11	1.92[1]	2.02[5]	1.15[5]
	median	9x3	IVOL	BHAR(0)	1.08	0.48[1]	0.50[1]	1.09	1.19[1]	0.10	1.06[10]	0.46[1]	0.43[1]	0.88	1.05[1]	0.18	-0.08
	worst	3x9	MW	BHAR(1)	-1.38	029[1]	0.27[1]	1.69[10]	-0.24	-1.93[5]	-1.34	0.26[1]	0.26[1]	2.00[1]	0.14	-1.86[5]	-0.07
Israel	best	9x12	MW	BHAR(0)	2.02[1]	0.20[1]	0.23[1]	0.22	1.81[1]	1.59[1]	1.66[1]	0.16[1]	0.16[1]	0.23	1.54[1]	1.31[1]	0.28
	median	9x12	EW	CAR(0)	0.05	0.23[1]	0.21[1]	1.31[1]	0.92[5]	-0.39	-0.21	0.19[1]	0.18[1]	1.39[1]	0.82[1]	-0.57[1]	0.18
	worst	3x3	EW	CAR(0)	-0.51[10]	0.92[1]	0.89[1]	2.24[1]	-0.08	-2.32[1]	-0.41[10]	0.75[1]	0.73[1]	2.13[1]	0.24	-1.89[1]	-0.43[1]

TABLE 13.3 (Continued)

COUNTRY		OPTIMAL			TSM						CSM						DIFFERENCE
		JxH	Weight	Construction	Momentum Raw return (%)	Cost – Loser (%)	Cost – Winner (%)	Loser (%)	Winner (%)	Momentum Net return (%)	Momentum Raw return (%)	Cost – Loser (%)	Cost – Winner (%)	Loser (%)	Winner (%)	Momentum Net return (%)	NET RETURN TSM – CSM (%)
Italy	best	12x6	MW	BHAR(0)	2.26[1]	0.21[1]	0.15[1]	-0.89	1.01[10]	1.90[1]	1.38[1]	0.15[1]	0.12[1]	0.11	1.22[5]	1.12[5]	0.78
	median	6x9	IVOL	BHAR(1)	1.19[1]	0.15[1]	0.13[1]	-0.15	0.76[10]	0.91[1]	0.98[1]	0.13[1]	0.12[1]	-0.18	0.55	0.73[5]	0.18
	worst	3x3	MW	CAR(0)	0.55	0.42[1]	0.38[1]	0.65	0.39	-0.26	0.21	0.37[1]	0.35[1]	0.90[10]	0.39	-0.51	0.25
Japan	best	3x12	MW	BHAR(0)	1.09[1]	0.12[1]	0.11[1]	-0.59	0.27	0.85[5]	0.24	0.10[1]	0.11[1]	0.16	0.20	0.04	0.81[1]
	median	3x6	MW	CAR(1)	0.24	0.24[1]	0.22[1]	0.08	-0.14	-0.22	-0.07	0.21[1]	0.20[1]	0.41	-0.07	-0.47	0.25[10]
	worst	3x3	EW	BHAR(0)	0.21	0.61[1]	0.60[1]	0.50	-0.51	-1.01[1]	-0.24	0.53[1]	0.51[1]	0.86[10]	-0.41	-1.27[1]	0.26
Netherlands	best	6x12	IVOL	BHAR(0)	2.17[1]	0.19[1]	0.12[1]	-0.84[10]	1.02[5]	1.86[1]	1.42[1]	0.14[1]	0.12[1]	0.10	1.26[1]	1.16[1]	0.70[5]
	median	6x12	IVOL	CAR(1)	1.05[1]	0.15[1]	0.13	-0.13	0.64[10]	0.77[1]	0.89[1]	0.13[1]	0.11[1]	0.31	0.96[1]	0.65[10]	0.12
	worst	6x3	MW	BHAR(1)	0.64	0.54[1]	0.44[1]	0.77	0.43	-0.34	-0.14	0.47[1]	0.37[1]	1.55[1]	0.57	-0.98[10]	0.64
New Zealand	best	12x6	MW	BHAR(0)	2.84[1]	0.28[1]	0.24[1]	-0.44	1.87[1]	2.31[1]	1.51[1]	0.25[1]	0.21[1]	0.14	1.19[1]	1.05[5]	1.26[10]
	median	12x9	MW	BHAR(1)	1.57[1]	0.19[1]	0.17[1]	0.45	1.65[1]	1.20[10]	0.76	0.18[1]	0.16[1]	0.74	1.16[1]	0.42	0.79
	worst	3x3	EW	BHAR(0)	0.81[5]	0.62[1]	0.61[1]	0.97[1]	0.55	-0.42	0.96[1]	0.54[1]	0.54[1]	1.02[1]	0.90[1]	-0.12	-0.30
Norway	best	6x12	MW	BHAR(0)	1.30[5]	0.22[1]	0.16[1]	0.71	1.63[1]	0.92	1.65[1]	0.18[1]	0.16[1]	0.45	1.77[1]	1.32[1]	-0.39
	median	3x12	EW	CAR(1)	0.71	0.23[1]	0.22[1]	1.26[1]	1.52[1]	0.26	0.55[5]	0.19[1]	0.19[1]	1.13[5]	1.29[1]	0.16	0.10
	worst	3x3	MW	BHAR(0)	0.08	0.85[1]	0.67	2.82[1]	1.37[1]	-1.44[5]	0.12	0.71[1]	0.66[1]	2.11[1]	0.87	-1.24[5]	-0.20
Portugal	best	6x12	MW	BHAR(0)	1.73[5]	0.14[1]	0.19[1]	-0.07	1.32[5]	1.40[10]	0.95	0.13[1]	0.12[1]	0.09	0.79	0.70	0.70
	median	6x3	IVOL	BHAR(1)	1.53[1]	0.47[1]	0.60[1]	-0.04	0.42	0.46	0.53	0.42[1]	0.53[1]	0.81[10]	0.39	-0.42	0.88[5]
	worst	3x3	EW	CAR(0)	-0.88[10]	0.59[1]	0.62[1]	2.13[1]	0.04	-2.09[1]	-0.63[10]	0.51[1]	0.51[1]	1.85[1]	0.20	-1.65[1]	-0.44
Singapore	best	3x9	MW	BHAR(0)	1.26[1]	0.26[1]	0.27[1]	0.51	1.24[10]	0.73	0.70[10]	0.23[1]	0.23[1]	0.70	0.92[10]	0.22	0.50
	median	9x9	EW	CAR(0)	0.82[10]	0.28%[1]	0.30[1]	0.59	0.82	0.23	0.26	0.25[1]	0.25[1]	0.97	0.73	-0.24	0.48[10]
	worst	3x3	MW	BHAR(1)	0.37	0.80[1]	0.81[1]	1.76[1]	0.53	-1.23[5]	-0.12	0.74[1]	0.70[1]	1.82[1]	0.26	-1.56[1]	0.33
Spain	best	12x6	EW	BHAR(0)	1.29[1]	0.20[1]	0.18[1]	0.25	1.16[1]	0.91[10]	1.00[1]	0.17[1]	0.15[1]	0.27	0.96[5]	0.68[5]	0.23
	median	12x6	MW	CAR(0)	0.35	0.20[1]	0.17[1]	0.69	0.67[10]	-0.02	0.76[10]	0.19[1]	0.15[1]	0.45	0.88[5]	0.43	-0.45
	worst	6x3	MW	BHAR(0)	-0.94	0.44[1]	0.40[1]	1.60[1]	-0.19	-1.78[1]	-0.63	0.38[1]	0.32[1]	1.38[1]	0.05	-1.33[1]	-0.46
Sweden	best	9x6	IVOL	CAR(0)	2.18[1]	0.44[1]	0.38[1]	0.14	1.50[1]	1.36[1]	1.39[1]	0.32[1]	0.27	0.62	1.42[1]	0.79[10]	0.56[5]
	median	3x12	EW	CAR(0)	1.01[1]	0.26[1]	0.26[1]	0.65	1.14[1]	0.49[10]	0.82[1]	0.19[1]	0.19[1]	0.65	1.09[1]	0.44[10]	0.05
	worst	3x3	EW	CAR(0)	1.02[5]	1.01[1]	1.03[1]	1.19[5]	0.17	-1.02[1]	0.96[1]	0.79[1]	0.77[1]	1.15[1]	0.54	-0.60[10]	-0.41
Switzerland	best	6x12	EW	BHAR(0)	1.42[1]	0.15[1]	0.12[1]	0.21	1.36[1]	1.15[1]	1.20[1]	0.12[1]	0.11[1]	0.33	1.30[1]	0.98[1]	0.18
	median	6x9	IVOL	BHAR(1)	1.04[1]	0.18[1]	0.16[1]	0.25	0.94[1]	0.69[1]	0.66[5]	0.15[1]	0.15[1]	0.58[10]	0.94[1]	0.36	0.34[10]
	worst	3x3	MW	BHAR(0)	0.05	0.49[1]	0.45[1]	1.01[1]	0.12	-0.89[1]	0.09	0.44[1]	0.43[1]	1.21[1]	0.44	-0.78[5]	-0.11
UK	best	12x3	IVOL	CAR(0)	2.15[1]	0.40[1]	0.39[1]	-0.13	1.22[1]	1.36[1]	1.85[1]	0.34[1]	0.31[1]	0.01	1.22[1]	1.20[1]	0.16
	median	3x12	IVOL	BHAR(1)	1.25[1]	0.16[1]	0.15[1]	-0.21	0.72[1]	0.93[1]	0.71[1]	0.15[1]	0.15[1]	0.17	0.58[10]	0.41[10]	0.52[1]
	worst	3x3	MW	BHAR(0)	0.31	0.63[1]	0.60[1]	1.44[1]	0.51	-0.93[5]	-0.10	0.58[1]	0.58[1]	1.60[1]	0.34	-1.26[1]	0.33
US	best	6x12	MW	BHAR(0)	0.42	0.15[1]	0.13[1]	1.04[1]	1.18[1]	0.14	0.70[5]	0.13[1]	0.13[1]	0.89[5]	1.34[1]	0.45	-0.31[5]
	median	3x9	EW	BHAR(0)	0.32	0.26[1]	0.24[1]	1.59[1]	1.41[1]	-0.18	0.04	0.23[1]	0.22[1]	1.75[1]	1.35[1]	-0.40	0.22[10]
	worst	3x3	IVOL	BHAR(0)	0.08	0.73[1]	0.66[1]	2.19[1]	0.89[1]	-1.30[1]	-0.38	0.65[1]	0.60[1]	2.36[1]	0.73[5]	-1.63[1]	0.33[10]

[10] = p–value of 0.10, [5] = p–value of 0.05, and [1] = p–value of 0.01

13.5.1 The profitability of momentum strategies

13.5.1.1 Time-series momentum There is clear evidence that time-series momentum has realised excellent performance across the majority of our 24 markets under the best implementation. On a before-transaction cost basis (raw returns), it yielded positive and significant returns in all 24 markets with the average monthly return across these markets being in excess of 1.8% per month or 25% p.a. On an after-transaction costs basis, it still yielded a positive return in all 24 markets with the positive return being significant in 19 markets. The average monthly returns after accounting for transactions costs fall to slightly in excess of 1.3% which equates with 17% p.a. Hence, the implementation costs reduce the annual returns by an average of approximately 8% p.a. across the 24 markets with Japan having the lowest implementation costs of approximately 3% p.a. and Australia the highest with approximately 13% p.a.

The apparent high transaction costs in some markets largely reflect the high turnover associated with implementing a momentum strategy. For example, the optimal implementation of a time series momentum strategy in Australia, before considering transaction costs, incorporates a holding period of three months. Hence, the maximum annual turnover for each of the winner and loser portfolios would be 400% (if we were to turn over every stock four times annually). In fact, the average annual turnover is 235% for the winner portfolio and 285% for the loser portfolio.[14]

When transaction costs are introduced, the only change in the implementation rules for the best time series momentum portfolios is to double the length of the holding period, from three months to six months. Thus, the maximum turnover with the longer holding period for each of the winner and loser portfolios is reduced from 400% to 200%. The actual average turnover for the winner portfolio is 175% (down from 235%) while it is 175% (down from 285%) for the loser portfolio. Hence, the extension of the holding period from three to six months results in a fall in turnover by approximately one-third, and thus significant savings in transaction costs. However, this comes at the expense of utilising a slightly less efficient implementation rule. Similar, but slightly lower, turnover figures apply to the cross sectional momentum strategy which is reflected in the slightly lower transaction costs associated with the implementation of this strategy.

Of course, not all traders would have the foresight to hit on the optimum set of implementation rules. Hence it is appropriate to examine how time-series momentum would perform under an 'average' implementation (as we have termed the median implementation). Under the average implementation, only 17 markets yield positive returns, with significance only arising in seven markets. One of the markets (Hong Kong) yields a significant negative return. The average monthly return across the 24 markets is slightly less than 0.3%, or 3.4% p.a. This compares with the average pre-transaction cost returns for the median implementation across the 24 markets of 11.6% p.a. The average annualised transaction cost of 8% for the median implementation is marginally higher than the costs for the optimum implementation, due to the median implementation exhibiting a slightly higher turnover.

---

[14]These are one-way figures and so a turnover of 235% means a turnover of 235% for both purchases and sales.

We see a much greater degradation in the performance of time-series momentum when we examine the worst implementation, with no market registering positive returns. In 17 markets, the returns are negative and significant. The average monthly raw return across all markets is -0.25% while the net returns are -1.25% per month. Hence, the transaction costs average 1% per month, approximately 50% higher than what they are for the best and median implementations.

In summary, we see that the profitability of time series momentum is largely eroded once we take account of the costs of implementing the strategy. Figure 13.1 shows the average net returns of the cross-sectional momentum strategy across the implementations for each of the markets. With the introduction of transaction costs, the average annual returns across all 192 implementations and across all 24 markets falls from 11.5% to 3%. The markets in which time series momentum would appear to be most viable on a net return basis are Italy, the Netherlands, New Zealand and the UK. The countries in which time series momentum is least viable are Australia, Greece, Hong Kong, Israel and the US. Our findings highlight the sensitivity of the viability of the momentum strategy to the implementation used.

Figure 13.1 reports the pooled average monthly before (raw)/after transaction cost (net) returns for 192 time-series momentum strategies for each market. The dashed lines show the average monthly returns across the 24 developed markets for both raw and net returns.

13.5.1.2 Cross-sectional momentum Cross-sectional momentum has the 'runs on the board', with many studies across various markets and time periods finding it to be a profitable investment strategy. The raw returns generated by cross-sectional momentum, using the best implementation, provide support for the findings in previous studies. Cross-sectional momentum is found to be profitable in all 24 countries, with raw returns averaging around 16.5% p.a. The after transactions cost (net) returns are positive in 23 markets, and significant in 20 markets. The average monthly returns across all markets are slightly less than 0.9% which yields an annualised return of around 11%. Hence, the average annual implementation costs across the 24 markets

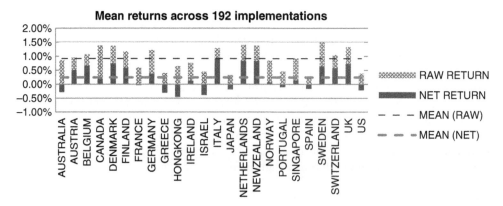

FIGURE 13.1 Average time-series momentum returns across implementations for each market.

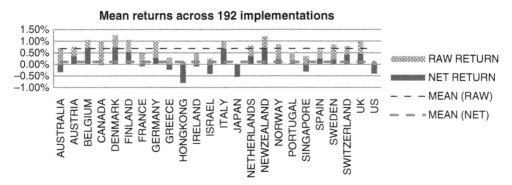

FIGURE 13.2   Average cross-sectional momentum returns across implementations for each market.

are 5.5%, substantially lower than the 8% cost for time-series momentum. This largely reflects the lower turnover required to implement a cross-sectional momentum strategy.

On a pre-transaction cost basis, with a median implementation, cross-sectional momentum realises a positive return in all countries other than Hong Kong and Japan. These positive returns are significant in 14 of these markets, and average approximately 8.5% per annum. This reduces to a positive performance in only 16 markets (seven significant) after transaction costs, with the average annual returns falling to slightly below 2%. Further degradation in performance is exhibited when we move to the worst implementation, with no markets recording positive net returns, and with 20 markets exhibiting significantly negative returns. The average annual return across the 24 markets with the worst implementation is slightly in excess of -16%.

In general, our findings question the viability of the cross-sectional momentum strategy after implementation costs are considered. Figure 13.2 shows the average net returns of the cross-sectional momentum strategy, across all implementations for each country. With the introduction of transaction costs, the average annual returns across all 192 implementations drop from approximately 8.5% to slightly in excess of 2%. The markets in which cross-sectional momentum appears to be most viable after accounting for transaction costs include Belgium, Denmark, Italy and New Zealand while those where viability appears least likely include Australia, Hong Kong, Israel, Japan, Singapore and the US.

It is worth commenting on the relatively poor performance of cross-sectional (and time-series) momentum in the US which contrasts with numerous studies that document positive performance in the US. This finding was observed by Hwang and Rubesam (2013) who noted that the performance of cross-sectional momentum is waning in the US market. Bird et al. (2016) attributed this drop-off in the performance of momentum in the US as not only a consequence of the poor performance of momentum during the Global Financial Crisis, but also because its performance did not subsequently recover to the extent that it has in most other markets.

This figure reports the average monthly raw and net returns for 192 cross-sectional momentum strategies for each market. The dashed line shows the average monthly returns across the 24 developed markets.

13.5.2 Comparing time-series and cross-sectional momentum strategies

An important focus of this chapter is on the relative performance of time-series and cross-sectional momentum. In the last column of Table 13.3, we present the difference between the net returns of these two strategies. Under the best implementation, time-series momentum outperforms cross-sectional momentum in 21 markets, with this outperformance being significant in seven markets. This is slightly inferior to the outperformance based on raw returns where time series momentum outperformed in all 24 markets (13 significant). The mean difference between the average raw returns generated by the two strategies across all 24 markets is an annualised 8.2%, or 5.7% pa after transaction costs. The difference is largely attributable to the lower turnover in the implementation of a cross-sectional momentum strategy.

Among median implementations, we find that time-series momentum continues to generate the higher return in 17 markets, with the difference being significant in seven markets. The average annual difference between the raw returns for the two momentum strategies is around 3%, or 1.75% p.a. on a net basis. As Bird et al. (2016) found when dealing with raw returns, any advantage enjoyed by time series momentum is eroded as one progresses from the best to the median implementation. With the worst implementation, there is almost an equal split between markets; time series momentum outperforms in 11 countries and cross sectional momentum outperforms in 13. Indeed, the two momentum strategies generate the nearly identical returns when measured on a net basis across the 24 markets and 192 implementations.

The general conclusion that we draw from our findings is that with the better implementations, the time-series approach delivers superior returns. This advantage erodes as one moves toward the less optimal implementations, but it still remains the preferable approach in the majority of markets for the majority of implementations.

Before moving on to examine more closely some of the implementation issues, it is interesting to reflect on our findings for the Japanese markets. Previous findings using cross sectional momentum have consistently found that momentum is not a profitable strategy in the Japanese market (e.g. Asness, 2012; Hanauer, 2014). We confirm these findings, with cross-sectional momentum yielding negative returns under the majority of the implementations examined. However, we also find that Japan is the only market where time-series momentum yields a significant higher return relative to cross-sectional momentum under the best, median and worst implementations. Our findings suggest that time-series momentum offers more potential to Japanese investors yielding a raw return of almost 1.1% per month, and a net return of 0.86% per month, under the best implementation.

13.5.3 Characteristics of the time-series and cross-sectional momentum portfolios

We discuss below the decision rules that were applied in the best, median and worst implementations that are reported in Table 13.3.

13.5.3.1 Formation and holding periods In the absence of implementation costs, Bird et al. (2016) found that the formation and holding periods for the best implementations were nine to twelve months and three months, respectively. They highlighted the importance for the aggregate of these two periods to be in harmony with the typical periodicity of a stock, which their analysis suggested to be around 15 months. Interestingly, with the introduction of implementation costs, the typical formation period under the best implementation reduces to six months while the typical holding period lengthens significantly to 12 months. Undoubtedly, this huge shift in the holding period represents an attempt to reduce turnover and so implementation costs. However, this lengthening of the holding period must be accommodated by a reduction in the formation period, so that the sum of the two (18 months) is not far out of synchronisation with the periodicity of the typical stocks (previously 15 months).

For the median implementation, the typical formation period is six months while the typical holding period is nine months. The introduction of transaction costs has again shortened the length of the formation period and extended the length of the holding period leaving the combined length of the two periods equivalent to what it was in the absence of implementation costs. With the worst implementation, we see that the typical formation and holding periods are both three months. These are portfolios that are not only entirely out of synchronisation with the oscillations of stocks in the market but also engender very high turnover and so implementation costs.

13.5.3.2 Weighting scheme and rebalancing strategy The weighting scheme and rebalancing strategy under the optimum implementation are much less sensitive to the introduction of implementation costs than the choice of formation and holding periods. In two out of every three markets, using market values provide the best weighting scheme under the best implementation where account is taken of implementation costs. Market value weights continue to be the most common for the worst implementations, although equal weighting appears relatively more common. Similarly, with the rebalancing strategy, a buy and hold strategy with no lag proves to be the most common across markets for both the best and worst implementations.

13.5.4 Summary of the impact of implementation costs on momentum strategies

Our findings have highlighted a sizable falloff in the apparent profitability of the two momentum strategies once account is taken of the costs of implementing these strategies. This is well illustrative by examining the proportion of implementations that generate positive returns across all 24 markets (i.e. $192 \times 24 = 4{,}608$ implementations). For time series momentum, the introduction of transaction costs saw this proportion drop from 94% to 66% while for cross sectional momentum it fell from 88% to 59%. In only six markets (Belgium, Denmark, Italy, the Netherlands, New Zealand and the UK), do time-series and cross-sectional momentum yield significant positive after-transaction costs returns under the majority of implementations.

13.6   RISK-ADJUSTED AFTER-TRANSACTION COSTS PERFORMANCE OF TIME-SERIES AND CROSS-SECTIONAL MOMENTUM STRATEGIES

In this section we use the after-transaction cost returns from previous section as the basis for calculating two risk-adjusted measures of performance: the Sharpe ratio and the Fama-French three-factor model.[15]

13.6.1   Time-series momentum strategies

Our findings are reported in Table 13.4 for the best, median and worst portfolio implementations discussed previously. If one was fortunate to choose the best implementation, then time-series momentum would benefit investors as it generates positive Fama-French alphas in all markets other than Hong Kong, Norway and the US. In ten markets significant positive alphas are generated under the best implementation of a time-series momentum strategy. The average annualised Fama-French alpha across the 24 markets is 11%, down from 17% without any risk-adjustment.

We see a sizable deterioration in the Fama-French alphas of the time-series momentum strategy when we look at the medium performing implementations. The alphas are positive in fewer than half of the markets (11), with six markets realising significant negative alphas. The average annualised Fama-French alpha across the 24 markets for the median implementations is -2%. Assuming that the median implementation is representative of the typical one chosen where the implementation is determined randomly, across all markets the time-series momentum strategy no longer offers outperformance. Not surprisingly, by the time the worst implementation is reached, time-series momentum does not realise positive Fama-French alphas in any markets, and significant and negative alphas are exhibited in 18 markets. The average annualised Fama-French alpha across the 24 markets for the worst implementations is -17.5%.

Across the 24 developed markets examined, the profits attributable to the time series momentum strategy are severely eroded with the introduction of transaction costs, and after adjusting for risk. Among the 192 implementations of time-series momentum over the 24 markets, 41% had a positive Fama-French alpha (7% significant) and 59% had a negative Fama-French alpha (24% significant). This represents a significant drop-off in performance compared to the after-transaction costs returns discussed previously where 66% (27% significant) were positive and 34% (9% significant) were negative. The performance findings were only marginally better for the Sharpe ratios, with approximately half of the strategies yielding a negative Sharpe ratio. This evidence suggests a further deterioration in the performance of time-series momentum when account is taken of the risks associated with the momentum portfolios.

Figure 13.3 contains the market-by market findings for the performance of time-series momentum as indicated by the Fama-French alphas calculated using after-transaction costs returns. Across the 24 markets, the average annual net return across all implementations is 3% whereas the average Fama-French alpha across the 24

---

[15]Since there is no powerful significance test for the Sharpe ratio, we concentrate our discussion more on the results from the Fama-French three-factor model.

TABLE 13.4 Risk-adjusted monthly momentum returns

		Time-series Momentum (TSM)			Cross-sectional momentum (CSM)			TSM - CSM		
		Net Return (%pm)	Sharpe ratio	FF alpha (%pm)	Net Return (%pm)	Sharpe ratio	FF alpha (%pm)	Net Return (%pm)	Sharpe ratio	FF alpha (%pm)
Australia	Best	1.33 **	0.11	0.79 *	0.57	0.02	0.18	0.76	0.10	0.61
	Median	-0.51	-0.17	-0.96 **	-0.20	-0.13	-0.69 *	-0.31	-0.04	-0.28
	Worst	-2.24 ***	-0.68	-2.64 ***	-1.97 ***	-0.56	-2.42 ***	-0.27 *	-0.12	-0.22
Austria	Best	1.05 **	0.09	0.21	0.93 ***	0.12	0.34	0.12	-0.03	-0.13
	Median	0.52	0.03	-0.15	0.41	0.02	* 0.24	0.11	0.01	0.09
	Worst	-0.63	-0.10	-1.32 *	-1.01 **	-0.16	-1.46 ***	0.37	0.06	0.15
Belgium	Best	1.19 **	0.10	0.97	1.47 ***	0.16	1.46 ***	-0.28	-0.06	-0.48
	Median	0.77 **	0.08	0.21	0.73 ***	0.10	0.23	0.04	0.03	-0.02
	Worst	-0.34	-0.08	-0.97	-0.75	-0.14	-1.22 ***	0.41	0.06	0.25
Canada	Best	2.28 ***	0.20	1.89 ***	1.13 *	0.09	0.91 *	1.14 ***	0.11	0.99 ***
	Median	0.07	-0.04	-0.45	0.09	-0.04	-0.24	-0.02	-0.01	-0.21
	Worst	-2.06 ***	-0.32	-2.22 ***	-1.91 ***	-0.30	-1.98 ***	-0.15	-0.02	-0.25
Denmark	Best	1.30 ***	0.21	0.84 ***	1.18 ***	0.21	0.57 **	0.12	0.00	0.27
	Median	0.69	0.04	0.34	0.90 **	0.07	0.47	-0.21	-0.04	-0.12
	Worst	-0.53	-0.11	-1.19 ***	-0.30	-0.09	-0.91 **	-0.23	-0.02	-0.28
Finland	Best	2.38 ***	0.17	0.18 **	1.25	0.09	0.73	1.13 *	0.08	0.11
	Median	0.57	0.03	0.22	0.42	0.02	0.17	0.16	0.01	0.05
	Worst	-0.60	-0.11	-0.84	-0.84	-0.18	-1.16 ***	0.24	0.07	0.32
France	Best	0.67	0.09	0.35	0.58	0.06	0.24	0.09	0.03	0.11
	Median	0.16	-0.03	-0.14	-0.04	-0.07	-0.28	0.20	0.04	0.14
	Worst	-1.87 ***	-0.27	-1.85 ***	-1.87 ***	-0.29	-1.84 ***	0.00	0.02	0.00
Germany	Best	1.00 *	0.09	0.32	1.07 ***	0.11	0.44	-0.08	-0.03	-0.12
	Median	0.35	0.01	-0.45 **	0.44 *	0.04	-0.32	-0.09	-0.02	-0.13
	Worst	-0.90 **	-0.19	-1.58 ***	-1.09 ***	-0.22	-1.73 ***	0.19	0.03	0.15
Greece	Best	1.40 *	0.07	0.45	1.12	0.04	0.36	0.28	0.03	0.09
	Median	-0.56	-0.17	-1.18 ***	0.00	-0.08	-0.53	-0.57	-0.09	-0.66 *
	Worst	-1.32 *	-0.16	-1.95 ***	-1.27 ***	-0.23	-1.99 ***	-0.05	0.07	0.04
Hong Kong	Best	0.65	0.04	-0.19	-0.12	-0.05	-0.47	0.77	0.09	0.28
	Median	-0.54 **	-0.22	-0.88 ***	-0.75 ***	-0.27	-1.02 ***	0.22	0.04	0.13
	Worst	-2.55 ***	-0.40	-2.45 ***	-2.36 ***	-0.38	-2.42 ***	-0.19	-0.02	-0.03
Ireland	Best	3.17 ***	0.18	2.88 ***	2.02 **	0.12	1.95 *	1.15 **	0.06	0.94
	Median	0.10	-0.02	0.09	0.18	-0.02	0.04	-0.08	0.00	0.05
	Worst	-1.93 **	-0.15	-1.72	-1.86 ***	-0.16	-1.88 *	-0.07	0.01	0.16
Israel	Best	1.59 ***	0.11	0.68	1.31 ***	0.09	0.73	0.28	0.02	-0.06
	Median	-0.39	-0.25	-1.12 ***	-0.57 ***	-0.34	-1.33 ***	0.18	0.09	0.21
	Worst	2.32 ***	-0.63	-2.96 ***	-1.86 ***	-0.60	-2.52 ***	-0.43 ***	-0.03	-0.44 **

(continued)

TABLE 13.4 (Continued)

		Time series Momentum (TSM)			Cross sectional momentum (CSM)			TSM – CSM		
		Net Profit (%pm)	Sharpe ratio	FF alpha (%pm)	Net Profit (%pm)	Sharpe ratio	FF alpha (%pm)	Net Profit (%pm)	Sharpe ratio	FF alpha (%pm)
Italy	Best	1.90 ***	0.14	0.013	1.12 **	0.09	-0.10	0.78	0.05	0.22
	Median	0.91 ***	0.09	-0.10	0.73 **	0.07	-0.10	0.18	0.02	0.00
	Worst	-0.26	-0.09	-0.95 **	-0.51	-0.13	-1.34 ***	0.25	0.04	0.39
Japan	Best	0.85 **	0.13	0.30	0.04	-0.01	-0.40	0.81 ***	0.14	0.70 ***
	Median	-0.22	-0.06	-0.55 **	-0.47	-0.12	-0.77 ***	0.25 *	0.05	0.22
	Worst	-1.01 ***	-0.23	-1.22 ***	-1.27 ***	-0.29	-1.43 ***	0.64	0.08	0.65
Netherlands	Best	1.86 ***	.27	1.41 ***	1.16 ***	0.21	0.81 ***	0.70 **	0.06	0.60 *
	Median	0.77	0.12	0.32	0.65	0.11	0.29	0.12	0.08	0.03
	Worst	-0.34	-0.06	-0.92	-0.98 *	-0.14	-1.57 ***	-0.64	-0.08	-0.65
New Zealand	Best	2.31 ***	0.18	2.13 ***	1.05 **	0.08	0.77	1.26 *	0.10	1.55 *
	Median	1.20 *	0.07	0.83	0.42	-0.01	-0.10	0.79	0.08	0.73
	Worst	0.42 *	-0.15	-0.95 ***	-0.12	-0.12	-0.63 *	-0.30	-0.04	-0.32
Norway	Best	0.92	0.05	-0.06	1.32 ***	0.12	0.53	-0.39	-0.07	-0.59
	Median	0.26	-0.04	-0.46	0.16	-0.08	-0.35	0.10	0.04	-0.11
	Worst	-1.44 **	-0.17	-1.92 ***	-1.24 ***	-0.19	-1.47 ***	0.20	0.03	-0.45
Portugal	Best	1.40 *	0.07	1.10	0.70	0.03	0.14	0.70	0.04	0.96
	Median	0.46	0.01	0.25	-0.42	-0.10	-0.61	0.88 **	0.11	0.86 *
	Worst	-2.09 ***	-0.31	-2.45 ***	-1.65 ***	-0.35	-1.99 ***	-0.44	0.04	-0046
Singapore	Best	0.73	0.08	0.11	0.22	0.02	0.33	0.50	0.06	-0.22
	Median	0.23	0.02	0.01	-0.24	-0.07	0.27	0.48 *	0.09	0.27
	Worst	-1.23 **	-0.15	-1.50 ***	-1.56 ***	-0.21	-1.52 ***	0.33	0.06	0.02
Spain	Best	0.91 **	+0.16	0.51	0.68 **	0.06	0.29	0.23	0.01	0.22
	Median	-0.02	0.07	-0.30	0.43	0.01	0.03	-0.45	-0.06	-0.33
	Worst	-1.78 ***	-0.05	-1.95 ***	-1.33 ***	-0.21	-1.50 ***	-0.46	0.01	-0.45
Sweden	Best	1.36 ***	0.15	1.04 ***	0.79 *	0.08	0.57	0.56 **	0.07	0.47 *
	Median	0.49 *	0.03	0.14	0.44	0.03	0.09	0.05	0.01	0.05
	Worst	-1.02 ***	-0.21	-1.40 ***	-0.60 *	-0.16	-0.95 ***	-0.41	-0.05	-0.45
Switzerland	Best	1.15 ***	0.16	1.09 ***	0.98 ***	0.22	0.77 ***	0.18	0.10	0.32
	Median	0.69 ***	0.13	0.55 **	0.36	0.05	0.27	0.34 **	0.08	0.28
	Worst	-0.89 ***	-0.18	-1.16 ***	-0.78 **	-0.15	-0.88 **	-0.11	-0.03	-0.27
UK	Best	1.36 ***	0.30	0.66 *	1.20 ***	0.20	0.55 *	0.16	0.10	0.11
	Median	0.93 ***	0.16	0.42 *	0.41 *	0.00	-0.14	0.52 ***	0.16	0.55 ***
	Worst	-0.93 **	-0.19	-0.79	-1.26 ***	-0.23	-1.36 ***	0.33	0.04	0.57 *
USA	Best	0.14	-0.02	-0.38	0.45	0.04	-0.07	-0.31 **	-0.06	-0.31 *
	Median	-0.18	-0.11	-0.37	-0.40	-0.15	-0.59 **	0.22 *	0.04	0.22
	Worst	-1.30 ***	-0.34	-1.29 ***	-1.63 ***	-0.34	-1.42 ***	0.33 *	0.00	0.13

* = p–value of 0.10, ** = p–value of 0.05, and *** = p–value of 0.01

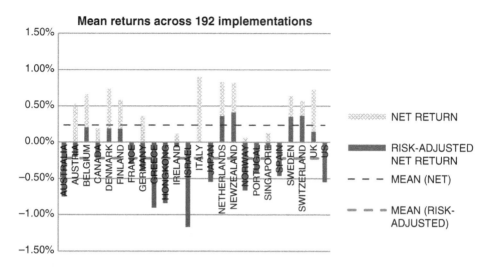

FIGURE 13.3 Average time-series momentum Fama-French alphas across markets.

markets is -2.5%. The markets where time-series momentum seems to still offer best investment opportunities include Belgium, Denmark, the Netherlands, New Zealand, Sweden and the UK. In these markets, more than 75% of the implementations yield a positive Fama-French alpha and Sharpe ratio. The markets in which time series momentum would seem to have least to offer on a risk-adjusted basis are Australia, Greece, Hong Kong, Israel, Japan, Norway, Spain and the US, where more than 80% of the implementations gave rise to a negative Fama-French alpha and Sharpe ratio.

Figure 13.3 plots the pooled average monthly after-transaction costs (net) returns and risk-adjusted net returns based on the Fama-French three-factor model for 192 time-series momentum strategies for each market. The dashed line shows the average monthly returns across the 24 developed markets.

13.6.2 Cross-sectional momentum

We now turn our attention to reviewing the performance of the three implementations of cross-sectional momentum reported in Table 13.4: the best, median and worst. If one was fortunate to choose the best implementation, then cross-sectional momentum would still seem to have much to offer investors as it generates positive Fama-French alphas in 18 markets with six markets enjoying significant positive alphas. The average annualised Fama-French alpha of the best implementations across the 24 markets is 6% which is down from 11% with no risk adjustment.

We see a sizable deterioration in the Fama-French alphas of the cross-sectional momentum strategy when considering median performing implementations. Alphas are positive in nine of the markets, with five of the other 15 markets realising significant negative alphas. The average annualised Fama-French alpha across the 24 markets for the median implementations is -3%. Not surprisingly, by the time the worst implementation is reached, cross-sectional momentum fails to realise positive Fama-French alphas in any markets, and generates significantly negative alphas in 23 markets. The average annualised Fama-French alpha across the 24 markets for the worst implementations is in excess of -20%.

Across the 192 implementations of cross-sectional momentum over the 24 markets, 34% had a positive Fama-French alpha (6% significant) and 66% had a negative Fama-French alpha (26% significant). This represents a significant drop-off in performance compared to the after-transaction costs returns for cross-sectional momentum discussed previously where 59% (23% significant) were positive and 41% (12% significant) were negative. The findings on performance using the Sharpe ratio are only marginally better with 60% of strategies generating a negative Sharpe ratio. Accounting for risk leads to a further deterioration in the performance of cross-sectional momentum.

Figure 13.4 contains the market-by market findings for the performance of time-series momentum as indicated by the Fama-French alphas, calculated using after-transaction costs returns. Across the 24 markets, the average annual net return across all implementations is slightly higher than 1% whereas the average Fama-French alpha across the 24 markets is -3.5%. Figure 13.4 indicates that cross sectional momentum seems to still offer some investment opportunities in a limited number of markets: namely, Belgium, Denmark, New Zealand, and Switzerland, while poor performance has been exhibited in: Australia, Greece, Hong Kong, Israel, Japan, Portugal, Singapore and the US.

Figure 13.4 plots the pooled average monthly after-transaction costs (net) returns and risk-adjusted net returns based on the Fama-French three-factor model for 192 cross sectional momentum strategies for each market. The dashed line shows the average monthly returns across the 24 developed markets.

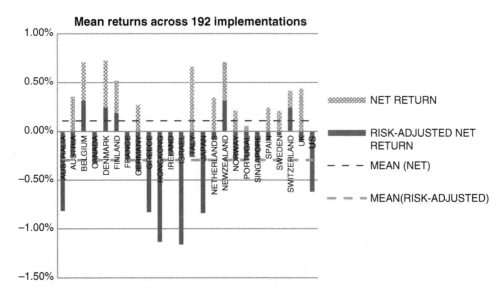

FIGURE 13.4   Average cross-sectional momentum Fama-French alphas across markets.

13.6.3 Comparing the performance of risk-adjusted time-series and cross-sectional momentum

We have seen the deterioration of the profitability of both time-series and cross-sectional momentum with the introduction of transaction costs and risk. However, the question still remains as to which is the better of the two momentum strategies. Bird et al. (2016) found that the market timing aspects of time-series momentum gave it an advantage but the question is whether this is maintained once account is taken of both implementation costs and risk. At first glance it appears that there is now very little difference between the performance of the two momentum strategies. The average annual return across all implementations, for all 24 markets is -2.6% for time-series momentum and -3.4% for cross-sectional momentum.

Although the overall picture suggests otherwise, it may be that an advantage for time-series momentum may still be maintained for some markets and for some implementations. Indeed, Bird et al. (2016) showed that that the real advantage of time-series momentum came with the better implementations. In order to investigate this, we return to Table 13.4 and examine the relative performance of the two momentum strategies under the best implementation. The time-series approach delivers the better return in 17 markets. The positive outperformance is significant in five of these markets and averages an annualised Fama-French alpha of slightly in excess of 3% across the 24 markets.

There is some small further deterioration in the relative performance of the two momentum strategies as we move to the median implementation. While time-series momentum still maintains an advantage in 16 markets, this difference is only significant in two markets and averages only 0.6% p.a. across the 24 markets. For the worst implementation, there is little to choose between the two momentum strategies. Each of the two strategies outperform on the basis of Fama-French alphas in 12 markets.

The general conclusion that we can draw is that much of the advantage that time-series momentum held over cross-sectional momentum is eliminated with the introduction of both transaction costs and risk. Although a relatively small proportion of its advantage remains under the best implementation, this advantage has largely disappeared with the median implementation and beyond.

13.6.4 Impacts of short-sale constraints

Starting with Jegadeesh and Titman (1993), momentum profits have been calculated as the aggregate of a long portfolio of winners and a short portfolio of losers. However, regulations in many markets restrict investors from shorting some or all of the stocks traded in a particular market. Alexander (2000) and Lesmond et al. (2004) argue that momentum studies are biased toward finding apparent anomalies because the strategies may not be implementable. The importance of this becomes apparent when one realises that the majority of the profits are attributed to the poor performance of the loser portfolios (Ali and Trombley, 2006). Jones and Lamont (2002) observe that overpriced shares tend to be expensive to short-sell. Furthermore, Chen et al. (2002) find that the majority of stocks have no short sale interest outstanding at any time and Barber and Odean (2008) find that only 0.29% of individual investors take short-selling positions. Together, this evidence suggests the profitability of the momentum strategies may be illusory and so momentum may not provide the challenge to the EMH that many would have us believe.

A counter to this evidence is that the momentum strategies may generate profits in the absence of any shorting. Griffin et al. (2005), in a study that covers 40 markets, find that small momentum traders can still generate profits without taking short positions. Fong et al. (2005) investigate momentum strategies in 24 countries and find that it is only buying stocks in winner portfolios that generate significant abnormal returns after considering the transaction costs. Phua et al. (2010) demonstrate that in Australia the continuation of momentum returns is mainly concentrated in past winners.

Given the difficulties of mimicking the short-sales approach as it applies in each of the 24 markets, we analyse the performance of the long-only (winner) portfolios. Our findings are presented in Table 13.5 for the best, median and worst implementations where we report, the excess returns of each portfolio (i.e. the portfolio's return minus that of its benchmark), the excess Sharpe ratio (i.e. the portfolio's Sharpe ratio minus that of its benchmark)[16] and the portfolio's Fama-French alpha. With the best implementations of time-series momentum, every market, apart from the US, yields a positive excess return, averaging almost 6% pa after transaction costs over the 24 markets. The equivalent return for the time-series momentum strategy (including shorting) was 17% p.a., suggesting about one-third of its performance came from the long-only portfolio. The equivalent results were not quite as good for cross-sectional momentum. In 19 markets, positive excess returns were realised from the long-only portfolio, and the average return over all 24 markets is slightly higher than 3.5% p.a. This compares with a return for cross-sectional momentum of 11% p.a. when short portfolios are allowed, again suggesting that the long-only portfolio contributes around one-third of the strategy's performance.

An analysis of net returns suggests that long-only momentum strategies may be profitable. With the introduction of risk to the time-series momentum portfolio, 19 markets generated a positive excess Sharpe ratio, averaging 0.12 across the 24 markets. The equivalent for cross sectional momentum was an average annualised Sharpe ratio of 0.11, which was positive in 17 markets. The findings are fairly similar when risk is measured via Fama-French factors, with 19 markets under time-series momentum and 16 markets under cross-sectional momentum yielding positive alphas.

Thus, there might be some profitability from momentum strategies under the best implementation, even in the event of a short-sale constraint. However, when we move to view the median implementations, we find that only six (seven) markets generate after-transaction costs excess returns using a time-series (cross-sectional) approach. For the median implementation of both time-series and cross-sectional strategies, the average annual return across the 24 markets is -2.5%. These findings carry over to the excess Sharpe ratios where there is only limited evidence of any positive values across the 24 markets for either form of momentum. The conclusion that we draw is that once we

---

[16]The benchmark portfolio is all stocks in the universe run in accordance with the portfolio construction used for the portfolio under consideration.

TABLE 13.5 Long-only momentum monthly returns

		Time series Momentum (TSM)			Cross sectional momentum (CSM)			TSM - CSM		
		Net excess Profit (%pm)	'Excess' Sharpe ratio	FF alpha (%pm)	Net Excess Profit (%pm)	'Excess' Sharpe ratio	FF alpha (%pm)	Net Profit (%pm)	Sharpe ratio	FF alpha (%pm)
Australia	Best	0.55	0.03	1.46 ***	−0.08	−0.04	0.90 ***	0.63	0.07	0.55 ***
	Median	0.06	−0.19	0.51 **	−0.07	−0.19	0.51 *	0.13	0.00	0.00
	Worst	−0.98	−0.17	−0.19	−0.97	−0.17	−0.18	−0.01	0.00	0.00
Austria	Best	0.23	0.05	0.50 *	0.23	0.04	0.57 ***	0.00	0.01	−0.07
	Median	0.04	0.01	0.33	0.13	0.03	0.27	−0.09	−0.02	0.06
	Worst	−0.39	−0.10	0.17	−0.83	−0.16	−0.39	−0.44	0.60	0.55 *
Belgium	Best	0.12	−0.04	0.07	0.64	0.08	0.72 ***	−0.42	−0.12	−0.65
	Median	−0.45	−0.09	0.49 *	−0.31	−0.03	0.67 ***	−0.12	−0.06	−0.18
	Worst	−0.98	−0.19	−0.02	−0.93	−0.18	−0.50	−0.05	−0.01	0.00
Canada	Best	0.72	−0.01	0.38	−0.09	−0.09	−0.16	0.81	0.08	0.54 **
	Median	0.60	0.01	−0.14	0.59	0.02	0.00	0.01	−0.01	−0.14
	Worst	−0.91	−0.25	−0.45	−0.89	−0.25	−0.41	−0.02	0.00	−0.04
Denmark	Best	0.50	0.10	0.79 ***	0.58	0.11	0.80 ***	−0.08	−0.01	−0.02
	Median	−0.12	−0.08	0.48	−0.06	−0.04	0.40 *	−0.06	−0.02	0.08
	Worst	−0.82	−0.19	−0.39	−0.54	−0.15	−0.23	0.18	−0.04	−0.16
Finland	Best	1.45	0.10	1.48 ***	0.54	0.01	0.33	0.91	0.09	1.15 **
	Median	0.09	−0.03	0.71 **	0.03	−0.02	0.62 **	0.06	−0.01	0.09
	Worst	−1.38	−0.16	−0.13	−1.33	−0.15	−0.16	−0.05	−0.01	0.02
France	Best	0.20	0.04	0.76 ***	0.14	0.02	0.65 ***	0.06	0.02	0.11
	Median	0.77	0.02	0.45 **	0.24	0.01	0.40 **	0.53	0.01	0.05
	Worst	−1.25	−0.21	−0.60 **	−1.56	−0.30	−1.10 ***	0.31	0.09	0.50
Germany	Best	0.65	0.09	0.21	0.57	0.07	0.28	0.08	0.01	−0.07
	Median	−0.20	−0.05	0.26 ***	−0.08	−0.02	0.40 ***	−0.12	−0.03	−0.14
	Worst	−1.72	−0.31	−0.25	−1.80	−0.33	−0.38 *	0.08	0.02	0.13
Greece	Best	0.08	−0.01	0.43	0.51	0.03	1.07 *	−0.43	−0.04	−0.64
	Median	−1.30	−0.14	−0.29	−0.94	−0.10	0.05	−0.36	−0.04	−0.34
	Worst	−1.53	−0.15	−0.18	−1.16	−0.12	0.08	−0.37	−0.03	−0.27
Hong Kong	Best	0.48	0.03	0.47	−0.43	−0.06	−0.25	0.91	0.09	0.72
	Median	−0.65	−0.08	0.36 *	−0.65	−0.08	0.33 *	0.00	0.00	0.03
	Worst	−2.29	−0.28	−0.48 *	−2.00	−0.25	−0.31	−0.29	−0.03	−0.16
Ireland	Best	1.29	0.07	0.80	1.12	0.06	0.87	0.17	0.01	−0.08
	Median	−0.42	−0.13	0.73 *	−0.56	−0.10	0.40	0.14	−0.03	0.33
	Worst	−1.85	−0.27	−1.21 **	−1.47	−0.23	−0.86	−0.38	−0.04	−0.34
Israel	Best	0.62	0.04	1.13 **	0.35	0.03	0.90 ***	0.27	0.01	0.24
	Median	−0.27	−0.04	0.67 ***	−0.37	−0.06	0.57 ***	0.10	0.02	0.10
	Worst	−1.75	−0.27	−0.28	−1.23	−0.22	0.06	−0.42	−0.05	−0.34 **

TABLE 13.5 (Continued)

		Time series Momentum (TSM)			Cross sectional momentum (CSM)			TSM – CSM		
		Net excess Profit (%pm)	'Excess' Sharpe ratio	FF alpha (%pm)	Net Excess Profit (%pm)	'Excess' Sharpe ratio	FF alpha (%pm)	Net Profit (%pm)	Sharpe ratio	FF alpha (%pm)
Italy	Best	0.66	0.08	0.16	0.87	0.12	0.47 **	-.21	-0.04	-0.31
	Median	-0.59	-0.08	0.81 ***	-0.59	-0.11	0.61 **	0.00	0.03	0.20
	Worst	-0.98	-0.14	-0.07	-0.96	-0.14	-0.13	-0.02	-0.12	0.07
Japan	Best	0.00	0.00	-0.61 ***	-0.07	-0.01	-0.61 ***	0.07	0.01	0.00
	Median	-0.85	-0.15	-0.81 ***	-0.78	-0.14	-0.71 ***	-0.07	-0.08	-0.10
	Worst	-1.22	-0.21	0 − 0.72 ***	-1.12	-0.20	-0.61 ***	-0.10	-0.11	-0.11
Netherlands	Best	0.25	0.01	0.58 ***	0.49	0.06	0.82 ***	-0.24	-0.05	-0.25
	Median	-0.13	-0.05	0.24	0.19	0.02	0.53 ***	-0.32	-0.07	-0.29
	Worst	-0.90	-0.18	-0.55	-0.77	-0.16	-0.53	-0.13	-0.02	-0.02
New Zealand	Best	0.82	0.04	1.27 **	0.14	0.00	0.52 ***	0.68	0.04	0.75
	Median	0.18	-0.06	1.00 **	-0.31	-0.10	0.41 *	0.49	0.04	0.58
	Worst	-0.92	-0.22	0.01	-0.57	-0.16	0.38 *	-0.35	-0.06	-0.37 **
Norway	Best	0.41	-0.01	0.00	0.55	0.03	0.22	0.14	0.04	-0.22
	Median	-0.39	-0.09	0.54 ***	-0.62	-0.09	0.41 ***	-0.23	0.00	0.14
	Worst	-0.54	-0.13	0.16	-1.04	-0.19	-0.54 *	-0.50	0.06	0.70 **
Portugal	Best	0.46	0.00	0.57	0.01	-0.05	-0.01	0.45	0.05	0.59
	Median	-0.27	-0.23	0.26	-0.30	-0.24	0.28	0.03	0.01	-0.02
	Worst	-1.22	-0.22	-0.12	-1.06	-0.17	-0.03	-0.16	-0.06	-0.09
Singapore	Best	0.14	0.00	-0.26	0.18	-0.01	-0.08	0.04	-0.04	0.18
	Median	-0.54	-0.12	0.12	-0.63	-0.13	-0.03	0.09	0.01	0.15
	Worst	-0.83	-0.16	-0.68 *	-1.10	-0.19	-0.93 ***	0.27	0.03	0.25
Spain	Best	0.45	0.08	1.03 ***	0.25	0.04	0.79 ***	0.20	0.04	0.24
	Median	-0.39	-0.03	0.32	-0.18	-0.04	0.40	-0.42	0.01	-0.08
	Worst	-1.25	-0.20	-0.58	-1.01	-0.17	-0.42	-0.24	-0.03	-0.16
Sweden	Best	0.35	0.05	0.96 ***	0.25	0.05	0.78 ***	0.10	0.00	0.18
	Median	-0.22	-0.01	0.67 ***	-0.06	-0.02	0.52 ***	-0.16	0.01	0.15
	Worst	-1.00	-0.19	-0.37	-0.63	-0.13	-0.03	-0.37	-0.06	-0.34 **
Switzerland	Best	0.57	0.10	0.83 ***	0.59	0.07	0.74 ***	0.02	0.03	0.09
	Median	0.17	-0.07	0.45 **	0.17	-0.06	0.46 ***	0.00	-0.01	-0.01
	Worst	-1.05	-0.24	-0.78 ***	-0.75	-0.18	-0.47 *	-0.30	-0.06	-0.30
UK	Best	0.61	0.12	1.45 ***	0.61	0.11	1.43 ***	0.00	0.01	0.01
	Median	0.48	0.13	1.02 ***	-0.17	0.13	0.88 ***	0.65	0.00	0.14
	Worst	-0.88	-0.21	0.06	-1.05	-0.21	-0.29	0.17	0.00	0.35 **
USA	Best	-0.34	-0.11	-0.71 ***	-0.18	-0.09	-0.55 **	-0.16	0.02	-0.16
	Median	0.36	-0.02	0.14	0.30	-0.04	0.01	-0.06	0.12	0.14
	Worst	-0.76	-0.19	-0.22	-0.31	-0.22	-0.30	-0.45	-0.03	0.08

* = p–value of 0.10, ** = p–value of 0.05, and *** = p–value of 0.01

are restricted to a long-only portfolio of stocks classified as winner, that there is little evidence of performance once account is taken of implementation costs and risk.

13.7 CONCLUSIONS

There has been a mountain of evidence produced over the last 30 plus years of market anomalies which question the efficiency of markets. As one might expect, the profitability of investments strategies based on these anomalies tend to erode once they have been identified. Momentum is the anomaly that has best stood the test of time in terms of maintaining its profitability since it was first 'identified' over 20 years ago. Most recently, Bird et al. (2016) confirmed this when they evaluated the performance of numerous implementations of both time-series and cross-sectional momentum across 24 markets. They found that both momentum strategies performed particularly well across most of the markets with the US being a notable exception. Further, they found time series momentum to generally be the better of the two momentum strategies largely due to the market timing element that it introduced into stock selection.

In this chapter, we evaluate the extent to which these apparent profits are exploitable as a medium for throwing evidence on market efficiency. The most obvious factor inhibiting their exploitation is transaction costs, especially given that momentum is a high turnover strategy. A second inhibiting factor is risk as maybe the higher returns are simply compensation for taking on more risk. A third factor is that most of the momentum profits come from shorting loser stocks, and such transactions are typically constrained in most markets.

The conclusion that we draw is that momentum profits significantly erode as we sequentially introduce transaction costs, risk, and constraints on short selling. We provide a summary of our findings in Table 13.6 where we report the average annual returns across the 24 markets for both time-series and cross-sectional momentum as we progressively introduce each of the encumbrances on strategy performance.

Tracing the erosion in performance with respect to the best implementation, there is about a one-third reduction in profitability with the introduction of transaction costs, a further 40% reduction when account is taken of risk. In addition, on average only around one-third of the profits come from the winner portfolio. Despite this dissipation in profitability, it still is apparent that both momentum methodologies when optimally implemented continue to offer small outperformance, even after taking into account the transactions costs, risk and restrictions on short-selling.

TABLE 13.6 Momentum profits at different levels

Implementation	Gross Returns (%pa)		Net Returns (%pa)		FF 3-factor α (%pa)		Long only excess net returns (%pa)	
	TSM	CSM	TSM	CSM	TSM	CSM	TSM	CSM
Best	25.0	16.5	17.0	11.0	11.0	6.0	6.0	3.5
Median	11.5	8.0	3.5	3.0	−2.0	−3.0	−2.5%	−2.5%

However, we see more evidence of how sensitive the exploitable profits are to the way that the momentum strategies are implemented when we consider the erosion in profits as we move to the median implementation. In this case, the average performance of both the time-series and cross-sectional momentum strategies across the 24 markets is negative once implementation costs and risk are taken into account. This performance would be further eroded in those markets where it is difficult to implement short portfolios. Overall, time-series momentum maintains a better performance compared to cross-sectional momentum but the magnitude of this outperformance is again eroded once one takes account of the encumbrances associated with implementation.

The performance reported in Table 13.6 is based on the average return across the 24 markets but there is a large variation in this performance across the markets. Hence there are several markets including Belgium, Denmark, New Zealand and Switzerland where in excess of 75% of the implementation of the momentum investment strategies generate exploitable investment opportunities. Equally there are several other markets such as Australia, Greece, Hong Kong, Israel, Japan and the US where exploitable profits are generated by less than 20% of the implementations considered.

In conclusion, it appears that the very enticing profits promised by the raw returns generated by the two momentum strategies are going to prove very difficult to exploit once account is taken of implementation costs, risk and restrictions on short sales. The implication being that momentum does not represent such a challenge to market efficiency as one might presume based upon the evidence presented in the academic literature. However, this does not mean that profits cannot ever be generated by those who pursue a momentum strategy. Indeed, the probability of a momentum strategy generating exploitable profits will depend on the form of momentum pursued (time-series momentum generally being preferable to cross-sectional momentum), how it is implemented (with the need being for the decision rules utilised to produce trading strategies that are in harmony with the behaviour of the market) and the market to which it is applied (with the best and worst markets being highlighted in previous discussion).

REFERENCES

Alexander, G. J. (2000). On back-testing 'zero-investment' strategies. *The Journal of Business,* **73**(2), 255–278.

Ali, A. and Trombley, M. A. (2006). Short sales constraints and momentum in stock returns. *Journal of Business Finance & Accounting,* **33**(3–4), 587–615.

Asness, C. (2012). Momentum in Japan: The exception that proves the rule. *The Journal of Portfolio Management,* **37**(4), 67–75.

Barber, B. M. and Odean, T. (2008). All that glitters: The effect of attention and news on the buying behavior of individual and institutional investors. *Review of Financial Studies,* **21**(2), 785–818.

Berkowitz, S. A., Logue, D. E. and Noser, E. A. (1988). The total cost of transactions on the NYSE. *The Journal of Finance,* **43**(1), 97–112.

Bird, R., Yeung, D. and Gao, X. (2016). Time-series and cross-sectional momentum strategies under alternative implementation strategies. *The Australian Journal of Management,* **42**(2). Available at: https://www.uts.edu.au/sites/default/files/FDG_Seminar_150408.pdf

Chen, J., Hong, H. and Stein, J. (2002), Breadth of ownership and stock returns. *Journal of Financial Economics*, **66**(2), 171–205.

Chordia, T., Subrahmanyam, A. and Qing T. (2014). Have capital market anomalies attenuated in the recent era of high liquidity and trading activity? *Journal of Accounting and Economics*, **58**(1), 41–58.

Chui, A. C., Titman, S. and Wei, K. J. (2010). Individualism and momentum around the world. *The Journal of Finance*, **65**(1), 361–392.

Conrad, J. and Kaul, G. (1998). An anatomy of trading strategies. *Review of Financial Studies*, **11**(3), 489–519.

Fama, E. F. (1998). Market efficiency, long-term returns, and behavioral finance. *Journal of Financial Economics*, **49**(3), 283–306.

Fama, E. F. and French, K. (1992). The cross-section of expected stock returns. *The Journal of Finance*, **47**(2), 427–465.

Fong, W. M., Wong, W. K. and Lean, H. H. (2005). International momentum strategies: a stochastic dominance approach. *Journal of Financial Markets*, **8**(1), 89–109.

Frazzini, A., Israel, R. and Moskowitz, T. (2015) Trading Costs of Asset Pricing Anomalies. Fama-Miller Working Paper; Chicago Booth Research Paper No. 14-05. Available at https:// papers.ssrn.com/sol3/papers.cfm?abstract_id=2294498

Goyenko, R. Y., Holden, C. W. and Trzcinka, C. A. (2009). Do liquidity measures measure liquidity? *Journal of Financial Economics*, **92**(2), 153–181.

Griffin, J. M., Ji, X. and Martin, J. S. (2005). Global momentum strategies. *The Journal of Portfolio Management*, **31**(2), 23–39.

Grundy, B. D. and Martin, J. S. (2001). Understanding the nature of the risks and the source of the rewards to momentum investing. *Review of Financial Studies*, **14**(1), 29–78.

Gulen, H. and Petkova, R. (2015). Absolute strength: Exploring momentum in stock returns. Available at SSRN: http://ssrn.com/abstract=2638004 or http://dx.doi.org/10.2139/ssrn .2638004

Hanauer, H. (2014). Is Japan different? Evidence on momentum and market dynamics. *International Review of Finance*, **14**(1), 141–160.

Hwang, S. and Rubesam, A. (2013). The disappearance of momentum. *The European Journal of Finance*, **21**(7), 584–607.

Ince, O. S. and Porter, R. B. (2006). Individual equity return data from Thomson Datastream: Handle with care! *Journal of Financial Research*, **29**(4), 463–479.

Jegadeesh, N. and Titman, S. (1993). Returns to buying winners and selling losers: Implications for stock market efficiency. *The Journal of Finance*, **48**(1), 65–91.

Jegadeesh, N. and Titman, S. (2000). Profitability of momentum strategies: An evaluation of alternative explanations. *The Journal of Finance*, **56**(2), 699–720.

Jegadeesh, N. and Titman, S. (2002). Cross-sectional and time-series determinants of momentum returns. *Review of Financial Studies*, **15**(1), 143–157.

Jensen, M. (1978). Some anonmalous evidence regarding market efficiency. *Journal of Financial Economics*, **6**(2–3), 95–101

Jones, C. M. and Lamont, O. A. (2002). Short-sale constraints and stock returns. *Journal of Financial Economics*, **66**(2), 207–239.

Keim, D. B. and Madhavan, A. (1997). Transactions costs and investment style: An inter-exchange analysis of institutional equity trades. *Journal of Financial Economics*, **46**(3), 265–292.

Lesmond, D. A., Ogden, J. P. and Trzcinka, C. A. (1999). A new estimate of transaction costs. *Review of Financial Studies*, **12**(5), 1113–1141.

Lesmond, D. A., Ogden, J. P. and Trzcinka, C. A. (2004). The illusory nature of momentum profits. *Journal of Financial Economics*, **71**(2), 349–380.

Li, X., Brooks, C. and Miffre, J. (2009). Transaction costs, trading volume and momentum strategies. Trading Volume and Momentum Strategies (18 May 2009).

Liu, M., Liu, Q. and Ma, T. (2011) The 52-week high momentum strategy in international stock markets, *Journal of International Money and Finance*, **30**, 180–204.

McLean, R. D., Pontiff, J. and Watanabe, A. (2009). Share issuance and cross-sectional returns: International evidence. *Journal of Financial Economics*, **94**(1), 1–17.

McLean, R. D. and Pontiff, J. (2016). Does academic research destroy stock return predictability?, *The Journal of Finance*, **71**(1), 5–32.

Moskowitz, T., Ooi, Y. H. and Pedersen, L. H. (2012). Time series momentum. *Journal of Financial Economics*, **104**(2), 228–250.

Novy-Marx, R. and Velikov, M. (2016), A taxonomy of anomalies and their trading costs. *Review of Financial Studies*, **29**(1), 104–147.

Phua, V., Chan, H., Faff, R. and Hudson, R. (2010). The influence of time, seasonality and market state on momentum: Insights from the Australian stock market. *Applied Financial Economics*, **20**(20), 1547–1563.

Sharpe, W. F. (1998). The Sharpe ratio. In P. L. Bernstein (ed.), *Streetwise–the Best of the Journal of Portfolio Management*, Princeton, NJ, Princeton University Press, 169–185.

CHAPTER 14

Time-Series Momentum in Credit: Machine Learning Approach

SHIVAM GHOSH, STEVE SATCHELL and NANDINI SRIVASTAVA

14.1 INTRODUCTION

In this chapter, we investigate applications of artificial intelligence to momentum strategies. We choose to include machine learning (ML) within the superset of ideas of artificial intelligence (AI). We recognise the enormity of both subjects; in particular artificial intelligence has both a philosophical and practical base which one needs to understand to deploy it to finance.

As a financial application we look at single index time-series momentum strategies. We investigate whether ML algorithms can improve risk-adjusted performance of the vanilla time-series momentum strategy – which simply goes long or short the index based on sign of past returns over a look back period. More specifically, we explore both linear regression methods with sparsity constraints like Lasso, Ridge and Elastic-Net, as well as non-linear classification methods like Random Forests and Neural Nets. We come to the conclusion that while standalone time series momentum strategies constructed via ML signals have Sharpe ratios comparable to vanilla time-series momentum, they do exhibit low correlation to the vanilla strategy. A result of this, low correlation is a potential diversification benefit from combining vanilla and ML signals. A risk parity combination of vanilla and ML signals has a Sharpe ratio in excess of 1.10 – almost twice that of an optimized vanilla strategy Sharpe of ~0.6 over the period 2006 to 2019. We next briefly summarize an outline of this chapter.

Section 14.2 is a brief exposition of some philosophical ideas around AI. In Section 14.3 we give a brief introduction to momentum, this is necessarily short since it is discussed elsewhere throughout the book. We highlight the fact that vanilla time-series momentum strategies have had poor returns recently across several asset classes.

This observation motivates a need for new signal definitions and ML is a natural direction to explore. In Section 14.4, we introduce Generalized Linear Models (GLM) to generate forward return signals for trading momentum. Section 14.5 discusses the intricate issue of training and hyper-parameter optimization of ML models. This is done in the context of GLM but has broader applicability to other ML algorithms. Results from GLM momentum signals are discussed in Section 14.6. Section 14.7 makes a foray into the realm of non-linear ML algorithms starting with Random Forests. Section 14.8 introduces Neural Nets and briefly outlines the procedure for training a single hidden layer Neural Net. Section 14.9 summarizes the main results from different vanilla and ML strategies and we conclude with final remarks in Section 14.10.

14.2   THE PHILOSOPHY OF ARTIFICIAL INTELLIGENCE

Here we provide a brief discussion on the philosophy of AI. We acknowledge an indebtedness to Ramón López de Mántaras (López de Mántaras, 2019) who provides a masterly summary of the topic.

At the most fundamental level, the ultimate goal of artificial intelligence (AI) is that a machine can have a type of general intelligence similar to a human's. These ideas find root in the Physical Symbol System (PSS) hypothesis – Allen Newell and Herbert Simon (Newell and Simon, 1976) formulated the PSS hypothesis according to which 'a physical symbol system has the necessary and sufficient means for general intelligent action'. The system consists of a set of entities called symbols that, through relations, can be combined to form larger structures and can be transformed by applying a set of processes. This hypothesis further implies that the nature of the underlying layer is unimportant as long as it allows symbols to be processed. López de Mántaras (López de Mántaras, 2019) recognises that AI is precisely the scientific field dedicated to attempts to verify this hypothesis for instance in the context of digital computers, that is, verifying whether a properly programmed computer is capable of general intelligent behaviour.

In fact, we find roots further back in the thinking of AI pioneers in the 1950s and even in Alan Turing's groundbreaking texts (Turing, 1948, 1950) on intelligent machines. Therein also lies a key distinction between the concepts of weak and strong AI, first introduced by philosopher John Searle (Searle, 1980). López de Mántaras (López de Mántaras, 2019) explains that the design and application of artificial intelligences that can only behave intelligently in a very specific setting is related to what is known as weak AI. It has been demonstrated in several areas that computers can perform specific tasks even better than humans for instance solving logical formulas, playing chess, medical diagnosis and other tasks related to decision making. These appeal to aspects of the mind through construction of programs to carry out functions to formulate and test hypotheses. Juxtaposed against weak AI is strong AI. Strong AI would imply that a properly designed computer does not simulate a mind but actually is one, and should, therefore, be capable of an intelligence equal, or even superior to human beings. As previously mentioned, the ultimate goal of AI is general intelligence. All strong AI will necessarily be general, but there can be general AIs capable of multitasking but not strong in the sense that, while they can emulate the capacity to exhibit general intelligence similar to humans, they do not experience states of mind. These concepts are important to layout to benchmark successes, failures and further developments in AI that will be adopted across multi-disciplinary fields and industries. Advances in the field of AI are manifestations of weak and specific AI predominantly so far.

A chronology on how these forms of AI manifested themselves in advances in models is useful. Early advances in AI were dominated by the symbolic model which is rooted in the PSS model. While it continues to be very important, it is now considered a classic top-down model architecture which is based on logical reasoning and heuristic searching as the pillars of problem solving. These early intelligent systems therefore did not require direct interaction with the real world, only perceiving the environment and acting upon it, for example learning and decision-making in autonomous robots. Analogous to the development for symbolic AI was the development of a biologically based approach called connectionist AI. Whilst connectionist systems are not incompatible with the PSS hypothesis, unlike symbolic AI that are modelled top down, these are modelled from the bottom up. The underlying hypothesis is that intelligence emerges from the distributed activity of a large number of interconnected units whose models closely resemble the electrical activity of biological neurons.

McCulloch and Pitts (1943) proposed a simplified model of the neuron based in the idea that it is essentially a logic unit and the model is a mathematical abstraction with inputs and outputs. An artificial neural network is created when outputs of each neuron are connected to the inputs of other neurons. López de Mántaras (2019) finds that, based on what was then known about the reinforcement of synapses among biological neurons, scientists found that these artificial neural networks could be trained to learn functions that related inputs to outputs by adjusting the weights used to determine connections between neurons. These models were hence considered more conducive to learning, cognition, and memory than those based on symbolic AI. Within these models, another biologically inspired model that is also compatible with the PSS hypothesis is evolutionary computation (Holland, 1975) derived from successes at evolving complex organisms which led some researchers from the early 1960s to consider the possibility of imitating evolution.

An even more important distinction came between corporeal and non-corporeal models. So far we have only referenced non-corporeal models. These models work from the programmers' descriptions of surroundings coded in a language to represent that information. AI experts like Rodney Brooks (Brooks 1991) initially proposed that it was not even important to generate internal representations of the world around an agent because the world is the best possible model of itself and the majority of intelligent behaviour emerged directly from the interaction of the agents with their surroundings, and didn't require any reasoning.

The strongest critique of these non-corporeal models is based on the idea that an intelligent agent will need a body to directly experience its surroundings. In 1965, philosopher Hubert Dreyfus affirmed that AI's ultimate objective – strong AI of a general kind – was unattainable (Dreyfus, 1965). Dreyfus argued that the brain processes information in a global and continuous manner, while a computer uses a finite and discreet set of deterministic operations, that is, it applies rules to a finite body of data. He further developed this in later articles and books (Dreyfus 1992) also argued that the body plays a crucial role in intelligence which allows interaction with the world, in the same manner as intelligence of living beings is derived from their situation in surroundings where they can interact through their bodies. According to Dreyfus (1992), AI must model all such aspects if it is to reach its ultimate objective of strong AI stating that achieving the ultimate goal of AI is not possible with the classic methods of symbolic, non-corporeal AI, implying that the PSS hypothesis is incorrect. This thinking has been the foundation of defining and measuring success in AI, which propounds that the corporeal approach with internal representation is essential for advancing toward general intelligences. Piaget's cognitive development theory (Inhelder and Piaget, 1958) proposes that AI is similar to human beings who follow a process of mental maturity in stages and the steps in this process could guide how to design intelligent machines. Such ideas have led to a new sub-area in AI called development robotics (Weng et al., 2001).

What has success been like in the context of such ideas against the ultimate goal of AI? Successes in systems like AlphaGO (Silver et al., 2016), Watson (Ferrucci et al., 2013), and advances in autonomous vehicles or image-based medical diagnosis have been possible due to successes in the capacity to analyse huge amounts of data and efficiently detect patterns. However as López de Mántaras (2019) affirms we have hardly advanced at all in the quest for general AI .and that current AI systems are examples of what Daniel Dennet called 'competence without comprehension' (Dennet, 2018). We've learnt that preconceived difficult tasks like diagnosing illnesses or playing superior chess have been quite easy and those that were conceived easy have turned out to have the most difficulties and the reason for this might have been exactly in this difficulty to equip machines with the knowledge that constitutes 'common sense'. Lines of research that might help contribute towards the acquisition of common-sense knowledge are development robotics or the mathematical modelling and learning of cause-and-effect relations, that is, the learning of causal, and thus asymmetrical, models of the world. Current deep-learning-based systems are capable of learning symmetrical mathematical functions but not asymmetrical relations and thus cannot distinguish cause from effects (Pearl and Mackenzie, 2018; Lake et al., 2017). Further today's deep-learning systems are significantly limited by what is known as 'catastrophic forgetting' such that if they have been trained to carry out one task and are then trained to do something different they completely forget what they learned for the previous task. Another important limitation is that they have no capacity to explain ('black boxes').

At the pinnacle of complex capacities are those that require interacting with unrestricted and not previously prepared surroundings and the design of such systems will require the integration of development in many areas of AI that will combine perception, representation, reasoning, action and learning. This is a very important AI problem as we are yet to figure out how to integrate all of these components of intelligence and will need cognitive architectures (Forbus, 2012) to integrate these components adequately. López de Mántaras (2019) believes that the most important research areas will be hybrid systems that combine the advantages of systems capable of reasoning on the basis of knowledge and memory use (Graves et al., 2016) with those of AI based on the analysis of massive amounts of data, that is, deep learning (Bengio, 2009). In the context of deep learning, it would be interesting to research how to endow these systems with an explicative capacity, which is essential to an intelligent system that can explain how it reached the proposed results and conclusion. Another area would be development of new learning algorithms that do not require enormous amounts of data for training from an efficiency point of view (see memristor-based neuromorphic computing in Saxena et al. [2018]). The quest for endowing machines with common sense has led to a new and very promising AI field known as computational creativity (Colton et al., 2009, 2015; López de Mántaras, 2016) where computers have begun to be creative agents themselves rather than 'tool-kits' such as in chess, music, the visual arts and narrative, among other creative activities. López de Mántaras (2019) makes the important point that the mental development needed for all complex intelligence depends on interactions with the environment and those interactions depend, in turn, on the body – especially the perceptive and motor systems. This, along with the fact that machines will not follow the same socialization and culture-acquisition processes as ours further reinforces the conclusion that, no matter how sophisticated they become, these intelligences will be different from ours. The existence of intelligences unlike ours, and therefore alien to our values and human needs, calls for reflection on the possible ethical limitations of developing AI (Weizenbaum, 1976).

14.3 VANILLA TIME-SERIES MOMENTUM

Momentum premium captures trends in asset prices by going long (short) on past winners (losers). Along with the three Fama-French factors – market beta, size and value, momentum helps to explain a significant cross-section of bond and equity returns (Cross-sectional R^2, a standard goodness-of-fit measure, are of the order of 7 to 25% (see Lewellen, 2015) i.e. cross-sectionally stocks/bonds with higher (lower) past returns also have higher (lower) future returns. Momentum risk premia have been empirically established across several markets – Equity, FX, Commodities and Sovereign debt (Moskowitz et al., 2012) and across several decades with Sharpe ratio ratios in the range of 0.6 to 0.7 (see Table 14.1) and cumulative wealth charts displayed in Figure 14.1.

In recent years, performance of momentum strategies has been underwhelming see Figure 14.2. One of the primary reasons has been CTA (Commodity Trading Advisor) crowding. As the strategy does well, it becomes increasingly attractive and more investors pile in, leading to crowding. As trends switch signs, there is mass exodus and

TABLE 14.1 Annualized returns and volatilities for time-series momentum strategies (TSMOM) from January 1985 to June 2019 (monthly returns). Annual returns are non-compounded.

	Ann Returns (%)	Ann. Vol (%)	Sharpe
Equity	18.4	27.0	0.68
Commodities	10.2	14.5	0.71
FX	12.0	18.2	0.66
Fixed Income	20.5	28.9	0.71
TSMOM	14.0	12.2	1.15

Source: Moskowitz et al., 2012 – AQR data portal (https://www.aqr.com/Insights/Datasets/Time-Series-Momentum-Factors-Monthly).

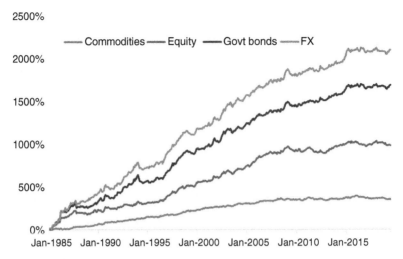

FIGURE 14.1   Cumulative wealth charts for Time Series Momentum
strategies across asset classes.
Source: Based on data from AQR Data Portal (https://www.aqr.com/
Insights/Datasets/Time-Series-Momentum-Factors-Monthly).

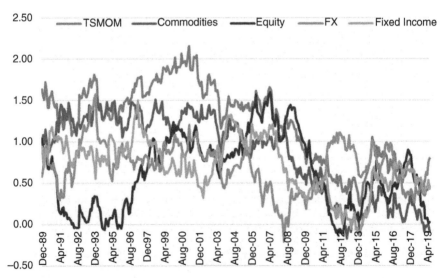

FIGURE 14.2   Rolling 5-year Sharpe ratios January 1990 to June 2019 (Monthly
returns, gross of transaction costs).
Source: Based on data from AQR data portal.

selling pressure leading to crashes. momentum is thus divergent in the sense that as the strategy does well, it gets increasingly crowded, as opposed to convergent strategies like value where investors take profit as value returns do well; demand for value assets declines and investors exit the trade.

Crowded momentum trades also stem from a relatively simplistic signal definition for the strategy which in many cases is sign of past returns over a look-back period. These look-back periods are optimized historically to deliver the best risk adjusted returns and are not adaptive to market regimes/changing conditions. The implication of this is that a vanilla estimate of the momentum signal may well estimate over a fixed period irrespective of market conditions. By contrast, an adaptive algorithm will adapt to market conditions. In volatile markets when trends are less persistent it might switch to a smaller look back horizon or decide to completely shut-off.

Furthermore, vanilla TSMOM (Time-Series Momentum) strategy performance is fairly sensitive to the choice of look back windows as shown for different developed market equity indices in Table 14.2. Looking at the Standard&Poor 500 Index (SPX), while the optimal Sharpe ratios correspond to a 252-day holding period, there is significant variance of Sharpe ratios as we move across the grid of the look-back window and holding periods with the lowest Sharpe ratios corresponding to a 21–42-day look-back period.

TABLE 14.2 SPX time-series momentum Sharpe ratio ratios across look-back periods (rows, in days) and holding periods (columns, in days). Daily returns data from January 2006 to June 2019

SPX	5	21	42	63
21	0.19	0.21	0.26	0.31
42	0.28	0.22	0.40	0.42
63	0.34	0.34	0.38	0.42
26	0.43	0.54	0.55	0.57
252	0.50	0.57	0.58	0.61
504	0.54	0.46	0.40	0.38
SX5E	5	21	42	63
21	−0.47	−0.29	−0.16	0.00
42	−0.42	−0.15	0.06	0.13
63	0.08	0.07	0.12	0.17
126	−0.08	0.17	0.19	0.17
252	0.14	0.09	0.05	0.05
504	0.05	0.06	0.00	0.00
UKX	5	21	42	63
21	−0.65	−0.65	−0.25	−0.05
42	−0.38	−0.20	0.06	0.10
63	−0.16	−0.16	0.04	0.07
126	−0.26	−0.02	0.08	0.10
252	−0.02	0.02	0.06	0.07
504	0.08	0.13	0.09	0.10

Source: Based on data from AlphaVantage

In this chapter, we explore the possibility of developing a suite of different signal definitions for a vanilla TSMOM strategy with the hope that they have low correlation to vanilla TSMOM and a respectable Sharpe ratio so that fusing these new strategies with vanilla TSMOM can potentially produce diversification benefits.

14.4 GENERALIZED LINEAR MODELS (GLM) – LASSO, RIDGE AND ELASTIC NET

In this section, we look in some detail at popular methods used in AI investigations. These are particularly suited to financial problems as in the three cases considered they are built around a linear factor model structure. By assuming that the fundamental process is linear we are limiting the efficacy of these techniques. However, the data do not know that they are linear so there is always scope for potential improvement. We return to this point in the conclusion in Section 14.10.

Recent advances in statistical learning have supplemented vanilla OLS regression with attributes that can help induce variable selection. For example, a simple L1 (absolute value) penalty term on the coefficients leads to Equation (14.1) and is equivalent to a sparseness constraint on the regressors. We have data through a look-back window of length T, across different look-back periods K.

$$C_{Lasso} = \left(\frac{1}{2T}\right) \sum_{i=1}^{T} (y_i - X_{ij}\beta_j)^2 + \alpha \sum_{j=1}^{K} |\beta_j| \qquad (14.1)$$

where y_i are a set of target values which will be estimated using a predictor matrix X of dimension $T \times K$ by minimizing C_{Lasso} via slope coefficient betas – a vector of length $K \times 1$. We have chosen $1/(2T)$ and α to be relative weights for the two terms in Equation (14.1). The first term in Equation (14.1) is the OLS objective minimizing least squares and the second term imposes a constraint on the cumulative L1 norm of the betas – i.e. it confines the slopes to a region in parameter space whose size is decided by the parameter α.

For a simple two-regressor predictor matrix ($K = 2$), the slopes β_1, β_2 are confined to a diamond shaped region shown in Figure.14.3. The size of the diamond box is controlled via α – a hyper-parameter of the model. For small values of α, the size of the diamond box is large and optimal betas obtained from minimizing Equation (14.1) are fairly close to the OLS objective. As α increases, the diamond box shrinks and the

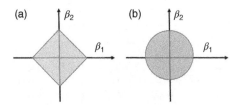

FIGURE 14.3 Parameter constraint regions for Lasso (a) and Ridge (b).

betas are forced to take values that confine them to within the diamond regions which may be quite different from the OLS outcome. They therefore begin deviating from their OLS limits. For very large values of α we get a simple constant intercept model. Thus, the tuning of α also allows us to regulate model complexity – small values allow for many non-zero slope coefficients and models are complex, very large values of α induce slope selection forcing very few relevant regressors to survive leading to simpler models. This competition between minimization of OLS L2 quadratic) norm with a sparsity constraint on the size of predictor coefficients is at the heart of model selection algorithms like Lasso. Whilst an interesting way to compute betas, it is fairly limited in its ability to even infer simple non-linear functional relationship between future and past returns.

Ridge is a close alternative to Lasso and differs in the form of the sparsity constraint on the slopes. Very similar techniques are used in econometrics where the procedure is called Ridge regression and is used to estimate models when multi-collinearity exists. Further applications of similar methods are also used in portfolio construction where one can carry out mean-variance optimization with a constraint on squared portfolio weights. The slopes are confined to a circle (hyper-sphere) in 2(K-dimensional) space. Formally, the Ridge objective function is given in Equation (14.2)

$$C_{Ridge} = \left(\frac{1}{2T} \right) \sum_{i=1}^{K} (y_i - X_{ij}\beta_j)^2 + \alpha \sum_{j=1}^{K} \beta_j^2 \qquad (14.2)$$

A combination of Lasso and Ridge which has both forms of L1 and L2 penalties for the magnitude of the predictor coefficients is called Elastic Net. Elastic Net has one additional parameter relative to Lasso and Ridge – the ratio of the relative weighting of the L1 to L2 norm – denoted by ρ.

Unlike linear regression where models are completely defined by a vector of linear coefficients, specification of generalized linear models like Lasso, Ridge and Elastic Net require setting values of additional hyper-parameters like α in Lasso, Ridge and (ρ, α) in the case of Elastic Net. Before discussing methods to set these parameters we first look at how model behaviour evolves as we vary these hyper-parameters.

Figure 14.4 shows results of a Lasso calculation on trading SPX momentum signal where the predictor matrix comprises non-overlapping monthly returns over last the 12 months and the target vector is 1 month future SPX returns. For different hyper-parameters values (shown on the horizontal axis on a log scale), the in-sample R^2 (the coefficient of determination/goodness-of-fit measure) and OOS model Sharpe ratio are plotted. Small values of α retain all predictors (size of region in Figure 14.3 is large) and the model fits well in-sample. However, a high in-sample R^2 corresponds to a low OOS Sharpe ratio of approximately 0.75 due to over fitting in-sample. On the far right, the model for high enough values of α is a constant intercept model that always goes long SPX and has a Sharpe ratio circa 0.85. This is the limit where the model under-fits and therefore again generalizes poorly OOS. In between these two limits of a complex and simple model lies an optimal specification of alpha that does not over/under-fit in sample and therefore has good OOS performance – this is characterized by a peak in the OOS Sharpe ratio corresponding to an optimal alpha of 0.08 and a strategy Sharpe ratio of 0.96.

In-sample Rsqr versus OOS sharpe

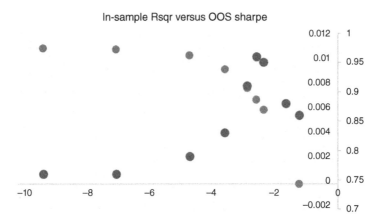

FIGURE 14.4   Evolution of in-sample R^2 (ranging from 0.0 to 0.012, right axis) and OOS (Out of Sample ranging from 0.75 to 1.0) Sharpe ratio as a function of Lasso hyper-parameter α plotted on a log scale along the horizontal axis.

The history (T) is typically divided into two periods – training and testing. The optimal alpha is acutely sensitive to lengths of training/testing periods that determine the correlation of past performance with future returns. In periods of high volatility, the model is likely to pick a high alpha that prevents any information from past look backs to filter into signal generation. On the other hand, in periods of calm when market trends are persistent, optimal alpha takes a small value and will allow larger look-back windows to determine the direction of future performance. To allow this dynamic calibration of alpha we now discuss methods for setting its value – a procedure commonly known in the Machine Learning literature as cross-validation (CV).

Before discussing CV we briefly digress to make some salient points regarding training ML algorithms, including linear models discussed earlier. While linear models like Lasso are simple to interpret, they usually have a large bias – i.e. they tend to oversimplify the problem since in effect we are approximating a non-linear function via a linear response. This bias does not go away even with an infinite training dataset. Despite this limitation, high-bias models do have an advantage. They exhibit low sensitivity to training datasets. In contrast, decision trees, which we discuss in Section 14.7, have low bias (since they can model non-linear responses) but have high variance as a consequence of over-fitting noise in the training dataset. Finding an optimal machine learning model is therefore both the art and science of navigating the complex landscape of ML hyper-parameters to optimize the bias-variance trade-off. The bias-variance competition is also nicely summarized in the following quote by Einstein – 'Everything should be made as simple as possible, but no simpler'. With this in mind, we move on to determining optimal GLM hyper-parameters.

14.5 DETERMINING OPTIMAL HYPER-PARAMETERS VIA CROSS-VALIDATION

Optimal hyper-parameters are determined using training, validation and testing procedures shown graphically in Figure 14.5. Each dot corresponds to an epoch where return data are available for training/testing. Lasso is trained on an expanding/rolling training dataset as shown in Figure 14.5. In practice, a series of models – each labelled by a choice of α are prepared by fitting them to the training dataset. Performance of each model is calibrated over a validation dataset. Our choice of validation metric is a simple R^2 between actual and forecasted returns. The best performing model, corresponding to the highest R^2, is picked based on performance over the cross-validation period. The optimal model is then used to generate true OOS predictions shown by the 'Testing' dots.

We now formally define our problem setup. In this example, our target variable is the index return over a forecasting horizon f – so we are forecasting a univariate variable. Lasso is trained on a set of target vectors comprising rolling index returns over period f along with a set of predictors consisting of non-overlapping monthly returns over a 12-month look-back period. The optimal alpha is determined via performance over the validation period, i.e. $\alpha_{opt} = \arg\max(2sq_{val}(\alpha))$, where $Rsq_{val}(\alpha)$ is the R^2 between the forecasted and actual returns over the cross-validation period for a given choice of α.

We now turn to our specific application. Based on this optimal alpha, we generate a series of return forecasts r_t^{fcast} over the testing period t which feeds into the final strategy return calculation as follows:

$$r_t^{Mom} = \frac{\sigma_T}{\sigma_{63d,t}} sign\left(r_{t-1}^{fcast}\right) r_t \tag{14.3}$$

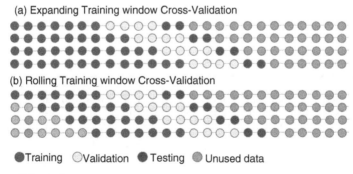

(a) Expanding Training window Cross-Validation

(b) Rolling Training window Cross-Validation

●Training ○Validation ● Testing ◐ Unused data

FIGURE 14.5 Schematic of training, validation and testing data splits for momentum signal generation.

Where σ_T is a target volatility which we set to 25%, $\sigma_{63d,t}$ is a 63-day standard deviation of daily returns and r_t is the 1-day index return on day t. To reduce sensitivity to strategy start date, we average final returns over f parally running Momentum portfolios that initiated trades with 1-day offsets relative to each other. This is analogous to the Jegadeesh and Titman rolling portfolio methodology (1993). In all results discussed in this chapter we set f to 21 days.

14.6   RESULTS: GENERALIZED LINEAR MODELS

We report results for both expanding and rolling window CV's for different choices of the training and validation window lengths and a 21-day holding period in Table 14.3. We also report statistics to gauge the accuracy of Lasso predictions. These are True Positive rates (TP: defined as the fraction of instances when forecasted and actual returns were both positive), True Negative rates (TN: defined as the fraction of instances when actual and forecasted returns were both negative), False Positive rates (FP: defined as the fraction of instances when the actual return was negative but the forecasted return was positive) and False Negative rates (FN: defined as the fraction of instances when the true return was positive but the forecasted return was negative). We also report prediction accuracy as the fraction of TP + TN over all TP + TN + FP + FN.

A first sense check is the scaling of OOS strategy Sharpe ratio versus prediction accuracy shown in Figure 14.6. The OOS Sharpe ratio increases with better forecasting accuracy which is hardly surprising but a good sense check to confirm model implementation. Average Lasso accuracy across different CV choices is 61%, the median Sharpe ratio is 0.51 with a significant variance – the highest Sharpe ratio is 0.75 and the lowest is 0.41. For reference, an optimal vanilla momentum strategy had a Sharpe ratio 0.57 during the same period with a 252-day look-back window and a 21-day holding period as shown in Table 14.2. Unfortunately, Lasso has a high (80%) correlation with the vanilla SPX TSMOM strategy and is therefore expected to have limited diversification benefits. Not surprisingly, we find very similar results from the Ridge and Elastic Net models –these are summarized in Table 14.3.

14.7   RANDOM FORESTS

Random Forests (RF) are predictive algorithms that allow a non-linear functional relationship between features (past returns in this case) and target variables (future returns). They are more competitive than the generalized linear models of the previous sections in cases where simple linear relationships fail to capture the dependence of target vectors on the feature matrix. RF rely on a series of decision/classification trees to produce target variable recommendations.

A decision tree solves a classification problem by growing nodes and branches based on a series of if-else statements. An example is a tree-based movie recommender system that picks movie choices given user-specific viewing history. For example, let's say the training set comprises of 100 movies belonging to each of two classes – 1(previously viewed) and 0 (not viewed). The feature matrix has a single column specifying

TABLE 14.3 Summary of strategy Sharpes for different ML algorithms – Lasso, Ridge, Elastic Net, Random Forests and Neural Networks. For each strategy we show the cross-validation choices for training the models (training_window = 1 for expanding and 0 for rolling, see Section 14.5), lengths of forecasting window, validation length and training window lengths in days. Also shown are accuracy metrics, strategy returns and volatility (both annualized and in %), max drawdowns and Sharpe ratios.

Lasso

Stra-tegy #	Index	Training_window	Forecast_window	Validation_length	Training_window_length	Val_metric	Return (%)	Vola-tility (%)	Sharpe	Draw-down (%)	TP (%)	FP (%)	TN (%)	FN (%)	Accu-racy (%)
1	SPX	0	21	84	273	R^{2}score	20.8	27.6	0.75	47	58	26	6.55	9	65
2	SPX	0	21	84	399	R^{2}score	16.8	26.2	0.64	84	58	28	5	9	63
3	SPX	0	21	84	525	R^{2}score	17.3	27.4	0.63	75	60	29	3	7	63
4	SPX	0	21	147	273	R^{2}score	17.6	26.6	0.66	85	57	26	6	10	63
5	SPX	0	21	147	399	R^{2}score	11.5	27.8	0.41	126	55	28	5	12	60
6	SPX	0	21	147	525	R^{2}score	11.9	27.5	0.43	124	56	28	5	11	61
7	SPX	1	21	84	273	R^{2}score	14.7	27.8	0.53	77	60	30	3	7	63
8	SPX	1	21	147	273	R^{2}score	16.3	27.8	0.59	70	61	29	3	6	64

Ridge

Stra-tegy #	Index	Training_window	Forecast_window	Validation_length	Training_window_length	Val_metric	Return (%)	Vola-tility (%)	Sharpe	Draw-down (%)	TP (%)	FP (%)	TN (%)	FN (%)	Accu-racy (%)
1	SPX	0	21	84	273	R^{2}score	16.3	26.5	0.62	42	54	25	7	13	62
2	SPX	0	21	84	399	R^{2}score	16.5	26.6	0.62	88	57	26	6	10	63
3	SPX	0	21	84	525	R^{2}score	16.1	27.5	0.59	84	59	28	4	8	63
4	SPX	0	21	147	273	R^{2}score	15.3	27.1	0.57	95	56	27	6	11	62
5	SPX	0	21	147	399	R^{2}score	12.2	27.5	0.45	116	54	26	7	13	61
6	SPX	0	21	147	525	R^{2}score	11.7	27.4	0.43	127	56	28	5	11	61
7	SPX	1	21	84	273	R^{2}score	15.0	27.8	0.54	77	60	30	3	7	63
8	SPX	1	21	147	273	R^{2}score	16.8	27.7	0.60	63	61	29	4	6	64

(continued)

TABLE 14.3 (Continued)

Elastic Net

Strategy #	Index	Training window	Forecast window	Validation length	Training window length	Val metric	Return (%)	Volatility (%)	Sharpe	Drawdown (%)	TP (%)	FP (%)	TN (%)	FN (%)	Accuracy (%)
1	SPX	0	21	84	273	R²score	16.8	26.8	0.63	57	57	27	6	10	63
2	SPX	0	21	84	399	R²score	16.2	26.6	0.61	93	58	28	5	9	63
3	SPX	0	21	84	525	R²score	14.7	27.3	0.54	82	58	29	4	9	62
4	SPX	0	21	147	273	R²score	15.0	26.9	0.56	86	57	27	6	10	62
5	SPX	0	21	147	399	R²score	11.8	27.5	0.43	120	54	26	6	13	60
6	SPX	0	21	147	525	R²score	12.3	27.5	0.45	119	56	28	5	11	61
7	SPX	1	21	84	273	R²score	14.6	27.8	0.53	84	60	30	3	7	63
8	Spx	1	21	147	273	R²score	16.9	27.7	0.61	61	61	29	3	6	64

Random Forests

Strategy #	Index	Training window	Forecast window	Validation length	Training window length	Val metric	Return (%)	Volatility (%)	Sharpe	Drawdown (%)	TP (%)	FP (%)	TN (%)	FN (%)	Accuracy (%)
1	SPX	0	21	126	504	accuracy_score	19.0	25.9	0.73	47	60	30	3	7	63
2	SPX	0	21	126	777	accuracy_score	14.2	25.6	0.55	57	60	31	2	7	62
3	SPX	0	21	252	504	accuracy_score	13.6	25.4	0.54	61	60	31	2	7	62
4	SPX	0	21	252	777	accuracy_score	13.9	25.7	0.54	55	61	31	2	6	63
5	SPX	1	21	126	504	accuracy_score	17.3	27.2	0.64	57	62	32	2	5	63
6	SPX	1	21	126	777	accuracy_score	17.3	27.2	0.64	57	62	32	2	5	63
7	SPX	1	21	252	504	accuracy_score	16.8	26.9	0.62	55	62	32	1	5	63
8	SPX	1	21	252	777	accuracy_score	16.8	26.9	0.62	55	62	32	1	5	63

Neural Networks

Strategy #	Index	Training_window	Forecast_window	Validation_length	Training_window_length	Val_metric	Return (%)	Volatility (%)	Sharpe	Drawdown (%)	TP (%)	FP (%)	TN (%)	FN (%)	Accuracy (%)
1	SPX	0	21	84	252	accuracy_score	3.4	24.6	0.14	61	48	26	7	19	56
2	SPX	0	21	84	504	accuracy_score	4.1	24.7	0.16	67	48	25	8	19	56
3	SPX	0	21	84	756	accuracy_score	4.7	24.9	0.19	59	52	28	5	15	57
4	SPX	0	21	84	1260	accuracy_score	16.6	26.0	0.64	59	60	30	3	7	63
5	SPX	0	21	147	252	accuracy_score	3.5	24.2	0.15	84	49	25	8	18	56
6	SPX	0	21	147	504	accuracy_score	2.3	25.0	0.09	79	49	26	7	18	56
7	SPX	0	21	147	756	accuracy_score	5.7	24.2	0.24	80	54	28	5	13	59
8	SPX	0	21	147	1260	accuracy_score	11.8	24.6	0.48	80	57	29	4	10	60
9	SPX	0	21	273	252	accuracy_score	9.2	23.7	0.39	54	55	28	5	12	60
10	SPX	0	21	273	504	accuracy_score	12.9	24.2	0.53	51	58	30	3	9	62
11	SPX	0	21	273	756	accuracy_score	12.1	25.3	0.48	51	59	31	2	8	61
12	SPX	0	21	273	1260	accuracy_score	19.8	23.0	0.86	51	55	25	8	12	63
13	SPX	1	21	84	252	accuracy_score	15.4	26.7	0.58	59	60	31	2	7	62
14	SPX	1	21	147	252	accuracy_score	9.3	25.8	0.36	80	55	29	4	12	59
15	SPX	1	21	273	252	accuracy_score	14.4	23.6	0.61	51	54	27	6	13	61

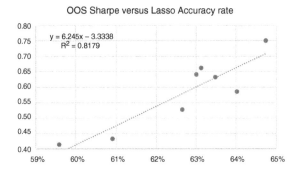

OOS Sharpe versus Lasso Accuracy rate

$y = 6.245x - 3.3338$
$R^2 = 0.8179$

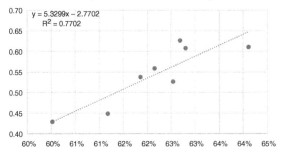

OOS Sharpe versus ElasticNet Accuracy rate

$y = 5.3299x - 2.7702$
$R^2 = 0.7702$

FIGURE 14.6 Scaling of Lasso momentum OOS Sharpe ratios with prediction accuracy (%) defined as the fraction of true predictions over the entire testing period length.

genres of each of the 100 movies in the training set. The target output is the solution to a binary classification problem that assigns a class (0 for no recommendation, 1 for recommendation) to a movie given its genre.

To produce this 1(0) classification the tree might start with a root node based on the if-else condition 'is genre horror?' The optimality of a split based on this if-else condition is determined by maximizing the fraction of samples belonging to a class at a given node. For example, if the root node based on the 'is genre horror?' condition splits in to 2 daughter nodes with configurations (50,0) and (0,50), the proportion of samples belonging to class 0 in (50,0) is 1 and to class 1 in (0,50) is 1. The split is therefore optimal and the decision tree concludes that the user only watches movies belonging to the horror genre. A less optimal split is (25, 25) for each of the two daughter nodes. In this case the proportion of samples belonging to each class is ½ in each daughter node and the split condition has been unsuccessful in learning a pure classification. Thus the split at every node is optimized to maximize proportion of samples belonging to a specific class.

Furthermore, each decision tree is trained via the above procedure using bootstrapping i.e. it is trained on a fraction of the training dataset (say 70%). Additionally, at each node of the decision tree only a randomly selected subsample of features is used to calculate the optimal split. Once a certain number of trees are trained, their OOS classification error (called the 'OOB score') is calculated on the remaining 30% of the training data. Number of trees and other hyper-parameters are varied until the OOB score converges and at this point the hyper-parameter optimized RF is ready to make predictions. The final RF recommendation is a majority vote from the forest of individual decision trees.

The RF estimator has lower variance relative to individual classification trees in the forest. This lower variance is a result of the bootstrapping procedure which creates low correlation of decisions across trees. The forest can then be treated as a collection of weakly correlated random variables. Invoking the Central Limit theorem (CLT) then makes it easy to see that the variance of the average decision across trees gets reduced by $1/B$ (presence of weak correlation between trees alters this CLT result), where B is the number of trees in the forest. However, the bias of a RF still equals the bias of an individual decision tree in the ensemble – akin to the mean of a sum of random variables being equal to the mean of an individual variable. Thus ensemble averaging algorithms like RF improve upon single decision trees via variance reduction.

Results from fitting RF to SPX data are summarized in Table 14.3. Highest and lowest Sharpe ratios are 0.73 and 0.54 respectively. More interestingly, the 0.73 Sharpe RF signal has a lower (65%) correlation with vanilla SPX TSMOM compared to the 80% correlation between GLM strategies and the vanilla signal. We therefore expect a combination of RF and vanilla TSMOM to have a higher Sharpe ratio relative to the two standalone strategies and we revisit this point in Section 14.9.

14.8 NEURAL NETWORKS

Neural Networks (or Neural Nets as they are popularly known) have a data training architecture inspired from human neural systems that comprise of a collection of nodes (neurons) and links (synapses). Here we present a brief exposition of the simplest, vanilla form of a neural net and refer the interested reader to the excellent source – 'Elements of Statistical Learning'

At the heart of a Neural net is a 2 step classification or regression procedure. In step 1, the feature matrix is mapped to a set of new variables via a non-linear transformation. This step is equivalent to a basis expansion of the input variables in terms of a set of non-linear functions whose parameters are learned from the training data-set. Step 2 of the net is a K-class classification problem that is solved by using a multivariate logit model trained on the non-linearly transformed variables from Step 1.

Figure 14.7 shows these steps in greater detail along with the architecture of a single hidden layer neural net. The input layer consists of the raw feature matrix variables X_i. These are mapped on to hidden layer variables Z_m via the transformation $Z_m = \sigma(A_{mj}X_j)$, where A_{mj} is a matrix of coefficients and σ is the non-linear sigmoid function $\sigma(x) = 1/(1 + e^{-x})$. The second step is a multivariate logit model that produces a classification probability $P(Y_i = k) = e^{B_{kj}Z_j} / \left(\sum_l e^{B_{lj}Z_j} \right)$, where B_{kj} is another matrix of coefficients (shown by black links and analogous to synaptic links) in Figure 14.7. The model is fitted to training data by matching the predicted classifications to training set classes by changing parameters $\{A_{mj}, B_{kj}\}$.

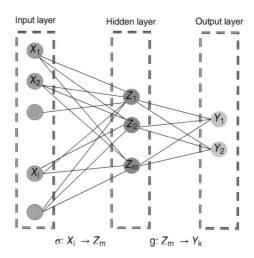

FIGURE 14.7 Architecture of a neural net showing three layers of neurons – the input layer on the far left, hidden layer in the middle and output layer on the far right.

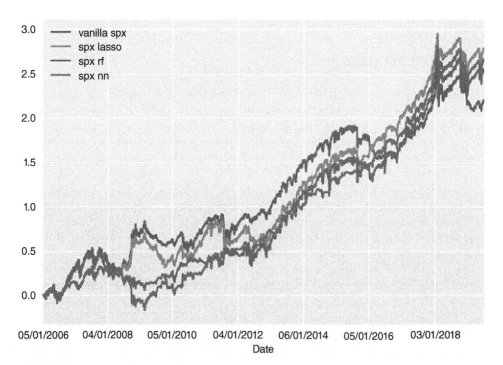

FIGURE 14.8 Cumulative wealth charts for vanilla SPX TSMOM ('vanilla spx'), Lasso trained TSMOM ('spx lasso'), Random Forest TSMOM ('spx rf') and 'neural net' TSMOM ('spx nn') for the period January 2006 to June 2019.
Source: AlphaVantage.

Neural Net Sharpe ratios for different training and cross-validation choices are shown in the bottom section of Table 14.3. The dispersion in risk adjusted performance for different training choices is the widest across strategies – maximum Sharpe ratio is 0.64 and minimum is 0.14. The correlation of the 0.64 strategy Sharpe ratio with vanilla SPX signal is only 33%! We next look at coupling these ML signals with a vanilla TSMOM strategy to form risk parity TSMOM portfolios.

14.9   RESULTS AND COMMENTS

We briefly summarize results from the various ML algorithms. Generalized Linear Models generated comparable Sharpe ratios to the vanilla strategy but were also highly correlated with it. Non-linear models RF and NN both had lower median Sharpe ratios but had lower correlations to the optimal vanilla TSMOM strategy. These results are summarized in Table 14.3. Cumulative wealth charts for the strategies listed in Table 14.3 are shown in Figure 14.8.

We now explore the central question of this chapter – Do ML signals offer sufficient diversification to enhance vanilla TSMOM strategies? To systematically answer

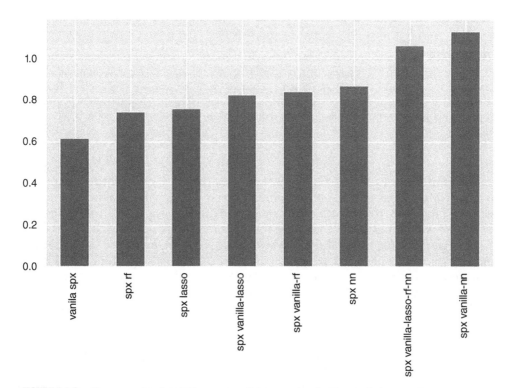

FIGURE 14.9   Sharpe ratios for different standalone and volatility scaled strategies.

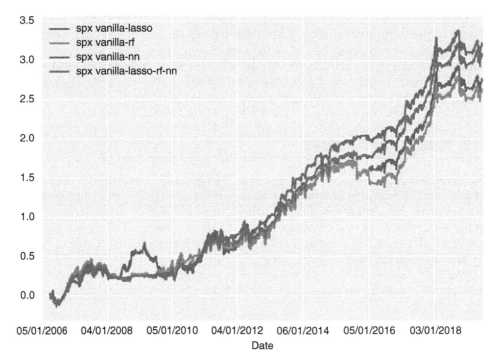

FIGURE 14.10　Cumulative wealth charts for hybrid TSMOM strategies coupling the vanilla TSMOM signal with ML signals. 'spx vanilla-lasso' is a risk parity weighted combination of vanilla TSMOM and Lasso. 'spx vanilla-rf' combined vanilla signal with the highest Sharpe RF signal and 'spx vanilla-nn' combines the highest Sharpe NN signal with vanilla TSMOM. 'spx vanilla-lasso-rf-nn' is a volatility scaled combination of vanilla, Lasso, RF and NN signals.

this question we construct two and four signal risk parity weighted portfolios coupling vanilla TSMOM returns with returns generated from ML signals for different strategies listed in Table 14.3. Returns for each strategy are inversely weighted by an estimate of its ex-ante volatility estimate and scaled to a target volatility of 25%.

Sharpe ratios for these different hybrid strategies are summarized in Figure. 14.9 and cumulative wealth charts are shown in Figure 14.10. Two- and four-signal hybrid strategies systematically improve on vanilla TSMOM Sharpe. Risk adjusted returns of 'spx vanilla-lasso-rf-nn' and 'spx vanilla-nn' are almost twice that of the vanilla TSMOM Sharpe. Rolling 1 year Sharpe ratios in Figure 14.11 indicate that these strategies have outperformed vanilla TSMOM during more recent risk-off episodes like the Q4 2018 sell-off and the early 2016 risk-off. They have also marginally outperformed vanilla TSMOM during the Euro zone crisis years 2011–2012. Finally, Figure 14.12 highlights the low correlation across the vanilla TSMOM and RF and NN signals. While Lasso has an almost perfect correlation with vanilla TSMOM, RF and NN pairwise

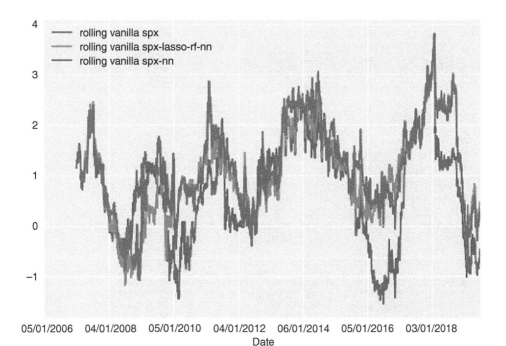

FIGURE 14.11 Rolling 1 year Sharpe ratio of 'vanilla spx','vanilla spx-lasso-rf-nn' and 'vanilla spx-nn' signals.

return plots with vanilla TSMOM exhibit crosses – indicating historical streams of both positively and negatively correlated returns.

14.10   CONCLUSION

We have discussed applications of Machine Learning/Artificial Intelligence to momentum strategies. We compared linear factor models like Lasso and Ridge with more complicated and non-linear models like Random-Forest and Neural Nets that are capable of inferring non-linear functional relationships between response and predictor variables. Our results suggest that ML signals generated from non-linear algorithms like Random Forests and Neural Nets are sufficiently well diversified relative to the vanilla TSMOM signal and can potentially add value in risk parity hybrid portfolios that combine vanilla and ML signals. While this appears to be a seemingly attractive proposition, it is worth bearing in mind the potential overfitting risks of models like RF and NN which have several free hyper-parameters and can be very sensitive to specific training histories. We have safeguarded against overfitting by following rigorous cross-validation procedures for hyper-parameter tuning, as well as using bagging

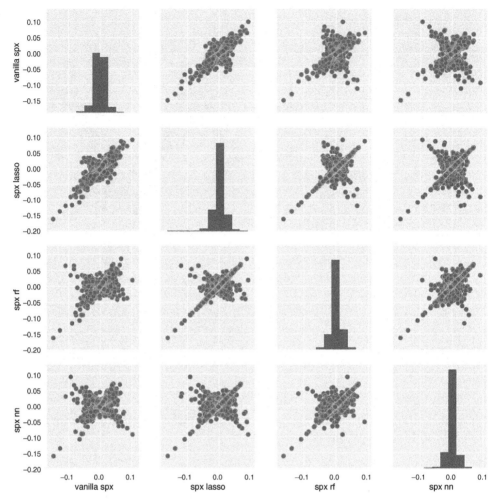

FIGURE 14.12   Correlograms of vanilla TSMOM and ML trained TSMOM strategies. Histograms of returns distribution are plotted along the diagonals. Pairwise regression of strategy returns are shown in off-diagonal boxes.

and ensemble methods like Random Forests which have lower variance and reduced sensitivity to training datasets compared to algorithms involving single decision trees.

While we have restricted our study to single index time-series momentum, an immediate venue for future exploration is cross-sectional momentum wherein a series of indices are trained on ML algorithms and indices with the highest long/short convictions are traded. We have also ignored turnover and transaction cost optimization in this analysis. We hope to report further results on both these fronts in the future.

REFERENCES

Bengio, Y. 2009. 'Learning deep architectures for AI'. *Foundations and Trends in Machine Learning* 2(1): 1–127.

Brooks, R.A. 1991. 'Intelligence without reason'. IJCAI-91 Proceedings of the Twelfth International Joint Conference on Artificial intelligence 1: 569–595.

Colton, S., Halskov, J., Ventura, D., Gouldstone, I., Cook, M., and Pérez-Ferrer, B. 2015. 'The Painting Fool sees! New projects with the automated painter'. International Conference on Computational Creativity (ICCC 2015): 189–196.

Colton, S., Lopez de Mantaras, R. and Stock, O. 2009. 'Computational creativity: Coming of age'. *AI Magazine* 30(3): 11–14.

Dennet, D.C. 2018. *From Bacteria to Bach and Back: The Evolution of Minds*. London: Penguin.

Dreyfus, H. 1965. *Alchemy and Artificial Intelligence*. Santa Monica: Rand Corporation.

Dreyfus, H. 1992. *What Computers Still Can't Do*. New York: MIT Press.

Ferrucci, D.A., Levas, A., Bagchi, S., Gondek, D. and Mueller, E.T. 2013. 'Watson: Beyond jeopardy!' *Artificial Intelligence* **199**: 93–105.

Forbus, K.D. 2012. 'How minds will be built'. *Advances in Cognitive Systems* 1: 47–58.

Graves, A., Wayne, G., Reynolds, M., Harley, T., Danihelka, I., Grabska-Barwińska, A., Gómez-Colmenarejo, S., Grefenstette, E., Ramalho, T., Agapiou, J., Puigdomènech-Badia, A., Hermann, K.M., Zwols, Y., Ostrovski, G., Cain, A., King, H., Summerfield, C., Blunsom, P., Kavukcuoglu, K. and Hassabis, D. 2016. 'Hybrid computing using a neural network with dynamic external memory'. *Nature* **538**: 471–476.

Holland, J.H. 1975. *Adaptation in Natural and Artificial Systems*. Ann Arbor: University of Michigan Press.

Inhelder, B. and Piaget, J. 1958. *The Growth of Logical Thinking from Childhood to Adolescence*. New York: Basic Books.

Jegadeesh, N. and Titman, S. 1993. 'Returns to buying winners and selling losers: Implications for stock market efficiency'. *Journal of Finance* 48(1): 65–91.

Lake, B.M., Ullman, T.D., Tenenbaum, J.B. and Gershman, S. J. 2017. 'Building machines that learn and think like people'. *Behavioral and Brain Sciences* 40:e253.

Lewellen, J. 2015. 'The cross-section of expected stock returns'. *Critical Finance Review* 4(1): 1–44.

López de Mántaras, R. 2016. 'Artificial intelligence and the arts: Toward computational creativity'. *In The Next Step: Exponential Life. Madrid: BBVA Open Mind*, 100–125.

López de Mántaras, R. 2019. '"The Future of AI: Toward Truly Intelligent Artificial Intelligences". Towards a New Enlightenment? A Transcendent Decade'. Madrid: BBVA Open Mind, 1-17.

McCulloch, W.S., and Pitts, W. 1943. 'A logical calculus of ideas immanent in nervous activity'. *Bulletin of Mathematical Biophysics* 5: 115–133.

Moskowitz, T., Hua, Y. and Pederson, L.H. 2012. 'Time series momentum'. *Journal of Financial Economics* 104(2): 228- 250.

Newell, A. and Simon, H.A. 1976. 'Computer science as empirical inquiry: Symbols and search'. *Communications of the ACM* **19**(3): 113–126.

Pearl, J. and Mackenzie, D. 2018. *The Book of Why: The New Science of Cause and Effect*. New York: Basic Books.

Saxena, V., Wu, X., Srivastava, I. and Zhu, K. 2018. 'Towards neuromorphic learning machines using emerging memory devices with brain-like energy efficiency'. Preprints: https://www.preprints.org/manuscript/201807.0362/v1.

Searle, J.R. 1980. 'Minds, brains, and programs'. *Behavioral and Brain Sciences* 3(3): 417–457.

Silver, D., Huang, A., Maddison, C.J., Guez, A., Sifre, L., ven den Driessche, G., Schrittwieser, J., Antonoglou, I., Panneershelvam, V., Lanctot, M., Dieleman, S., Grewe, D., Nham, J., Kalchbrenner, N., Sutskever, I., Lillicrap, T., Leach, M., Kavukcuoglu, K., Graepel, T., and Hassabis, D. 2016. 'Mastering the game of Go with deep neural networks and tree search'. *Nature* 529(7587): 484–489.

Turing, A.M. 1948. 'Intelligent machinery'. National Physical Laboratory Report. Reprinted in: *Machine Intelligence 5*, B. Meltzer and D. Michie (eds.). Edinburgh: Edinburgh University Press, 1969.

Turing, A.M. 1950. 'Computing machinery and intelligence'. Mind LIX(236): 433–460.

Weizenbaum, J. 1976. *Computer Power and Human Reasoning: From Judgment to Calculation.* San Francisco: W.H. Freeman and Co.

Weng, J., McClelland, J., Pentland, A., Sporns, O., Stockman, I., Sur, M. and Thelen, E. 2001. 'Autonomous mental development by robots and animals'. *Science* 291: 599–600.

CHAPTER 15

Momentum and Business Cycles

BYOUNG-KYU MIN

15.1 INTRODUCTION

Jegadeesh and Titman (1993) show that statistically and economically significant profits accrued to the simple momentum strategy of buying prior winner stocks (those with high recent performance) and selling prior loser stocks (those with low recent performance). Subsequent works have confirmed and refined the momentum effect. Jegadeesh and Titman (2001) report that momentum remains significant even after the period studied in Jegadeesh and Titman (1993). Rouwenhorst (1998) and Chui, Titman and Wei (2010) provide international evidence in momentum. Asness, Moskowitz and Pedersen (2013) find momentum effects in other asset classes. Both rational and behavioral explanations have been suggested for momentum. Rational risk-based explanations propose that winner stocks are riskier than loser stocks thus momentum profits are realizations of risk premium (see, for example, Berk, Green and Naik, 1999; Johnson, 2002; Sagi and Seasholes, 2007). Behavioral explanations suggest that investors' irrational under-reaction to firm-specific information drives momentum (see, for example, Barberis, Shleifer and Vishny, 1998; Daniel, Hirshleifer and Subrahmanyam, 1998; Hong and Stein, 1999).

Whereas the cross-sectional aspects of momentum have been studied extensively, considerably less attention has been accorded to time variation of momentum profits. It is important to examine time variation of momentum payoffs, since it provides implications for the source of momentum profitability. For instance, Lakonishok, Shleifer and Vishny (1994) suggest that a strategy would be fundamentally risky if, first, there are at least some states of the world in which a strategy underperforms, and second, these periods of underperformance are, on average, 'bad' states, in which the marginal utility of wealth is high, rendering the strategy unattractive to risk-averse investors. Simply put, we pay for a premium to purchase an insurance which provides monetary compensation when we face an accident (i.e., in bad state when we need most). In a similar vein, if an asset (or strategy) delivers loss in 'bad' state when investors need most, an investor should require premium as a compensation for bearing this downside risk.

Whether periods in which momentum strategies yield negative profits are, in fact, 'bad' economic states when the marginal utility of consumption is high is a focus of this chapter. Prior studies that have explored this research question have reached different conclusions consequent to using different classifications of economic states. The various measures of economic states employed in the literature are discussed and interpreted here, with a particular focus on Min and Kim (2016), who propose that the expected market risk premium is a right measure of the marginal utility of consumption, and show that momentum strategies deliver significantly negative profits during 'bad' economic states in which investors demand the highest market risk premium. Alternative strands of the literature showing momentum profits to depend on market-wide measures of investor overconfidence and sentiment, supporting behavioral explanations, are also reviewed.

15.2 MOMENTUM, BUSINESS CYCLES AND REALISED MARKET RETURN

Chordia and Shivakumar (2002) is the first study which shows that momentum profits are related to business cycles. Chordia and Shivakumar (2002) use the expansionary and recessionary periods as classified by the National Bureau of Economic Research (NBER), and examine the profitability of momentum strategies across different business cycles. Table 15.1 presents results of their study for the period from July 1926 to December 1994. Momentum payoffs are positive in each of the ten, and statistically significant in four, of the postwar expansionary periods. In contrast, only one of nine postwar contractionary periods had statistically significant positive momentum profits. Averaged across periods, momentum profits are reliably positive at 0.53% per month (t-value = 2.35) for the expansionary, but negatively statistically insignificant at -0.72% (t-value = -0.92) for the contractionary, period. The study further shows that momentum payoffs can be predicted by lagged macroeconomic variables, and that once stock returns are adjusted for predictability based on macroeconomic variables, momentum profits are no longer significant.

Subsequent studies, however, identify other considerations to which Chordia and Shivakumar's (2002) results appear not to be robust. Griffin, Ji and Martin (2003) find that macroeconomic variables considered in Chordia and Shivakumar do not predict momentum payoffs in international markets, and further point out that skipping a month between the ranking and holding periods, a common procedure for mitigating microstructure-induced biases, renders the relation between momentum and NBER classification of business cycles more modest. Cooper, Gutierrez and Hameed (2004) report that a multifactor macroeconomic model used by Chordia and Shivakumar fails to explain momentum after controlling for market frictions (standard price screens and skip-month returns). Min and Kim (2016) also show that average momentum profits are no longer negative during NBER contractionary periods after excluding January when momentum exhibit negative profits.[1]

---

[1]Momentum payoffs are known to exhibit January seasonality, being negative in January and positive in other months (Jegadeesh and Titman, 1993; Grundy and Martin, 2001; George and

TABLE 15.1 Momentum profits classified by NBER business cycles

Expansionary Periods		Contractionary Periods	
Jul 1926 – Oct 1926	1.89	Nov 1926 – Nov 1927	0.81
	(1.09)		(0.59)
Dec 1927 – Aug 1929	2.12	Sep 1929 – Mar 1933	-2.52
	(3.09)		(-1.10)
Apr 1933 – May 1937	-1.94	Jun 1937 – Jun 1938	-1.60
	(-1.38)		(-0.48)
Jul 1938 – Feb 1945	-0.94	Mar 1945 – Oct 1945	-1.03
	(-0.85)		(-1.39)
Nov 1945 – Nov 1948	1.42	Dec 1948 – Oct 1949	0.24
	(2.46)		(0.21)
Nov 1949 – Jul 1953	0.60	Aug 1953 – May 1954	1.43
	(1.64)		(0.96)
Jun 1954 – Aug 1957	0.90	Sep 1957 – Apr 1958	0.80
	(2.78)		(0.35)
May 1958 – Apr 1960	0.85	May 1960 – Feb 1961	1.03
	(1.57)		(0.91)
Mar 1961 – Dec 1969	1.10	Jan 1970 – Nov 1970	-0.42
	(2.67)		(-0.16)
Dec 1970 – Nov 1973	1.33	Dec 1973 – Mar 1975	-2.34
	(1.51)		(-0.74)
Apr 1975 – Jan 1980	0.24	Feb 1980 – Jul 1980	0.56
	(0.50)		(0.39)
Aug 1980 – Jul 1981	0.89	Aug 1981 – Nov 1982	2.60
	(0.80)		(2.79)
Dec 1982 – Jul 1990	1.36	Aug 1990 – Mar 1991	-4.22
	(3.36)		(-0.76)
Apr 1991 – Dec 1994	0.34		
	(0.37)		
Mean	0.53		-0.72
	(2.35)		-0.92

The table reports the average raw monthly momentum profits classified into the various expansionary and contractionary periods as determined by the NBER. *t*-statistics are reported in parenthesis.
Source: Chordia and Shivakumar (2002)

Griffin, Ji and Martin (2003) explore whether time variation of momentum payoffs is related to economic conditions. They adopt the approach suggested by Lakonishok, Shleifer and Vishny (1994) who analyse value and growth strategies. Griffin, Ji and Martin define economic states in terms of realised market excess returns or GDP growth. Specifically, they identify good states as periods with high ex post

---

Hwang, 2004). It suggests that that the relation between momentum profits and NBER contractionary periods could be attributed to the January effect in momentum payoffs.

TABLE 15.2   Momentum profits classified by NBER business cycles

Panel A: GDP Growth States			
	GDP < 0		GDP > 0
Average profit	0.31		0.92
(*t*-stat)	(0.38)		(5.58)
	Lowest	2	3	Highest
Average profit	0.90	1.58	0.25	0.65
(*t*-stat)	(1.92)	(5.80)	(0.69)	(2.27)

Panel B: Aggregate Stock Market States			
	MKT < 0		MKT > 0
Average profit	1.04		0.32
(*t*-stat)	(4.95)		(1.26)
	Lowest	2	3	Highest
Average profit	1.23	0.99	1.24	-1.11
(*t*-stat)	(4.55)	(4.39)	(6.30)	(-1.96)

The table reports the average raw monthly momentum profits classified into various economic states. Panel A reports the results when economic states are defined based on quarterly real GDP growth. Panel B reports the results when economic states are defined based on value-weighted stock market index returns. *t*-statistics are reported in parenthesis. The sample period is from April 1960 to December 2000.
Source: Griffin, Ji and Martin (2003)

market excess returns or GDP growth, and bad states as periods with low ex post market excess returns or GDP growth. Results of the study, presented in Table 15.2, show that monthly momentum profits are both positive at 0.92% (t-value = 5.58) in periods of positive GDP growth and at 0.31% (t-value = 0.38) in periods of negative GDP growth. When economic states are classified on the basis of quartiles of GDP growth, average momentum profits are again positive across all four GDP growth states. Results from using market return for classifying economic states show that momentum payoffs are even more strongly positive during periods of negative market excess returns than during periods of positive market excess returns. Average momentum profits are positive and statistically significant at 1.04% per month (t-value = 4.95) when market returns are negative. They are positive but lower and statistically insignificant at 0.32% (t-value = 1.26) when market returns are positive. Results remain unchanged when four regimes using the market return quartiles are used. Griffin, Ji and Martin therefore conclude that time variation of momentum payoffs is not related to economic states as proxied by realized GDP growth or market return. In related work, Liew and Vassalou (2000) find that, whereas the size factor (SMB) and value factor (HML) of the Fama-French model can predict future GDP growth, momentum does not contain information predictive of future economic growth.

15.3 MOMENTUM AND EXPECTED MARKET RISK PREMIUMS

Griffin, Ji and Martin (2003) define economic states in terms of the *realised* market excess returns or GDP growth and have failed to provide evidence that momentum payoffs are related to downside risk. However, *ex-post* realised market excess return is at best a very noisy measure for marginal utility or business cycles. It is well documented in the macroeconomic literature that the ex-post market excess return does not have substantial predictive power for business cycles. Further, the standard asset pricing theory predicts that investors demand an *ex-ante* risk premium for holding risky securities, and that risk premium is countercyclical (Merton, 1973; Campbell and Cochrane, 1999; Bansal and Yaron, 2004). Many studies point out that realised returns are a noisy measure of expected returns or expected risk premium (Blume and Friend, 1973; Sharpe, 1978; Elton, 1999; Campello, Chen and Zhang, 2008).[2] Petkova and Zhang (2005) argue that aggregate economic conditions are more precisely measured by macroeconomic variables, such as default and term spread and short-term interest rate, commonly used to model expected market risk premium. Suggesting that it is hence reasonable to expect their inferences to have led Griffin, Ji and Martin (2003) to the incorrect conclusion, Min and Kim (2016) make a case for reevaluating the riskiness of momentum strategies using the expected market risk premium as a measure of the state of the economy.

Being unobservable, the expected market risk premium must be estimated. Macroeconomic variables known to predict excess market returns and capture fluctuations in economic conditions include the default spread (DEF), term spread (TERM), and three-month T-bill rate (RF) as well as the variable CAY, constructed by Lettau and Ludvigson (2001) to capture movements in the consumption-aggregate wealth ratio.[3] The default spread is the yield spread between Moody's BAA and AAA corporate bonds, and the term spread is the yield spread between ten- and one-year government bonds. Data on bond yields are obtained from the Federal Reserve Bank of St. Louis. Consistent with the frequency of the CAY, quarterly data are used to estimate the market risk premium. Use of these variables is motivated by the time-series predictability literature.

Following Fama and French (1989) and Ferson and Harvey (1991), the expected market risk premium is estimated by regressing the (quarterly) market excess return

---

[2]Elton (1999) shows that realised returns can deviate significantly from expected returns, and also questions the common practice of using realised returns as a proxy for expected returns in asset-pricing tests.

[3]The three-month T-bill rate, known to be negatively related to future market returns, can act as a proxy for expectations of future economic growth (Fama, 1981; Fama and Schwert, 1977); the default spread is known to track long-term business conditions, being higher during recessions and lower during expansions (Keim and Stambaugh, 1986; Fama and French, 1989); the term spread is closely related to short-term business cycles identified by the NBER (Fama and French, 1989); and the CAY is superior to other popular forecasting variables in predicting future stock market returns over short horizons (Lettau and Ludvigson, 2001).

from time $t - 1$ to t, $R^e_{m,t}$, on the (quarterly) macroeconomic variables known at time $t - 1$:

$$R^e_{m,t} = \beta_0 + \beta_1 DEF_{t-1} + \beta_2 TERM_{t-1} + \beta_3 RF_{t-1} + \beta_4 CAY_{t-1} + \varepsilon_t \qquad (15.1)$$

The expected market risk premium, $EMRP_t$, is the fitted value from Equation (15.1):

$$EMRP_t = \hat{\beta}_0 + \hat{\beta}_1 DEF_{t-1} + \hat{\beta}_2 TERM_{t-1} + \hat{\beta}_3 RF_{t-1} + \hat{\beta}_4 CAY_{t-1}. \qquad (15.2)$$

Following Petkova and Zhang (2005), economic states are classified based on the expected market risk premium as follows: state 'peak' includes the 10% of periods with the lowest expected risk premium; 'expansion' state represents the remaining periods in which the premium is below its average; 'recession' state represents the periods in which the premium is above its average but still below the 10% of periods with the highest premium; and 'trough' state represents the 10% of periods with the highest expected market risk premium. This sorting procedure is consistent with the stock market return predictability literature, which shows expected market risk premium to be higher in bad times and correlated with business cycle (Fama and Schwert, 1977; Fama and French, 1989). The classification is also consistent with modern asset pricing theories that feature the countercyclical price of risk (Campbell and Cochrane, 1999; Zhang, 2005). Figure 15.1 plots a time-series of the estimated expected market risk premium together with the contractionary period (the shaded region) defined by the NBER. Consistent with the earlier mentioned theoretical and empirical studies, the figure demonstrates that the estimated expected market risk premium exhibits strong countercyclical variation over business cycles, becoming, for example, especially high during the period of the recent financial crisis.

The construction of a momentum portfolio follows Jegadeesh and Titman (1993). A list of all common stocks (with CRSP share-code of 10 or 11) listed on NYSE and AMEX is obtained from the Center for Research in Security Prices (CRSP) monthly file. The sample period is from January 1960 to December 2011. All stocks are ranked into deciles based on their 6-month ranking period returns (months t - 7 through t - 2). To control for short-term return reversal and avoid microstructure bias, one month is skipped between the end of the ranking period and the beginning of the holding period. Decile portfolios are formed by equally weighting all firms in the decile ranking. The momentum profit is the return of the top decile portfolio (the winners) less the return of the bottom decile portfolio (the losers). Momentum portfolios are formed every month and held for the subsequent 6-month period, from t through $t + 5$. Thus, portfolios have overlapping holding period returns.

Table 15.3 presents average momentum profits conditional on the economic states classified by the expected market risk premium. Several noteworthy findings are observed. First, the winner portfolios significantly underperform the loser portfolios in the 'trough' state when marginal utility of wealth is especially high, the averages of raw, CAPM and Fama-French momentum profits being large and statistically significantly negative at –2.23% (*t*-value = –2.90), –2.08% (*t*-value = –2.74), and –2.06% (*t*-value

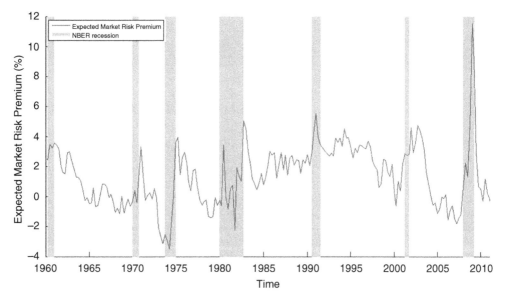

FIGURE 15.1 Time-series of the expected market risk premium.
The figure is a time-series plot of the quarterly expected market risk premium, which is estimated as a following model: $R^e_{m,t} = \alpha + \beta Z_{t-1} + e_{m,t}$, where Z_{t-1} is a vector representing conditioning variables that include the default spread, term spread, three-month T-bill rate and CAY. The shaded regions are the contractionary periods defined by the NBER. The sample period is from 1960 :Q1 to 2011 :Q4.
Source: Min and Km (2016)

= –2.81) per month, respectively.[4] Second, the payoffs to momentum strategies tend to positively covary with macroeconomic conditions, as reflected in average raw monthly momentum profits of 1.86%, 1.10%, 0.87%, and –2.23%, respectively, across the 'peak', 'expansion', 'recession' and 'trough' states, showing a monotonically decreasing pattern as economic state worsens. The difference between 'non-trough' and 'trough' momentum profits is large and statistically significant at 3.30% per month (with a *t*-statistic of 4.10). The results from the risk-adjusted profits indicate that payoffs to momentum trading strategies show a monotonically increasing pattern when macroeconomic distress risk is diminished. Differences between 'non-trough' and 'trough' momentum profits are statistically significant for all cases considered.

In the four scatter plots in Figure 15.2 corresponding to different economic states, the *x*-axis represents the expected market risk premium and the *y*-axis momentum

---

[4]We test robustness with alternative classifications of the 'trough' state using different threshold values, specifically, the 15%, 7% and 5% of periods with the highest expected market risk premium. Although results are similar under these different classifications, stronger negative momentum profits are observed when the 'trough' state is more finely sliced and classified, as, for example, the 5% of periods with the highest expected market risk premium for which the average raw monthly momentum profit is more strongly negative at –4.32% (*t*-value = –4.01).

TABLE 15.3 Momentum profits and economic states

	Peak	Expansion	Recession	Trough	Non-trough vs Trough
Average profit	1.86	1.10	0.87	-2.23	3.30
(*t*-stat)	(2.43)	(2.97)	(2.30)	(-2.90)	(4.10)
CAPM alpha	1.64	1.11	1.08	-2.08	3.23
(*t*-stat)	(2.15)	(3.02)	(2.85)	(-2.74)	(4.05)
Fama-French alpha	1.81	1.43	1.36	-2.06	3.50
(*t*-stat)	(2.46)	(4.02)	(3.68)	(-2.81)	(4.53)

The table reports the average raw monthly momentum profits, CAPM alphas, and Fama-French alphas conditional on the economic states. The economic states are classified based on the expected market risk premium, which is estimated as a following model: $R_{m,t}^{e} = \alpha + \beta Z_{t-1} + e_{m,t}$, where Z_{t-1} is a vector representing conditioning variables that include the default spread, term spread, three-month T-bill rate, and CAY. State 'peak' is defined as the lowest 10% periods of the expected risk premium; state 'expansion' represents the remaining periods with the premium below its average; state 'recession' represents the periods with the premium above its average except the 10% highest; and state 'trough' represents the highest 10% periods of the expected market risk premium. The difference of momentum profits between 'non-trough' and 'trough' is reported in the last column. Panel A reports the results for the Jegadeesh and Titman (1993) momentum construction, while Panel B reports the results for the Fama and French (1996) construction. The sample period is from January 1960 to December 2011.
Source: Min and Kim (2016)

profits. Most of WML portfolio returns reside in the positive range during the 'peak' state, shift down, but for the most part remain positive, in the 'expansion' state, become biased towards negative values in the 'recession' state, and during the 'trough' state about half of momentum profit observations turn negative and the volatility of the profits soars. When momentum trading strategies lose money, they clearly lose a significant amount, as much as 84% in a quarter.

The relation between momentum strategies and economic distress risk is even more explicit in the time-series of quarterly profits of the momentum strategy and estimated market risk premium plotted in Figure 15.3, which clearly shows large negative returns when the predicted market risk premium is highest. The periods in which momentum trading generates the most strongly negative quarterly profits – –84%, –83%, –53%, and –45% occurring in 2009:Q2, 1991:Q1, 2009:Q3, and 1975:Q1, respectively – coincide with the estimated 'trough' state.

Given that a number of studies have found momentum profits to be negative in January and positive during other months (e.g., Jegadeesh and Titman, 1993; Grundy and Martin, 2001; George and Hwang, 2004),[5] it is incumbent to investigate whether significant negative momentum profits in the 'trough' state might be attributable to this 'January effect'.

---

[5]Grinblatt and Moskowitz (1999) suggest as one possible explanation for the January effect in momentum profits tax-loss selling of the loser stocks in December that results in the price of such stocks to rebounding (and thus generating negative momentum profits) in January.

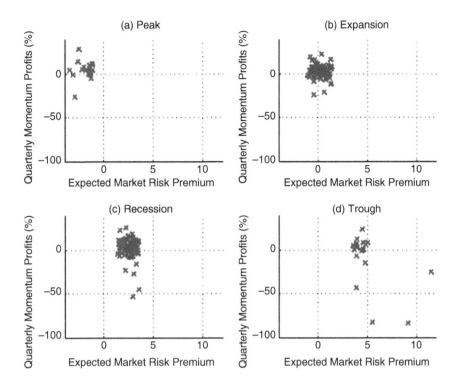

FIGURE 15.2 Expected market risk premium and momentum profits.
The figure shows scatter plots of quarterly momentum profits against the expected market risk premium across different economic states. The expected market risk premium is estimated as a following model: $R_{m,t}^e = \alpha + \beta Z_{t-1} + e_{m,t}$, where Z_{t-1} is a vector representing conditioning variables that include the default spread, term spread, three-month T-bill rate, and CAY. State 'peak' is defined as the lowest 10% periods of the expected risk premium; state 'expansion' represents the remaining periods with the premium below its average; state 'recession' represents the periods with the premium above its average except the 10% highest; and state 'trough' represents the highest 10% periods of the expected market risk premium. The sample period is from 1960 :Q1 to 2011 :Q4.
Source: Min and Kim (2016)

Table 15.4 reports average momentum profits conditional on the four economic states across two periods: January and non-January months. That momentum generates negative profits in all economic states during January is consistent with the literature. Our primary interest is the results for non-January months. The results for non-January months mirror the essential features drawn from the overall samples; that is, negative payoffs of momentum strategies are skewed towards the 'trough' states in which investors require the highest risk premium. Specifically, during 'trough' states excluding January, momentum strategies still deliver large negative profits: –1.72% (*t*-statistic of –2.28) per month. These negative profits are still sizable in magnitude, albeit with

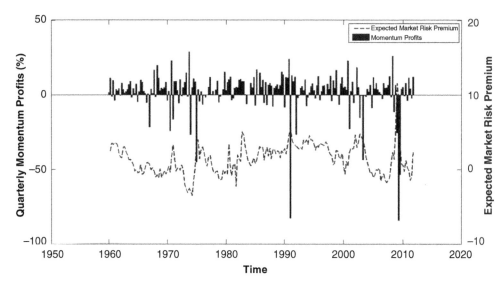

FIGURE 15.3   Time-series of momentum profits with the expected market risk premium.
The figure is time-series plots of quarterly momentum profits (bar graph) from the Jegadeesh
and Titman (1993) momentum construction and the expected market risk premium (dashed
line). The expected market risk premium is estimated as a following model:
$R^e_{m,t} = \alpha + \beta Z_{t-1} + e_{m,t}$, where Z_{t-1} is a vector representing conditioning variables that include
the default spread, term spread, three-month T-bill rate, and CAY. The sample period is from
1960 :Q1 to 2011 :Q4.
Source: Min and Kim (2016)

weaker statistical significance. Differences between 'non-trough' and 'trough' momentum payoffs also remain statistically significant for all cases considered. The results in
Table 15.4 suggest that the finding that winner stocks underperform loser stocks in
extremely bad economic states cannot be attributable to the January effect.

One possible concern about the findings presented here is the potential for
'look-ahead' bias due to the fact that the expected market risk premium is estimated
using the full sample. This concern can be addressed by performing an out-of-sample
estimation in which the parameters in Equation (15.1) are re-estimated for every
period using only data available up to time $t-1$. This analysis complements prior
evidence of the robustness of the relation between the expected market risk premium
and momentum profits.

The recursive out-of-sample forecast of the market risk premium is formed as
follows. The initial coefficient estimates are obtained over the 20-year period from
1960:Q1 to 1979:Q4. The first out-of-sample quarter is 1980:Q1. The quarterly observation of 1980:Q1 is added to the initial period and Equation (15.1) is re-estimated
to obtain an out-of-sample forecast for 1980:Q2. The process is repeated to the end
of the sample, 2011:Q4. The predicted market risk premium at time t is thus obtained
using the estimated coefficients from the most recent in-sample regression (i.e., from
1960:Q1 to time $t-1$) and realizations of the lagged instrumental variables at time t.

TABLE 15.4 Momentum profits and economic states: January versus non-January months

	Peak	Expansion	Recession	Trough	Non-trough vs Trough
		January			
Average profit	-2.24	-4.43	-8.11	-6.73	0.82
(*t*-stat)	(-0.98)	(-3.38)	(-6.84)	(-2.97)	(0.34)
CAPM alpha	-2.28	-4.45	-7.72	-6.70	0.97
(*t*-stat)	(-1.01)	(-3.42)	(-6.53)	(-2.97)	(0.41)
Fama-French alpha	-1.07	-2.89	-6.46	-6.97	2.62
(*t*-stat)	(-0.48)	(-2.21)	(-5.45)	(-3.15)	(1.10)
		Non-January			
Average profit	2.32	1.51	1.75	-1.72	3.42
(*t*-stat)	(3.07)	(4.21)	(4.72)	(-2.28)	(4.29)
CAPM alpha	2.10	1.52	1.92	-1.59	3.34
(*t*-stat)	(2.79)	(4.27)	(5.16)	(-2.11)	(4.22)
Fama-French alpha	2.10	1.66	2.02	-1.53	3.39
(*t*-stat)	(2.84)	(4.74)	(5.52)	(-2.08)	(4.37)

The table reports the average raw monthly momentum profits, CAPM alphas and Fama-French alphas conditional on the economic states across two separate periods, January and non-January months. The economic states are classified based on the expected market risk premium, which is estimated as a following model: $R^e_{m,t} = \alpha + \beta Z_{t-1} + e_{m,t}$, where Z_{t-1} is a vector representing conditioning variables that include the default spread, term spread, three-month T-bill rate and CAY. State 'peak' is defined as the lowest 10% periods of the expected risk premium; state 'expansion' represents the remaining periods with the premium below its average; state 'recession' represents the periods with the premium above its average except the 10% highest; and state 'trough' represents the highest 10% periods of the expected market risk premium. The difference of momentum profits between 'non-trough' and 'trough' is reported in the last column. Panel A reports the results for the Jegadeesh and Titman (1993) momentum construction, while Panel B reports the results for the Fama and French (1996) construction. The sample period is from January 1960 to December 2011.
Source: Min and Kim (2016)

Figure 15.4 compares the out-of-sample and in-sample estimates of the market risk premium by plotting their time-series (depicted as solid and dashed lines, respectively) for the period 1980:Q1 to 2011:Q4. The plot reveals two interesting facts. The first, that the magnitude of fluctuation is greater in the out-of-sample than that in the in-sample estimate, should not come as a surprise as the recursively estimated coefficients tend to exhibit greater variation than the coefficients estimated using the full sample. Second, and more important, the out-of-sample and in-sample estimates of the market risk premium strongly co-move, their correlation being 0.83. Of even greater interest is that periods in which the out-of-sample estimate of the risk premium is especially high are essentially identical to those identified by the in-sample estimate. This suggests that classifying economic states on the basis of the out-of-sample estimate is unlikely to identify states different from those identified by the in-sample estimate.

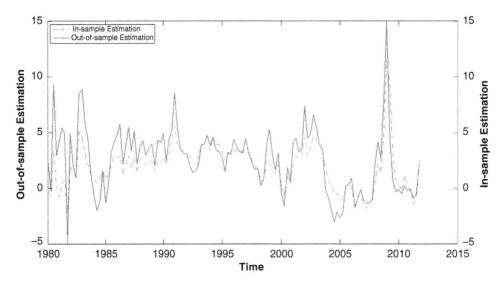

FIGURE 15.4 Out-of-sample and in-sample estimates of the expected market risk premium. The figure is time-series plots of the out-of-sample estimate of the expected market risk premium (solid line) and in-sample estimate of the expected market risk premium (dashed line). The sample period is from 1960 :Q1 to 2011 :Q4.
Source: Min and Kim (2016)

The robustness of out-of-sample estimation of the market risk premium is assessed by redefining the economic states using the out-of-sample estimate of the expected market risk premium. Averages of raw, CAPM-adjusted, and Fama-French-adjusted profits conditional on each state are presented in Table 15.5. The results presented in Table 15.5 confirm momentum profits to be negative and statistically significant when investors require the highest risk premium. In 'trough' states, momentum strategies yield significant negative monthly profits of –2.39%. Similar results are obtained for the benchmark risk-adjusted profits. Differences between 'non-trough' and 'trough' momentum profits are again large and statistically significant for all cases considered. These findings suggest that the evidence is robust to the out-of-sample estimation of the expected market risk premium for defining the economic states.

Out-of-sample estimation of the market risk premium has important implications for traders seeking to develop a strategy that enhances momentum profitability. The foregoing analysis suggests that when the next period of the expected market risk premium estimated using information observable at time $t - 1$ is especially high, there is a greater likelihood that a momentum strategy will lose money in the next period. One way to modify a momentum strategy to enhance profitability is thus to develop a conditional momentum strategy that reverses the momentum trading rule (i.e., buy loser stocks and sell winner stocks) when the next period is expected to be a 'trough' state; if loser stocks outperform winner stocks in the next period, the conditional momentum strategy can turn losses into profits. When the next period of the expected market risk premium is not forecasted to be high, a trader can maintain the original trading

TABLE 15.5 Momentum profits and economic states based on the out-of-sample estimate of the expected market risk premium

	Peak	Expansion	Recession	Trough	Non-trough vs Trough
Average profit	2.11	1.24	1.10	-2.39	3.63
(*t*-stat)	(1.59)	(2.24)	(2.18)	(-2.78)	(3.90)
CAPM alpha	2.11	1.21	1.35	-2.28	3.62
(*t*-stat)	(1.61)	(2.21)	(2.66)	(-2.67)	(3.93)
Fama-French alpha	1.79	1.59	1.55	-2.25	3.84
(*t*-stat)	(1.40)	(2.92)	(3.10)	(-2.70)	(4.24)

The table reports the average raw monthly momentum profits, CAPM alphas and Fama-French alphas conditional on the economic states based on the out-of-sample estimate of the expected market risk premium. The recursive out-of-sample forecasts of the market risk premium is as follows. The initial coefficient estimates are obtained over the 20-year period from 1960:Q1 to 1979:Q4 from the following model: $R^e_{m,t} = \alpha + \beta Z_{t-1} + e_{m,t}$, where Z_{t-1} is a vector representing conditioning variables that include the default spread, term spread, three-month T-bill rate and CAY. The first out-of-sample quarter is 1980:Q1. Subsequently, the quarterly observation of 1980:Q1 is added to the initial period. The regression model is re-estimated, and an out-of-sample forecast for 1980:Q2 is obtained. This process is repeated until the end of the sample, 2011:Q4. By implementing this approach, the predicted market risk premium at time *t* is obtained using the estimated coefficients from the most recent in-sample regression (i.e., from 1960:Q1 to time *t-1*) and the realizations of the lagged instrumental variables at time *t*. Then, the economic states are re-defined using the out-of-sample estimate of the expected market risk premium as in Table 15.3. Panel A reports the results for the Jegadeesh and Titman (1993) momentum construction, while Panel B reports the results for the Fama and French (1996) construction. The sample period is from January 1960 to December 2011.
Source: Min and Kim (2016)

rule (i.e., buy winner stocks and sell loser stocks). Note that the proposed strategy is conditional on economic conditions and a real-time implementable strategy.[6]

15.4 MOMENTUM, OVERCONFIDENCE AND SENTIMENT

This section discusses alternative strands of literature that suggest that time variation of momentum payoffs is related to market-wide measures of investor overconfidence and

---

[6]The proposed trading strategy is based on the *time-series* relation between momentum profits and economic conditions as measured by the expected market risk premium. On the other hand, prior studies document the *cross-sectional* relation between momentum profits and firm characteristics. One can propose other simple trading rules by combining the cross-sectional and time-series aspects of the momentum effect. For instance, the momentum strategy conditional on both firm size and the expected market risk premium could be one such modified strategy. That is, a trader could consider small stocks, rather than the entire stock universe, in forming a dynamic momentum strategy; a trading rule being either to buy or sell 'small stocks winners' and 'small stocks losers', depending on the forecasted market risk premium.

sentiment, supporting behavioral explanations. Cooper, Gutierrez and Hameed (2004) show that momentum payoffs are related to the lagged three-year market return, which they term market state. They suggest that market state can proxy for aggregate over-confidence given that investors on the whole have long positions in the stock market and overconfidence tends to be greater following market gains (Gervais and Odean, 2001). Cooper, Gutierrez and Hameed (2004) find that following an UP market state when the lagged three-year market return is positive, average momentum payoffs are positive and significant at 0.93% per month (t-value = 8.41). In contrast, following a DOWN market state when the lagged market return is negative, average momentum payoffs are negative and insignificant at –0.37% (t-value = –0.65). That momentum is stronger following an UP market when aggregate overconfidence is greater is consistent with the behavioral model of Daniel, Hirshleifer and Subrahmanyam (1998), in which an increase in overconfidence strengthens overreaction, which in turn generates return momentum.

A subsequent study by Sagi and Seasholes (2007), however, proposes a rational asset pricing model that can also reproduce the market state dependent momentum profits that Cooper, Gutierrez and Hameed (2004) attribute to a behavioral explanation. Winner stocks that have performed well would have more growth options than loser stocks that have performed poorly. Since growth options are riskier than assets in place, winner stocks are expected to have higher expected returns than loser stocks. Sagi and Seasholes further posit that following up markets, firms are better poised to exploit their growth options, leading to higher momentum. Following down markets, firms are closer to the point of financial distress, resulting in lower momentum. Kim, Roh, Min, and Byun (2014) provide supporting evidence that winners have higher growth options and lower leverage than losers and that market-wide growth options are greater and leverage is lower in the expansion state. As such, winner stocks are risker and thus earn higher returns than loser stocks during expansion periods, supporting risk-based explanations.

Antoniou, Doukas and Subrahmanyam (2013) show that time variation of momentum profits is related to investor sentiment. Using the orthogonalized Conference Board consumer confidence index with respect to macroeconomic variables, they find that average momentum payoffs are significantly positive at 2% during optimistic periods, but it is lower and insignificantly positive at 0.34% during pessimistic periods. As an explanation for this relation between momentum and sentiment, Antoniou, Doukas and Subrahmanyam combine the Hong and Stein (1999) arguments with cognitive dissonance. In the model of Hong and Stein, private information diffuses slowly, generating under-reaction to information, leading to price momentum. Cognitive dissonance, insofar as it might account for investors underreacting more strongly when the information received contradicts prevailing market-wide sentiment, would predict that during optimistic (pessimistic) sentiment, bad (good) news among loser (winner) stocks would diffuse gradually, and loser and winner stocks consequently be underpriced during optimistic and pessimistic periods, respectively. Short sale constraints would generate asymmetric price correction of underpriced winner and loser stocks, it being relatively easy to arbitrage away underpriced winner stocks, but costly to short underpriced loser stocks. Momentum payoffs are thus predicted to be more pronounced when sentiment is optimistic.

Relatedly, Stambaugh, Yu and Yuan (2012) also show that momentum payoffs, including other well-known 10 market anomalies, are larger following periods of high sentiment. Combining the presence of market-wide sentiment together with the notion that short-sale constraints render overpricing more likely than underpricing (á la Miller, 1977), they suggest that sentiment-driven overpricing can explain sentiment-dependent momentum profits.

15.5 SUMMARY AND CONCLUSIONS

We discuss the intertemporal aspects of momentum profits. Chordia and Shivakumar (2002) show that momentum profits are related to business cycles classified by NBER, but subsequent studies (Griffin, Ji and Martin, 2003; Min and Kim, 2016) document that this relation becomes rather modest when skipping a month between ranking and holding periods, and that the relation is not robust after controlling for the January seasonality in momentum payoffs. Griffin, Ji and Martin (2003), classifying economic states by realised market excess return, failed to find evidence that momentum strategies generate negative loss during bad economic states. Motivated by both theoretical and empirical asset pricing studies, Min and Kim (2016), however, argue that the realised excess market return is a poor measure of marginal utility or business cycle and suggest instead the market expected risk premium as a right measure of marginal utility or business cycle. Showing momentum strategies to generate significantly negative profits when the expected market risk premium is especially high, they suggest that momentum strategies are fundamentally risky investments. Cooper, Gutierrez and Hameed's (2004) finding that momentum payoffs are dependent on market state, which can be viewed as a proxy for investors' aggregate overconfidence, supports Daniel, Hirshleifer and Subrahmanyam's (1998) behavioral model. Antoniou, Doukas and Subrahmanyam's (2013) finding that momentum profits are observed mainly during optimistic periods is consistent with Hong and Stein's (1999) behavioral model, extended with cognitive dissonance.

ACKNOWLEDGEMENT

This chapter largely builds on Min and Kim (2016).

REFERENCES

Antoniou, C., J. A. Doukas and A. Subrahmanyam. 2013. 'Cognitive Dissonance, Sentiment, and Momentum'. *Journal of Financial and Quantitative Analysis* **48**, 245–275.

Asness, C. S., T. J. Moskowitz and L. H. Pedersen. 2013. 'Value and Momentum Everywhere'. *Journal of Finance* **68**, 929–985.

Bansal, R. and A. Yaron. 2004. 'Risks for the Long Run: A Potential Resolution of Asset Pricing Puzzles'. *Journal of Finance* **59**, 1481–1509.

Barberis, N., A. Shleifer and R. Vishny. 1998. 'A Model of Investor Sentiment'. *Journal of Financial Economics* **49**, 307–343.

Berk, J. B., R. C. Green and V. Naik. 1999. 'Optimal Investment, Growth Options, and Security Returns'. *Journal of Finance* **54**, 1553–1608.

Blume, M. E. and I. Friend. 1973. 'A New Look at the Capital Asset Pricing Model'. *Journal of Finance* **28**, 19–33.

Campbell, J. Y. and J. H. Cochrane. 1999. 'By Force of Habit: A Consumption-Based Explanation of Aggregate Stock Market Behavior'. *Journal of Political Economy* **107**, 205–251.

Campello, M., L. Chen', and L. Zhang. 2008. 'Expected Returns, Yield Spreads, and Asset Pricing Tests'. *Review of Financial Studies* **21**, 1297–1338.

Chordia, T. and L. Shivakumar. 2002. 'Momentum, Business Cycle and Time-Varying Expected Returns'. *Journal of Finance* **57**, 985–1019.

Chui, A. C. W., S. Titman and K. C. J. Wei. 2010. 'Individualism and Momentum around the World'. *Journal of Finance* **65**, 361–392.

Cooper, M. J., R. C. Gutierrez and A. Hameed. 2004. 'Market States and Momentum'. *Journal of Finance* **59**, 1345–1365.

Daniel, K., D. Hirshleifer and A. Subrahmanyam. 1998. 'Investor Psychology and Security Market Under- and Overreactions'. *Journal of Finance* **53**, 1839–1885.

Elton, E. J. 1999. 'Expected Return, Realized Return, and Asset Pricing Tests'. *Journal of Finance* **54**, 1199–1220.

Fama, E. F. 1981. 'Stock Returns, Real Activity, Inflation, and Money'. *American Economic Review* **71**, 545–565.

Fama, E. F. and K. R. French. 1989. 'Business Conditions and Expected Returns on Stocks and Bonds'. *Journal of Financial Economics* **25**, 23–49.

Fama, E. F. and G. W. Schwert. 1977. 'Asset Returns and Inflation'. *Journal of Financial Economics* **5**, 115–146.

Ferson, W. and C. R. Harvey. 1991. 'The Variation of Economic Risk Premiums'. *Journal of Political Economy* **99**, 285–315.

George, T. J. and C. Hwang. 2004. 'The 52-Week High and Momentum Investing'. *Journal of Finance* **59**, 2145–2176.

Gervais, S. and T. Odean. 2001. 'Learning to be Overconfident'. *Review of Financial Studies* **14**, 1–27.

Griffin, J. M., S. Ji and J. S. Martin. 2003. 'Momentum Investing and Business Cycle Risk: Evidence from Pole to Pole'. *Journal of Finance* **58**, 2515–2547.

Grinblatt, M. and T. Moskowitz. 1999. *The Cross Section of Expected Returns and Its Relation to Past Returns: New Evidence*. Working paper, University of California, Los Angeles.

Grundy, B. D. and J. S. Martin. 2001. 'Understanding the Nature of Risks and the Sources of Rewards to Momentum Investing'. *Review of Financial Studies* **14**, 29–78.

Hong, H. and J. Stein. 1999. 'A Unified Theory of Underreaction, Momentum Trading, and Overreaction in Asset Markets'. *Journal of Finance* **54**, 2143–2184.

Jegadeesh, N. and S. Titman. 1993. 'Returns to Buying Winners and Selling Losers: Implications for Stock Market Efficiency'. *Journal of Finance* **48**, 65–91.

Jegadeesh, N. and S. Titman. 2001. 'Profitability of Momentum Strategies: An Evaluation of Alternative Explanations'. *Journal of Finance* **56**, 699–720.

Johnson, T. C. 2002. 'Rational Momentum Effects'. *Journal of Finance* **57**, 585–607.

Keim, D. B. and R. F. Stambaugh. 1986. 'Predicting Returns in the Stock and Bond Markets'. *Journal of Financial Economics* **17**, 357–390.

Kim, D., T.-Y. Roh, B.-K. Min', and S.-J. Byun. 2014. 'Time-Varying Expected Momentum Profits'. *Journal of Banking and Finance* **49**, 191–215.

Lakonishok, J., A. Shleifer', and R. Vishny. 1994. 'Contrarian Investment, Extrapolation, and Risk'. *Journal of Finance* **49**, 1541–1578.

Lettau, M.', and S. Ludvigson. 2001. 'Consumption, Aggregate Wealth, and Expected Stock Returns'. *Journal of Finance* **56**, 815–849.

Liew, J. and M. Vassalou. 2000. 'Can Book-to-market, Size and Momentum be Risk Factors that Predict Economic Growth?' *Journal of Financial Economics* **57**, 221–245.

Merton, R. 1973. 'An Intertemporal Capital Asset-Pricing Model'. *Econometrica* **41**, 867–887.

Miller, E. M. 1977. 'Risk, Uncertainty and Divergence of Opinion'. *Journal of Finance* **32**, 1151–1168.

Min, B.-K. and T. S. Kim. 2016. 'Momentum and Downside Risk'. *Journal of Banking and Finance* **72**, S104–S118.

Petkova, R. and L. Zhang. 2005. 'Is Value Riskier than Growth?' *Journal of Financial Economics* **78**, 187–202.

Rouwenhorst, K. G. 1998. 'International Momentum Strategies'. *Journal of Finance* **53**, 267–284.

Sagi, J. S. and M. S. Seasholes. 2007. 'Firm-Specific Attributes and the Cross Section of Momentum'. *Journal of Financial Economics* **84**, 389–434.

Sharpe, W. F. 1978. 'Capital Asset Pricing Theory: Discussion'. *Journal of Finance* **33**, 917–920.

Stambaugh, R. F., J. Yu. and Y. Yuan. 2012. 'The Short of it: Investor Sentiment and Anomalies'. *Journal of Financial Economics* **104**, 288–302.

Zhang, L. 2005. 'The Value Premium'. *Journal of Finance* **60**, 67–103.

CHAPTER 16

Momentum as a Fundamental Risk Factor

CHRISTOPHER TINKER

16.1 INTRODUCTION

Equity-based momentum strategies lie at the core of many structured products and commodity trading advisers (CTA) or managed futures funds, with trend-following strategies being the most popular. The use of past returns as a source of trading signals for both momentum and contrarian trading has been well documented and the persistent outperformance of momentum trading strategies has been shown by Lempérière et al. (2014) and Hurst et al. (2017) over long time periods. The key difference is one of duration. In examining the overreaction of US equity markets, De Bondt and Thaler (1985, 1987) and Lakonishok et al. (1994) find evidence of outperformance of a contrarian strategy with a holding period of three to five years. By contrast, Jegadeesh and Titman (1993, 2001) amongst many others have consistently found a momentum strategy to be profitable over a 3 to 12 month holding period in the US equity market, over a range of formation time periods.

For the most part, both momentum and long-run mean reversion continue to be considered market anomalies. Indeed, with Gene Fama's famous (1998) observation of momentum to be the 'one outstanding anomaly in market behavior', where performance is considered to be behavioural and not a risk factor, momentum continues to be treated in much of the literature as a trading process as opposed to an investment process. However, with more than three-quarters of US mutual funds found to be operating as momentum investors between 1974 and 1984 according to a study by Grinblatt et al. (1995) and with momentum increasingly regarded as a robust source of abnormal returns across asset classes, geographies and time periods, it is no surprise that analysis of momentum as a potential investment return strategy as well as momentum as a risk factor have become a more central focus in recent years.

In part this is due to the increased interest in the study of alternative risk premia (ARPs) – see Fung and Hsieh (2001) and Potters and Bouchaud (2006) – and growing interest in factor investing by institutional investors, where momentum strategies were typically less common, given the typically longer-term investment horizons of institutions such as pension funds and sovereign wealth funds. Much of the recent work on the topic of momentum is focused upon returns to a momentum strategy or portfolio in the form of a factor-based analysis. Indeed, as Roncalli (2017) observes, carry, momentum and value are three risk premia that are now considered essential for strategic risk allocation in order to diversify traditional risk premia portfolios.

Historically, with momentum has outperformed as a strategy, and is now increasing in importance for risk analysis. The fact that short-term momentum is not explicable under the Fama-French three-factor model according to their own study (Fama and French, 1996) poses a dilemma for those whose factor-based investment approach is driven by the cross-sectional, realised return methodology characteristic of many existing factor models.

Whilst the concept of momentum as an anomaly in market behaviour appears to be true in such an environment (and where realised returns are used as a proxy for expected returns), this may not be the case under a different forecasting environment of expected returns: one that is more stock-level and time-series based. If forecasted expected returns are both time varying and a function of cash flow news, and the implied cost of capital can be determined from the model, the dynamics of the relationship between the return on capital and the cost of capital on a stock-by-stock basis can be evaluated. The implied Sharpe ratios for different assets can then form the basis for portfolio construction.

Intuitively, analysing momentum as a risk premium as a function of changes in forecast expected returns (and implied Sharpe ratios) at the asset level is also consistent with other risk premium approaches where the level and dispersion of Sharpe ratios forms a major part of the portfolio construction process. Although Fama and French (1996) determined in their analysis of asset pricing anomalies that the alternative approach of Lakonishok et al. (1994) with their use of fundamental ratios to categorise glamour and value stocks did not add more information to the process than their own three-factor model, their acknowledgement of the three-factor model's failure to deal with momentum suggests that the classification approach to value used by Lakonishok et al. (1994) could be used in conjunction with a forward looking expectations model to try and produce a more integrated approach.

One consequence of the decision to treat momentum as an anomaly is that much of the work on momentum strategies treats it as a behavioural phenomenon and arguably outside the normal framework of factor analysis. This is not unreasonable given the relative importance of news flow and market response over shorter-term investment horizons. Even if we move to a forward-looking, stochastic pricing model for expected returns, this can still operate under a behavioural framework. The behavioural literature on investor sentiment, over-and under-reaction, herding, and trend chasing provides a broad line of analysis to be followed. One common approach taken is that of the Heterogeneous Agent Model (HAM) – see Day and Huang (1990), Lux (1995) and Brock and Hommes (1998) – where heterogeneous agents are seen to act within a largely efficient, forward-looking, marginal utility framework, and respond to marginal information (news flow) via the price mechanism. Examples of work in this area with continuous time models include He and Li (2012) and He and Zheng (2016).

The task of extending the analysis into an applied environment to allow the momentum risk premium to be integrated into formal risk models is certainly made easier by the use of continuous-time-series analysis. However, the difficulty of integrating traditional and alternative risk premia in order to improve portfolio diversification lies in the non-linearity of the relationships between them. Traditional mean-variance diversification (Markowitz, 1952), focused upon optimizing portfolio volatility, cannot be applied and Lempérière et al. (2017) point out that these risk premia also possess different levels of skewness. Recent work on the momentum risk premium itself (Jusselin et al., 2017) extends the earlier studies of Fung and Hsieh (2001), Potters and Bouchaud (2006) and Bruder and Gaussel (2011), and suggests that an options-based approach to the quantification of momentum, both in terms of a risk premium and the measurement of its effectiveness as a signal or strategy, could provide the best means of quantifying the theoretical approach via a continuous time record of actual signal returns.

It is, therefore, this framework of a continuous-time-series behavioural model, combined with a stochastic stock level model of expected returns and implied volatilities that provides for momentum-based stock level selection and risk management and ultimately feeds into an options-based momentum strategy that is developed through the rest of the chapter. Empirical returns to the momentum strategy developed under this framework are then used to quantify the validity of the approach and help determine its effectiveness as a contributory tool for risk modeling and portfolio construction.

16.2 DEFINING MOMENTUM AS A STRATEGY

Definitions of momentum are wide ranging but at a broad level, a momentum strategy seeks to use information gathered in a portfolio formation period and use this to select a portfolio of assets – the momentum portfolio – which is then held for a holding period. Whilst momentum per se is not asset class specific, the focus of this chapter is on momentum in equities, so all references to asset prices, returns, variances, values, portfolios or strategies refer to listed equities.

Perhaps the best-known version of a momentum portfolio is the cross-sectional momentum strategy, whereby the momentum portfolio is formed by buying the formation period winners and selling the formation period losers and maintaining this portfolio for the holding period. The winners/losers are selected on the basis of relative past performance over the formation period with the top decile of performance/bottom decile of performance over the formation period forming the winners/losers portfolios respectively. Jegadeesh and Titman (1993, 2001) found this to be profitable over a 3 to 12 month holding period in the US equity market over a range of time periods and their $J \times K$ trading model is the default model for constructing cross sectional model portfolios. Explanations as to why this might be the case tend to look to both firm-specific factors such as systematic risk, firm size, industry factors and topics such as reaction to earnings announcements – see Conrad and Kaul (1998).

The behavioural explanations cover topics relating to shifts in investor sentiment and perceptions of risk but tend to focus upon the concept of momentum and contrarian investment strategies being a market over- or under-reaction to information. Jegadeesh and Titman (1993) determined a 3 to 12 month holding period for the cross-sectional portfolio, but the idea that rather than being a short-term non-persistent response to news, that stock prices adjust slowly to information, requiring the examination of longer-term horizons was argued by Fama (1998).

Moskowitz et al. (2012) took a different approach to the stock selection process of the formation period, using the stock level time-series past return as the only selection criteria and making the portfolio selection one based on absolute, not relative returns. Because of this, a time-series momentum strategy requires a separately determined set of rules in order to form the winner and loser portfolios with a particular focus in their analysis upon ex ante stock level volatility as a scalar for the portfolio constituents.

The success of any trend-following momentum strategy requires a significant price trend in either direction when compared to its volatility. This is a reason why shorter-term momentum strategies often have poorer profit and loss (P&L) outcomes. Shorter-term trends are harder to estimate and, whilst a long only investor merely needs to be convinced about the positive nature of expected returns, the momentum trader needs to be convinced of the likelihood of a significant trend taking place.

The seminal momentum life cycle (MLC) hypothesis of Lee and Swaminathan (2000) has been widely used as a framework of analysis. Their hypothesis is that stocks experience periods of investor favouritism and neglect, which can be captured by examining their trading volumes. They propose that there is an empirical link between trading volume, intermediate horizon momentum and long-term reversal and which is a function of what they describe as a momentum life cycle, illustrated in Figure 16.1.

For Lee and Swaminathan (2000), a stock with positive price and/or earning momentum (past winner) would be on the left hand side of the cycle, whereas a stock

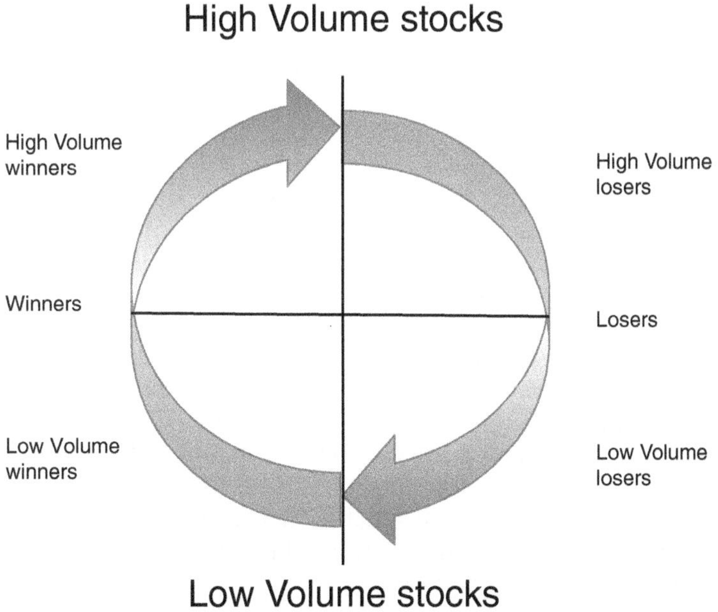

FIGURE 16.1 The momentum life cycle. Source: Lee and Swaminathan (2000).

with negative price and/or earning momentum (past loser) would be on the right hand side of Figure 16.1. In terms of what moves stocks around this cycle, an initial observation was to observe that low volume stocks tend to act more like value stocks, and high-volume stocks act more like glamour (growth) stocks. Growth stocks that experience positive news move up the cycle, but eventually disappoint the market and are 'torpedoed'. Stocks that disappoint begin a downward slide (in volume), and eventually experience general neglect. If they fall far enough in price, they may become attractive to contrarian investors.

In terms of persistence of trend and eventual reversal, their results suggest that low volume stocks generally outperformed high volume stocks and that, amongst winners, low volume stocks exhibit more persistence. Amongst losers, high volume stocks showed more persistence.

Their categorisation of the MLC characterizes high volume winners and low volume losers as *late stage* momentum stocks (at the top of the MLC), in the sense that their price momentum is more likely to reverse in the near future. Conversely low volume winners and high volume losers are *early stage* momentum stocks (at the bottom of the MLC), in the sense that their momentum is more likely to persist in the near future.

16.3 A NEW FRAMEWORK

The separation into glamour/value like characteristics is interesting in that they propose another possibility: that the variation in trading volume – and hence movement around the cycle – captures investors' disagreement about a stock's intrinsic value. Our earlier point about Lakonishok et al. (1994) and their use of fundamental ratios to categorise glamour and value stocks is worth revisiting here. If so-called glamour stocks tend to be high growth stocks that are more likely to be valued on intangible metrics (as opposed to tangible metrics applied to value stocks) then a greater disagreement among investors about their intrinsic values could lead to higher trading volumes and a stock level stochastic pricing model, designed to calculate those differing levels of intrinsic value would enable those disagreements to be quantified. Interpreted in this context, early stage momentum stocks tend to have less investor disagreement, whereas late stage momentum stocks tend to have more investor disagreement.

Lee and Swaminathan (2000) go on to identify the limitations of their analysis at a stock level, making the point that:

> For individual firms, things are far less deterministic than the figure implies. Individual firms do not necessarily exhibit expectation cycles of the same frequency. Nor does each firm need to pass through all phases of the cycle each time. The turning points for individual firms may appear random and difficult to pinpoint, even though the portfolios in each quadrant conform to the predictions of the MLC hypothesis.

Whilst subsequent analysis of the volume effect by Scott et al. (2003) found that, after adjusting for growth, the momentum effect was largely explicable by news and not volume, the argument in favour of the MLC remains valid. Despite their own caveats regarding the limitations of analysis at a stock level, it is Lee and Swaminathan's contention that it is the variation in belief about the intrinsic value of a stock amongst investors that is key. An investor's decision to buy (or not to buy) a stock is likely to be dependent on a view of the expected return available and not simply a view of a level of intrinsic value. Taking on board the importance of variance in trend, following strategies outlined by Dao et al. (2016) and many others, we can restate their view as one of the momentum cycle being potentially driven by differentiated views about the implied Sharpe ratios of the asset through time.

16.4 FROM REALISED RETURNS TO FORECAST RETURNS

Early empirical literature, such as Jegadeesh and Titman (1993, 2001), showed that the use of momentum trading strategies based upon over- or underreaction to past returns was profitable, but the holding period was relatively short (3 to 12 months) and the time horizon variable. This meant that the lengths of both the formation and the holding periods are critical to the formation of an effective momentum strategy. In addition to this, the state of the market is also of importance. Griffin et al. (2003) and Hou et al. (2009) find that momentum strategies are not profitable in down markets but are profitable in up markets.

The need for a successful momentum strategy to have more effective implementation rules and timing signals more aligned at an individual stock level is also noted by Bird et al. (2017), and Chapter 13 of this book. In their multi-country, comparative performance analysis of both cross-sectional and time-series momentum strategies, they conclude that either a nine or twelve-month formation period, and a three-month holding period produced the better investment outcomes. This is consistent with a slow adjustment in prices to new information, but an eventual over-shooting.

If quarterly news flow with respect to a company's future cash flows (earnings, revenues, etc.), and the implications that this news flow has on investor perceptions of intrinsic value, appears to be a significant influence on the momentum cycle it prompts a new approach to the question of price action. Why should views of implied volatility and expected returns become conflicted amongst investors at different stages of the MLC and the overall market cycle? The partial or incomplete integration of news by investors into their updated views on intrinsic value would appear to be one answer. If, as Scott et al. (2003) suggest, investors do incorporate regular news into their forecasts of expected returns, then the variability of expected returns over time and the role they play in stock price movements noted by Cochrane (2011) suggests that a behavioural, expected returns framework is best placed to examine the drivers of a momentum strategy.

16.5 EXAMINING BEHAVIOUR

The emergence of ARP models has moved momentum into the spotlight for more traditional long only or contrarian style investors (such as pension funds or sovereign wealth funds). Multifactor investing treats momentum as one of the factors (alongside, value, size, low beta and quality). In this setting, we retain the core framework and behavioural underpinning of the MLC; summarised as follows:

Share prices typically oscillate around their (fair) intrinsic values, and investors have differing levels of agreement as to that intrinsic value at different stages of the MLC. When all types of investor agree on the intrinsic value of the share, there is generally a low(er) level of transaction, and a stock can be expected to trend in line with its expected return outlook. The MLC categorisation for these stocks is early stage momentum. However, when the consensus around intrinsic value breaks down, then the implication is that the expected return for the stock will change for one or both groups of investors. This means that the stock moves around the cycle into a late stage price momentum stage with the effect that shorter-term momentum moves and a higher risk of reversal will then occur.

It is immediately clear that, if we consider the primary driver of the momentum cycle to be related to changes in expectations of future value, the traditional approach of examining momentum as a function of realised returns is no longer sufficient. Both the (short-term) momentum investor and the (long-term) fundamental/contrarian investor are considered to base their decisions on an updating model of future value (and by implication forecast expected returns) driven by news flow. If momentum is to be treated as a factor by investors, then asset selection and position management of the momentum portfolio will require a systematic set of implementation rules and signals derived from forecast stock level expected returns and implied volatilities.

In one sense, this is no different from any other factor portfolio selection process based around forecast expected returns and implied Sharpe ratios. However, given the relatively short time frames involved, these will need to be re-estimated with a higher degree of frequency than other factor portfolios might require. The need to model the behavioural actions of momentum explicitly, in terms of information evaluation and adjustment points, to the adoption of bounded rationality models such as the one proposed by Hong and Stein (1999) or heterogeneous agent models (HAM) (Chiarella et al., 2006), which treat the market as an expectations feedback system. Among others, Day and Huang (1990), Lux (1995) and Brock and Hommes (1998) study the interactions of heterogeneous investors with different rules based behaviours in relation to trading. Agent decisions are based upon their own predictions of endogenous variables, allowing the simultaneous existence of different beliefs related to expected returns and fundamental asset prices.

Chiarella et al. (2006) use a two-agent chartist and fundamentalist model of the market. Chartists examine the price in relation to past returns, whilst the fundamentalists model their view of the price with respect to their perceived estimate of fundamental value. When chartists expectations change sufficiently fast, the stability of the market equilibrium is lost, with a supercritical bifurcation that leads to self-sustaining price fluctuations. The idea of periodic bifurcations or breakdowns of the existing status quo is widespread amongst the literature and is central to the process of signal generation. Identifying the breakdowns and recoveries of the momentum trading signals through the identification of these bifurcations enables a momentum strategy to move from a trading approach based upon a fixed holding period to one based upon forecast expected returns.

In applying the HAM framework to the practical creation of momentum portfolios and analysis of the momentum risk premium, we frame the manner by which marginal fundamental-based information (both public and private) being received by the market has an impact on both the share price, and profitability of various trading strategies. The framework is not restricted to a single strategy but allows for the possibility of multiple strategies. For example, when an asset is identified as being appropriate for a momentum portfolio, it may simultaneously be appropriate for a fundamental portfolio based upon other factor characteristics – low volatility, value, quality, size – due to the measured absolute and relative signals.

The HAM framework we adopt here allows for asset price fluctuations to be regarded as an endogenous, heterogeneous process with bounded rationality; operating in an otherwise largely efficient pricing and information market along the lines proposed by He and Li (2012). The benefit of their approach is that the impact of marginal private and public information on the profitability of various strategies can be specified. Thus, a set of implementation rules can be established for the strategy and a credible signal testing regime can be constructed, based upon the post-signal performance of the share price. Both entry and exit signals can be evaluated on a time-series basis and cross-sectional basis in order to evaluate the effectiveness of the fundamental signal process.

We start with He and Li's (2012) four agent model, consisting of fundamentalist, contrarian, momentum and market maker strategies. A set of excess demand equations are described for each strategy, based upon the trading rules implied and this, in turn allows for a continuous time, stochastic system model of the price mechanism to be specified.

A fundamentalist operates a mean reverting strategy whereby he buys a stock when the current price $P(t)$ is below their measure of fundamental price $F(t)$ and vice versa. This is the same measure referred to as intrinsic value by Lee and Swaminathan (2000) but we will retain the reference to fundamental price $F(t)$ used by He and Li (2012). They assume for simplicity that excess demand is proportional to the degree to which the current price $P(t)$ diverges from the fundamental price $F(t)$:

$$D_f(t) = \beta\_f \, [F(t) - P(t)], \tag{16.1}$$

where $\beta_f > 0$ is a constant parameter measuring the speed of mean reversion of $P(t)$ to $F(t)$.

Momentum and contrarian traders are considered to operate on the basis of their estimate of market price trends. However, their response to the public information provided by the price trend leads to contrasting actions: the momentum trader will observe a price in excess of a price trend $\mu_m(t)$ and believe that this price trend will continue so will buy the stock, whilst the contrarian will observe the price trend $\mu_c(t)$ and if the price moves to be greater than, the trend, will anticipate a mean reversion in the price and take a short position. Note that the price trend for momentum traders and contrarians does not have to be the same.

He and Li (2012) write the excess demand with respect to the two strategies as follows

$$D_m(t) = g_m(P(t) - \mu_m(t)),$$

$$D_c(t) = g_c(\mu_c(t) - P(t)), \tag{16.2}$$

where the demand function $g_i(x)$ satisfies

$$g_i(0) = 0, \quad g_i'(x) > 0, \quad g_i'(0) = \beta_i > 0, \quad xg_i''(x) < 0 \quad \text{for } x \neq 0, i = m, c. \tag{16.3}$$

and the parameter β_i represents the extrapolation rate of the price trend when the deviation from the trend is small.

Following Chiarella (1992) they model this as an S-shaped excess demand function, re-designating $g_i(x) = \tanh(\beta_i x)$ whose slope levels off as the magnitude of $|x|$ increases.

The default price trend used is a moving average,

$$\mu_i(t) = \frac{1}{\tau_i} \int_{t-\tau_i}^{t} P(s)ds, \quad i = m, c, \tag{16.4}$$

Where $\tau_i \geq 0$ represents the time horizon of the moving average and where τ_m and τ_c do not have to be equal.

This means that the aggregate market excess demand that the market maker faces – weighted by the population weights of the three categories – is given by

$$\alpha_f D_f + \alpha_m D_m + \alpha_c D_c \tag{16.5}$$

and that the price $P(t)$ at time t is set according to aggregate excess demand.

$$dP(t) = \mu[\alpha_f D_f + \alpha_m D_m + \alpha_c D_c]dt + \sigma_M dW_M(t) \tag{16.6}$$

Where $\mu > 0$ represents the speed of adjustment by the market maker, $W_M(t)$ is a standard Wiener process capturing random excess demand and $\sigma_M \geq 0$ is a constant.

Based upon Equations (16.1) to (16.6), He and Li (2012) set out the following stochastic delay integro-differential system

$$dP(t) = \mu \left[\begin{array}{l} \left[\alpha_f \beta_f (F(t) - P(t)) + \alpha_m \tanh\left(\beta_m \left(P(t) - \frac{1}{\tau_m} \int_{t-\tau_m}^{t} P(s)ds \right) \right) \right] \\ + \alpha_c \tanh\left(-\beta_c \left(P(t) - \frac{1}{\tau_c} \int_{t-\tau_c}^{t} P(s)ds \right) \right) \end{array} \right] dt$$

$$+ \sigma_M dW_M(t) \tag{16.7}$$

Where the fundamental price *F(t)* is exogenously determined. We will use the stochastic pricing model specified elsewhere in the chapter to determine this input in the test environment.

He and Li (2012) make several observations at this point. Firstly, the importance of the fundamental price *F(t)*. In the absence of market noise and in the situation where the fundamental price is a constant, then $F(t) \equiv \overline{F}$ and $P(t) = \overline{F}$ represents the fundamental, steady state of the system.

Thus, we have

$$
dP(t) = \mu \left[\begin{array}{l} \alpha_f \beta_f (F(t) - P(t)) + \alpha_m \tanh \left(\beta_m \left(P(t) - \frac{1}{\tau_m} \int_{t-\tau_m}^{t} P(s)ds \right) \right) \\ + \alpha_c \tanh \left(-\beta_c \left(P(t) - \frac{1}{\tau_c} \int_{t-\tau_c}^{t} P(s)ds \right) \right) \end{array} \right] \tag{16.8}
$$

In the absence of a momentum trader (e.g. a world consisting only of contrarians and fundamentalists), the continuous adjustment of the market price by the market means that the impact of the contrarian upon the price becomes insignificant over a small time frame, leaving the price environment stable and profitability independent of the time horizon. However, the lack of momentum trading in the market limits the degree of price over-reaction and hence the profitability of contrarian traders.

Where fundamental views dominate, momentum traders are unlikely to have much impact. However, in a situation where it is the momentum traders that dominate – e.g. where no contrarians operate – the market is stable at small time horizons and profitable for the momentum trader. However, the market can become unstable at long horizons, leading to riskier profits for the momentum trader. Hence, their time horizon is important, and both in the short- and long-term, it is the strength of the momentum trend that is important for the profitability of the momentum trade.

16.6 THE MOMENTUM TRADER AS A BYSTANDER

In this model, the momentum trader is a passive participant. Because our approach is based upon the impact of news flow on the fundamental price *F(t)* and, by extension, expected returns, the momentum trend is neither initiated nor concluded by the momentum trader himself. Once he has identified his point of entry – a break above a moving average line for example – then his profitability is dependent upon a reversal *not* happening during his holding period. Under the HAM model described earlier, the momentum trader's excess demand is positively correlated with the extrapolation of the price trend and the degree of price divergence from the underlying price trend. The impact of news flow on the momentum trader arises only via the price mechanism. The reversal phase of the momentum cycle is driven by the fundamental/contrarian investor in response to the degree of divergence that the price is exhibiting from the perceived fundamental price *F(t)*. This is consistent with the concept of divergence in investor views of intrinsic value increasing though the value cycle as proposed by Lee and Swaminathan (2000).

Whilst this initial model does not deal with the implementation rule for establishing a potential momentum phase, it nevertheless does provide us with a straightforward means of signaling the end of a momentum phase. At the early stage of the momentum phase, the contrarian does not participate and his demand function is assumed to be zero.

$$g_c(x) = \tanh(\beta_c x) = 0 \tag{16.9}$$

However, as the momentum phase continues, the value of this becomes positive. When the excess demand from the contrarian investor outweighs that of the momentum investor, $\alpha_c \tanh(\beta_c x) > \alpha_m \tanh(\beta_m x)$ and the phase is ended.

In terms of the model, when

$$0 > \left[\alpha_m \tanh \left(\beta_m \left(P(t) - \frac{1}{\tau_m} \int_{t-\tau_m}^{t} P(s)ds \right) \right) + \alpha_c \tanh \left(-\beta_c \left(P(t) - \frac{1}{\tau_c} \int_{t-\tau_c}^{t} P(s)ds \right) \right) \right] \tag{16.10}$$

the momentum phase has ended. We can use the nature of the S-shaped demand function to identify this point directly from the value of the second term changing sign so that

$$\tanh(\beta_c x_{t-1}) < 0 > \tanh(\beta_c x_t) \text{ and}$$

$$\tanh(\beta_c x_{t-1}) > 0 > \tanh(\beta_c x_t) \tag{16.11}$$

provide the closure points for the short-momentum/long-momentum trades respectively.

It is not that these strategies are operating as continuous alternatives, but that there will be times when one or more of the agents is absent from the market; allowing the performance of one or other strategy to win out. For example, a positive momentum phase may be initiated by a fundamental signal that the fundamental price $F(t)$ and therefore the future expected returns are increasing. If, as a result of this, the price also moves to a premium to the momentum trader's view of value such that:

$$(F(t) - P(t)) > 0 < \left(\beta_m \left(P(t) - \frac{1}{\tau_m} \int_{t-\tau_m}^{t} P(s)ds \right) \right) \tag{16.12}$$

then if the contrarian holds a similar view to the fundamentalist with regard to $F(t)$ he will be absent from the market and the price will continue to rise. Unless or until the contrarian re-enters the market as a seller – either because the market price $P(t)$ is no longer at a discount to the fundamental price $F(t)$ or because of new information suggesting that $F(t)$ may no longer be increasing or may be at risk of falling, the price will move in line with the momentum trader.

Identifying the movement in and out of the market by different agents holds the key to understanding the evolution of the momentum phase of the market. If these movements in and out of the market are driven by differential opinion as to the level of intrinsic value, then identifying the transmission method from news flow to the determination of intrinsic value will provide the timing signals to determine the initiation and duration of the momentum cycle.

It is also the case that, although we are looking for the impact of news on the fundamental value $F(t)$, for significant periods of time, the marginal investor is unlikely to act on anything other than a largely stable view of the expected return. Under a continuous time-series framework, and in conditions where pricing is stable with respect to fundamental measure of value, the contrarian has little need to participate. In a market where pricing is mostly efficient (and therefore mis-pricing is mostly absent), the combination of the fundamentalist, the market maker and the short-term trader provide for a relatively stable market. Only in conditions of extreme divergence from the fundamental perception of value would the contrarian step in and, given that the fundamental value of the fundamentalist and the contrarian are considered to be the same under this framework, there is no reason to suggest that a fundamentalist would not buy on the same terms as the contrarian.

This raises the question as to the role of the contrarian in the model, except as a counterbalance to the momentum trader when momentum trading is dominant. It also raises the question as to why momentum trading would ever become the dominant activity in the market? When markets are stable, the price will trade around the fundamental price and in line with expected returns: both short-term news-related/ noise trading and fundamental investors will ensure that this remains the case. Unless momentum is considered a spontaneous phenomenon, then we see momentum traders as following after a price event. As a result, it must be the response of the fundamental investor (in the form of the contrarian) to news flow that potentially changes the perceived value of fundamental value, $F(t)$ and it is the change to that fundamental value that establishes the momentum trade. The contrarian in this model is not the longer-term contrarian of the overreaction hypothesis of De Bondt and Thaler (1985, 1987) and Lakonishok et al. (1994), with a holding period of three to five years. Instead, the contrarian is a shorter-term fundamental investor with a view of fundamental value $F(t)$ similar to but not necessarily identical to that of the long-term investor, whose view of fundamental value is influenced by cash-flow-related news.

16.7 EXTENDING THE MODEL

In terms of the He and Li's (2012) model, this implies that the demand functions of the fundamental investor and the contrarian contained in the demand equation (16.8) can be expressed as:

$$D_f(t) = \beta_f[F_l(t) - P(t)] \text{ and}$$

$$D_c(t) = \alpha_c \tanh(-\beta_c(P(t) - F_s(t))) \tag{16.13}$$

where $F_l(t), (F_s(t)$ are the long-term and short-term investor measures of value, respectively.

The constraint of the fundamental price being constant is therefore relaxed; that is $F(t) \neq \overline{F}$ and $P(t) \neq \overline{F}$. When this occurs, the contrarian's focus is no longer upon a slope of the price line and the extrapolation of the current price from that underlying trend but upon the divergence of $F_s(t)$ from $P(t)$ and the potential mispricing where $F_s(t + 1) > F_s(t) > P(t)$. Given the assumption of the short- and long-term fundamentalist investor that the price will converge to the fundamental price $F_i(t)$, he can assume that $P(t+1) > P(t)$ and so his forecast expected return is positive. Under conditions of a variable level of $F_i(t)$ and the arrival of marginal new information relating to the value of $F_i(t)$, the role of the short-term fundamental investor is to see a mis-pricing in terms of a potential change in expected return, $P(t+1) - P(t)$ as a result of a change in $P(t) - F_s(t)$.

He and Zheng (2016) extend the HAM to one closer to this idea of a dynamic determination of fundamental value; examining trading and switching behaviour under conditions of information uncertainty. This update also suits our purposes. The shift from assuming agents have complete information and have their identities (chartist/fundamentalist) exogenously determined as proposed by Brock and Hommes (1998) to one where agents can choose their strategy based upon the combination of both public and private information about the asset concerned has two consequences that are beneficial to our approach. It extends the analysis of switching behaviour from an exogenous probability approach to an endogenous one. This means that the share of agents in each group is not fixed, but a function of both past asset prices and the significance of recent cash-flow signals. Secondly, the decision to switch between a fundamental, long-run mean reversal strategy and a shorter-term momentum model allows for both states to exist in the model simultaneously but with time varying patterns of optimal trading and information uncertainty.

The advantage of using this approach is that, provided that the data relating to return expectations is measurable in continuous form, the dynamics of heterogeneous agents can be modeled under the framework of long-run market stability, and localised equilibrium with respect to expected returns, variances and correlations. Cash flow news events affect different agents' levels of certainty around their preferences for following one of the two strategies given a level of uncertainty over fundamental value.

16.8   SHORT-TERM VERSUS LONG-TERM INVESTORS

Unlike the chartist model of Chiarella et al. (2006) and the momentum trader in He and Li (2012), the assumption that we make is that the alternative strategy to the fundamentalist is a short-term investor, who has a fundamental view based upon more than just public information (recent price action). This is because although the short-term investor may rely on recent price action for some or all of his trading signals, his risk decisions are made on the basis of information that he also holds with respect to the fundamental valuation $F_s(t)$ and $F_l(t)$ made by both short-term and long-term investors.

$F_s(t)$ and $F_l(t)$ may well be identical (or close to it) under stable conditions as the information set for all agents is relatively well informed (although still uncertain). The endogenously determined status and switching of trading strategies of He and Zheng (2016), where switching by agents between being a chartist or a fundamentalist is based upon a long-term view of fundamental value, can be adapted to one where it is the shorter-term view $F_s(t)$ that is observed. The same information set provides the long-term fundamentalist and the short-term fundamental trader with potentially differing levels of underlying value and expected return.

Under their information uncertainty framework, the momentum trader remains one whose view is based upon a public information reference price. However, the heterogeneous nature of agents is neither predetermined nor random. Instead it is a function of incomplete (uncertain) information about the fundamental value of the asset, leading to differentiated perceptions of value and to agents following competing strategies. Each agent receives a private signal on the fundamental value, μ (equivalent to $F_S(t)$ in the prior model).

$$x_{i,t} = \mu + \varepsilon_{i,t} \tag{16.14}$$

where the noise term is independent and normally distributed with mean 0 and standard deviation of σ_x across agents through time. The precision of agents' signals is set as $\alpha = 1/\sigma_x^2$, leaving private signals to be normally distributed with a mean of μ and a variance of $1/\alpha_x$.

All agents have a constant absolute risk aversion (CARA) utility function,

$$U(W_{i,t}) = -\exp(-A W_{i,t}) \tag{16.15}$$

where A is the common risk aversion coefficient and $W_{i,t}$ is the Wealth of agent i at time t.

Whilst He and Zheng (2016) go on to model a switching strategy between the chartist/ momentum trader and the fundamentalist; optimizing the utilities of both and determining the optimum strategy to be followed, for the purposes here we only need to take advantage of the uncertainty framework they describe to model the likely event of a marginal entry of an agent into the market.

The agent's optimal demand is described as

$$q_{i,t} = \frac{E(p_t|x_{i,t}, I_{t-1}) - p_{t-1}}{A \, Var(p_t|x_{i,t}, I_{t-1})} \tag{16.16}$$

where $E(p_t|x_{i,t}, I_{t-1})$ is the agent's prediction about the price and $Var(p_t|x_{i,t}, I_{t-1})$ the variance of the risk asset, conditional on both the public information of price history I_{t-1} and the agent's own signal $x_{i,t}$.

Under this framework, agent demand is independent of wealth, is an increasing function of the predicted price change and a decreasing function of price volatility – in effect it is proportional to the implied Sharpe ratio of the investment opportunity.

Given that both the current and the future expected levels of fundamental value are a function of the marginal private signal of the agent and the signals of other agents that are already reflected in the current price, the agent's expected return will be similarly determined. From Equation (16.13) we see that, since the fundamental investor believes that over the period $(t \to \tau)$ the future price will converge to the *expected* fundamental value at time τ, $F(\tau)$ the agent's expected return over $(t \to \tau)$,

$$R_\tau = E_t(R_{\tau-t}) + \varepsilon_t = (F_s(\tau) - F_s(t)) + (P(t) - F_s(t)) \tag{16.17}$$

where $E_t(R_{\tau-t}) = F_S(\tau) - F_S(t)$ the expected return in period (t, τ), conditional on the information set available at t and the unexpected return, and

$\varepsilon_t = P(t) - F_s(t)$ is the divergence between the current level of fundamental value and the price.

From Equation (16.16) the predicted price and variance of the fundamental strategy becomes:

$$E^f(p_t|x_{i,t}, I_{t-1}) = (1 - \gamma)p_{t-1} + \gamma \frac{\alpha_\mu \overline{\mu} + \alpha_x x_{i,t}}{\alpha_\mu + \alpha_x} \tag{16.18}$$

$$Var^f(p_t|x_{i,t}, I_{t-1}) = \gamma^2 Var(\mu|x_{i,t}, I_{t-1}) = \frac{\gamma^2}{\alpha_\mu + \alpha_x} \tag{16.19}$$

where $\gamma \in (0,1)$ is a constant and where $\frac{\alpha_\mu \overline{\mu} + \alpha_x x_{i,t}}{\alpha_\mu + \alpha_x}$ and $\frac{1}{\alpha_\mu + \alpha_x}$ are agent i's posterior updating of the mean and variance of the fundamental value $F_S(t)$ of the risk asset, conditional on the private signal $x_{i,t}$.

The optimal demand for the fundamental strategy is therefore

$$q_{i,t}^f = \frac{\alpha_\mu \overline{\mu} + \alpha_x x_{i,t} - (\alpha_\mu + \alpha_x)p_{t-1}}{A\gamma} \tag{16.20}$$

By contrast, the decision to be a chartist/momentum investor is independent of the marginal private information,

$$E^c(p_t|x_{i,t}, I_{t-1}) = p_{t-1} + \beta(p_{t-1} - v_t), \qquad Var^c(p_t|x_{i,t}, I_{t-1}) = \sigma_{t-1}^2 \tag{16.21}$$

where following the earlier construction v_t is a reference price or price trend, β measures the extrapolation of the price deviation from the price trend and σ_{t-1}^2 is a prediction of the variance of the asset price.

The optimal demand for this momentum strategy is then

$$q_{i,t}^c = \frac{\beta(p_{t-1} - v_t)}{A\sigma_{t-1}^2} \tag{16.22}$$

Given that the model is designed to provide for an optimal decision between the two strategies, this suggests that a threshold value for the private signal exists where the agent is indifferent between being a fundamental investor or a chartist. In such circumstances, a fundamental strategy would be followed.

By modeling a standard normal probability density function, He and Zheng (2016) show that if the private signal is in the tails of an expected distribution of $x_{i,t}$ around the mean, then a fundamental strategy is preferred; otherwise the momentum strategy is selected. In other words, as the degree of mispricing increases with respect to $|p_{t-1} - \mu|$ the choice of the momentum strategy decreases, leading to the mean reversion observed earlier.

The tail of the distribution of returns, based on the distribution of the private signal with respect to the fundamental price, becomes of particular interest when seeking to move the analysis into the portfolio level, and in terms of providing risk adjusted expected return forecasts. However, what we aim to identify here are the threshold points at which the information set of the market prompts the price to move due to the change in demand from the fundamentally driven investor. This is the point of divergence of the price from the fundamental value at which the tails of the returns distribution start to reward the agent to act as a fundamental investor as opposed to a momentum trader.

The idea that there is a maximum or minimum range for a momentum trade with respect to the fundamental value is consistent with the idea of uncertainty with respect to future expected returns. He and Zheng (2016) create value functions for the two strategies and define the threshold level $\overline{x}_t$ as the point of indifference between strategies so that $x_{i,t} = \overline{x}_t$.

Solving for $\overline{x}_t$ yields

$$x_t^{\pm} = \frac{1}{\alpha_x} \left[(\alpha_{\mu} + \alpha_x)\, p_{t-1} - \alpha_{\mu}\overline{\mu} \pm \frac{\beta\sqrt{\alpha_{\mu} + \alpha_x}}{\sigma_{t-1}}(p_{t-1} - v_t) \right] \qquad (16.23)$$

Defining $x_t^m = \min(x_t^{\pm})$ and $x_t^M = \max(x_t^{\pm})$, if the agents signal of value falls in the interval (x_t^m, x_t^M) then they treat the investment as a momentum trade based upon their current information considered to be broadly aligned with the fundamental value held by the market.

If order to quantify this in the form of a probability distribution with respect to the threshold levels of x_t^m *and* x_t^M and quantify the distribution of returns, given that $x_{i,t} \sim N\left(\mu, 1/\alpha_x\right)$ He and Zheng (2016) modify Equation (16.23) by letting,

$$y_{i,t} = \sqrt{\alpha_x}(x_{i,t} - \mu), \qquad y_{i,t}^{\pm} = \sqrt{\alpha_x}(x_{i,t}^{\pm} - \mu),$$

then,

$$y_t^{\pm} = \frac{1}{\sqrt{\alpha_x}} \left[(\alpha_{\mu} + \alpha_x)\, p_{t-1} - \alpha_{\mu}\overline{\mu} \pm \frac{\beta\sqrt{\alpha_{\mu} + \alpha_x}}{\sigma_{t-1}}(p_{t-1} - v_t) \right] \qquad (16.24)$$

By denoting

$$y_t^m = \sqrt{\alpha_x}(x_t^m - \mu), \quad y_t^M = \sqrt{\alpha_x}(x_t^M - \mu)$$

the standard normal probability density and cumulative probability functions are then denoted, respectively, as

$$\phi(x) = \frac{1}{\sqrt{2\pi}}\, e^{-x^2/2} \quad, \Phi(x) = \int_{-\infty}^{x} \phi(y)dy \qquad (16.25)$$

and the momentum trade falls into the interval (y_t^m, y_t^M).

The distribution of possible returns is hence one bounded within a normal distribution around the relationship between the expected future price and expected future value.

Clearly, when the price is sufficiently far away from the level of value that the fundamental investor perceives the asset to possess based upon his private information, he enters the market as a fundamental investor to buy/sell the stock in the manner of a contrarian. It is, however, unlikely that, absent an information shock, this is the role that a marginal investor would undertake unless his information was significantly at odds with the current market equilibrium.

Indeed, intuition would suggest that when the agent's private signal is close to the mean fundamental value, both the expected return, $E_t(R_{\tau-t})$ and the unexpected return, ε_t are likely to be small. Similarly, if $p_{t-1} = v_t$ all agents would follow a fundamental strategy as there would be no demand for the momentum strategy. In these circumstances, private information is less valuable than when the signal is at a distance from the mean. The short-term investor may simply choose to act as a momentum investor, so long as the expected return β implied by the measure of value is either relatively attractive and/or the level of implied volatility σ^2_{t-1} is low. The Sharpe ratio of the momentum opportunity needs to be attractive enough to encourage the fundamental investor to enter the position; otherwise, there may be no incentive for any marginal investor – short- or long-term – to enter the market.

Nevertheless, because an agent can enter the market and act upon both public information I_{t-1} and his private information $x_{i,t} = \mu + \varepsilon_{i,t}$ at any time t, it is highly likely to be the private information that leads to the marginal entry in the absence of a public information shock. By contrast, when the divergence in terms of perceived fundamental value is small and there is less noise in the private information, even though the fundamental information is more accurate, its lack of value to the fundamental trader may lead to an increase in popularity of the momentum strategy. However, if the information does not cause the Sharpe ratio of the position to improve, it will ultimately lead to an increase in instability and volatility and a potential loss to the investor.

16.9 THE IMPACT OF THE SHORT-TERM INVESTOR

By definition, the arrival of the marginal fundamental investor means that the shorter-term momentum trader risks losing money. For any existing trade that currently runs counter to the marginal investor's preferences, but benefits from the arrival of the marginal investor, the risk arises when the marginal news flow is consistent with an existing position. This is the momentum trader as bystander. There may also be instances where the entry of the marginal investor is independent of information directly related to the underlying measure of value. This can be a function of changing sentiment towards a stock or news flow relating to potential cheap or expensive opinion expressed by third parties or be news flow relating to corporate actions. An announcement of a share buyback programme, announcement/payment of a special dividend or the announced listing of a stock in an index/ETF for the first time would be examples of this but these can be considered to act with a sufficiently high pace of convergence to not make the case for inclusion under any preference scenario.

The private information that is relevant to the momentum trader is the information that changes the market equilibrium price of the stock by changing the perceived value of $F_S(t)$ with respect to $P(t)$ in the mind of the fundamental investor to a sufficient degree that a move into a fundamental trade takes place. The fact that the directional move of the fundamental trader can be either for or against his interests means that if the same information were available to the momentum trader in the form of a signal that the price had reached the boundary of the interval (y_t^m, y_t^M), then the momentum trader's risk of loss could be guarded against. Equally, for the momentum trader to know the degree to which the Sharpe ratio of the expected return is consistent with his existing position would help to ensure that a potential reversal trade was mitigated.

In this sense, the marginal fundamental investor is not 'switching' to be a momentum trader with no independent private information – it is simply the case that private information leads to a (different) level of fundamental value. In the situation where he sees his 'contrarian' trade as aligned with that of the momentum trader, this is because his level of value $F_S(t)$ is at a premium to $P(t)$ whilst that of the momentum trader is currently at a discount. It is also likely to be the case that if periodic news flow reinforces an existing trend, a confirmation of the trend is sufficient to see the price move towards the boundary of the range (y_t^m, y_t^M).

The arrival of the short-term investor, in the form of a contrarian, is a price point at which an existing momentum investor reaches an inflection point in terms of his risk of loss. However, it also marks the point at which the reversal in that trade may pave the way for a new momentum trade to take place in the reverse direction. The early momentum phase under the momentum cycle framework of Lee and Swaminathan (2000) can be considered to be a result of the reversal of a prior directional trade resulting from a change in the perceived value of the fundamental investor. For a momentum trader, the direction of the price move is not a condition of the trade's ability to deliver a return. In fact, it is the move in the price (and more importantly the strength of the resulting price trend that evolves from it) that encourages the establishment of a new momentum trade in the first place.

16.9.1 Short-term versus long-term

The naive assumption that the marginal investor makes is that, in an equilibrium market, both the long-term investor and the short-term investor have a view of fundamental value that is not inconsistent with the current price and implied expected return and therefore with the short-term investor himself. Under this approach, all agents (including momentum traders) exist in equilibrium, so long as the (long-term) expected return assumption – implicit or explicit – of each agent is similar. Agents may have different views about price variance based on either realised or implied volatility and depending on their risk appetite but provided that their implied Sharpe ratios are stable, then price action becomes largely a function of alpha not beta risk and individual agents act according to non-fundamental factors.

This is rationalised by the fact that the contrarian investor does not act to address any mispricing when the market is in equilibrium and will only do so when he identifies that a mispricing is significant. This will tend to take the form of an ex post response to cash-flow news if, as a result, the undershoot / overshoot of the price is sufficient to leave a persistent mispricing relative to a revised view of long-term fundamental value $F_s(t)$. In fact, in an informationally efficient market, the likelihood of the contrarian being the only agent to take advantage of any mispricing is small. All three agents will hold a similar long-term fundamental value in mind, so the bounded rationality of the approach suggests that an equilibrium is restored within a relatively discrete period of time.

For short-term agents, their view of expected returns is largely driven by the investment horizon over which cash-flow news in likely to impact the expectations of their peers in relation to expected returns. Their own time horizons and those of their short-term peers are dominated by relatively near-term information – typically fundamental cash flow expectations out to two years – whereby both absolute and inter-temporal information shocks can change the perceived view of both short-term risk and longer-term value. This is likely to be dominated by corporate reported results and significant external news information.

Both the short and the long-term investor operate on the basis that this shorter-term information is part of – but not all of – the longer-term investor's information set in terms of the formation of their expectation of fundamental value $F_l(t)$. They pay attention to the data out to two years but will only integrate any significant cash-flow news into their expectations of longer-term fundamental value if that information changes their view of where long-term fundamental value lies. However, even if the mispricing in the short term is only expected to be small, the long-term fundamental strategy may, nonetheless yield a lower utility than the short-term momentum strategy such that long-term investors are also motivated to follow into the momentum strategy.

From an expected return standpoint, the standard return equation takes the expanded form described by Elton (1999)

$$R_t = E(R_{t-1}) + I_t + \varepsilon_t \tag{16.26}$$

where I_t is a significant information event related to cash flow news. If I_t is mostly zero but occasionally large, then it takes the form of a jump model. However, under a continuous time model, if I_t is incorporated as news in the individual agent's model of fundamental value and expected return, then the individual agent will combine this with the public information of price history available in order to determine an updated model of expected return for the asset and an updated measure of risk.

16.10   THE MOMENTUM RISK PREMIUM

Under this framework, the appearance of momentum and the emergence of the momentum risk premium occurs when, as a result of a cash-flow news related information event, the future expected returns of the short-term and the long-term investor diverge to a sufficient degree that the existing price equilibrium is lost. The bifurcation event that occurs leads short term investors to believe that, because their view of fundamental value $F_s(t)$ is now changed, that the long-term investor view of fundamental value $F_l(t)$ is going to be similarly updated. They are, in effect anticipating that a model of fundamental value based upon a shorter-term time series will feed through to a longer-term model that leads to a permanent change in the longer-term expected returns of the longer-term investor. In the early stage of this cycle, price action is not directionally constrained, and the implied change in future fundamental value does not need to be explicitly quantified. The price action can be either in accordance with – or contrary to – the current trend in expected returns and in the latter case, is likely to be accompanied by an increase in short-term volatility.

Thus, a significant cash-flow event may lead to either a price correction or a period of price momentum. In order to evaluate whether the impact is liable to be the former or the latter, a view of the past/current trend in both longer-term and shorter-term expected returns and implied future cash flows is required, along with a measure of the degree to which the post-event price has diverged from the current trend. A stochastic model of the price formation process is required for the next stage of the process. Given this, an estimation of the impact that the news event might have on longer-term fundamental value and the future implied cost of capital will allow the potential duration and extent of the potential excess return to be determined. The final stage of the process is to identify when the equilibrium is restored – i.e. when the short-term and longer-term forecasts of implied future cash flows realign.

The resulting signal can be used in two distinct ways – at the individual stock level and at the portfolio construction and risk management level. The information set of the marginal short-term investor is an information signal for the momentum trader as bystander, or the stock position manager in an active portfolio environment. The risk appetite of the marginal investor towards any stock has a direct impact on the existing owner. At a portfolio level, most investors include momentum strategies as part of their investment process. Position risk management of these strategies benefit from the systematic nature of the signal provided since both the absolute and relative momentum conditions of all portfolio members can be quantified at any point in time. Using the momentum signal as a basis for portfolio construction is also of value. If a portfolio manager uses Sharpe ratios for portfolio construction purposes; either for ranking or diversification, then a measure of the stability of those Sharpe ratios is clearly a valuable risk-management tool. For overall management of portfolio risk exposure to style, volatility, turnover and skew, the momentum risk premium signal adds value in the form of quantifying the individual stock level impact on all these measures.

16.10.1   Required – a forecast of time-series expected returns

The dataset required to evaluate this model is as follows.

1. A continuous time series of fundamentally determined expected returns and the associate risk profile of those expected returns for both the short-term and the longer-term investor.
2. Implied Sharpe ratios in the form of continuous time series
3. A model of implied future cash-flows driving the expected return model that allows for the discrete modeling of the impact of differential time frames of risk and expected return.
4. A normalised measurement of the covariance of the two expected return series, such that both a significance signal and a bifurcation signal can be extracted in a continuous time series format.
5. A normalised time series of the trend in expected returns.

The clear issue here is the need for a credible, continuous time series of stock-level expected returns. The wide variability of expected returns over time and the role they play in stock price movements – a point made by Cochrane (2011) in his seminal

Presidential address to the American Finance Association – is well recognised. However, using realised returns as a proxy for expected returns is inconsistent with the forward-looking framework of changing expected returns that is required. If realised returns are used as a basis for such forecast expected returns, the fact that individual stock prices are subject to large, unpredictable information shocks to either cash flow or investor sentiment means that the variance in measurement errors will also be large, limiting their attractiveness as proxies for expected returns.

Several theoretical and empirical present value-based models do exist, where the equity price is expressed as the expected sum of its future cash flows discounted at an appropriate rate. Since both expected returns and implied discount rates are unobservable independent variables in any pricing model, they need to be estimated in proxy form from the models. Lee et al. (2019) develop an empirical framework for evaluating the relative performance of five classes of expected return proxies (ERPs) from the literature. Unlike the earlier work of Easton and Monahan (2005), their process allows for the evaluation of both cross-sectional and time-series variance in returns. Their analysis confirms the relatively poor performance of 'factor based' ERPs derived from CAPM and the Fama-French Four factor model, that are dependent upon slope regressions from (monthly) realised returns and factor premiums estimated from time-series averages. By contrast, the non-factor-based classes of implied cost of capital (ICC), characteristic-based expected return (CER) and a fitted implied cost of capital model (FICC) using the ICCs instead of returns as the dependent variable are significantly more robust.

Lee et al. (2019) identify that in a time series analysis, the factor based models have between three and five times the standard deviation of the non-factor-based proxies. For time series analysis, the fitted ICC model performs the best, lending support for the argument in favour of characteristic based, fitting methodologies designed for removing noise from their underlying measures.

16.11   THE APOLLO ASSET PRICING MODEL

The stochastic pricing model used here is the Apollo Asset pricing model, written by the author and produced commercially by Libra Investment Services (2010) Ltd. The model conforms to the definitional classes of both a CER and a FICC model described by Lee et al. (2019). As well as determining time-varying forecasts of fundamental value, it provides both forecasts of expected returns and measures of implied volatility over a range of forecast horizons. Covering 7,000 global stocks on a continuous basis since its inception in 2004, its present-value-based approach uses a multi-factor vector of forward looking fundamental expectations, from which an implied forecast of future cash flows is derived using a maximum likelihood estimation approach. This is then used to generate a time series of expected returns using Fama-MacBeth regressions, in a method that is broadly similar to the characteristic based approach of Lewellen (2015). The implied cost of capital derived from the Apollo process is constructed by making the ICC the dependent variable. This 'fitted ICC' result enables explicit proxies of the two unobservable components of the standard asset pricing model to be generated as time series at the single asset level.

The model can be formally described as a continuous ARMA/GARCH-J model in that it is a continuous model that treats stock returns as auto-regressive processes with non-constant volatility and adjusts for price jumps.

As a first step, the Apollo model uses a set of market generated forecast cash flow measures (Earnings, Cash Flow, Book Value, Sales and EBITDA) for each firm in the system (sourced from the FactSet estimates database on a continuous basis since 2004) and at each moment in time and uses a maximum likelihood estimation technique (MLE) to generate a robust, generalized, proxy measure of future cash-flows, updated on a daily basis (Apollo FV). The use of multiple factors not only helps to reduce forecast errors but allows the use of the implied factor parameters to demonstrate the time varying relative importance of the factors driving the forecast. This provides an important insight into the changing nature of individual firm characteristics in the eyes of investors.

When Apollo FV is coupled with prices, it then allows for the implied cost of capital (ICC) to be backed out. The implied market discount rate that the market applies that future cash flow (expected return) is then able to be derived from the regression. The price is now the start point and the analytical focus of Apollo is the sources of price variation which can be derived from the time series analysis of the independent variables (the Apollo FV and the expected return). The main source of potential alpha – the unexpected return – is the forecast error of the model. The better the model, the smaller the error term and the more useful the expected return forecast in predicting future actual returns and quantifying firm level risk premia.

The current price is a function of a vector of the cash flow proxy forecasts that represent the investor information set available to investors, and the discount rate applied to those cash-flow forecasts at the current point in time. From this daily data set, a Fama-MacBeth (FM) regression process is run to determine the way this discount rate has varied over time. The slope of the FM regression provides the expected return or discount rate. The systematic nature of this approach means that any stock can be analysed on a time-series basis but that stock level forecasts and indicators can also be aggregated to a portfolio, sector or market level with no loss of signal significance.

16.12 MOMENTUM ALPHA

Even before we calculate the momentum signal itself, the process of determining the implied future value as a continuous time series provides our trader-as-bystander (or the active position holder) with valuable information as to the stock level risk-reward environment. The availability of a measure of future value as a daily time series from the Apollo data base for any stock in the system (for illustrative purposes we have used Pfizer in the accompanying figures) means that we can not only calculate $|p_{t-1} - \mu_t|$ and plot the relationship between the current price and the measure of FV (FV is shown in Figure 16.2 alongside the price), but we can replace the measure of future value μ, with the Apollo Fair value (FV) in Equation (16.24) to calculate the levels of (y_t^m, y_t^M) explicitly and plot the FV range (Figure 16.3).

The range – and the relationship that the current share price has to it – has several useful properties that can be exploited for the purposes of risk management and signal generation. As outlined earlier in the behavioural analysis, the range (y_t^m, y_t^M)

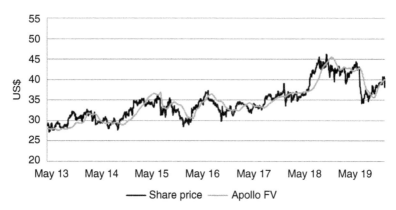

FIGURE 16.2   Apollo FV for Pfizer. Source Libra Investment Services (2010) Ltd.

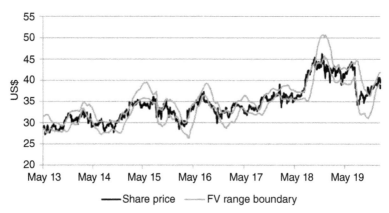

FIGURE 16.3   Apollo FV range for Pfizer. Source Libra Investment Services (2010) Ltd.

represents the region wherein expectations of fundamental value are relatively closely aligned with the current price and within which momentum traders operate in normal market conditions. Our momentum trader now has a guide to his upside/downside risk reward, independent of the marginal investor's position. This is the 'momentum alpha trading zone' and the potential alpha upside and downside of any existing or potential portfolio position can be evaluated on a potential risk of loss basis. The position of the current share price within that zone can be standardized so that the normal trading range is between 0 and 100% (Figure 16.4) and then the output normalised using a z-score (Figure 16.5).

A bifurcation breakout on either boundary provides a trigger flag that the marginal investor may now be an influence on future returns. This is not in itself a decision signal, as other flags may confirm or contradict the actions of the marginal investor implied by the bifurcation. The close of the bifurcation, however, does provide a signal. In this instance, the movement of the *tanh* of the normalised range % score through zero (change of sign) points to an ending of the breakout phase.

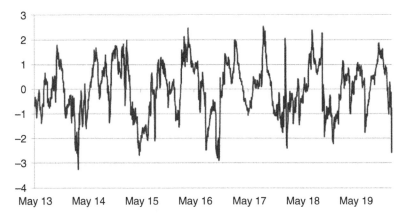

FIGURE 16.4 Apollo FV range % score for Pfizer. Source Libra Investment Services (2010) Ltd.

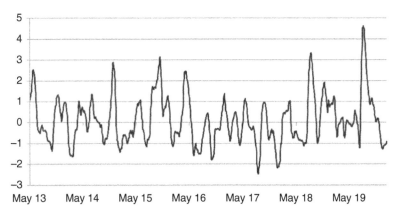

FIGURE 16.5 Apollo FV range width (normalised) for Pfizer. Source Libra Investment Services (2010) Ltd.

Two other properties relating to the FV range are of value to the trader. The first is the width of the range as a measure of volatility and, in particular the time series of the range width in a normalised form. Any significant change in implied volatility from this series in the form of a threshold breach (setting the threshold to a 95th percentile score in terms of the normalised distribution for instance) will provide risk position flags and signals on a daily basis for position monitoring purposes. Sharp spikes in short-term volatility are a clear risk to momentum investors regardless of trend direction and can be modeled as flags, whilst a persistent narrowing (widening) in short-term volatility is a signal of an increase (decrease) in trend strength.

The final property is the trend of the FV range itself (Figure 16.6), measured as the rolling regression (slope) of the midline of the FV Range. On a risk-reward basis, the stronger the initial trend, the more likely the momentum trade is to be taken up. Conversely, as the trend weakens, the potential downside increases for any level of $P(t)$. This

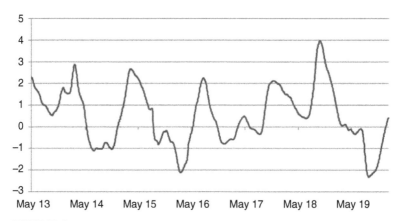

FIGURE 16.6 Apollo FV range trend (normalised) for Pfizer. Source Libra Investment Services (2010) Ltd.

is true for both long and short positions. In a forward-looking risk reward environment, the direction and strength of the initial trend are important flags as to the likely position and scale of existing momentum traders.

A normalised measure of the trend and a *tanh* bifurcation signal provide the flag and signal relating to the implied strength of short-term expected returns.

The degree of correlation between these signals can be significant – a drop in volatility combined with a strengthening trend and a positive (>50%) range position within a trend are all likely to occur at the same time. Consequently, investors or traders exposed to short-term momentum alpha can use the range of signals and flags for timely position management.

One of the underlying assumptions of the model is that with a forecast horizon of a rolling 24-month window, the measure of expected cash flow will reflect a relatively steady state growth rate. This, in turn means that whilst there is undoubtedly an impact on total expected returns from cash flow news, it will be far more likely to impact upon unexpected returns and may also be inter-temporal in nature – that is to say, the timing of expected cash flows may vary over the forecast horizon – a delay in expected revenues from one period to another for example. The impact in relation to expected returns from regular cash flow news is liable to be more muted. To the extent that news flow may increase/decrease investor confidence over the short term, this may be considered a discount rate effect as opposed to a cash flow effect.

However, when cash flow news does change investor perceptions of fundamental value, the price response can be significant and the implied level of expected returns will rise (fall), even as unexpected returns fall (rise) in response to price action.

So long as any changes in cash flow growth assumptions are slow moving, it is not unreasonable to treat the outlook for expected returns over short-term and longer-term return horizons as constant. However, at more extended investment horizons, the importance of cash flow news becomes more significant. A slower but more persistent view of fundamental value can be developed to better describe the fundamental value likely to be held by the longer-term fundamental investor.

In order to achieve this, we run predictive regressions to extend the separate cash-flow measure forecasts out to 60 months. We employ the same multi-factor regression technique to generate a longer-term measure of future cash flow, which reduces the short-term noise in the forecasts, but captures potential longer-term growth impacts from cash flow news. This measure - Apollo Intrinsic Value is generated as a daily time series in parallel with the Apollo FV. By using the regression slopes of these two time series, we can compare the implied expected returns of the two investor groups. By modeling the change in relative risk over both time frames, we can generate a signal that captures the behavioural processes described above.

16.13   BETA MOMENTUM

Once again we take the HAM model approach of He and Li (2015) outlined at Equations (16.14) to (16.25) as a basis and make the assumption of an otherwise largely efficient pricing and information market that generates time varying expected return forecasts consistent with the Apollo asset pricing model.

Start with the standard return equation

$$R_t = E_{t-1}(R_t) + \varepsilon_t,$$

where R_t is the return in period t, $E_{t-1}(R_t)$ is expected return at t conditional on the information set available at $t-1$ and ε_t is unexpected return.

The Apollo signal focuses on the momentum implied by the change in expected return. At this point, momentum of unexpected returns is assumed to take the form of a stationary Brownian time series with mean zero and captured by the Apollo FV range. Its conditions can be observed using the price efficiency measure which can be used as a complementary signal for short-term trading purposes.

For any given time period, we can use the regression slopes of the Apollo FV and Apollo Intrinsic value in the formula above to generate an estimate of R_t. However, in terms of identifying a measure of momentum, we use the two regression slopes as separate inputs into a covariance calculation. This allows us to model the impact of cash flow news within the uncertainty of the forecast horizon, under the conditions where two separate agents take the inputs with different risk functions to their forecasts of fundamental value and expected returns.

In effect we model news flow risk, as both the target price implied by the anticipated future cash flows and the investor's level of private sentiment towards that target price (i.e. the willingness to change the implied cost of capital demanded as compensation for that future cash flow) are impacted by the news.

Under our framework – news flow risk over the time from t-1 to t will evolve according to

$$d\mu_t = r\mu_t dt + \sigma_\mu \mu_t \, dB_t^\mu, \tag{16.27}$$

where μ_t is the implied value at time, t, r is the risk-free rate, B_t^μ is a Brownian motion, risk neutral martingale process where $E_t[B_t^\mu] = 0$, and $\sigma_\mu > 0$ reflects the anticipated volatility of μ_t.

News risk consists of shocks that lead to the potential revision of the future value of the expected value of the price at time t. For the purposes of the determination of momentum, we treat there as being two, distinct measures of μ existing in a heterogeneous agent model of the market – the short-term measure, $F_s(t)$ which we now call Fair value (FV) and the long-term measure $F_l(t)$ which we refer to as Intrinsic value (IV).

The news flow information set is identical for each measure of value, but we assume that the agents integrate the information differently such that the Brownian motions are not identical and that

$$E_t[dB_t^{FV} dB_t^{IV}] = \rho dt \tag{16.28}$$

where $\rho \in [-1, 1]$ and is the correlation between the two martingales.

We also want to measure this in terms of differential expected returns as opposed to a target price over a specific time period. Because the expected return for the long-term investor is equal to the slope of the intrinsic value line and the short-term investor's expected return is equal to the slope of the Fair Value line the risk parameter, κ takes the form

$$\kappa = (\sigma_{FVs}^2 - 2\rho\sigma_{FVs}\sigma_{IVs} + \sigma_{IVs}^2) \tag{16.29}$$

where σ_{FVs} and σ_{IVs} are the implied volatilities of the slopes of the FV regression line and the intrinsic value regression line, respectively. By analysing the combination of period-dependent expected returns and their associated implied volatilities in this way, we create a stability measure of the relationship between the Sharpe ratios of the two investor groups with respect to the same asset. Note that the levels of the two Sharpe ratios are not explicitly calculated as part of the process – it is enough to use their relative variance and covariances of the expected returns in order to generate the signal.

Because of the stock level, time-series nature of the process, the duration of the signal is not fixed in the calculation and it is somewhat dependent upon the initial state of the FV range (alpha) trend with respect to the news flow. This initial state is, in itself an important determinant of where the stock exists on the momentum cycle of Lee and Swaminathan (2000). An early stage momentum signal in the form of a trend reversal has a higher degree of risk than a late stage signal, which is supportive of an existing trend. Additionally, a weak existing trend may leave sufficient uncertainty in the mind of the investor that what might at first appear to be a beta momentum signal quickly reverts to being an alpha signal; leaving the position at risk of moving to the lower (upper) range boundary and into an unprofitable position. As a result, early stage momentum signals tend to be of longer duration on average but tend to display a higher degree of kurtosis on a cross-sectional analysis than later stage momentum signals where existing trends are likely to be reinforced. This is discussed in more detail in the results section.

16.14 BETA SIGNAL

Once the time series κ is generated, a rolling, normalised score is calculated, in a manner similar to that described for the alpha signals.

$$z = \frac{\kappa - \overline{\kappa}}{\sigma_\kappa} \tag{16.30}$$

In order to generate the Beta momentum signal, the threshold level for a significance signal is set at the equivalent of the 95th percentile of the normalised distribution of the measure Z. On a break of the significance level (equivalent to a Z score of 1.645), the relationship between the implied Sharpes of the short-term investor and the long-term investor is no longer stable, and the marginal investor is likely to enter the market in the direction implied by the news flow. Note that this signal does not discriminate as to what the current trend status or strength is, although the absolute level of the signal is likely to be consistent with direction (above +1.645 buy, below -1.645 sell).

The measure of the existing trend is a simple filter that can be applied to the process by creating an additional signal of a normalised measure of the FV trend G_{FV}, itself in a manner similar to the FV range trend outlined earlier.

$$G_{FV} = \frac{FV_s - \overline{FV}_s}{\sigma_{FV_s}} \tag{16.31}$$

In order to calculate the potential inflection points and momentum flags, a robust, fixed score normalisation of G_{FV} in the form of a *tanh* estimator is employed.

$$\widehat{S_G} = 0.5[tanh[G_{FV}]] + 1. \tag{16.32}$$

This is the classic calculation introduced by Hampel where a switch point is set at 0.5. For the purpose of generating a Boolean (1,0) signal as a pass-through, the calculation is simplified to:

$$\widehat{S_G} = tanh[G_{FV}] \tag{16.33}$$

The close long signal and the close short signal are triggered by the tanh measure going through zero from a negative or positive value under the terms identified in the calculation specifications given earlier. Given the high degree of robustness that tanh signals possess, the expectation that a close short signal will be followed shortly by a positive momentum flag and vice versa is high.

We now have a range of short-term alpha signals and implied Sharpe ratio related beta signals for a momentum risk premium measure or momentum strategy.

16.15 MOMENTUM STRATEGIES

We have moved a long way from simply treating momentum as a function of price. The ability to select stocks based upon a momentum signal creates a portfolio of assets that, in an ARP world, has a discrete set of risk characteristics. It is this ability of a momentum strategy to actively contribute to overall portfolio construction and risk management that is central to the evolution of the ARP approach. Fung and Hsieh (2001) established a framework suggesting that trend-following strategies have nonlinear, option like structures, similar to a look-back straddle option with a convex payoff. The convexity of the payoff was confirmed by Potters and Bouchaud (2006) whose analysis of the probability distribution of trend followers concluded that the fraction of winning trades (hit rate) was highest when asset volatility was low; decreasing rapidly as volatility increases. Given that the hit rate in low volatility periods was 50%, their conclusion was that trend followers lost more often than they gained but that the average gain was higher than the average loss.

Whilst not explicitly momentum based, in their paper on dynamic investment strategies, Bruder and Gausell (2011) developed an option-like framework, which decomposes the return of a strategy into an option profile – the intrinsic value of the option – and a trading impact; equivalent to its time value. The continuous-time, trend following model they developed confirmed the prior model conclusions of Fung and Hsieh (2001) and Potters and Bouchaud (2006): a convex option profile, positive skewness, a sub 50% hit rate with an average gain larger than the average loss.

Dao et al. (2016) extend the relationship to the term structure of realised volatility and showed that 'the performance of the trend is positive when the long term volatility is larger than the short term volatility'. The conclusion they draw – the need for trend followers to manage short-term volatility in order to maintain the required positive skewness and convexity corresponds to the reality of the modern ARP approach. As Roncalli (2017) notes, 'the main motivation of momentum investing is diversification, not performance. The convexity of trend-following strategies mitigates the risk of diversified portfolios in bad times'. This allows the non-linear nature of risk to be managed by using a momentum portfolio alongside a carry or value strategy to perform the role of risk management of skewness of risk.

Burgues et al. (2017) explore the role that trend following may contribute to diversification in ARP and differentiate between pay-out diversification and correlation diversification. They conclude that momentum helps to mitigate risk in bad times but that the pay out is very different from a diversification exposure to bonds. The argument is therefore that understanding the momentum risk-return trade off on a standalone basis is less important than analysing the momentum risk premium in the context of the construction of an alternative risk premia portfolio. In this regard, momentum investing is a time-varying beta strategy and with the need for beta strategy diversification only in bad times, the convex nature of the momentum portfolio may fit well into an overall ARP strategy.

In order to evaluate our momentum signal's potential contribution to this process, we need to move on from a simple returns-based back-test of the signal and establish a framework within which our signal can be placed. In their detailed study of the momentum risk premium, Jusselin et al. (2017) seek to explore the nature of how a portfolio of momentum stocks might behave in an ARP environment. Extending the single asset case (Bruder and Gaussel, 2011) they model and calculate the P&L of a trend-following strategy composed of two terms; an option profile and a trading impact. They assume the trend is time varying and unobservable and adopt the principle that the trend is an exponential weighted moving average (EWMA). We follow a similar framework to theirs and use it to examine our own trend process.

Assume the asset price S_t follows a geometric Brownian motion with constant volatility but with a time-varying trend:

$$dS_t = \mu_t S_t + \sigma_t S_t dW_t$$
$$dy_t = \gamma dW_t^\star \tag{16.34}$$

where μ_t is the unobservable trend and that the exposure of the strategy is proportional to the estimated trend of the asset.

Under the assumption that the best returns estimation between times t and $t + dt$ is $\hat{\mu}dt$, Bruder and Gaussel (2011) apply the optimal Merton strategy and the exposure to the risky asset can be defined as

$$e_t = m\frac{\hat{\mu}_t}{\sigma^2} \tag{16.35}$$

where σ is the annualised volatility of the underlying risk asset and m is a risk tolerance parameter.

This can be rewritten as

$$e_t = \alpha\hat{\mu}_t$$

where the optimal Markovitz allocation, $\alpha = \frac{m}{\sigma^2}$

Next, defining $dy_t = dS_t/S_t$ to obtain

$$dy_t = \mu_t dt + \sigma\, dW_t \tag{16.36}$$

Bruder and Gaussel (2011) show that the dynamics of the investor's P&L are:

$$\frac{dV_t}{V_t} = e_t\frac{dS_t}{S_t} = \alpha\mu_t dy_t \tag{16.37}$$

and then apply Ito's lemma to the process in continuous time in order to determine the following two term construction:

$$ln\frac{V_T}{V_0} = \frac{\alpha}{2\lambda}(\hat{\mu}_T^2 - \hat{\mu}_0^2) + \alpha\sigma^2 \int_0^T \left(\frac{\hat{\mu}_t^2}{\sigma^2}\left(1 - \frac{\alpha\sigma^2}{2}\right) - \frac{\lambda}{2} \right) dt \tag{16.38}$$

The return of the trend following strategy is therefore composed of the two terms:

$$ln\frac{V_T}{V_0} = G_{0,T} + \int_0^T g_t dt \tag{16.39}$$

where the short-run component (the option profile) is:

$$G_{O,T} = \frac{\alpha}{2\lambda}(\hat{\mu}_T^2 - \hat{\mu}_0^2) \tag{16.40}$$

and the long-run component (the trading impact) is:

$$g_t = \alpha\sigma^2 \left(\frac{\hat{\mu}_t^2}{\sigma^2}\left(1 - \frac{\alpha\sigma^2}{2}\right) - \frac{\lambda}{2} \right). \tag{16.41}$$

The option profile corresponds to the trend directional signal, G_{FV}, whilst the trading impact signal directly relates to the momentum signal, Z.

Jusselin et al. (2017) identify that the frequency parameter that they take from the Kalman filtering equation in terms of:

$$d\widehat{\mu}_t = \lambda dy_t - \widehat{\mu}_t dt \tag{16.42}$$

means that

$$dy_t = \frac{1}{\lambda} d\widehat{\mu}_t + \widehat{\mu}_t dt \tag{16.43}$$

They go on to show that the average duration of the EWMA estimator, τ as equal to the inverse of the frequency parameter,

$$\lambda = \frac{1}{\tau} \tag{16.44}$$

For example, if the duration of the estimator is three months, then λ would be equal to four. Jusselin et al. (2017) find an optimal value for λ equal to 2.3, meaning that the optimal average duration is close to five months.

This is important in two ways. The EMEA estimator, τ, is equal to the ratio of the asset volatility and the trend volatility.

$$\tau = \frac{\sigma}{\gamma} \tag{16.45}$$

A high value of τ is indicative of a situation where the volatility of the asset dominates the volatility of the trend. Thus, a longer-term trend would be appropriate. This confirms the views of Dao et al. (2016) that 'the performance of the strategy is positive when the long term volatility is larger than the shorter term volatility'. Given that short-term strategies exhibit less convexity than longer-term ones, trend followers need to be convinced that not only do significant price trends need to exist but that they need to be significant in relation to volatility.

16.15.1   The option model

The option profile is related to the square of the observed trend and vanishes quickly along with the measured trend. A worst case scenario would then be that the measured trend falls to zero leading to an upper limit of $\frac{\alpha}{2\lambda} \widehat{\mu}_0^2$

However, if the initial measured trend is assumed to be $\widehat{\mu}_0 = 0$ then the option profile is always positive.

16.15.2   The trading impact

Unlike the option model, the trading impact is cumulative and its P&L impact is dependent upon $\frac{\widehat{\mu}_t^2}{\sigma^2}$ - which is equivalent to the square of the measured Sharpe ratio. Jusselin et al. (2017) estimate the hit ratio for a range of Sharpe ratios and moving average durations. Their analysis shows that when the Sharpe ratio is below 0.35, the hit ratio of the trend-following strategy is below 50%. The expected gain is an increasing concave function of the absolute value of the Sharpe ratio such that the effect of a rising Sharpe ratio is amplified by the trend-following strategy.

16.15.3   A forward-looking framework

Under the options-based framework, the role of the realised Sharpe ratio is important as a relative measure of the strength of the trend. However, given the lack of any insight into future, implied volatility may be a limitation for a momentum strategy – even where the expected return is high. Jusselin et al. (2017) find that a stock with a strong trend and high volatility is not necessarily as attractive as a stock with a medium trend and very low volatility. The momentum risk premium is a trade-off between trend and volatility but its use at a portfolio level varies in terms of the portfolio construction. Jussselin et al. (2017) argue that a time-series momentum portfolio prefers independent as opposed to positively or negatively correlated assets and would ideally hold a small number of high Sharpe ratio assets. A cross-sectional momentum portfolio, by contrast, is more sensitive to the dispersion of Sharpe ratios, and seeks highly correlated assets. For a time-series portfolio, weight diversification reduces the gains to the portfolio, whilst the cross-sectional portfolio benefits from weightings.

Ultimately, though, this options-based academic framework is theoretical. Asset prices do not follow simple, predictable geometric Brownian motions – they are discontinuous and incorporate jumps. Trend estimation needs to be undertaken at the asset level. The assumption that the measured Sharpe ratio can not only provide a measure of relative trend strength but also provide a scalar for the expected P&L of the trading impact component of the momentum strategy is also problematic in practice, as past returns have long been identified as a relatively poor estimator of future returns.

16.15.4   Implied Sharpe ratios

We introduce an implied Sharpe ratio based upon forecast expected returns from asset level cash flow forecasts. A measure of implied volatility is required in a practical environment. It is also desirable to maintain the ability to manage short-term volatility in order to preserve the convex nature of the momentum strategy. Given that the estimator of the trend used in the options framework is the ratio of the trend volatility to the asset volatility, an explicit estimate of both short-term and long-term implied volatility can be used to identify both an ex-ante and a real time trend persistence estimator for risk managing a momentum strategy.

16.15.5   Construction

Utilising the Apollo dataset, we adopt the two-component forward-looking framework implied by the options model of Bruder and Gaussel (2011). However, instead of leaving the trend as unobservable and estimated via an EWMA, we determine the trend directly from the signals generated by the model. We also employ the forward-looking measures of asset level implied volatility and implied expected returns derived from the Apollo asset pricing model to determine the actual value of the implied Sharpe ratio over different investment horizons. Under the option framework of Jusselin et al. (2017), the two key elements required are the realised volatility and the realised Sharpe ratio. Since a trend-following strategy has a negative vega, (the amount that an option contract's price changes in response to the change in the implied volatility of the underlying asset) the momentum risk premium is negatively related to volatility. As Dao et al. (2016) observe, the performance of trend-following momentum strategies are a direct result of the difference between realised short-term and long-term volatilities.

In a mostly efficient market, share prices will tend to move in line with expected returns; assuming those expected returns are credible. This is the core asset pricing model formula of present value. However, because time-series forecasts of both expected return and implied volatility are explicitly generated in the forecast process, we observe that the variance in longer-term implied volatility has a significantly longer cycle than that of the expected return. This variance in expected return is, in effect, the main driver of the momentum signal. For the purposes of both generating and analysing the momentum signal itself, we can use the observed trend and volatility of expected returns explicitly.

Under the Bruder and Gaussel (2011) framework, the 'option' profile is related to the square of the observed trend and vanishes quickly along with the measured trend. Under our adapted approach, the trigger signal to enter a momentum trade takes the form of a gamma signal of the forecast expected return, G_{FV}. If the observed trend is positive (negative), then a significant positive (negative) cash-flow news event sufficient to change the gamma of the expected return will generate both a positive (negative) option and a positive (negative) trading impact. The entry signal is therefore a significance indicator of the change in forecast expected returns sufficient to see a shift in the existing steady state equilibrium of price formation with respect to expected returns.

A simple reversal of the price back to the underlying observed trend is likely to be the natural consequence of an end phase of the momentum trade. Whilst the duration of the signal is not fixed, the typical duration of such a phase should be in line with the observed theoretical EMEA from the option pricing models. This would appear to be the case as our analysis shows that the average holding period of a late momentum signal is 131 calendar days, 4 ½ months.

However, the situation will clearly occur whereby a positive (negative) cash-flow news signal will occur that is contrary to the current observed trend. Under these circumstances, the significance of news flow with respect to the trading impact is the focus, not the option. A simple reversal of the price back to the underlying observed trend is likely to be the natural consequence of an end phase of the momentum trade. What we are actively measuring though, is the situation where we do not simply reverse back to the underlying trend – that is more the framework of the trading alpha signal analysis – but the idea that a signal of sufficient momentum impact occurs to allow a new, early momentum phase to take hold. The reversal phase is obviously within this period as, for a new momentum phase to occur the price has to move to a premium to the underlying level of value. Failure to do so would simply mark the move as a simple reversal. The typical duration of an early momentum phase is slightly longer at 141 days according to our test results.

Given that the cumulative impact on the P&L is related to the squared Sharpe ratio, even if the implied change in expected returns is significant, it is the increase in return volatility that is likely to see the trading impact dominate the observed trend, for P&L purposes. In fact, unlike the situation whereby the trading impact is coincident with the observed trend, the amplitude of the trading impact during a reversal means that the payoff is unlikely to be convex.

The signal can be further conditioned based on minimisation of volatility in the form of explicitly modelling the estimator duration using the implied volatilities of both the trend and the asset and optimising on a preferred likely duration. The components of a momentum strategy could then be optimised; ranking the universe of available assets by the implied Sharpe ratio prior to selection. However, these are portfolio construction decisions designed for cross-sectional performance analysis of a strategy. They would not allow the effectiveness of the momentum signal to be analysed in time-series form and so do not feature in the following results.

16.16   RESULTS

Given the behavioural nature of the momentum signal that we are seeking to analyse, the trigger for opening a position is largely exogenous and cash-flow news related, whilst the close signal is endogenous and time dependent with a convex pay-off structure. The current trend in existing returns is a key (stock) component of the signal. When the exogenous news event (flow) occurs, it impacts upon the current trend to either reinforce or run counter to the existing status quo. Therefore, the price response will inevitably vary; depending on the strength, direction and level of the existing trend.

The importance of being able to separate momentum and reversal should not be underestimated. One of the major difficulties with traditional momentum trading strategies is that if the trigger for entry into the position is simply a function of recent price performance, there is no discrimination as to the nature of the price action. For the purposes of the test, we simply categorise a reversal as an early momentum trade. The risk involved in following this approach is that short-term reversals back to underlying trends may not continue into a reversal of the actual trend itself. This leads to a reinstatement of the prior trend and resulting in a loss on the initial position. In these circumstances a close signal under the condition $|p_{t-1} - \mu_t = 0|$ would be better to treat this as a simple reversal trade. However, the decision to implement such a close signal is not one that is made at the initial entry time and argues for the use of the conditional alpha momentum signals at the point that the price has returned to FV. The relevant measures of FV range slope, percentile value and volatility would all impact on the trade decision maker.

The details of how the entry and exit signals are developed is covered in earlier sections and the test process is conducted as follows:

An entry signal is generated when the signal exceeds a preset threshold. At this point, the existing fundamental 'equilibrium' is in potential transition to a new higher/lower state. During this period, a trading impact occurs leading to a variation in delta. The initial impact upon the current expected return trend will be relatively small, with the bulk of any price action taking the form of an unexpected return. However, depending upon the directional impact with respect to the existing trend, this could be either a momentum move or a reversal. The close signal is the Boolean 'cross through zero' of the *tanh* measure of the normalized momentum signal.

Under the option-based framework that we have adopted for the analysis, two separate impact measures combine to give the overall return: the *option impact* which is the 'stock' component and the *trading impact* which is the 'flow' component of the signal. By separating the signal into these two components, we can examine the different outcomes of cash-flow related price action under different 'stock' conditions and differentiate the momentum and reversal phases in continuous time.

The gamma of the option impact is directional with respect to the stock's existing delta (its existing trend of expected returns). This means that when expected returns are trending positively, the option impact of positive cash flow news is reinforcing the existing trend – positive gamma – and the trading impact of the cash flow news is also positive with respect to the positive option. By contrast, when the news flow is directionally opposite to the existing trend (the delta of the stock), then the option impact and the trading impact are conflicting, and we are not in a momentum phase but a (potential) reversal.

The Apollo data set employed for the test contains 7,000 global stocks and provides daily data for from January 2004. The subset used covered the S&P500 universe from January 2004 to October 2019; separated into two daily time series – 2004-2009 (Period 1) and 2010-2019 (Period 2). Similar tests were carried out for the EuroStoxx 600 and the Nikkei 225 with qualitatively similar results.

Every entry signal generated opens a 'trade' at price (S) and time (t), S_t which is recorded at the closing price of S_{t+1}. When a close signal is generated, at $t + n$, the price at $S_{t+(n+1)}$ is used to calculate the annualized log return of the position. A secondary signal, G_{FV} that measures the strength and direction of the current expected return (in the form of a Z score) is used for the categorisation of the current trend. The final results were winsorised in order to manage data outliers that resulted from the annualisation of the log returns.

Four paired signals (entry and exit) were generated at the stock level: Open long early momentum trade (OLEM), Close long early momentum trade(CLEM), Open Long late momentum trade (OLLM); Close long early momentum trade (CLLM).

Open short early momentum trade (OSEM), Close short early momentum trade(CSEM), Open short late momentum trade (OSLM), Close short early momentum trade (CSLM) (see Table 16.1).

TABLE 16.1 Return portfolios

Growth trend	Cash flow news impact direction	Open position	Close position	Option impact	Trading impact	
Positive trend	Positive	OLLM	CLLM	+	+	Pos. momentum ++
Positive trend	Negative	OSEM	CSEM	+	−	Neg. reversal +/−
Negative trend	Positive	OLEM	CLEM	−	+	Pos. reversal −/+
Negative trend	Negative	OSLM	CSLM	−	−	Neg momentum -/-

Four trading strategies are tested across both periods and are recorded as flows to produce 8 different portfolios. For example, we denote 'Early Momentum Long position in period 1' as EML1, and 'Late Momentum short position in period 2' as LMS2, and so on.

The results of the portfolio tests are set out below. The hit rate is defined as a positive annualized log return (to either short or long) to a signal 'trade' greater than zero.

The overall hit rate is specified for the both periods and across all four trading strategies. The overall number of signals is listed for each period.

Note that, because a stock price may be in excess of the open trade threshold at time (t) on more than one stamp date, multiple trades in the same stock may be open at any one point in time. However, because the close signal is Boolean, all existing trades will be closed at the same time.

Performance is calculated as the annualized log return of each trade using FactSet, standard bourse closing prices on $t + 1$ in the manner described above. Average returns and the standard deviation of returns are calculated across each portfolio along with the average duration of the trades (Table 16.2).

In order to examine the principle of convexity and varying duration, each portfolio is broken down into weekly periods and the distributions of returns, hit rates and volatility, re-examined. The results are displayed in Figures 16.7–16.18.

TABLE 16.2 Average portfolio performance results

		EML1	EML2	LML1	LML2	EMS1	EMS2	LMS1	LMS2
Count	('000s)	33	66	69	126	5	8	50	60
Hit Rate	(av)%	56	67	54	63	45	46	50	41
Average return	%	13.7	19.8	13.2	16.6	22.4	20	14.8	19
Volatility of returns	St Dev.	0.49	0.41	0.49	0.42	0.75	0.56	0.59	0.51
Duration	days	151	138	103	134	131	151	130	131

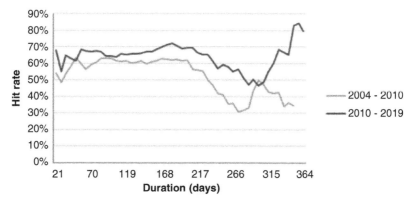

FIGURE 16.7 Hit rates for EM long portfolios.
Source: Libra Investment Services (2010) Ltd.

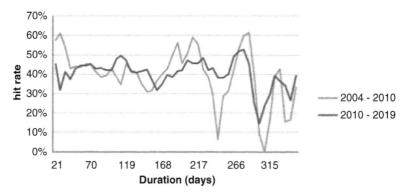

FIGURE 16.8 Hit rates for EM short portfolios.
Source: Libra Investment Services (2010) Ltd.

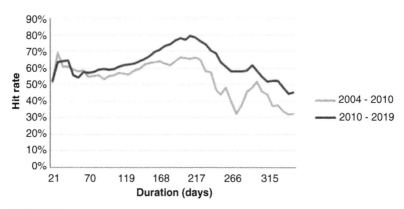

FIGURE 16.9 Hit rates for LM long portfolios.
Source: Libra Investment Services (2010) Ltd.

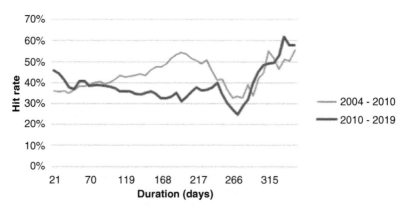

FIGURE 16.10 Hit rates for LM short portfolios.
Source: Libra Investment Services (2010) Ltd.

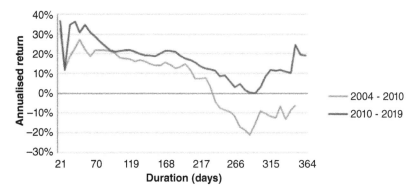

FIGURE 16.11 Returns for EM long portfolios by duration.
Source: Libra Investment Services (2010) Ltd.

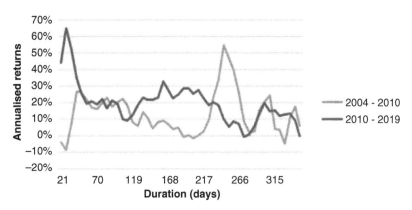

FIGURE 16.12 Returns for EM short portfolios by duration.
Source: Libra Investment Services (2010) Ltd.

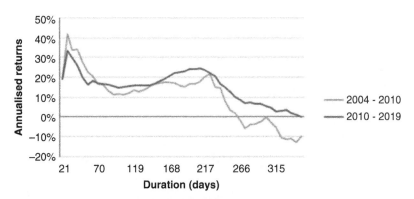

FIGURE 16.13 Returns for LM long portfolios by duration.
Source: Libra Investment Services (2010) Ltd.

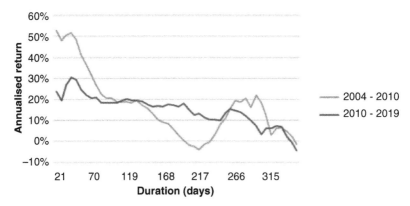

FIGURE 16.14 Returns for LM short portfolios by duration.
Source: Libra Investment Services (2010) Ltd.

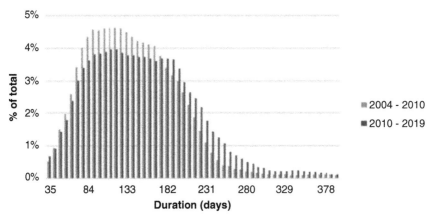

FIGURE 16.15 Duration of EM long portfolios.
Source:: Libra Investment Services (2010) Ltd.

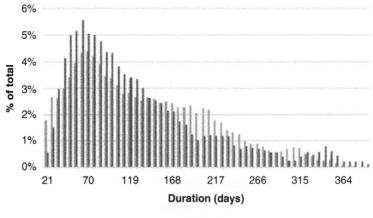

FIGURE 16.16 Duration of EM short portfolios.
Source:: Libra Investment Services (2010) Ltd.

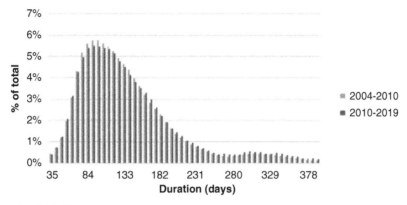

FIGURE 16.17 Duration of LM long portfolios.
Source: Libra Investment Services (2010) Ltd.

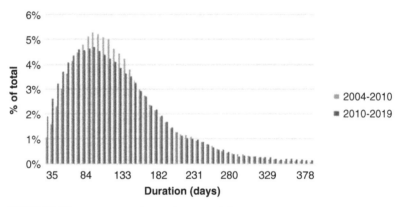

FIGURE 16.18 Duration of LM short portfolios.
Source: Libra Investment Services (2010) Ltd.

16.17 ANALYSIS OF RESULTS

At the aggregate level, the results, whilst different for the two periods concerned, remain broadly consistent throughout. Distributions in terms of duration show similar patterns around the average holding period. The distinction in terms of kurtosis and skewness between early and late momentum are retained both long- and short-term. This is clear from Figures 16.14–16.18. From a coverage point of view, we observe a significantly higher number of long trades (both early and late momentum) than shorts – see Table 16.2. The hit rates for the long momentum portfolios are ahead of the assumed 50% hit rate at the aggregate level, as can be seen in Figures 16.7 and 16.9. The short portfolios are less attractive on this measure, with an insignificant success rate

TABLE 16.3 Average portfolio performance results

	Period	EML1	EML2	LML1	LML2	EMS1	EMS2	LMS1	LMS2
Count	1–63	4761	5411	8555	10010	1564	1268	12931	7628
Hit Rate (%)	1–63	58.8	66.7	57.0	57.5	45.7	42.0	37.8	39.9
Average return (%)	1–63	13.2	24.8	10.7	12.5	8.1	16.4	21.2	13.3
Volatility of returns (%)	1–63	57.8	54.5	60.9	55.8	71.2	68.7	83.5	68.1
Duration (days)	1–63	57	48	61	50	52	44	54	47
Count	64–126	11427	26216	22670	60365	1483	2728	18993	26550
Hit Rate (%)	64–126	61.6	65.3	56.3	59.5	39.8	44.5	41.9	37.5
Average return (%)	64–126	13.0	16.6	6.6	10.5	13.6	8.1	8.3	11.3
Volatility of returns (%)	64–126	51.9	44.8	48.5	44.5	55.2	56.5	71.2	52.8
Duration (days)	64–126	109	96	107	95	105	92	107	95
Count	127–189	10627	23743	11627	37048	716	1860	10793	16931
Hit Rate (%)	127–189	61.6	69.4	63.4	68.1	40.5	38.8	48.5	34.4
Average return (%)	127–189	10.3	15.4	11.5	13.4	6.2	15.3	−0.2	11.9
Volatility of returns (%)	127–189	44.0	36.1	40.5	36.0	44.5	52.3	66.0	42.1
Duration (days)	127–189	171	156	166	153	166	157	167	153
Count	189–	6302	11144	6757	18441	713	2288	6385	9569
Hit Rate (%)	189–	46.6	63.5	47.5	66.2	37.9	42.5	46.5	36.7
Average return (%)	189–	−6.6	8.4	−2.0	11.3	13.2	7.2	1.7	7.2
Volatility of returns (%)	189–	39.8	32.0	40.5	30.6	37.6	45.4	42.7	33.7
Duration (days)	189–	248	225	275	253	273	248	261	242

observed (Figures 16.8 and 16.10.) Average returns to the short portfolios are in fact positive, although significantly lower than their long portfolio counterparts, as shown in Table 16.2, Figure 16.12 and Figure 16.14.

Given that one of the aims of the momentum risk signal is to try to retain a positive convexity to a portfolio of momentum stocks, the fact that the average holding periods are consistent with realised historic analysis – around five months - is reassuring. The relatively low kurtosis and limited skew of the late momentum portfolio duration distributions, compared to the fatter-tailed and slightly longer average duration of the early momentum portfolios is also consistent with our objective of differentiating via a signal stock at the individual asset level that can be aggregated into a momentum risk portfolio with common characteristics.

Whilst the duration patterns are visible on the charts, summary statistics are put into four sub-periods for relative comparison and can be seen in Table 16.3.

From a hit rate and returns point of view, the convexity of the late momentum portfolios is apparent: returns deteriorate through time. This is not the case with the early momentum portfolios, although the limited number of available results at longer horizons suggests caution in extending this as a significant point of difference. Situations in which reversals lead to the establishment of opposing trends over time bear similarity to the buying of cheap, out-of-favour stocks and holding them until an improvement in sentiment arises.

The hit rates and returns themselves are also significantly more attractive over shorter holding periods, where hit rates can be as high as 80% for long momentum portfolios (see Figure 16.9). When these returns are aligned with the frequency distributions of the different portfolios, a persistent pattern of relatively high portfolio density around the average holding periods is observed, offering higher hit rates and greater excess returns to the signal in both EM and LM phases.

For the short signal, the appearance of average negative returns only appears at longer horizons where the lower frequency of outcomes is an issue. However, the fact that at no point do we see the long portfolios provide negative average returns and that the spread in returns between the long and short portfolios would still provide a positive result for a sorted portfolio

The negative impact on the results is most likely to be upon the performance of the short momentum signal, as reversals back to rising trends are not only more frequent than reversals back to falling trends, but the actions of marginal investors are more likely to be deep (cheap) value buyers as opposed to expensive value sellers/ shorters. The results would support this assumption, with lower overall hit rates for the short-term signals. However, for the long-momentum trader, the establishment of a short-term sell signal is still a valuable information point and further tests could be conducted based on the combination of beta and alpha momentum-related signals in a model portfolio.

16.18   CONCLUSIONS

With momentum long regarded as an anomaly, the observation that the momentum trader may largely operate as a passive bystander raises the question as to why momentum arises at all. Our proposal is that it is the marginal fundamental investor who, by virtue of cash-flow related news, establishes a view of expected returns and implied future volatility that both change through time. Whilst the shorter term investor has traditionally been treated as a trader; only in possession of public, price-related information, we assume that there are shorter-term (out to 12 months) fundamentalists who hold a view on fundamental value in much the same way as longer-term (three to five year) investors. Under stable market conditions, the share price will tend to trade in line with fundamentals and both investor groups will hold largely similar views of where fundamental value lies.

When cash-flow related news arrives that has a direct impact on expected returns, the situation may arise where the views and opinions of the short- and long-term fundamental investors diverge. The initial recognition of this divergence, followed by an eventual confirmation of a restoration of relative stability of expected returns (and the price realignment with the revised expected returns), provide the entry and exit signals that we test. In effect, we are analysing the stability of two implied Sharpe ratios: one belonging to the short-term investor and the other to the long-term investor. The correlation between these two information sets is never equal to one, but any cash-flow news led breakdown in the stability of the relationship between them is a potential source of price adjustment in the direction of the news flow concerned.

While every investor's buy signal can be different, there tends to be much more uniformity in their sell signals. We model this using multiple entry signals in our tests for individual assets, but a single point of exit for all of the open trades in the asset. This helps explain the 'up escalators and down elevators' psychology of trading markets. Far from being passive bystanders, short-term traders can actively benefit from knowing how the information set that the fundamental investor has might impact on their open positions. The risk of reversal is ever present for the momentum trader, so any information relating to the marginal risk appetite of the fundamental investor is of value. Knowledge that fundamental investors are buying into the short-term investor's existing position – or prompting traders to follow into the trade that is established by the LT investor may prove valuable. Likewise, the forecasting of a reversal signal is critical for the short-term investor, as it can pre-empt their own exit signal and improve profitability.

This is also the case within the fundamental investor group itself. For long-term investors knowing the likelihood of their decision being followed into by ST traders is a clear benefit. A value investor who buys/sells when no one else is, will only see trading support when the trader's buy/sell signal is triggered – return into a FV range for example. These signals are both level dependent and regime dependent. The trends of value, shifts in volatility and tradeoff between risk and reward are all important.

REFERENCES

Bird, R., Gao, X. and Yeung, D. (2017) Time-series and cross-sectional momentum strategies under alternative implementation strategies. *Australian Journal of Management* **42**(2): 230–251.

Brock, W. and Hommes, C. (1998) Heterogeneous beliefs and routes to chaos in a simple asset pricing model, *Journal of Economic Dynamics and Control*, **22**, 1235–1274.

Bruder, C.B. and Gaussel, N. (2011) *Risk-Return Analysis of Dynamic Investment Strategies*, Working Paper, Lyxor Asset Management.

Burgues, A., Knockaert, A., Lezmi, E., Malongo, H., Roncalli, T. and Sobotka, R. (2017) *The Quest for Diversification – Why Does It Make Sense to Mix Risk Parity, Carry and Momentum Risk Premia?*, Working Paper, Amundi Asset Management, Paris.

Chiarella, C. (1992) The dynamics of speculative behavior, *Annals of Operations Research* **37**, 101–123.

Chiarella, C., Dieci, R. and Gardini, L. (2006) Asset price and wealth dynamics in a financial market with heterogeneous agents, *Journal of Economic Dynamics and Control*, **30**, 1775–1786.

Cochrane, J. H. (2011) Presidential Address, Discount rates, *Journal of Finance*, **66**(4), 1047–1108.

Conrad, J. and Kaul, G. (1998) Anatomy of trading strategies, *Review of Financial Studies*, **11**(3), 489–519.

Dao, T.-L., Nguyen, T.-T., Deremble, C., Lempérière, Y., Bouchaud, J.-P. and Potters, M. (2016) *Tail Protection for Long Investors: Trend Convexity at Work*, Working Paper, Amundi Asset Management, Paris.

Day, R. and Huang, W. (1990) Bulls, bears and market sheep, *Journal of Economic Behavior and Organization*, **14**, 299–329.

De Bondt, W.F.M. and Thaler, R. (1985) Does the stock market overreact? *Journal of Finance*, **40**(3), 793–805.

De Bondt, W.F.M. and Thaler, R. (1987) Further evidence on investor overreaction and stock market seasonality. *Journal of Finance*, **42**(3), 557–581.

Easton, P.D. and Monahan, S.J. (2005) An evaluation of accounting-based measures of expected returns, *The Accounting Review*, **80**, 501–538.

Elton, E. (1999) Expected return, realized return, and asset pricing tests, *Journal of Finance*, **54**, 1199–1220.

Fama, E.F. (1998) Market efficiency, long-term returns, and behavioral finance, *Journal of Financial Economics*, **49**(3), 283–306.

Fama, E.F. and French, K.R. (1996) Multifactor explanations of asset pricing anomalies, *Journal of Finance*, **51**, 55–84.

Fung, W. and Hsieh, D.A. (2001) The risk in hedge fund strategies: Theory and evidence from trend followers, *Review of Financial Studies*, **14**(2), 313–341.

Griffin, J.M., Ji, X. and Martin, J.S. (2003) Momentum investing and business cycle risk: Evidence from Pole to Pole, *The Journal of Finance*, **58**, 2515–2547.

Grinblatt, M., Titman, S. and Wermers, R. (1995) Momentum investment strategies, portfolio performance, and herding: A study of mutual fund behavior, *American Economic Review*, **85**(5), 1088–1105.

He, X.-Z. and Li, K. (2012) Heterogeneous beliefs and adaptive behaviour in a continuous-time asset price model, *Journal of Economic Dynamics and Control*, **36**(7), 973–987.

He, X.-Z. and Li, K. (2015) Profitability of time series momentum, *Journal of Banking and Finance*, **53**, 140–157.

He, X.-Z. and Zheng, H. (2016) Trading heterogeneity under information uncertainty, *Journal of Economic Behavior and Organization*, **130**, 64–80.

Hong, H. and Stein, J.C. (1999) A unified theory of underreaction, momentum trading, and overreaction in asset markets, *Journal of Finance*, **54**(6), 2143–2184.

Hou, K., Xiong, W. and Peng, L. (2009) *A Tale of Two Anomalies: The Implications of Investor Attention for Price and Earnings Momentum.* Working Paper, Ohio State University.

Hurst, B., Ooi, Y.H. and Pedersen, L.H. (2017) A century of evidence on trend-following investing, *Journal of Portfolio Management*, **44**(1),15–29.

Jegadeesh, N. and Titman, S. (1993) Returns to buying winners and selling losers: Implications for stock market efficiency, *Journal of Finance*, **48**(1), 65–91.

Jegadeesh, N. and Titman, S. (2001) Profitability of momentum strategies: An evaluation of alternative explanations, *Journal of Finance*, **56**(2), 699–720.

Jusselin, P., Lezmi, E., Malongo, H., Masselin, C., Roncalli, T. and Dao, T.-L. (2017) *Understanding the Momentum Risk Premium: An In-Depth Journey Through Trend-Following Strategies*, Working Paper, Amundi Asset Management, Paris.

Lakonishok, J., Shleifer, A. and Vishny, R.W. (1994) Contrarian investment, extrapolation, and risk, *Journal of Finance*, **49**, 1541–1578.

Lee, C. and Swaminathan, B. (2000) Price momentum and trading volume, *Journal of Finance*, **55**(5), 2017–2069.

Lee, C.M.C., So, E.C. and Wang, C.C.Y. (2019) *Evaluating Firm-Level Expected-Return Proxies.* Working Paper, Harvard Business School.

Lempérière, Y., Deremble, C., Nguyen, T.-T., Seager, P., Potters, M. and Bouchaud, J.-P. (2017) Risk premia: Asymmetric tail risks and excess returns, *Quantitative Finance*, **17**(1), 1–14.

Lempérière, Y., Deremble, C., Seager, P., Potters, M. and Bouchaud, J-P. (2014), Two centuries of trend following, *Journal of Investment Strategies*, **3**(3), 41–61.

Lewellen, J. (2015) The cross-section of expected returns, *Critical Finance Review*, **4**, 1–44.

Lux, T. (1995) Herd behaviour, bubbles and crashes, *Economic Journal*, **105**, 881–896.

Markowitz, H.M. (1952) Portfolio selection, *Journal of Finance*, 7(1), 77–91.

Moskowitz, T.J., Ooi, Y.H. and Pedersen, L.H. (2012) Time series momentum, *Journal of Financial Economics*, **104**, 228–250.

Potters, M. and Bouchaud, J.-P. (2006) Trend followers lose more often than they gain, *Wilmott Magazine*, **26**, 58–63.

Roncalli, T. (2017) *Keep Up The Momentum*, Working Paper, Amundi Asset Management, Paris.

Scott, J., Stumpp, M. and Xu, P. (2003) News, not trading volume, builds momentum, *Financial Analysts Journal*, **59**(2), 45–54.

CHAPTER 17

Momentum, Value and Carry Commodity Factors for Multi-Asset Portfolios

STEFANO CAVAGLIA, LOUIS SCOTT, KENNETH BLAY and VINCENT DE MARTEL

17.1   INTRODUCTION

To date, smart beta or factor-based strategies have been offered in the marketplace as stand-alone strategies providing a return enhancement to a passive, market-capitalization weighted allocation to a base (equity or fixed income) asset or providing a moderate, alternative source of total return. The cost effectiveness, scalability and potential Sharpe ratio improvements offered by these strategies have been particularly appealing to both asset owners and investment managers.

This chapter aims to provide a *complementary* perspective on mainstream factor-based products by focusing on the *strategic* or long-run allocation to factors in a *portfolio context*. We will examine how specific asset class factors can be used as instruments to enhance an investor's ability to attain specific goals. This broad formulation suggests a more customized approach to incorporating factor investments into portfolios in a way that focuses on targeting relevant client-specific goals. We cannot realistically address all issues corresponding to customising factor allocations in this chapter. Instead, we focus on a few key mainstream issues and goals to illustrate the characteristics of such an approach. In particular, we will review how factors can enhance investors' ability to attain their long-run wealth accumulation (and decumulation) goals and how the (over time) transition path to attaining their goals is impacted. The goals-based approach provides greater appreciation for the tendency of some factors to generate positive payoffs in adverse market environments. Mitigating downside risk allows the investor to subsequently reap the compounding benefits of exposures to traditional mixtures of equities and fixed income assets thus enhancing the likelihood of attaining the desired goal; evidence supporting this view can be found in Scott and Cavaglia (2017).

The portfolios (and strategies) we consider are comprised of two components: a base asset and a long-short factor overlay. This construct allows one to identify the return contribution to each component and their interaction over time. It also permits an explicit and separate assessment of the benefits from factor exposures on the long side and factor exposures on the short side. From a holistic perspective, this represents a more general formulation of portfolio construction; current, mainstream products can be viewed as constrained versions of the general solution.[1] Our construct is well aligned with empirical finance theory. As eloquently stated by Gene Fama (1996):

> *The typical multifactor-efficient portfolio of the ICAPM[2] combines an MVE[3] portfolio with hedging portfolios that mimic uncertainty about consumption-investment state variables*

This is echoed by John Cochrane (1999):

> *A typical investor then picks a point which gives him the best possible portfolio – trading off mean, variance, and recession sensitivity – that is available. Investors want to hold multifactor efficient rather than mean-variance efficient portfolios.*

In this context, the factor overlay portfolio is a completion portfolio to underlying assets that may be targeted to help achieve certain objectives. Note that the composition of a stand-alone maximum Sharpe ratio factor portfolio is likely to be quite different than that of the completion portfolio as it would fail to explicitly account for the correlation of the factors with the underlying assets.

In this chapter we will consider simple portfolio construction rules applied to commodity factor premia. In future work we will consider other asset class premia and more sophisticated portfolio construction rules. Thus, we provide a first pass at reviewing a long run, *strategic* allocation to factors in a *portfolio context,* and our analysis is organized in the following sections:

1. Methodology and key research questions
2. Commodity factors – insights from the historical data
3. Wealth accumulation strategies and rebalancing considerations
4. Wealth decumulation strategies
5. Long/short versus long only strategies
6. Completion portfolios versus maximum Sharpe ratio portfolios

---

[1] For instance, investors may be restricted from shorting and hence may be constrained into a long only exposure to factor.
[2] Intertemporal Capital Asset Pricing Model (ICAPM)
[3] Mean-variance efficient (MVE)

17.2 METHODOLOGY AND KEY RESEARCH QUESTIONS

We follow and adapt the research of Scott and Cavaglia (2017) who examined the impact of equity risk factors on goals-based, capital accumulation strategies. The construct is as follows:

- Artee (our aspiring retiree) invests in a passive, fully invested strategy in a reference base asset that is held over a period of 20 years.
- The above strategy is compared to an alternative strategy comprised of the base asset with a factor overlay. The overlay provides $1 long and $1 short for every dollar of the base asset exposure; this is akin to a 200/100 portfolio typically applied in a portable alpha context. In keeping with more mainstream strategies, we also show our results for a 130/30 product.[4]
- The base assets we consider are 100% global equities, 100% global bonds, and a 60/40 equities-bonds mix.
- The commodity premia we consider are momentum, carry, value and a portfolio that holds equal weights in each.[5]
- We assume that the overlay exposures are adjusted to the drifting base asset exposures on a monthly basis.

The key research questions we will aim to address are:

- To what extent does the overlay enhance Artee's ability to attain their wealth accumulation (or retirement income) goal?
- Is the journey over time to attaining the desired goal smoother or more turbulent due to the factor overlay?
- What role do shorts play in these results? How does a long/short overlay compare to a long only overlay that is hedged for market exposure? Similarly, how does a long/short overlay compare to a short only overlay that is hedged for market exposure?
- How do commodity premia interact with different underlying base assets?
- How sensitive are the results to alternative views about the future persistence of the historical returns of the factor premia?

In order to tackle these questions, we apply block bootstrap simulations to the historical returns for the base assets and for the premia to generate terminal wealth distributions from investing $1 across alternative investment strategies over 20-year horizons. Block bootstraps are used to preserve any serial correlation and dependence in the data.[6]

---

[4]These constructs can be easily implemented with futures. For instance, for $100 of initial investment $10 are used to buy futures on margin providing a notional exposure of $100 to the base asset. The remaining $90 can be invested in a long/short strategy that could exhibit varying leverage; for simplicity we assume the long/short gross exposure to be either $200 (for the 200/100) or $60 (for the 130/30.

[5]The construction of these factors is outlined in the Appendix.

[6]Scott and Cavaglia (2017) provide a more technical motivational and methodological expose of the block bootstrap approach. In their 2017 study they use quarterly data blocks. Our results are not overly sensitive to alternative blocks sizes of up to 12 months. Politis and Romano (1992) and Politis (2003) provide relevant analytical foundations.

The length of the investment horizon is representative of a long investment horizon but arbitrary. The broad qualitative conclusions we present would still hold; however, the orders of magnitude of the statistics we present would be magnified (reduced) with longer (shorter) horizons.

Some notes and caveats:

- The intertemporal problem that Artee aims to solve in our example is extremely simple. We concede that a full, intertemporal asset-liability framework is more complete; see for instance, Wilcox, Horvitz, and DiBartolomeo (2008), and Das et al. (2019a, 2019b).
- The long/short overlay should not be construed as championing hedge funds. Rather, the overlay provides a very effective representation of a range of smart beta strategies. Indeed, conventional smart beta strategies can be viewed as a mixture of a passive exposure plus a risk premia exposure. In practice, a long only smart beta product is a constrained version of a passive exposure plus some fraction of the overlay. The 130/30 strategy can be similarly viewed as a constrained version of the 200/100 construct we present.
- We concede that our portfolio construction is rudimentary, indeed in our future paper will wish to account for a full risk budgeting approach, dynamic factor allocations, and alternative portfolio rebalancing strategies.

17.3 COMMODITY FACTORS – INSIGHTS FROM THE HISTORICAL DATA

For our analysis, we use historical return data for the period of July 1998 to May 2019 for the returns to the momentum, carry and value commodity factor strategies.[7] We compute the equal-weight (EQW) strategy which represents a portfolio whose capital is equally weighted across the strategies. For each strategy we report the long/short return and the contribution from the longs and from the shorts separately. Clearly the long contribution will be significant in up markets and conversely the short contribution will be significant in down markets. In order to correct for 'market' effects we regress the long and the short returns onto the commodity market, the equity market and the bond market; we believe that accounting for these three factors will capture most of the systematic 'risk on' and 'risk off' market effects.[8] We then obtain beta-adjusted returns which we label 'hedged'. Broadly, the long and short components of each of the factors have a beta exposure to the commodity market of approximately 0.4 and to the equity market of 0.3; once these effects are accounted for the exposure to the

---

[7]While returns are reported gross of transaction costs, factors strategies are implemented with futures making these costs negligible.

[8]The commodity market is proxied by the S&P GSCI index, the equity market is proxied by the MSCI World index, and the bond market is proxied by the FTSE World Government Bond index (WGBI).

fixed income market is economically small.[9] Failure to make these corrections may account for the strongly touted view by Blitz et al. (2014) that the short side of risk premia brings marginally small benefit to the investor, and hence that long only, smart beta strategies carry most of the benefit of the premium. Our results will provide an alternative perspective.

In Tables 17.1 and 17.2 we report summary statistics for the risk premia. We show average monthly returns through the sample as well as under different environments (up/down) – for bonds, equities and commodities. These statistics suggest the following:

- The premia have different payoff profiles relative to the underlying base asset. For instance, carry and value tend to be profitable in extremely bullish bond markets; the converse holds for momentum. They tend to be less profitable in extremely adverse equity markets.
- The above suggests that the composition of a completion factor portfolio may be very different for a multi-asset defensive portfolio relative to a multi-asset growth portfolio. Controlling for the level of expected returns, we would expect a tilt to commodity momentum to best complement a base portfolio of equities; similarly, we would expect a tilt to commodity value to best complement a base portfolio of bonds.
- The hedged returns across the longs and the shorts for each strategy have similar mean returns in contrast to the raw or unhedged returns that favour the long side. This suggests that we may need to consider the role of shorts in a strategy based on factor premia.[10]

TABLE 17.1   Summary statistics (July 1998 to May 2019)

| | | | | Cross Premia Correlations | | | | Moments | | |
| | | | Carry | Mom | Value | EQW | Average | Volatility | |
	Bonds	Equities	Comm	L/S	L/S	L/S	L/S	(%)	(%)	AR Coeff
Bonds	1.00							0.33	0.86	
Equities	−0.29	1.00						0.55	4.40	
Commodities	−0.21	0.36	1.00					0.20	6.55	
Carry L/S	−0.07	0.06	−0.05	1.00				0.94	3.89	−0.11
Mom L/S	0.04	−0.02	0.07	0.43	1.00			0.68	3.51	0.01
Value L/S	−0.07	0.09	−0.10	0.31	0.08	1.00		1.14	3.67	−0.02
EQW L/S	−0.05	0.06	−0.04	0.82	0.69	0.65	1.00	0.92	2.66	

Source: Invesco, MSCI, FTSE, S&P

---

[9]The long/short implementation of the factors results in negligible exposures to commodity, equity and fixed income market exposures as evidenced in the correlations shown in Table 17.1. However, an analysis of the characteristics of the long and short components independently requires that we remove (hedge) the impact of the influences of these exposures.

[10]The ubiquitous equity value premium provides an interesting illustration of our insight. The MSCI World Value index for the period July 1990 to May 2019 returned 7.35% per annum,

TABLE 17.2 Summary statistics – longs, shorts and long/short (July 1998 to May 2019)

| | Carry Returns | | | | | |
| | Actual returns | | | Hedged returns | | |
	Longs (%)	Shorts (%)	L/S (%)	Longs (%)	Shorts (%)	L/S (%)
Average	0.70	0.24	0.94	0.45	0.47	0.94
Volatility	4.48	4.82	3.89	3.97	4.46	3.89
Bonds up	0.24	0.63	0.86	0.28	0.59	0.86
Bonds down	1.55	−0.47	1.08	0.77	0.24	1.08
Equities up	1.90	−1.01	0.89	0.41	0.35	0.89
Equities down	−1.16	2.18	1.02	0.52	0.65	1.02
Commodities up	2.81	−1.90	0.92	2.08	−1.22	0.92
Commodities down	−1.88	2.85	0.97	−1.54	2.54	0.97

| | Momentum Returns | | | | | |
| | Actual returns | | | Hedged returns | | |
	Longs (%)	Shorts (%)	L/S (%)	Longs (%)	Shorts (%)	L/S (%)
Average	0.56	0.12	0.68	0.34	0.34	0.68
Volatility	4.05	3.90	3.51	3.69	3.48	3.51
Bonds up	0.37	0.46	0.82	0.40	0.42	0.82
Bonds down	0.90	−0.49	0.42	0.24	0.19	0.42
Equities up	1.48	−0.99	0.49	0.22	0.30	0.49
Equities down	−0.89	1.86	0.97	0.54	0.40	0.97
Commodities up	2.37	−1.48	0.89	1.74	−0.84	0.89
Commodities down	−1.65	2.08	0.43	−1.36	1.79	0.43

| | Value Returns | | | | | |
| | Actual returns | | | Hedged returns | | |
	Longs (%)	Shorts (%)	L/S (%)	Longs (%)	Shorts (%)	L/S (%)
Average	0.75	0.39	1.14	0.50	0.60	1.14
Volatility	4.09	4.49	3.67	3.55	4.16	3.67
Bonds up	0.31	0.69	1.01	0.35	0.66	1.01
Bonds down	1.54	−0.17	1.38	0.78	0.49	1.38
Equities up	1.89	−0.67	1.22	0.43	0.59	1.22
Equities down	−1.03	2.04	1.01	0.62	0.62	1.01
Commodities up	2.63	−1.49	1.14	1.91	−0.86	1.14
Commodities down	−1.55	2.68	1.13	−1.22	2.39	1.13

Source: Invesco, MSCI, FTSE, S&P

marginally outperforming the MSCI World index over the same period which returned 7.27% per annum. Over this same period the Fama-French report a long/short global value return of 2.82% per annum. The lower performance of the long strategy relative to the long/short strategy illustrates what is often referenced as a 'transfer' loss; in this case it is material.

TABLE 17.3 Summary statistics – performance across regimes

	Contraction (%)	Expansion %	Recovery (%)	Slowdown %	All Periods %
Bonds	0.66	0.13	0.18	0.43	0.33
Equities	−1.32	0.60	1.27	0.79	0.55
60/40 E/B	−0.53	0.42	0.83	0.65	0.46
Commodities	−2.08	0.68	0.04	0.59	0.20
Mom L/S	0.69	0.90	0.21	0.70	0.68
Carry L/S	0.52	0.78	1.88	0.82	0.94
Value L/S	0.67	1.20	2.20	0.81	1.14
EQW L/S	0.63	0.96	1.43	0.77	0.92

Source: Invesco, MSCI, FTSE, S&P

- The premia exhibited low correlation to one another and to the base assets, equities and bonds; thus, a maximum Sharpe ratio portfolio of factor premia could provide an attractive strategy for holders of such base assets.
- The volatility of risk premia strategies was lower than that of equities but higher than that of bonds. This may, of course, change depending on the leverage used.
- We report the first order autoregressive coefficients for each factor premia; as in Scott and Cavaglia (2017) we find economic evidence of serial correlation supporting the need to use a block bootstrap when undertaking simulations.

To provide an economic perspective on this analysis we examine the performance of factors under different regimes that capture the cyclicality of the cash flow drivers that are priced in the marketplace. We partition our historical sample period into four regimes – contraction, expansion, recovery and slowdown. De Longis (2019), De Longis and Ellis (2019), and Polk, Haghbin, and De Longis (2019) provide an extensive discussion of the methodology for identifying the state variables and their economic interpretation. In Table 17.3 we report the performance of our factor premia in each regime. The data suggest the following:[11]

- Commodities (as reflected in the S&P GSCI index) performed best in expansion and slowdown, i.e. when growth is above trend, when demand is typically strong and inelastic supply leads to rising prices. This is also in line with the general view that cyclical commodities are a coincident indicator of economic growth, not a leading indicator like equities.
- The commodity value factor performed best in recovery and expansion. The strong performance in recovery is a confirmation of value reversals following cyclical turning points. These observations are consistent with stylized facts relating to value in the equity market.
- Momentum performed best in recovery and worst in contraction. This price-based dynamic is similar to what we see in equities where cyclical turning points are negative for momentum and late upswings are positive (i.e. expansion).

---

[11]We are grateful to Alessio De Longis for guiding us through these observations.

Taken together, these observations suggest that there is significant time variation in the performance of factor premia. This time variation may be linked to the stage of the economic cycle. These stylized facts need to be considered in the total portfolio context for investors holding some combination of equities or bonds as base assets.

17.4   WEALTH ACCUMULATION STRATEGIES AND REBALANCING CONSIDERATIONS

We first consider the performance of alternative 200/100 premia overlay portfolios that are fully exposed to either momentum, carry or value. Additionally, we consider an overlay that is comprised of an equal weighted allocation to the three factors. Each month the long/short exposures of the overlay are adjusted to allow for drift due to market movement in the underlying base assets, the long exposures of the factor premia and the short exposures of the factor premia to maintain the 200/100 targeted allocation. The rebalancing frequency is arbitrary, and we will explore the performance impact of altering that frequency.

The 200/100 portfolio construct may represent more risk than some investors may be willing to bear and may not be feasible due to leverage and or short sale constraints. Hence, we also examine a 130/30 portfolio construct that is a more mainstream strategy but one that nonetheless reaps some of the benefits of the short side of the factor premia strategies.

The present analysis will focus on comparing empirically obtained distributions of terminal wealth. For each strategy considered we run 10,000 simulations. Each simulation provides a hypothetical return series over a 20-year period that can be summarized with an accumulated wealth level at the end of the period. In this first hypothetical construct, we assume that the expected returns to the premia equal the historical returns of the premia; namely, we make no adjustment for the market's 'discovery' of the factors. Hence the historical data are applied 'as is' to the bootstrap simulation. Our framework however allows us to adjust the forward-looking expected returns. For instance, one might argue that the historical returns for the premia we have reported represent an unusual historical episode and are higher than what one would expect in the long run. One might also argue that the 'discovery' of the factors might place some downward pressure on future returns. Hence, a conservative estimate for the strategic, expected returns is about 5% – a midpoint between the return of equities and on bonds.[12] We opt for an agnostic approach and postulate that for all our commodity premia. This assumption can be incorporated in our analysis by adjusting the mean historical returns of the data while preserving their cross correlation across assets and their mean relative performance in extreme market conditions. It should be noted that the expected return assumption of 5% is approximately equivalent to a 50% haircut on the historical returns of these strategies.

---

[12]As previously noted, the factor premia have a volatility that is between that of bonds and equities,

As previously suggested, the strategic focus of our analysis is well characterized by goals-based investment strategies; these strategies typically do not focus on returns but rather on investors' desire to attain a given goal. The goal could thus be a target wealth level required to support a future retirement income stream. Investors typically view deviations from the goal in an asymmetric fashion. Falling short of the goal is extremely undesirable while exceeding the goal is viewed as a 'nice to have'. Formal utility functions have been postulated based on a variety of empirical methods – see the excellent survey of Warren (2019). However, our results here permit a review of possible outcomes captured in the empirically estimated distribution of terminal wealth. Thus, in this chapter, we will provide a qualitative assessment of how alternative investment strategies impact the distribution of terminal wealth for a wealth accumulation strategy.

It is well known that *during* the transition to retirement, clients may question the merits of their strategy when experiencing adverse environments. The largest drawdown experienced over the 20-year transition to retirement is one metric that we may consider. However, our experience suggests that this extreme tail statistic may be difficult for many investors to fathom. Rather, we suggest constructing an analogous measure. Namely the historical simulations can be utilized to create alternative 12-month return histories. These 12-month return histories can in turn be sorted into deciles and compared across strategies.

We reference Table 17.4 to illustrate our results for a 200/100 overlay strategy with equities as a base asset. The first panel of Exhibit 17.4 provides the average value of each decile of the terminal wealth distribution. Thus, $1 invested in a global equity portfolio may be worth $0.81 after 20 years in the worst-case scenario captured by the bottom decile. Referencing the 5th decile of the distribution $1 invested in equities would have accrued, on average, to $2.74 in 20 years' time. An overlay comprised entirely of the momentum factor onto the base equity strategy would have provided $11.78, on average, for the 5th decile; this assumes that the expected return for momentum equals 0.68% per month which is the historic return earned. Similarly, an overlay comprised of the momentum factor onto the base equity strategy would have provided $6.29, on average, for the 5th decile; this assumes that the expected return for momentum equals 0.42% per month which results from the 5% per annum return assumption.

The second panel of Table 17.4 provides the average value of each decile of the distribution of 12-month returns. Thus, $1 invested in a global equity portfolio may suffer, on average, a 29.15% loss in the transition to retirement in the worst-case scenario captured by the bottom decile. Referencing the 5th decile of the distribution $1 invested in equities earned, on average, 9.80% over one year in the transition to retirement. An overlay comprised entirely of the momentum factor onto the base equity strategy earned 21.53%, on average, for the 5th decile; this assumes that the expected return for momentum equals 0.68% per month which is the historical return earned. Similarly, an overlay comprised of the momentum factor onto the base equity strategy earned 17.81%, on average, for the 5th decile; this assumes that the expected return for momentum equals 0.42% per month which results from the 5% per annum return assumption.

Tables 17.5 to 17.9 report results for alternative base assets and across the alternative investment strategies we consider. Table 17.10 reports the historical volatility of the strategies. Broadly the results suggest the following:

TABLE 17.4 Base asset - global equities

		Terminal Wealth Distribution: 200/100 Strategy							
Reference		Expected Premia Returns: Historical				Expected Premia Returns: 5%			
Decile	Base ($)	Base + Mom ($)	Base + Carry ($)	Base + Value ($)	Base + EQW ($)	Base + Mom ($)	Base + Carry ($)	Base + Value ($)	Base + EQW ($)
1	0.81	2.59	4.18	6.60	5.10	1.38	1.19	1.18	1.53
2	1.38	4.96	8.25	13.04	9.59	2.64	2.36	2.33	2.89
3	1.83	7.04	11.84	18.88	13.31	3.75	3.40	3.39	4.02
4	2.26	9.27	15.79	25.05	17.12	4.95	4.54	4.50	5.18
5	2.74	11.78	20.24	32.34	21.51	6.29	5.83	5.83	6.51
6	3.26	14.80	25.90	41.40	26.87	7.91	7.47	7.47	8.14
7	3.93	18.96	33.28	52.73	33.80	10.14	9.61	9.53	10.26
8	4.87	24.70	43.82	69.86	43.38	13.22	12.67	12.66	13.18
9	6.32	34.24	63.06	102.54	59.51	18.34	18.26	18.63	18.11
10	10.89	68.38	136.64	228.21	118.21	36.70	39.76	41.74	36.12

Source: Invesco, MSCI

		Transition Path: 12-Month Returns: 200/100 Strategy							
Reference		Expected Premia Returns: Historical				Expected Premia Returns: 5%			
Decile	Base (%)	Base + Mom (%)	Base + Carry (%)	Base + Value (%)	Base + EQW (%)	Base + Mom (%)	Base + Carry (%)	Base + Value (%)	Base + EQW (%)
1	−29.15	−20.00	−17.32	−19.34	−18.72	−22.54	−22.46	−26.17	−23.57
2	−13.27	−1.85	−0.48	−1.24	−1.20	−4.91	−6.56	−9.48	−7.00
3	−3.12	3.50	8.48	9.59	7.10	0.28	1.90	0.54	0.85
4	2.99	6.47	7.22	15.39	9.58	3.17	0.71	5.89	3.19
5	9.80	21.53	20.78	27.09	23.18	17.81	13.52	16.72	16.08
6	13.19	27.10	30.64	29.44	29.08	23.22	22.84	18.89	21.67
7	16.28	32.17	32.85	25.41	30.05	28.15	24.93	15.17	22.58
8	18.60	31.71	37.46	35.89	34.95	27.70	29.29	24.86	27.23
9	22.46	37.85	34.79	41.39	37.90	33.66	26.76	29.95	30.02
10	33.04	41.35	53.79	61.41	51.88	37.07	44.73	48.50	43.27

Source: Invesco, MSCI

- For all base assets the overlays considered enhance accumulated wealth and enhance the transition to retirement. This holds across the distribution of outcomes
- This holds both for the 200/100 strategy and the 130/30 strategy
- This holds both when we assume the expected return on factor premia to equal their historical value and to equal a fixed 5% per annum level
- Overlays can mitigate extremely undesirable outcomes as for instance suffering a net capital loss over a 20-year period when fully invested in the equity market or suffering a loss over any 1-year period when invested in government treasury bonds.

TABLE 17.5 Base asset - global equities

| | Terminal Wealth Distribution: 130/30 Strategy | | | | | | | | |
| Reference | Expected Premia Returns: Historical | | | | Expected Premia Returns: 5% | | | |
Decile	Base ($)	Base + Mom ($)	Base + Carry ($)	Base + Value ($)	Base + EQW ($)	Base + Mom ($)	Base + Carry ($)	Base + Value ($)	Base + EQW ($)
1	0.81	1.25	1.45	1.65	1.47	1.04	1.00	0.98	1.03
2	1.38	2.17	2.55	2.91	2.56	1.80	1.75	1.73	1.79
3	1.83	2.89	3.41	3.90	3.43	2.39	2.35	2.32	2.39
4	2.26	3.62	4.29	4.89	4.27	3.00	2.95	2.92	2.98
5	2.74	4.38	5.19	5.95	5.18	3.63	3.57	3.55	3.61
6	3.26	5.28	6.25	7.21	6.25	4.37	4.30	4.30	4.36
7	3.93	6.43	7.66	8.81	7.58	5.32	5.27	5.26	5.29
8	4.87	7.96	9.55	10.97	9.42	6.60	6.57	6.56	6.58
9	6.32	10.43	12.69	14.60	12.41	8.65	8.74	8.73	8.67
10	10.89	18.26	22.55	26.52	21.96	15.14	15.54	15.88	15.36

Source: Invesco, MSCI

| | Transition Path: 12-Month Returns: 130/30 Strategy | | | | | | | | |
| Reference | Expected Premia Returns: Historical | | | | Expected Premia Returns: 5% | | | |
Decile	Base (%)	Base + Mom (%)	Base + Carry (%)	Base + Value (%)	Base + EQW (%)	Base + Mom (%)	Base + Carry (%)	Base + Value (%)	Base + EQW (%)
1	−29.15	−26.46	−25.71	−26.23	−26.12	−27.17	−27.13	−28.17	−27.48
2	−13.27	−9.96	−9.63	−9.72	−9.77	−10.82	−11.33	−12.06	−11.41
3	−3.12	−1.17	0.22	0.57	−0.13	−2.10	−1.66	−2.01	−1.93
4	2.99	3.98	4.22	6.63	4.93	3.00	2.28	3.90	3.06
5	9.80	13.27	12.95	14.81	13.68	12.21	10.86	11.90	11.66
6	13.19	17.20	18.10	17.89	17.73	16.11	15.92	14.91	15.65
7	16.28	20.72	20.92	19.06	20.23	19.60	18.70	16.05	18.11
8	18.60	22.44	23.90	23.60	23.31	21.30	21.63	20.48	21.13
9	22.46	26.82	26.05	27.94	26.93	25.65	23.74	24.73	24.70
10	33.04	35.60	38.94	41.05	38.51	34.35	36.41	37.54	36.09

Source: Invesco, MSCI

- The complementarity of momentum to a base investment in equities is well illustrated by its impact on terminal wealth and on the transition path when assuming factor premia returns are 5% per annum.
- When we assume factor premia returns to be 5%, all factors improve the terminal wealth outcome with bonds as a base asset. However, carry exhibits the strongest benefit in the tail of the transition periods; note how the bottom decile return for bonds is negative but is most enhanced by carry.

TABLE 17.6 Base asset: global bonds

| | Terminal Wealth Distribution: 200/100 Strategy | | | | | | | | |
| Reference | | Expected Premia Returns: Historical | | | | Expected Premia Returns: 5% | | | |
Decile	Base ($)	Base + Mom ($)	Base + Carry ($)	Base + Value ($)	Base + EQW ($)	Base + Mom ($)	Base + Carry ($)	Base + Value ($)	Base + EQW ($)
1	1.70	3.61	6.45	10.45	8.78	1.92	1.85	1.87	2.65
2	1.87	5.30	9.49	15.42	11.69	2.83	2.73	2.77	3.53
3	1.97	6.47	11.68	19.02	13.61	3.45	3.36	3.42	4.12
4	2.05	7.65	13.85	22.39	15.32	4.08	3.99	4.03	4.64
5	2.13	8.83	16.03	25.80	16.99	4.71	4.62	4.65	5.14
6	2.21	10.17	18.47	29.77	18.79	5.44	5.32	5.37	5.69
7	2.29	11.75	21.46	34.51	20.87	6.28	6.19	6.23	6.32
8	2.38	13.85	25.26	40.69	23.55	7.41	7.29	7.36	7.14
9	2.51	17.06	31.33	49.82	27.27	9.13	9.05	9.02	8.28
10	2.78	25.79	47.91	75.95	36.45	13.82	13.87	13.80	11.08

Source: Invesco, FTSE

| | Transition Path: 12-Month Returns: 200/100 Strategy | | | | | | | | |
| Reference | | Expected Premia Returns: Historical | | | | Expected Premia Returns: 5% | | | |
Decile	Base (%)	Base + Mom (%)	Base + Carry (%)	Base + Value (%)	Base + EQW (%)	Base + Mom (%)	Base + Carry (%)	Base + Value (%)	Base + EQW (%)
1	−1.11	6.98	12.63	9.06	9.28	3.66	5.83	0.05	2.91
2	0.45	12.48	12.59	15.44	13.42	9.01	5.79	5.95	6.83
3	1.51	15.75	16.23	14.22	15.27	12.19	9.23	4.83	8.59
4	2.50	7.60	12.05	20.27	13.11	4.27	5.28	10.42	6.55
5	3.23	9.72	19.86	21.90	17.15	6.33	12.66	11.92	10.37
6	4.17	14.56	15.01	22.05	17.21	11.03	8.07	12.06	10.42
7	4.98	14.93	17.69	21.13	18.07	11.40	10.60	11.21	11.24
8	5.89	16.01	18.42	22.57	19.05	12.44	11.30	12.54	12.17
9	7.10	22.22	30.34	21.25	24.70	18.48	22.56	11.32	17.51
10	8.85	22.85	18.25	18.62	19.89	19.09	11.14	8.89	12.96

Source: Invesco, FTSE

Table 17.10 highlights the result that a 200/100 strategy entails a significantly higher level of portfolio volatility than that borne by a base asset that is fully invested in equities. However, the 130/30 strategy entails a more moderate increase in volatility and provides significant wealth enhancements.

There is an extensive literature suggesting that rebalancing strategies automatically generate rebalancing returns by 'buying low and selling high' see Erb and Harvey (2006). Cuthbertson et al. (2016) have questioned this claim noting that predictability in the underlying asset returns is a necessary supporting condition; they suggest that

TABLE 17.7 Base asset: global bonds

	Terminal Wealth Distribution: 130/30 Strategy								
Reference	Expected Premia Returns: Historical				Expected Premia Returns: 5%				
Base	Base + Mom	Base + Carry	Base + Value	Base + EQW	Base + Mom	Base + Carry	Base + Value	Base + EQW
Decile	($)	($)	($)	($)	($)	($)	($)	($)	($)
1	1.70	2.39	2.92	3.33	3.06	1.98	2.01	1.99	2.14
2	1.87	2.78	3.37	3.86	3.46	2.30	2.32	2.30	2.41
3	1.97	3.01	3.64	4.18	3.69	2.49	2.50	2.49	2.58
4	2.05	3.21	3.87	4.45	3.88	2.66	2.66	2.65	2.71
5	2.13	3.39	4.09	4.70	4.07	2.81	2.81	2.81	2.84
6	2.21	3.58	4.31	4.97	4.25	2.97	2.96	2.96	2.97
7	2.29	3.79	4.55	5.24	4.45	3.14	3.13	3.13	3.11
8	2.38	4.02	4.83	5.58	4.69	3.33	3.32	3.33	3.27
9	2.51	4.35	5.21	6.02	5.00	3.60	3.58	3.60	3.49
10	2.78	5.07	6.06	7.00	5.65	4.20	4.17	4.18	3.94

Source: Invesco, FTSE

	Transition Path: 12-Month Returns: 130/30 Strategy								
Reference	Expected Premia Returns: Historical				Expected Premia Returns: 5%				
Base	Base + Mom	Base + Carry	Base + Value	Base + EQW	Base + Mom	Base + Carry	Base + Value	Base + EQW
Decile	(%)	(%)	(%)	(%)	(%)	(%)	(%)	(%)	(%)
1	−1.11	1.17	2.69	1.94	1.91	0.22	0.78	−0.67	0.09
2	0.45	3.84	3.91	4.83	4.18	2.86	1.97	2.15	2.32
3	1.51	5.55	5.69	5.13	5.45	4.56	3.73	2.45	3.56
4	2.50	3.99	5.25	7.55	5.58	3.01	3.30	4.81	3.70
5	3.23	5.14	7.96	8.64	7.24	4.15	5.96	5.87	5.33
6	4.17	7.19	7.26	9.31	7.92	6.19	5.27	6.52	6.00
7	4.98	7.93	8.69	9.68	8.78	6.91	6.67	6.89	6.84
8	5.89	8.93	9.48	10.74	9.72	7.91	7.45	7.92	7.77
9	7.10	11.55	13.64	11.29	12.17	10.51	11.54	8.46	10.17
10	8.85	12.94	11.59	11.84	12.12	11.89	9.52	9.00	10.13

Source: Invesco, FTSE

rebalancing returns are more closely tied to volatility drag. We examine the impact of alternative rebalancing frequencies on median terminal wealth; namely we allow the notional value of the overlay to deviate from the notional value of the base asset due to market drift and accrued profit and losses and reset them at predetermined intervals of 3 months, 6 months, and 12 months rather than our assumed one month frequency. The analysis is restricted to global equities as a base asset and to a 200/100 overlay. Our results are presented in Table 17.11. We find that less frequent rebalancing is beneficial and leads to a higher terminal wealth over a simulation period of 20 years; this

TABLE 17.8   Base asset: global 60/40 equity/bond

| | | Terminal Wealth Distribution: 200/100 Strategy | | | | | | | |
| | Reference | Expected Premia Returns: Historical | | | | Expected Premia Returns: 5% | | | |
Decile	Base ($)	Base + Mom ($)	Base + Carry ($)	Base + Value ($)	Base + EQW ($)	Base + Mom ($)	Base + Carry ($)	Base + Value ($)	Base + EQW ($)
1	1.33	3.66	6.03	9.63	7.74	1.95	1.73	1.72	2.33
2	1.81	5.91	10.02	15.94	11.97	3.15	2.88	2.86	3.62
3	2.12	7.67	13.26	21.12	15.03	4.10	3.81	3.80	4.55
4	2.39	9.42	16.42	26.27	18.06	5.03	4.73	4.73	5.47
5	2.67	11.36	19.88	31.89	21.11	6.07	5.73	5.75	6.39
6	2.93	13.52	23.91	38.15	24.59	7.23	6.90	6.89	7.45
7	3.27	16.14	28.86	45.91	28.78	8.63	8.33	8.30	8.73
8	3.69	19.73	35.62	56.78	34.22	10.56	10.29	10.29	10.39
9	4.28	25.23	46.84	75.72	42.82	13.51	13.56	13.74	13.02
10	5.78	41.85	82.98	137.46	67.81	22.44	24.09	25.07	20.67

Source: Invesco, MSCI, FTSE

| | | Transition Path: 12-Month Returns: 200/100 Strategy | | | | | | | |
| | Reference | Expected Premia Returns: Historical | | | | Expected Premia Returns: 5% | | | |
Decile	Base (%)	Base + Mom (%)	Base + Carry (%)	Base + Value (%)	Base + EQW (%)	Base + Mom (%)	Base + Carry (%)	Base + Value (%)	Base + EQW (%)
1	−15.79	−5.56	−0.90	−4.46	−3.43	−8.52	−6.95	−12.44	−9.11
2	−5.57	4.13	7.01	7.97	6.33	0.89	0.51	−0.96	0.12
3	0.29	5.21	8.31	13.70	8.92	1.95	1.74	4.34	2.58
4	4.01	11.60	13.51	17.31	14.06	8.15	6.66	7.67	7.44
5	7.82	22.10	16.87	21.07	19.98	18.36	9.83	11.15	13.04
6	9.06	21.40	28.69	21.78	23.88	17.68	21.01	11.81	16.74
7	10.38	24.94	27.83	25.82	26.16	21.12	20.19	15.55	18.90
8	12.00	25.03	24.04	26.97	25.41	21.20	16.60	16.61	18.19
9	13.91	28.17	32.66	30.90	30.47	24.26	24.75	20.25	22.98
10	19.89	26.61	34.54	46.83	35.74	22.74	26.53	34.99	27.97

Source: Invesco, MSCI, FTSE

holds for all overlays – those based on a single factor and those based on a portfolio of factors. One possible explanation for this result is that the premia have a defensive characteristic. Hence, when the equity market experiences adverse conditions a strategy of less frequent rebalancing would have resulted in above average protection (via leverage) and hence provide the diversification benefit. This explanation would beg the question of whether the strategy implied significant time variation in the risk borne by the investor; a detailed review of this issue is beyond the scope of this paper but will be explored in future work.

TABLE 17.9 Base asset: global 60/40 equity/bond

	Terminal Wealth Distribution: 130/30 Strategy								
Reference	Expected Premia Returns: Historical				Expected Premia Returns: 5%				
Base	Base + Mom	Base + Carry	Base + Value	Base + EQW	Base + Mom	Base + Carry	Base + Value	Base + EQW
Decile	($)	($)	($)	($)	($)	($)	($)	($)	($)
1	1.33	2.00	2.34	2.66	2.39	1.66	1.61	1.58	1.67
2	1.81	2.81	3.31	3.77	3.35	2.32	2.28	2.25	2.34
3	2.12	3.33	3.95	4.51	3.97	2.76	2.72	2.69	2.77
4	2.39	3.81	4.53	5.16	4.53	3.15	3.11	3.08	3.16
5	2.67	4.25	5.08	5.82	5.06	3.52	3.49	3.47	3.53
6	2.93	4.76	5.67	6.55	5.64	3.94	3.90	3.91	3.93
7	3.27	5.36	6.41	7.37	6.33	4.44	4.41	4.40	4.42
8	3.69	6.10	7.34	8.44	7.20	5.05	5.05	5.04	5.03
9	4.28	7.15	8.71	10.07	8.48	5.93	6.00	6.02	5.92
10	5.78	9.87	12.24	14.39	11.78	8.18	8.43	8.61	8.23

Source: Invesco, MSCI, FTSE

	Transition Path: 12-Month Returns: 130/30 Strategy								
Reference	Expected Premia Returns: Historical				Expected Premia Returns: 5%				
Base	Base + Mom	Base + Carry	Base + Value	Base + EQW	Base + Mom	Base + Carry	Base + Value	Base + EQW
Decile	(%)	(%)	(%)	(%)	(%)	(%)	(%)	(%)	(%)
1	−15.79	−12.76	−11.46	−12.41	−12.19	−13.59	−13.13	−14.68	−13.78
2	−5.57	−2.76	−1.99	−1.60	−2.12	−3.68	−3.83	−4.12	−3.88
3	0.29	1.70	2.61	4.19	2.82	0.74	0.69	1.53	0.98
4	4.01	6.23	6.73	7.89	6.94	5.23	4.75	5.14	5.04
5	7.82	11.95	10.34	11.71	11.33	10.90	8.30	8.87	9.35
6	9.06	12.56	14.50	12.81	13.28	11.50	12.39	9.95	11.27
7	10.38	14.52	15.37	14.84	14.91	13.45	13.24	11.93	12.87
8	12.00	15.81	15.51	16.37	15.90	14.73	13.38	13.42	13.85
9	13.91	18.00	19.18	18.86	18.67	16.91	16.99	15.85	16.58
10	19.89	21.99	24.09	27.47	24.50	20.85	21.82	24.27	22.30

Source: Invesco, MSCI, FTSE

17.5   WEALTH DECUMULATION STRATEGIES

We have examined the impact of a factor overlay for wealth accumulation strategies *to retirement*. We now consider Artee's investment strategy while drawing on his savings *through* the retirement period. Estrada and Kritzman (2018) provide a goals-based framework to analyze this problem using a quantity called the coverage ratio, defined as $C_t = Y_t/L$ where Y is the number of years withdrawals are sustained by a strategy, both during and after the retirement period and L is the length of the retirement period being considered. They invoke mainstream assumptions of a 30-year retirement period

TABLE 17.10 Annual volatility of alternative strategies

Long/Short Premia

	Base Asset (%)	Strategy: 200/100				Strategy: 130/30			
		Base + Mom (%)	Base + Carry (%)	Base + Value (%)	Base + EQW (%)	Base + Mom (%)	Base + Carry (%)	Base + Value (%)	Base + EQW (%)
Equities	15.25	19.28	20.94	20.70	18.28	15.60	16.01	16.05	15.66
Equity/Bond 60/40	8.88	14.92	16.52	16.08	13.14	9.54	9.95	9.95	9.44
Bonds	2.97	12.63	13.59	12.83	9.53	4.79	4.84	4.66	3.95

Long-Hedged Premia

	Base Asset (%)	Strategy: 200/100				Strategy: 130/30			
		Base + Mom (%)	Base + Carry (%)	Base + Value (%)	Base + EQW (%)	Base + Mom (%)	Base + Carry (%)	Base + Value (%)	Base + EQW (%)
Equities	15.25	19.79	20.65	19.71	19.43	15.68	15.84	15.74	15.68
Equity/Bond 60/40	8.88	15.52	16.41	15.23	14.92	9.65	9.81	9.64	9.59
Bonds	2.97	13.24	13.93	12.55	12.29	4.94	4.96	4.65	4.62

Short-Hedged Premia

	Base Asset (%)	Strategy: 200/100				Strategy: 130/30			
		Base + Mom (%)	Base + Carry (%)	Base + Value (%)	Base + EQW (%)	Base + Mom (%)	Base + Carry (%)	Base + Value (%)	Base + EQW (%)
Equities	15.25	19.46	21.63	21.04	20.03	15.68	15.91	15.88	15.74
Equity/Bond 60/40	8.88	14.98	17.75	16.95	15.72	9.60	9.98	9.89	9.69
Bonds	2.97	12.41	15.70	14.67	13.29	4.67	5.49	5.21	4.88

Source: Invesco, MSCI, FTSE

and a 4% real withdrawal rate per annum. We thus define the coverage ratio we use for our assessment as the proportion of periods over which Artee's savings supports a 4% real spending rate over 30-year periods. We assume that Artee is primarily concerned with not running out of money to fund expenditures and aspires for a coverage ratio of 1; values above 1 are perceived to be desirable, but not nearly to the extent (on absolute basis) that values below 1 are perceived as highly undesirable. Estrada and Kritzman (2018) postulate a kinked utility function of the following form to capture Artee's preferences:

$$u(c) = \begin{cases} \dfrac{C^{1-\gamma}-1}{1-\gamma} & \text{for } C \geq 1 \\ \dfrac{1^{1-\gamma}-1}{1-\gamma} - \lambda(1-C) & \text{for } C < 1 \end{cases}$$

TABLE 17.11 Median terminal wealth outcomes for various rebalancing frequencies

Rebalancing Frequency	Equity + Mom ($)	Equity + Carry ($)	Equity + Value ($)	Equity + EQW ($)
1 month	14.37	34.15	52.09	29.65
3 months	18.85	44.71	66.92	40.47
6 months	20.66	49.26	73.19	45.29
12 months	20.79	53.25	75.41	47.93

Source: Invesco, MSCI, FTSE

Where λ the coefficient of risk aversion is assumed to equal 0.9999 and γ the linear penalty coefficient is set to equal 10.[13]

We apply the above to our simulation framework; our focus in this context is the effect of alternative strategies on the distribution of the coverage ratio and how this is valued given the assumed kinked utility function. The nominal, historical returns to the base assets and the factor premia are converted to real returns by applying the OECD inflation rate. We consider our previous overlay strategies 200/100 and 130/30. We assume that expected real returns either will equal historical real returns or that expected real returns will equal 4%.[14] We only apply the equal weighted portfolio of factor premia as the overlay portfolio.

Our simulation results are provided in Tables 17.12 to 17.14. We report summary statistics for the distribution of the coverage ratio as well as an expected utility. The results support the beneficial effect of the overlay for all base assets. We find that coverage ratios are significantly enhanced and hence investors reap significant utilitarian benefits from these enhancements.

17.6 LONG/SHORT VERSUS LONG ONLY STRATEGIES

As we have previously noted there is limited evidence in the literature documenting the relative efficiency of long/short factor premia strategies versus long only factor premia strategies. For completeness, we extend our analysis to consider alternative exposures:

- Long a factor – financed by borrowing
- Long a hedged factor financed by borrowing
- Short a factor – financed by borrowing
- Short a hedged factor financed by borrowing
- Long/Short a factor – self financed

---

[13] As γ approaches 1, utility equals the natural logarithm of the coverage ratio; hence, a γ value of 0.9999 effectively implies the use of a log-wealth utility function for the coverage ratios above 1.
[14] The later assumption is the equivalent of our assumption of 5% nominal returns in Section 17.4 allowing for an inflation of 1%.

TABLE 17.12 Coverage ratios with global equities as base asset

200/100 Strategy: expected return = historical

	Mean	25th Percentile	50th Percentile	75th Percentile	Utility
Base	31.08	0.86	10.84	39.68	1.21
Base + EQW	800.44	200.75	448.87	911.00	5.94

200/100 Strategy: expected return = 4%

	Mean	25th Percentile	50th Percentile	75th Percentile	Utility
Base	34.02	0.85	10.53	39.43	1.25
Base + EQW	176.42	22.40	76.43	191.99	3.59

130/30 Strategy: expected return = historical

	Mean	25th Percentile	50th Percentile	75th Percentile	Utility
Base	32.12	0.86	10.97	40.81	1.19
Base + EQW	95.90	14.12	52.65	121.08	3.10

130/30 Strategy: expected return = 4%

	Mean	25th Percentile	50th Percentile	75th Percentile	Utility
Base	30.82	0.84	12.10	39.93	1.17
Base + EQW	52.64	2.20	25.99	66.98	2.11

Source: Invesco, MSCI

TABLE 17.13 Coverage ratios with global bonds as base asset

200/100 Strategy: expected return = historical

	Mean	25th Percentile	50th Percentile	75th Percentile	Utility
Base	3.20	0.94	1.76	4.69	0.09
Base + EQW	349.54	184.01	294.77	437.41	5.64

200/100 Strategy: expected return = 4%

	Mean	25th Percentile	50th Percentile	75th Percentile	Utility
Base	3.18	0.94	2.00	4.69	0.08
Base + EQW	54.88	21.66	43.06	74.09	3.46

130/30 Strategy: expected return = historical

	Mean	25th Percentile	50th Percentile	75th Percentile	Utility
Base	3.24	0.95	1.93	4.77	0.22
Base + EQW	28.86	19.77	27.21	35.68	3.26

130/30 Strategy: expected return = 4%

	Mean	25th Percentile	50th Percentile	75th Percentile	Utility
Base	3.14	0.93	1.87	4.63	0.04
Base + EQW	11.52	5.65	10.53	16.10	1.99

Source: Invesco, FTSE

TABLE 17.14   Coverage ratios with a 60/40 equity/bond portfolio as base asset

200/100 Strategy: expected return = historical

	Mean	25th Percentile	50th Percentile	75th Percentile	Utility
Base	16.00	0.97	9.25	22.96	1.40
Base + EQW	560.28	236.19	430.73	738.32	5.99

200/100 Strategy: expected return = 4%

	Mean	25th Percentile	50th Percentile	75th Percentile	Utility
Base	16.06	0.99	9.91	22.89	1.51
Base + EQW	103.68	30.64	67.95	139.51	3.87

130/30 Strategy: expected return = historical

	Mean	25th Percentile	50th Percentile	75th Percentile	Utility
Base	16.13	1.44	10.28	23.06	1.55
Base + EQW	60.37	27.21	49.01	81.36	3.64

130/30 Strategy: expected return = 4%

	Mean	25th Percentile	50th Percentile	75th Percentile	Utility
Base	16.96	1.97	12.24	23.88	1.66
Base + EQW	32.87	9.58	25.71	46.54	2.66

Source: Invesco, MSCI, FTSE

We consider a 200/100 strategy with equities as a base asset. We do not want to impose any ex-ante assumptions on the alternative sources of the premia returns (longs vs shorts); hence our analysis must assume that expected returns (longs, shorts and long/short) will equal historical returns for our simulations. Hedge returns are obtained as previously expounded. We review single factor overlays (momentum, carry and value) and an equal weighted portfolio of the factors.

In Table 17.15 we present the distribution of terminal wealth across all the strategies and the multiple possible factor overlays. In Table 17.16 we present the historical volatility of each of these alternative strategies. The results suggest:

- The overlays increased total volatility relative to the volatility of the base asset.
- The volatility of the long (short) overlay to a base equity allocation provided the highest (lowest) volatility. This is consistent with the systematic exposure embedded in a long (short) position.
- The volatility of the long/short overlay to a base equity allocation was generally lower than that of overlays exploiting long-hedged or short-hedged factor exposures; this supports the diversifying benefits of long/short exposures.
- The terminal wealth of the long/short overlays dominated all other factor overlays (long, long hedged, short and short hedged).

In brief then, if one were to run a 'horse race' across overlay strategies, the long/short combination would be expected to provide the highest reward to risk enhancement to the base asset investment. The large gap in accumulated wealth between the long/short and long hedged (or short hedged) suggests important capital allocation considerations when assessing taking on additional units of risk.

TABLE 17.15 Terminal wealth distributions

		Base + Momentum Overlay					Base + Value Overlay			
Decile	Base ($)	L/S ($)	Long ($)	Long Hedged ($)	Short ($)	Short Hedged ($)	L/S ($)	Long ($)	Long Hedged ($)	Short ($)	Short Hedged ($)
1	0.81	2.59	1.45	0.98	1.18	1.17	6.60	1.93	2.04	2.07	2.02
2	1.38	4.96	2.81	1.77	2.04	2.19	13.04	3.93	3.73	3.65	3.82
3	1.83	7.04	4.03	2.46	2.74	3.08	18.88	5.86	5.24	4.96	5.40
4	2.26	9.27	5.39	3.19	3.47	4.04	25.05	7.98	6.85	6.33	7.09
5	2.74	11.78	6.92	3.99	4.27	5.15	32.34	10.37	8.60	7.86	9.06
6	3.26	14.80	8.69	4.93	5.20	6.50	41.40	13.25	10.63	9.66	11.41
7	3.93	18.96	11.12	6.16	6.37	8.18	52.73	17.27	13.30	11.94	14.47
8	4.87	24.70	14.62	7.93	7.96	10.60	69.86	23.14	17.11	15.17	18.90
9	6.32	34.24	20.75	10.84	10.60	14.74	102.54	34.16	23.85	20.66	26.70
10	10.89	68.38	42.56	20.56	18.94	29.37	228.21	78.43	47.73	39.08	55.18

		Base + Carry Overlay					Base + EQW Overlay			
Decile	Base ($)	L/S ($)	Long ($)	Long Hedged ($)	Short ($)	Short Hedged ($)	L/S ($)	Long ($)	Long Hedged ($)	Short ($)	Short Hedged ($)
1	0.81	4.18	1.81	1.90	1.35	1.33	5.10	1.82	1.66	1.62	1.58
2	1.38	8.25	3.60	3.43	2.49	2.63	9.59	3.57	2.97	2.82	2.97
3	1.83	11.84	5.20	4.71	3.43	3.76	13.31	5.17	4.10	3.78	4.16
4	2.26	15.79	6.98	6.05	4.41	4.96	17.12	6.92	5.27	4.77	5.40
5	2.74	20.24	9.10	7.66	5.54	6.45	21.51	8.91	6.59	5.90	6.93
6	3.26	25.90	11.60	9.48	6.88	8.15	26.87	11.31	8.12	7.20	8.70
7	3.93	33.28	14.91	11.77	8.58	10.44	33.80	14.43	10.04	8.77	10.86
8	4.87	43.82	19.82	14.92	10.99	13.76	43.38	19.02	12.70	10.98	14.03
9	6.32	63.06	28.50	20.55	15.07	19.70	59.51	27.21	17.36	14.78	19.70
10	10.89	136.64	62.36	39.78	29.33	41.61	118.21	58.05	33.00	26.82	39.42

Source: Invesco, MSCI

TABLE 17.16 Historical annual volatility

Strategy	L/S (%)	Long (%)	Long Hedged (%)	Short (%)	Short Hedged (%)
Base + Mom	19.3	24.6	19.8	15.1	19.5
Base + Carry	20.9	26.3	20.6	17.8	21.7
Base + Value	20.7	25.4	19.7	17.2	21.0
Base + EQW	18.3	25.0	19.4	15.9	20.1

Source: Invesco, MSCI

17.7 COMPLETION PORTFOLIOS VERSUS MAXIMUM SHARPE RATIO PORTFOLIOS

Our analysis is partly inspired by the Canadian Pension Plan Investment Board's total portfolio approach; see Raymond (2009). Our base asset is akin to what they label as 'the reference portfolio'. As previously suggested, the construction of our overlay portfolio does not exploit the correlation structure of the factors with the reference portfolio. This also holds for a maximum Sharpe ratio portfolio. In a follow up paper we plan to examine these issues in greater depth. However, we offer a first look at these matters by comparing the composition of the completion portfolio to that of the maximum Sharpe ratio portfolio.

We assume that global equities are the base asset and that the expected returns across premia are the same. Hence a maximum Sharpe ratio portfolio will be obtained through a minimum variance construct across the premia. We assume that long/short strategies are held 'long'; namely we do not sell, for instance, the 'carry' strategy. Similarly, the overlay portfolio is obtained by minimizing risk across the premia and the fixed, given exposure in the base asset. In both instances the ratio of gross exposure to net asset value is constrained to 2.

In Table 17.17, we report factor premia exposures and associated portfolio statistics for three strategies – an equal weighted, maximum Sharpe ratio, and the overlay. The overlay portfolio has a greater allocation to momentum than the maximum Sharpe ratio portfolio and this is not surprising given the countercyclical properties of this factor. Additionally, we note that the overlay portfolio has a lower total correlation with the base asset than the maximum Sharpe ratio portfolio leading to a lower total portfolio risk. Though the maximum Sharpe ratio portfolio differs from the overlay portfolio the differences in portfolio weights and resulting impact on volatility are relatively small. This would suggest that a max Sharpe ratio portfolio is reasonably efficient from a total portfolio perspective. One should be careful in not generalizing this observation. Our sampled premia exhibit near zero correlation with the base asset; hence there is little scope for alternative portfolio weights to optimally impact outcomes when we assume expected returns to be equal across premia.

Our analysis on completion portfolios is preliminary. We need to more explicitly incorporate risk budgeting considerations more formally as well as consider alternative base assets that exhibit exposures to both alpha and beta risks.

TABLE 17.17 Commodity premia with equities as base asset

	Momentum	Carry	Value	Correlation with Base	Equity Market Volatility (%)	Overlay Portfolio Volatility (%)	Total Portfolio Volatility (%)
Equal weight	0.33	0.33	0.33	0.06	15.24	9.21	18.29
Maximum Sharpe	0.44	0.15	0.41	0.05	15.24	8.97	18.08
Total Portfolio no shorts	0.54	0.10	0.36	0.04	15.24	9.08	18.01

Source: Invesco, MSCI

17.8　CONCLUSIONS

We focus here on the key insights derived from our analysis:

- A factor overlay of commodity premia can be applied – even in a conservative fashion – to enhance the likelihood that Artee's goals will be attained. This holds whether Artee's reference portfolio is either all equities, all bonds or some mix of the two.
- The factor overlay is also expected to smooth out the transition to attaining the goals. In particular, worst outcomes are mitigated by the overlay.
- These results hold just as well over the decumulation or retirement stage of Artee's journey.
- A factor overlay utilizing commodity premia is expected to provide the reward-to-risk ratio that is highest when implemented via a long/short strategy rather than a long or a short strategy that are hedged for systematic market effects.
- A maximum Sharpe ratio portfolio of commodity risk premia is quite close and similar to an optimal completion portfolio that accounts for the correlation of the premia with the base asset.
- Results improved when the rebalancing frequency between the base asset and the overlay was lowered, even in the absence of transaction costs. This result reinforces the idea that factor overlays need to be analyzed in a broader portfolio context.
- Our analysis will need to be extended in several dimensions:
  - We will consider other asset class premia as we have noted that any one premium co-moves very differently with alternative base assets.
  - We will review the construction and composition of the overlay factor portfolio in a more rigorous risk budgeting framework; our early findings imply that long/short strategies may offer a more attractive return benefit than long only strategies and imply that the composition of the factor portfolio may be sensitive to the underlying base asset.
  - We will consider more dynamic factor allocation strategies that incorporate broad macroeconomic conditions as determinants of capital allocation across factors.

We are confident that we have highlighted key attributes of a framework that will enable us to apply a total portfolio approach over multiple investment horizons. We believe this is quite novel and heretofore unexplored in the investment community.

APPENDIX: COMMODITY FACTOR PORTFOLIO CONSTRUCTION

To start, commodity factors should satisfy the same three properties as equity (or indeed currency or bond) factors. First, factor definitions should be intuitive and driven by a fundamental understanding of commodity markets instead of empirical results, in order to minimize the risk of data mining. Second, factors should offer positive returns over time[15]; though achieving the highest in-sample return is never the goal. Third, factors used in a multi-factor commodity strategy should be differentiated in their information content. In other words, there should be no strong positive correlation among them.

With these properties in mind, we construct three cross-sectional factors: momentum, value and carry - using 20 commodity futures. The commodity futures universe in this chapter is similar to that of the S&P GSCI Commodity Index, with some modifications due to liquidity considerations.

We exclude six of 24 commodities (lead, sugar, cotton, lean hogs, live cattle and feeder cattle) in the index and include two additional commodities (soybean oil and soy meal). The resulting commodity universe of 20 commodities includes six energy commodities (crude oil, Brent crude oil, heating oil, gasoil, natural gas and gasoline), two precious metals (gold and silver), four industrial metals (copper, aluminum, zinc and nickel), and eight agricultural commodities (cocoa, coffee, corn, wheat, red wheat, soybeans, soybean oil and soymeal).

17.A.1   MOMENTUM FACTOR

Momentum was first proposed as a factor by Jegadeesh and Titman in their 1993 seminal paper. It is based on the assumption of short-term price continuation i.e. stocks with the highest intermediate-term returns (winners) will outperform stocks with the worst past performance (losers) for up to 12 months. Much later, momentum strategies were applied to commodity futures markets e.g. by Pirrong (2005), Erb and Harvey (2006) and Miffre and Rallis (2007), and similar positive returns were observed.

Rather than raw one-year returns, a common measure in the literature, we define momentum in terms of risk-adjusted returns.[16] Volatility can vary widely across commodities and focusing on risk-adjusted returns will avoid simply selecting assets with extreme volatilities.

We construct the momentum factor portfolio by ranking the 20 commodities by their risk-adjusted momentum signals, going long the top 40% and short the bottom 40%. These thresholds were chosen to balance the desire to have some buffer between long and short assets and to avoid concentrating risk in a small number of positions; however, a range of definitions produces similar results. We apply the same ranking process to the carry and value factors.

17.A.2   CARRY FACTOR

A significant body of research supports the notion that the futures price curve, also called the term structure, contains information about the market and its related eco-

---

[15]The rationale for a return premium generally falls into one of three categories: behavioural anomaly, compensation for a specific risk, or market structure related.
[16]We construct all factors in this chapter with a simple prior and then test the parameter for robustness. In the case of momentum, the definition is twelve-month return relative to twelve-month volatility. A range of different parameters yields similar results.

nomic fundamentals.[17] All things equal, one should expect an upward-sloping term structure since the futures curve needs to embed the costs of holding the asset (e.g., financing and storage costs). However, the curve will shift to a downward-sloping profile when market participants ascribe greater value to immediate delivery. This is generally referred to as the convenience yield.

For many assets, carry and momentum are negatively or, at best, weakly correlated. For example, a bond with weak momentum will likely have improved carry. Commodities are different, as the same basic phenomena drive both momentum and carry. For example, when demand for a commodity outstrips supply, we should expect the price of a commodity to rise. At the same time, the term structure will almost certainly respond with positive carry (also described as backwardation). Our research shows a 0.38 correlation between carry and momentum over the past 20 years.[18]

17.A.3   VALUE FACTOR

Value is often viewed as the natural complement to momentum, given its contrarian nature. Conrad and Kaul (1998) concluded that contrarian strategies tend to perform well over long horizons while momentum strategies perform better over short-to-intermediate horizons. In recent years, a number of researchers have explored applying both momentum and value (reversal) metrics in the asset selection process. We construct the momentum and value factors separately in order to benefit more fully from the available diversification among factors.

Asness, Moskowitz, and Pederson (2013) proposed a quite reasonable definition of value for commodities: the five-year change in spot returns.[19] Such a definition possesses the virtues of simplicity, negative correlation to momentum, and a least some degree of efficacy. The challenge is that it also has a material negative exposure to carry. Fundamentally, this makes sense. Assets generally fall due to a surplus of supply over demand, a situation generally accompanied by sizable negative carry (also known as contango). This means that, for commodities unlike most other assets, value and carry will tend to have a negative correlation.

While a negative correlation between factors is certainly attractive, negative loadings on a factor with positive expected returns is not. Therefore, we augment the definition described earlier in the section by neutralizing the negative loadings on carry using negative carry for an asset as a hurdle to its classification as an undervalued asset.

---

[17]Fama and French (1989), Swanson and White (1995), and McCallum and Wu (2005).

[18]For the purposes of this chapter we define carry as the difference in price between the contract that is closest to expiration and the next available contract. Alternative definitions provide similar results.

[19]Unlike stocks and bonds, commodities have no series of future cash flows to be discounted and used for valuation. Therefore, a simpler definition based on the change in real spot prices is reasonable.

For example, an asset with -10% annualized carry must have fallen more over the past five years to be considered inexpensive than one without negative carry. The resulting definition has a near-zero correlation with both momentum and carry while providing a far more compelling return profile.

17.A.4   FROM COMMODITY FACTORS TO FACTOR PORTFOLIOS

For each of the three cross-sectional factor definitions, we apply a risk parity framework to create each factor strategy. Both the long and short side of each factor strategy are weighted according to each asset's volatility and correlation characteristics. In this case, more volatile, highly correlated assets will tend to receive smaller weights than less volatile uncorrelated assets. In our experience a risk parity approach helps to improve portfolio diversification versus a simple 1/n allocation approach, particularly when there are wide variations in the characteristics of the asset universe. In addition to the allocation framework, we have also included a risk target (10%) for both the long and short side of each factor strategy.

17.A.5   FACTOR CONSTRUCTION

The goal of factor construction is to isolate the performance of the factor in question and therefore minimizing idiosyncratic risk exposures. In a relatively small investment universe, such as we have with commodities, standard approaches to portfolio construction can result in risk concentration, especially when some of the assets possess vastly different volatilities than the average. For example, a highly volatile asset like natural gas can have an outsized impact on results in an equally weighted approach. Likewise, a weighting scheme based on ordinal rank presents difficulties due to both the small number of assets and the wide range of volatilities.

As a result, we use a risk parity framework for long/short factor construction. The process has two steps. First, we calculate the long side asset weights such that each individual asset has the same marginal risk contribution to the long-side portfolio. We apply the same process to create the short-side portfolio. Second, we scale the long and short sides so that each has the same marginal risk contribution to the factor portfolio.

A key input to this risk parity framework is the asset covariance matrix, which determines both the correlation structure of commodity assets and the risk estimation of individual assets. Investors need to balance two considerations when deciding how to construct the covariance matrix. A shorter-term matrix will tend to have greater accuracy on average but will tend to be wrong at inconvenient times. A longer-term matrix will have the opposite properties along with lower turnover unrelated to changes in the factors. We have a bias toward the latter in order to incorporate the full-cycle behavior of the assets and therefore apply a matrix with a seven-year half-life.

REFERENCES

Asness, C.S., Moskowitz, T.J. and Pedersen, L.H., 2013, 'Value and Momentum Everywhere', *Journal of Finance*, **68**(3), 929–985.

Blitz, David, Joop Huij, Simon Lansdorp and Pim van Vliet, 2014. 'Factor Investing: Long-Only versus Long-Short'. *SSRN Working Paper*.

Cochrane, John, 1999. 'Portfolio Advice in a Multifactor World', *Federal Reserve Bank of Chicago Economic Perspectives*, **23**, 59–78.

Conrad, J. and Kaul, G., 1998 'An Anatomy of Trading Strategies', *The Review of Financial Studies*, **11**(3), 489–519.

Cuthbertson, Keith, Simon Hayley, Nick Motson and Dirk Nitzche, 2016, 'Diversification Returns, Rebalancing Returns and Volatility Pumping', *Caas Business School Working Paper*.

Das, Sanjiv, Daniel Ostrov, Anand Radhakrishnan and Deep Srivastav, 2019a. 'A New Approach to Goals Based Wealth Management'. *Santa Clara University Working Paper*.

Das, Sanjiv, Daniel Ostrov, Anand Radhakrishnan and Deep Srivastav, 2019b. 'Dynamic Portfolio Allocation in Goals-Based Wealth Management'. *Santa Clara University Working Paper*.

De Longis, Alessio, 2019, 'Dynamic Asset Allocation Through the Business Cycle: A Macro Regime Approach, *Invesco Investment Solutions Manuscript*.

De Longis, Alessio and Dianne Ellis, 2019, 'Market Sentiment and the Business Cycle: Identifying Macro Regimes Through Investor Risk Appetite', *Invesco Investment Solutions Manuscript*

Erb, Claude and Campbell Harvey, 2006, 'The Strategic and Tactical Value of Commodity Futures', *Financial Analyst Journal*, **62**(2), 69–97.

Estrada, Javier and Mark Kritzman, 2018, 'Evaluating Retirement Strategies: A Utility Based Approach', *SSRN Working paper no. 3135125*.

Fama, Eugene, 1996, 'Multifactor Efficiency and Multifactor Asset Pricing', *Journal of Financial and Quantitative Analysis*, **31**(4), 441–465.

Fama, E.F. and French, K.R., 1989, 'Business Conditions and Expected Returns on Stocks and Bonds,' *Journal of Financial Economics*, **25**, 23–49.

Jegadeesh, Narasimhan and Sheridan Titman, 1993, 'Returns to Buying Winners and Selling Losers: Implications for Stock Market Efficiency', *Journal of Finance*, **48**(1), 65–91.

McCallum, A.H. and Wu, T., 2005, 'Do Oil Futures Prices Help Predict Future Oil Prices?', *Federal Reserve Bank of San Francisco Economic Letter* **2005-38**, https://ssrn.com/abstract=1967966 (accessed 23 June 2020).

Miffre, J. and Rallis, G., 2007, 'Momentum Strategies in Commodity Futures Markets,' *Journal of Banking & Finance*, **31**(6), 1863–1886.

Pirrong, C. 2005, 'Momentum in Futures Markets', *Working Paper*, University of Houston, https://ssrn.com/abstract=671841 (accessed 23 June 2020).

Politis, D.N. , 2003, 'The Impact of Bootstrap Methods on Time Series Analysis', *Statistical Science*, **18**(2), 219–230.

Politis, D.N. and Romano, J.P.,1992, 'A circular block-resampling procedure for stationary data', in Exploring the Limits of Bootstrap (R. LePage and L. Billard, eds.) Wiley, New York, 263–270.

Polk, Christopher, Mo Haghbin and Alessio De Longis, 2019, 'Time-Series Variation in Factor Premia: The Influence of the Business Cycle', *SSRN Working Paper 3377677*

Raymond, Donald, 2009, 'Integrating Goals, Structure, and Decision-Making at Canada Pension Plan Investment Board', *SSRN Working Paper 1131414*.

Scott, Louis and Stefano Cavaglia, 2017. 'A Wealth Management Perspective on Factor Premia and the Value of Downside Protection', *Journal of Portfolio Management*, Spring, 1–9.

Swanson N. R. and White, H., 1995, 'A Model-Selection Approach to Assessing the Information in the Term Structure Using Linear Models and Artificial Neural Networks,' *Journal of Business and Economic Statistics,* **13**(3), 265–275.

Warren, Geoffrey, 2019. 'Choosing and Using Utility Functions in Forming Portfolios', *Australian National University Working Paper.*

Wilcox, Jarrod, Jeffrey Horvitz and Dan DiBartolomeo, 2008, Investment Management for Taxable Private Investors. Charlottesville, VA, *The Research Foundation of CFA Institute.*

Index

Please note that page references to Figures will be followed by the letter 'f', to Tables by the letter 't'; References to Notes will contain the letter 'n' following the Note number